International Adaptations
of the MMPI-2

The publication of this book was assisted by a bequest
from Josiah H. Chase to honor his parents,
Ellen Rankin Chase and Josiah Hook Chase,
Minnesota territorial pioneers.

International Adaptations of the MMPI-2

Research and Clinical Applications

James N. Butcher, Editor

University of Minnesota Press

Minneapolis

London

Copyright 1996 by the Regents of the University of Minnesota

Published by the University of Minnesota Press
111 Third Avenue South, Suite 290, Minneapolis, MN 55401-2520
Printed in the United States of America on acid-free paper

Library of Congress Cataloging-in-Publication Data

International adaptations of the MMPI-2 : research and clinical
    applications / James N. Butcher, editor.
        p.   cm.
    Includes bibliographical references.
    ISBN 0-8166-2632-4 (alk. paper)
    1. Minnesota Multiphasic Personality Inventory.   I. Butcher,
James Neal, 1933-   .
BF698.8.M5158   1996
155.2′83—dc20   95-35024

The University of Minnesota is an equal-opportunity educator and employer.

Contents

Tables

Figures

Preface

In the early 1970s, when Paolo Pancheri, from the University of Rome, and I began the international MMPI project that culminated in the publication of our *Handbook of Cross-National MMPI Research* in 1976, we mistakenly believed that there were only a few projects and publications exploring the cross-cultural use of the MMPI that we would need to incorporate. However, we quickly learned that even then there were hundreds of publications on the instrument and numerous ongoing projects in several countries. Since the publication of the handbook, the international use of the MMPI has expanded broadly to many additional countries. The international scene in personality assessment has become considerably busier and more diverse over the past two decades, especially with the publication of the MMPI-2 in 1989. I anticipate that future developments will continue at an ever increasing pace.

Many factors account for the extensive development of the MMPI-2 in international contexts.

1. A number of countries have undergone rapid political-economic changes and have become more open to adapting Western technology. Mental-health professionals in several countries that were traditionally not open to psychological testing are now incorporating assessment procedures derived in the West. With the end of the cold war new international friendships and working alliances began forming. Several chapters in this book (e.g., the chapters on Russia and the People's Republic of China) are clear examples of the "new world order" and could not have been written just a few short years ago. At the end of the Cultural Revolution, psychologists from the People's Republic of China made contacts with American psychologists with the goal of developing an East-West scientific interchange. One of their aims was to adapt clinical tests, such as the MMPI, for their mental health uses since they did not have the financial and professional resources to develop new instruments. Testimony to the remarkable robustness of the

MMPI in clinical assessment across cultures is provided by the large number of studies done in China in the late 1980s (Cheung & Song, 1989).

2. Communications between mental-health professionals from different countries have continued to broaden, and more effective procedures and professional practice models have been shared. As a result, working psychological assessment instruments and procedures from one context are being adapted in other settings.

3. Technological developments over the past two decades have shortened the distances between people around the world, allowing more efficient research collaboration. When Pancheri and I were working on our handbook we had great difficulty communicating because the mail between the United States and Italy was so unreliable that correspondence and data were routinely lost between Minneapolis and Rome. Telephone calls, though more reliable, were prohibitively expensive and had to be very brief.

Fax machines, computer-based communication (the Internet), and increasingly reliable, though expensive, express mail delivery between countries make it possible to communicate quickly, even on an hourly or daily basis if demands of a particular project require it.

4. The publication of two new MMPI instruments made translation and adaptation much easier and more immediately rewarding for psychologists from other countries. The MMPI-2 for adults was published in 1989 (Butcher, Dahlstrom, Graham, Tellegen, & Kaemmer, 1989), and the MMPI-A for adolescents (Butcher, Williams, Graham, Archer, Tellegen, Ben-Porath, & Kaemmer, 1992) appeared three years later. The revised versions are being adapted internationally much more rapidly than was the original MMPI, as a result both of the rapid expansion of applied psychology internationally and of improvements introduced in the new MMPI instruments. The revised and new items are much easier to translate; the new norms are based on a more diverse sample of Americans and have proven to be a closer match to normals from other countries; and there is a broader range of relevant scales with which to assess clinical problems.

Scope of the Volume

One of the primary goals of this volume is to discuss cross-national personality assessment research and to explore the applicability of the MMPI-2 in a number of countries. A second goal is to describe a number of specific clinical adaptations of the MMPI-2 that have been initiated by psychologists in other countries, illustrating the increasing use of the instrument around the world. A third goal is to provide, in some detail, an overview of the expanding clinical research base of the MMPI-2 that has been accumulating through the work of scholars around the world. The chapters on adaptations of the MMPI-2 vary considerably in the type and amount of information presented. Some projects are quite far along and have fully adapted a translation, developed separate norms, and conducted clinical validation research. Others have just begun the process and provide information about development and efforts at preliminary clinical application. Each project has also taken a distinctive direction as a result of the research and clinical interests of the translation staff and the availability of resources. However, all the projects provide mental-health professionals interested generally in international test adaptation and specifically in the MMPI-2 with informative test-application strategies.

The book is divided into five parts. Several general methodological issues are introduced in the early chapters, followed by descriptions of the international projects grouped roughly geographically. In part I, the opening chapter addresses cross-cultural psychological issues and the need to adapt psychological tests in developing countries. Chapter 2 presents a number of issues and practical problems related to translation of personality inventories. Information from several translation projects is used to illustrate and provide some detail about how translation problems were dealt with in two quite different cultural contexts with somewhat different translation strategies. The third chapter by Kyunghee Han and me addresses models for testing the equivalence of psychological tests in cross-national settings.

In part II, we begin our survey of international applications of the MMPI-2 with an exploration of Asian and Southeast Asian research programs. In chapter 4, Noriko K. Shiota, Steven S. Krauss, and Lee Anna Clark describe the development of the Japanese version of the MMPI-2 and provide a model translation and adaptation program. This work is followed in chapter 5 by Kyunghee Han's detailed discussion of the development of a Korean translation of the MMPI-2. Next, the extensive research program to develop a Chinese version of the MMPI-2 in the People's Republic of China and Hong Kong is described by Fanny M. Cheung, Weizheng Song, and Jianxin Zhang. Chapter 7 by Col. La-Or Pongpanich of the Royal Thai Army and the Bangkok Army Hospital describes the translation procedures and a number of research projects that have centered on the Thai version of the MMPI-2. The remaining three chapters in part II address "international" applications within the United States. Bao-Chi Nguyen Tran, in chapter 8, describes the Vietnamese version of the MMPI-2; Amos S. Deinard and his colleagues present a description of and early empirical research on the Hmong version of the MMPI-2; and Stanley Sue and his colleagues describe the use of the MMPI-2 with Asian Americans and the importance of considering the individual's level of acculturation in MMPI-2 based assessment.

In part III, we continue our survey of international applications of the MMPI-2 by exploring research in Spanish-speaking countries, beginning with a description of the exemplary project of Fernando J. Rissetti and his colleagues from Chile (chapter 11). Rissetti and his colleagues have tested more than 40,000 individuals during the 18 years that their MMPI (now MMPI-2) project has been under way.

In chapter 12 Maria Martina Casullo and her colleagues from Buenos Aires describe the adaptation of the MMPI-2 in Argentina. In the following chapter Emilia Lucio-G.M. and Isabel Reyes-Lagunes present their extensive research project on the MMPI-2 in Mexico and Nicaragua. The Hispanic version of the MMPI-2 for the United States is the subject of chapter 14. José J. Cabiya, from the Center for Caribbean Studies, discusses his validational and clinical research on the Garcia-Peltoniemi/Azán translation as well as its use in San Juan. Finally, we close part III (and begin our focus on European MMPI-2 projects) with the extensive research project developed by Alejandro Avila-Espada and Fernando Jimenéz-Gómez from Salamanca, Spain, in chapter 15.

Part IV begins with the Flemish/Dutch translation of the MMPI-2. Hedwig Sloore, a long-time MMPI researcher and advocate from Belgium, and Jan Derksen, from Holland, teamed up to develop the Flemish/Dutch translation (chapter 16). Chapter 17 concerns the translation and adaptation of the MMPI-2 into Norwegian by Bjorn Ellertsen, Odd E. Havik, and Rita R. Skavhellen. Sölvína Konráòs, in chapter 18, provides a detailed account of the translation and adaptation of the MMPI-2 into "Old Norse" for use in Iceland. The Russian-language MMPI-2 project initiated by Victor S. Koscheyev, former director of the Specialized Center for the Disaster Medicine "Protection" in Moscow, and Gloria R. Leon is described in chapter 19. The French version of the MMPI-2, by Isabelle Gillet, Mireille Simon, and J. D. Guelfi, is described in chapter 20. Chapter 21 presents the Italian adaptation done by Paulo Pancheri, Saulo Sirigatti, and Massimo Biondi. The final two chapters in part IV report preliminary MMPI-2 development projects in Greece and Turkey. Anna Kokkevi from the University of Athens describes earlier work on the original MMPI in Greece and introduces the reader to the development of the Greek MMPI-2. Işık Savaşır from the University of Haceteppe and Meral Çulah from Iowa State University describe the Turkish MMPI-2.

Part V presents three projects in which the MMPI-2 has been adapted for use in Middle Eastern countries. Abdalla M. Soliman (chapter 24), an Egyptian-born and -trained psychologist who has taught in both Kuwait and the United Arab Emirates, developed the Arabic version of the MMPI-2 that will likely be used throughout the Arabic-speaking world. In chapter 25, Moshe Almagor and Baruch Nevo from the University of Haifa describe the translation and standardization of the Hebrew version of the MMPI-2. Finally, Elahe Nezami from the University of California and Reza Zamani from the University of Teheran are collaborating to develop a Farsi version of the MMPI-2 for use in Iran. Early clinical application of these translations reveals the MMPI-2 to be a valuable means of assessing clinical patients in these countries.

Throughout this volume our goal is to provide both research information and clinical case material to illustrate the clinical utility of the MMPI-2 in other countries. To this end, several appendixes are included: Appendix A provides a description of the MMPI-2 validity, clinical, and content scales to serve as a reference guide for readers who are becoming familiar with the MMPI-2. Appendix B offers a list of MMPI-2 translation projects and translators. Appendix C reports the results of an item-endorsement study giving the percentage of subjects responding "true" to each MMPI item. These data reveal a high degree of similarity in responses to items concerning symptoms of psychopathology between different cultures. Appendix D provides a comparison of item-response data from a number of translation projects compared with the American normative sample or the U.S. college data set.

This book is a clear example of cross-national research collaboration and bears witness to the fact that such collaboration is not only possible but can thrive when the scientific communities and environmental circumstances are in synchrony. Although the editor of this volume provided impetus for some of the projects presented here and assumed the overall responsibility of organizing and reporting the diverse projects, the individual contributors provided the energy and industry to make the projects viable. This book is truly a cross-cultural effort and would not have become a reality without the extensive effort and commitment of the collaborators.

A number of people have contributed substantially to organizing material for this book. Linda Fresquez and Eli Smith deserve much gratitude for tracking information, typing manuscripts, organizing tabular material, and aiding substantially in the communication process among authors. Lynn Allen, Russ Morfit, and Brad Roper contributed substantially to data analysis during the project. Russ deserves special thanks for his dogged determination to produce the profile graphs by computer. Beverly Kaemmer deserves special thanks for her support of this difficult project and for having confidence that my somewhat far-flung collection of research efforts would actually come to fruition. And Lydia Ericson contributed substantially to the project by managing the office in my absences, assisting with the communication of international project collaborators, and coordinating the MMPI-2 Workshop & Symposium programs which provided some financial support for these translation programs. Carolyn and Holly deserve special thanks for their tolerance of my absence during this project.

J. N. B.

References

Butcher, J. N., & Pancheri, P. (1976). *Handbook of cross-national MMPI research*. Minneapolis: University of Minnesota Press.

Cheung, F. M., & Song, W. Z. (1989). A review on the clinical applications of the Chinese MMPI. *Psychological Assessment*, 1, 30–237.

Part I

Methodological Issues

Chapter 1

Understanding Abnormal Behavior Across Cultures: The Use of Objective Personality Assessment Methods

James N. Butcher

Mental-health professionals in other countries are discovering a growing need for developing mental-health services that require the use of reliable, valid psychological instruments. Psychologists have learned that well-constructed psychological tests can, with care, be translated and adapted for use in their own countries.

Psychological evaluations of individuals from different cultural backgrounds are becoming more common in clinical psychology today. In the United States, individuals from different cultural backgrounds (e.g., refugees) are frequently being evaluated with psychological tests developed in the United States. Moreover, psychological tests developed in Western nations are finding wider adaptation and application in other countries. Rapid communication of information and increased travel from one country to another have reduced the geographic distance between people. Many professionals outside the West are adapting techniques developed in Western countries for use in their own countries to assess emotional disorders.

This book is devoted to an exploration of international adaptations of the most widely used personality test in the United States, the MMPI-2, which is now being widely adapted for use in other countries. It may seem to some that clinical tests developed in one country cannot easily be adapted to other languages and cultures. The diffusion of psychological technology across diverse languages and cultures raises a number of questions. It is important to recognize that these intercultural test adaptations require careful and extensive work before the process can be considered complete. This book presents cross-cultural test adaptations that have been accomplished with considerable success. We will begin by examining the rationale and empirical basis for translating and adapting psychological tests in other countries before surveying the diverse test adaptations.

The Cross-Cultural Perspective in Psychology

Several general factors important to cross-cultural psychology must be considered before one can appreciate how psychological tests are used in diverse cultures. We will first examine issues central to understanding psychopathology in cross-cultural contexts.

Mode of Cross-Cultural Study

The similarities and differences between cultural groups and the way in which cultural factors are viewed by researchers are important factors. A strategic variable to address concerns how cross-cultural research can be studied. *Emic* and *etic* approaches to understanding cross-cultural data have evolved to clarify broad strategies for examining cross-cultural data (Headland, Pike, & Harris, 1990). Harris (1976) defines *etics* as "domains or operations whose validity does not depend upon the demonstrations of conscious or unconscious significance or reality in the minds of natives" and *emics* as "domains or operations whose validity depends upon distinctions that are real or meaningful (but not necessarily conscious) to the natives themselves." The emic approach seeks to understand a culture on its own terms, without reference to outside perspectives or judgments. In personality psychology, this distinction parallels the *idiographic* approach contrasted to the *nomothetic* described by Allport (1937). He generally preferred to understand individuals on their own terms without reference to others. The etic approach corresponds to Allport's nomothetic view of science as a comparative strategy. Both approaches are valuable in understanding people from different cultures and both have their particular limitations. Emic descriptions provide rich and important insights about cultures, but are not readily translatable into data that allow for rigorous scientific comparisons.

For empirical cross-cultural science to proceed, it is necessary to compare different cultures on the same or generally equivalent measures using etic strategies. Etic approaches may erroneously (and ethnocentrically) assume that some phenomena are common across all cultures and inappropriately impose the same categories of comparison across groups. Cautions have been urged about this problematic use of etic measures to understand emic phenomena, referred to as the *pseudoetic* strategy (Triandis, Malpass, & Davidson, 1972). The emic-etic issue pervades many cross-cultural comparisons. Cross-cultural experts disagree about preferred strategies for resolving the conflict, express skepticism about the prospects for reconciliation, and question whether any dichotomy really exists (Segall, 1986).

The approach followed in this book is more consistent with an etic approach and views the study of psychopathology cross-culturally as an effort to explore universals (or at least widely found constructs) that have demonstrated equivalence. It presents the view that similar behavioral dimensions reflected in objective test indices can be considered comparable behavioral patterns across diverse cultures.

Intercultural Similarity of National Groups: A Basis for Scientific Study

People from diverse cultures, even those cultural groups that might at first appear to be very distinct and irrevocably different from us, often turn out to be quite similar in terms of customs, behaviors, and personality characteristics. There is considerably more commonality between human cultural groups today than there are notable differences—at least when it comes to the study of psychopathology. An important consideration in cross-cultural psychology involves the need to understand the relative homogeneity of the populations (even seemingly disparate cultures) to be studied. Today, most national groups actually share considerable common heritage, including many traditional attitudes and beliefs. Even groups with seemingly differing cultural backgrounds, such as those in the East and in the West, cannot be assumed to be "different," since past centuries have seen great interchanges of ideas and beliefs as well as of material goods. Comparisons between cultural groups should be based on a clear understanding of the preexisting conditions of common characteristics.

Generalizability of Constructs across Cultures

The foregoing considerations bear directly on the next point. People from many cultures show considerable similarity in motivation, interests, and personality characteristics. However, before cross-cultural research can proceed effectively one must ensure that the variables being studied (e.g., traits) operate the same way in all cultures under study. For example, if one is studying the personality variable of "interpersonal aggressiveness," it is important to determine if the components of the traits in question and the meanings of them in each culture are generally equivalent. Ensuring the equivalence of processes and variables under study is a basic problem in the cross-cultural study of behavior.

Appropriate concerns about the definition of variables under study are important. Cross-cultural researchers need to be aware that some variables from highly different cultures may differ in form and quantity across groups, making it inappropriate to engage in comparisons of essentially different variables. It is usually important to establish cross-cultural similarity before any observed differences can be evaluated. In the study of abnormal behavior cross-culturally, a good example of the equivalence problem is found in the syndrome of depression. Depression has been observed to be manifested somewhat differently across cultures (Good & Kleinman, 1985; Marsella, 1978) and is composed of different characteristics

(Butcher & Pancheri, 1976); thus, comparing "depressed" patients from different cultures can result in erroneous conclusions.

Conducting Research across Language or Cultural Boundaries

Language and cultural barriers may complicate efforts to adapt psychological measures across cultures. All phases of a test adaptation project require close attention and sensitivity to possible cultural differences. An informative example of the types of errors that can occur in cross-cultural research was reported by Butcher and Pancheri (1976):

> A few years ago, a graduate student research assistant (a non-United States citizen of a non-Christian religious faith) was frantically attempting to complete a required number of follow-up interviews before the end of fall quarter in a United States university. The research involved a brief interview with the parent and a longer inquiry and observation of the child. For several days she had had difficulty scheduling the program with one family but was pleased that her unannounced visit on the morning of December 25 at last found them at home! This unfortunately true anecdote underscores the importance of a sensitive understanding of significant cultural influences. A smoothly operated research investigation requires close collaboration with behavioral scientists from the culture under investigation. To conduct competent and generalizable cross-culture or cross-national research (or any research for that matter) one must have an intimate knowledge of the subject population, research instruments, research methodology, and the current political, social, and economic situation. (p. 17)

Multinational studies require that researchers exercise judgment and cultural awareness so that situations like the preceding example do not destroy working relationships that have been developed. This book, in many respects, is not a cross-cultural study since the separate contributions are from psychologists who are actually *from* the countries in which the research was conducted, not Americans who were visiting those countries. For example, the research in Chile was essentially designed, organized, and carried out by Chilean psychologists; the work in China, by the Chinese; and so forth. This volume reports a collection of international research and clinical projects organized around a central theme—the use of translated versions of the MMPI-2. In many ways this volume represents an ideal multicultural study since it involves equal participation by psychologists from many different cultures on similar projects. It was, of course, a cross-cultural collaboration, and issues central to cross-cultural investigations were observed. The importance of international research collaboration in cross-cultural investigations has been described by a number of authors (Manaster & Havighurst, 1972; Campbell, 1968; Brislin, Lonner, & Thorndike, 1973; Norbeck, Price-Williams, & McCord, 1968; Berrien, 1970).

Abnormal Psychology in Cultural Context

An important task of the cross-cultural psychopathologist is to formulate working definitions of mental health and illness that will make possible the identification of abnormality. Two important traditions exist in the mental-health field when cross-cultural comparisons of psychopathology are involved.

The *relativistic* approach to defining abnormal behavior was first described by anthropologists such as Boas, Benedict, Mead, and Sapir in the 1930s and 1940s. This perspective maintains that the assignment of "abnormal" status to persons or behaviors is always a social act, carried out on the basis of cultural values or beliefs. Since, according to this view, norms for acceptable and unacceptable behavior vary, it is not possible to establish any universal standards for the identification of abnormality. The criteria for psychopathology may change at different times, may vary in different circumstances, and may not be shared by different cultural or subcultural groups (Tseng & Hsu, 1980). Western investigators who employ their own culture-bound definitions of mental illness in cross-national research may be committing the error referred to as "psychiatric imperialism" (Marsella, 1979; Torrey, 1972) by assuming that their own essentially arbitrary norms of human behavior can be used as definitive standards in other cultures (Yap, 1951). According to this position, a strict application of a Western-derived psychiatric diagnostic system might result in misclassifying unfamiliar behavior patterns such as the following:

> For instance, if a Hindu fakir behaves much like a catatonic schizophrenic in Britain, he need not necessarily be insane, since not only can he begin or stop his apparently catatonic behavior at will, but such behavior has a recognizable place, and possesses some degree of social approbation, in his own culture. Similarly, the Siberian shaman may fall into a state of partial hysterical dissociation . . . but this state he voluntarily seeks, and in doing so he obtains authority and respect from his tribe. (Yap, 1951, p. 315)

The relativistic research strategy has some theoretical validity and is very easy to implement. However, Draguns (1977b) cautioned that its advantages are outweighed by the methodological complexity of interpreting results obtained with shifting and variable criteria.

A second approach to the definition of abnormality advocates the use of a single set of diagnostic criteria, for example, those developed in a particular (e.g., Western) psychiatric tradition to apply to other groups. According to this view, a professional has the authority to define clinical abnormality even if others in the community perceive the person as normal or as serving a useful function in society (Honigmann, 1968). This absolutist approach proceeds from the assumption that Western concepts of psychiatric impairment and of diagnostic categories have utility and cross-cultural constancy (Draguns, 1977b).

This view, although not universally endorsed, merits careful examination. First, there is substantial methodological value in establishing consistent procedures for collecting data on the nature and distribution of mental illness throughout the world. Also, there is evidence that the discrepancy between Western and non-Western diagnostic criteria may not be as great as the relativist school has suggested. While the patterning of specific disorders may vary, most of the behaviors regarded as abnormal in Western societies are also considered disordered or deviant wherever they occur throughout the world (Marsella, 1979; Murphy, 1976; Wittkower & Dubreuil, 1968; Yap, 1969). For example, Murphy (1976) pointed out that "almost everywhere a pattern composed of hallucinations, delusions, disorientation, and behavioral aberrations appears to identify the idea of 'losing one's mind'" (p. 1027), although the content and presumed etiology of these manifestations are dependent on cultural beliefs. Murphy (1976) further noted that "rather than being simply violations of the social norms of particular groups . . . symptoms of mental illness are manifestations of a type of affliction shared by virtually all mankind" (p. 1027). If such is the case, the adoption of a single set of criteria to facilitate the study of psychopathology is a justifiable research strategy, whose value can ultimately be assessed with reference to the utility of the information it yields.

A third approach to studying abnormal behavior appears to be replacing both the relativist and the absolutist frameworks. A number of writers have held that it is possible to distinguish between intrapsychic or personal maladjustment and culture-bound, socially defined deviance (Draguns, 1977b, 1980; Kennedy, 1973). They have suggested that the former can be evaluated on a pancultural basis with reference to functional concepts such as "adjustment," "efficiency," and "goal attainment" (Draguns, 1980; Marsella, 1979; Yap, 1951). Draguns (1977b) suggested that each of the current standards for distinguishing normal from abnormal behavior provides only a partial view and that more precise, comprehensive criteria are required. He recommended that the field of cross-cultural psychopathology would benefit from clear, unambiguous standards of disturbance that are cross-culturally acceptable; measures that embody this concept in a manner applicable across cultures; and demonstrations of the equivalence of these measures in different cultural environments.

The study of the classification process and the rates of abnormal behavior disorders cross-culturally has been influenced by two contrasting approaches. One view maintains that the categories of psychological disturbance described in Western classification systems provide a universally valid basis for naming and studying abnormal behavior cross-culturally. Proponents of this position maintain that psychiatric disorders are analogous to physical diseases and are likely to be distributed and manifested in similar patterns throughout the world. Other, more moderate advocates consider that Western nosological systems only provide a convenient framework for detecting and comparing mental disorders found in different cultures. In general, this view holds that it is possible to discover universals of psychological disturbances, which support the hypotheses derived from the study of Western populations.

The second view focuses on the study of psychological disorders within their own cultural context without reference to how well they conform to the traditional psychiatric nomenclature. This approach derives from an anthropological tradition and emphasizes the unique manifestations of mental illness that are thought to reflect specific cultural meanings (Phillips & Draguns, 1969). According to this view, Western diagnostic categories are likely to be culture bound and are thus unlikely to accommodate disorders found in other cultures.

Most of the research in cross-cultural psychopathology has involved the universalist approach of the psychiatric-medical tradition. The application of psychiatric diagnostic concepts across cultures is an important topic and has recently been explored and summarized by Butcher, Narikiyo, and Vitousek (1992).[1] The general conclusion to be derived from the extensive research on the psychiatric-medical perspective has been that no conclusive answer is now available regarding the cross-cultural distribution and manifestation of psychiatric disorders or the generalizability of psychiatric diagnoses across cultures. Abandoning the psychiatric-medical approach would clearly eliminate many methodological and conceptual problems. However, a purely culture-specific strategy would sacrifice much of the value of cross-cultural research along with its flaws. If classification research can be faulted for often making inappropriate comparisons of dissimilar data, culture-specific research runs the risk of making any comparative analyses impossible. It is not possible, nor is it desirable, to seemingly resolve this controversy by affirming the correctness of one position or the other. Phillips and Draguns (1969) aptly pointed out that "these two divergent conceptual orientations . . . are mutually complementary rather than antagonistic" (p. 24)—that the field of cross-cultural psychopathology is legitimately concerned both with universal principles and with the relationship between a particular culture and the kind of psychopathology its members manifest.

Research on cross-cultural psychopathology has yielded two kinds of general findings that document both universal and cultural components (Draguns, 1985). Large-scale investigations have demonstrated that the same major disorders do exist in a variety of cultures (WHO, 1973). Considerable research has also demonstrated that culture influences the rates, manifestations, course, and outcome of mental disorders (Butcher & Pancheri, 1976; Marsella & Kameoka, 1989). The extreme positions that psychopathology is universally identical or that each culture produces only unique and incomparable disorders are not tenable. Instead, there seems to be a recognizable core of central features of psychopathology that are molded into a variety of manifestations by cultural influences (Draguns, 1985). The existence of both views calls for an interactionist theoretical perspective (Good & Kleinman, 1985; Weiss & Kleinman, 1988). Both approaches are necessary to address the fundamental tasks of cross-cultural research: the identification of core features of psychopathology with respect to stable human attributes, and the elaboration of the impact of culture on the occurrence, definition, and experience of mental illness (Weiss & Kleinman, 1988).

Clinical diagnosis of course suffers from other problems that limit its generalizability across cultures. Psychiatric diagnosis is dependent on interview data and on the clinician's subjective appraisal of the symptomatic status of the patient. Reliability and validity of clinical diagnosis are often considered suspect. It has not been uniformly considered the most objective means of collecting and summarizing mental health symptomatic data.

In this chapter, a more objective means of characterizing psychological problems and symptoms in clinical settings will be described. In this approach, symptoms and behaviors are delineated by psychological tests that incorporate direct symptom appraisal rather than relying upon the clinician's inferences about the person's problems.

Assessment of Abnormal Behavior across Cultures

Objective Personality Tests

Early cross-cultural personality research typically used projective techniques such as the Rorschach or Thematic Apperception Test because the ambiguous test stimuli (e.g., inkblots) were thought to be devoid of cultural content, providing a "culture-free" test of personality. However, low reliability, lack of demonstrated validity, and the extensive time required to administer, score, and interpret projective techniques made them somewhat difficult and expensive to use (Lindsey, 1961). Also, there is no evidence that projective techniques can provide informative measures of psychopathology across cultures (Draguns, 1984).

The cross-cultural use of objective instruments to assess personality and psychopathology has increased markedly in recent times (Sundberg & Gonzales, 1981). Extensive cross-cultural research has been conducted on the California Psychological Inventory, Spielberger's Trait-State Anxiety Scale, the Strong Vocational Interest Blank, the Internal-External Locus of Control Scale, and the Minnesota Multiphasic Personality Inventory (MMPI) and MMPI-2 (Butcher & Clark, 1979; Pongpanich, 1982). The cross-cultural use of personality tests has demonstrated that many paper-and-pencil inventories can provide useful information, if the item content and the measurement constructs are appropriate and relevant to the culture studied and the instrument is carefully translated and adapted for the new culture. Most tests used cross-culturally today were not developed as cross-cultural research instruments but were adapted in other countries to provide effective personality measures for intracultural use with a target population.

The most widely translated and adapted clinical tests of personality are the MMPI and MMPI-2. They have been used on all continents and have been translated into dozens of languages (Draguns, 1984). Butcher et al. (1992) pointed out several reasons for this broad international use:

- The MMPI and MMPI-2 have an objective scoring and interpretation format that can be readily automated.
- The inventory has well-established validity for a wide range of clinical problems (see Appendix A for a description of widely used MMPI-2 scales).
- The MMPI-2 is the recent revision of the MMPI, in which outdated, objectionable, and awkwardly worded items have been revised or eliminated, and new contemporary norms, more appropriate for cross-cultural comparisons, were developed (Butcher, Dahlstrom, Graham, Tellegen, and Kaemmer, 1989; Tellegen & Ben-Porath, 1992).
- A number of useful self-study resources or interpretive guides are available (e.g., Butcher, 1990; Butcher & Williams, 1992; Butcher, Graham, Williams, and Ben-Porath, 1990; Graham, 1990), and the MMPI instruments are, relative to other approaches to personality assessment, easy to learn.
- The MMPI/MMPI-2 item pool has great clinical relevance for diverse cultures. The items appear to reflect psychopathology in all cultures studied to date.
- The MMPI and MMPI-2 have been shown to provide useful clinical diagnostic information in a wide range of countries that are culturally different from the United States (Manos, 1985; Savasir and Erol, 1990).

Psychologists in many countries in which clinical psychological assessment is beginning to develop as a discipline are finding that adaptation of existing measures, such as the MMPI-2, allows them to efficiently incorporate the broadly studied constructs and objective assessment in their own culture.

Illustrations of MMPI Generalizability across Different Cultures

In this section, we will illustrate the utility of the MMPI in classifying clients who have similar psychological problems but come from quite diverse national backgrounds. We will examine one type of patient with severe mental-health problems (paranoid schizophrenia) from a number of countries to illustrate how the original MMPI profiles typify similar mental-health problems. The profile type is a 6-8/8-6, a code type typically found among individuals with features of paranoid schizo-

12   James N. Butcher

Table 1-1. Personality Characteristics of the 6-8/8-6 MMPI Profile Type

Historical Features:	May have a history of psychological disorder; may have relatives with a history of schizophrenia; schizoid lifestyle possible; poor achievement history
Symptomatic Picture:	Appear as tense, withdrawn, apathetic; guilty; depressed, and autistic; may be delusional, hallucinating, or show other elements of active psychotic process; they are negativistic, suspicious, moody, irritable, or may show flat affect; in interview they may be tangential and circumstantial; they tend to use projection and vague intellectualization as defenses, although these mechanisms tend not to work well—they often appear lacking in workable defenses; they appear to withdraw into fantasy under even mild stress; 6-8s are often preoccupied with the occult—and may be involved in food fads or strange activities; thought disorder is likely; feelings of ego deterioration; inadequacy; and have problems concentrating
Interpersonal Relationships:	Disturbed personal relations; they are suspicious of others; they avoid close relationships; they are viewed as unfriendly and have poor social skills; have little or no sense of humor; have low social interest; are introverted and often reclusive; appear negativistic in social relations
Diagnostic Possibilities:	DSM-IV Axis I: Schizophrenia; Paranoid Schizophrenia DSM-IV Axis II: Schizoid or Paranoid Personality
Behavioral Projection:	Personality decompensation and disorganization likely; acute symptomatic disturbance with delusions and hallucinations
Treatment Possibilities:	Hospitalization may be necessary if they are considered a threat to themselves and/or others; outpatient treatment complicated by regressed or disorganized behavior; day treatment often effective at managing activities; major tranquilizers to control psychotic thinking often helpful; long-term, marginal adjustment is a problem; thus frequent brief "management" therapy contacts helpful; insight-oriented treatment may exacerbate problems and result in regression
Hypotheses for Further Study:	Is hospitalization required—is patient dangerous to self or others?

phrenia. The research literature on the 6-8/8-6 code type presents a picture of severe and long-standing psychological problems.

Now let's examine a number of cases and research samples from several different countries of the same profile type.

The first case is an Italian paranoid schizophrenic reported in Butcher and Pancheri (1976). This case history described a man who manifested severe psychopathology widely found among paranoid schizophrenic patients:

Male, age 27, never married. He works as a teacher in a junior high school in a small town in southern Italy (Calabria). The patient was referred to the outpatient service of the Institute of Psychiatry of the University of Rome, Italy (IPUR), by his parents because he had attempted suicide twice in the previous fifteen days,

MMPI

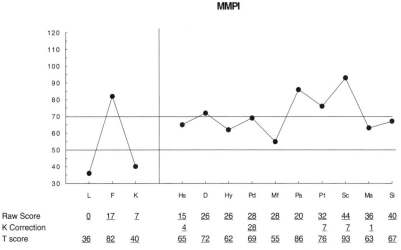

	L	F	K		Hs	D	Hy	Pd	Mf	Pa	Pt	Sc	Ma	Si
Raw Score	0	17	7		15	26	26	28	28	20	32	44	36	40
K Correction					4			28			7	7	1	
T score	36	82	40		65	72	62	69	55	86	76	93	63	67

Figure 1-1. Original MMPI Profile of a 27-Year-Old Paranoid Schizophrenic School Teacher from Italy

without any apparent reason. His parents told the doctor that in the last two months the patient, an introverted, closed man, broke off relations with his few friends, left his job, and started saying "strange things." Four days before admission, he insulted and slapped his mother without any apparent motivation. During the interview with the doctor, the patient was diffident, suspicious, and very anxious. He said that he attempted suicide because he could no longer stand the threats he had received for several months. He said that everyone in town says he is homosexual and that from time to time he hears strange voices insulting him overtly. He thinks that in the last few months his body has changed, especially his hands and face, and that this is probably because someone has been putting something in his food. After the interview, the patient was admitted to the male ward of the IPUR for treatment. During the first four days of hospitalization, he was silent, withdrawn, and very anxious. On the fifth day he completed the MMPI; then a phenothiazine treatment was started. The patient was discharged after two months of treatment. He was no longer delusional or hallucinating, and he criticized his past psychiatric behavior. Discharge diagnosis: paranoid schizophrenia, acute.

The MMPI was taken in Italian and the profile was plotted according to the U.S. norms. The profile, provided in Figure 1-1, shows the clear features of paranoid schizophrenic patients from inpatient psychiatric settings in the United States. When interpreting this profile one would find the descriptive personality and symptomatic correlates shown in Table 1-1 to be quite appropriate for the Italian patient.

MMPI

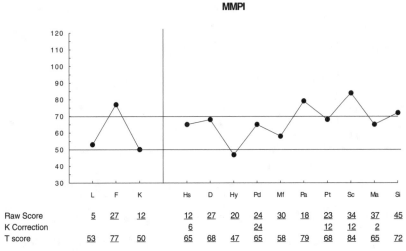

		L	F	K	Hs	D	Hy	Pd	Mf	Pa	Pt	Sc	Ma	Si
Raw Score		5	27	12	12	27	20	24	30	18	23	34	37	45
K Correction					6			24			12	12	2	
T score		53	77	50	65	68	47	65	58	79	68	84	65	72

Figure 1-2. Original MMPI Profile of a 31-Year-Old Paranoid Schizophrenic from Santiago, Chile

The second case (see Figure 1-2), provided by Rissetti and his colleagues from Santiago, Chile, is a Chilean paranoid schizophrenic:

The patient, a 31-year-old Chilean man, was found wandering the streets of Santiago, Chile, completely nude and claiming to be Jesus Christ. He was brought to the emergency service of a local hospital and admitted to the psychiatric unit. In addition to his delusional behavior, he was hallucinating and showed severe disturbance of thought and affect. After a few days on the service, he was administered the Spanish (Chilean) version of the MMPI. His MMPI profile shown in Figure 1-2 is plotted against the American norms. His acute psychotic state, showing clear features of paranoid schizophrenia, is reflected in the resulting MMPI profile.

The symptoms expressed by this psychologically disturbed Chilean patient appear quite similar to those of the Italian paranoid schizophrenic patient. The MMPI profile features resemble the configuration and elevation shown in the Italian patient's profile in Figure 1-1. The symptoms described in Table 1-1 that had been derived on psychiatric patients in the United States (e.g., see Gilberstadt & Duker [1965]) appear to provide an appropriate description of the Chilean patient, who also appears to be suffering from a paranoid schizophrenic disorder.

The data presented in Figure 1-3 indicate that paranoid schizophrenics in India produce MMPI profiles similar to those found in psychiatric facilities in the United States. The MMPIs were obtained from a study in which the MMPI was administered in the English language to clients from India. The MMPI profile in Figure 1-3 is plotted against American norms. The group mean profile of the 17 paranoid

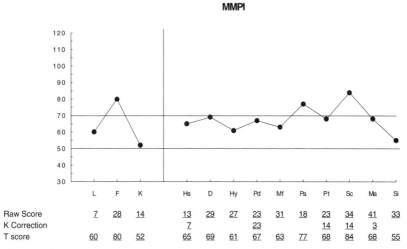

Figure 1-3. A Group Mean MMPI Profile of 17 Paranoid Schizophrenic Women from India

schizophrenics from India shows the familiar 6-8/8-6 group profile that we saw in the previous cases (Thatte, Manos, & Butcher, 1987).

In 1982, La-Or Pongpanich translated the MMPI into Thai and began using the inventory in the Bangkok Army Hospital for assessment of clinical patients admitted to the facility. The group mean profile obtained from the first patients admitted to the hospital with an independently obtained clinical diagnosis of paranoid schizophrenia is shown in Figure 1-4 (men) and Figure 1-5 (women). The Thai language version of the MMPI was administered to the patients and the profiles were plotted on the United States norms. The MMPI profiles obtained on the Thai paranoid schizophrenics resemble quite closely profiles obtained from schizophrenics in the United States and the other profiles reported above.

After the Cultural Revolution in China was over and economic and educational interchange with the West resumed, psychologists began an MMPI translation and adaptation project in the People's Republic of China. The research team at Beijing University adapted the Hong Kong version of the original MMPI (Cheung, 1985). The goal of one of the first projects in China was to determine if the MMPI detected psychopathology. The mean clinical profile of a group of paranoid schizophrenic women from Beijing is shown in Figure 1-6. The pattern of clinical scale scores closely resembles the scores of paranoid schizophrenics in several other countries. A research group in Shanghai, China, also conducted a study of paranoid schizophrenics and reported the results shown in Figure 1-7. Cheung and Song (1989) provided a summary of the extensive research on the MMPI in the People's Republic of China since it was introduced there in the early 1980s.

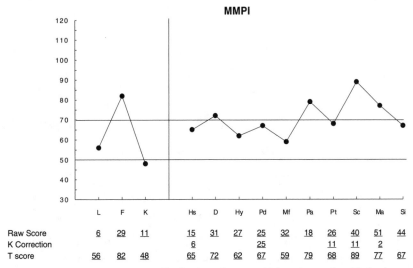

Figure 1-4. A Group Mean MMPI Profile of Eight Male Paranoid Schizophrenics from Thailand

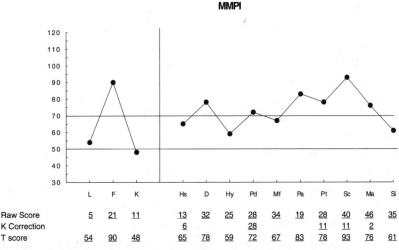

Figure 1-5. A Group Mean MMPI Profile of Six Female Paranoid Schizophrenics from Thailand

Finally, the robustness of the MMPI in detecting psychological disorders across different cultural settings is shown in Figure 1-8. Thatte et al. (1987) conducted a study on groups of patients from India, the United States, and Greece who had previously been diagnosed (not using the MMPI) as having DSM-III-R diagnoses of schizophrenic disorder. The highly similar clinical scale profiles are provided in Figure 1-8. Although these individuals had taken the MMPI in quite different hospital settings (the Greek patients were administered the Greek version of the

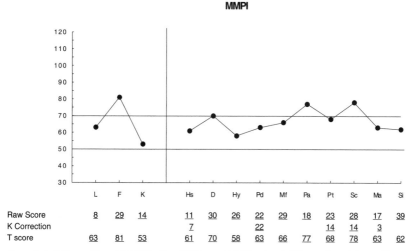

Figure 1-6. A Group Mean MMPI Profile of 45 Paranoid Schizophrenic Women from Beijing, China

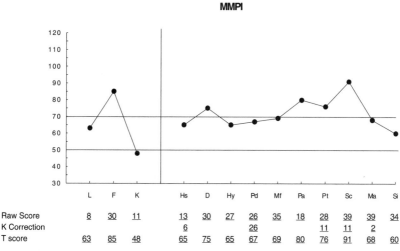

Figure 1-7. A Group Mean Profile of Schizophrenics from Shanghai, China

test) and all profiles were plotted on the norms developed in the United States, their clinical profiles are quite similar in configuration.

The similarity of the high-point scores for similarly diagnosed patient groups across several national groups demonstrates the generalizability of MMPI scores across cultures. All of the profiles shown in these studies were plotted on United States norms. In each country, more culture-specific information would be expected to emerge when the MMPI scores are standardized in target populations.

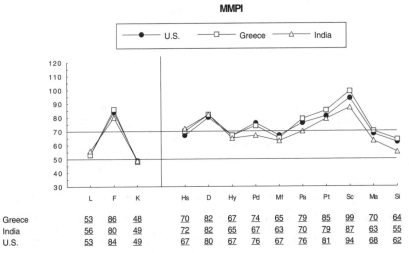

Figure 1-8. Mean MMPI Profiles of Schizophrenic Disorder Patients (*DSM-III-R*) from the United States, Greece, and India (Thatte et al., 1987)

Problems Involved in Cross-Cultural Assessment

Before an instrument can be successfully applied in another culture, problems inherent in the cross-cultural application of psychological tests need to be resolved.

Before a test adaptation is initiated, the test translator must deal with a number of preliminary issues. For example, it must be determined whether a required test-taking task is relevant to the target culture and whether responses to the items are likely to be equivalent across cultures. Lonner (1985) pointed out that cross-cultural test adapters must be aware of possible cultural variations in response sets and must be prepared to evaluate and compensate for possible differences. For example, in some cultures individuals may simply respond to questions out of politeness and then give only socially desirable answers. Others, unfamiliar with psychological tests, may respond in a careless manner. Test adapters may naively assume that test takers in other cultures are equally comfortable with the standardized verbal limited-option format of many Western measures (Draguns, 1984). In one country, true-false tests were referred to by some subjects as "American tests," usually in a less than complimentary manner. Finally, the problem of illiteracy in some countries may preclude the use of written test materials. It may be possible, once a test is translated, to develop a tape-recorded version to allow easier administration to those with marginal reading skills.

Research conducted across a language barrier often proves difficult. Problems may be encountered in all phases of the research collaboration, from initial correspondence to elicit cooperation,[2] to the development of equivalently translated instructions for each language of the study, to the dissemination of results in scientific papers. A great deal has been written about problems of translation (Brislin, 1970; Brislin, 1986; Brislin et al., 1973; Werner & Campbell, 1970). Therefore, a full chapter (chapter 2) is devoted to the important issues pertaining to translation.

The most important psychometric quality of a psychological test is that it validly measure the qualities it is supposed to measure in the new culture. There is evidence (Gough, 1965) that some personality concepts, e.g., socialization, may operate across widely divergent groups. However, other personality type constructs, e.g., leadership potential, may have culturally specific meaning. Gregariousness is an example of a concept that may be difficult to study across cultures. Americans have allegedly been obsessed by the need to "belong" (Horney, 1937) while the Melanesian people who inhabit Dobu Island show no inclination toward gregariousness outside their biological family. They reportedly show little or no social feelings toward others, even their spouses, but instead are hostile and belligerent. Cattell and Warburton (1961) reported that the concepts of anxiety and introversion-extroversion were so congruent in the United States and England that it was correct to use the same concepts to describe individuals in both groups in the two countries. However, they found that the trait of dominance is more instrumental in England and that "dispositional timidity" plays a larger role in the pattern of anxiety in the United States. Thus, even ostensibly similar groups across cultures may possess some personality traits that may require careful scrutiny to determine points of equivalence and difference.

The adaptation of personality tests, such as the MMPI, in other countries has often involved the development of new norms for the target populations for which the test is intended (Abe, Sumita, & Kuroda, 1963; Butcher & Pancheri, 1976; Cheung, 1985; Pucheu & Rivera, 1976; Rissetti, Butcher, Agostini, Elgueta, Gaete, Margulies, Morlans, & Ruiz, 1979; Rissetti & Maltes, 1985; Manos, 1981, 1985; Clark, 1985). However, many translators and clinicians have found that, before developing special norms for new populations, they can usefully employ the American norms as *itinerant norms* (Butcher & Garcia, 1978). In some countries tests can be effectively interpreted using the U.S. norms, since the local populations do not differ appreciably from test takers in the United States (Butcher & Pancheri, 1976; Rissetti et al., 1979).

It is important that new test translations undergo a careful, rigorous evaluation to determine what normative adaptations need to be made for the new culture. Research should involve the study of both normal and clinical samples to determine if the items and scales are operating as intended.

Once tests are translated, there are several useful means of validating them in cross-cultural adaptation. First, the translated and adapted test must be shown to measure in the target culture the same constructs in the same way it does in the culture of origin. It needs to have demonstrated *content validity*. Content validation may be sufficient to initiate the development of a test in a new culture, but additional information is needed to ensure the equivalence of the test in the new culture. A second approach to the validation of the measure in a new culture might be ensuring *factorial validity*, that is, to determine if the factor structure of the measures is equivalent in the target culture (i.e., that the items and scales maintain generally the same factors in the target population as in the population of origin; see Ben-Porath, 1990; Brislin et al., 1973; Butcher & Pancheri, 1976). See chapter 3 for an extended discussion of cross-cultural validational methods. Finally, the most important validational strategy involves ensuring *predictive validity*, that is, determining whether the scales actually predict the expected behavior in the target population (Savaşır & Erol, 1990). We will evaluate the methods cross-cultural personality researchers employ to assess cross-cultural validity in several subsequent chapters describing adaptation projects in other countries.

Summary

The cross-national use of psychological tests has increased greatly in recent years as psychologists in other countries adapt Western psychological tests for use in their countries. This chapter has addressed the process by which psychologists attempt to understand abnormal behavior from a cross-cultural perspective and reviews a number of issues that influence our interpretation of behavior across different cultural groups: the emic-etic distinction; the necessity of determining the equivalence of concepts and measures in cross-cultural comparisons; and the need to take into account the fact that most cultures have a great deal of commonality as well as difference.

Approaches to understanding abnormal behavior were discussed and several perspectives for viewing behavioral problems were presented. The relativistic approach versus the absolutist position was described along with the more conciliatory approach, which assumes that it is possible to distinguish between intrapsychic deviancy and culture-bound deviancy and to evaluate both from a broad cultural perspective. The research literature on using clinical diagnostic procedures in the study of abnormal behavior in cross-cultural context was summarized. Issues related to the limitation of psychiatric diagnosis in cross-cultural psychology were described.

This chapter presented the view that the use of objective personality scales can add interesting information to the cross-cultural study of abnormal behavior. MMPI test results illustrated how similar patients from different nations produce similar profiles. Methodological issues in adapting psychological tests in other languages and cultures were discussed and validation procedures suggested.

Notes

1. For a more extensive exploration of issues in clinical diagnosis see: Al-Issa, 1982; Boyd & Weissman, 1982; Butcher, 1982; Carpenter, Strauss, & Bartko, 1974; Cooper, Kendell, Gurland, Sartorius, & Farkas, 1969; Dohrenwend & Dohrenwend, 1974; Draguns, 1973; Draguns, 1980; Draguns, 1984; Fabrega, 1974, 1982, 1987; Feighner, Robins, Guze, Woodruff, Winokur, & Munoz, 1972; Good & Kleinman, 1985; Kendell, 1975; Kennedy, 1973; Kinzie, 1974: Kleinman, 1977; Leighton, Lambo, Hughes, Leighton, Murphy, & Macklin, 1963; Marsella, 1978; Marsella, 1979; Marsella, 1980; Marsella, Kinzie, & Gordon, 1933; Marsella, Sartorius, Jablensky, & Fenton, 1985; Murphy, 1976; Prince, 1983; Prince & Tcheng-Laroche, 1987; Sen & DeJesus Mari, 1986; Stevens & Wyatt, 1987; Swartz, 1985; Torrey, 1987; Tseng, Di, Ebata, Hsu, & Yahua, 1986; Westermeyer, 1985; Westermeyer, 1987a, 1987b; Westermeyer, 1988; Wittkower & Dubreuil, 1968; Wittkower & Fried, 1959; World Health Organization, 1973; Yap, 1967; Zubin, 1969.

2. Butcher and Pancheri (1976) report an incident of intercultural miscommunication that illustrates the need for clear, careful communication. One American researcher tells the story of writing a Japanese psychologist some time ago to solicit a brief bit of cooperation on some ratings. He received a fairly prompt and courteous reply that the psychologist would be glad to do so, and he was instructed to send $50,000 by return mail to cover expenses.

References

Abe, M., Sumita, K., & Kuroda, M. (1963). *A manual of the MMPI, Japanese Standard Edition.* Kyoto: Sankyobo.

Al-Issa, I. (1982). Does culture make a difference in psychopathology? In I. Al-Issa (Ed.), *Culture and psychopathology* (pp. 3–29). Baltimore: University Park Press.

Allport, G. W. (1937). *Personality: A psychological interpretation.* New York: Holt.

Ben-Porath, Y. S. (1990). Cross-cultural assessment of personality: The case for replicatory factor analysis. In J. N. Butcher & C. D. Spielberger (Eds.), *Recent advances in personality assessment.* Hillsdale, NJ: Erlbaum.

Berrien, F. K. (1970). A superego for cross-cultural research. *International Journal of Psychology, 5,* 1–9.

Boyd, J., & Weissman, M. (1982). Epidemiology. In E. Paykel (Ed.), *Handbook of affective disorders.* New York: Guilford.

Brislin, R. W. (1970). Back-translation for cross-cultural research. *Journal of Cross-Cultural Psychology, 1,* 185–216.

Brislin, R. W., Lonner, W. J., & Thorndike, R. (1973). *Cross-cultural research methods.* New York: Wiley.

Brislin, R. W. (1986). The wording and translation of research instruments. In W. J. Lonner & J. W. Berry (Eds.), *Field methods in cross-cultural research* (pp. 137–164). Beverly Hills: Sage.

Butcher, J. N. (1982). Cross-cultural research methods in clinical psychology. In P. Kendall & J. N. Butcher (Eds.), *Handbook of research methods in clinical psychology.* New York: Wiley, Interscience.

Butcher, J. N. (1990). *MMPI-2 in psychological treatment.* New York: Oxford University Press.

Butcher, J. N. (1991). Psychological evaluation of refugees. In J. Westermeyer, C. L. Williams, & A. N. Nguyen, (Eds.), *Mental health of refugees* (DHHS Publication No. {AD} 91–824). Washington, DC: U.S. Government Printing Office.

Butcher, J. N., & Clark, L. A. (1979). Recent trends in cross-cultural MMPI research and application. In J. N. Butcher (Ed.), *New developments in the use of the MMPI.* Minneapolis: University of Minnesota Press.

Butcher, J. N., Dahlstrom, W. G., Graham, J. R., Tellegen, A. M., & Kaemmer, B. (1989). *MMPI-2: Manual for administration and scoring.* Minneapolis: University of Minnesota Press.

Butcher, J. N., & Garcia, R. (1978). Cross-national application of psychological tests. *Personnel and Guidance, 56,* 472–475.

Butcher, J. N., Graham, J. R., Williams, C. L., & Ben-Porath, Y. S. (1990). *Development and use of the MMPI-2 content scales.* Minneapolis: University of Minnesota Press.

Butcher, J. N., Narikiyo, T., & Vitousek, K. B. (1992). Understanding abnormal behavior in cultural context. In P. Sutker & H. Adams (Eds.), *Handbook of psychopathology* (2nd ed.). New York: Plenum Press.

Butcher, J. N., & Pancheri, P. (1976). *Handbook of cross-national MMPI research.* Minneapolis: University of Minnesota Press.

Butcher, J. N., & Williams, C. L. (1992). Essentials of MMPI-2 and MMPI-A interpretation. Minneapolis: University of Minnesota Press.

Campbell, D. T. (1968). A cooperative multinational opinion sample exchange. *Journal of Social Issues, 24,* 245–258.

Carpenter, W. T., Strauss, J. S., & Bartko, J. J. (1974). The diagnosis and understanding of schizophrenia, Part I: Use of signs and symptoms for the identification of schizophrenia patients. *Schizophrenia Bulletin, 11,* 37–49.

Cattell, R. B., & Warburton, F. W. (1961). A cross-cultural comparison of patterns of extroversion and anxiety. *British Journal of Psychology, 52,* 3–15.

Cheung, F. M. (1985). Cross-cultural considerations for the translation and adaptation of the Chinese MMPI in Hong Kong. In J. N. Butcher & C. D. Spielberger (Eds.), *Advances in personality assessment* (Vol. 4). Hillsdale, NJ: Erlbaum.

Cheung, F. M., & Song, W. Z. (1989). A review of clinical applications of the MMPI in China. *Psychological Assessment: A Journal of Clinical and Consulting Psychology, 1,* 230–237.

Clark, L. A. (1985). A consolidated version of the MMPI in Japan. In J. N. Butcher and C. D. Spielberger (Eds.), *Advances in personality assessment* (Vol. 4). Hillsdale, NJ: Erlbaum.

Cooper, J., Kendell, R., Gurland, B., Sartorius, N., & Farkas, T. (1969). Cross-national study of diagnosis of the mental disorders: Some results from the first comparative investigation. *American Journal of Psychiatry, 125,* 21–29.

Dohrenwend, B., & Dohrenwend, B. (1974). Social and cultural influences on psychopathology. *Annual Review of Psychology, 25,* 417–452.

Draguns, J. G. (1973). Comparisons of psychopathology across cultures: Issues, findings, directions. *Journal of Cross-Cultural Psychology, 4,* 9–47.

Draguns, J. G. (1977). Problems of defining and comparing abnormal behavior across cultures. *Annals of the New York Academy of Sciences, 285,* 664–679.

Draguns, J. G. (1980). Psychological disorders of clinical severity. In H. C. Triandis & J. G. Draguns (Eds.), *Handbook of cross-cultural psychology* (Vol. 6). Boston: Allyn & Bacon.

Draguns, J. G. (1984). Assessing mental health and disorder across cultures. In P. B. Pedersen, N. Sartorius, & A. J. Marsella (Eds.), *Mental health services: The cross-cultural context* (pp. 31–58). Beverly Hills: Sage.

Draguns, J. G. (1985). Psychological disorders across cultures. In P. Pedersen (Ed.), *Handbook of cross-cultural counseling and therapy* (pp. 55–62). Westport, CT: Greenwood Press.

Fabrega, H., Jr. (1974). Problems implicit in the cultural and social study of depression. *Psychosomatic Medicine, 36,* 377–398.

Fabrega, H., Jr. (1982). Culture and psychiatric illness: Biomedical and ethnomedical aspects. In A. J. Marsella & G. M. White (Eds.), *Cultural conceptions of mental health and therapy* (pp. 39–68). Boston: D. Reidel.

Fabrega, H., Jr. (1987). Psychiatric diagnosis: A cultural perspective. *Journal of Nervous and Mental Disease, 175,* 383–394.

Feighner, J. P., Robins, E., Guze, S. B., Woodruff, R. A., Winokur, G., & Munoz, R. (1972). Diagnostic criteria for use in psychiatric research. *Archives of General Psychiatry, 26,* 57–63.

Gilberstadt, H., & Duker, J. (1965). *A handbook of clinical and actuarial MMPI interpretation.* Philadelphia: W. B. Saunders Company.

Good, B., & Kleinman, A. (1985). Epilogue: Culture and depression. In A. Kleinman & B. Good (Eds.), *Culture and depression*. Berkeley: University of California Press.

Gough, H. G. (1965). Cross-cultural validation of a measure of asocial behavior. *Psychological Reports, 17,* 379–387.

Graham, J. R. (1990). *The MMPI-2*. New York: Oxford University Press.

Greene, R. L. (1987). Ethnicity and MMPI performance: A review. *Journal of Consulting and Clinical Psychology, 55,* 497–512.

Harris, M. (1976). History and significance of the emic/etic distinction. *Annual Review of Anthropology, 5,* 329–350.

Headland, T. N., Pike, K. L., & Harris, M. (1990). *Emics and etics: The insider/outsider debate*. Newbury Park, CA: Sage.

Honigmann, J. J. (1968). The study of personality in primitive societies. In E. Norbeck, D. Price-Williams, & W. M. McCord (Eds.), *The study of personality: An interdisciplinary appraisal*. New York: Holt, Rinehart & Winston.

Horney, K. (1937). *The neurotic personality of our time*. New York: Norton.

Kendell, R. E. (1975). *The role of diagnosis in psychiatry*. Oxford: Blackwell Scientific Publications.

Kennedy, J. (1973). Cultural psychiatry. In J. J. Honigmann (Ed.), *Handbook of social and cultural anthropology*. Chicago: Rand-McNally.

Kinzie, J. D. (1974). A summary of literature on epidemiology of mental illness in Hawaii. In W. S. Tseng, J. G. McDermott, Jr., & T. W. Maretzki (Eds.), *People and cultures in Hawaii*. Honolulu: University of Hawaii.

Kleinman, A. (1977). Depression, somatization and the "new cross-cultural psychiatry." *Social Science and Medicine, 11,* 3–10.

Leighton, A. H., Lambo, T. A., Hughes, C. C., Leighton, D. C., Murphy, J. M., & Macklin, D. B. (1963). *Psychiatric disorder among the Yoruba*. Ithaca, NY: Cornell University Press.

Lindsey, G. (1961). *Projective techniques and cross-cultural research*. New York: Appleton-Century-Crofts.

Lonner, W. J. (1985). Issues in testing and assessment in cross-cultural counseling. *The Counseling Psychologist, 13,* 599–614.

Manaster, G. J., & Havighurst, R. J. (1972). *Cross-national research: Social psychological methods and problems*. New York: Houghton-Mifflin.

Manos, N. (1981). *Translation and adaptation of the MMPI in Greece*. Paper presented at the International Conference on Personality Assessment, Honolulu.

Manos, N. (1985). Adaptation of the MMPI in Greece: Translation, standardization, and cross-cultural comparisons. In J. N. Butcher and C. D. Spielberger (Eds.), *Advances in personality assessment* (Vol. 4). Hillsdale, NJ: Erlbaum.

Marsella, A. J. (1978). Thoughts on cross-cultural studies on the epidemiology of depression. *Culture, Medicine, and Psychiatry, 2,* 343–357.

Marsella, A. J. (1979). Cross-cultural studies of mental disorders. In A. J. Marsella, R. Tharp, & T. Ciborowski (Eds.), *Perspectives in cross-cultural psychology*. New York: Academic Press.

Marsella, A. J. (1980). Depression experience and disorder across cultures. In H. Triandis & J. G. Draguns (Eds.), *Handbook of cross-cultural psychology* (Vol. 6). Boston: Allyn & Bacon.

Marsella, A. J., & Kameoka, V. A. (1989). Ethnocultural issues in the assessment of psychopathology. In S. Wetzler (Ed.), *Measuring mental illness: Psychometric assessment for clinicians* (pp. 229–256). Washington, DC: American Psychiatric Press.

Marsella, A. J., Kinzie, D., & Gordon, P. (1973). Ethnic variations in the expression of depression. *Journal of Cross-Cultural Psychology, 4,* 435–458.

Marsella, A. J., Sartorius, N., Jablensky, A., & Fenton, F. R. (1985). Cross-cultural studies of depressive disorders: An overview. In A. Kleinman & B. Good (Eds.), *Culture and depression*. Berkeley: University of California Press.

Murphy, J. M. (1976). Psychiatric labeling in cross-cultural perspective. *Science, 191,* 1019–1028.

Norbeck, E., Price-Williams, D., & McCord, W. (1968). *The study of personality: An interdisciplinary approach.* New York: Holt, Rinehart & Winston.

Phillips, L., & Draguns, J. (1969). Some issues in intercultural research on psychopathology. In W. Caudill & T. Y. Lin (Eds.), *Mental health research in Asia and the Pacific.* Honolulu: East-West Center Press.

Pongpanich, L. O. (1982). Use of the MMPI in Thailand. Personal Communication.

Phillips, L., & Draguns, J. G. (1971). Classification of behavior disorders. *Annual Review of Psychology, 22,* 447–482.

Prince, R. H. (1983). Is anorexia nervosa a culture-bound syndrome? *Transcultural Psychiatric Research Review, 20,* 299–300.

Prince, R., & Tcheng-Laroche, F. (1987). Culture-bound syndromes and international disease classifications. *Culture, Medicine, and Psychiatry, 11,* 3–19.

Pucheu, C., & Rivera, O. (1976). The development of a method of detecting psychological maladjustment in university students. In J. N. Butcher & P. Pancheri (Eds.), *Handbook of cross-national MMPI research.* Minneapolis: University of Minnesota Press.

Rissetti, F. J., Butcher, J. N., Agostini, J., Elgueta, M., Gaete, S., Margulies, T., Morlans, I., & Ruiz, R. (1979). *Translation and adaptation of the MMPI in Chile: Use in a university student health service.* Paper given at the 14th Annual Symposium on Recent Developments in the Use of the MMPI, St. Petersburg, Florida.

Rissetti, F. J., & Maltes, S. G. (1985). Use of the MMPI in Chile. In J. N. Butcher and C. D. Spielberger (Eds.), *Advances in personality assessment* (Vol. 4). Hillsdale, NJ: Erlbaum.

Sartorius, N., Jablensky, A., & Shapiro, R. (1978). Cross-cultural differences in short-term prognosis of schizophrenic psychosis. *Schizophrenia Bulletin, 4,* 102–113.

Savaşir, I., & Erol, N. (1990). The Turkish MMPI: Translation, standardization, and validation. In J. N. Butcher and C. D. Spielberger (Eds.), *Advances in personality assessment* (Vol. 8). Hillsdale, NJ: Erlbaum.

Segall, M. H. (1986). Culture and behavior: Psychology in global perspective. *Annual Review of Psychology, 37,* 523–564.

Sen, B., & DeJesus Mari, J. (1986). Psychiatric research instruments in the transcultural setting: Experiences in India and Brazil. *Social Science and Medicine, 23,* 277–281.

Stevens, J. R., & Wyatt, R. J. (1987). Similar incidence of worldwide schizophrenia: Case not proven. *British Journal of Psychiatry, 151,* 131–132.

Sundberg, N. D., & Gonzales, L. R. (1981). Cross-cultural and cross-ethnic assessment: Overview and issues for clinical and community psychology. In P. McReynolds (Ed.), *Advances in psychological assessment* (Vol. 5). San Francisco: Jossey-Bass.

Swartz, L. (1985). Anorexia nervosa as a culture-bound syndrome. *Social Science and Medicine, 20,* 725–730.

Tart, C. J. (1975). Some assumptions of orthodox Western psychology. In C. J. Tart (Ed.), *Transpersonal psychologies.* New York: Harper.

Tellegen, A., & Ben-Porath, Y. S. (1992). The new uniform T-scores for the MMPI-2; Rationale, derivation, and appraisal. *Psychological Assessment, 4,* 145–155.

Thatte, S., Manos, N., & Butcher, J. N. (1987, July). *Cross-cultural study of abnormal personality in three countries: United States, India, and Greece.* Paper given at the 10th Annual Conference on Personality Assessment, Brussels, Belgium.

Torrey, E. F. (1972). *The mind game: Witch doctors and psychiatrists.* New York: Emerson Hall.

Torrey, E. F. (1987). Early manifestations and first contact incidence of schizophrenia in different cultures: Commentary. *British Journal of Psychiatry, 151,* 132.

Triandis, H. C., Malpass, R. S., & Davidson, A. R. (1972). Psychology and culture. In P. H. Mussen (Ed.), *Annual Review of Psychology, 24,* 355–378.

Tseng, W. S., Di, X., Ebata, K., Hsu, J., & Yuhua, C. (1986). Diagnostic pattern for neuroses in China, Japan, and the United States. *American Journal of Psychiatry, 43,* 1010–1014.

Tseng, W. S., & Hsu, J. (1980). Minor psychological disturbances of everyday life. In H. C. Triandis & J. G. Draguns (Eds.), *Handbook of cross-cultural psychology* (Vol. 6). Boston: Allyn & Bacon.

Weiss, M. G., & Kleinman, A. (1988). Depression in cross-cultural perspective: Developing a culturally informed model. In P. R. Dasen, J. W. Berry, & N. Sartorius (Eds.), *Health and cross-cultural psychology* (pp. 179–206). Beverly Hills: Sage.

Werner, O., & Campbell, D. (1970). Translating, working through interpreters, and the problem of decentering. In R. Narroll and R. Cohen (Eds.) *A handbook of methods in cultural anthropology.* New York: American Museum of Natural History.

Westermeyer, J. (1985). Psychiatric diagnosis across cultural boundaries. *Hospital and Community Psychiatry, 38,* 160–165.

Westermeyer, J. (1987a). Clinical considerations in cross-cultural diagnosis. *Hospital and Community Psychiatry, 38,* 160–165.

Westermeyer, J. (1987b). Cultural factors in clinical assessment. *Journal of Consulting and Clinical Psychology, 55,* 471–478.

Westermeyer, J. (1988). Some cross-cultural aspects of delusions. In T. F. Oltmanns & B. A. Maher (Eds.), *Delusional beliefs* (pp. 212–229). New York: Wiley.

Wittkower, E., & Dubreil, G. (1973). Psychosocial stress in relation to mental illness. *Social Science and Medicine, 7,* 691–704.

Wittkower, E. D., & Dubreuil, G. (1968). Cultural factors in mental illness. In E. Norbeck, D. Price-Williams, & W. M. McCord (Eds.), *The study of personality: An interdisciplinary appraisal.* New York: Holt, Rinehart, & Winston.

Wittkower, E. D., & Fried, J. (1959). A cross-cultural approach to mental illness. *American Journal of Psychiatry, 116,* 423–428.

World Health Organization (1973). *International pilot project on schizophrenia.* Geneva, Switzerland: Author.

Yap, P. M. (1951). Mental diseases peculiar to certain cultures: A survey of comparative psychiatry. *Journal of Mental Science, 97,* 313–327.

Yap, P. M. (1967). Classification of the culture-bound reactive syndromes. *Australian, New Zealand Journal of Psychiatry, 1,* 172–179.

Yap, P. M. (1969). The culture-bound reactive syndromes. In W. Caudill & T. Lin (Eds.), *Mental health research in Asia and the Pacific.* Honolulu: East-West Center Press.

Zubin, J. (1969). Cross-national study of diagnosis of the mental disorders: Methodology and planning. *American Journal of Psychiatry, 125,* (Suppl), 12–20.

Chapter 2

Translation and Adaptation of the MMPI-2 for International Use

James N. Butcher

This chapter is devoted to providing a rationale and describing procedures for translating and adapting personality tests, specifically the MMPI-2, into languages and for use in countries different from the culture in which they were developed. We will address general problems of translating personality tests into other languages and cultures, focus upon specific problems with adapting MMPI-2 items, explore various strategies for translating and adapting the MMPI-2 with a particular emphasis on solving item translation problems, and finally will address problems of cultural adaptation and the possible need for specific national norms in adapting the MMPI-2 in international contexts.

Mirza (1976) provided a very insightful description of the often difficult task of the test translator:

> Thus the translator, in most cases, has a more difficult job than the original author. The author generally has a wide vocabulary from which to choose as he constructs the test. His act of creation is free from the constraint of conforming to an original. The translator, on the other hand, is required to produce the same effects that resulted from the first effort. The author might have inadvertently produced certain side effects. A perfect translation demands that not only the polish but also the blemishes of the original be reproduced. (p. 56)

The task of test translation is often a difficult one, requiring both meticulous care and sharp judgment to capture the psychological meaning in the translated language. In the next section, we will explore several general issues that need to be carefully considered before a translation of the MMPI-2 is undertaken.

General Strategies for Test Item Translation

Translation of item content is one of most important and most basic aspects of cross-cultural test adaptation. It is essential that the translation developer obtain an equivalent rendering of the test stimuli to ensure that the translated version of the test provides the same information as the original instrument does in the United States. In the past this important and ideal requirement for test adaptation was often only partially achieved. Some translations of the original MMPI were less than optimal. For example, a number of translators simply translated the items literally without sufficient checking to ensure item equivalency. These inadequate early translations, with some item wordings that bore little resemblance to the English original, came to be widely used for many years. One version of the original MMPI, for example, was very sloppily translated into another language by undergraduate students in an English-speaking university as a class project. Unfortunately, this version of the test was published without any further study.

Cross-cultural researchers have often held differing viewpoints with respect to the translation strategy to use for personality inventory items. Recommended strategies have ranged from considering it impossible to adequately translate items developed in one culture into a second language and culture (Triandis, Malpass, & Davidson, 1972) to the opposite extreme of encouraging test adapters to translate item content with as little change in linguistic structure or meaning as possible. Fridja and Jahoda (1966), for example, held that translation and adaptation problems can never be satisfactorily resolved to provide equivalent measures. Instead, they suggested that investigators construct comparable forms of the items to be used in different cultural settings. Triandis et al. (1972) argued against test translation on grounds that equivalence usually cannot be obtained. They concluded that even a perfect linguistic version of a test instrument does not provide sufficient assurance that similar responses by subjects have the same frequency in both languages.

Although supporting the general goal of personality inventory translation, Campbell (1968) and Werner and Campbell (1970) considered it important to modify or "decenter" items on a test to make the content appropriate to the target culture. The decentering approach to test translation has the aim of achieving a "loyalty of meaning and equal familiarity and colloquialness in each language" (Werner & Campbell, 1970, p. 398). This approach assumes that there is no correct translation of an item into another language, that there are a number of possible appropriate phrasings in the target language. Furthermore, the sentences of the target language have multiple equivalents in back-translation into the source language. A decentered translation is seen as one possible *set* of equivalent sentences of the source language corresponding to a similar *set* in the target language. The decentering approach is intended to eliminate the distinction between source and target language and make the two language versions of the instrument more equivalent. Decentering necessarily requires longer versions of translated text, but advocates of this approach believe that the process results in more equivalent translations. Some decentered tests have been developed. For example, Brislin

(1970) described the translation of the Marlow-Crowne Social Desirability Scale into Chamorro. However, the final product was considered to be an inequivalent scale, not measuring the same constructs in the target language.

Sechrest, Fay, & Zaida (1972) observed that the process of decentering has two clear disadvantages that limit its utility in cross-national test adaptation. First, inventories that have been decentered are usually longer and more cumbersome. Second, decentering places a severe limitation on the number of languages with which one can work because it requires a multilingual rather than a bilingual translator, and it is unlikely that there are many cultures in which multilingual translators are available.

The decentering procedure for translating text may have greater value if a particular concept is being studied in two diverse cultures and a scale to measure it is being simultaneously developed in both languages. The procedure ascertains that subjects in *both* cultures are responding to the *same* item content. This procedure has considerably less utility when working with an established instrument, such as the MMPI-2, since it is not possible to modify the meaning of the original measuring instrument. Moreover, much of the value of translating the MMPI-2 into another language is to maintain or capture the same clinical diagnostic information in other cultures. Decentering would not enable researchers to relate their findings to the original culture if the test items were drastically altered.

With respect to translating an established inventory, like the MMPI-2, approaches that modify test stimuli drastically would not be acceptable. Hathaway (1970), one of the developers of the original MMPI, had earlier advanced the view that personality psychologists using tests like the MMPI would gain more from their investigations if they did not radically modify the test content in developing translations. He believed that if one could develop close translations a new and more powerful method for assessing personality across cultures would be available.

Furthermore, Hathaway was not in favor of developing new norms in other countries since he considered the "norm" to be a scale, analogous to a yardstick, that should remain constant to allow for comparison. A number of factors have been found to be important in the task of translating MMPI-2 items. Several cross-cultural researchers have provided guidance to the would-be test translator: Brislin (1970); Brislin, Lonner, and Thorndike (1973); Butcher and Pancheri (1976); Egli (1991); Lonner (1967); Mirza (1976); Rosen (1958); Sechrest, Fay, and Zaidi (1972); and Werner and Campbell (1970).

Experience Requirements of the Test Translator

To successfully convey the original meaning of text in the target language, it is necessary that the translator have a high degree of familiarity with both the source and target languages. Formal or dictionary language is often not the language of the prospective test respondent (Sechrest et al., 1972) and therefore cannot be depended upon as the "final authority" for a problematic phrase or word. The adequacy and utility of a translation will depend to a great extent on the inclusion of terms that refer to "real" experiences that are familiar in both cultures. For some languages, it may be necessary to alter the level of difficulty or readability of some items to convey the meanings of the original items (Mirza, 1976).

What language skills are required to develop an effective test translation? Ervin and Osgood (1954) described the nature of bilinguality and bilinguals' use of language that provides insight into the task of determining if one's linguistic skills in source and target languages are sufficient for translating test items. They distinguished between "true" bilinguals (those for whom two sets of linguistic signs, languages A and B, come to be associated with two different sets of meanings) and individuals for whom the two languages are simply two different systems for coding the same meaning. They considered the context in which languages are acquired to be the most important element in the determination. Lambert, Havelka, and Crosby (1958) supported the ideas advanced by Ervin and Osgood. In a study on bilinguality, they showed that the functional separation of the bilinguals' two languages is influenced by the context in which they acquired the languages. Bilinguals who acquired their language skills in geographically different cultural settings accounted for the overall difference in the translated equivalents in their groups. These were individuals who had spent at least a year living in the culture of the second language. Lambert et al. concluded that "bicultural" experience would particularly enhance true bilinguality.

Researchers translating the MMPI-2 have tended to vary in terms of the criteria of bilinguality they chose (see chapters 2, 3, and 4 in Butcher and Pancheri [1976] and several later chapters in this book on the translation projects in various countries to get an idea of the criteria used in MMPI-2 translation projects). In most cases, researchers have applied more stringent criteria than those proposed by Lambert et al.

Need for Linguistic Equivalence

The initial challenge facing a test translator involves the requirement of linguistic equivalence. The translated version of the test items must accurately convey the meaning of the items employed in original developmental research for the test. It is necessary for the translator to ensure that the items convey the same meaning in both the target and the source language, to ensure content validity.

Awareness of Potential Problems Arising from Extreme Cultural Differences

In general, the more different from the original language and culture in which an instrument is being translated, the more challenge the translator experiences in adapting the instrument, given the requirement of content validity. Rosen (1958) pointed out that "the greater the distance between a pair of cultures, the greater will be the problems of translation and adaptation, and the more need for time, careful collaboration, expert knowledge, and empirical check" (p.7). Brislin (1970) also concluded that the greater the distance between the source and target cultures or languages, the greater the translation error rates between different language versions.

Mirza (1976) pointed out that the line between translation and modification in cross-cultural translation was "pretty thin" since the search for linguistic and cultural equivalents inevitably leads to changes in both form and content. He indicated:

> No two languages have a point-to-point correspondence of linguistic symbols. In general, the modifications involved in the translation of a psychological inventory can be divided into the following categories: formal modification, transformal modification, and radical modification. (p. 62)

Formal Modifications. Mirza found that formal modifications were unavoidable accompaniments of the translation process. For the most part, they are usually confined to the lexical and grammatical requirements of the new language, which may differ greatly from the original. An example in the translation from English into Urdu is the problem of making a sentence equally valid for both sexes without making it too cumbersome. Ordinarily, gender determines the conjugation of verbs and the declension of qualifying words in an Urdu sentence. The solution was to avoid, where possible, beginning sentences with the subject "I."

Transformal Modifications. According to Mirza, modifications that reshape the content to suit the new conditions without radically changing the subject matter are called transformal. For example, items that had a religious theme based upon Christianity had to be transformed to Islam to make them appropriate for subjects in Pakistan.

Radical Modifications. When cultural differences make it impossible to retain the original form and content of an item, a radical modification is needed. Usually, a new item is required to replace the original one.

Psychological Equivalence in the Context of Item Alteration

When two cultures or languages are very different, it may be very difficult to achieve complete equivalence of meaning for some words or expressions. Test items may need to be altered to make them relevant to the new culture. Issues of content equivalence have been described by several writers (Butcher, Narikiyo, & Vitovsek, 1992; Brislin, 1970, 1986; Brislin, Lonner, & Thorndike, 1973; Flaherty, Gaviria, Pathak, Mitchell, Wintrob, Richman, & Birz, 1988; Marsella & Kameoka, 1989). It has been suggested that any problematic items be eliminated or replaced by more meaningful equivalents (Rosen, 1958; Mirza, 1976; Sechrest et al., 1972). Equivalence of alternatively worded statements needs to be evaluated before the new statement can be assumed to replace the original. Methods for appraising equivalence, such as item response congruence analysis and factor analysis, will be discussed in chapter 3.

When adapting a psychological test in a different culture it is important to obtain *psychological equivalence* of test items and not simply to provide a literal translation. For example, a literal translation of an item might make the item meaningless in a different language. Test item content can be changed to reflect the underlying psychological dimension measured in the original version of the test scores. There are many safeguards to developing effective adaptations, such as back-translation, use of key informants to verify linguistic and social appropriateness, and pretesting the translated items on a bilingual sample (Draguns, 1984) to facilitate content equivalence.

Rendering Obscure or Rare Expressions into the Target Language

Translators often encounter the problem of choosing between phrasings for rare and sophisticated expressions that are exact equivalents of the original terms or more frequently used but less equivalent expressions. Rosen (1958) preferred the use of the more familiar but perhaps more awkward expression, since this makes the test understandable and acceptable to a wider range of subjects. Simply worded sentences are also recommended by Brislin (1970) and Werner and Campbell (1970). Frequently, the words to be translated have a number of possible definitions, and it is difficult to catch the proper nuance of the original. The solution recommended by Brislin (1970), Sechrest et al. (1972), and Rosen (1958) is to use several words in attempting to convey the original meaning. Redundancy to preserve meaning is preferred over using a shorter but less accurate translation.

Avoiding Abstract Terms

In translating inventory items, it is best to use concrete rather than abstract terms if possible (Brislin, 1970; Lonner, 1967; Werner & Campbell, 1970). Very general translations are more difficult to understand, and the use of vague, abstract terminology promotes a lack of congruence between translation and original. For some languages, translators have the option of choosing basic, common expressions or highly polished academic language. If possible, the language used should be understandable by the majority of the intended population.

Adding Explanation to Clarify Meaning

Some expressions in items comprising personality scales may be problematic because they may be interpreted figuratively in one culture and literally in another. In such cases, an explanation should be added to the item that will specify the intention of the original version (Rosen, 1958). This will make the item more equivalent in meaning.

José Cabiya (1993), from San Juan, Puerto Rico, after attempting to adapt various Spanish versions of the MMPI-2 for use with Puerto Ricans, concluded that the Hispanic version of the MMPI-2 by Rosa Garcia and Alex Azan would work well in Puerto Rico with only slight modification. Rather than change the booklet, he concluded that an eight-word glossary of terms that clarify some colloquial Spanish expressions could be provided to individuals taking the test. This is somewhat analogous to suggestions made by Butcher and Williams (1992) for testing adolescents. Although most adolescents who can read at a sixth-grade level can understand the items in the MMPI-A, a few items contain terms with which they might not be familiar. A glossary of potentially difficult terms was provided for test administrators to use in cases where subjects have marginal reading ability.

Explaining Difficult-to-Translate Idioms

Idiomatic expressions in the original language do not always have equivalents in the target language, and so are translated into nonidiomatic substitutes. The opposite occurs when the target language has an idiom to express the nonidiomatic content of the original item. Several writers—Brislin (1970), Rosen (1958), Sechrest et al., (1972), Werner and Campbell, (1970)—have suggested strategies for dealing with idioms to convey accurately the intended meaning. The recommendations are that the translator should use *both* the idiom and a literal translation of the item, the latter provided in parentheses. Although this procedure usually makes the items longer, and possibly more complex, this appears to be the most effective strategy available.

Avoiding Changing Meaning by Shifting Verb Tenses

Verb tenses in test items are often problematic for the translator. In some languages tense and gender are employed with greater precision than they are in English. The use of a particular tense in a translation may, therefore, not convey the meaning of the original item. Rosen (1958) suggested that two tenses could be used in the translated version (one in parentheses) to convey the exact meaning of the original. Brislin (1970) and Werner and Campbell (1970) favor repeating nouns rather than using pronouns and avoiding the passive tense, hypothetical phrasing, and the subjunctive mood.

Culturally Problematic or Nonequivalent Expressions

One problem that occurs in the translation of objective personality tests is that some items are found to be inappropriate or nonequivalent culturally. This is perhaps the most complicated aspect of test translation, potentially requiring radical item modification or substitution and possibly resulting in nonequivalent items in the target language. Translators need to be intimately familiar with the target culture (as well as the original one) and exercise considerable judgment in modifying items since decisions about item content are to a great extent subjective.

One type of item change involves modifying content in an effort to preserve the psychological meaning of the item in the new language. This change requires finding new, appropriate content that is meaningful in the target culture—for example, prominent persons or historical events in the culture, or life experiences that are unique to it.

Some items are so inappropriate that they require a complete substitution because the item has different behavioral connotations in the second culture. For example, in the United States the item "I like to cook" is considered a feminine interest item. In Italy, however, cooking is not considered unmasculine and should not be scored in the feminine direction (Rosen, 1958). A literal translation of the item would be linguistically correct but psychologically meaningless. Rosen recommended that such items be replaced by new ones that retain the psychological connotation of the original item but are culturally appropriate.

Special Translation Issues for the MMPI-2 and MMPI-A

The original version of the MMPI had some characteristics that made it difficult to translate into other languages. Because the inventory was constructed in the late 1930s, some of the language used in the items was out-of-date and unfamiliar to many translators. In addition, the MMPI item pool contained a number of items, particularly the religion items and several interest items, that were "culture bound" and not easily translatable into other languages. And some of the original MMPI item content was highly objectionable to people taking the test—for example, items referring to sex or to bowel and bladder habits. Many of these items had, over the years, not proved very useful for assessing clinical problems. In fact, the majority did not score on any of the clinical scales. Among them were several—e.g., "I like Lincoln better than Washington"—that caused translators much difficulty. Another problem for translators was the awkward phrasing and complex syntax of some of the original items.

One aspect of the revision of the MMPI resulting in publication of the MMPI-2 in 1989 (Butcher, Dahlstrom, Graham, Tellegen, & Kaemmer) and the publication of a new version for adolescents, the MMPI-A, in 1992 (Butcher, Williams,

Graham, Archer, Tellegen, Ben-Porath, & Kaemmer) was the revision or elimination of cumbersome, out-of-date, or objectionable items. Translators have discovered that the MMPI-2 and MMPI-A are much easier to translate than was the original MMPI because many troublesome items have been either deleted or modified.

Content Substitution

Even though much of the item content that test-takers found objectionable was eliminated in the MMPI-2 and MMPI-A, there are still a few items (particularly those involving sexual behavior) that prove somewhat problematic in some cultures. For example, in translating the MMPI-2 into Arabic, Soliman wrestled with the question of whether to include items referring to sex in the Arabic version of the MMPI-2 since the topic itself is considered inappropriate for individuals in the target countries. He was unable to find substitutes that would have the same psychological meaning for Arabic test-takers and decided simply to leave the items in the booklet and allow subjects the option of not responding to them if they were offended by the content. Similarly, Kokkevi, in translating the MMPI-A into Greek, considered the item containing "marijuana" to be inappropriate for adolescents since the drug is unavailable in Greece.

There is considerable need for caution in deleting items or radically altering content. Researchers may forget or not be aware of the changes that were made and may be confronted with confusing results simply because the items being compared across cultures are actually different in content and could not be expected to elicit similar endorsement.

Clarification of Qualifying Statements

The MMPI-2 and MMPI-A contain a number of qualifiers that require special care in translating them: "frequently"; "sometimes"; "usually"; "a few"; "every few days or oftener."

Difficult-to-Translate Expressions

Slang or colloquial expressions may be difficult to translate:
Item 91 "muscles twitching and jumping"
Item 158 "put on a stunt"
Item 269 "gossip"
Item 357 "to be in on"
Item 388 "spells of the blues"
Item 393 "keeping people in the dark"
Item 423 "go out of my way"

Double Negatives

Many MMPI items were initially worded with double negatives to balance "true-false" responding (i.e., to avoid having all pathological items endorsed "true"). These items have proved difficult for translators. (Actually, in many languages double negatives are used when in English the single negative occurs. This creates a problem for personality tests that employ a true-false format.) One suggestion for handling double negatives was proposed by Rosen (1958). He recommended that problematic items be clarified by adding an explanation that would reduce the confounding effects of the double negative.

A possible alternative solution to the problem of double negatives involves changing the item from the negative to the positive. Han (1993) conducted an empirical evaluation of this strategy. She reworded many of the double negative statements and administered the alternatively worded statements along with the regular item wording. She concluded that the alternative wording did not satisfactorily convey the meaning of the original items and so retained the double negatives to preserve the equivalent meaning of the Korean and English language forms.

Procedures for Test Translation

Many approaches have been taken in structuring MMPI-2 translation projects, each of which is an attempt to obtain highly equivalent translations for the target language. The chapters in this book will provide details of these different approaches. There are general guidelines that can be followed in developing a translation program that can help ensure that the translation will be equivalent to the original. (See Table 2-1 for a suggested step-by-step procedure for translating the MMPI-2 and MMPI-A.)

Direct Translations

Perhaps the most common approach to translation, particularly for earlier translations of the original MMPI, and by far the least adequate approach is direct translation of the items. The bilingual translator simply translates the material from one language to the other without completing a back-translation to cross-check item meaning. This procedure is limited by the experience, background, and linguistic ability of the translator. A poor translation results if the translator is relatively unskilled in one of the languages, is insufficiently familiar with the culture of either language group, or uses awkward or idiosyncratic language. The direct translation method, especially when it is done by a single translator, is quite likely to result in an inadequate translation. Warnings by Werner and Campbell (1970), Anderson (1967), and Sechrest et al. (1972) against limiting translation efforts to the direct translation approach should be heeded. Unfortunately, this rudimen-

Table 2-1. A Suggested Translation Procedure for the MMPI-2 and MMPI-A

Step one: The translation
In translating the MMPI-2 or MMPI-A, it is desirable to use translators who have a high degree of facility in both English and the target language. (At least five years living in each country or equivalent experience is recommended.)

It is desirable in arriving at a working translation to use at least two translators who independently translate from English to the target language. Care should be taken to ensure that linguistic equivalence is maintained as closely as possible.

Once the initial translators have translated the items, they should discuss their translations and compare the item renderings. In cases where there is disagreement, the translators should discuss the possible meanings and arrive at the "best" translation.

This process should be followed until all items have been agreed upon.

Step two: Back-translation
A back-translation is essential to obtaining an equivalent translation. In the back-translation stage, an independent bilingual translator (experienced in both languages) translates the items back into English.

Step three: Comparison of the English and back-translated versions
The back-translated version of the items should be compared with the English language version to determine if the item meanings have been maintained in the translation. Experience with back-translation of the MMPI-2 suggests that about 10 to 15 percent of the items fail the back-translation evaluation. These items need to be retranslated and again back-translated until the meanings are equivalent.

Step four: Study of equivalency
After a satisfactory translation and back-translation have been completed it is necessary to evaluate the meaning of the test in the new culture. One recommendation is for a *bilingual test-retest study.* This research involves administering the test to individuals in the target language and culture and determining the acceptability and validity of the instrument in the target language.

Step five: Study to determine the adequacy of the American norms
In this step, a study of normals in the target country is conducted to determine how normal (nonclinical subjects) score on the clinical scales. Groups of college students are ideal since they tend to be readily available and, as a group, usually produce relatively normal range MMPI-2 profiles compared with the American norms. Moreover, there is a considerable amount of data available on college student subjects from many countries.

Step six: Development of norms for the target country
If it is determined that the American norms are too different for application in the target country, then a representative sample of nonclinical normals should be collected to serve as a basis for the new norms. The normative sample should be made up of about 500 men and 500 women. Norms should be derived according to the method that generated uniform T scores for the MMPI-2 normative study.

Step seven: Study to determine the utility of the translated instrument in clinical settings
The translated version should be researched in clinical settings to determine if the scales are operating in the target country for clinical assessment as they do in the United States.

tary approach is apparently quite common. The author recently received a telephone call from an appeals judge in the United States asking whether it is appropriate for a psychologist to administer the MMPI-2 by having a bilingual person sit down with a patient and translate the items on the spot as the patient answers them in his or her own language.

Committee Approach to Translation

Many translation projects are team or committee efforts. Including several translators on a project is a useful way of improving a direct translation. A team of bilinguals translate the items independently from one language to the other and, after completing their tasks, collaboratively produce the best composite translation. For example, the translation team in one country (Russia) employed 15 bilinguals in the initial translation phase to obtain the most linguistically equivalent MMPI-2. This approach can be a great improvement over the solitary translator method since it reduces the possibility of error and diminishes the impact of individual biases on the final product. Brislin (1970) observed that this procedure can be flawed if committee members are hesitant to challenge more "powerful" members of the committee or are reluctant to "criticize" each other's work.

Back-Translation Method

Regardless of how the items are originally translated into the target language, a useful method for improving a translation by detecting errors and biases is back-translation. Back-translation, discussed by Butcher and Pancheri (1976), Rosen (1958), Werner and Campbell (1970), Brislin (1970), Sechrest et al. (1972), and Brislin, Lonner, and Thorndike (1973), is recommended as an important step toward developing an equivalent translation. In this procedure, one or more bilinguals translate from the source or carrier language to the target language (and culture). The translated material is then translated back into the source language, most often by different bilinguals. The two versions (the original and the retranslated form) are then compared and checked for discrepancies by a third person (not necessarily a bilingual). If items in the two forms appear to differ in meaning, further translation efforts may be necessary. If the two source-language versions are identical, no additional work is required. Today, back-translation is considered an essential part of any translation project. In our experience over several language translation projects, about 10 to 15 percent of initially translated items require retranslation.

Brislin (1970) cautioned that back-translation might fail to detect some instances of nonequivalence. He pointed out that there are several factors besides good translation that could create apparent equivalence between the source, target, and back-translated versions. For example, translators may share an incorrect set of rules for translating nonequivalent words or phrases; some translators may be particularly adept at making good sense out of a poorly written target version in the back-translation; or the grammatical structure of the source language may be retained in the translation, resulting in a target version that was easy to back-translate but worthless because of the poor sentence structure in the target language.

Sechrest et al. (1972) concluded that back-translation does not necessarily solve all translation problems. Any time a back-translation is done, some discrepancies result. A judgment must then be made about whether the two versions are equivalent. Discrepancies can also occur because the original text is poor. Another possible source of problems is that lack of equivalence may result because a satisfactory word, phrase, or concept does not exist in the target language.

However, most authorities conclude that successive translations and back-translations will result in better approximations of the original text (Butcher & Pancheri, 1976; Sechrest et al., 1972; Triandis et al., 1972; Werner & Campbell, 1979).

Conducting a Pretest Field Study

Conducting a field test of provisional MMPI-2 translations may provide valuable information concerning the understandability and acceptability of the translated test. In the pretest study, an interviewer might select a random sample of items or text and have subjects respond to the content. If time permits, the psychologist might conduct an inquiry about each item. If the respondents' answers or comments are unusual and suggest that the intent of the item is not being conveyed, then further questions could be asked to correct misinterpretation (Brislin, 1970; Mirza, 1976). The field study, particularly if item response data were collected, could also shed light on whether intragroup language or cultural differences produce different reactions to the test content.

An important step in the translation of a personality inventory is the evaluation of item properties as well as the determination of how scales operate. Rosen (1958) suggested that endorsement frequencies be used as an empirical check on translation. The percentage of true responses for each item in the target population could be compared with those of a relevant sample from the source group. Items that have "extreme" endorsement differences could be studied further to determine if the differences are the result of translation problems. The item content could be modified with qualifying phrases, substitutions, etc., to bring the endorsement percentages in line with those of the source population. This is a more appropriate suggestion for empirically developed instruments than for "content" based inventories since endorsement percentage is the building block for scales and indices.

Bilingual Retest Method

An important procedure for evaluating the accuracy and adequacy of a translation of a test such as the MMPI-2 with an established empirical base is the bilingual retest technique. In this method of verifying the adequacy of a translation, both the original English language form and the translated version are administered to a selected group of bilinguals who are familiar with both cultures (Rosen, 1958). This method allows the translation team, using the scores from the two tests, to conduct an alternate form test-retest study (Prince & Mombour, 1967). That is, the resulting test scores can be utilized to contrast scale differences or to compare profile similarity. Moreover, if the bilingual test-retest sample is large enough, analyses could be conducted at the item level to determine if there are discrepant item translations. It is possible then to determine if modifying or eliminating items is required.

A number of past studies have employed some variant of the bilingual procedure to gain information about a translation. Gordon and Kikuchi (1966) noted that this type of analysis was useful if the subjects are sufficiently fluent in both languages and knowledgeable about both cultures. Anderson (1967) found that simply possessing a background in two languages does not mean that the individual thinks similarly in both. The true bilingual not only uses both languages with facility but also uses them independently, linking them for purposes of translation by parallel responses from both languages to various environmental stimuli. However, some bilinguals may have a set of concepts that spans both languages—they may then transfer word meanings from one language to the other, but the true connotations of the concepts as they exist in the two cultures will not be represented.

The bilingual technique for checking translation adequacy of inventory items has been used in a number of studies. Lonner (1967) translated the Strong Vocational Interest Blank into German using a bilingual sample for checking equivalence. He obtained a median correlation of .80 between responses to the SVIB in English and responses in German—the latter respondents were from Germany, Austria, and Switzerland, and were highly fluent in English. He surmised that this evidence, though not conclusive, suggested that the translation was probably equivalent. Spreen and Spreen (1963) used a bilingual sample's responses to MMPI items to revise a German translation of the MMPI that had been done earlier by Sundberg (1956). Other studies (Butcher & Gur, 1974; Glatt, 1969; Manos, 1985) have employed bilingual responses to evaluate translations of the original MMPI. Several translation projects in this book have employed the bilingual test-retest design to evaluate the equivalence of a translation (e.g., Tran, chapter 8; Deinard et al., chapter 9; and Konráòs, chapter 18).

Development of Culturally Appropriate Norms

After a satisfactory translation and back-translation have been completed and the translator/adaptor has determined that the items have been successfully translated, it is necessary to evaluate whether the test works in the new culture as it does in the original. As described above, a *bilingual test-retest study* is likely to provide valuable information about whether the MMPI-2 is measuring the same things in both languages. A number of additional measures can be taken to further evaluate the instrument in the target language. A very valuable evaluation could be obtained by administering the translated version to a sample of normals whose performance on the scales in other countries has been well established. For example, the translated version of the test could be administered to large groups of college students and evaluated against the U.S. norms and against other college students in other countries. Groups of college students are ideal to use in determining the adequacy of the test to measure personality in the target country since they tend to be readily available to many researchers, are accustomed to taking tests, and, as a group, usually produce relatively normal-range MMPI-2 profiles when compared with the American norms. Moreover, a considerable amount of information has accumulated on the MMPI-2 with college student subjects from many countries (see Appendix C).

Another type of investigation could be conducted to further evaluate the MMPI-2 in the target country. The translated version could be administered to patients with known diagnostic problems in clinical settings to determine if the scales are assessing clinically in the target country as they do in the United States.

Development of Norms for the Target Country

If it is determined that use of the U.S. norms in the target country produces results that are too disparate from other known groups, then new norms for the target country should be developed. For this purpose, a representative sample of normals should be collected to serve as a basis for the new norms. It is desirable to have a rather large sample of nonclinical subjects for use in developing the new norms, for example, 500 men and 500 women. Norms should be derived according to the same method that was used to generate the MMPI-2 norms in the United States, that is, uniform T scores for the MMPI-2 normative study (Tellegen & Ben-Porath, 1992). A computer program (called the UT PAK) that can be used to derive uniform T scores in the target culture can be obtained from the University of Minnesota Press.

Summary

This chapter was devoted to exploring the requirement that tests be translated in a manner that produces the most equivalent form of the instrument in the target country. A number of general strategies for test translation, such as decentering, were surveyed and evaluated. The translation strategy for verbal tests like the MMPI-2 and MMPI-A involves keeping the item content in the target version as parallel to the original version as possible. This is an important requirement since the primary goal in the translation program is to capture the same scale meanings in the target language and culture. Therefore, close rendering and linguistic equivalence are seen as desirable when the structure of the language permits. Content deviation is recommended only when no equivalent expressions are present in the target language. A number of practical issues concerning MMPI-2 and MMPI-A item translation were discussed and special problems that occur with some items were highlighted.

Several ways of structuring MMPI-2 and MMPI-A translation projects were discussed. Important requirements in any translation program include performing a back-translation and developing equivalency evaluations such as a field test of item wordings (such as those by Mirza [1976] and Han [1993]) and bilingual test-retest studies (such as those conducted by Butcher & Gur [1974] and Tran [1992]). Moreover, it is important that the translated version be administered to groups in the new culture with known personality or symptomatic characteristics. For example, it is desirable to test groups such as college students or clearly diagnosed patient groups where test performance in other countries has been extensively studied.

The test translator needs to study how the new translation performs in the target culture to determine if new norms need to be developed for the test.

References

Abe, M. (1955). On the personality inventory. *Bulletin of Tohoku Institute of Correctional Science, 1,* 161–162.

Abel, T. (1974). *Psychological testing in cultural contexts.* New Haven: College and University Press.

Anderson, R. (1967). On the comparability of meaningful stimuli in cross-cultural research. *Sociometry, 30,* 124–136.

Brislin, R. W. (1970). Back translation for cross-cultural research. *Journal of Cross-Cultural Psychology, 1,* 185–216.

Brislin, R., Lonner, W. J., & Thorndike, R. M. (1973). *Cross-cultural research methods.* New York: Wiley Interscience.

Brislin, R. W. (1986). The wording and translation of research instruments. In W. J. Lonner & J. W. Berry (Eds.), *Field Methods in cross-cultural research* (pp. 137–164). Beverly Hills: Sage.

Butcher, J. N., & Gur, R. (1974). A Hebrew translation of the MMPI: An assessment of translation adequacy and preliminary validation. *Journal of Cross-cultural Psychology, 5,* 220–228.

Butcher, J. N., & Williams, C. L. (1992). *MMPI-2 and MMPI-A: Essentials of clinical interpretation.* Minneapolis: University of Minnesota Press.

Butcher, J. N., & Pancheri, P. (1976). *A handbook of cross-national MMPI research.* Minneapolis: University of Minnesota Press.

Butcher, J. N., Narikiyo, T., & Vitovsek, K. B. (1992). Understanding abnormal behavior in cultural context. In P. Sutker & H. Adams (Eds.), *Handbook of psychopathology* (2nd ed.) New York: Plenum Press.

Cabiya, J. (1993) Personal communication.

Campbell, D. T. (1968). A cooperative multinational opinion sample exchange. *Journal of Social Issues, 24,* 245–258.

Carlson. R. (1971). Where is the person in personality research? *Psychological Bulletin, 75,* '03-'19.

Cattell, R. B., & Warburton, F. W. (1961). A cross-cultural comparison of patterns of extroversion and anxiety. *Irish Journal of Psychology, 52,* 3–15.

Comrey, A. L. (1960). Comparison of certain personality variables in American and Italian groups. *Educational and Psychological Measurement, 20,* 541–550.

Comrey, A. L., & Nencini, R. (1961). Factors in MMPI responses of Italian students. *Educational and Psychological Measurement, 1,* 657–662.

Draguns, J. G. (1984). Assessing mental health and disorder across cultures. In P. B. Pedersen, N. Sartorius, & A. J. Marsella (Eds.), *Mental health services: The cross-cultural context* (pp. 31–58). Beverly Hills: Sage.

Egli, E. (1991). Bilingual workers. In J. Westermeyer, C. L. Williams, & A. N. Nguyen, (Eds.), *Mental health of refugees* (DHHS Publication No. [AD] 91–824). Washington, DC: U.S. Government Printing Office.

Ervin, S. M., & Osgood, C. E. (1954). Second language learning and bilingualism. *Journal of Abnormal and Social Psychology, 59,* 139–146.

Flaherty, J. A., Gaviria, F. M., Pathak, D., Mitchell, T., Wintrob, R., Richman, J. A., & Birz, S. (1988). Developing instruments for cross-cultural psychiatric research. *Journal of Nervous and Mental Disease, 176,* 257–263.

Fowler, R. D. (1967). Computer interpretation of personality tests: The automated psychologist. *Comprehensive Psychiatry, 8,* 455–467.

Fowler, R. D. (1969). Automated interpretation of personality test data. In J. N. Butcher (Ed.), *MMPI: Research developments and clinical applications.* New York: McGraw-Hill.

Fowler, R. D., & Blaser, P. Around the world in 566 items. Paper given at the 7th Annual Symposium on Recent Developments in the Use of the MMPI, Mexico City, 1972.

Fridja, N., & Jahoda, G. (1966). On the scope and methods of cross-cultural research. *International Journal of Psychology, 1,* 109–127.

Glatt, K. N. (1969). An evaluation of the French, Spanish and German translations of the MMPI. *Acta Psychologica, 29,* 65–84.

Gordon, L. V., & Kikuchi, A. (1966). American personality tests in cross-cultural research: A caution. *Journal of Social Psychology, 69,* 179–183.

Han, K. (1993). Translation and adaptation of the MMPI-2 in Korean. Unpublished doctoral dissertation. University of Minnesota, Minneapolis.

Hathaway, S. R. (March, 1970). Research pertinent to the Spanish American cross-validation of the MMPI. Paper given at the 5th Annual Symposium on Recent Developments in the Use of the MMPI, Mexico City.

Lambert, W., Havelka, J., & Crosby, C. (1958). Language acquisition. *Journal of Abnormal and Social Psychology, 56,* 239–244.

Lonner, W. (1967). Cross-cultural measurement of vocational interests. Unpublished doctoral dissertation, University of Minnesota, Minneapolis.

Manos, N. (1985). Adaptation of the MMPI in Greece: Translation, standardization, and cross-cultural comparison. In J. B. Butcher & C. D. Spielberger (Eds.), *Advances in personality assessment. Volume 4* (pp. 159–208). Hillsdale, NJ: Lawrence Erlbaum Press.

Marsella, A. J., & Kameoka, V. A. (1989). Ethnocultural issues in the assessment of psychopathology. In S. Wetzler (Ed.), *Measuring mental illness: Psychometric assessment for clinicians* (pp. 229–256). Washington, D. C.: American Psychiatric Press.

Mirza, L. (1976). Translation and standardization of the MMPI for Pakistan. In J. N. Butcher and P. Pancheri (Eds.), *A handbook of cross-national MMPI research.* Minneapolis: University of Minnesota Press.

Prince, R., & Mombour, W. A. (1967). A technique for improving linguistic equivalence in cross-cultural surveys. *International Journal of Social Psychiatry, 13,* 229–237.

Putsch, R. W. (1985). Cross-cultural communication: The special case of interpreters in health care. *Journal of the American Medical Association, 254,* 3344–3348.

Rosen, E. (1958). Translation and adaptation of personality tests for use in other cultures. Unpublished manuscript. University of Minnesota.

Sechrest, L., Fay, T., & Zaida, S. (1972). Problems of translation in cross-cultural research. *Journal of Cross-Cultural Psychology, 1,* 41–56.

Spreen, O., & Spreen, G. (1963). The MMPI in a German speaking population: Standardization report and methodological problems of cross-cultural interpretations. *Acta Psychologica, 21,* 265–273.

Sundberg, N. D. (1956). The use of the MMPI for cross-cultural personality study: A preliminary report on the German translation. *Journal of Abnormal and Social Psychology, 52,* 281–283.

Tellegen, A., & Ben-Porath, Y. S. (1992). The new uniform T-scores for the MMPI-2: Rationale, derivation, and appraisal. *Psychological Assessment, 4,* 145–155.

Tran, P. (1992). Unpublished manuscript.

Triandis, H. C., Malpass, R. S., & Davidson, A. R. (1972). Psychology and culture. In P. H. Mussen (Ed.), *Annual Review of Psychology, 24,* 355–378.

Werner, O., & Campbell, D. (1970). Translating, working through interpreters, and the problem of decentering. In R. Naroll and R. Cohen (Eds.), *A handbook of methods in cultural anthropology.* New York: American Museum of Natural History.

Chapter 3

Methods of Establishing Cross-Cultural Equivalence

James N. Butcher and Kyunghee Han

An important goal of cross-cultural psychology is to evaluate the universality or specificity of a psychological concept or to explain differences and similarities in the behaviors of people from different cultures (Poortinga & Malpass, 1986). A fundamental assumption of cross-cultural research is that there is a "dimensional identity" (Frijda & Jahoda, 1966) or "common underlying process" (Campbell, 1964) that encourages researchers to describe cultures in an identical categorical system. This assumption can be confirmed by establishing cross-cultural equivalence (Berry, 1980) of a measurement instrument. Without evidence of equivalence at several different levels, no observed cross-cultural differences can be reliably interpreted.

We will identify and compare four types of equivalence: conceptual, functional, metric, and scalar. A number of methods for evaluating cross-cultural equivalence will also be discussed. The most rigorous of these methods, evaluating factorial similarity (congruence coefficients, factor score correlation, and confirmatory factor analysis) and applying Item Response Theory, will be presented in some detail.

Equivalence in Cross-Cultural Research

Conceptual Equivalence

The first requirement for making cross-cultural comparisons is conceptual equivalence of the constructs involved. For example, the construct "love" is not conceptually equivalent when it means different things in different cultures. Conceptual equivalence is perhaps the vaguest of the types of equivalence because it is the most general. However, several approaches to operationalizing conceptual equivalence have been introduced. Some authors (Irvine & Carroll, 1980; Hui & Triandis, 1983) attempt to explain this equivalence in the context of the construct validation process (Cronbach & Meehl, 1955). A more detailed explanation of the validation of a construct through its nomological network will be discussed later. Important to establishing the cross-cultural equivalence of personality measurement instruments such as the MMPI-2 is the assurance that the underlying dimensions (e.g., traits, symptom patterns) are present in the cultures being compared.

Functional Equivalence

Functional equivalence exists when the function of a behavior is equivalent to that of a behavior in another culture, regardless of whether the manifest behavior is the same (Berry, 1980). For example, the act of smiling in Asia and America lacks functional equivalence because Asians smile frequently when they are embarrassed. In the case of a personality measure such as the MMPI, when personality characteristics measured by one scale are highly related to those measured by another scale in a different culture, it can be said that these two scales, though manifestly different, are functionally equivalent across cultures.

The most commonly used statistical method to evaluate functional equivalence is examination of an instrument's internal structure via inter-item or inter-scale correlations and reduced space analyses (e.g., principal components analysis, factor analysis; Van de Vijver & Poortinga, 1982). Similar correlational patterns or factor structures suggest the same qualitative relationships among variables across cultures (Poortinga, 1989). Concepts with functional equivalence can be considered universal in a qualitative sense, but are not necessarily so in a quantitative sense unless evidence of metric equivalence is obtained across cultures.

Metric Equivalence

Metric equivalence exists when an instrument possesses similar psychometric properties in data obtained from more than one culture. There is little agreement among authors on a precise definition and measurement of metric equivalence. Some authors (e.g., Angoff, cited in Hui & Triandis, 1985; Berry, 1980; Irvine, 1979) define metric equivalence loosely as psychometric properties that are similar in two (or more) sets of data from two (or more) cultures. These authors employ relatively simple methods to evaluate metric equivalence, including: similarity of item difficulty or preference value by rank order or absolute value; item-scale correlations; correlation among rankings of item difficulty or preference (termed the "response pattern method"); and correlations between or factor analysis of items or scales. These authors consider any psychometric data, including inter-item correlations or factor analysis (methods previously discussed as useful for evaluating functional equivalence) as useful for evaluating metric equivalence.

Other authors use metric equivalence in a stricter sense, but it may mean different things. Authors at the University of Illinois have applied Item Response Theory (IRT) to the evaluation of metric equivalence (measurement or item equivalence; e.g., Drasgow, 1984; Hulin, 1987; Hulin, Drasgow, & Parsons, 1983; Hulin & Mayer, 1986), arguing that the above classical statistics depend on sub-populations with different distributions of the traits, which is problematic for the use of these statistics. They argue that the use of classical statistics is appropriate when making within-group comparisons, but not for between-group compar-isons. Van de Vijver and Poortinga (1982) hold that metric equivalence can be es-tablished if one demonstrates that common metrics exist in both cultures. For ex-ample, their conception of metric equivalence requires that the difference between score values of 1 and 11 in culture A is twice the difference between score values of 20 and 25 in culture B. Intracultural score differences can then be compared across cultures, although cross-cultural comparisons of absolute scores may be meaningless. Metric equivalence allows for quantitative comparisons within (or across, according to IRT theorists) cultures. However, it does not allow for absolute value comparisons across the cultures.

One simple means of establishing metric equivalency with an MMPI-2 transla-tion involves studying the item endorsement properties among similar groups of people. In this book, many of the investigators have included item response data on college populations in their countries on the assumption that many demo-graphic factors would be constant for samples of subjects who are attending col-leges or universities in their own country. Item frequency data for a number of these samples are presented in Appendixes B and C. These national samples on which there are comparable data were analyzed in the same way using a computer analysis program developed specifically for that purpose. The computer program, ITCOM, was originally developed in Fortran in collaboration with Paul Mauger for the Butcher and Pancheri (1976) cross-national MMPI handbook. The program was substantially modified for use on an IBM PC by Brad Roper. The ITCOM program provides a comparison of item endorsement percentages for samples from two different groups, giving the researcher a ready picture of the items that are similarly endorsed and those that differentiate the two samples (see Figure 3-1). For example, Figure 3-1 shows how the Dutch normal men (see chapter 16) com-pare with the U.S. male normative sample on item responses. Most of the items are endorsed in a similar direction by both the Dutch and U.S. normals. Item re-sponse differences at or below 25% are considered negligable. Item endorsement data from a number of different countries are reported in Appendix D.

Item comparison data, as discussed in chapter 2, can provide information about possible differences between groups in two different cultures. For example, if re-sponses to an item produce an extremely different endorsement pattern between two cultures, several possible reasons can be further evaluated to (a) determine if the translation of the item has introduced problems that result in extreme item response differences; (b) analyze cultural differences between two groups. Items

```
100
 98  -  99
 96  -  97
 94  -  95
 92  -  93
 90  -  91                    Dutch men (N=681) vs U.S. Normative men (N=1,138)
 88  -  89
 86  -  87
 84  -  85
 82  -  83
 80  -  81
 78  -  79
 76  -  77
 74  -  75
 72  -  73
 70  -  71
 68  -  69
 66  -  67
 64  -  65
 62  -  63
 60  -  61
 58  -  59
 56  -  57
 54  -  55
 52  -  53
 50  -  51  353
 48  -  49
 46  -  47  61
 44  -  45  119
 42  -  43  335
 40  -  41  112  217  269  341  357
 38  -  39  384
 36  -  37
 34  -  35  264  423  449
 32  -  33  153  232  279  373
 30  -  31  100  214  259  359  362  376  458
 28  -  29  220  410  418  420  439  557  560
 26  -  27  29   47   76   89  184  197  487
 24  -  25  50   55  121  199  203  266  272  286  290  297  344  434  456
 22  -  23  87  110  113  130  132  391  396  481
 20  -  21  16   37   41  200  205  284  342  496  504  550
 18  -  19  5   25   35   67   68  107  120  157  287  337  345  385  401  416  422  426  477  541
 16  -  17  10   14   19   51   86  163  178  189  194  209  211  256  293  302  346  350  390  453  511  542
 14  -  15  27   77  109  123  128  137  160  201  215  218  238  285  305  306  347  363  375  398  425
            429  558
 12  -  13  26   45   56   79  103  127  135  141  191  216  225  226  242  245  280  304  330  339  348  354
            366  367  374  377  403  411  430  438  513  525  532  545  556  567
 10  -  11  15   20   21   64   71   85   93  151  185  187  210  251  257  271  274  278  283  301  313  428
            452  464  492  552
  8  -   9  49   80   94  102  115  124  139  174  176  183  230  235  249  263  265  275  281  316  320
            326  328  338  358  361  380  382  399  406  409  427  436  448  460  467  470  474  490  507
            510  521  522  528  533  535  538  543  544
  6  -   7  7   11   18   32   33   43   63   73   83   92  108  118  122  131  167  171  173  181  188  196  206
            221  224  227  228  231  241  248  250  253  254  255  261  268  270  273  299  308  309  318
            321  327  352  379  394  408  412  417  419  443  444  465  473  482  486  488  508  509  531
            537  547  548  551  554  566
  4  -   5  13   17   22   44   46   58   69   82   88   91  104  105  129  140  146  147  148  150  152  154  156
            158  164  169  192  202  207  212  219  223  229  233  237  239  243  244  260  262  267  277
            292  296  310  340  343  349  351  368  372  389  400  407  413  431  433  446  451  459  466
            472  480  483  489  495  499  505  514  534  549  563  564
  2  -   3  6   8    9   12   23   24   30   31   36   39   52   53   54   57   59   66   70   75   78   81   84   95   96  111  114
            116  117  142  145  149  155  159  161  165  168  170  175  180  190  193  195  204  208  234
            240  258  276  288  295  298  300  315  317  319  333  356  360  369  370  371  381  383  388
            393  397  402  404  405  414  415  421  424  435  437  440  441  442  454  455  461  462  463
            471  475  491  494  500  503  506  512  517  518  519  526  527  529  539  540  546  553  559
            561  562  565
  0  -   1  1   2    3    4   28   34   38   40   42   48   60   62   65   72   74   90   97   98   99  101  106  125  126  133
            134  136  138  143  144  162  166  172  177  179  182  186  198  213  222  236  246  247  252
            282  289  291  294  303  307  311  312  314  322  323  324  325  329  331  332  334  336  355
            364  365  378  386  387  392  395  432  445  447  450  457  468  469  476  478  479  484  485
            493  497  498  501  502  515  516  520  523  524  530  536  555
```

Figure 3-1. ITCOM Print-out of Item Response Differences between Dutch Normative Men (N = 681) and American Men (N = 1,138)

that are endorsed very differently by two groups (i.e., greater than 25%) might be studied further to examine potential cultural differences with respect to symptom checking. Two methods have been employed for evaluating extreme item differences with the MMPI. First, the content of the items is analyzed rationally to determine if particular themes characterize the different items. Or, the items might be more formally subjected to a factor analysis (if sample sizes permit) to describe the extreme item differences.

Scalar Equivalence

Scalar equivalence, the most stringent kind of equivalence, is ideally suited to cross-cultural comparison but is the most difficult to achieve. Mean score differences cannot be interpreted as true cultural differences until the researcher has established scalar (i.e., the same degree, intensity, or magnitude) equivalence for the instrument. Scalar equivalence has been established if we can say that, for example, two persons who have MMPI T scores of 75 on the Si scale are socially introverted to approximately the same degree.

Researchers who have developed MMPI-2 translations in other cultures typically assume that the scales are generally equivalent in the target country. That is, translators usually assume that there is "transplant validity" for the scales (Butcher & Garcia, 1978). Scalar equivalence can be demonstrated simply once the translation is complete by administering the inventory to well-defined groups and confirming that the scales are operating properly in the new culture. An important early investigation in the adaptation of a test is to administer the inventory to groups of "normals" to determine whether the scale scores are within the normal range. In some cases (e.g., Norway) the initial administration of the MMPI-2 to normal subjects produced responses so similar to the responses of the U.S. normative sample that developing norms for the Norwegian translation of the MMPI-2 was considered unnecessary. In other countries (for example, Holland) a more traditional normative strategy was followed. Derksen, De Mey, Sloore, and Hellenbosch (1993) computed T scores based on normative data collected in Holland even though the mean scores of the target group of "normals" fell close to the U.S. norms (i.e., within the Standard Error of Measurement).

When comparable groups of "normals" produce similar scale scores, the translator can be somewhat assured that the scales are operating in a similar way in both cultures. It is, of course, desirable with a clinical instrument like the MMPI-2 to further explore scale meanings in clinical samples. In most MMPI-2 translation programs, the cross-cultural practitioner begins to use the instrument with clinical cases immediately—in most cases the inventory was translated to provide clinical information on patients. And in most cases the practitioner simply adopts interpretation strategies and scale meanings for the target culture. Even though this clinical-experiential approach is very valuable for gaining a "clinical feel" for the inventory in the new language and culture, it is desirable to collect more field data to ensure potential test users that the scales are measuring the same clinical constructs in the new culture. It would, for example, be very desirable to test known patient groups such as schizophrenics, depressives, pain patients, or criminals to determine if they perform as similar groups do in the United States (see the empirical evaluation of cross-cultural psychopathology provided by Butcher and Pancheri in 1976 with the original MMPI).

It is important to recognize that these approaches provide only indirect evidence of scalar equivalence. Similar scale scores across groups do not prove identical scale origin and metric. However, the property of scalar equivalence has been notoriously difficult to establish, and more direct techniques (such as Van de Vijver and Poortinga's application of generalizability theory, 1982) have not been widely accepted. Therefore, indirect methods can be employed until agreement exists about more sophisticated techniques.

Multistrategy Approach

Van de Vijver and Poortinga (1982) summarized the differences between the above equivalences in this way:

> In sum, conceptual universals refer to molar, theoretical concepts without any reference to measurement scales; functionally equivalent universals are concepts for which empirical referents have been specified and that are measured in quantitatively the same way in each culture; metrically equivalent universals are concepts that have the same metric but not the same scale origin across cultures, and strictly equivalent universals have the same scale with the same origin in each culture. (p. 391)

It is not easy to draw clear boundaries between the four equivalences because of multiple and ambiguous definitions and multiple and overlapping measurement methods. Hui and Triandis (1985) argue that establishing more abstract types (e.g., conceptual equivalence) is a prerequisite for considering more specific types (e.g., scalar equivalence). According to their arguments, one can first improve an instrument by proper translation techniques, and then establish conceptual equivalence and functional equivalence by constructing a nomological network or by factor analysis. After that, response pattern methods, application of IRT, or regression methods can be used to test item/metric equivalence and scalar equivalence.

The most controversial approach to evaluating conceptual equivalence has been the process of construct validation, as outlined by Cronbach and Meehl (1955). They describe construct validity as the process of forming a nomological network. The construction of this network is accomplished by correlating variables of interest with measures of other psychological constructs. Some researchers attempt to establish conceptual equivalence by showing similar patterns of correlations among variables and constructs in both cultures.

Establishing conceptual equivalence by a nomological network is not simple, however. Suppose one adapts an instrument such as the MMPI into a culture and attempts to establish its conceptual equivalence by correlating each scale with scale scores from the Multidimensional Personality Questionnaire (Tellegen, 1982) or with psychiatric diagnoses (based on the *DSM-IV*). This would require establishing cross-cultural equivalence of the other two instruments. If there are no well-established nomological networks in the source culture, simultaneous development of extensive, fully articulated nomological networks in both cultures is required, which is difficult, perhaps even impossible, in practical terms (Hulin, Drasgow, & Parsons, 1983).

Not only is the above procedure difficult, but little agreement exists about the stage in cross-cultural research at which this method should be used. It is difficult to believe it would be used in the first stage of cross-cultural comparison. If items have been translated unsatisfactorily or if they function differently across cultures, correlations between that variable and external variables would not be similar across the two cultures. For this reason, the above methods might best be used in the final stage of cross-cultural comparison. Drasgow (1984, 1987) makes a noteworthy contribution here. He refers to metric equivalence and construct validation by a nomological network as "measurement equivalence" (defined as identical relations between observed test scores and the latent attribute measured by the test across subpopulations) and "relational equivalence," respectively, and claims that

> Measurement equivalence should be examined first. . . . Equivalence of relations with external variables can be studied if the test provides equivalent measurement. Note that nonequivalent relations with some external variable would not be the fault of the test; test revision would not be appropriate because the test already provided equivalent measurement. (p. 134)

It is probably not fruitful to argue whether a certain method measures either functional equivalence or metric equivalence, or whether a certain method should be used before another method, because it is clear that each is important and complementary to the others. As Malpass and Poortinga (1986) point out, equivalence should be seen as a conceptual rather than as a measurement problem. They argue that it is more important to use multiple methods to evaluate equivalence than to determine which particular method measures which kind of equivalence.

Methods of Measuring Cross-Cultural Equivalence

In recent years, important advances have been made in the development of sophisticated statistical methodologies to evaluate equivalence. Such methodologies include (a) factor similarity indices (Barrett, 1986; Everett & Entrekin, 1980; Eysenck, 1987; Eysenck, Barrett, & Eysenck, 1985; McCormick, Green, & Walkey, 1987; Watkins, 1989), used to examine the similarity of underlying factors across instruments to evaluate functional equivalence; and (b) Item Response Theory (Ellis, Becker, & Kimmel, 1993; Ellis, Minsel, & Becker, 1989; Hulin, 1987;

Hulin, Drasgow, & Parsons, 1983; Hulin & Mayer, 1986), which can be applied to evaluate item equivalence, translation equivalence, and metric or measurement equivalence.

Factor Similarity Indices

The most extensively used method for evaluating equivalence in the area of cross-cultural research on psychological tests is factor analysis (Ben-Porath, 1990; Butcher & Pancheri, 1976; Brislin, Lonner, & Thorndike, 1973; Irvine, 1979). It allows researchers to examine the underlying dimensions (Eysenck & Eysenck, 1983) or latent structure (Davenport, 1990; Poortinga, 1981; Thurstone, 1947) of personality measurements across cultures. If an instrument possesses a different structure across groups, it could be argued that it measures different traits in those groups and it would therefore be meaningless to discuss mean differences (Finn, 1984). Until structural similarity is demonstrated, an adapted test should not be considered a valid indicator (Butcher, Narikiyo, & Vitousek, 1992) and no further evaluative steps should be taken.

In traditional exploratory factor analysis, matrices of factor loadings are visually inspected for similarities. However, subjective inspection may not provide a sufficiently accurate evaluation of similarity. Several authors warn against subjectively determining factor similarity, agreeing that factor convergence must be objectively demonstrated (Barrett, 1986; Ben-Porath, 1990; Hui & Triandis, 1985; Nunnally, 1978; Poortinga, 1989). These authors suggest a number of indices of factor comparison for cross-cultural research. In the following sections, the most common methods for evaluating factor similarity will be discussed: congruence coefficients, factor score correlation, and confirmatory factor analysis.

The Congruence Coefficient. Tucker's congruence coefficient (1951) has been extensively used because its calculation is very simple. Burt (1948) and Wrigley and Newhaus (1955) independently developed the same index under the terms "unadjusted correlation" and "degree of factorial similarity," respectively. This measure is the sum of the cross products of the loadings for the two factors under consideration, divided by the square root of the product of the sums of the squared loadings. The congruence coefficient represents an index of agreement or similarity between two factor loadings, ranging from +1 for perfect agreement (or −1 for perfect inverse agreement) to zero for no agreement whatsoever. If one compares four-factor solutions of a ten-variable instrument between two samples, the computation of the congruence coefficient would involve manipulation of two 10 x 4 matrices, ultimately resulting in a 4 x 4 congruence coefficient matrix. In this final matrix, there are four diagonal values and 12 off-diagonal values.

Although both measure the relatedness of scores on a pair of vectors, the Pearson correlation coefficient and the congruence coefficient are different in two ways. First, in calculating the congruence coefficient, vectors are not deviations from their corresponding means, and summations are made over variables rather than individuals (Derogatis, Serio, & Cleary, 1972; for a more detailed discussion of this point, see Cattell, 1978). Second, the Pearson correlation measures the degree to which vectors are related under permissible transformations for an interval scale, whereas the congruence coefficient measures the degree to which vectors are related under permissible transformations for a ratio scale (Davenport, 1990). Consider as an example the sets of loadings obtained on four variables in Study A and Study B: .2, .3, .1, .5 and .1, .15, .05, .25, respectively. Each factor loading for Study B can be produced by multiplying the corresponding loadings of Study A by .5. In this example, both the Pearson correlation coefficient and the congruence coefficient are equal to one. Consider as a second example two sets of factor loadings whose values are as follows: .2, .3, .1, .5 and .7, .8, .6, 1.0. In this example the points are separated by a constant of .5 (interval scale). The congruence coefficient is now .95, whereas the Pearson correlation coefficient is still equal to one.

There are several drawbacks to the use of congruence coefficients. First, they are insensitive to differences in mean levels of factor loadings because they reflect similarity in terms of the pattern of the columns of factor loadings (Derogatis et al., 1972). Pinneau and Newhaus (1964) also point out that the congruence coefficient tends to overestimate similarity when the sign of all loadings is predominantly the same and the level of the loadings is approximately the same. Several studies have examined the distribution of the congruence coefficient and the effects of various parameters on the magnitude of the congruence coefficient (Davenport, 1990; Korth, 1978; Korth & Tucker, 1975; Nesselroade & Baltes, 1970; Nesselroade, Baltes, & Labouvie, 1971). The results of these studies demonstrate that the size of congruence coefficients varies with number of variables, number of extracted factors, and, to a lesser degree, sample size. Tucker (1951) shows that as the number of factors approaches the number of variables, very high congruence values can be obtained. Therefore, a conservative interpretation of congruence coefficients is required, especially when the difference between the number of factors and variables is small.

Second, the congruence coefficient gives inflated values for noncorrespondent factor pairs. One reason is that the loadings on two orthogonal factors may become correlated after rotation. If intrastructure congruence between factors 1 and 2 for Sample A is high and the structures between Sample A and Sample B are equivalent, it is expected that there would be a similar degree of interstructure congruence between factor 1 for Sample A and factor 2 for Sample B (Davenport, 1990).

Finally, there is a problem with testing for significance (Davenport, 1990). The decision of whether a given congruence coefficient is high had been subjective until Korth and Tucker (1975) developed critical values for making decisions about a given congruence coefficient. According to Davenport (1990), however, too often the magnitude of the congruence coefficient is significant for factors that are known to differ. The formula for the congruence coefficient indicates that it is expected to be zero when the pair of vectors is orthogonal. However, critical values (Korth & Tucker, 1975) were developed for independent vectors, a less stringent condition, which increases the probability of Type I errors. For a more detailed discussion of this point, see Davenport (1990) and Barrett (1986).

The Factor Score Correlations. The factor score correlations, also called the "comparability coefficient" (Everett & Entrekin, 1980), were first suggested by Nunnally (1978). These authors distinguish between factor similarity and factor loading similarity. Factors are linear combinations of variables, whereas factor loadings are correlations of variables with factors. Geometrically, factors are reference vectors placed in the data space; factor loadings represent projections of the variable vectors on the reference vectors. The congruence coefficients measure factor loading similarity and the factor score correlations measure factor similarity.

Factor score correlations are correlations between two sets of factor scores. One set of factor scores is derived from the standard scores and factor score weights from its own sample; the other set of factor scores is derived from standard scores of its own sample, but factor score weights from the other sample are used. This is done for each sample. The average correlation is taken as the factor score correlation for this factor pair. A matrix of factor score correlations is constructed by computing the factor score correlation for each pair of factors across samples.

A more detailed explanation of the computation of the factor score correlation may be helpful here. Factor score correlations are derived in the following manner:

$$\text{Matrix of Factor Score Correlations} = \frac{r\text{FS1,FS1*} + r\text{FS2,FS2*}}{2 \text{ (the number of samples)}},$$

where FS1 = Z1 * FSW1; FS2 = Z2 * FSW2; FS1* = Z1 * FSW2; FS2* = Z2 * FSW1. One matrix of factor scores from sample 1 (FS1) is derived by multiplying standard scores on the variables (Z1) by factor score weights (FSW1) from sample 1. The factor score weight matrix (FSW1) is the product of the factor loading matrix and the inverse of the correlation matrix. The other matrix of factor scores from sample 1 (FS1*) is derived by multiplying the standard score matrix of the variables (Z1) from sample 1 by the factor score weight matrix (FSW2) from sample 2. The two matrices of factor scores for sample 2 can be calculated in the same manner as for sample 1.

One advantage of using factor scores is that, unlike factor loadings, they will be uncorrelated across the factors extracted from the same solution, and thus may present a somewhat clearer convergent-discriminant pattern (Watson, Clark, & Tellegen, 1984).

Confirmatory factor analysis (CFA). A major criticism of the factor comparison methods discussed above is that they tend to give high coefficients of similarity even when substantial differences exist between the matrices (Bijnen, Van der Net, & Poortinga, 1986; Poortinga, 1989). A more promising method in which the fit of data to an a priori specified model is assessed was developed by Jöreskog (1971). This method examines the similarities and differences in factor structures among different groups through maximum likelihood confirmatory factor analysis. This procedure provides a more elegant solution for the problem of relating factors when raw data are available for groups (Gorsuch, 1983).

To use this technique in cross-cultural research, the researcher first needs information about the number of factors that appear repeatedly in the source culture, information about the relationships between these factors, and the size of the factor loadings themselves. The researcher then extracts factors with these predetermined characteristics from the data of the target culture and tests the goodness of fit of the model. A significant chi-square leads to the rejection of the hypothesis that the model fits the data and therefore to the rejection of the hypothesis of equivalent dimensions across cultures. Like any complex statistical technique, there are a number of problems in the use of CFA. The most serious problem intrinsic to CFA concerns the assessment of goodness-of-fit indices that are strongly influenced by sample size (Harris & Harris, 1971; Marsh and Hocevar, 1985; Watkins, 1989). That is, a relatively good fit based on a large sample size may result in a significant chi-square statistic. When there are many variables and degrees of freedom, the chi-square value will nearly always be statistically significant, even when there is a reasonably good fit to the data.

To summarize: The congruence coefficient is easiest to calculate, but it is insensitive to the mean level of loadings and is influenced by the sign of the loadings. The factor score correlation may present a somewhat clearer convergent-discriminant pattern. The CFA is the most involved, but it seems to provide the most sophisticated solution. While it is adequate when a single index of similarity or goodness of fit is all that is required, it is unable to indicate just which factors within the structure are well replicated and which are not. In other words, a factor-by-factor comparison is impossible (Walkey & Green, 1990). Also, the adequacy of the goodness-of-fit test is doubtful. It appears that there is little consensus about the best single index to report the degree of factor similarity. What, then, is the best way to compare factor structures across cultures? Most authors recommend employing several of them simultaneously when comparing factors because each method has drawbacks and advantages.

Application to Studies of the Factor Structure of the MMPI-2

When correlation matrices using non–K-corrected raw scale scores for the three validity and ten clinical scales of the MMPI are subjected to principal components analyses with varimax rotation, four factors typically emerge in U.S. samples. These four factors have been labeled Anxiety (General Psychopathology or General Maladjustment), Repression (Overcontrol), Social Introversion, and Masculinity-Femininity. Cross-cultural studies with the MMPI and the MMPI-2 have also shown that factors derived from samples in other cultures replicate the U.S. factors fairly well when the same factor analytic method is employed (Butcher & Pancheri, 1976; Clark, 1982; Shiota, 1989).

Although MMPI validity and clinical scales have shown fairly stable four-factor structures across cultures, two major problems have been identified concerning cross-cultural factor analysis: limitations of scale-level factor analysis and the failure to use objective factor comparison indices (Ben-Porath, 1990). Several authors (Guilford, 1952; Shure & Rogers, 1965) have warned against using inter-scale factor analysis because MMPI validity and clinical scales are highly correlated with each other owing to item overlap. However, item factor analysis is not always the best solution because it requires extremely large samples and extensive computer resources. Ben-Porath (1990) recommends using intra-scale factor analysis as an alternative. He argues that because MMPI interpretations rely on both single scale elevation and configural relations between the scales, both inter- and intra-scale factor analyses should be conducted in cross-cultural research. Another advantage of using intra-scale factor analysis is that translation errors can be uncovered. If there is a drastic change in loading for an item, it may indicate either translation error or true cultural differences for that item (Eysenck & Eysenck, 1983). In either case, it provides the researcher extra information for evaluating item equivalence.

Conducting an intra-scale factor analysis is not without difficulties. Few authors have attempted to factor analyze each MMPI scale separately (see Comrey, 1957a, 1957b, 1957c, 1958a, 1958b, 1958c, 1958d, 1958e, 1958f; Comrey & Marggraff, 1958). It is necessary to reach agreement regarding the intra-scale factor structures of the MMPI instruments within the United States before cross-cultural comparisons can be made.

A simpler solution than that of item factor analysis or intra-scale factor analysis is the use of MMPI scales that are homogeneous in structure and content. Johnson, Butcher, Null, and Johnson (1984) derived 21 factor scales from the full MMPI item pool using 11,138 psychiatric patients. As one might expect, however, an attempt by Costa, Zonderman, Williams, and McCrae (1985) to replicate this 21-factor solution using normals was not entirely successful because a different type of research sample was used. The Costa et al. (1985) study is the first published study to analyze the entire MMPI item pool with a psychologically normal sample of a large size. They reported nine interpretable components and suggested the use of nine factor scales as MMPI research scales. Unfortunately, neither the 21 factor scales nor the nine factor scales can be used with the MMPI-2 because a number of original MMPI items were deleted in the MMPI-2. In total, 32 items of the 309 items on the 21 factor scales were dropped. As a temporary solution, MMPI-2 content scales may be useful for cross-cultural applications because they are homogeneous, internally consistent, and easily interpretable in terms of content (Butcher, Graham, Williams, & Ben-Porath, 1990).

A final problem with cross-cultural factor analytic research on the MMPI has been the widespread failure to use objective factor comparison indices (Ben-Porath, 1990). Two authors to date have used congruence coefficients to evaluate similarities in factor structures: between the Japanese MMPI and the original MMPI (Clark, 1982); and between the Japanese MMPI-2 and the American MMPI-2 (Shiota, 1989).

Item Response Theory

A number of traditional procedures are useful for examining the quality of a translation: back translation, bilingual responses, item extremity or item endorsement frequencies, descriptive statistics at the scale level, and item loadings on factors. Some argue that no matter how rigorous the translation process or the follow-up using standard testing methods based on classical test theory, the psychometric equivalence of the scales may still be questionable (Ellis et al., 1989; Hulin et al., 1983). Traditional methods do not ensure the adaptation's measurement equivalence, in the sense that individuals with equal standing on the trait measured, but sampled from different subpopulations, have equal expected observed test scores (Drasgow, 1987). Recently, researchers have attempted to apply IRT to the problem of evaluating measurement equivalence of a translation. The following section reviews basic concepts of IRT and outlines steps for applying IRT to the evaluation of translation or item/measurement/metric equivalence of the MMPI-2 across cultures.

Basics of IRT. IRT assumes a specified relationship between a person's response to an item and the trait (in theta units) being measured by the test. This relationship can be expressed graphically in an S-shaped curve, referred to as an item characteristic curve (ICC), which displays the conditional probabilities of response to an item for different levels of the latent trait to be measured. In general, the higher the theta, the greater the probability of a response in a specified direction (Ellis et al., 1989; Weiss & Yoes, 1988).

The three parameters that usually describe this item response function (IRF) are referred to as the "a, b, and c" parameters of the item—the discrimination, difficulty (or extremity), and pseudoguessing parameters, respectively. The "a" parameter is an index of item discrimination and is similar, in some respects, to the item-test correlation of classical test theory. Higher values of "a" are associated with items that are better able to discriminate between trait values. The difficulty parameter ("b") indicates the level of theta necessary for an individual to have a probability of .50 of responding in a given direction to the item. In IRT, high values of item difficulty are associated with items that have low endorsement probabilities. The pseudoguessing parameter ("c") represents the probability of keyed response for individuals with very low trait levels. When we describe a test item in terms of all three parameters, we are using a three-parameter model. If we assume that the c parameter is zero, and use the a and b parameters to describe the IRF, we are using a two-parameter model. When we describe items only in terms of their item difficulties, we have a one-parameter (Rasch) model (Weiss & Yoes, 1988).

IRT requires two specific assumptions before it can be applied to the analysis of item responses. It must be assumed that all items assess a single latent trait, that is, that the item pool is unidimensional. The second assumption is that the probabilities of specified responses at different levels of the underlying trait can be fit adequately by some IRT model.

Applications of IRT to Evaluation of MMPI-2 Measurement Equivalence. The first step in applying IRT to the evaluation of MMPI-2 item/translation/measurement/metric equivalence is to produce unidimensional scales that include as many of the 567 items as possible. Carter and Wilkinson (1984) have applied a one-parameter latent trait model to the MMPI validity and clinical scales. Their analyses showed that poorly fitting items were found on all scales but scale L. Their findings indicate that most of the validity and clinical scales of the MMPI do not satisfy the assumptions of IRT. The MMPI-2 content scales, however, may be likelier candidates for IRT applications because they were developed rationally and were designed to possess high internal consistency (Butcher et al., 1990). Ben-Porath, Waller, Slutske, and Butcher (1988) performed an IRT applicability analysis of the depression (DEP) and cynicism (CYN) content scales, and found that they fit well with a two-parameter logistic model. This suggests that the application of IRT to the MMPI-2 content scales is feasible. However, the MMPI-2 content scales involve only part (323 items) of the MMPI-2 item pool. Thus their examination via IRT does not allow for translation evaluation of a substantial portion of the MMPI-2 item pool. Ultimately, factor scales derived from item factor analysis of the entire item pool will be most useful for IRT application with the MMPI-2.

The second step in IRT application involves an examination of the unidimensionality of each factor scale for each culture. Although research (Dragow & Parsons, 1983) has suggested that IRT is fairly robust to violations of unidimensionality, it is prudent to examine the latent structure of an item pool to ascertain whether it is sufficiently unidimensional to permit further analyses.

To date, two methods have been widely used to assess scale unidimensionality. One method entails examination of the eigenvalues generated by a factor analysis of the reduced matrix of tetrachoric item intercorrelation. If (a) the first eigenvalue is large compared to the second and (b) the second eigenvalue is not much larger than any of the others, then the items are considered relatively unidimensional (Lord, 1980). The second method, referred to as modified parallel analysis (Drasgow & Lissak, 1983), was derived from Humphreys and Montanelli's (1975) parallel analysis, designed to determine the proper number of factors to retain in factor analysis. In modified parallel analysis, eigenvalues of the reduced tetrachoric correlation matrix are first obtained. Then IRT item and person parameters are estimated and used to generate a truly unidimensional data set, termed the "synthetic data" set. Eigenvalues from the correlation matrix of the synthetic data are then obtained and compared to those of the real data set. The difference between the second eigenvalues of the two sets of data is used as an indicator of the extent of multidimensionality in the real data set. The unidimensionality assumption of IRT is considered violated when the second eigenvalue of the real data is substantially larger than the second eigenvalue of the synthetic data (Drasgow & Lissak, 1983).

Third, provided that the item pool of each MMPI-2 scale is sufficiently unidimensional, the researcher must then select an IRT model. If there is a reason to expect response styles to cause individuals with very low trait levels to respond to items in the keyed direction, a three-parameter model might be considered. However, a two-parameter model has been shown to provide reasonably accurate approximations to item response data in the personality domain (Reise & Waller, 1990). A method of checking the fit of a model to actual item response data is discussed in Hulin et al. (1983).

The final stage of IRT application involves fitting the selected IRT model to the cross-cultural data. Computer programs such as LOGIST (Wood & Lord, 1976; Wood, Wingersky, & Lord, 1976), BILOG (Mislevy & Bock, 1986), or BISCAL (Wright & Mead, 1976; for estimating one-parameter models) are used to estimate parameter values. Chi-square statistics are often computed to test the hypotheses simultaneously that the parameters (a, b, and c) are identical across the two groups. If these parameters are similar, an item is said to provide equivalent measurement of the latent trait theta across groups.

If an item has different item characteristics in each cultural sample, it is said to exhibit differential item functioning (DIF; Hambleton & Swanmonathan, 1985;

Lord, 1980). If all items across two translations of a test possess the same item parameters, scale scores from either translation can be compared because they are in the same metric. This, however, does not mean that a given score has the same relative standing in each culture. Different test norms may exist for each culture (Hulin et al., 1983). Further, metric equivalence does not imply conceptual equivalence. It is still necessary to investigate cross-cultural equivalence of the nomological network containing the construct of interest. The goals of using IRT in evaluating translation adequacy are to ensure equivalent observed score metrics across translations and to ensure that any differences in norms have not been created artifactually by the translation process.

When translated items display DIF, there are, in general, two possible sources: (a) translation problems and (b) cultural differences. Hulin proposed that DIF due to item extremity differences indicates translation problems, whereas DIF due to item discrimination differences indicates cultural differences (Hulin, 1987). A study by Ellis et al. (1989) provided some support for this position. DIF items due to translation error can be corrected by retranslating, administering items, and analyzing the effects of retranslation.

Although successful application of IRT produces a test with the property of measurement equivalence, there are at least two major limitations to this approach. First, a very large number of items and subjects are required for stable estimation of parameters (Hulin, Lissak, & Drasgow, 1982). The procedures are also very time-consuming and computation-intensive when applied to an inventory with a large number of items, such as the MMPI-2. The need for intensive examination of 567 pairs of ICCs, retranslation and readministration of DIF items, and reexamination of these ICCs is not easily met, and is hardly an incentive to learn and apply IRT.

Second, IRT application does not provide a definitive explanation for the source of DIF. There are no adequate statistical procedures that will differentiate between the possible causes of discrepancy between ICCs. Like other methods of analysis, deciding whether DIF is due to translation problems or cultural differences rests on subjective judgment. Items with DIF due to translation errors may sometimes be corrected and retested for DIF. If corrections successfully eliminate DIF, the item may return to the item pool, thus maintaining the integrity of the original test. Items with DIF due to cultural differences remain problematic, and caution is needed in interpreting mean scale differences between cultures. Despite these limitations, application of IRT appears to represent a great stride forward in the evaluation of translation equivalence. It is hoped that continuing developments will encourage its use in cross-cultural contexts.

References

Barrett, P. (1986). Factor comparison: An examination of three methods. *Personality and Individual Differences, 7,* 327–340.

Ben-Porath, Y. S. (1990). Cross-cultural assessment of personality: The case of replicatory factor analysis. In J. N. Butcher & C. D. Spielberger (Eds.), *Recent advances in personality assessment: Vol. 8* (pp. 27–48). Hillsdale, NJ: Erlbaum.

Ben-Porath, Y. S., Waller, N. G., Slutske, W. S., & Butcher, J. N. (1988, August). *A comparison of two methods for adaptive administration of MMPI-2 content scales.* Paper presented at the American Psychological Association Annual Convention, Atlanta, GA.

Berry, J. W. (1980). Introduction to methodology. In H. C. Triandis & J. W. Berry (Eds.), *Handbook of cross-cultural psychology: Vol. 2* (pp. 1–28). Boston: Allyn & Bacon.

Bijnen, E. J., Van der Net, T. Z. J., & Poortinga, Y. H. (1986). On cross-cultural comparative studies with the Eysenck Personality Questionnaire. *Journal of Cross-Cultural Psychology, 17,* 3–16.

Brislin, R. W., Lonner, W. J., & Thorndike, R. M. (1973). *Cross-cultural research methods.* New York: Wiley.

Burt, C. L. (1948). The factorial study of temperamental traits. *British Journal of Psychology* (Statistical Section), *1,* 178–203.

Butcher, J. N., & Garcia, R. (1978). Cross-national study of personality. *Personnel and Guidance Journal, 56,* 472–475.

Butcher, J. N., Graham, J. R., Williams, C. L., & Ben-Porath, Y. S. (1990). *Development and use of the MMPI-2 content scales.* Minneapolis: University of Minnesota Press.

Butcher, J. N., Narikiyo, T., & Vitousek, K. B. (1992). Understanding abnormal behavior in cultural context. In P. B. Sutker & H. E. Adams (Eds.), *Comprehensive handbook of psychopathology* (2nd ed., pp. 83–105). New York: Plenum Press.

Butcher, J. N., & Pancheri, P. (1976). *A handbook of cross-national MMPI research.* Minneapolis: University of Minnesota Press.

Campbell, D. T. (1964). Distinguishing differences of perception from failures of communication in cross-cultural studies. In F. S. C. Northrop & H. H. Livingston (Eds.), *Cross-cultural understanding* (pp. 308–336). New York: Harper & Row.

Carter, J. E., & Wilkinson, L. (1984). A latent trait analysis of the MMPI. *Multivariate Behavioral Research, 19,* 385–407.

Cattell, R. B. (1978). *The scientific analysis in behavioral and life sciences.* New York: Plenum Press.

Clark, L. A. (1982). A consolidated version of the MMPI in Japan: Development of the translation and evaluation of equivalence (Doctoral dissertation, University of Minnesota, 1982). *Dissertation Abstracts International, 42,* 2702B.

Comrey, A. L. (1957a). A factor analysis of the items on the MMPI hypochondriasis scale. *Educational and Psychological Measurement, 17,* 568–577.

Comrey, A. L. (1957b). A factor analysis of the items on the MMPI depression scale. *Educational and Psychological Measurement, 17,* 578–585.

Comrey, A. L. (1957c). A factor analysis of the items on the MMPI hysteria scale. *Educational and Psychological Measurement, 17,* 586–592.

Comrey, A. L. (1958a). A factor analysis of the items on the MMPI F scale. *Educational and Psychological Measurement, 18,* 621–632.

Comrey, A. L. (1958b). A factor analysis of the items on the MMPI K scale. *Educational and Psychological Measurement, 18,* 633–639.

Comrey, A. L. (1958c). A factor analysis of the items on the MMPI psychopathic deviate scale. *Educational and Psychological Measurement, 18,* 91–98.

Comrey, A. L. (1958d). A factor analysis of the items on the MMPI paranoia scale. *Educational and Psychological Measurement, 18,* 99–107.

Comrey, A. L. (1958e). A factor analysis of the items on the MMPI psychasthenia scale. *Educational and Psychological Measurement, 18,* 293–300.

Comrey, A. L. (1958f). A factor analysis of the items on the MMPI hypomania scale. *Educational and Psychological Measurement, 18,* 313–323.

Comrey, A. L., & Marggraff, W. (1958). A factor analysis of the items on the MMPI schizophrenia scale. *Educational and Psychological Measurement, 18,* 301–311.

Costa, P. T., Zonderman, A. B., Williams, R. B., Jr., & McCrae, R. R. (1985). Content and comprehensiveness in the MMPI: An item factor analysis in a normal adult sample. *Journal of Personality and Social Psychology, 50,* 289–296.

Cronbach, L. J., & Meehl, P. E. (1955). Construct validity in psychological tests. *Psychological Bulletin, 52,* 281–302.

Davenport, E. C., Jr. (1990). Significance testing of congruence coefficients: A good idea? *Educational and Psychological Measurement, 50,* 289–296.

Derksen, J., De Mey, H., Sloore, H., & Hellenbosch, G. (1993). *MMPI-2: Handleiding bij afname, scoring en interpretatie.* Nijmegen: The PEN Test Publishers.

Derogatis, L. R., Serio, J. C., & Cleary, P. A. (1972). An empirical comparison of three indices of factorial similarity. *Psychological Reports, 30,* 791–804.

Drasgow, F. (1984). Scrutinizing psychological tests: Measurement equivalence and equivalent relations with external variables are the central issues. *Psychological Bulletin, 95,* 134–135.

Drasgow, F. (1987). Study of the measurement bias of two standardized psychological tests. *Journal of Applied Psychology, 72,* 19–29.

Drasgow, F., & Lissak, R. I. (1983). Modified parallel analysis: A procedure for examining the latent dimensionality of dichotomously scored item responses. *Journal of Applied Psychology, 68,* 363–373.

Drasgow, F., & Parsons, C. K. (1983). Application of unidimensional item response theory models to multidimensional data. *Applied Psychological Measurement, 7,* 189–199.

Ellis, B. B., Becker, P., & Kimmel, H. D. (1993). An item response theory evaluation of an English version of the Trier Personality Inventory (TPI). *Journal of Cross-Cultural Psychology, 24,* 133–148.

Ellis, B. B., Minsel, B., & Becker, P. (1989). Evaluation of attitude survey translations: An investigation using item response theory. *International Journal of Psychology, 24,* 665–684.

Everett, J. E., & Entrekin, L. V. (1980). Factor comparability and the advantages of multiple group factor analysis. *Multivariate Behavioral Research, 15,* 165–180.

Eysenck, H. J. (1987). Cross-cultural comparisons: The validity of assessment by indices of factor comparison. *Journal of Cross-Cultural Psychology, 17,* 506–515.

Eysenck, H. J., Barrett, P., & Eysenck, S. B. G. (1985). Indices of factor comparison for homologous and non-homologous personality scales in 24 different countries. *Personality and Individual Differences, 6,* 503–504.

Eysenck, H. J., & Eysenck, S. B. G. (1983). Recent advances in the cross-cultural study of personality. In J. N. Butcher & C. D. Spielberger (Eds.), *Advances in personality assessment: Vol. 2* (pp. 41–69). London: Erlbaum.

Finn, S. E. (1984). A partial cross-sequential analysis of personality ratings on 400 men (Doctoral dissertation, University of Minnesota, 1984). *Dissertation Abstracts International, 45,* 2685B.

Frijda, N. H., & Jahoda, G. (1966). On the scope and methods of cross-cultural research. *International Journal of Psychology, 1,* 110–127.

Gorsuch, R. L. (1983). *Factor analysis* (2nd ed.). Hillsdale, NJ: Erlbaum.

Guilford, J. P. (1952). When not to factor analyze. *Psychological Bulletin, 49,* 26–37.

Hambleton, R. K., & Swanmonathan, H. (1985). *Item response theory: Principles and the applications.* Boston: Kluwer-Nijhoff.

Harris, M. L., & Harris, C. W. (1971). A factor analytic interpretation strategy. *Educational and Psychological Measurement, 31,* 589–606.

Hui, C. H., & Triandis, H. C. (1983). Multistrategy approach to cross-cultural research: The case of locus of control. *Journal of Cross-Cultural Psychology, 14,* 65–83.

Hui, C. H., & Triandis, H. C. (1985). Measurement in cross-cultural psychology: A review and comparison of strategies. *Journal of Cross-Cultural Psychology, 16,* 131–152.

Hulin, C. L. (1987). A psychometric theory of evaluation of item and scale translations: Fidelity across languages. *Journal of Cross-Cultural Psychology, 18*, 115–142.

Hulin, C. L., Drasgow, F., & Parsons, C. K. (1983). *Item response theory: Application to psychological measurement.* Homewood, IL: Dow Jones Irwin.

Hulin, C. L., Lissak, R. I., & Drasgow, F. (1982). Recovery of two- and three-parameter logistic item characteristic curves: A Monte Carlo study. *Applied Psychological Measurement, 6*, 249–260.

Hulin, C. L., & Mayer, L. J. (1986). Psychometric equivalence of a translation of the job descriptive index into Hebrew. *Journal of Applied Psychology, 71*, 894.

Humphreys, L. G., & Montanelli, R. G., Jr. (1975). An investigation of the parallel analysis criterion for determining the number of common factors. *Multivariate Behavioral Research, 10*, 193–205.

Irvine, S. H. (1979). The place of factor analysis in cross-cultural methodology and its contribution to cognitive theory. In L. H. Eckensberger, W. L. Lonner, & Y. H. Poortinga (Eds.), *Cross-cultural contributions to psychology: Vol. 2* (pp. 300–341). Amsterdam: Swets & Zeitlinger.

Irvine, S. H., & Carroll, W. K. (1980). Testing and assessment across cultures: Issues in methodology and theory. In H. C. Triandis & J. W. Berry (Eds.), *Handbook of cross-cultural psychology: Vol. 2* (pp. 181–244). Boston: Allyn & Bacon.

Johnson, J. H., Butcher, J. N., Null, C., & Johnson, K. N. (1984). Replicated item level factor analysis of the full MMPI. *Journal of Personality and Social Psychology, 47* (1), 105–114.

Jöreskog, K. G. (1971). Simultaneous factor analysis in several populations. *Psychometrika, 36*, 409–426.

Korth, B. A. (1978). A significance test for congruence coefficients for Cattell's factors matched by scanning. *Multivariate Behavioral Research, 13*, 419–430.

Korth, B. A., & Tucker, L. R. (1975). The distribution of chance congruence coefficients from simulated data. *Psychometrika, 40*, 361–372.

Lord, F. (1980). *Applications of item response theory to practical testing problems.* Hillsdale, NJ: Erlbaum.

Malpass, R. S., & Poortinga, Y. H. (1986). Strategies for design and analysis. In W. J. Lonner & J. W. Berry (Eds.), *Field methods in cross-cultural research* (pp. 47–84). Newbury Park, CA: Sage.

Marsh, H. W., & Hocevar, D. (1985). Application of confirmatory factor analysis to the study of self-concept: First- and higher order factor models and their invariance across groups. *Psychological Bulletin, 97*, 562–582.

McCormick, I. A., Green, D. E., & Walkey, F. H. (1987). A multiple replication of the Eysenck Personality Inventory identified using a two-step confirmation and the factor replication procedure, FACTOREP. *Personality and Individual Differences, 8*, 285–287.

Mislevy, R. J., & Bock, R. D. (1986). PC BILOG: Item analysis and test scoring with binary logistic models [Computer program]. Mooresville, IN: Science Software.

Nesselroade, J. R., & Baltes, P. B. (1970). On a dilemma of comparative factor analysis: A study of factor matching based on random data. *Educational and Psychological Measurement, 30*, 935–948.

Nesselroade, J. R., Baltes, P. B., & Labouvie, E. W. (1971). Evaluating factor invariance in oblique space: Baseline data generated from random numbers. *Multivariate Behavioral Research, 6*, 233–241.

Nunnally, J. C. (1978). *Psychometric theory* (2nd ed.). New York: McGraw-Hill.

Pinneau, S. R., & Newhaus, A. (1964). Measures of invariance and comparability in factor analysis for fixed variables. *Psychometrika, 29*, 271–281.

Poortinga, Y. H. (1981). Psychometric approaches to intergroup comparison: The problem of equivalence. In S. H. Irvine & J. W. Berry (Eds.), *Human assessment and cultural factors* (pp. 237–257). New York: Plenum Press.

Poortinga, Y. H. (1989). Equivalence of cross-cultural data: An overview of basic issues. *International Journal of Psychology, 24*, 737–756.

Poortinga, Y. H., & Malpass, R. S. (1986). Making inferences from cross-cultural data. In W. J. Lonner & J. W. Berry (Eds.), *Field methods in cross-cultural research* (pp. 17–46). Newbury Park, CA: Sage.

Reise, S. P., & Waller, N. G. (1990). Fitting the two-parameter model to personality data. *Applied Psychological Measurement, 14*, 44–58.

Shiota, N. K. (1989). Japanese MMPI-2: Inventory adaptation and equivalence evaluation using Japanese and American college samples (Doctoral dissertation, University of Minnesota, 1989). *Dissertation Abstracts International, 50,* 5335B.

Shure, G. H., & Rogers, M. S. (1965). Note of caution on the factor analysis of the MMPI. *Psychological Bulletin, 63,* 14–18.

Tellegen, A. (1982). *Brief manual for the differential personality questionnaire.* Minneapolis: University of Minnesota Press.

Thurstone, L. L. (1947). *Multiplefactor analysis: A development and expanding of the vectors of mind.* Chicago: University of Chicago Press.

Tucker, L. R. (1951). *A method for synthesis of factor analysis studies.* Personal Research Section Report No. 984. Washington, DC: Department of the Army.

Van de Vijver, F. J. R., & Poortinga, Y. H. (1982). Cross-cultural generalization and universality. *Journal of Cross-Cultural Psychology, 13,* 387–408.

Walkey, F. H., & Green, D. E. (1990). The factor structure of the Eysenck Personality Inventory revealed in the responses of Australian and New Zealand subjects. *Personality and Individual Differences, 11,* 571–576.

Watkins, D. (1989). The role of confirmatory factor analysis in cross-cultural research. *Journal of Psychology, 24,* 685–701.

Watson, D., Clark, L. A., & Tellegen, A. (1984). Cross-cultural convergence in the structure of mood: A Japanese replication and a comparison with U. S. findings. *Journal of Personality and Social Psychology, 47,* 127–144.

Weiss, D. J., & Yoes, M. E. (1988). Item response theory. In R. K. Hambleton & J. Zaal (Eds.), *New developments in testing: Theory and applications.* North-Holland Publishing Company.

Wood, R. L., & Lord, F. M. (1976). *A user's guide to Logist* (Research memorandum 76–4). Princeton, NJ: Educational Testing Service.

Wood, R. L., Wingersky, M. S., & Lord, F. M. (1976). Logist-A computer program for estimating examinee ability and item characteristic curve parameters [Computer program]. Princeton, NJ: Educational Testing Service. (Research memorandum 76-6)

Wright, B. D., & Mead, R. J. (1976). BISCAL: Calibrating rating scales with the Rasch model [Computer program]. Chicago: Chicago Statistical Laboratory, Department of Education, University of Chicago. (Research memorandum, no. 23)

Wrigley, C. S., & Newhaus, J. O. (1955). The matching of two sets of factors. *American Psychologist, 10,* 418–419.

Part II

Adaptations in Asia and Southeast Asia

Chapter 4

Adaptation and Validation of the Japanese MMPI-2

Noriko K. Shiota, Steven S. Krauss, and Lee Anna Clark

The original MMPI became one of the most widely used assessment instruments throughout the world (Butcher & Pancheri, 1976; Butcher & Spielberger, 1985; Lubin, Larsen, & Matarazzo, 1984; Lubin, Larsen, Matarazzo, & Seever, 1985; Piotrowski & Lubin, 1990). With its revision and reintroduction as the MMPI-2 (Butcher, Dahlstrom, Graham, Tellegen, & Kaemmer, 1989), a new era in the rich history of the MMPI has begun both in the United States and internationally. To further the international transition into this new era, we adapted the MMPI-2 for use with the Japanese. In this chapter we describe how the Japanese MMPI-2 was developed and present data evaluating its psychometric equivalence to the U.S. MMPI-2.

Development of the Japanese MMPI-2 follows a long and prolific tradition of adapting the MMPI for use in Japan. The first translation of the original MMPI was done in 1950, within a decade of its publication in the United States (Clark, 1985). Since then, as many as 15 different Japanese translations or adaptations have been produced (Hidano, cited in Butcher & Pancheri, 1976). However, most of these Japanese versions did not follow currently accepted practices for adapting a psychological instrument for cross-cultural use, and rarely was there any attempt to demonstrate a translation's psychometric equivalence to the original MMPI. Without establishing such equivalence, the meaningfulness of any cross-cultural comparisons using one of these instruments remained in doubt. Moreover, the ex-

This chapter is based on a dissertation submitted to the University of Minnesota in partial fulfillment of the requirements for the degree of Doctor of Philosophy. The research was supported in part by the Jessamine-Allen Dissertation Grant from the University of Minnesota, the MMPI-2 Restandardization Project, and a grant from the University of Minnesota Computer Center. We wish to thank Professor Tadashi Hidano for his invaluable assistance. Thanks also goes to James Butcher for his generous support and encouragement and to Chizuko Saeki for her help in evaluating the Japanese translation.

istence of so many versions with different psychometric properties slowed the advance of MMPI research in Japan because comparisons across studies were difficult to make.

In 1979, many of the Japanese MMPI translators and researchers in Japan, along with MMPI researchers from the United States, met in Japan to discuss the several issues that arise from having multiple versions of the MMPI (Clark, 1985). Overall, the conferees agreed that having a single, reliable, and well-validated Japanese version of the MMPI would be both useful and desirable. They therefore agreed to cooperate with research efforts to compare existing translations, with the further goal of producing a version that combined the strongest aspects of each. The result of this research was the Consolidated Version of the Japanese MMPI (see Clark, 1985, for further details regarding the development of this instrument). Clark subsequently demonstrated that the Consolidated Version is conceptually equivalent to the original MMPI and is reliable for use in cross-cultural and clinical investigations (Clark, 1985). The Japanese MMPI-2 draws heavily on the advances made in the Consolidated Version and, therefore, can be considered an extension of it.

Adaptation Procedure

The present study was conducted concurrently with the U.S. MMPI Restandardization Project, and therefore used both the experimental version of the MMPI-2 (MMPI-AX) and the Biographical and Life Events questionnaires used in that project. The MMPI-AX contained 704 items: 550 from the original MMPI, of which 82 were reworded, and 154 new provisional items. The Japanese adaptation of the MMPI-2 was, therefore, derived from the Japanese translation of the MMPI-AX. The two supplementary instruments were also translated into Japanese and used to elicit detailed information on demographic background and recent life changes. The following section describes the adaptation procedures and the methods used for data collection.

MMPI-2

The translation of the MMPI-2 into Japanese and the evaluation of the translation's psychometric equivalence to the original closely followed the procedures recommended by cross-cultural methodologists for culturally adapting an inventory (Berry, 1980; Brislin, Lonner, & Thorndike, 1973; Butcher & Clark, 1979; Butcher & Pancheri, 1976). The translation took into account both the linguistic and conceptual equivalence of the items. However, when these two considerations conflicted, conceptual equivalence was given priority over linguistic equivalence. Moreover, maximizing understandability and "naturalness" in Japanese was considered very important.

With these principles in mind, the 154 provisional items of the MMPI-AX were translated by the first author (NKS). Another bilingual Japanese psychologist independently evaluated the accuracy and naturalness of the translations and suggested modifications. The translations were then evaluated by two bilingual psychologists, one Japanese and one American, and a few items were further reworded to make them sound even more natural. The 550 original items had been translated previously into Japanese and field tested for the Consolidated Version of the Japanese MMPI (Clark, 1985). Therefore, these items were not retranslated for this study; the Consolidated Version translations of them were used.

No newly translated items needed drastic cultural adaptation. However, some items needed elaboration or clarification while others required minor adjustments. For example, "I really like playing rough sports (such as football or soccer)" was elaborated in Japanese to include " . . . (such as soccer, rugby, or American football)" because in Japan rugby is popular and football is known as "American football." Another item, "I have a drug or alcohol problem," was changed to read "I have a problem with drugs or alcohol and am troubled by it." This was done because prior work on the Consolidated Version showed that this type of change produces similar item endorsement frequencies between Japanese and Americans, whereas a direct translation does not.

The accuracy of the final translation of the Japanese MMPI-2 was evaluated in two back-translation studies into English. The Japanese items were first submitted to four Japanese bilinguals for back-translation, with each person taking a part of the task. The two English versions—the original English items and the items back-translated into English from Japanese—were then compared for discrepancies. No discrepancies due to inaccurate translation were noted. However, as expected, minor differences emerged in which the back-translation used synonyms or similar phrases rather than the exact wording of the original item. A second back-translation study in which the items were submitted to two bilinguals, one Japanese and one American, produced results similar to the first study and again identified no discrepancies due to inaccurate translation of the items into Japanese.

The Biographical and Life Events Questionnaires

The Biographical and Life Events questionnaires were translated by the first author and checked for accuracy by a bilingual Japanese psychologist. These forms were not subject to the rigorous adaptation work described above since they were fairly brief and their content was straightforward. The Biographical Questionnaire asked for information on personal and family background, and the Life Events Questionnaire inquired about life changes within the past six months. The life changes included events that are very stressful, such as the death of a spouse or family member, as well as less stressful events, such as a change in social activities or recreation. Because some of the Japanese psychologists who consulted on the study found certain items in these questionnaires to be excessively invasive by Japanese standards or irrelevant for the college students who were to serve as subjects, shortened forms of the questionnaires were prepared. These short forms were used by schools that declined the use of the full forms.

Data Collection

The MMPI-AX and the Biographical and Life Events questionnaires were administered to a sample of Japanese college students and results were compared to those from an American college sample.

Exclusion Criteria

An identical set of exclusion criteria were used for the Japanese and American samples. A subject's protocol was excluded if (1) one of the three forms was incomplete or missing, (2) MMPI results indicated invalidity, or (3) subjects were currently in psychiatric treatment. Invalidity was determined through the use of three indicators: (1) omission of 15 or more items, (2) scoring 25 or higher on the standard F scale, or (3) scoring 25 or higher on the F Back (F_B) Scale.

Japanese sample

Data were collected from an initial sample of 1,356 Japanese college students from eight universities and colleges in the metropolitan Tokyo area: Aoyama University, Gakushuin University, International Christian University, Jitsen Women's College, Keio University, Komazawa University, Meiji University, and Tsuda School of Business. The MMPI-AX was printed in a booklet form and standard MMPI instructions were used. Subjects' protocols were identified by numbers; no names were obtained and all information was kept confidential. Test administration for the Japanese sample was done during class time; the length of the classes varied from school to school, but most classes lasted approximately 1 and 1/2 hours. Although most of the subjects were able to complete the materials during the allotted time, 8% of the subjects were not able to complete all the questionnaires. Subjects were not allowed to take the forms with them to complete elsewhere. Applying the exclusion criteria outlined above eliminated 18% (n = 232) of the initial sample. Thus, the final Japanese sample consisted of 1,070 subjects: 563 men (52.62%) and 507 women (47.38%). The mean age for the men was 20.63 (s.d. = 1.74; range = 18–36) and the mean age for the women was 19.79 (s.d. = 1.48; range = 18–37).

American Sample

The comparison group for the current study initially consisted of 1,513 American college students who participated in the U.S. MMPI Restandardization Project.

Data for the project was collected at four American academic institutions: Kent State University, the University of Minnesota, the University of North Carolina, and the United States Naval Academy (Butcher, Graham, & Dahlstrom, 1989; Butcher, Graham, Dahlstrom, & Bowman, 1989; Butcher, Graham, Dahlstrom, & Bowman, 1990). The exclusion criteria eliminated 13% (n = 210) of the initial sample. The final American sample consisted of 1,312 individuals: 515 men (39%) and 797 women (61%). The mean age for the men was 19.77 (s.d. = 2.39; range = 17–37) and the mean age for the women was 19.82 (s.d. = 3.42; range = 17–48).

Sample Differences

Although the two national samples were similar in age, they differed in gender distribution, with the Japanese having approximately equal numbers of men and women and the U.S. sample having more women than men. Additional differences from the Biographical and Life Events questionnaires were found for both alcohol and drug use (Shiota, 1989/1990). The level of alcohol consumption was less for the Japanese subjects than the American subjects, especially for the women. Although the question was not asked of every Japanese subject, drug use among the Japanese college students nonetheless appears to be considerably lower than among the Americans.

Results and Discussion

The Japanese MMPI-2 was examined at three conceptual levels—the item, the scale, and the factorial structure—and the Japanese data were compared to those from the U.S. college sample to determine the psychometric equivalence of the Japanese and original MMPI-2. The Japanese MMPI-2 was also compared to the Consolidated Version of the Japanese MMPI to examine the effects due to revising the MMPI. Further, because the items forming the validity and ten clinical scales remained nearly identical between the Consolidated Version and the Japanese MMPI-2, comparing these versions can also be viewed as a replication of previous MMPI findings among Japanese college students.

Scale Level Comparisons

To investigate the equivalence of the Japanese and original MMPI-2, it is first necessary to compare group profile means and standard deviations. The scale level comparisons were done on three sets of scales: (1) basic validity and clinical scales, (2) supplementary scales, and (3) newly developed content scales.

Basic Validity and Clinical Scales. As presented in Table 4-1, the MMPI-2 basic scale means and standard deviations for the Japanese men and women are highly similar. Examination of the mean profiles based on K-corrected T scores for males

Table 4-1. MMPI-2 Basic Scales Means and Standard Deviations for a Japanese College Sample

Scale	Men (N = 563)		Women (N = 507)	
	Mean	S.D.	Mean	S.D.
L	3.45	2.22	3.31	2.11
F	6.14	4.12	5.41	3.71
K	15.09	4.97	14.73	4.55
Hs	6.36	4.11	6.31	4.16
D	20.12	5.56	20.94	5.32
Hy	22.34	4.90	22.26	4.61
Pd	18.26	4.58	17.59	4.52
Mf	27.12	4.07	33.75	3.94
Pa	11.40	3.46	11.11	3.41
Pt	15.37	7.71	15.57	7.90
Sc	15.79	8.23	15.30	8.15
Ma	17.58	4.60	17.22	4.20
Si	27.35	8.70	28.31	8.42

Note: Values are raw scores without K-correction.

(Figure 4-1) and females (Figure 4-2) shows that all scales lie close to a T score of 50, with only Pt and Sc for men and F, Mf, and Sc for women deviating more than 5 T scores from this value. However, the largest T score is still a modest 58. Therefore, unlike the high elevations on most earlier Japanese adaptations of the MMPI (Clark, 1985), the present scales are well within the normative T-score range for both men and women.

The basic validity and clinical scale profiles for the Japanese and American college samples were also very similar. Figures 4-3 and 4-4 show the group mean profiles for the American men and women, respectively. Comparing the male groups between the national samples, scales Ma and D showed the largest differences, with a gap of close to 7 T scores. Although relatively small, these may reflect actual cultural differences. Japanese men, lower on Ma and higher on D, may be less active and energetic relative to their college-aged peers in the United States. The largest difference between the two female groups was also observed on Ma, with the American women scoring 4 T scores higher than the Japanese. As with the men, this difference suggests that Japanese women may also be less active and energetic than college women in the U.S. However, it should be noted that scale Ma for both Japanese groups was well within the normative range and did not deviate meaningfully from a T score of 50.

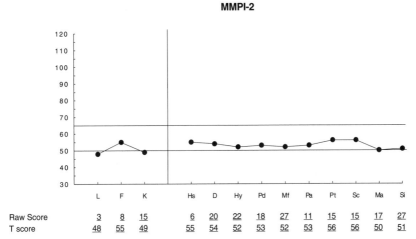

Figure 4-1. Group Mean K-Corrected MMPI-2 Profile for Japanese Men

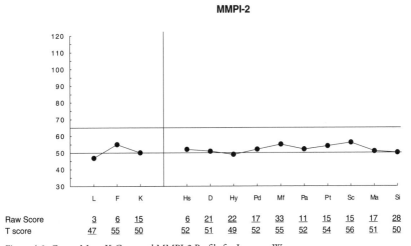

Figure 4-2. Group Mean K-Corrected MMPI-2 Profile for Japanese Women

When comparing the basic scales across the two Japanese versions of the MMPI—the Consolidated Version and the Japanese MMPI-2—most scales differed by only 1 or 2 raw score points and the group mean profiles were very similar (Figures 4-5 and 4-6 present the Consolidated Version group mean profiles for men and women respectively). Thus, although not on the same individuals, the similarity in scale means and standard deviations of the two versions suggests that the basic scales of the MMPI are highly replicable across Japanese college student samples.

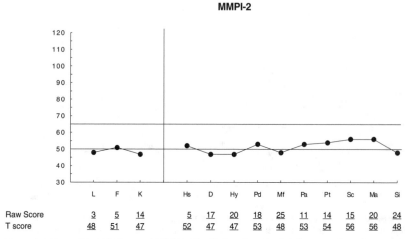

Figure 4-3. Group Mean K-Corrected MMPI-2 Profile for a Sample of College Men from the United States (Butcher et al., 1990)

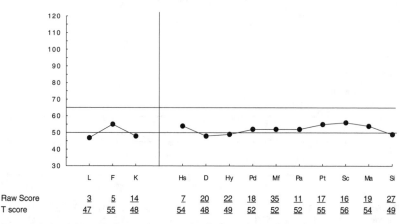

Figure 4-4. Group Mean K-Corrected MMPI-2 Profile for a Sample of College Women from the United States (Butcher et al., 1990)

Supplementary Scales. As presented in Table 4-2, comparisons of the supplementary scales between the Japanese men and women showed that the raw scores differed across gender by no more than 2 points on any scale, and on eight scales—Repression (R), F Back (F$_B$), True Response Inconsistency (TRIN), Variable Response Inconsistency (VRIN), Over-Controlled Hostility (O-H), Dominance (Do), Social Responsibility (Re), and College Maladjustment (Mt)—the raw score means were nearly identical. The standard deviations of the supplementary scales were also quite similar across gender.

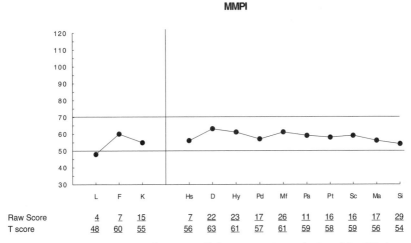

Figure 4-5. Group Mean K-Corrected MMPI Profile for Japanese Men on the Consolidated Version

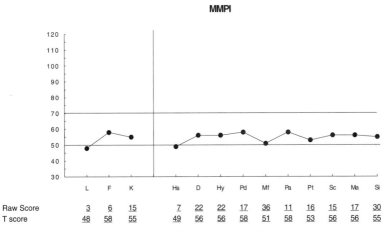

Figure 4-6. Group Mean K-Corrected MMPI Profile for Japanese Women on the Consolidated Version

The Japanese and American samples also showed similar raw score means and standard deviations and similar T scores on the MMPI-2 supplementary scales. The only scales that showed a between-nation difference of greater than 2 points were R and F_B. The Japanese men were 3.70 and the women 2.45 higher on R than their American counterparts. Similarly, the Japanese men were 2.95 and women 2.47 higher on F_B than their American counterparts. This difference on F_B could be due to the pressure that some Japanese students may have experienced as they rushed to complete the MMPI-2 in the allotted time. However, all group means for both national samples were within normal limits.

Table 4-2. MMPI-2 Supplementary Scales Means and Standard Deviations
for a Japanese College Sample

| Scale | Men (N = 563) | | Women (N = 507) | |
	Mean	S.D.	Mean	S.D.
A	13.97	7.98	15.14	8.16
R	17.20	4.57	17.54	4.00
Es	35.44	5.39	33.77	5.03
Mac-R	20.26	3.66	19.11	3.33
F_B	5.83	3.97	5.69	3.85
TRIN	7.38	1.80	7.59	1.62
VRIN	7.41	3.24	7.05	2.70
O-H	12.37	2.86	12.81	2.69
Do	14.93	2.93	14.88	2.71
Re	19.44	3.26	20.00	3.03
Mt	14.47	7.03	14.77	7.29

Note: Values are raw scores.

Content Scales. As presented in Table 4-3, the Japanese men and women scored similarly on the 15 new content scales with all but one scale, Fears (FRS), differing by less than 1 raw score point and 3 T-score points. Even on FRS, the difference was only 2 raw score and 4 T-score points. Furthermore, T scores for all scales were between 49 and 59 for both genders, indicating that the Japanese groups do not deviate clinically when the MMPI-2 American norms are applied.

Between the two national groups, many scales showed very similar means and only slight differences. Scales that showed the most difference between the two groups of males were Low Self-Esteem (LSE), Negative Treatment Indicators (TRT), Work Interference (WRK), and FRS, in which they differed by approximately 3 raw score points and 5 to 9 T-score points. The remaining 11 content scales differed by only 1 to 2 raw score points and 2 to 3 T-score points. Similar findings apply to the two female groups. Seven scales differed by no more than 1 raw score point and 3 T-score points. Only two scales, TRT and LSE, showed a difference of 3.14 and 2.80 raw score points and 6 and 5 T-score points, respectively. All other scales differed by between 1 to 2 raw score points and 2 to 5 T-score points. Overall, most content scales showed very similar means and only slight differences across the two national groups. True cultural differences suggested by these results are that Japanese college students compared to their American counterparts may have a slightly lower opinion of themselves or are more self-effacing, and they may feel less comfortable discussing their problems with others.

Table 4-3. MMPI-2 Content Scales Means and Standard Deviations for a Japanese College Sample

Scale	Men (N = 563)		Women (N = 507)	
	Mean	S.D.	Mean	S.D.
ANX	6.73	4.39	6.62	4.34
FRS	5.91	3.74	8.09	4.10
OBS	6.58	3.66	6.92	3.53
DEP	8.35	5.46	8.85	5.93
HEA	6.22	4.41	5.90	4.26
BIZ	3.49	2.64	3.18	2.38
ANG	5.89	3.26	5.68	3.15
CYN	9.50	4.21	9.04	4.23
ASP	7.71	3.49	6.63	3.40
TPA	8.75	3.76	8.54	3.55
LSE	7.63	4.57	8.64	5.07
SOD	7.85	4.57	7.12	4.42
FAM	6.50	3.59	6.67	3.65
WRK	11.23	5.75	11.96	5.66
TRT	8.44	3.96	8.96	4.27

Note: Values are raw scores.

Factorial Structure Comparisons

Examination of the factorial structure of the Japanese MMPI-2 in comparison to that of the original MMPI-2 is essential to evaluating the equivalence of the instruments. If the factor structures of the two versions of the MMPI-2 are similar when identical factoring procedures are used, then it is likely that the Japanese adaptation has maintained the same or similar psychological meaning as the items and scales of the original.

Studies on the MMPI factor structure have repeatedly found two main factors that have been variously labeled Anxiety and Repression (Welsh, 1956; Eichman, 1961, 1962) or Ego Resiliency and Ego Control (Block, 1965). The first factor—Anxiety or Ego Resiliency—reflects general maladjustment. This factor is usually represented by high loadings on Pt and Sc on one pole and K on the opposite pole. The second factor—Repression or Ego Control—is typically defined by high loadings on scales Hs, D, and Hy at one pole and moderate loadings on Ma at the other pole. However, two main factors are usually found only when scales Mf and Si are excluded from the analyses. When the three validity and *all ten* clinical scales (including Mf and Si) are included in the correlation matrix used for factoring, four meaningfully interpretable factors usually emerge (Johnson, Butcher, Null, & Johnson, 1984). They are frequently labeled Anxiety, Repression, Masculinity-Femininity, and Social Introversion (Johnson et al., 1984).

Before the use of factor analysis can be justified to demonstrate equivalence of instruments across cultures, methodological issues need to be addressed. There is a lack of consensus on what methods to use to factor analyze data for cross-cultural studies (Guilford, 1975). Studies differ in the variables included (all or only some of the scales), the methods used to estimate communalities, the criterion used to determine the number of factors to extract, the rotational procedures applied, and the populations studied (clinical, community, or college). Even with the same instrument, such as the MMPI, different structures can emerge from factor analytic studies when different methodological choices are made.

Ben-Porath (1990) suggests that newly adapted instruments should be evaluated through the use of replicatory factor analysis. This approach requires that the methods for estimating communalities and for extracting and rotating factors be the same for both the original and the adapted instruments. Only when identical methods are used can factorial structures found in two cultures with the same instrument be directly compared. Such an approach is used in the current study. The factor analyses began by producing separate male and female correlation matrices using non–K-corrected scale scores for the three validity and ten clinical scales of the MMPI-2. The correlation matrices were then subjected to principal components analyses (ones in the diagonals) with varimax rotation (Kaiser, 1958).

Applying the Kaiser-Guttman criterion (Guttman, 1954; Kaiser & Caffrey, 1965) of retaining factors with eigenvalues greater than 1.0 indicated that three factors should be extracted for both men and women. However, the eigenvalue for the fourth factors approached 1.0 for men (eigenvalue = .86) and women (eigenvalue = .97), suggesting four factors may also be appropriate for both genders. Applying a "scree" test (Cattell, 1966) could justify the extraction of four factors for both men and women since the data showed minor breaks after the first, second, and third factors and relatively level slopes beginning after the fourth factors. Consequently, both three- and four-factor solutions were derived from the two national samples. However, the results of the four-factor solution were more clearly interpretable than those of the three-factor solution, and therefore, the discussion below will focus only on that solution. The three-factor solution is discussed in Shiota (1989/1990).

To compare the degree to which factors converged across data sets, coefficients of congruence (Gorsuch, 1983; Wrigley & Neuhaus, 1955) were computed. For this coefficient to reach unity, the rank order, scatter, and magnitude of the loadings must be identical across the data sets being compared.

Table 4-4. Factor Loadings on Four Factors Extracted from the Japanese MMPI-2

Scales	Factor 1 M	Factor 1 F	Factor 2 M	Factor 2 F	Factor 3 M	Factor 3 F	Factor 4 M	Factor 4 F
L	−02	11	06	−08	−74	−74	−12	01
F	72	56	46	52	01	21	−15	−18
K	−24	−05	−40	−52	−78	−73	−06	−01
Hs	61	75	47	33	−12	06	23	−03
D	25	50	78	71	−29	−20	26	12
Hy	51	82	15	−05	−61	−36	37	07
Pd	72	66	19	26	05	28	12	10
Mf	15	12	19	06	11	−06	89	96
Pa	72	66	11	16	−03	19	22	27
Pt	51	45	63	64	40	50	24	10
Sc	69	54	48	52	41	56	13	−03
Ma	66	43	−28	−28	49	70	−07	−12
Si	11	09	91	91	17	13	06	07
Percentage of total variance explained								
	27.0	26.1	21.8	22.0	17.3	19.1	9.4	8.3

Note: Scales loading ≥ .40 are underlined. Decimal points have been omitted.

Japanese MMPI-2 Factor Structure. For the Japanese sample, the four-factor solution (Table 4-4) produced distinct and clearly interpretable factors corresponding to those found in other cross-cultural studies using the MMPI (Butcher & Pancheri, 1976). The first factor appears to reflect general maladjustment, and is characterized by scales Pa, Pd, Hs, Hy, F, Sc, Ma, and Pt, with D loading for men only. The second factor unequivocally represents social introversion with extremely high Si loadings (.91) for both men and women and moderate positive loadings for F, D, Pt, and Sc and moderate negative loadings for K for both men and women. The third factor appears to be a repression or ego control factor, defined by scales Ma, Sc, and Pt at one pole and L, K, Hy, and D at the opposite pole. The fourth factor is clearly a masculinity-femininity dimension with a high loading for Mf for both men (.89) and women (.96) and low loadings for all other scales.

The loadings on the four factors are strikingly similar between the Japanese men and women, and the coefficients of congruence for the four factors range from .89 to .98 (Table 4-6). This indicates that the factors that emerged from the four-factor solutions are highly similar across gender and suggests that the person-

Table 4-5. Factor Loadings on Four Factors Extracted from a U.S. College Sample

Scales	Factor 1		Factor 2		Factor 3		Factor 4	
	M	F	M	F	M	F	M	F
L	−14	01	04	−07	<u>71</u>	<u>−79</u>	−36	−21
F	<u>77</u>	<u>56</u>	35	<u>45</u>	−02	21	06	−38
K	<u>−41</u>	−05	−34	<u>−75</u>	<u>74</u>	−47	04	07
Hs	<u>64</u>	<u>70</u>	<u>49</u>	32	16	07	09	−07
D	24	<u>62</u>	<u>75</u>	<u>50</u>	29	−24	28	20
Hy	27	<u>80</u>	15	−37	<u>71</u>	−18	<u>43</u>	12
Pd	<u>66</u>	<u>70</u>	22	22	−04	25	38	−11
Mf	10	09	20	05	−07	06	<u>84</u>	<u>88</u>
Pa	<u>61</u>	<u>69</u>	11	18	10	14	<u>45</u>	13
Pt	<u>60</u>	<u>53</u>	<u>57</u>	<u>71</u>	−39	31	21	−02
Sc	<u>78</u>	<u>59</u>	<u>43</u>	<u>60</u>	−27	37	17	−22
Ma	<u>77</u>	28	−32	04	−34	<u>69</u>	−11	<u>−40</u>
Si	15	14	89	89	−21	−20	10	13

Note: Scales loading ≥ .40 are underlined.   Decimal points have been omitted.
Source: Butcher, Graham, Dahlstrom, & Bowman (1989).

Table 4-6. Coefficients of Congruence Comparing Japanese and American Males and Females across the Four Factors Extracted from the MMPI-2

Groups	Factor 1	Factor 2	Factor 3	Factor 4
Japanese Men vs. Women	95	98	93	89
American Men vs. Women	87	86	78	66
Japanese Men vs. American Men	98	99	99	91
Japanese Women vs. American Women	99	95	94	87

Note: Decimal points have been omitted.

ality structure of the Japanese men and women are alike when measured with the MMPI-2.

Comparison of the Japanese and American Factor Structures. The four-factor solution derived from the American college MMPI-2 is consistent with the four factors found in other MMPI factor analytic studies (Johnson et al., 1984). The factor structures that emerged in the Japanese data are nearly identical to the structures obtained in the U.S. college sample using the MMPI-2 (Table 4-5). Between the Japanese and American men, only Hy on the first factor and Pd and Pa on the fourth factor showed mild differences in factor loadings. For Hy on the first factor, Japanese men loaded .51 and American men .27, and for Pd and Pa on the fourth factor, Japanese men loaded .12 and .22, respectively, while the American men loaded .38 and .45. However, these differences do not alter the interpretation of the factors across the two national groups and are relatively minor as evidenced by the extremely high coefficients of congruence that range from .89 to .98 between the two male samples (Table 4-6) across the four factors.

Between the Japanese and American women there was also very little difference in factor loadings. The largest differences were for the loadings of Ma and Hy on the second factor: Ma and Hy loaded -.28 and -.05, respectively, in the Japanese female sample, but .04 and -.37 in the American sample. However, because these two scales do not strongly mark the second factor in either of the female samples, these differences in loadings do not alter how the factor is interpreted in the two national groups. Overall, the coefficients of congruence across the four factors for the two female samples (Table 4-6) were also extremely high, ranging from .87 to .99.

It is important to note that the coefficients of congruence comparing males and females within the American sample (Table 4-6) for the four factors are slightly lower (.66 to .87) than the coefficients of congruence across the two national samples for both men and women. Thus between-culture differences are less than the within-culture difference found in the U.S. sample. However, the between-culture differences are similar to the within-culture difference for the Japanese sample. Taken together, these comparisons clearly demonstrate that the Japanese adaptation of the MMPI-2 has maintained the same or very similar psychological meaning as the original version and that factorial invariance and dimensional equivalence have been achieved.

Comparison of the Two Japanese Versions. The Japanese MMPI-2 factor structure can also be compared to the factors obtained from the Consolidated Version of the Japanese MMPI to identify changes in the structure due to revision of the instrument. However, differences between the MMPI and MMPI-2 validity and clinical scales are due primarily to reworded items that did not necessitate retranslation into Japanese. Thus, a more appropriate way to view a comparison between these two Japanese versions is that it provides a replication of the MMPI factor structure in Japan.

As detailed elsewhere (Shiota, 1989), the three- and four-factor solutions obtained from the Japanese MMPI-2 were very similar to those obtained with the Consolidated Version of the Japanese MMPI. The coefficients of congruence for the four-factor solutions for men were .97, .99, .94., and .94 respectively across the four factors and for women were .92, .98, .92, and .82. Overall, then, the factor structure of the standard validity and clinical scales is very stable across Japanese college samples.

Item Level Comparisons

Comparing item endorsement frequencies (IEF) in the two national samples provides another means of investigating the equivalence of the Japanese MMPI-2 to the original. The percent of each national sample who responded "True" to an item was determined separately for males and females (see Appendix C for Japanese IEFs). Items with a 15% or greater endorsement difference between the national samples for both males and females were identified. These items have been called "extreme items" by Butcher and Pancheri (1976) and may indicate (1) a translation problem, (2) a cultural difference, or (3) a sample difference.

Comparison of Japanese and American IEFs. The results of the Japanese and American MMPI-2 IEFs indicate that the vast majority of items were endorsed at similar frequencies across the national samples. Between the Japanese and American male groups 162 items showed a 15% or greater difference in endorsement, and between the female groups 166 items showed such a difference. However, only 107 items replicated a 15% or greater endorsement difference across genders and therefore should be designated as "extreme." Importantly, only 55 of these "extreme" items are scored on any of the three validity or ten clinical scales (the others score on supplementary or content scales). As presented in Table 4-7, scales L (7%) and Hs (6%) contained the lowest percentages of extreme items, whereas scales K (27%), Mf (23%), Pd (22%), and Ma (22%) contained the highest percentages. Japanese and American male samples differed most on scales Pd (38% of the items deviating by more than 15%), Mf (38%) and Ma (35%), whereas the two female samples differed most on scales K (37%) and Si (35%).

Extreme items for the supplementary and content scales of the Japanese MMPI-2 were also examined (see Table 4-7). Among the content scales, Anxiety (ANX), Health Concerns (HEA), Bizarre Mentation (BIZ), Social Discomfort (SOD), and Depression (DEP) contained only small percentages (< 9%) of extreme items. By contrast, Cynicism (CYN), Antisocial Practices (ASP), Negative Treatment Indicators (TRT), and Low Self-Esteem (LSE) contained high percentages (33–43%). Although a future study of items in the supplementary and content scales is needed to determine whether the "extreme" items obtained in this study are due to translation, sampling, or culture, given the committee approach to translation (including two back-translation checks) and the sample composition (students from eight and four universities for the Japanese and American

Table 4-7. Number and Percentage of Extreme Items per Scale in the Japanese MMPI-2

Validity Scale	%	Supplementary Scale	%	Content Scale	%
L	7	A	13	ANX	0
F	12	R	24	FRS	26
K	27	Es	13	OBS	13
Hs	6	MacR	16	DEP	9
D	11	F_B	20	HEA	3
Hy	18	TRIN	15	BIZ	4
Pd	22	VRIN	16	ANG	13
Mf	23	O-H	18	CYN	43
Pa	13	Do	24	ASP	36
Pt	10	Re	17	TPA	21
Sc	10	Mt	12	LSE	33
Ma	22			SOD	8
Si	17			FAM	24
				WRK	18
				TRT	35

Note: "Extreme items" had a 15% or greater difference in endorsement between Japanese and Americans for both males and females.

samples respectively), it is most likely that these item endorsement differences reflect true cultural differences. Overall, however, the comparison of the "extreme" items between the Japanese and Americans on the MMPI-2 provide further evidence that the Japanese adaptation of the instrument is generally an equivalent measure to the original.

IEFs between Genders. Item endorsement comparisons can also be made between genders within cultures. The Japanese men and women differed on 50 items, of which 28 were scored on the validity or clinical scales. The American men and women differed on a much larger 91 items, of which 57 were scored on the validity or clinical scales. As expected, only scale Mf showed appreciable gender differences in item endorsement rates, with this scale showing the highest percentage of endorsement difference in both cultures. Overall, Japanese men and women showed fewer large differences (>15%) in item endorsement rates across more scales than that found between the American men and women. Thus, Japanese men and women show fewer gender differences across items than do American men and women.

Comparison of the Two Japanese Versions. When the frequency of "extreme" items from the Japanese MMPI-2 is compared to the number obtained from the Consolidated Version of the Japanese MMPI (Clark, 1985), scales K, Pa, Pt, and Si, which contained the highest percentages of extreme items in the Consolidated Version (33%, 23%, 23%, and 21%, respectively), all show lower percentages (27%, 13%, 10%, and 17%, respectively) with the MMPI-2. Although four scales (F, Pd, Mf, and Ma) show an increase in the number of extreme items for the Japanese MMPI-2, the differences are very minor, representing at most a difference of three items on any scale.

The reasons for the Consolidated Version showing more "extreme" items than the Japanese MMPI-2 may involve the use of different reference groups. The Consolidated Version was compared to the U.S. MMPI normative data collected in the mid 1940s, decades before the Consolidated Version data was collected in Japan, while the Japanese MMPI-2 data were compared to an MMPI-2 college sample collected contemporaneously with the Japanese data. Thus, the use of a more contemporary (mid 1980s) and demographically appropriate (i.e., college students) comparison group may have reduced the number of "extreme" items present in the Japanese MMPI-2 data.

Cultural Differences on the MMPI-2

The findings of the present study support several characterizations of how the Japanese differ vis-à-vis Americans. Although ignoring individual differences, popular and scholarly characterizations of Japanese often have emphasized their tendency to maintain harmony with others within their group (Nakane, 1970). Relationships between superiors and inferiors are carefully cultivated and maintained by using self-effacing and polite expressions that serve to reinforce group harmony in everyday life. This cultural tendency toward maintaining harmony through polite restraint is also believed to be reflected in the personality of the Japanese.

The present study suggests that Japanese college students are more conventional and formal and lead more careful and cautious lifestyles, whereas American college students are more informal, dominant, and daring. The restraint shown by Japanese students is consistent with the need for social restraint required to successfully function within a highly structured and role-dominated society. Rather than interpreting the results as indicating that Japanese students are overly restrained, a more appropriate interpretation may be that American students are more carefree and less constrained.

Whereas popular and scholarly characterization of the Japanese emphasize their desire to maintain social harmony, this proclivity should not be confused with a tendency toward high sociability or extroversion. The present study showed only a small difference on Si; this small difference is probably due to the two national groups differing on outgoingness but not differing on attributes such as being hypersensitive and uncomfortable around others, which are also measured by Si. In contrast, Ma showed consistent and larger differences across culture for each gender. Extroversion as viewed by Eysenck (Eysenck & Eysenck, 1985) includes not only the trait of gregariousness but also traits such as being lively, assertive, dominant, and adventuresome, traits that are tapped by Ma. Thus the difference on Ma may reflect a tendency for the Americans to be more extroverted, dominant, and assertive than the Japanese. The higher score for the Japanese on LSE suggests that the Japanese may have slightly lower self-esteem or may have learned to be socially more self-effacing than Americans. Furthermore, lower scores on TRT for the Japanese suggest that they are less comfortable discussing personal problems with others. Despite these findings, it should be emphasized that the personality *structure* of the Japanese and Americans as measured by the MMPI-2 is nearly identical, and the mean level differences on specific traits are small.

Conclusion

The present study adapted the newly developed MMPI-2 into Japanese following procedures recommended by cross-cultural methodologists. Since demonstration of psychometric equivalence is required before meaningful cross-cultural comparisons can be made, the present study contrasted the performance of the MMPI-2 in a Japanese college sample with its performance in a comparable American sample.

The comparisons revealed that the validity, clinical, supplementary, and content scales all perform similarly in Japan and the United States; that the factorial dimensions measured by the Japanese MMPI-2 are nearly identical to those measured by the U.S. MMPI-2; and that the majority of the items were endorsed in similar frequencies by the two national groups. Taken together, these factors indicate that the Japanese adaptation of the MMPI-2 demonstrates equivalence to the original MMPI-2.

Now that the psychometric equivalence of the Japanese MMPI-2 has been demonstrated, its clinical utility needs to be established by administering the instrument to psychiatric populations. This would enable researchers to investigate the ability of the Japanese MMPI-2 to contribute to differential psychiatric assessment. For the MMPI-2 to be clinically useful in Japan, elevations on the scales must be demonstrated to be associated with symptomatic or syndromal psychopathology. That is, external correlates of MMPI-2 code types need to be established for Japan. It is hoped that the current successful adaptation of the MMPI-2 will enhance clinical assessment with Japanese populations and contribute to advancing cumulative cross-cultural research.

References

Ben-Porath, Y. S. (1990). Cross-cultural assessment of personality: The case for replicatory factor analysis. In J. N. Butcher & C. D. Spielberger (Eds.), *Recent advances in personality assessment: Vol 8.* Hillsdale, NJ: Erlbaum.

Berry, J. W. (1980). Introduction to methodology. In H. C. Triandis & J. Berry (Eds.), *Handbook of cross-cultural psychology: Vol 2.* Boston: Allyn and Bacon.

Block, J. (1965). *The challenge of response sets: Unconfounding meaning, acquiescence, and social desirability in the MMPI.* New York: Appleton-Century-Crofts.

Brislin, R. W., Lonner, W. L., & Thorndike, R. M. (1973). *Cross-cultural research methods.* New York: Wiley.

Butcher, J. N., & Clark, L. A. (1979). Recent trends in cross-cultural MMPI research and application. In J. N. Butcher (Ed.), *New developments in the use of the MMPI.* Minneapolis: University of Minnesota Press.

Butcher, J. N., Dahlstrom, W. G., Graham, J. R., Tellegen, A., & Kaemmer, B. (1989). *Manual for the restandardized Minnesota Multiphasic Personality Inventory: MMPI-2. An administrative and interpretive guide.* Minneapolis: University of Minnesota Press.

Butcher, J. N., Graham, J. R., & Dahlstrom, W. G. (1989). [Archival file of U.S. College Biographical and Life Events Questionnaires]. Unpublished raw data.

Butcher, J. N., Graham, J. R., Dahlstrom, W. G., & Bowman, E. (1989). [Archival file of MMPI-AX]. Unpublished raw data.

Butcher, J. N., Graham, J. R., Dahlstrom, W. G., & Bowman, E. (1990). The MMPI-2 with college students. *Journal of Personality Assessment, 54,* 1–15.

Butcher, J. N., & Pancheri, P. (1976). *A handbook of cross-national MMPI research.* Minneapolis: University of Minnesota Press.

Butcher, J. N., & Spielberger, C. D. (1985). *Advances in personality assessment: Vol 4.* Hillsdale, NJ: Erlbaum.

Cattell, R. B. (1966). The scree test for the number of factors. *Multivariate Behavioral Research, 1,* 245–256.

Clark, L. A. (1985). A consolidated version of the MMPI in Japan. In J. N. Butcher & C. D. Spielberger (Eds.), *Advances in personality assessment: Vol 4.* Hillsdale, NJ: Erlbaum.

Eichman, W. J. (1961). Replicated factors on the MMPI with female NP patients. Journal of Consulting Psychology, 25, 55–60.

Eichman, W. J. (1962). Factored scales for the MMPI: A clinical and statistical manual. *Journal of Clinical Psychology, 18,* 363–395.

Eysenck, H. J., & Eysenck, M. W. (1985). *Personality and individual differences: A natural science approach.* New York: Plenum Press.

Gorsuch, R. L. (1983). *Factor analysis* (2nd ed.). Hillsdale, NJ: Erlbaum.

Guilford, J. P. (1975). Factors and factors of personality. *Psychological Bulletin, 82,* 802–814.

Guttman, L. A. (1954). Some necessary conditions for common-factor analysis. *Psychometrika, 19,* 149–161.

Johnson, J. H., Butcher, J. N., Null, C., & Johnson, K. N. (1984). Replicated item level factor analysis of the full MMPI. *Journal of Personality and Social Psychology, 47,* 105–114.

Kaiser, H. K. (1958). The varimax criterion for analytic rotation in factor analysis. *Psychometrika, 22,* 187–200.

Kaiser, H. K., & Caffrey, J. (1965). Alpha factor analysis. *Psychometrika, 30,* 1–14.

Lubin, B., Larsen, R. M., & Matarazzo, J. (1984). Patterns of psychological test use in the United States, 1935–1984. *American Psychologist, 39,* 451–454.

Lubin, B., Larsen, R. M., Matarazzo, J., & Seever, M. (1985). Psychological assessment services and psychological test usage in private practice and military settings. *Psychotherapy in Private Practice, 4,* 19–29.

Nakane, C. (1970). *Japanese society.* London: Weidenfeld & Nicolson.

Piotrowski, C., & Lubin, B. (1990). Assessment practices of health psychologists: Survey of APA Division 38 clinicians. *Professional Psychology Research and Practice, 21,* 99–106.

Shiota, N. K. (1990). Japanese MMPI-2: Inventory adaptation and equivalence evaluation using Japanese and American college samples (Doctoral dissertation, University of Minnesota, 1989). *Dissertation Abstracts International, 50,* 5353B.

Welsh, G. S. (1956). MMPI profiles and factors A and R. *Journal of Clinical Psychology, 21,* 43–47.

Chapter 5

The Korean MMPI-2

Kyunghee Han

The MMPI, developed in the United States and widely used in many other countries as a clinical personality test, has been used in Korea as a clinical assessment and research instrument for almost three decades (Kim et al., 1989). Although the validity of the original MMPI is well documented by research data in the United States and other countries, systematic information regarding the instrument's adaptability and validity for the Korean culture has been lacking.

To evaluate the usefulness of the MMPI and MMPI-2 for Koreans, this chapter will begin with a discussion of personality and psychopathological characteristics that may be unique to Koreans.

Personality and Psychopathological Characteristics of Koreans

An aspect of cross-cultural research that often receives little attention is an understanding of the culture and people under study. This is often due to lack of time or availability of information about the target culture as well as the complexity and ambiguity that characterizes investigation of these areas. Clearly it may be impractical and unnecessary to review and compare the history and research of all personality domains across two cultures when one is interested in examining a single construct. However, it is very common for such studies to be conducted without introducing any information regarding the cultural background of the subjects under study. Typically, researchers attempt to explain existing cultural differences after discrepancies across cultures have been revealed. Without an a priori knowledge about the cultures, artifactual differences may be interpreted as real cultural

I would like to express my appreciation to James Butcher and Nathan Weed for reading earlier versions of this manuscript and for making valuable suggestions. I thank Noriko Shiota for access to her Japanese data set, and Beverly Kaemmer from the University of Minnesota Press for providing MMPI-2 computer answer sheets and access to the American college data set.

differences. Thus, an understanding of cultural differences may lead to a more accurate interpretation of results of cross-cultural studies (Butcher, Narikiyo, & Vitousek, 1992).

Many recent ethnic studies conducted on Pacific/Asian cultures have been limited to specific populations, primarily Chinese and Japanese, with other East Asian groups, such as Koreans, receiving little attention (Kitano & Sue, 1973). Westerners generally are not knowledgeable about Korea or Koreans and frequently assume that all Asians are alike. Regrettably, research findings on Asians are often generalized across the various Asian subgroups. China, Japan, and Korea once shared a sociocultural background, but in recent history these countries have been influenced by the West to varying degrees. The heterogeneity of the Asian population makes any simple generalization tenuous at best (Bond & Cheung, 1983; Foley & Fuqua, 1988; Nakane et al., 1988; Reischauer, 1988).

In this section I will attempt to identify and discuss potentially unique personality and psychopathological characteristics of Koreans. It may be appropriate here to indicate briefly the scope of the discussion. First, it is not intended as a complete description of personality and psychopathological characteristics of Koreans. Only personality and psychopathological aspects unique to Koreans are identified and discussed. Second, this section does not purport to provide a complete explanation for all the phenomena that are interpreted as characteristics of Koreans. For these phenomena there are no doubt many determinants. Finally, much of the following discussion is historical rather than empirical. However, an understanding of this material is important for guiding and understanding Korean cross-cultural research.

Philosophy, Values, and Religions of Koreans

Foreigners who come to Korea and observe Koreans' behavior carefully might be surprised to discover how naturally they can change their philosophical and value systems on different occasions. Paek (1990) illustrates this point:

> In contemporary Korea, the average person will reveal some degree of Western rationalism and Christian thought in his office, school or public affairs. Confucian elements predominate, however, on New Years Day, in home life, and in ancestor worship ceremonies, and in senior-junior relationships which are often determined by age. During aging, or at the abrupt loss of a beloved one, or at funerals, a Buddhist element becomes prominent. And when helpless, in despair or during unbearable trauma, Koreans readily depend on the shamanistic elements. (p. 29)

According to Yum (1987a), there are three main roots of Korean philosophical and value systems: (a) Confucianism, which originated in China; (b) shamanism, which is a strictly Korean belief system that evolved from prehistoric periods; and

(c) Mahayana Buddhism, which originated in India but was imported to Korea through China.

Confucianism. Confucianism is a compendium of wisdom pertaining to human action, consistent with the basic worldview of Asian cultures, upon which persons draw for guidance (Kang & Pearce, 1983). Some scholars believe that Confucianism is the most pragmatic of the philosophies that made an impact on Korea and that it is the most important philosophy underlying the Korean collective personality. It was the official ideology of the Yi dynasty (1392-1910) and was thoroughly institutionalized and systematically diffused to the people. Korean society was more literally Confucian than was China itself during that period (Osgood, 1951). Keeping and sometimes suffering from Confucianism for five hundred years has produced a unique mode of thinking for Koreans.

The Confucian concept *uye-ri* is central to an understanding of the development and maintenance of Korean interpersonal relationships. This term has three major meanings. The first relates to justice, righteousness, duty, morality, and integrity. The second, to obligation, a debt of gratitude, and faithfulness. The third meaning concerns the proper relationships between people, such as *uye-ri* between lord and retainer or *uye-ri* between friends. *Uye-ri* governs blood relations, regional relations, and school relations. Even though the practice of *uye-ri* can create warm and lasting human relationships in Korea, it sometimes creates seemingly irrational or unethical behavior because Koreans usually put the highest value on maintaining good relationships with people within an in-group. For example, employers sometimes pay more attention to what school an applicant graduated from or whose relative he or she is than to professional qualifications. *Uye-ri* is not based on universal, rational logic but on a specific group principle or group spirit (Yum, 1987b).

Yi (1983) points out that in a Confucian state the concepts of "home" and "family" are stronger than those of "state" and "society." One's relationship with one's parents is regarded as the starting point of all relationships. *Hyo* (filial piety; a repayment to parental kindness) encompasses not only one's immediate parents but also previous generations. A stranger in Korea is defined as a person whom one would not greet when encountered. Some foreigners visiting Korea are perplexed that Koreans are talkative and easily engaged in conversation with one another but on the other hand quiet and even rude toward strangers. This is because Confucian teaching says little about an individual's conduct in public (Yum, 1987b; Smart, 1977). One Korean writer (Smart, 1977) has written that "there is no doubt that we are a courteous Oriental country, but this courteousness lies within the wall and amongst people we know" (p. 27).

Shamanism. Confucianism, which is the product of a patriarchal and strongly male-dominated society in China, considers women important only for bearing children and perpetuating the family. It could be said that Confucianism fulfilled the needs of men, whereas shamanism was developed to fulfill the needs of women. Shamanism is considered a source of the Korean nation's "spiritual energy," preceding the foreign influences of Confucianism and Buddhism (Kendall, 1981). Lee (1975) points out that at present more than half the Korean population still adheres to shamanistic practices. For the past several centuries, shamans have almost always been female (the female shaman is called *mudang* or *masin*) and their clientele are almost all women, which indicates that shamanistic thought in Korea is closely associated with women and their home lives. Harvey (1976) describes the shaman as "a household therapist" giving divinations and advice to her female clients. When the Yi dynasty was established, shamanism allied itself with Confucianism to complement the lack of religiosity in the latter. Since then, Confucianism and shamanism have complemented each other, together forming a unique system for Korean daily life (Lee, 1975).

In Korean shamanism, restless ancestors, ghosts, and angry household gods are believed to bring affliction to the home: illness, financial loss, and domestic strife. It is the main purpose of the shamanistic ceremonies (*kut*) to protect and keep the peace at home by feasting and entertaining the spirits (Kendall, 1988; Lee, 1975). Shamanistic healing ceremonies are still performed in rural areas. According to a survey by Kim and Won (Kim, 1974), 44.5% of rural Koreans preferred supernatural treatment of psychoses to other methods of treatment. Kim (1973) acknowledges various psychotherapeutic elements at work in *kut:* catharsis, suggestion, hypnosis, and transference. Even though shamanistic rituals have been disappearing in urban settings, a basic shamanistic orientation has not vanished from Korean life but is manifest in different contexts and other forms of expression (Lee, 1975). For example, it is very common to observe middle-aged women consulting with a shaman when they have to make major decisions such as setting a wedding date for their children or setting dates for moving their households. They may seek information from a shaman when they wonder about the gender of an unborn grandchild, when they name newborn grandchildren, and when they wonder about causes of failure in the family business.

Buddhism. Even though Confucian thought has exerted a prominent influence on social aspects of Korean life, Buddhism has exerted the most profound religious influence. The main principle of original Buddhism is that worldly attachment is a source of suffering and that this world is an illusion. This is not consistent with Confucianist thought, which emphasizes human relationships. Therefore, Buddhism in Korea, through its interaction with Confucianism and Korean indigenous shamanism, was transformed into something less metaphysical and more oriented to the present, capable of bringing about well-being and happiness to the believer and his or her family (Yum, 1987a).

Yum (1987a) describes two impacts of Buddhism on Korean communication: (a) the importance of silence and distrust of words; and (b) its egalitarian aspect. In Buddhism, written or spoken communication is incomplete and incapable of conveying true meaning. The highest level of communication is believed to occur only when one "speaks without the mouth" and when one "hears without the ears." Therefore, mind reading is regarded as an important communication skill. Unlike Confucian ethics, which emphasize hierarchy and the distinction between different relationships, Buddhism teaches benevolence to all living creatures. Koreans are polite only to insiders because strangers are considered to be beyond the realm of properly prescribed human relationships (the influence of Confucianism). They can be rude to strangers, but Buddhism alleviates the distinction between insiders and outsiders by saying that even a casual brushing together of clothes means a predestined relationship. According to Yum, "Buddhism makes egalitarian communication possible, a communication that cuts across social status or group boundaries, which would otherwise have no place in a purely Confucianist society" (1987a, p. 84).

Psychopathology

Han. Elderly Koreans often use the terms *han,* "*han* of poverty," "*han* of women," "*han* of family," or "*han* of country" in everyday conversation. The concept of *han* is somewhat similar to the French "chagrin" and to the English "lamentation," "heartburning," or "grudge." Min and Lee (Prince, 1989) described the term *han* as "something accumulated, precipitated, and formed in mass in the depth of mind in Korean people as they have experienced emotional frustration" (p. 143). Historically, it is associated with repeated military invasions, political and social suppression, and chronic poverty. Korean psychoanalysts speak of it as Koreans' repressed instinctual demands, and inhibited and neglected internal drives for acceptance of wider, outer demands (Paek, 1990). They believe that this results in both personal and collective *han,* which passes down through families and generations. In addition to its association with historical incidents, women in particular are thought to suffer from birth the "*han* of women." An announcement of the birth of a daughter is often received with regret because, in traditional Korean society, sons inherit the family line, but daughters are "raised for others" and are considered outsiders once they have married. Arnold and Kuo (1984) conducted a comparative study of the gender preference of parents across seven Asian countries and the United States. It was found that the two countries with the strongest preference for sons were Korea and Taiwan, with Korea's preference being the greatest.

According to Paek (1990), *han* has become more tangible and concentrated with the traumas of the twentieth century. Poverty and the loss of the nation, in particular, are believed to have resulted in a psychological phenomenon called the "*han* of family." Sons usually try to placate decades of family *han* by becoming successful. This in turn gives rise to a "big man complex," which is considered nearly universal among contemporary Korean males. Kook (1986) writes that Koreans are generally short-tempered and prefer speed to elaboration because they are anxious to be big and successful as quickly as possible. In Korea, some parents sacrifice themselves to support children and their education. In turn, they expect their children to be successful. The failure of most Koreans to achieve "big" is thought to result in widespread psychopathology, including severe guilt feelings (for not having fulfilled filial duty), inferiority complexes (for having fallen behind others), anxiety, and even paranoid thoughts (fear of being ridiculed).

Somatization. Kim (1974) writes that the main psychological problems of Koreans are characterized by a tendency toward projection and somatization. Koreans' tendency to project is believed to stem from the disease concepts in shamanism and oriental medicine known as *han-bang* (Chinese or herb medicine). Shamanist society considers emotional and physical illness diseases over which one has no control, their causes being attributed to supernatural beings. The essence of the disease concept in *han-bang* is also projective in that people believe that most emotional problems are caused by somatic problems.

Two kinds of cultural tradition, *han-bang* and Confucianism, are regarded as precursors for Korean's somatization. First, because of a strong dependency on the disease concepts of *han-bang*, the distinction between the psyche and the body is vague in the minds of Koreans. According to *han-bang*, every organ has a specific symbolic function. For example, the heart is a reservoir of pleasure, ideation, and spirit. Therefore, anxiety is thought to originate from dysfunction of the heart. Second, people in a Confucianistic society are not allowed to express hostile feelings. The only culturally approved way to express their emotions is through somatic complaints (Kim, 1974).

The tendency to somatize is also prominent in other Asian cultures with similar cultural backgrounds. Cross-cultural studies with samples of Asians or Asian Americans have consistently shown that they tend to somatize their psychosocial distress more than do Caucasian Americans or other non-Asians (Kleinman, 1977; Marsella, Kinzie, & Gordon, 1973; Sue & Sue, 1974; Sue & Sue, 1987; Sue, Wagner, Ja, Margullis, & Lew, 1976; White, 1982). White (1982) states that several factors contribute to the phenomenon of somatization and consequently to the underutilization of mental heath services: (a) social stigma; (b) modes of expression and communication of emotion; (c) psychological repression or suppression; and (d) socioeconomic or educational differences. According to Yamamoto and Acosta (1982), the stigma of mental illness remains so great for Asian Americans that, even among individuals of the third or fourth generation, there is hesitation to admit to psychological problems. A study by Sue et al. (1976) also showed that Asian Americans are more likely to feel that mental illness is associated with organic or somatic variables and that mental health involves the avoidance of morbid thoughts.

A study by Cheung (1982) does not support the above notion, however. Her results indicated that among Chinese in urban Hong Kong, reports of psychological symptoms were higher than those of psychophysiological and physiological symptoms. But a detailed investigation of individual items on the subscales used reveals that items expressing behaviors and states that interfered with task achievement such as "can't get going" and "memory not all right" were endorsed more often than items indicating pure emotions or personality traits such as "bothered by nervousness" and "feel somewhat apart."

Hwa-byung. *Hwa-byung* is a Korean folk illness well known to Korean mental health workers. *Hwa* refers to "fire" or "anger" and *byung* means "sickness." Thus, *hwa* and *byung* together become "fire-illness" or "anger-illness." Fire is one of the basic elements (evolutive phase) in the Korean and Chinese cosmologies. According to Chinese medical theory, the harmonious interaction of the five elements, together with maintaining a balance between *yin* (the female, cold, dark principle) and *yang* (the male, hot, light principle), are fundamental in matters of health and sickness. An excess of the fire element manifests behaviorally in the expression of anger, whereas pent-up anger disturbs the fire element to such a degree that serious illness may appear (Lin, 1983). The most conspicuous complaints of *hwa-byung* are gastrointestinal, such that the patient feels or believes that there is a mass struck in the epigastrium (upper stomach). Associated symptoms include shortness of breath, palpitations, and fear of impending death. It may later develop into a chronic picture of pressure in the epigastrium, indigestion, diffuse muscle and joint pains, fatigue, and general malaise (Prince, 1989). According to Min and Lee (Prince, 1989), "typical complaints were feelings of heat sensations in the body, boiling, fire or burning sensation in the chest or epigastrium, and pushing up, rising up or stretching of something hot in the chest. Frequently they had to take off their clothes or go out, or could not stay in a hot bath or closed room because of feeling excessively hot" (p. 143). Lee (Prince, 1989) argues that *hwa-byung* is due to suppression and somatization of anger resulting from initial traumatic shocks in family life and that it should be seen as a psychosomatic disorder combined with anxiety and depression. He states that *hwa-byung* is most common in lower-class, married, middle-aged or elderly women who had or have serious family problems, such as conflicts with their husbands, in-laws, or children as well as financial difficulties.

Alcoholism. Lee et al. (1990a, 1990b) conducted studies of psychiatric epidemiology to estimate the lifetime prevalence of specific mental disorders in Korea by means of version III of the Diagnostic Interview Schedule (DIS-III). Authors compared their results with the lifetime prevalence of specific psychiatric disorders in St. Louis, Missouri (Robins et al., 1984). In comparing the results from a sample of 5,100 Koreans and a sample of 3,004 Americans, the most dramatic finding is the very high prevalence of alcohol abuse or dependence among men in Korea. The overall lifetime prevalence of alcohol abuse or dependence for men was 43%, both in Seoul and in rural Korea, whereas the rate was 29% in St. Louis. The prevalence of all other psychiatric disorders as diagnosed by DIS-III was lower in Korea than in St. Louis.

Racial differences in alcoholism had previously been explained on cultural grounds (i.e., Chinese moderate drinking habits and low rates of alcoholism are due to cultural patterns of alcohol use and family stability) until the pioneering studies of Wolff (1972) and Ewing, Rouse, and Pellizari (1974). These investigators found that the flush response, which is very common among Oriental people, is similar to the alcohol-disulfiram (antabuse) reaction and suggest that the flush response may serve as an endogenous protection against excessive use of alcohol among Oriental populations. According to Agarwal, Harada, and Goedde (1981), the decreased activity of aldehyde dehydrogenase (ALDH) is important in the postalcohol flush. In a comparison study of flush response between Koreans and Taiwan Chinese, Park et al. (1984, cited in Prince, 1990a) found that the number of fast flushers among the Chinese was much higher than among the Koreans. This result led them to hypothesize that fast flushing may play a more important role in preventing alcohol abuse among Chinese than it does among Koreans.

In addition to biological explanations, some sociocultural factors unique to Koreans should be taken into consideration in the interpretation of these results. Yamamoto et al. (Prince, 1990b) note that Koreans have been called the "Irish of the Orient" because of their long history of rebellion against other nations seeking to control them and because of their proclivity to alcohol, whereas the Chinese are sometimes called the "Jews of the Orient" because of their temperate use of alcohol and strong family orientation. Lee et al. (1990a) point out that in modern Korean culture drinking is regarded as a means to facilitate social interaction. It is very common to observe a group of men in a bar, drinking heavily, singing, and dancing together. However, solitary drinking is rare in Korea. Kim (1976) notes that the admission rates of alcoholics to psychiatric wards are low partly because alcoholism is seldom seen as symptomatic of illness. The general public is highly tolerant of alcoholism and does not see alcoholics as needing psychiatric attention.

The Korean MMPI/MMPI-2

When one evaluates an instrument adopted into a new culture, one needs to understand the target culture and its people, and to be able to evaluate the applicability of foreign concepts to the new culture. However, it is also important to consider the development and use of the instrument in the new culture.

The Korean MMPI

First Version. The MMPI was first translated into Korean in 1963 by Bum-Mo Chung, Chung-kyoon Lee, and Wee-kyo Chin (Chung, Lee, & Chin, 1963). Unfortunately, no sources are available to examine how the MMPI was translated. The only psychometric data available are means, standard deviations, reliability coefficients, and intercorrelations among MMPI validity and clinical scales from a sample of males.

Aside from a lack of information about this translation, there appear to be two major difficulties with the translation of the MMPI items. First, 55 items are keyed in the opposite direction from the original MMPI: 53 negatively phrased items were translated positively; one positively phrased item was translated negatively; and one positively phrased item was translated positively with the opposite meaning. Some modifications (formal modifications; Butcher & Pancheri, 1976) are an unavoidable part of translation, because of lexical and grammatical differences in the new language. In particular, Koreans usually have difficulty answering complex negative sentences. Therefore, the 53 items that were rewritten in the positive direction might create less confusion or ambiguity for Koreans. However, no explanation for these or other modifications was provided in the test manual. For someone who has administered the Korean MMPI and scored scales using the English MMPI scoring, it is potentially a great source of confusion and error.

Second, several items were mistranslated or modified awkwardly. Following are examples of mistranslation: "I would like to be a journalist" (204) was translated to "I like to be an artist"; "At times I hear so well it bothers me" (341) was translated "I hear so well the sound of bothering me." Following are examples of awkward modifications: "I used to like drop-the-handkerchief" (70) was modified to "I tend to be passive in relationships"; "I go to church almost every week" (95) was modified to "I wash my face every day"; "Children should be taught all the main facts of sex" (199) was translated "Children need home education"; "I think Lincoln was greater than Washington" (513) was translated "The 1919 Independence Movement is worth commemorating." Butcher and Pancheri (1976) recommend that some items with cultural and religious bias be reshaped to suit the new conditions without radically changing the subject matter. However, the modifications from "drop the handkerchief" to "passivity in relationships," from "go to church almost every week" to "wash face every day," and from Lincoln versus Washington to the 1919 Independent Movement are serious distortions of the original meaning of these MMPI items.

Second Version. The second Korean MMPI translation was published in 1989 by a team of seven psychologists (Kim et al., 1989). Once again, the authors did not provide information on how the items were translated or whether the translation was evaluated for accuracy. The only information available about the translation is the names of the translators. An informal review of this new version reveals that it is more faithful to both the wording and the meaning of the original MMPI items than were the items of the first Korean MMPI. The most notable change is that in the new version no items have meanings opposite the original items. All the items were keyed in the same direction as the original items.

Items 70, 95, and 513, which were translated and modified inappropriately in the old version, remain incorrect in the new version. Item 513, "I think Lincoln was greater than Washington," was translated to "I think General Lee Sun-Shin is greater than King Sejong." King Sejong was responsible for creating Korean written language and had many cultural interests. General Lee Sun-Shin is known for his success as a warrior. It can easily be argued that the placement of these two names should be switched within the item. Four more items that did not preserve the original meanings were found: "Everything tastes the same," "I like poetry," "I like to know important people because it makes me feel important," and "A large number of people are guilty of bad sexual conduct" were translated to "Everything is dry and uninteresting," "I like to write poetry," "I like to get acquainted with some important people," and "There are a lot of people who feel guilty because of bad sexual conduct," respectively.

To summarize, the MMPI has been used extensively with Koreans since it was translated and adapted in the early 1960s. However, in both versions of the Korean MMPI, there is no discussion of how items were translated and whether efforts were made to evaluate the accuracy of the translation and the adequacy of the instrument for Korean culture. Several incorrect translations seem to suggest that these investigators did not use basic procedures such as back-translation to evaluate the adequacy of the translation.

Overview of the Korean MMPI-2 Development Project. The goals of this project (Han, 1993) were (a) to adapt the MMPI-2 for use in Korea and (b) to evaluate its cross-cultural applicability. The task of inventory adaptation was undertaken by the present author in 1989 just after a revised and updated form of the MMPI (MMPI-2) had been developed by the MMPI Restandardization Committee (Butcher, Dahlstrom, Graham, Tellegen & Kaemmer, 1989).

The first task of the project was to create an adequate Korean translation of the MMPI-2. The second was to determine whether this new Korean version of the MMPI-2 was equivalent to the original. To evaluate equivalence, data on the new version were collected and analyzed at several levels: (a) Its internal structure was examined through factor congruence coefficients and factor score correlations and compared with data on American and Japanese college samples; (b) equivalence was studied at the scale level, including comparing MMPI-2 scale means and skewness of scale distributions; (c) equivalence was also investigated at the item level, including comparing item endorsement frequencies and percentages, intercorrelations of item endorsement percentages, and "extreme items" across cultures, and examing items that best discriminate Koreans from Americans and Japanese. The reliability of the Korean MMPI-2 was examined via test-retest, and investigation of the validity of the Korean MMPI-2 was conducted by correlating clinical scales with peer ratings.

Development of the Korean MMPI-2

Measurement Instruments and Translation. The first decision to be made before translating the MMPI-2 was whether an entirely new translation had to be done since most of the original MMPI items were retained in the MMPI-2 to maintain continuity. After reviewing the first Korean version, it was decided to translate all 567 items of the MMPI-2 because there were too many translation errors and outdated or ambiguous item wordings in that version. Although there are now two versions of the Korean MMPI, only the first version was available in 1989 when the author began adapting the MMPI-2. While collecting data in 1990, it was discovered that a second version of the original MMPI items had just been developed. Unfortunately, neither this author nor the University of Minnesota Press had knowledge of that second version.

Several translation problems arose during the translation process, requiring general strategies for their solution. The first and most important decision to be made was what approach to follow in doing the translation. Tests may be literally translated with little or no content change, or they may be modified through item substitution to fit local behavioral norms. For the Korean translation of the MMPI-2 it was decided to try to maintain the meaning of the MMPI-2 items as closely as possible. Therefore, only items considered completely irrelevant or meaningless in the Korean culture were altered substantially. No items needed drastic cultural adaptation, but a few required minor content change. Some professions, illnesses, and activities have no exact equivalent in Korea. Examples are "forest ranger" (item 69), "journalist" (191), "flirt" (189), "law enforcement" (126), and "breaking out on skin" (194). "Forest ranger" was translated as "someone who looks after the forest or mountain"; "journalist" was translated as "someone who works at a newspaper company, a magazine company, or broadcasting station"; "flirt" was translated as "laugh and talk over nothing with the opposite sex"; "I believe in law enforcement" was expanded as "The law should be upheld and anyone who breaks it should be punished"; and "breaking out on skin" was modified as "pimples, acne, or swelling."

The second problem encountered was idiomatic expressions in several MMPI-2 items. For example, there were no equivalent idioms in Korean for the following English phrases: "get a raw deal from life" (17), "had it in for" (42, 99), "beating criminals at their own game" (406), "one hundred percent sold on" (439), and "drive a hard bargain" (537). These items were translated nonidiomatically or idiomatically with the most appropriate Korean idiom in an effort to convey the meaning as best as possible.

The third problem was passive sentences. It is unusual for Koreans to use the passive voice. Although there was some variation by item, most of the passive sentences were translated as active sentences. For example, "I am liked by most people who know me" (78) was translated as "most people who know me like me." Several items included the phrase, "it makes me . . ." For example, "It makes me impatient" (136), "It makes me uncomfortable" (158), "It makes me feel like" (347), "It makes me nervous" (375), and "It makes me angry" (461) were all translated as "I am" or "I feel."

A fourth problem was associated with personal and possessive pronouns. Most of the original MMPI-2 items start with "I" or "my." Koreans use "our" instead of "my" so "we" or "our" was substituted for "I" or "my" depending on the context.

A final problem that arose during the translation was the many negatively phrased items. Koreans usually have difficulty answering complex negative sentences. However, positively rewritten items might create a shift in the response pattern of the subjects, even if they might create less confusion or ambiguity for Koreans. The strategy followed in these cases was to include both forms of the items and to examine empirical differences in the response pattern of the subjects.

Following the above general guidelines, the translation was accomplished in seven stages: (1) The present author and one bilingual independently translated the MMPI-2 from English into Korean. The bilingual was a Korean graduate student of history at the University of Minnesota. She had experience teaching English and translating questionnaires. (2) Both translators compared the two versions and resolved the discrepancies between them. (3) A third bilingual student, in pre-med at the University of Minnesota, who had lived in the United States for 10 years, compared common items between the first Korean version of the MMPI and the Korean version of the MMPI-2. He was instructed to select the items that were more accurate and natural in wording and to substitute items or portions of items if he found them unsatisfactory. (4) The present author reviewed the selected items and made minor changes. (5) The Korean items were submitted to a fourth bilingual student for back-translation into English. This back-translator was a 24-year-old undergraduate student at the University of Minnesota who had come to the United States eight years earlier. She spoke English fluently and had a great deal of translation experience. (6) The two English versions, the original items and the back-translated items, were examined for discrepancies by an American psychologist who was one of the members of the MMPI Restandardization Committee and is an expert in MMPI cross-cultural work. (7) Resolving these discrepancies resulted in a revision of the corresponding Korean items. Of the total MMPI-2 item pool, 20 items were judged as nonequivalent in the two English versions. The 20 inadequate items were reviewed and retranslated. The corrected versions of these items were reviewed by the same back-translator. This time the back-translation produced acceptable items.

A second measure used in the Korean MMPI-2 development project was a peer rating form. Most of the items on this form were adapted from the spouse rating form used in the MMPI Restandardization Project. This form, adapted from the Katz Adjustment Scale (KAS; Katz, 1968), consists of 110 four-point items on which the subject is asked to rate the degree to which a descriptive statement applies to his or her spouse. Of these 110 items, 56 items were selected that were relevant to Korean culture, appropriate for rating peers, and would serve well as prototypical correlates of MMPI-2 clinical scales. Twenty-four additional items, suggested by the MMPI-2 clinical scale descriptors listed in Graham (1987), were written by the present author to serve as Korean MMPI-2 scale correlates. The 80 items were then translated into Korean by the present author. The translation of this questionnaire was checked for accuracy by a bilingual graduate student. The items were not subjected to back-translation since they were fairly brief and straightforward.

All subjects in the development project were also administered 24 positively translated MMPI items that are negatively phrased in the original MMPI-2 and in the Korean version of the MMPI-2. As stated earlier, the purpose of administering this questionnaire was to see if a shift in the response pattern of the subjects could be attributed to the direction of the phrasing.

Data collection. Data collection was conducted in Korea from August to November 1990; 726 Korean college students (295 men and 431 women) from eight universities participated in the study, including students from Dongah University, Ehwa Women's University, Goshin University, Jeonnam University, Kyungnam University, Kyungseung University, Seoul National University, and Sookmyung Women's University.

Subjects were recruited to participate in the study either by personal contacts or by advertisement on a school bulletin board. Subjects were requested to bring a friend to the testing if possible. When subjects arrived at the test site, those who arrived alone were instructed to sit on one side of the classroom and those who came with a friend were asked to sit with their friends.

Students (187 men and 352 women) who participated with friends were administered 24 rewritten MMPI-2 items, the Korean version of the MMPI-2, and a peer rating form. Each of these subjects was instructed to rate his or her friend on the peer rating form. For participating, each student received a payment of 7,000 won, roughly $10. Students who came to the test session by themselves were not given a peer rating form (105 men and 72 women), and each received 5,000 won, roughly $7, for participating. Some subjects (61 men and 88 women) from this initial testing were administered the MMPI-2 a second time about one week later to evaluate test-retest reliability. Each student in the test-retest group received an additional 5,000 won ($7) for participating.

Subjects were eliminated from the study if their MMPI responses included 15 or more "cannot say" responses, a raw score of 25 or greater on F, or a raw score of 25 or greater on the F Back scale (F_B). The final Korean normative group consisted of 683 subjects (284 men and 399 women). In the test-retest group, 11 subjects were eliminated because of invalid profiles (2 men and 4 women), mismatched identification numbers (1 man and 1 woman), or an outlying D_2 value (1 woman, 8 s.d. above the mean), leaving 140 (58 men and 82 women) valid subjects. The D_2 index (Wiggins, 1973) is equal to the sum of the squared differences between corresponding T-score values for the eight basic clinical scales and serves as an index of profile stability across two administrations. After removing invalid cases, 519 (184 men and 335 women) subjects remained for the validity study. Among a total of 519 subjects, only 394 (147 men and 247 women) who claimed to have a very or extremely close relationship with their friends were included in further analyses.

A decision that had to be made before the Korean data were analyzed was whether positively rewritten items that were negatively phrased in the original MMPI-2 and the Korean version of the MMPI-2 changed the response pattern of the subjects. Table 5-1 presents item endorsement percentages of negatively and positively phrased items for the Korean and American college samples. As expected, percentages of true responses to a negatively written item are not the same as percentages of false responses to the same positively phrased item. In 16 items (66.7%) for males and 15 items (63%) for females, endorsement percentage differences to negatively written items between Korean and American samples are less than item endorsement differences between Koreans' false endorsement of the positively written items and Americans' true endorsement of the negatively written items. It was also discovered that Koreans tend to answer false to the positively phrased items more often than true to the negatively phrased items. On five items for both sexes, the percentages of false responses to the positively

Table 5-1. Item Endorsement Percentages of the Negatively (N) and Positively (P) Written Items for the Korean (K) and American (A) College Samples

Item#	Men N		Men P	Women N		Women P
	K	A	K	K	A	K
20	88	88	94	70	79	77
33	41	52	44	44	57	49
47	79	77	93	79	76	92
57	69	76	93	59	70	50
63	53	45	54	32	20	36
91	68	84	46	59	88	37
117	78	83	89	78	82	95
142	87	89	95	90	90	96
152	56	77	57	30	57	31
159	88	82	92	77	65	79
163	45	77	42	18	52	13
164	49	89	29	17	77	09
176	68	83	76	44	69	40
177	62	90	73	51	89	63
184	06	33	07	05	25	09
208	57	72	53	49	64	38
220	46	11	60	21	05	37
245	52	32	57	46	28	48
255	65	80	57	48	80	40
295	70	87	78	67	86	72
321	57	65	54	45	49	46
385	72	81	85	43	52	58
401	66	83	72	58	73	65
453	75	65	79	55	29	56

Note: Values are percentage of true responses.

phrased items are more than 10 points greater than the percentages of true responses to the negatively phrased items. However, on only one item for both sexes did the percentages of true responses to the negatively phrased item exceed 10 points more than the percentages of false responses to the positively phrased item.

Table 5-2 presents item-scale correlations between negatively written items and their scales, correlations between positively written items and their scales, and internal consistency of those scales. Four scales were selected for tabular presentation since each one included five or more positively written items. For each of these scales the item-scale correlations of the negatively written items are generally higher than those of the positively written items.

Table 5-3 shows test-retest correlations for both negatively and positively phrased items in the Korean sample. The mean phi coefficients of the negatively written items are .49 for males and .61 for females, whereas the mean phi coefficients of the positively written items are .58 for males and .67 for females. This result suggests that positively phrased items have higher response consistency over time than do the negatively phrased items.

To summarize, direction of phrasing affects item endorsement patterns, item-scale correlations, and response consistency. In comparisons of endorsement percentages, negatively written items in the Korean sample are more similar than positively phrased items to those in the American sample. Negatively phrased items have higher item-scale correlations but less stability over time than positively phrased items. Given the conflicting merits of each approach and the goal of literal continuity with the original MMPI-2, it was decided not to change the original negative phrasing.

Psychometric Evaluation of the Korean MMPI-2

Several types of analyses were performed to determine whether the Korean version of the MMPI-2 was equivalent to the original MMPI-2. The performances of the Korean college sample were compared to those of American (515 men and 797 women) and Japanese (563 men and 507 women) college samples.

Comparisons of Internal Structure. The first level of analysis for examining equivalence of the Korean MMPI-2 was a comparison of its internal structure against that of the two other national samples. Examining the underlying dimensions or latent structure is the fundamental procedure for cultural comparisons. If an instrument has different structures between groups, it could be argued that it measures different traits in the different groups and would therefore not be meaningful in a discussion of mean differences (Finn, 1984). Therefore, assurance that the instrument is measuring similar dimensions, traits, or factors is required before any further steps can be taken.

Table 5-2. Item-Scale Correlations and Internal Consistency of the Negatively (N) and Positively (P) Written Items for the Four Scales for the Korean College Samples

		Item-Scale Correlations			
		Men		Women	
Scale	Item#	N	P	N	P
Hs	20	.13	.14	.21	.29
	47	.29	.23	.29	.33
	57	.33	.32	.38	.34
	91	.35	.34	.40	.29
	117	.09	.14	.22	.10
	152	.36	.43	.36	.35
	164	.37	.35	.25	.19
	176	.33	.38	.50	.43
	208	.41	.49	.35	.33
	255	.30	.24	.30	.33
	Alpha	.77	.77	.81	.80
D	20	.09	.03	.03	.06
	33	.27	.25	.20	.17
	117	−.04	−.07	−.05	−.06
	142	.05	.04	.13	.03
	245	.02	.08	.09	.15
	Alpha	.66	.67	.66	.67
Hy	47	.23	.22	.20	.26
	91	.19	.26	.28	.15
	152	.25	.36	.30	.31
	159	.01	.02	.05	.05
	164	.29	.21	.23	.12
	176	.24	.24	.41	.36
	208	.31	.28	.22	.23
	Alpha	.57	.57	.60	.58
HEA	20	.13	.08	.22	.29
	33	.27	.30	.38	.40
	47	.30	.26	.30	.41
	57	.31	.30	.35	.32
	91	.38	.40	.38	.25
	117	.15	.17	.21	.10
	142	.27	.19	.24	.20
	159	.08	.08	.16	.18
	164	.37	.31	.23	.15
	176	.31	.35	.48	.39
	255	.33	.22	.33	.32
	295	.39	.36	.35	.40
	Alpha	.78	.77	.83	.82

Note: Data from subjects who responded "cannot say" to an item on a scale were deleted for that scale. The minimum number of subjects in the above analyses was 271 males and 354 females for the negatively written items and 268 males and 324 females for the positively written items. Internal consistency estimates are coefficient alphas, based on the total item membership of each scale.

Table 5-3. Test-Retest Correlations of the Negatively (N) and Positively (P) Written Items for the Korean College Samples

Item#	Men (N = 58)		Women (N = 82)	
	N	P	N	P
20	.57	.86	.66	.79
33	.46	.58	.69	.63
47	.21	.48	.40	.59
57	.52	.33	.52	.73
63	.68	.57	.63	.65
91	.44	.55	.35	.59
117	.33	.48	.47	.85
142	.31	.38	.63	.56
152	.65	.69	.70	.56
159	.19	.78	.70	1.00
163	.53	.60	.72	.68
164	.67	.51	.48	.28
176	.62	.58	.68	.71
177	.47	.51	.51	.61
184	.58	.60	.74	.58
208	.45	.43	.55	.62
220	.70	.67	.52	.72
245	.57	.56	.75	.80
255	.36	.41	.40	.54
295	.38	.59	.53	.58
321	.34	.61	.83	.77
385	.44	.46	.73	.70
401	.61	.81	.72	.84
453	.62	.77	.66	.67
Median	.50	.58	.64	.66
Mean	.49	.58	.61	.67

Note: Retest interval was one week for both samples.

Table 5-4. Factor Loadings on the Four Factors Extracted from MMPI-2 Basic Scales for Korean (K; N = 284), American (A; N = 515), and Japanese (J; N = 563) Male College Samples

Scale	Factor 1			Factor 2			Factor 3			Factor 4		
	K	A	J	K	A	J	K	A	J	K	A	J
L	09	–15	–03	05	02	03	81	71	74	09	–36	–12
F	75	73	69	–04	42	50	–35	01	02	11	07	–15
K	–23	–38	–22	–02	–41	–44	85	72	76	13	03	–06
Hs	27	58	58	09	56	51	–30	18	15	80	11	23
D	24	15	20	62	75	78	–21	32	32	58	30	26
Hy	23	24	49	03	15	16	23	72	62	90	44	36
Pd	54	64	71	–06	28	22	–32	–02	–03	47	38	13
Mf	48	08	15	29	20	19	05	–07	–10	19	84	89
Pa	80	59	71	03	16	15	02	11	04	23	45	22
Pt	50	54	47	28	64	68	–65	–37	–37	35	22	24
Sc	60	73	67	08	51	53	–62	–24	–38	35	18	13
Ma	25	81	68	–75	–22	–22	–41	–34	–49	14	–12	–07
Si	32	12	11	73	89	91	–43	–23	18	16	11	07
% variance	21.2	25.9	25.5	12.8	22.3	23.6	22.6	15.8	17.1	18.6	12.2	9.4

Note: Decimal points are omitted. Highest loadings for each scale are underlined.

Factor analyses were carried out in the following manner. Intercorrelation matrices of non–K-corrected raw scores for the three validity and 10 clinical scales for each of the three national samples were submitted to a principal component analysis with varimax rotation, separately by gender. Each of the correlation matrices of the 15 content scales for each sample were also subjected to a principal components analysis with varimax rotation. The "eigenvalues greater than one" criterion and scree test suggested three- and four-factor solutions for the validity and clinical scales, and two- and three-factor solutions for the content scales. However, only the four-factor solution for the 13 basic scales and the two-factor solution for the 15 content scales will be discussed here because these factor solutions showed far better convergence than did the three-factor solutions within the U.S. samples (Han, 1993). These factor solutions were also more interpretable and supported by prior research (Butcher & Pancheri, 1976; Shiota, 1989; Tonsager & Finn, 1992). To determine the degree of similarity of the factor solutions, two indices of factorial (or factor loading) similarity, congruence coefficients, and factor score correlations were computed across the six samples.

Table 5-5. Factor Loadings on the Four Factors Extracted from MMPI-2 Basic Scales for Korean (K; N=399), American (A; N=797), and Japanese (J; N=507) Female College Samples

Scale	Factor 1			Factor 2			Factor 3			Factor 4		
	K	A	J	K	A	J	K	A	J	K	A	J
L	11	02	17	05	−09	−18	<u>72</u>	<u>79</u>	<u>71</u>	21	21	00
F	42	<u>55</u>	<u>52</u>	08	48	<u>57</u>	<u>−70</u>	−20	−16	−02	−37	−17
K	04	−02	03	−10	<u>−78</u>	<u>−63</u>	<u>84</u>	43	<u>64</u>	04	06	−01
Hs	<u>82</u>	<u>69</u>	<u>73</u>	11	35	37	−27	−05	−06	−07	−08	−03
D	<u>50</u>	<u>61</u>	48	<u>69</u>	<u>51</u>	<u>70</u>	−22	25	28	16	21	12
Hy	<u>93</u>	<u>81</u>	<u>85</u>	02	−35	−07	10	16	29	07	10	06
Pd	<u>51</u>	<u>69</u>	<u>63</u>	03	24	34	<u>−56</u>	−26	−28	11	−11	11
Mf	03	09	12	06	04	05	08	−06	07	<u>95</u>	<u>88</u>	<u>96</u>
Pa	<u>50</u>	<u>69</u>	<u>64</u>	−02	21	22	−49	−13	−21	30	12	28
Pt	37	<u>50</u>	38	30	<u>74</u>	<u>74</u>	<u>−78</u>	−29	−42	18	−01	11
Sc	42	<u>57</u>	48	12	<u>63</u>	<u>63</u>	<u>−83</u>	−35	<u>−50</u>	04	−22	−02
Ma	20	27	39	<u>−70</u>	09	−15	<u>−51</u>	<u>−68</u>	<u>−77</u>	12	−41	−11
Si	06	13	07	<u>76</u>	<u>91</u>	<u>93</u>	−49	16	−06	09	11	08
% variance	21.8	26.3	24.1	13.0	24.9	26.0	32.5	13.3	17.3	8.8	9.7	8.3

Note: Decimal points are omitted. Highest loadings for each scale are underlined.

Tables 5-4 and 5-5 present scale factor loadings and percentage of variance. The order of factors has been rearranged as necessary to make the factors maximally comparable to each other and to the other data sets. In the three male samples, the first factor is characterized by scales F, Pd, Pa, Pt, and Sc. Hs and Ma also have moderate to high loadings on this factor in the American and Japanese samples. In the female sample, the neurotic scales load on this factor more highly than do the psychotic scales. This factor is usually referred to as general maladjustment.

The second factor is represented by the D and Si scales in all samples. Scales Pt and Sc also load on this factor in American and Japanese male and female samples, with Hs also loading on this factor in American and Japanese male samples and K loading negatively on this factor in American and Japanese female samples. Ma has a high negative loading on this factor in the Korean male and female samples. This factor can be labeled social introversion.

The third factor, labeled repression or ego control, is characterized by high loadings on L and K, with Hy loading highly in the American and Japanese male samples and Pt and Sc loading negatively in the Korean male sample. For females, this factor is characterized by high loadings on L and K (except American females) and moderate to high negative loadings on Ma. For Korean females this factor also includes some psychotic scales.

The last factor is characterized solely by Mf for all samples, except the Korean male sample, and can be considered masculinity-femininity. A neuroticism factor, instead of a masculinity-femininity factor, was found in the Korean male factor structure. To explore this exception further, the Korean male sample was split randomly in halves 10 times. Each of 20 sample halves was submitted to a principal components analysis with varimax rotation of four factors. Only nine of the 20 factor structures had factor loadings above .70 for the Mf scale. Among these nine structures, only three evidenced a pure masculinity-femininity factor (a high factor loading by Mf and low loadings by all other scales). The other six factor structures also included high loadings on the Pa scale (5) or the neurotic scales (1). This suggests that the idiosyncratic neuroticism factor for Korean males is stable and not due to sampling error.

For the male factor structures, convergence between American and Japanese men for the four factors are extremely high, with congruence coefficients (CC) of .98, 1.00, .99, and .92 and factor score coefficients (FSC) of .98, .99, .97, and .92 (see Table 5-6). Overall, when one compares Korean males with American or Japanese males, the first three factors appear to be somewhat similar. The CC and FSC range from .64 to .91. It is puzzling that unlike the FSC, the CC for the fourth factor between Korean males and American and Japanese males are quite high (.65 and .61), considering that completely different scales appear to load on this factor. However, since CC are also fairly high among the noncorresponding intrastructure factors, it is not surprising to find such high CC for the noncorresponding interstructure factors. The FSC provide values that are more consistent with visual inspection.

For females, the factor structures between American and Japanese subjects are again very similar. The CC for the four factors are .99, .97, .96, and .87, while the FSC are .97, .95, .96, and .93. On the first and fourth factors, Korean and Japanese females show high convergence (CC of .98 and .94; FSC of .95 and .94). Only on the first factor do Korean and American women have high convergence (CC of .97 and FSC of .95). Overall, however, the Korean female sample has similar factor structures to American and Japanese females.

It is surprising to note here that the CC and FSC within the American samples (males versus females) and within the Japanese samples (males versus females) are lower than the CC and FSC between the American and Japanese college samples for each gender (American males versus Japanese males; American females versus Japanese females). (Han [1993] further showed that the factor convergence of the

Table 5-6. Congruence Coefficients and Factor Score Correlations between Four Factors Extracted from MMPI-2 Basic Scales for Korean, American, and Japanese Male and Female College Samples

Scale		KM F1	KM F2	KM F3	KM F4	AM F1	AM F2	AM F3	AM F4	JM F1	JM F2	JM F3	JM F4	KF F1	KF F2	KF F3	KF F4	AF F1	AF F2	AF F3	AF F4	JF F1	JF F2	JF F3	JF F4
KM	F1	**.640**																							
	F2	.241	**.803**																						
	F3	-.539	-.142	**.800**																					
	F4	.623	.302	-.325	**.328**																				
AM	F1	**.879**	-.082	-.704	.644	**.977**																			
	F2	.712	**-.644**	.756	.650	.598	**.993**																		
	F3	-.106	.111	.281	.318	-.258	-.135	**.972**																	
	F4	.674	.405	-.577	.651	.453	.492	.040	**.924**																
JM	F1	**.912**	-.026	-.644	.744	**.976**	.601	-.072	.550	**.976**															
	F2	.711	**.720**	.796	.626	.592	**.998**	-.141	.473	.591	**.998**														
	F3	-.189	.172	-.194	.220	-.369	-.154	**.985**	-.026	-.190	-.158	**.985**													
	F4	.527	.438	-.322	.608	.315	.462	.064	**.916**	.401	.444	-.158	**.916**												
KF	F1	**.742**	.193	-.255	.952	**.759**	.636	.574	.226	**.857**	.620	-.190	.401	**.946**											
	F2	.283	**.971**	**.939**	.341	.021	.797	.317	.132	.059	.798	-.158	.444	.520	**.971**										
	F3	-.761	-.121	.006	-.426	-.861	-.689	-.389	-.225	-.775	-.690	-.689	-.689	-.262	.181	**.803**									
	F4	.538	.297	-.439	.291	.247	.284	.751	.838	.322	.280	.673	.826	-.087	.243	.135	**.807**								
AF	F1	**.850**	.219	-.830	.911	**.843**	.697	.638	.087	**.922**	.683	.019	.087	**.966**	.164	-.634	.313	**.974**							
	F2	.686	**.510**	.782	.365	.657	**.896**	.291	-.516	.578	**.902**	.087	-.516	.139	**.954**	-.847	.181	.294	**.612**						
	F3	-.385	.422	.181	-.121	-.651	-.108	-.228	-.102	-.524	-.104	-.516	-.102	-.021	.139	.754	-.003	.358	.422	**.839**					
	F4	-.001	.525	-.349	.091	-.320	.092	.648	.763	-.239	.079	.839	.814	-.131	.089	.243	.682	-.093	.525	.181	**.682**				
JF	F1	**.823**	.127	-.783	.909	**.834**	.621	.597	.156	**.923**	.606	.081	.156	**.987**	.634	-.555	.329	**.983**	.127	-.349	.091	**.987**			
	F2	.724	**.625**	.858	.511	.649	**.963**	.417	-.362	.610	**.966**	.140	-.362	.967	.967	-.823	.191	.530	**.727**	.625	-.783	.634	**.967**		
	F3	-.441	.319	.011	-.100	-.693	-.239	-.150	-.044	-.551	-.237	-.053	-.546	-.277	-.285	-.237	.020	-.150	.319	**.858**	-.100	-.277	-.546	**.858**	
	F4	.395	.392	.246	.246	.083	.240	.807	.896	.160	.226	.778	.962	.198	.435	.319	.939	.143	.392	.011	.246	.198	.111	.014	**.063**

Note: Values below diagonal are congruence coefficients; values above diagonal are factor score correlations; values of corresponding factors are given in boldface. KM: Korean males, AM: American males, JM: Japanese males, KF: Korean females, AF: American females, JF: Japanese females.

Table 5-7. Factor Loadings on the Two Factors Extracted from MMPI-2 Content Scales for Korean (K; N = 284), American (A; N = 515), and Japanese (J; N = 563) Male College Samples

Scale	Factor 1			Factor 2		
	K	A	J	K	A	J
ANX	76	73	81	44	44	34
FRS	49	54	48	22	20	09
OBS	64	62	71	47	54	45
DEP	80	81	79	36	33	35
HEA	56	60	58	16	25	17
BIZ	32	46	30	55	55	57
ANG	27	27	25	72	78	71
CYN	23	23	22	78	82	82
ASP	03	17	−00	78	81	80
TPA	27	22	22	75	82	80
LSE	82	79	80	27	28	27
SOD	70	70	68	−25	−04	−08
FAM	51	49	36	52	51	54
WRK	80	79	79	42	42	44
TRT	78	73	67	41	43	48
% variance	34.4	34.5	32.6	26.6	28.7	27.0

Note: Decimal points are omitted. Highest loadings for each scale are underlined.

basic scales between American and Japanese female college samples exceeded that between the American normative females and the American female college sample.)

Careful inspection of Table 5-6 reveals some interesting aspects of the two similarity indices (discussed in greater depth elsewhere in this volume [Butcher & Han, chapter 3]). First, the two similarity indices give different values for the same factor comparisons. As discussed in Butcher and Han, the CC and FSC measure different similarities: the CC measure a factor loading similarity; the FSC measure a factor similarity. Therefore, the two similarity indices frequently give different values. Second, as expected, compared to the FSC, CC for the noncorresponding factor pairs were very high, indicating the lack of a convergent-discriminant factor pattern.

The two factor solutions on the 15 content scales are given in Table 5-7 and 5-8. The first factor, labeled negative emotionality (Tonsager & Finn, 1992), is primarily represented by scales ANX, OBS, DEP, HEA, LSE, SOD, WRK, and TRT for all samples. The second factor, labeled impulsivity, is characterized by scales

Table 5-8. Factor Loadings on the Two Factors Extracted from MMPI-2 Content Scales for
Korean (K; N = 399), American (A; N = 797), and Japanese (J; N = 507) Female College Samples

Scale	Factor 1				Factor 2		
	K	A	J		K	A	J
ANX	73	74	79		44	43	36
FRS	27	30	27		13	36	17
OBS	64	69	75		41	44	36
DEP	82	79	83		30	36	32
HEA	45	45	48		32	40	26
BIZ	35	36	33		62	64	56
ANG	25	30	39		70	70	65
CYN	28	26	23		78	83	82
ASP	11	08	04		76	81	78
TPA	12	22	20		82	79	77
LSE	82	84	84		23	25	16
SOD	65	64	71		–14	–04	–09
FAM	41	46	46		53	51	48
WRK	82	81	83		33	41	37
TRT	80	77	68		35	40	45
% variance	31.6	32.4	33.9		25.9	28.7	24.5

Note: Decimal points are omitted. Highest loadings of each factor are underlined.

BIZ, ANG, CYN, ASP, TPA, and FAM. The CC and FSC for the two factors are
extremely high, ranging from .98 to 1.00 in factor comparisons across six samples
(see Table 5-9). They clearly indicate that the factor structures of the content scales
are identical in the college samples cross-nationally.

To summarize, factor structure of the basic scales between American and Japanese
samples was so similar for each gender that factor convergence cross-nationally
was even higher than that between samples within the United States for each gender.
Factor convergence between Korean females and American and Japanese females
was moderate to high. A neuroticism factor, rather than a masculinity-femininity
factor, emerged in the Korean male structure. For the content scales, a two-factor
solution emerged with extremely high convergence across all six samples.

Scale-Level Comparisons. Two analyses were performed to examine the equivalence
of the Korean MMPI-2 to the original at the scale level: a comparison of MMPI-2
scale mean profiles and a comparison of skewness of linear and uniform T scores.

Table 5-9. Congruence Coefficients and Factor Score Correlations between Two Factors Extracted from MMPI-2 Content Scales for Korean, American, and Japanese Male and Female College Samples

Scale		KM (N = 284)		AM (N = 515)		JM (N = 563)		KF (N = 399)		AF (N = 797)		JF (N = 507)	
		F1	F2	F1	F2	F1	F2	F1	F2	F1	F2	F1	F2
KM	F1		.000	**.996**	.009	**.997**	.040	**.994**	.005	**.989**	.035	**.995**	.006
	F2	.634		.005	**.995**	-.018	**.994**	.022	**.993**	.009	**.986**	.026	**.994**
AM	F1	**.995**	.657		.000	**.995**	.033	**.989**	.007	**.984**	.050	**.988**	.010
	F2	.665	**.993**	.686		-.013	**.992**	.023	**.991**	.011	**.982**	.036	**.990**
JM	F1	**.995**	.612	**.991**	.644		.000	**.988**	-.021	**.985**	-.002	**.993**	-.027
	F2	.643	**.992**	.664	**.995**	.616		.060	**.987**	.072	**.977**	.058	**.991**
KF	F1	**.990**	.636	**.987**	.664	**.988**	.649		.000	**.995**	.022	**.995**	.011
	F2	.624	**.991**	.650	**.993**	.602	**.991**	.622		-.018	**.994**	.015	**.994**
AF	F1	**.994**	.657	**.989**	.686	**.990**	.669	**.998**	.644		.000	**.995**	-.009
	F2	.677	**.985**	.706	**.991**	.656	**.983**	.668	**.991**	.688		.024	**.994**
JF	F1	**.990**	.638	**.984**	.671	**.991**	.650	**.993**	.627	**.997**	.670		.000
	F2	.625	**.990**	.650	**.993**	.599	**.995**	.625	**.994**	.644	**.991**	.623	

Note: Values below diagonal are congruence coefficients; values above diagonal are factor score correlations; values of corresponding factors are given in boldface.
KM: Korean males, AM: American males, JM: Japanese males, KF: Korean females, AF: American females, JF: Japanese females.

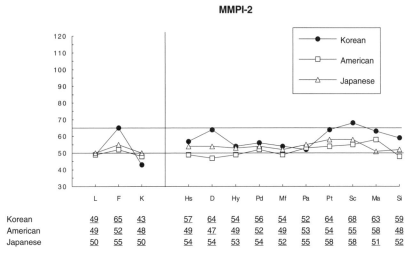

	L	F	K	Hs	D	Hy	Pd	Mf	Pa	Pt	Sc	Ma	Si
Korean	49	65	43	57	64	54	56	54	52	64	68	63	59
American	49	52	48	49	47	49	52	49	53	54	55	58	48
Japanese	50	55	50	54	54	53	54	52	55	58	58	51	52

Figure 5-1. Group Mean K-Corrected MMPI-2 Standard Scale Profile for Korean Men Compared with Japanese and American Men

Mean basic scale profiles of the three national samples are presented in Figures 5-1 and 5-2, plotted against American norms. The most general observation that can be made about Koreans' mean profiles is that, with the exception of scales L and K, all mean scores fall above the mean of the American normative sample. In the male sample the most elevated scale is Sc, whose mean falls near a T score of 70. The next four highest scores are on scales F, D, Pt, and Ma. Relative to the Japanese and American college samples, means on scales D and Sc are the highest, with Korean men scoring 10 or more T-score points higher.

Findings from the female college sample comparisons are similar to those from the male samples. Overall, the highest scale means, which are above a T score of 70, are on scales F and Sc. The next four highest scores are on scales Hs, D, Pt, and Ma. Relative to American and Japanese female college samples, means on scales F, Hs, D, Pt, and Sc are the highest, with Korean women scoring 10 or more T-score points higher. The mean score on F is 17 T-score points above the American female college mean.

The scales that show mean T-score differences of five or fewer points in both sexes are L, K, Pd, Mf, and Pa between Korean and American samples and L, Hs, Pd, Mf, and Pa between Korean and Japanese samples. For both men and women, the lowest clinical scale scores are on scales Mf and Pa, with means of 54 and 52 for men and 56 and 54 for women, respectively. The validity and clinical scales configurations between American and Japanese samples for men and women are very similar.

Mean MMPI-2 content scale profiles for the three national samples are pre-

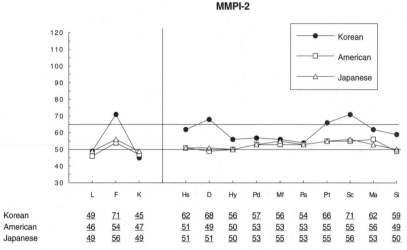

	L	F	K	Hs	D	Hy	Pd	Mf	Pa	Pt	Sc	Ma	Si
Korean	49	71	45	62	68	56	57	56	54	66	71	62	59
American	46	54	47	51	49	50	53	53	53	55	55	56	49
Japanese	49	56	49	51	51	50	53	55	53	55	56	53	50

Figure 5-2. Group Mean K-Corrected MMPI-2 Standard Scale Profile for Korean Women Compared with Japanese and American Women

sented in Figures 5-3 and 5-4. Examination of these profiles reveals that all mean scores fall above the means of the U.S. normative sample. On average, the elevations are one standard deviation above the normative sample mean. In the Korean-American comparison, scales FRS, OBS, DEP, HEA, LSE, SOD, WRK, and TRT for men and FRS, OBS, DEP, HEA, SOD, and TRT for women represent the highest mean score differences, with Koreans scoring 9 to 12 points higher. Content scales with T-score differences of 3 or fewer points for both sexes are ASP and CYN. In the Korean-Japanese male comparison, no scales show T-score differences of 9 or more points. In the Korean-Japanese female comparison, the scales that show T-score differences of 9 or more points are OBS, HEA, and SOD. The content scales with T-score differences of 3 or fewer points for both sexes are CYN, LSE, and TRT.

One of the new features of the MMPI-2 is the inclusion of uniform T scores (UT scores). UT scores have the advantage of being percentile comparable across scales, unlike linear T scores (LT scores). Additionally, UT scores were designed to retain the positively skewed shape of the MMPI-2 LT scores since it was believed that the positively skewed distribution is an accurate reflection of the distribution of psychopathological characteristics in the population. (Butcher et al., 1989; Tellegen & Ben-Porath, 1992). It is therefore important to examine the two characteristics of MMPI-2 scale distributions, percentile comparability across scales, and positive skewness.

A brief description of the characteristics of UT scores is appropriate before dis-

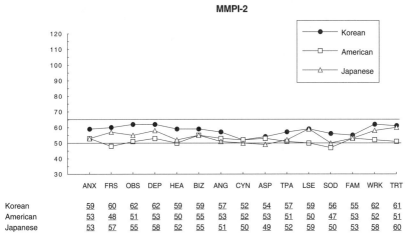

Figure 5-3. Group Mean MMPI-2 Content Scale Profile for a Sample of Korean Men Compared with Japanese and American Men

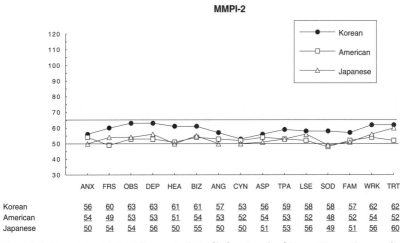

Figure 5-4. Group Mean MMPI-2 Content Scale Profile for a Sample of Korean Women Compared with Japanese and American Women

cussing cross-cultural comparisons. Traditionally, raw scores on MMPI scales were converted to standardized T scores with a mean of 50 and a standard deviation of 10. These T scores were linear transformations of the raw-score distributions, retaining the positive skew found in all the clinical scales with the original norms and also retaining the wide variation in range across the scales.

For the MMPI-2, a UT score transformation developed by Tellegen was adopted (Tellegen & Ben-Porath, 1992; Butcher et al., 1989). The UT scores have

Table 5-10. Skewness of the Linear (LT) and Uniform (UT) T Scores of MMPI-2 Clinical Scales for Korean (N = 284), American (N = 515), and Japanese (N = 563) Male College Samples

Scale	Korean Men		American Men		Japanese Men	
	LT	UT	LT	UT	LT	UT
Hs	0.704	0.396	1.287	0.645	1.045	0.517
D	0.043	-0.140	1.220	1.014	0.524	0.323
Hy	0.373	0.616	0.528	0.954	0.599	0.927
Pd	0.131	0.150	0.638	0.687	0.324	0.379
Pa	0.514	0.652	0.566	0.700	0.440	0.558
Pt	0.136	0.148	0.679	0.601	0.444	0.402
Sc	0.281	0.225	0.985	0.724	0.662	0.415
Ma	-0.089	0.300	0.101	0.548	0.275	0.788
Mean	0.262	0.293	0.751	0.734	0.539	0.539
S.D.	0.261	0.261	0.394	0.165	0.242	0.214
Range	0.793	0.792	1.186	0.466	0.770	0.604

Note: Values are non–K-corrected T scores; T scores are based on MMPI-2 normative adult sample.

a distribution that approximates the typical linear T-score distribution of MMPI-2 clinical scales. The distribution is a positively skewed composite (or prototype) of 16 distributions, namely, the non–K-corrected linear T-score distributions of the eight MMPI-2 clinical scales (omitting scales 5 and 0) for both normative gender groups. A series of composite T-score values (corresponding to percentiles) is used as the uniform standard in deriving regression formulas and look-up tables for individual scales. UT scores have the advantage of being percentile comparable, unlike linear T scores used in the original MMPI, while retaining the familiar shape of linear T scores.

Skewness is an index of the symmetry of a distribution. The normal curve is perfectly symmetrical and has a skewness of zero. If a skewness value is positive, the distribution is skewed to the right, indicating that most scores fell to the left of (below) the mean, with extreme values to the right of (above) the mean. In skewed distributions, the mean is always pulled toward the skewed (pointed) end of the curves. If the skewness value is negative, the distribution is skewed to the left, indicating that most scores fell to the right of (above) the mean (Guilford & Fruchter, 1981).

Tables 5-10 and 5-11 present LT and UT score skewness statistics for the eight non–K-corrected clinical scales for men and women for the three national

Table 5-11. Skewness of the Linear (LT) and Uniform (UT) T Scores of MMPI-2 Clinical Scales
for Korean (N = 399), American (N = 797), and Japanese (N = 507) Female College Samples

Scale	Korean Women		American Women		Japanese Women	
	LT	UT	LT	UT	LT	UT
Hs	0.660	0.586	0.895	0.445	1.332	0.766
D	0.193	0.279	0.563	0.705	0.637	0.838
Hy	0.354	0.547	0.111	0.399	0.668	1.027
Pd	0.436	0.536	0.592	0.745	0.352	0.491
Pa	0.589	0.755	0.497	0.682	0.353	0.578
Pt	0.062	0.127	0.452	0.403	0.573	0.516
Sc	0.271	0.232	0.755	0.444	0.820	0.529
Ma	0.040	0.293	0.065	0.485	0.130	0.541
Mean	0.326	0.419	0.491	0.539	0.608	0.661
S.D.	0.229	0.216	0.287	0.146	0.365	0.195
Range	0.620	0.628	0.830	0.346	1.202	0.536

Note: Values are non–K-corrected T scores; T scores are based on MMPI-2 normative adult sample.

college samples. These T scores are based on U.S. norms. For all six samples, mean skewnesses are positive. The rank of the mean UT score skewnesses are as follows: American men (.73), Japanese women (.66), American women (.54), Japanese men (.54), Korean women (.42), and Korean men (.29). Examination of standard deviations and ranges of skewnesses (across scales) provides information about how similar scale distributions are across scales (i.e., percentile comparability). As expected, for American men and women, the standard deviations of the UT score skewnesses are much smaller than those of the LT score skewnesses, clearly indicating that UT scores are more percentile comparable across scales than are linear T scores. The superiority of UT scores over LT scores is evident also in Japanese women. However, for Japanese men and Korean men and women, UT distributions across scales are nearly as variable as LT distributions.

Differences at the scale level in both means and skewnesses clearly indicate that the U.S. MMPI-2 normative sample is not an appropriate reference group for Koreans and that special norms need to be developed for interpreting profiles from a Korean population. Therefore, it was decided to develop UT scores normed on Korean subjects.

UT scores for Koreans were developed in the following manner. Following Tellegen and Ben-Porath (1992), a composite distribution containing 101 proto-

Table 5-12. Skewness of the Linear (LT) and Uniform (UT) T Scores of MMPI-2 Clinical Scales Based on Korean College Norms: Korean Male (N = 284) and Female (N = 399) College Sample

Scale	Men		Women	
	LT	UT	LT	UT
Hs	.713	.806	.668	.721
D	.093	.814	.275	.670
Hy	.339	.836	.401	.715
Pd	.206	.777	.431	.715
Pa	.499	.696	.611	.616
Pt	.128	.776	.086	.748
Sc	.270	.785	.327	.714
Ma	.060	.731	.107	.769
Mean	.286	.778	.363	.709
S.D.	.224	.045	.211	.047
Range	.653	.140	.582	153

Note: Values are non–K-corrected T scores.

typical (or averaged) linear T-score values corresponding to percentiles (0.5, 1.0, 2.0, . . . , 98.0, 99.0, 99.5) was derived from the eight clinical scales in the U.S. MMPI-2 adult normative sample. This prototype served as a target for deriving Korean UT scores. First, a series of interpolated raw score values corresponding to a series of 52 composite integer T-score values (ranging from 31 to 82) was derived from the raw score frequency distribution. It was assumed that the 52 integer composite T scores are more equally spaced over the underlying scale continuum than are the 101 composite T scores corresponding to a series of percentile values. Second, the raw scores were transformed into scores that approximate or predict the composite T-score values. The goal of this step was to derive for each scale the regression weights and intercept for the UT score equation as follows:

$$UT = B_0 + B_1X + B_2D_2 + B_3D_3,$$

where X is the raw score, B_0 is the intercept, B_1, B_2, B_3 are regression weights, and D = (C – X) if X < C, otherwise D = 0, C equaling the value of X that corresponds to a composite T score of 60. For more details about the rationale behind this equation, see Tellegen and Ben-Porath (1992). Finally, UT scores were obtained by inserting the B weight and B_0 intercept into the above equation and calculating UT scores for each possible raw score value.

Table 5-12 shows the skewnesses of the LT and UT scores developed for the

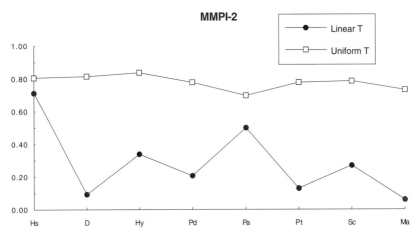

Figure 5-5. Comparison of Skewness for Uniform and Linear Distributions of Korean College Men

Korean college sample. The skewnesses of the linear T scores are very different across scales, ranging from .13 to .71 (mean = .29) for men and .09 to .67 for women (mean = .36). However, the skewnesses of the UT score distributions cluster closely around a mean of .78 for men and .71 for women. Examination of standard deviations and ranges of the skewness of the linear and uniform T scores clearly indicates that the UT distributions are more similar in skewness than are the linear T distributions. Figures 5-5 and 5-6 illustrate these findings in a striking fashion.

In summary, examination of the skewnesses of the UT and LT scores developed for the Korean college samples showed that the range of the skewnesses of the UT scores was smaller than that of the LT scores, indicating more percentile comparability across scales with UT scores.

Item-Level Comparisons. Mean profile comparisons in the previous section showed that Koreans had elevated mean scores on most of the clinical and content scales. The next questions to be asked concern the items that contribute to the mean scale elevations and the items that discriminate Korean samples from other national samples. Item-level comparisons among the three national samples were conducted in four ways. First, item endorsement frequencies and percentages were examined. Second, intercorrelations of item endorsement percentages among the national samples were compared. Third, extreme items across cultures were examined. Finally, items that best discriminate Koreans from Americans and Japanese were identified and grouped by content categories.

Items distinguishing the three national samples were examined by comparing individual item endorsement frequencies across Korean, American, and Japanese samples. Items with endorsement percentage differences greater than 50% were

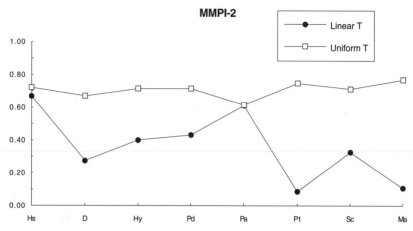

Figure 5-6. Comparison of Skewness for Uniform and Linear Distributions of Korean College Women

identified. Between the Korean and American samples, 8 items for males and 11 items for females were found. The most extreme item was item 495 (66% difference for males and 73% difference for females), on which 80% of the Korean males and 84% of the Korean females indicated that they believe that people should keep personal problems to themselves. Between the Korean and Japanese samples, 5 items for men and 11 items for women had endorsement differences of over 50%. For men the most extreme item was item 494, on which 93% of the Koreans and 31% of the Japanese indicated that their main goals in life are within reach. For women the most extreme item was item 12, on which 17% of the Koreans and 89% of the Japanese indicated that their sex lives were satisfactory (although 59% of the Korean women did not answer that item). The high endorsement rate on this item by Japanese women may be due to the wording in the Japanese translation (Clark, 1982). Between the American and Japanese samples, 3 items for men and 5 items for women had endorsement differences of over 50%. For both men and women, the most extreme item was item 359, on which 80% of American men and women and 17% and 12% of Japanese men and women, respectively, reported that they enjoyed the excitement of a crowd.

Table 5-13 presents intercorrelations of item endorsement percentages among the six samples. Within the same culture, male and female item endorsement patterns are very similar. The correlation between males and females is .90 for Koreans, .90 for Americans, and .94 for Japanese.

Item endorsement patterns between American and Japanese samples are fairly similar. The correlations of endorsement percentages between American and Japanese samples are .85 within gender for both males and females. The correlations between the Korean sample and the American sample are somewhat lower

Table 5-13. Correlations of True Item-Endorsement Percentages
between Korean, American, and Japanese College Samples

	KM (N = 284)	KF (N = 399)	AM (N = 515)	AF (N = 799)	JM (N = 563)	JF (N = 507)
KM						
KF	.90					
AM	.74	.59				
AF	.73	.70	.90			
JM	.78	.67	.85	.82		
JF	.73	.73	.77	.85	.94	

Note: KM: Korean males, KF: Korean females, AM: American males, AF: American females, JM: Japanese males, JF: Japanese females.

Table 5-14. Number and Percentage of Extreme Items between Korean, American, and Japanese College Samples on MMPI-2 Basic Scales

Scale	Korean vs. American		Korean vs. Japanese		American vs. Japanese	
	# of extreme items/ # in scale	%	# of extreme items/ # in scale	%	# of extreme items/ # in scale	%
L	1/15	7	0/15	0	0/15	0
F	4/60	7	5/60	8	1/60	2
K	6/30	20	7/30	23	2/30	7
Hs	4/32	13	3/32	9	0/32	0
D	17/57	30	11/57	19	2/57	4
Hy	12/60	20	9/60	15	2/60	3
Pd	12/50	24	8/50	16	2/50	4
Mf	7/56	13	4/56	7	4/56	7
Pa	4/40	10	3/40	8	0/40	0
Pt	13/48	27	6/48	13	1/48	2
Sc	17/78	22	13/78	17	1/78	1
Ma	11/46	24	7/46	15	4/46	9
Si	19/69	28	17/69	25	4/69	6

but still high, .74 for males and .70 for females. It is noteworthy that correlations between American and Japanese samples cross-gender are even higher than those between Korean and Japanese males (.78) and Korean and Japanese females (.73).

Item endorsement differences among the three national samples were further examined to determine if any of the MMPI-2 validity and clinical scales contained a disproportionate number of "extreme" items (Butcher & Pancheri, 1976). Extreme items between cultures were arbitrarily defined as those that differ by 25% or greater between the two cultures for both genders. With these criteria, 98 items between Korean and American samples, 73 items between Korean and Japanese samples, and 32 items between American and Japanese samples were identified. Table 5-14 presents the number and percentage of extreme items on each of the 13 basic scales. In the comparison between Korean and American samples, the percentage of extreme items on the basic scales ranged from 7% (scales L and F) to 30% (scale D). Between Korean and Japanese samples, the percentage of extreme items ranged from 0% (scale L) to 25% (scale Si). Between American and Japanese samples, the discrepancies were fairly small. The percentages of extreme items ranged from 0% (scales L, Hs, and Pa) to 9% (scale Ma).

Table 5-15 presents the number and percentage of extreme items on each of the 15 content scales. Overall, the content scales have higher percentages of extreme items than did the basic scales. The scale that contained the highest percentage of extreme items in both the Korean/American comparison (38%) and the Korean/Japanese comparison (31%) was OBS. CYN (13%) and LSE (13%) contained the highest percentages of extreme items between the American and Japanese samples.

The final item-level study examined the content of the MMPI-2 items that discriminate best between the Korean sample and the American and Japanese samples. Items with a 25% or greater endorsement percentage difference between Korean and American groups and between Korean and Japanese groups were selected: 125 items between the Korean and American male groups, 137 items between the Korean and American female groups, 100 items between the Korean and Japanese male groups, and 119 items between the Korean and Japanese female groups had endorsement differences of 25% or greater. Of those items only 41 overlap across the four comparisons. The five scales that contain the highest percentages of these items are OBS (25%, 4 items), Si (16%, 11 items), D (16%, 9 items), DEP (15%, 5 items), and Sc (12%, 9 items).

Table 5-16 presents these items grouped according to content categories. The content categories were derived by the present author on the basis of face validity. The five content categories with the largest number of items are interpersonal and social attitudes (10); depressive affect (5); obsessiveness-compulsiveness (5); rare sensory experience (4); and health concern-somatization (4).

Table 5-15. Number and Percentage of Extreme Items between Korean, American, and Japanese College Samples on MMPI-2 Content Scales

Scale	Korean vs. American		Korean vs. Japanese		American vs. Japanese	
	# of extreme items/ # in scale	%	# of extreme items/ # in scale	%	# of extreme items/ # in scale	%
ANX	2/23	9	2/23	9	0/23	0
FRS	8/23	35	1/23	4	2/23	9
OBS	6/16	38	5/16	31	0/16	0
DEP	9/33	27	5/33	15	1/33	3
HEA	3/36	8	3/36	8	0/36	0
BIZ	2/23	9	2/23	9	1/23	4
ANG	2/16	13	4/16	25	0/16	0
CYN	4/23	17	4/23	17	3/23	13
ASP	3/22	14	2/22	9	1/22	5
TPA	4/19	21	3/19	16	1/19	5
LSE	6/24	25	6/24	25	3/24	13
SOD	8/24	33	6/24	25	2/24	8
FAM	5/25	20	3/25	12	2/25	8
WRK	9/33	27	4/33	12	2/33	6
TRT	7/26	27	4/26	15	3/26	12

Test-Retest Reliability. Table 5-17 shows test-retest correlation coefficients for the Korean sample and American college sample (from Butcher, Graham, Dahlstrom, and Bowman, 1990). No test-retest data are available for the Japanese college sample. Coefficients are comparable and generally high, ranging from .66 (Hy and Pa) to .87 (Sc) for Korean males, .66 (Pa) to .92 (Pt) for Korean females, .62 (K) to .87 (Si) for American males, and .73 (L) to .91 (Si) for American females. For both cultures the median test-retest correlations for the female samples (.85 for Koreans and .81 for Americans) were higher than those for the male samples (.75 for Koreans and .78 for Americans). We used Fisher Z transformation and Bonferroni correction and found that no test-retest correlations for the Korean sample are significantly different from those for the American sample at the p<.05 level (corrected to p<.004 per comparison).

Table 5-18 presents test-retest correlations for the Korean MMPI-2 content scales. No data were available for cross-cultural comparisons. Examination of

Table 5-16. Items That Discriminate the Korean Sample from American and Japanese Samples by Content Categories

Item #	Item Contents and Categories
Interpersonal and Social Attitudes (10)	
46[a]	I prefer to pass by school friends, or people I know but have not seen for a long time, unless they speak to me first.
49[b]	I am a very sociable person.
161[a]	I frequently have to fight against showing that I am bashful.
189[b]	I like to flirt.
278[b]	I get all the sympathy I should.
310[a]	Often I cross the street in order not to meet someone I see.
338[a]	People often disappoint me.
359[c]	I enjoy the excitement of a crowd.
374[a]	Most people will use somewhat unfair means to get ahead in life.
495[a]	I believe that people should keep personal problems to themselves.
Depressive Affect (5)	
56[a]	I wish I could be as happy as others seem to be.
95[b]	I am happy most of the time.
148[b]	I have never felt better in my life than I do now.
215[a]	I brood a great deal.
348[a]	I often think, "I wish I were a child again."
Obsessiveness-Compulsiveness (5)	
135[a]	I have often lost out on things because I couldn't make up my mind soon enough.
309[a]	I usually have to stop and think before I act even in small matters.
402[a]	I often must sleep over a matter before I decide what to do.
482[a]	I usually have a hard time deciding what to do.
553[a]	Much of what is happening to me now seems to have happened to me before.
Rare Sensory Experience (4)	
106[b]	My speech is the same as always (not faster or slower, no slurring or hoarseness).
168[a]	I have had periods in which I carried on activities without knowing later what I had been doing.
177[b]	My hands have not become clumsy or awkward.
229[a]	I have had blank spells in which my activities were interrupted and I did not know what was going on around me.
Health Concern-Somatization (4)	
149[a]	The top of my head sometimes feels tender.
164[b]	I seldom or never have dizzy spells.
173[b]	I can read a long while without tiring my eyes.
388[b]	I very seldom have spells of the blues.
Family Problems (2)	
217[a]	My relatives are nearly all in sympathy with me.
300[a]	I have reason for feeling jealous of one or more members of my family.
Lack of Self-Esteem (2)	
475[a]	Often I get confused and forget what I want to say.
485[a]	I often feel that I'm not as good as other people.

continued on next page

Table 5-16 (*continued*)

Mental Dullness (2)

38[a]   I have had periods of days, weeks, or months when I couldn't take care of things because I couldn't "get going."

170[a]   I am afraid of losing my mind.

Work Problems (2)

364[a]   I feel like giving up quickly when things go wrong.

566[a]   When I am sad or blue, it is my work that suffers.

Anger (1)

430[a]   I am often sorry because I am so irritable and grouchy.

Fears (1)

154[a]   I am afraid when I look down from a high place.

Habits (1)

502[a]   I have some habits that are really harmful.

Sexual Attitudes (1)

12[b]   My sex life is satisfactory.

Unclassified (1)

156[a]   I am never happy unless I am roaming or traveling around.

[a]The Korean sample has the highest percentage of true responses.
[b]The Korean sample has the lowest percentage of true responses.
[c]The Japanese sample has the lowest percentage of true responses.

Tables 5-17 and 5-18 reveals that, on average, test-retest correlations for the MMPI-2 clinical scales are somewhat lower than those for the content scales.

External Validation of the Korean MMPI-2. Information on the external validity of the Korean MMPI-2 clinical scales was obtained from ratings of subjects by their friends. These ratings cover a broad range of both desirable and undesirable behaviors about which a friend would likely have information. Only subjects who claimed to have a very close relationship with their friends were included in these analyses. The mean length of time that the friends had known the subjects was 2.7 years for men and 2 years for women.

Effectiveness of the peer rating data as external correlates for the clinical scales may be limited for two reasons. First, compared to couples, even very close friends might not share enough intimate moments to be able to rate each other on a wide variety of aspects of personality and interpersonal behavior. A second limitation is related to the restricted range of rating. According to Butcher, Graham, Williams, and Ben-Porath (1990), variance of psychological "normals" on clinical scales and ratings are somewhat restricted in psychopathological expression. As a result, restricted variances in the two sets of scores likely had attenuating effects on the correlations between the clinical scales and the behavioral data. Nevertheless, these

Table 5-17. Test-Retest Correlations of MMPI-2 Basic Scales
for Korean and American[a] College Samples

Scale	Men		Women	
	Korean (N = 58)	American (N = 42)	Korean (N = 82)	American (N = 79)
L	.75	.77	.87	.73
F	.74	.67	.85	.79
K	.82	.62	.82	.75
Hs	.80	.80	.85	.88
D	.85	.85	.80	.74
Hy	.66	.68	.79	.80
Pd	.69	.82	.87	.84
Mf	.71	.79	.69	.84
Pa	.66	.76	.66	.81
Pt	.86	.78	.92	.85
Sc	.87	.79	.89	.88
Ma	.73	.78	.80	.79
Si	.85	.87	.88	.91
Median	.75	.78	.85	.81
Mean	.77	.77	.82	.82

Note: Retest interval was one week for both samples.
[a]Source: Butcher, Graham, Dahlstrom, & Bowman (1990).

data are believed to serve an important role in the validation of the Korean version of the MMPI-2.

Table 5-19 lists behavioral correlates for the clinical scales. For each clinical scale, it lists the three peer rating items with the highest obtained correlation. Scores on Hs are related to ratings of rebelliousness, complaints of physical symptoms, and talking to oneself. Women who scored high on scale Hs were viewed as worrying about their health, complaining a great deal about their physical symptoms, and being neat, orderly, or organized.

On scale D, high-scoring males were viewed as being uncomfortable around members of the opposite sex, avoiding contact with people, and acting very shy. Women with high D scores were viewed by their friends as not being cheerful, worrying about their health, and having a lack of interests and not being involved in many activities.

Table 5-18. Test-Retest Correlations of the MMPI-2 Content Scales
for the Korean College Sample

Scale	Men (N = 58)	Women (N = 82)
ANX	.85	.88
FRS	.76	.86
OBS	.79	.86
DEP	.86	.91
HEA	.77	.90
BIZ	.78	.83
ANG	.81	.86
CYN	.82	.83
ASP	.80	.81
TPA	.79	.81
LSE	.89	.91
SOD	.84	.88
FAM	.78	.85
WRK	.89	.92
TRT	.79	.87
Median	.80	.86
Mean	.81	.87

Note: Retest interval was one week.

Both males and females high on Hy were rated by their friends as complaining of physical problems. In addition, males were rated as being cheerful and thinking others are talking about them. Females were seen by their friends as worrying about health and being perfectionistic.

Behavioral correlates for scale Pd for males and females contain similar elements—unconventionality, misconduct, and rebelliousness. However, there were some differences in the expression of those aspects for each gender. Men scoring high on Pd were viewed by their friends as having stormy family relationships, wearing strange or unusual clothes, and lying or cheating. Women who scored high on Pd were rated as restless, rebellious, and not being passive and obedient to superiors.

Behavioral ratings of friends for females did not provide much information that discriminated scales Pa, Pt, and Sc. This is perhaps due to the fact that the indi-

Table 5-19. Behavioral Correlates for the MMPI-2 Clinical Scales Derived from Peer Ratings: Korean College Sample

	Men (N = 147)		Women (N = 247)	
	Peer Rating Items	r	Peer Rating Items	r
Hs	is rebellious	.25	worries about health a great deal	31
	complains of headaches, stomach		complains of headaches, stomach	
	trouble, or other ailments	.23	trouble, or other ailments	.28
	talks to self	.19	neat, orderly, or organized	18
D	uncomfortable around members		is cheerful	−.20
	of the opposite sex	.31	worries about health a great deal	.19
	avoids contact with people		has a wide range of interests;	
	for no reason	.29	involved in many activities	−.17
	acts very shy	.23		
Hy	is cheerful	.23	complains of headaches, stomach	
	complains of headaches, stomach		trouble, or other ailments	.27
	trouble, or other ailments	.19	perfectionistic	.24
	thinks other are talking about him/her	.17	worries about health a great deal	.23
Pd	has stormy family relationships	.32	is restless	.28
	wears strange or unusual clothes	.24	is rebellious	.28
	lies or cheats	.20	is passive and obedient to superiors	−.23
Pa	uncomfortable around members		feel mistreated or picked on	.26
	of the opposite sex	.24	whines and demands special attention	.25
	wears strange or unusual clothes	.21	gives up too easily	.22
	feels isolated, alienated	.20		
Pt	gets very excited or happy for little		gives up too easily	.26
	or no reason	.24	feel mistreated or picked on	.23
	acts very shy	.22	talks about committing suicide	.23
	is rebellious	.22		
Sc	gets very excited or happy for little		talks about committing suicide	.28
	or no reason	.25	gives up too easily	.26
	talks back to others	.25	feel mistreated or picked on	.22
	has stormy family relationships	.23		
Ma	energetic, talkative	.29	talks back to others	.21
	is rebellious	.27	acts without thinking	.18
	enjoys parties, entertainments, or		whines and demands special attention	.17
	having friends over	.24		
Si	uncomfortable around members		has a wide range of interests; involved	
	of the opposite sex	.35	in many activities	−.22
	gets along well with others	−.26	is cheerful	−.22
	enjoys parties, entertainments, or		enjoys parties, entertainments, or	
	having friends over	−.25	having friends over	−.20

viduals rated were college students, not psychiatric patients; responses on these scales were somewhat restricted. Females with elevations on these three scales were described by their friends as feeling mistreated or being picked on, and giving up too easily. Females high on Pt and Sc were viewed by their friends as talking about committing suicide. Males high on Pa were rated as being uncomfortable around women, wearing strange clothes, and feeling isolated and alienated. High Pt and Sc males were described as getting excited or being happy for no reason, being rebellious, and having stormy family relationships.

On scale Ma, high-scoring males were viewed as being energetic, talkative, and rebellious and enjoying parties. Women with high Ma scores were viewed by their friends as talking back to others, acting without thinking, and whining and demanding special attention.

Both males and females who scored high on Si were described by their friends as displaying socially introverted behavior. Both sexes were rated as not enjoying parties or having friends over. In addition, high Si males were viewed by their friends as feeling uncomfortable around women and not getting along with others. High Si females were viewed as not being cheerful, having a lack of interests, and not being involved in many activities.

To summarize, the behavioral correlates identified in this section are highly informative concerning the validity of the Korean MMPI-2 clinical scales despite some methodological limitations. The above findings strongly suggest that the clinical scales of the Korean version of the MMPI-2 performed comparably to the American version in predicting relevant behaviors.

Summary and Discussion

Reliability and Validity of the Korean Version of the MMPI-2

Many projects translating objective personality inventories into other languages have not been overly concerned with demonstrating the equivalence of the two most fundamental and important aspects of the test—its reliability and external validity. Korean test-retest correlations for the validity and clinical scales compare favorably with test-retest data obtained on the American MMPI-2. For both cultures, median test-retest correlations for female samples are higher than those for the male samples. Similar to findings in the American normative samples (Butcher, Dahlstrom, Graham, Tellegen, & Kaemmer, 1989), Korean test-retest correlations for the content scales are higher than those for the basic scales.

Perhaps most important for clinical use of a personality assessment instrument is providing evidence of external validity. If scales on an instrument do not predict what they are supposed to, they are useless regardless of how internally consistent or repeatable scores on the scales might be. In cross-cultural research, the main criterion for judging the success of inventory adaptation is demonstrating similar external validity of the translated instrument.

Examination of the external validity of the Korean MMPI-2 clinical scales obtained from ratings of subjects by their friends revealed very promising results. No detailed cultural comparisons were made on the external validity of the Korean MMPI-2 in the previous section because validity data were not gathered for the American college sample. However, a major source of MMPI-2 validity information is provided by behavioral spouse ratings obtained on part of the adult normative sample collected on the MMPI Restandardization Project (Butcher et al., 1989). Behavioral correlates for the MMPI-2 clinical scales derived from the couples' ratings are listed in Butcher (1990) and compare favorably to the Korean external correlates.

Correlates for Hs in both Korean and American samples centered on worries over health or complaints of physical symptoms. Women and men with high D scores in both cultures were viewed by their friends or spouses as generally maladjusted, not being cheerful, worrying about their health, having a lack of interests, not being involved in many activities, and avoiding contact with people. For both cultures, males and females high on Hy were reported to complain of physical problems and were rated as being cheerful or socially outgoing. Behavioral correlates for scale Pd for males and females in both cultures contain similar elements—unconventionality, misconduct, and rebelliousness. Although Korean correlates for scales Pa, Pt, and Sc suffered due to restricted range, Korean females and American males and females who were high on scale Pa were described as externalizing blame, and Korean females high on Pt and Sc were reported by their friends to talk about committing suicide. On scale Ma, high-scoring males and females in both cultures were viewed as being talkative, talking back to others, acting without thinking, and whining and demanding special attention. Males and females in both cultures who scored high on Si were described as displaying socially introverted behavior. They were rated as not enjoying parties, having a lack of interests, and not being involved in many activities.

It is surprising to find that behavioral correlates of the MMPI-2 clinical scales derived from two different sources of ratings—peer ratings (for the Korean sample) and spousal ratings (for the American sample)—are so similar. It is even more surprising given the differences between Korean and American samples in mean level of scale elevation and item endorsement patterns.

Uniform T Scores

For the Korean sample, UT distributions based on American norms were as variable as LT distributions. Thus, it would appear that the U.S. MMPI-2 normative sample is not the most appropriate reference group for Koreans, and special norms are needed for interpreting profiles from a Korean population. Therefore, it was decided to develop UT scores for the Korean MMPI-2 based on the available item response data.

As expected, the UT scores developed for the Korean college samples shared the characteristics of the American UT scores: positive skewness and percentile comparability across scales. However, a question can be raised regarding the appropriateness of the American composite (or prototypic) distribution for developing UT scores for Koreans. As discussed earlier, both Korean LT score distributions (or raw score distributions) based on American norms and those based on Korean norms were less positively skewed than was the American LT score distribution. By adopting the positively skewed composite distribution derived for Americans, we force the Korean prototypic distribution to fit the prototypic American distribution. As a result, this UT transformation assigns higher T scores for Koreans at upper percentile levels than would the LT or UT transformations using a Korean-based prototypic distribution. If UT scores were derived using a Korean composite distribution, they would be expected to have T-score values and percentiles closer to LT score values. In doing so, the UT distribution would be less positively skewed than the American UT distribution, but would still be percentile comparable across scales.

An advantage to using composite T scores derived from the American normative samples with the Korean MMPI-2 is that UT distributions across cultures are the same, which makes cross-cultural comparison easier and more meaningful. Therefore, I believe that a UT transformation using American composite distributions can be used in Korea until further normative research can evaluate whether a Korea-specific UT transformation should be used and would be more appropriate.

Internal Structure of the MMPI-2

Factor analyses of the content scales showed that a two-factor solution for the content scales replicated very well in other cultures as well as in the United States. However, the validity and clinical scales did not possess as stable an internal structure even within U.S. samples. It was particularly surprising to find that the factor convergence of the basic scales between American and Japanese female college samples exceeded that between the American normative females and the American female college sample.

The robustness of the two-factor solution for the content scales requires some comment. It might be argued that reducing the number of factors increases factor stability. Content scales may have yielded high convergence across samples simply because the number of factors extracted for the content scales (2) was smaller than for the basic scales (4). However, it should be noted that, overall, the three-factor solution for the basic scales (see Han, 1993) showed lower convergence than did the four-factor solutions, although there was some variation. This result demon-strates that an inappropriate reduction of factors can make factors less comparable across samples. Furthermore, a comparison of three-factor solutions for the basic and content scales revealed that overall, three factors for the content scales yielded higher convergence across samples than did three factors for the basic scales. As discussed earlier in this volume (Butcher & Han, chapter 3), the basic scales might be a poorer candidate for examining the internal structure of the MMPI-2 because scales are correlated highly with each other, owing partly to item overlap. The con-tent scales, on the other hand, are more internally consistent, and few items over-lap across scales. Are the basic scales, then, not a reliable source for examining the internal structure of the MMPI-2? There is at least some evidence (Han, 1993) for the stability of the factor structure of the basic scales, depending on the sample. For example, factor convergence was found to be high between genders for Koreans with a three-factor solution, for Japanese with a four-factor solution, and between American and Japanese college samples for each gender with both a three- and four-factor solution.

A remaining problem with these factor analysis results lies in their interpreta-tion when there is low factor convergence. In spite of the factor structure differ-ences between American normative females and American college females, there is little doubt that the MMPI-2 basic scales measure the same constructs in both American female samples. Similarly, when factor structure differences are iden-tified across cultures we should not be quick to claim that the scales measure dif-ferent constructs. In conclusion, although the content scales provide unequivocal evidence for factor invariance, the basic scales also add some information about the factor structure of the MMPI. Owing to its robustness, it is recommended that factor invariance of the content scales be considered a minimum condition for further investigation of the internal structures of the MMPI-2. However, both sets of scales should be used for exploring the internal structure of the instrument.

Scale Mean Differences

If we assume that both Korean and Japanese versions of the MMPI-2 are equiva-lent to the original, any mean differences should reflect cultural differences. In light of this, it is puzzling to find that the two Asian cultures, Korean and Japan-ese, differ so remarkably, more so even than do the American and Japanese sam-ples. Internal structure of the MMPI-2 for Japanese and American samples was identical, and scale mean differences and item endorsement differences between Japanese and American samples were very small. Does this result indicate that Japanese are more like Americans than they are like Koreans? There are at least two factors to be considered in the interpretation of these results: translation differ-ences and response sets.

Clark (1982), who developed the consolidated version of the Japanese MMPI, took a liberal approach in the translation. One of the goals she set forth in translating items for the consolidated version was to minimize item endorsement differences between American and Japanese data. By contrast, a relatively conservative approach to translation was adopted for the Korean version of the MMPI-2. Only items considered completely irrelevant or meaningless in the Korean culture were altered substantially. Therefore, as Clark has stated, it is difficult to compare the three cultures directly using the Japanese version of the MMPI-2, since it has been, in effect, partially renormed as well as culturally adapted in the process of translation.

The Chinese version of the MMPI-2 may be a better candidate for comparison since the Korean and Chinese versions are very similar in translation approach, and the two cultures, Korean and Hong Kong, have similar cultural backgrounds (Cheung, 1985). Data from a small sample of Hong Kong college students (123 men and 162 women [Cheung, 1993]) may answer some questions about Koreans' performance on the MMPI-2. Like Korean students, these Hong Kong college students had very elevated scores on scales F, D, Pt, and Sc. Hong Kong male students had even more elevated scores on those scales than did the Korean male students. Cheung (1985) attributed the elevated profiles and discrepant item endorsements evident in the Hong Kong sample to cultural differences in social norms and values, rather than to psychopathology. The similarity of the Korean mean profiles to the Chinese mean profiles suggests strongly that different approaches in translation procedures will produce quite different results even when applied to two similar cultures.

Response set is another consideration in interpreting these results. A test designed to measure personality through self-report very often suffers from method bias. In some cultures people tend to flatter themselves, and in others people tend toward self-deprecation (Triandis & Brislin, 1984). As described earlier, compared to Americans, Koreans are pessimistic and self-effacing. Different ways of responding to the test have an impact on test results. Unfortunately, the Korean MMPI-2 development project did not attempt to evaluate the effects of response set. In the future, it would be useful to include other measures with different formats (e.g., ratings or interview) to examine method bias. If a number of different methods converge on the same results, confidence in those results will increase.

Future Directions

It is evident from the preceding discussion that the Korean version of the MMPI-2 is as reliable and valid as the original MMPI-2. However, the sample used in the present study is relatively small and does not sufficiently represent the general Korean adult population. To make possible a comparison of Korean MMPI-2 profiles with an appropriate normative group, a Korean MMPI-2 normative project should be an immediate goal for future research. Ideally, a normative sample should match the population census in terms of age, educational level, socioeconomic background, and geographic distribution. Data from clinical settings should be collected, since the utility of the Korean MMPI-2 will ultimately be determined by its efficacy with psychiatric populations. It will be important to determine whether the Korean MMPI-2 can be used as effectively as the U.S. MMPI-2 to differentiate disturbed persons from normals and to make clinically useful distinctions among individuals manifesting various types of psychopathology. If individual scales do not function well in Korean clinical settings, it may also be necessary to create additional or alternate scales that are more sensitive to specific cultural phenomena to supplement the instrument in its present form.

References

Agarwal, D. P., Harada, S., & Goedde, H. W. (1981). Racial differences in biological sensitivity to ethanol: The role of alcohol dehydrogenase and aldehyde dehydrogenase isoenzymes. *Alcoholism: Clinical and Experimental Research, 5,* 12–16.

Arnold, F., & Kuo, E. C. Y. (1984). The value of daughters and sons: A comparative study of the gender preference of parents. *Journal of Comparative Family Studies, 15,* 209–318.

Bond, M. H., & Cheung, T. (1983). College students' spontaneous self-concept: The effect of culture among respondents in Hong Kong, Japan, and United States. *Journal of Cross-Cultural Study, 14,* 153–171.

Butcher, J. N. (1990). *The MMPI-2 in psychological treatment.* Oxford: Oxford University Press.

Butcher, J. N., Dahlstrom, W. G., Graham, J. R., Tellegen, A., & Kaemmer, B. (1989). *Manual for the restandardized Minnesota Multiphasic Personality Inventory: MMPI-2. An administrative and interpretive guide.* Minneapolis: University of Minnesota Press.

Butcher, J. N., Graham, J. R., Dahlstrom, W. D., & Bowman, E. (1990). The MMPI-2 with college sample. *Journal of Personality Assessment, 54,* 1–15.

Butcher, J. N., Graham, J. R., Williams, C. L., & Ben-Porath, Y. S. (1990). *Development and use of the MMPI-2 content scales.* Minneapolis: University of Minnesota Press.

Butcher, J. N., Narikiyo, T., & Vitousek, K. B. (1992). Understanding abnormal behavior in cultural context. In P. B. Sutker, & H. E. Adams (Eds.), *Comprehensive handbook of psychopathology* (2nd ed., pp. 83–105). New York: Plenum Press.

Butcher, J. N., & Pancheri, P. (1976). *A handbook of cross-national MMPI research.* Minneapolis: University of Minnesota Press.

Cheung, F. M. (1982). Psychological symptoms among Chinese in urban Hong Kong. *Social Science Medicine, 16,* 1339–1344.

Cheung, F. M. (1985). Cross-cultural considerations for the translation and adaptation of the Chinese MMPI in Hong Kong. In J. N. Butcher & C. D. Spielberger (Eds.), *Advances in personality assessment: Vol. 4* (pp. 131–158). Hillsdale, NJ: Erlbaum.

Cheung, F. M. (1993). [Archival file of the Chinese version of the MMPI-2]. Unpublished raw data.

Chung, B., Lee, C., & Chin, W. (1963). *MMPI manual.* Seoul: Korean Testing Center.

Clark, L. A. (1982). A consolidated version of the MMPI in Japan: Development of the translation and evaluation of equivalence (Doctoral dissertation, University of Minnesota, 1982). *Dissertation Abstracts International, 42,* 2702B.

Ewing, J., Rouse, B. A., & Pellizari, E. D. (1974). Alcohol sensitivity and ethnic background. *American Journal of Psychiatry, 131,* 206–210.

Finn, S. E. (1984). A partial cross-sequential analysis of personality ratings on 400 men (Doctoral dissertation, University of Minnesota, 1984). *Dissertation Abstracts International, 45,* 2685B.

Foley, J. B., & Fuqua, D. R. (1988). The effects of status configuration and counseling style on Korean perspectives of counseling. *Journal of Cross-Cultural Psychology, 19,* 465–480.

Graham, J. R. (1987). *The MMPI: A practical guide* (2nd ed.). New York: Oxford University Press.

Guilford, J. P., & Fruchter, B. (1981). *Fundamental statistics in psychology and education.* London: McGraw-Hill.

Han, K. (1993). The use of the MMPI-2 in Korea: Inventory adaptation, equivalence evaluation, and initial validation. (Unpublished doctoral dissertation, University of Minnesota, 1993).

Harvey, Y. K. (1976). The Korean Mudang as a household therapist. In W. P. Lebra (Ed.). *Culture bound syndromes, ethnopsychiatry, and alternate therapies* (pp. 189–198). Honolulu: University of Hawaii Press.

Kang, K. W., & Pearce, W. B. (1983). Reticence: A transcultural analysis. *Communication, 8,* 79–106.

Katz, M. M. (1968). A phenomenological typology of schizophrenia. In M. M. Katz, J. O. Cole, & W. E. Barton (Eds.), *The role and methodology of classification in psychiatry and psychopathology.* (Public Health Service Publication #1584). Washington, DC: U.S. Government Printing Office.

Kendall, L. (1981). Supernatural traffic: East Asian shamanism [Review of the book *Six Korean women: The socialization of shamans*]. *Culture, Medicine, and Psychiatry, 5,* 171–191.

Kendall, L. (1988). Healing thyself: A Korean shaman's afflictions. *Social Science Medicine, 27,* 445–450.

Kim, H. (1974). East Asia [Review of *Folk psychiatry in Korea and psychoanalytic consideration of Korean shamanism*]. *Transcultural Psychiatric Research Review, 11,* 40–42.

Kim, K. (1973). Shamanist healing ceremonies in Seoul. *Korean Journal, 13* (4), 41–47.

Kim, K. (1974). Culture and mental illness in Korea. *Korean Journal, 14* (2), 4–8.

Kim, K. (1976). A review of Korean cultural psychiatry. *Transcultural Psychiatric Research Review, 13,* 101–114.

Kim, Y., Kim, J., Kim, Z., Rho, M., Shin, D., Yum, T., & Oh, S. (1989). *Damyunjeok Insungkyumsa Shilshi Yokang* [MMPI Manual]. Seoul: Korea Guidance.

Kitano, H., & Sue, S. (1973). The model minorities. *Journal of Social Issues, 29,* 1–31.

Kleinman, A. M. (1977). Depression, somatization and the "new cross-cultural psychiatry." *Social Science and Medicine, 11,* 3–10.

Kook, H. (1986). Hankookinun ywae sheadurunga? [Why does Korean in a hurry?]. In S. W. Yoon (Ed.), *Hankookin Hankookbyung* [Korean and Korean illness] (pp. 111–119). Seoul: Il-yeum.

Lee, C., Kwak, Y., Yamamoto, J., Rhee, H., Kim, Y., Han, J., Choi, J., & Lee, Y. (1990a). Psychiatric epidemiology in Korea: Part 2: Urban and rural differences. *The Journal of Nervous and Mental Disease, 178,* 247–252.

Lee, C., Kwak, Y., Yamamoto, J., Rhee, H., Kim, Y., Han, J., Choi, J., & Lee, Y. (1990b). Psychiatric epidemiology in Korea: Part 1: Gender and age differences in Seoul. *The Journal of Nervous and Mental Disease, 178,* 242–246.

Lee, J. (1975). Shamanistic thought and traditional Korean homes. *Korean Journal, 15* (11), 43–51.

Lin, K. M. (1983). Hwa-Byung: A Korean culture-bound syndrome? *American Journal of Psychiatry, 140,* 105–107.

Marsella, A. J., Kinzie, D., & Gordon, P. (1973). Ethnic variations in the expression of depression. *Journal of Cross-Cultural Psychology, 4,* 435–458.

Nakane, Y., Ohta, Y., Uchino, J., Takada, K., Yan, H. Q., Wang, X. D., Min, S. K., & Lee, H. Y. (1988). Comparative study of affective disorders in three Asian countries: 1. Differences in diagnostic classification. *Acta Psychiatrica Scandinavica, 78,* 698–705.

Osgood, C. (1951). *The Koreans and their culture.* New York: Ronald.

136   Kyunghee Han

Paek, S. (1990). Modernization and psychopathology in Korea. *Korean Journal, 30* (8), 27–31.

Prince, R. H. (1989). Western pacific [Review of *A case study of hwabyung*]. *Transcultural Psychiatric Research Review, 26,* 137–147.

Prince, R. H. (1990a). General and theoretical issues. [Review of *Somatic complaint syndromes and depression: The problem of cultural effects on symptomatology*]. *Transcultural Psychiatric Research Review, 27,* 31–36.

Prince, R. H. (1990b). Pacific [Review of *Alcoholism abuse among Korean and Taiwanese and flushing response, ALDH negativity, and Asian alcohol abuse*]. *Transcultural Psychiatric Research Review, 27,* 131–141.

Reischauer, E. O. (1988). *The Japanese today.* Cambridge: The Belknap Press of Harvard University Press.

Robins, L. N., Helzer, J. E., Weissman, M. M., Orvaschel, H., Gruenberg, E., Burke, J. D., & Regier, D. A. (1984). Lifetime prevalence of specific psychiatric disorders in three sites. *Archives of General Psychiatry, 41,* 949–958.

Shiota, N. K. (1989). Japanese MMPI-2: Inventory adaptation and equivalence evaluation using Japanese and American college samples (Doctoral dissertation, University of Minnesota, 1989). *Dissertation Abstracts International, 50,* 5335B.

Smart, C. E. (1977). Manners private and public. *Korean Journal, 17* (2), 25–27.

Sue, D., & Sue, S. (1987). Cultural factors in the clinical assessment of Asian American. *Journal of Counseling and Clinical Psychology, 55,* 479–487.

Sue, S., & Sue, D. W. (1974). MMPI comparisons between Asian-American and non-Asian students utilizing a student heath psychiatric clinic. *Journal of Counseling Psychology, 21,* 423–427.

Sue, S., Wagner, N., Ja, D., Margullis, C., & Lew, L. (1976). Conceptions of mental illness among Asian and Caucasian-American students. *Psychological Reports, 38,* 703–708.

Tellegen, A., & Ben-Porath, S. Y. (1992). The new uniform T scores for the MMPI-2: Rationale, derivation, and appraisal. *Psychological Assessment, 4,* 145–155.

Tonsager, M. E., & Finn, S. E. (1992, May). *MMPI-2 content and clinical scale correlations: Implications for interpretation.* Paper presented at the meeting of the 27th Annual Symposium on Recent Developments in the Use of the MMPI (MMPI-2), Minneapolis, MN.

Triandis, H. C., & Brislin, R. W. (1984). Cross-cultural psychology. *American Psychologist, 39,* 1006–1016.

White, G. M. (1982). The role of cultural explanations in "somatization" and "psychologization." *Social Science and Medicine, 16,* 1519–1530.

Wiggins, J. S. (1973). *Personality and prediction: Principles of personality assessment.* Reading, MA: Addison-Wesley.

Wolff, P. (1972, January). Ethnic differences in alcohol sensitivity. *Science,* pp. 449–450.

Yamamoto, J., & Acosta, F. X. (1982). Treatment of Asian Americans and Hispanic Americans: Similarities and differences. *American Academy of Psychoanalysis, 10,* 585–607.

Yi, S. U. (1983). On the criticism of Confucianism in Korea. In Korean National Commission for UNESCO (Ed.), *Main current Korean thought* (pp. 112–146). New York: Pace International Research.

Yum, J. O. (1987a). Korean philosophy and communication. In D. L. Kincaid (Ed.), *Communication theory: Eastern and western perspectives* (pp. 71–85). San Diego: Academic Press.

Yum, J. O. (1987b). The practice of Uye-Ri in interpersonal relationships. In D. L. Kincaid (Ed.), *Communication theory: Eastern and western perspectives* (pp. 87–98). San Diego: Academic Press.

Chapter 6

The Chinese MMPI-2:
Research and Applications in Hong Kong
and the People's Republic of China

Fanny M. Cheung, Weizheng Song, and Jianxin Zhang

Use of Personality Assessment in Chinese Societies

Researchers and clinicians in Chinese societies have been very interested in personality assessment for the past 20 years. Tsoi and Sundberg (1989) surveyed the assessment activities of clinical psychologists in Hong Kong and found that the most popular personality measures were the House-Tree-Person technique, the Thematic Apperception Test, and the Minnesota Multiphasic Personality Inventory (MMPI). A survey of the use of psychological tests by mental health professionals in the People's Republic of China (PRC) from 1979 to 1989 (Dai, Zheng, Ryan, & Paolo, 1993) showed that objective personality tests were more commonly used than projective techniques. The most popular personality tests were the Eysenck Personality Questionnaire (EPQ) for Adults and Children and the MMPI.

The popularity of objective personality assessment in clinical settings is related to the role of clinical psychologists as well as to the availability of instruments. In Hong Kong, where the role and training of clinical psychologists closely model that of the United Kingdom because of its colonial links, psychological assessment is a major activity of clinical psychologists (Tsoi & Sundberg, 1989). This has also been true of clinicians in the PRC since psychology was resumed in the late 1970s. However, psychoanalysis is still not readily accepted, and projective techniques that require more intensive training are seldom used. Most test users in the People's Republic are medical professionals who have little training in clinical psychology and psychological assessment. Instead, there is a strong interest in the use of psychometrically based instruments. The major English language personality

We would like to express our appreciation to James Butcher for his continuing support of our work with the Chinese MMPI and MMPI-2. Our work has been partly funded by the Research Grant Council of the University and Polytechnic Grants Committee of the Hong Kong Government in Hong Kong and by the Academia Sinica in the People's Republic of China.

inventories, including the MMPI, 16-PF, California Psychological Inventory (CPI), and EPQ, have been translated into Chinese in the PRC in the past 15 years. Local norms have been collected for many of these tests (Dai et al., 1993). The relative convenience of administering objective personality scales and the "scientific authenticity" of test scores contribute to their widespread use by clinicians.

While personality researchers in China have relied heavily on translations of English language personality inventories such as the CPI and Edwards Personal Preference Schedule (EPPS) (Cheung, Conger, Hau, Lew, & Lau, 1992), in Taiwan the clinical use of personality assessment has been influenced by Y. Ko, a pioneer of clinical psychology there. Concerned about the length and cultural appropriateness of the MMPI, Ko (1978) developed the Ko's Mental Health Questionnaire (KMHQ) based on the MMPI. However, the development of the KMHQ is ongoing, and its application has been limited primarily to a small circle of clinical psychologists trained by Ko in Taiwan.

In Singapore, where the development of clinical psychology is still in its early stages, the Chinese version of the MMPI translated by Cheung (1985) in Hong Kong has been adapted for use (Boey, 1985). Owing to the small community of clinical psychologists in Singapore, objective personality assessment has not been developed to the extent it has been in the other Chinese societies.

Although objective personality assessment has been found useful by Chinese mental health professionals, there are limitations that need special attention. Paper-and-pencil tests require a minimum level of literacy from the respondent. The overall literacy level of the Chinese population is generally lower than that in developed countries in the West. Especially for the older and less educated Chinese, completing a lengthy questionnaire is an unfamiliar task. Also, they are cautious about revealing their private feelings and perceptions to others, especially concerning such matters as sexual behavior. For example, Song (1991) reported that 24 items on the original MMPI were answered by less than 5% of the Chinese subjects in the PRC.

Given these factors, it is important to consider the validity of individual profiles. Without checking for validity, it would be difficult to ascertain whether the respondents' profiles are indeed true reflections of their personality characteristics. The experience of the authors in research applications of a number of personality measures is that as many as 20% of the research subjects have to be eliminated owing to careless or inconsistent responding. Hence it is important that the tests used include validity measures.

The MMPI has a number of advantages for use in China. It contains validity scales; it provides comprehensive coverage of personality characteristics that are important to clinical applications; and it has been widely researched and applied in Hong Kong and the People's Republic of China. This chapter reviews the use of the Chinese MMPI, reports the adaptation of the Chinese MMPI-2 and its preliminary results, and compares the results for the two versions.

The Chinese MMPI

The Hong Kong version of the MMPI was translated in 1976. Subsequent revisions were made on the basis of item analysis, which identified items showing extreme discrepancies in endorsement percentage between the Hong Kong and the American normative samples (Cheung, 1985). The People's Republic of China version of the MMPI was based on the Hong Kong translation (it was compared with the 1979 Hong Kong version), modified slightly to adapt items to the social and cultural conditions in the PRC. Abbreviated Chinese characters were used in printing the PRC version (National MMPI Coordinating Group, 1982). For items on which the two translated versions differed in meaning, two American MMPI researchers (J. N. Butcher and R. D. Fowler) were consulted. Subsequent adjustments were made in both translations.

Item endorsement patterns on the two Chinese versions were very similar. Song, Cui, Cheung, and Hong (1987) compared the endorsement rates of college students in Beijing, Hong Kong, and the United States. The number of discrepant items between Beijing and Hong Kong subjects was 106 (18.7% of all items) for males and 129 (22.8%) for females, using 20% discrepancy in endorsement as the criterion. The percentage of discrepant items between Chinese and U.S. college students was much higher, with 40.5% and 42.8% for the comparison between Beijing and U.S. males and females, respectively, and 30.7% and 36.0% for the comparison between Hong Kong and U.S. males and females, respectively.

Empirical studies on the Chinese MMPI in Hong Kong and in the PRC have shown that the instrument's psychometric properties and cross-cultural equivalence are good, and that it has useful clinical applications (Cheung, 1985; Cheung & Song, 1989; Cheung, Zhao, & Wu, 1992; Song, 1985; Zhou & Zhao, 1992; Zhou, Zhao, & Jiang, 1989).

Cultural Considerations in the Use of the Chinese MMPI

Although the translation equivalence of the Chinese MMPI was found to be satisfactory, when the U.S. norms were used, elevations were found on a number of the basic scales even among normal subjects (Cheung, 1985; National MMPI Coordinating Group, 1989; Song, 1985). In particular, the mean T scores for normal subjects in both Hong Kong and the PRC on scales F, 2, 7, and 8 are in the upper 60s, close to the cutoff criterion of 70. It would be misleading to interpret these elevations as indicating the presence of psychopathology on the basis of the U.S. T scores without taking into consideration the cultural context.

Cheung pointed out that the elevated scores on the MMPI scales among normal Chinese people may be a reflection of the acceptability in China of certain behaviors that may be considered pathological in the United States. Many of the items endorsed by a higher percentage of Chinese subjects were also rated as more desirable by college students in Hong Kong compared with desirability ratings by American college students (Cheung, 1985). The content of the items that were rated differently on scales 2 and 8 related to social behavior and interpersonal relationships, attitudes of nonchalance and stoicism, acceptance of low arousal and low activity level, emphasis on hard work and careful planning, admission of physical illness, fears and psychological problems, and inclination toward modesty. On the other hand, self-disclosure concerning sexual matters was regarded more negatively and such items might be left unanswered by more than 10% of normal respondents.

Similarly, elevations on the F scale when U. S. norms are used may be explained by the large number of items on that scale that were endorsed differently by Chinese and American subjects. Only 27 of the 64 items on the F scale were actually "infrequent items," that is, endorsed by fewer than 10% (the basis of item selection on the F scale) of the normal male and female subjects in Hong Kong. When scored on the U.S. norms, the average T score for normal Hong Kong subjects is 68. In the PRC, the number of "infrequent items" on the F scale was 19 for males and 22 for females (Cheung, Song, & Butcher, 1991). The average T score for normal male subjects is 77; that for females is 70. The conventional practice of invalidating an MMPI profile on the basis of a high F score or the F minus K index would tend to discard too many cases who may not be dissimulating or responding randomly.

Given the high F score among normal Chinese subjects, researchers of the Chinese MMPI have used the TR index (Dahlstrom, Welsh, & Dahlstrom, 1975, Appendix C) instead of a high F score or the F minus K index to screen out invalid profiles. For clinical use, an infrequency scale was developed using < 10% endorsement rate for both Hong Kong and PRC normal subjects as the item selection criterion (Cheung et al., 1991). This scale is scored according to the local norms. Scores for normal subjects, patients, and subjects who deliberately fake bad are significantly different from one another.

National norms have also been developed in the PRC (National MMPI Coordinating Group, 1989), and T scores derived from this norm are generally more moderate. When using these Chinese norms, the peaks on scales F, 2, 7, and 8 disappear. The code types of 28/82 or 78/87 that predominate among psychiatric subjects when the U. S. norms are used are replaced by code types that are more akin to code types typical of specific psychiatric diagnoses (Cheung, Zhao, & Wu, 1992; Lo, 1991). However, with the Chinese norms, the overall elevation of T scores among patients becomes more restricted, with few clinical scale scores over an average T score of 65. The PRC researchers recommended using a T score of 60 instead of 70 as the cutoff point on the Chinese norms (National MMPI Coordinating Group, 1989). Cheung (in press; Cheung, Zhao, & Wu, 1992) suggested a compromise strategy of scoring the Chinese MMPI profile on both the U.S. and the PRC norms and comparing the two profiles when interpreting.

In addition to cultural differences, one possible explanation for the elevations on the Chinese MMPI is the cohort difference between the original U.S. norms, which were developed in the late 1940s, and the contemporary sample of Chinese people. This possibility may be examined in studies of the Chinese version of the MMPI-2, which is based on contemporary American norms.

The Chinese MMPI-2

The Chinese version of the MMPI-2 was developed in an extended collaboration between the researchers in Hong Kong and those in the PRC. The initial Chinese translation was developed by the first author in Hong Kong. For items retained from the original MMPI, minor refinements were made on some of the translations where difficulties in comprehension were detected in previous applications. New items written for the MMPI-2 content scales were translated and went through the standard back-translation procedure. These new Chinese items were then given to 50 undergraduate students in Hong Kong who were asked to rate the items in terms of comprehension and ambiguity. The translation was further refined on the basis of their feedback.

As a check on the accuracy of translation, the preliminary results of the item endorsement patterns of Hong Kong college students were compared with those of U.S. college students. The meanings of those items with large differences in item endorsement percentages were checked with James Butcher when the first author was visiting Minnesota. More appropriate Chinese translations were substituted following discussion of the implicit meanings of the items. The purpose of this exercise was to ascertain if the translation was accurate, not to examine the cultural equivalence of item responses. Some items were endorsed by the Hong Kong and American students at extremely different rates, representing not translation inaccuracy but actual differences in beliefs or behavior.

The Hong Kong translation of the MMPI-2 was then given to the PRC researchers, who adapted it for the mainland. Given the economic developments in China since the 1980s, some items that were considered irrelevant at the time the original MMPI was translated are no longer so, for example, going to dances, being an auto racer, and criminals being freed through the arguments of a smart lawyer. The deletion of many original MMPI items with religious and sexual content also meant there was less content of a sensitive nature in the MMPI-2.

However, the length of the 567-item inventory continues to be a problem in testing. Whereas the PRC researchers often used only the first 399 items of the original MMPI in their research or clinical applications, the inclusion of the additional items for the content scales does not permit a simple approach to shortening the test. And the need to screen out invalid profiles remains important, especially when older and less educated subjects are tested.

MMPI-2 Results with Normal Chinese Subjects

Given the overlap of the majority of items on the clinical scales, one would expect the raw scores of the Chinese subjects on the MMPI-2 to be similar to those found on the original MMPI. However, with the new U.S. norms, it was expected that the T scores of Chinese subjects on the MMPI-2 would be lower, hence closer to the American means.

In Hong Kong, the Chinese MMPI-2 was administered to several groups of university students and a smaller group of nonstudents of mixed age and educational level. After screening out invalid profiles with the Chinese Infrequency Scale (ICH raw score over 10) and VRIN and TRIN criteria revised for Chinese subjects (VRIN raw score over 13 and TRIN raw score below 6 and above 13)—to be discussed in a later section—149 males and 184 females constitute the student group. Their ages range from 18 to 24. For the nonstudent group, there are 40 valid male cases with a mean age of 34, and 36 female cases with a mean age of 33 (based on Lo, 1993). The educational level of the nonstudent group ranges from grade 6 to university. The raw scores, standard deviations, and K-corrected T scores for the Hong Kong student groups based on the U.S. norms are listed in Table 6-1. Those for the nonstudent groups are listed in Table 6-2.

In the PRC, the National MMPI Coordinating Group, consisting of psychologists and doctors in different geographical regions of China, was mobilized to collect data on the Chinese MMPI-2. After invalid protocols were screened out with ICH, VRIN, and TRIN, the national normative sample consists of 1,106 males and 1,108 females from all seven major geographical regions of China. The educational level of the subjects ranges from primary to postgraduate, the majority of them being junior and senior high school graduates. Ages range from 18 to 70. The sample was selected to match the national population statistics in terms of geographical distribution, marital status, education, and age. The mean raw scores, standard deviations, and K-corrected T scores for the PRC normal subjects based on the U.S. norms are listed in Table 6-3.

The pattern of scores for the Hong Kong and the PRC subjects is very similar. On most of the clinical scales, the U.S. T scores fall within one standard deviation of the American norms. No scale score among the PRC males and females exceeds a T score of 70 except for F_B. However, on the scales that were elevated on the original Chinese MMPI, the T scores remain high relative to the new MMPI-2

Table 6-1. MMPI-2 Raw Scores and K-Corrected T Scores (Based on U.S. Norms) for Hong Kong Normal College Adults

	Male (N = 149)				Female (N = 184)			
	Raw Score		T Score		Raw Score		T Score	
Scale	Mean	SD	Mean	SD	Mean	SD	Mean	SD
L	4.2	2.4	52.9	10.4	4.3	2.2	53.6	10.4
F	9.0	7.1	62.7	16.9	8.2	5.9	64.8	16.2
K	12.7	4.5	44.5	9.7	12.3	3.9	44.1	8.5
Hs	9.3	5.0	60.9	11.0	10.6	4.9	60.2	9.3
D	24.5	5.7	63.0	11.4	26.2	6.0	62.3	12.7
Hy	24.1	5.2	57.4	12.0	24.9	5.1	56.1	11.4
Pd	19.8	5.1	56.9	11.4	18.7	4.6	55.0	10.1
Mf	26.1	4.2	50.1	9.4	33.2	4.4	56.8	10.6
Pa	12.4	3.9	58.3	13.6	12.4	3.9	57.5	13.7
Pt	21.2	8.8	64.6	12.8	21.6	8.8	62.2	11.7
Sc	22.9	11.3	65.2	14.0	22.2	10.6	63.6	12.2
Ma	18.5	4.7	53.6	11.0	17.8	4.4	53.8	10.1
Si	33.8	9.3	59.2	10.9	34.9	9.2	57.5	10.0
F_B	6.3	5.7	67.5	20.1	6.6	5.0	67.8	17.5
VRIN	7.5	2.8	59.2	10.6	7.9	2.8	61.4	11.2
TRIN	9.0	1.4	58.0	8.0	8.8	1.4	58.2	6.8
ANX	9.7	5.0	59.9	11.6	10.0	5.2	57.6	11.7
FRS	6.3	3.7	58.3	12.3	8.6	3.9	55.8	10.9
OBS	8.2	3.5	60.4	11.5	8.2	3.5	58.1	11.3
DEP	11.8	6.1	64.1	10.6	12.0	6.2	61.7	10.4
HEA	8.7	5.6	58.4	12.1	10.2	5.3	58.8	10.5
BIZ	5.0	3.9	60.1	13.1	4.9	3.5	60.5	10.7
ANG	5.7	3.5	50.1	10.3	6.4	3.3	52.3	10.8
CYN	11.3	4.0	52.5	7.7	10.8	3.7	53.2	7.1
ASP	10.2	3.5	54.9	8.7	9.1	3.0	57.5	8.2
TPA	9.2	3.6	52.7	10.6	10.1	3.5	58.5	12.1
LSE	8.8	5.4	61.9	13.5	9.1	5.1	59.0	11.9
SOD	11.0	5.4	57.0	11.9	10.0	5.0	55.1	10.2
FAM	8.0	4.2	57.6	11.7	8.3	4.2	55.6	11.1
WRK	13.1	6.6	61.2	12.4	14.1	6.5	60.1	12.2
TRT	10.2	4.9	64.4	12.1	9.9	5.0	61.9	12.0

Table 6-2. MMPI-2 Raw Scores and K-Corrected T Scores (Based on U.S. Norms) for Hong Kong Normal Nonstudent Adults

	Male (N = 40)				Female (N = 36)			
	Raw Score		T Score		Raw Score		T Score	
Scale	Mean	SD	Mean	SD	Mean	SD	Mean	SD
L	5.5	2.6	58.8	11.6	6.4	2.4	63.4	12.1
F	9.2	4.9	64.4	15.2	7.9	4.4	64.5	14.8
K	13.3	4.2	45.8	8.9	13.6	5.0	46.2	12.3
Hs	8.6	5.0	59.2	11.1	8.5	4.5	56.0	8.9
D	24.4	4.8	62.8	9.3	26.2	5.2	62.0	10.9
Hy	22.5	5.7	54.0	12.4	22.3	5.7	51.5	11.0
Pd	19.9	4.5	57.1	10.1	17.4	4.9	52.4	10.7
Mf	24.2	4.1	46.4	8.2	31.1	3.5	61.9	8.5
Pa	11.8	4.1	56.3	15.1	11.1	3.5	53.2	12.0
Pt	18.8	8.1	61.2	11.7	17.2	7.4	56.2	9.9
Sc	20.4	9.5	62.3	11.7	19.1	8.9	59.9	10.4
Ma	17.8	4.4	51.9	9.9	16.4	4.7	50.8	10.9
Si	34.0	8.1	59.4	9.5	34.4	7.1	57.1	7.9
F_B	6.0	4.6	66.9	18.2	6.4	3.5	67.2	13.8
VRIN	8.2	2.8	62.1	11.0	8.0	3.0	62.1	11.8
TRIN	9.2	2.0	59.7	9.3	9.4	1.4	58.1	7.7
ANX	8.3	4.5	56.5	10.1	8.1	5.1	53.6	11.2
FRS	6.2	3.6	58.1	11.4	8.2	3.3	54.4	9.6
OBS	6.6	3.5	55.2	11.2	6.8	3.2	53.5	9.3
DEP	10.8	5.5	62.4	9.5	10.0	4.7	58.1	8.1
HEA	8.5	5.3	57.9	12.0	8.2	4.5	54.7	9.4
BIZ	4.2	2.6	57.3	9.7	4.5	3.2	58.5	11.1
ANG	5.7	3.2	50.2	9.4	6.2	3.0	51.6	9.8
CYN	11.8	4.0	53.5	7.7	11.5	4.6	54.7	8.8
ASP	10.9	4.0	57.3	10.5	9.1	3.5	57.8	9.7
TPA	8.9	3.9	52.5	10.9	8.6	3.9	53.8	12.4
LSE	8.2	4.9	60.3	12.3	8.0	3.9	56.3	8.6
SOD	10.7	4.2	56.1	9.1	10.3	4.0	55.4	8.1
FAM	8.0	4.5	57.4	12.3	8.3	4.0	55.5	10.2
WRK	11.1	5.8	57.3	11.0	11.2	5.0	54.6	8.9
TRT	9.8	5.1	63.2	12.9	9.3	3.9	60.4	9.2

Table 6-3. MMPI-2 Raw Scores and K-Corrected T Scores (Based on U.S. Norms)
for PRC Normal Adults

	Male (N = 40)				Female (N = 36)			
	Raw Score		T Score		Raw Score		T Score	
Scale	Mean	SD	Mean	SD	Mean	SD	Mean	SD
L	6.0	2.8	60.6	12.6	5.8	2.8	60.9	13.9
F	9.3	4.6	64.8	13.9	9.0	4.5	68.3	15.2
K	14.1	5.0	47.3	11.2	13.3	4.9	45.6	12.1
Hs	8.3	4.6	56.1	12.0	9.5	4.9	55.3	12.2
D	24.3	5.0	62.8	10.0	26.6	5.0	63.0	10.7
Hy	22.2	5.7	53.2	12.6	23.2	5.8	52.7	12.8
Pd	18.6	4.6	52.5	10.1	17.9	4.6	51.3	10.0
Mf	24.4	4.1	46.9	8.3	30.0	3.9	64.5	9.2
Pa	11.7	3.6	55.9	13.0	12.2	3.9	57.0	13.6
Pt	15.8	8.0	57.2	12.0	17.4	8.2	55.8	11.4
Sc	19.5	9.2	62.7	12.1	20.6	9.7	62.3	11.7
Ma	17.8	5.1	51.0	11.5	16.6	4.9	49.7	10.7
Si	32.3	7.3	57.4	8.6	35.4	7.5	58.1	8.2
F_B	7.1	4.8	71.1	19.0	8.1	5.2	73.4	18.9
VRIN	8.3	2.6	62.2	10.4	8.5	2.6	64.1	10.6
TRIN	9.1	2.0	61.5	9.1	9.1	2.0	62.5	9.4
ANX	7.3	4.2	54.1	9.8	8.1	4.5	53.2	9.9
FRS	7.0	3.9	60.6	12.9	10.7	4.2	62.0	12.6
OBS	5.4	3.6	51.5	11.8	6.1	3.6	51.6	10.9
DEP	9.6	5.2	60.4	9.1	10.8	5.6	59.6	9.5
HEA	8.4	4.8	57.6	11.1	9.5	5.0	57.4	10.3
BIZ	4.1	3.6	56.6	12.7	4.2	3.6	57.8	11.8
ANG	5.9	3.0	50.8	9.2	6.6	3.2	52.8	10.2
CYN	11.8	4.2	53.7	8.4	11.9	4.5	55.7	8.7
ASP	8.8	3.9	51.7	9.2	8.0	3.3	54.7	8.8
TPA	10.7	3.5	57.1	10.8	11.0	3.3	61.5	12.2
LSE	8.6	4.5	61.4	11.0	9.8	4.6	60.6	10.5
SOD	9.5	4.4	53.6	9.2	10.2	4.6	55.4	9.4
FAM	7.0	3.9	54.8	10.5	7.4	3.9	53.1	10.0
WRK	11.2	5.7	57.7	10.8	12.1	5.8	56.5	10.7
TRT	9.9	4.5	63.7	10.9	10.4	4.5	63.1	10.7

cutoff of 65. Clinical scales 2 (D) and 8 (Sc) averaged over 60. For the validity scales, including the F scales and especially scale F_B and the new validity scale, VRIN, the average T scores all exceed 60. On the content scales, the elevated scales are DEP and TRT. In addition, FRS is very elevated among the PRC sample, whereas WRK is elevated among the Hong Kong university students who have little working experience. High scores on both DEP and TRT in the United States are associated with lack of interest in things, lack of energy, and being fearful of the future (Butcher, Graham, Williams, & Ben-Porath, 1990). These characteristics are consistent with the Chinese sociocultural context in which low arousal level and restraint are considered positive. In the PRC and particularly in Hong Kong during the transitional period before sovereignty will be returned to China in 1997, uncertainty about the future is a political reality.

Test-Retest Reliability of the Chinese MMPI-2

Small groups of university students in Hong Kong and in the PRC took the Chinese MMPI-2 twice to investigate the test-retest reliability of the scales. In Hong Kong, the sample consists of 25 males and 25 females who took the tests one week apart. Two males were eliminated from the analysis owing to invalid profiles in either of the two trials. The results are listed in Table 6-4.

For the Hong Kong subjects, the test-retest reliability coefficients for the clinical and the content scales are all very high, with most of the coefficients over 0.80. Among the clinical scales, the lowest coefficient is obtained on Ma (0.74) and the highest is obtained on Si (0.94). Among the content scales, the lowest coefficient is found on TPA (0.70) while the highest is found on SOD (0.95). Only among the validity scales are lower test-retest reliability coefficients obtained, such as TRIN (0.42) and VRIN (0.59). It is understandable that social discomfort and social introversion, being stable personality characteristics, should be measured more consistently over time, whereas response style characteristics may vary from one trial to another.

In the PRC, 40 university students in Beijing took the Chinese MMPI-2 twice with a one-week interval. The test-retest reliability coefficients range from 0.69 (Pd) to 0.91 (D) on the clinical scales and 0.71 (TPA) to 0.90 (FRS) on the content scales. Most of the coefficients exceed 0.80. Among the validity scales, only VRIN had a lower reliability coefficient of 0.58 (Table 6-4).

Translation Equivalence of the Chinese MMPI-2

The original English as well as the Chinese translation of the MMPI-2 were given to 30 college students at the foreign language institute in Beijing. These students were proficient in both English and Chinese. The two language versions were ad-

Table 6-4. Test-Retest Reliability and Bilingual Equivalence of MMPI-2 Scales for Hong Kong and PRC Normal Subjects

| | HK | PRC | |
| | Test-retest Correlation (N = 48) | Bilingual Correlation (N = 30) | Test-retest Correlation (N = 40) |
Scale			
L	.67	.56	.74
F	.65	.50	.82
K	.68	.65	.83
Hs	.82	.50	.84
D	.89	.60	.91
Hy	.83	.59	.73
Pd	.81	.52	.69
Mf-m	.82	.76	.72
Mf-f	.82	.72	.73
Pa	.78	.61	.70
Pt	.93	.80	.86
Sc	.88	.75	.89
Ma	.74	.60	.86
Si	.94	.74	.90
ANX	.85	.76	.89
FRS	.91	.82	.90
OBS	.79	.82	.86
DEP	.89	.74	.77
HEA	.81	.59	.87
BIZ	.75	.63	.83
ANG	.80	.56	.82
CYN	.78	.67	.73
ASP	.89	.55	.73
TPA	.70	.57	.71
LSE	.85	.60	.89
SOD	.95	.67	.87
FAM	.83	.67	.83
WRK	.85	.83	.88
TRT	.86	.79	.75
FB	.87	.72	.75
VRIN	.59	.31	.58
TRIN	.42	-.06	.77

Table 6-5. Factor Loadings of MMPI-2 Basic Scales for PRC Normal Male Subjects

Scale	Factor			
	1	2	3	4
L	−.65	.28	−.06	.20
F	.67	.39	.17	.14
K	−.76	.25	−.39	−.01
Hs	.21	.76	.26	.10
D	−.02	.69	.56	.09
Hy	−.20	.87	−.07	.19
Pd	.55	.53	−.11	.08
Mf	.03	.14	.10	.92
Pa	.51	.37	−.04	.48
Pt	.79	.21	.42	.15
Sc	.84	.26	.27	.20
Ma	.83	−.05	−.28	.07
Si	.16	.10	.89	.06

Factor	Eigenvalue	% of Variance	Cumulative %
1	5.08	39.1	39.1
2	2.59	19.9	59.0
3	1.31	10.1	69.1
4	0.85	6.5	75.6

ministered two weeks apart. The correlations between the English and Chinese versions for the MMPI-2 scales are also listed in Table 6-4.

The correlation coefficients for the English and Chinese versions ranged from 0.50 to 0.83 on the clinical and content scales. The average correlation for the clinical scales is 0.64 and for the content scales 0.68. Compared to the overall test-retest reliability of the Chinese version, the translation equivalence of the Chinese MMPI-2 is found to be acceptable.

Factor Structure of the Chinese MMPI-2

A principal components analysis was run on the MMPI-2 basic scale scores of the PRC male and female subjects. Following varimax rotation, four factors were extracted for both the male and the female groups. The loadings for the four factors are listed in Tables 6-5 and 6-6.

The patterns of factor loadings for male and female subjects are very similar. Factor 1 is characterized by high positive loadings on Sc, Ma, Pt, Pa, Pd, and F

Table 6-6. Factor Loadings of MMPI-2 Basic Scales for PRC Normal Female Subjects

	Factor			
Scale	1	2	3	4
L	−.52	.44	−.09	−.29
F	.76	.28	.14	−.11
K	−.69	.36	−.42	−.02
Hs	.34	.72	.22	−.01
D	.63	.67	.59	.11
Hy	.01	.90	−.10	.16
Pd	.61	.41	−.03	.25
Mf	.01	.14	.08	.94
Pa	.67	.40	.00	.12
Pt	.80	.13	.47	.05
Sc	.89	.15	.29	−.02
Ma	.83	−.15	−.21	−.03
Si	.12	.03	.91	.06

Factor	Eigenvalue	% of Variance	Cumulative %
1	5.14	39.5	39.5
2	2.41	18.6	58.1
3	1.35	10.4	68.5
4	1.00	7.7	76.2

and negative loadings on L and K. This may be labeled the psychoticism factor. Factor 2 is loaded primarily on the neurotic triad (Hs, D, and Hy), with moderate loading on Pd for both males and females, and may be labeled the neuroticism factor. For both males and females, Factor 3 is loaded highly on Si and moderately on D, and may be labeled the social introversion factor. Factor 4 is dominated by a single high loading on Mf, the masculinity-femininity factor. These four factors are very consistent with the factors found on the clinical scales of the MMPI and MMPI-2.

MMPI-2 Studies with Clinical Samples

The Chinese MMPI-2 was administered to a number of patient groups in the PRC and in Hong Kong. In Hong Kong, Lo (1993) compared the scale scores of 62 schizophrenic patients (31 males and 31 females) with 62 normal subjects (31 males and 31 females) matched for demographic backgrounds. For the male subjects, the scores for the schizophrenic patients are significantly higher (p < 0.01 level) on F, 6 (Pa), 8 (Sc), and 9 (Ma) among the basic scales and on ANX, FRS, DEP, BIZ, TPA, LSE, WRK, and TRT among the content scales. For the female subjects, the scores for the schizophrenic patients are significantly higher (p < 0.01 level) on F, 4 (Pd), 6 (Pa), 7 (Pt), 8 (Sc), and 9 (Ma) among the basic scales and ANX, FRS, DEP, HEA, BIZ, LSE, WRK, and TRT among the content scales. The average T scores for scales 6 (Pa), 7 (Pt), and 8 (Sc) are 73, 72, and 81, respectively, for the male schizophrenic patients and 81, 67, and 80 for the female patients (Table 6-7). Scales F and F_B are extremely elevated above an average T score of 90. On the content scales, BIZ, TRT, FRS and DEP are all elevated.

Lo further used discriminant function analysis to compare the usefulness of the content scales in discriminating between schizophrenic patients and normal subjects. The discriminant power of the content scales was found to be comparable to that of the basic scales, and no significant difference was found between the classification hit rates of the two sets of discriminant functions.

The Chinese MMPI-2 was also used to assess a small group of neurotic patients who were accepted into psychotherapy at a psychiatric outpatient clinic in Hong Kong. There were 10 male and 32 female patients whose diagnoses included depression, anxiety, and obsessive-compulsive disorders. They took the Chinese MMPI-2 before they began psychotherapy. Their average scores on the MMPI-2 are listed in Table 6-8.

For the Hong Kong neurotic patients, all of the clinical scales are elevated higher than T scores of 65 except for scales 5 (Mf), 9 (Ma), and, in the case of the males, scales 1 (Hs) and 4 (Pd). The highest elevations are on scales 2 (D), 8 (Sc), and 7 (Pt) with T scores ranging from 73 to 84. Both the F and the F_B scales are extremely elevated. Among the content scales, the most elevated scales are DEP, ANX, HEA, TRT, and LSE, which are higher than a T score of 70. Compared to the slight elevations found on some of the clinical scales among normal adults in Hong Kong, the scale elevations among the neurotic patients exceed those of normals by a T-score range of 10 to 20 points.

In the PRC, the psychiatric sample consists of 194 (119 male and 75 female) schizophrenic patients, 110 (65 male and 45 female) neurotic patients, and 98 (56 male and 42 female) patients with affective disorders who had been admitted to mental hospitals in different regions of the country. Some of the neurotic patients were attending outpatient clinics. The psychiatric diagnoses were made by the attending doctors based on the criteria set by the Chinese Medical Association (1981), which are based on the third edition of the *Diagnostic and Statistical Manual of Mental Disorders* (*DSM-III;* American Psychiatric Association, 1980), the ICD-9 Classification of Mental Disorders (*Manual of the International Statistical Classification of Diseases, Injuries, and Causes of Death,* Vol. 1; World Health Orga-

Table 6-7. MMPI-2 Raw Scores and K-Corrected T Scores (Based on U.S. Norms)
for Hong Kong Schizophrenic Patients

	Male (N = 34)				Female (N = 35)			
	Raw Score		T Score		Raw Score		T Score	
Scale	Mean	SD	Mean	SD	Mean	SD	Mean	SD
L	6.9	2.6	64.9	12.0	6.8	2.8	65.5	14.1
F	18.0	8.4	89.6	23.1	19.5	10.7	95.9	24.9
K	12.6	5.7	43.1	14.5	11.6	6.0	40.3	17.4
Hs	11.6	6.2	65.5	13.3	12.4	6.4	63.3	12.6
D	26.4	6.5	66.8	12.5	28.3	6.5	66.7	13.9
Hy	25.1	6.8	60.0	15.6	26.1	7.3	59.5	15.4
Pd	22.1	5.7	62.1	12.6	22.6	6.4	64.0	14.4
Mf	25.5	3.5	49.0	6.9	30.2	3.9	64.2	9.4
Pa	16.4	5.6	72.9	20.6	18.9	5.9	80.9	21.4
Pt	24.0	10.4	68.9	15.3	25.1	11.1	66.7	15.4
Sc	32.0	12.3	76.1	15.1	34.1	14.8	76.9	16.7
Ma	21.6	6.1	62.1	14.7	22.3	5.0	65.1	13.1
Si	34.7	6.6	60.2	7.6	34.9	9.1	57.5	9.9
F$_B$	15.4	8.9	96.1	24.7	15.3	8.8	94.7	24.6
VRIN	10.0	2.6	68.7	9.7	8.4	2.0	63.7	8.5
TRIN	11.7	3.2	72.6	18.7	11.3	2.6	70.1	18.3
ANX	12.1	4.4	65.5	10.2	12.7	5.9	63.8	13.5
FRS	11.0	3.6	73.8	11.8	12.3	4.4	66.6	13.2
OBS	8.6	4.4	61.9	14.5	8.9	4.9	61.1	16.1
DEP	16.1	7.3	71.4	12.9	16.6	8.4	69.1	14.3
HEA	12.1	6.7	65.4	13.9	14.3	7.7	66.2	15.2
BIZ	10.4	5.9	78.4	20.6	10.9	6.3	78.1	18.6
ANG	6.9	3.5	53.6	10.8	7.0	4.2	54.6	14.5
CYN	13.8	4.7	58.3	9.7	13.3	4.9	58.9	10.3
ASP	11.4	4.6	58.9	12.8	10.7	4.2	62.6	12.5
TPA	11.2	4.1	59.3	13.2	11.0	4.4	62.1	15.2
LSE	12.4	6.0	70.9	15.3	12.1	6.3	66.5	15.2
SOD	11.7	3.5	58.0	7.4	10.8	4.2	56.4	8.7
FAM	10.1	4.7	63.4	12.7	10.5	6.1	61.3	15.7
WRK	16.1	6.6	66.6	12.4	16.5	7.7	64.8	14.9
TRT	14.1	4.7	73.9	11.6	13.3	5.8	70.4	14.1

Table 6-8. MMPI-2 Raw Scores and K-Corrected T Scores (Based on U.S. Norms) for Hong Kong Neurotic Patients

| | Male (N = 10) | | | | Female (N = 32) | | | |
| | Raw Score | | T Score | | Raw Score | | T Score | |
Scale	Mean	SD	Mean	SD	Mean	SD	Mean	SD
L	3.5	1.7	50.0	7.5	5.0	2.4	56.8	12.1
F	12.8	6.0	75.6	18.5	15.5	7.4	88.5	22.1
K	8.4	4.5	31.9	15.7	10.4	3.9	38.6	11.9
Hs	14.2	6.8	62.8	16.7	19.9	5.3	75.1	11.3
D	29.6	7.9	72.8	15.8	36.1	5.5	83.6	12.0
Hy	27.3	7.1	65.2	16.7	34.1	5.6	77.6	13.0
Pd	23.2	3.5	57.4	7.9	26.8	4.9	69.7	12.0
Mf	29.3	5.1	57.2	11.0	33.2	3.5	56.7	8.7
Pa	14.4	4.6	65.8	17.1	17.3	4.4	75.2	16.0
Pt	28.8	9.5	72.8	20.3	32.0	6.6	77.7	8.9
Sc	31.5	11.5	73.5	16.6	36.2	11.1	81.7	13.3
Ma	21.9	6.1	58.7	14.1	19.2	3.7	54.1	9.0
Si	38.2	11.3	64.2	13.3	40.2	6.6	63.2	7.3
F_B	10.8	6.2	85.8	24.1	14.9	7.6	96.1	23.3
VRIN	6.8	2.8	56.6	10.9	7.4	2.4	59.5	10.0
TRIN	10.0	2.0	59.9	13.6	9.7	2.0	62.7	10.9
ANX	14.7	5.7	72.0	13.5	17.4	3.9	74.8	9.2
FRS	6.7	3.0	59.5	9.4	11.8	4.6	65.3	13.7
OBS	10.2	4.4	67.4	14.8	10.2	3.0	64.7	9.8
DEP	18.7	6.6	76.0	11.4	21.0	6.5	76.6	10.8
HEA	13.5	7.8	68.5	15.4	19.6	6.6	76.6	12.2
BIZ	6.2	4.0	64.4	13.4	7.5	4.7	68.3	13.6
ANG	9.0	3.7	60.6	11.6	9.5	3.3	62.9	11.5
CYN	12.4	4.1	55.1	9.6	13.2	4.0	58.1	8.4
ASP	10.4	2.4	54.9	7.0	9.9	2.8	59.9	8.0
TPA	11.1	4.6	59.8	15.1	11.4	3.2	63.0	11.5
LSE	12.1	6.3	70.3	15.9	13.8	5.0	70.1	12.8
SOD	13.4	5.5	62.4	13.3	13.3	4.4	61.9	9.4
FAM	11.2	3.7	66.2	10.2	14.0	4.9	70.2	12.9
WRK	18.1	9.3	69.9	17.8	18.1	5.7	67.8	11.2
TRT	13.6	5.9	72.9	14.7	14.9	5.1	74.2	12.4

nization, 1977), and the Chinese Journal of Nervous and Mental Disease Editorial Committee (1986). The patients took the Chinese MMPI-2 within three weeks of treatment. The average MMPI-2 scale scores for the male and female patients with schizophrenia, neurotic disorders, and affective disorders are listed in Tables 6-9, 6-10, and 6-11, respectively.

The profile of the patients with affective disorders is marked by elevations above T scores of 70 on scales 8 (Sc), 2 (D), 7 (Pt), and 6 (Pa). Both the F and F_B scales are extremely elevated. Elevations on the content scales are slightly more moderate on DEP, TRT, LSE, HEA, ANX, and FRS.

The schizophrenic patients' profile is characterized by elevations on scales 8 (Sc), 6 (Pa), and 2 (D). The F scales are likewise extremely elevated. However, there is no significant elevation of the content scales. The profile of the PRC schizophrenic patients seems to be less disturbed than that found in Hong Kong. Owing to the variable source of the PRC sample, there are some questions about the duration of treatment received by the patients prior to the administration of the Chinese MMPI-2. The reliability of the patient selection will be checked at a later stage of validation research.

The PRC neurotic patient profile is likewise less elevated than those found for a smaller group of neurotic patients in Hong Kong. Moderate elevations are found on scales 8 (Sc), 7 (Pt), and 2 (D) and for females scale 6 (Pa) as well. As in the other psychiatric profiles, the F scales are extremely elevated.

Among the hospitalized patients in the PRC, the most disturbed profile is found among the patients with affective disorders. For both male and female patients, significant differences (p < 0.01 level) are found between this group and the schizophrenic and neurotic patients on most of the clinical scales, including 1 (Hs), 2 (D), 3(Hy), 7(Pt), 8 (Sc), and 0 (Si). On the content scales, they scored higher on ANX, OBS, DEP, HEA, ANG, ASP, TPA, LSE, SOD, WRK, and TRT.

Comparisons between the Chinese MMPI and MMPI-2

Generally, the U.S. uniform T scores obtained on the basic scales of the Chinese MMPI-2 are lower than those obtained on the Chinese MMPI. For normal subjects, most of the scales averaged below a T score of 60 except for scales F, 2 (D), 7 (Pt), and 8 (Sc), the same scales that were found to be elevated and close to the cutoff point of 70 on the Chinese MMPI. However, although the absolute T scores for these scales on the Chinese MMPI-2 are lower, they are also close to the new cutoff point of 65 used in the MMPI-2.

Before the availability of the new MMPI-2 U.S. norms, there were questions about whether the elevations found on the Chinese MMPI might be due to the cohort differences between the original American MMPI normative sample and a contemporary Chinese sample. In Cheung, Zhao, and Wu's (1992) study of Chi-

154   Fanny M. Cheung et al.

Table 6-9. MMPI-2 Raw Scores and K-Corrected T Scores (Based on U.S. Norms) for PRC Schizophrenic Patients

	Male (N = 119)				Female (N = 75)			
	Raw Score		T Score		Raw Score		T Score	
Scale	Mean	SD	Mean	SD	Mean	SD	Mean	SD
L	6.8	2.8	64.1	12.4	7.4	3.5	68.6	16.9
F	12.6	5.7	74.9	17.2	13.6	6.2	82.9	18.6
K	14.6	5.7	47.7	14.1	14.9	5.3	49.0	13.6
Hs	10.2	4.9	61.1	13.2	10.7	5.1	60.0	12.0
D	27.1	5.5	68.0	10.7	28.6	5.1	67.2	11.0
Hy	25.7	6.5	61.3	15.0	26.1	6.1	59.1	13.7
Pd	20.1	4.8	56.4	11.7	20.1	4.6	57.8	10.3
Mf	26.5	4.0	51.1	7.9	30.1	4.2	64.2	10.5
Pa	14.9	4.0	67.7	14.7	16.4	4.8	71.9	17.3
Pt	19.2	8.5	65.4	12.2	19.0	9.0	62.3	9.8
Sc	24.5	10.4	72.1	13.3	25.3	11.7	72.2	12.4
Ma	18.5	5.6	53.0	12.4	17.9	5.6	53.8	12.2
Si	32.8	7.4	58.1	8.7	34.0	6.0	56.5	6.6
F_B	9.4	5.5	80.4	21.7	11.0	6.8	83.3	22.5
VRIN	8.7	2.6	63.9	10.1	8.8	2.8	65.0	11.0
TRIN	9.7	2.2	64.9	10.7	10.0	2.2	66.0	11.0
ANX	8.7	4.2	57.5	9.9	8.9	4.7	55.2	10.5
FRS	8.5	3.9	65.4	12.6	10.7	4.2	62.0	12.5
OBS	6.1	4.0	53.8	12.9	6.2	4.0	52.2	12.1
DEP	11.6	5.7	63.9	10.0	11.8	5.9	61.1	10.1
HEA	10.3	5.2	61.9	11.4	11.0	5.7	60.2	11.7
BIZ	6.2	4.4	64.1	15.0	6.6	5.3	64.9	16.4
ANG	6.2	3.2	51.7	9.1	5.8	3.5	50.4	10.9
CYN	10.5	5.5	51.9	10.4	10.0	5.6	52.5	10.9
ASP	7.4	4.1	48.5	9.3	6.5	4.2	50.8	11.4
TPA	9.9	4.0	55.2	12.2	10.2	4.2	59.5	14.6
LSE	9.5	4.8	63.5	12.2	10.0	5.0	61.0	11.9
SOD	10.2	4.5	55.2	9.6	10.5	4.0	55.9	8.2
FAM	8.0	4.2	57.4	11.6	8.9	5.0	57.0	12.9
WRK	12.0	5.8	59.1	11.1	12.6	5.8	57.3	10.8
TRT	10.6	4.7	65.2	11.5	10.7	5.0	63.7	12.1

Table 6-10. MMPI-2 Raw Scores and K-Corrected T Scores (Based on U.S. Norms) for PRC Neurotic Patients

Scale	Male (N = 65)				Female (N = 45)			
	Raw Score		T Score		Raw Score		T Score	
	Mean	SD	Mean	SD	Mean	SD	Mean	SD
L	6.4	3.2	62.7	14.2	6.5	3.0	63.8	13.7
F	12.3	4.7	73.9	14.2	14.3	6.6	86.0	21.6
K	14.0	5.1	46.9	11.6	13.8	5.5	46.9	13.2
Hs	10.0	4.8	60.1	13.0	12.3	6.2	62.2	13.2
D	26.2	7.7	66.1	15.1	29.2	7.6	68.6	16.5
Hy	25.0	6.6	59.6	15.7	26.5	6.9	60.1	15.7
Pd	20.9	4.5	57.6	10.7	21.3	4.7	59.7	11.9
Mf	25.8	2.8	49.5	5.9	30.0	3.7	64.5	9.1
Pa	14.0	3.9	64.3	14.4	17.0	4.1	74.1	15.2
Pt	19.7	8.9	65.2	15.4	23.6	11.2	68.5	14.8
Sc	24.6	9.0	71.2	12.5	30.0	11.8	77.5	13.3
Ma	19.1	6.3	54.6	15.1	19.8	5.2	57.9	12.7
Si	32.6	9.5	57.8	11.1	34.9	9.3	57.6	10.2
F_B	9.4	5.5	80.2	20.7	13.8	7.7	92.0	24.4
VRIN	8.9	2.4	64.8	9.2	8.0	2.6	62.0	10.9
TRIN	9.8	2.2	63.6	10.2	10.7	2.4	69.1	12.0
ANX	9.4	4.8	59.1	11.2	11.3	5.7	60.7	12.9
FRS	7.6	4.2	62.6	14.0	10.8	5.0	62.5	15.0
OBS	6.4	4.2	54.8	13.9	7.5	4.7	56.5	14.8
DEP	11.9	5.8	64.3	9.9	15.2	7.4	67.0	12.5
HEA	10.1	4.6	61.6	10.2	12.6	7.1	63.4	13.6
BIZ	5.5	4.5	62.1	15.1	7.0	4.8	66.4	14.9
ANG	6.7	3.5	53.2	10.1	7.1	3.3	54.6	11.0
CYN	11.5	4.8	53.4	9.3	12.2	5.3	56.4	10.7
ASP	7.7	3.7	49.4	8.8	7.5	3.6	53.3	9.5
TPA	10.2	4.2	56.4	12.6	10.3	4.1	59.8	14.0
LSE	9.8	4.7	64.3	11.7	11.2	5.5	64.1	13.0
SOD	9.4	4.5	53.5	9.4	10.6	5.4	56.5	11.5
FAM	8.2	4.6	58.0	12.8	9.6	4.9	58.9	12.8
WRK	13.2	5.8	61.5	10.8	14.6	7.5	61.7	14.4
TRT	10.8	4.8	65.7	11.9	12.6	5.1	68.3	12.5

Table 6-11. MMPI-2 Raw Scores and K-Corrected T Scores (Based on U.S. Norms)
for PRC Affective Disorder Patients

	Male (N = 56)				Female (N = 42)			
	Raw Score		T Score		Raw Score		T Score	
Scale	Mean	SD	Mean	SD	Mean	SD	Mean	SD
L	5.5	2.6	58.6	12.2	6.1	2.6	62.0	12.2
F	15.2	7.2	81.9	18.9	15.2	6.1	88.6	19.6
K	12.6	4.5	43.7	11.2	11.7	4.9	42.7	10.7
Hs	14.9	5.8	69.9	12.5	15.7	6.2	67.8	12.4
D	33.2	6.6	79.9	12.6	33.4	5.7	77.6	12.5
Hy	29.7	5.8	70.7	13.9	29.3	6.5	66.3	15.3
Pd	22.5	4.1	59.9	9.1	21.4	5.6	58.0	13.2
Mf	26.2	3.9	50.5	8.1	29.9	3.7	65.0	9.0
Pa	16.6	4.8	73.9	17.4	16.8	5.1	73.3	18.5
Pt	27.1	9.7	78.3	15.5	27.5	9.8	72.0	14.1
Sc	31.2	12.0	80.3	16.2	31.9	11.5	77.2	14.2
Ma	18.3	5.0	51.2	10.8	19.8	4.9	56.6	11.7
Si	38.7	9.5	64.9	11.0	38.5	8.5	61.6	9.3
F_B	11.8	7.5	86.6	22.5	13.5	7.0	91.8	22.6
VRIN	8.1	2.6	61.6	9.7	8.3	3.0	63.3	12.2
TRIN	9.8	2.0	62.4	8.5	10.2	2.0	63.8	10.9
ANX	13.6	5.6	69.1	13.5	14.0	5.3	66.9	12.4
FRS	8.4	4.8	65.1	15.9	12.9	4.6	68.5	13.7
OBS	8.7	4.2	62.3	14.1	8.8	3.7	60.3	11.6
DEP	16.7	6.2	72.6	10.6	16.9	6.7	69.7	11.4
HEA	14.2	6.0	69.9	12.2	15.7	6.8	69.2	12.8
BIZ	6.3	5.2	64.4	17.8	7.0	4.6	66.7	13.9
ANG	7.8	3.2	56.6	10.1	8.3	2.8	58.5	10.2
CYN	12.5	5.4	55.7	11.2	13.3	4.7	58.5	9.7
ASP	8.4	4.2	50.8	10.3	8.5	3.6	56.0	9.8
TPA	11.3	3.7	59.3	12.1	11.9	3.6	65.3	12.8
LSE	12.8	6.0	72.1	15.2	12.7	5.1	67.8	12.3
SOD	12.6	5.4	60.6	12.1	11.8	5.6	58.9	11.8
FAM	9.3	4.8	61.1	13.2	9.4	5.2	58.4	13.4
WRK	17.0	7.1	68.4	12.9	17.4	6.6	66.5	12.9
TRT	13.3	5.2	72.1	12.7	13.8	4.9	71.3	11.9

nese neurotic patients, the MMPI profiles were scored on the basis of the Chinese norms and the original MMPI norms as well as the MMPI-2 uniform T scores. For both the MMPI and MMPI-2 U.S. norms, Chinese neurotic patients peaked on scales 2 (D) and 8 (Sc), as is characteristically found among normal Chinese subjects. The use of the contemporary U.S. norms did not remove these characteristic peaks, which suggests that the elevations on these scales are more likely caused by cultural rather than cohort differences.

Similarly, the results obtained from the Chinese normal subjects on the Chinese MMPI-2 further support the presence of cultural differences in the pattern of responses on some of the scales. The same set of scales found to be elevated on the Chinese MMPI using U.S. norms is found to be similarly elevated on the Chinese MMPI-2 despite the lower overall score level. However, with the lower cutoff point of 65 on the MMPI-2, these elevated scores obtained by normal subjects still approach the American cutoff point.

The elevations found among normal subjects on scale F in the Chinese MMPI as well as in the Chinese MMPI-2 are further extended to the F_B scale, a new scale assessing deviant responses to items located in the later part of the MMPI-2 booklet. The T scores obtained by the Chinese normal sample on F_B are even higher than those on the F scale. These two scales, which are derived from empirical response rates of the American normative sample, would overestimate invalidity among normal Chinese subjects, although they are able to discriminate between Chinese normal subjects and psychiatric patients. Instead, the infrequency (ICH) scale developed by Cheung, Song, and Butcher (1991) is a better indicator of infrequent responses than the F or F_B scales on both the Chinese MMPI and the Chinese MMPI-2.

On the other hand, the new validity scales, TRIN and VRIN, in the MMPI-2 are found to be applicable with Chinese subjects. However, the raw score cutoff points suggested in the manual for TRIN and VRIN would have eliminated too many subjects. Profiles of over 21% of the normal PRC sample and 39% of the psychiatric patients would be invalidated using these criteria. Instead, a slightly higher raw score cutoff point of 14 or less in the case of VRIN and scores between 5 and 14 in the case of TRIN, in addition to an ICH raw score of 10 or less, are used to determine the validity of the Chinese MMPI-2. With these modified cutoff criteria, 8.6% of the PRC normative sample and 14.6% of the clinical sample are invalidated. The availability of these two validity scales to identify carelessness and inconsistency replaces the previous practice of using the TR index (Dahlstrom, Welsh, & Dahlstrom, 1975, Appendix C), which consists of 16 pairs of repeated items, as the major validity indicator for the Chinese MMPI.

The clinical utility of the Chinese MMPI-2 in discriminating psychiatric patients from normal subjects is similar to that found for the Chinese MMPI. Despite the elevations found on scales F, 2 (D), 7 (Pt), and 8 (Sc) among normals, psychiatric patients score significantly higher than normal subjects on most of the clinical scales. The pattern of scale elevations on the clinical scales also discriminates between patients with schizophrenic, neurotic, and affective disorders. The addition of the content scales provides further information on behavioral and personality characteristics to differentiate between different criterion groups.

Advantages and Limitations in the Use of the Chinese MMPI-2

Initial studies and applications of the Chinese MMPI-2 have shown that, like the Chinese MMPI, it is useful as an assessment instrument. In addition, modifications in the wording of some of the items and the elimination of items related to sex and religion have improved the translation of the Chinese version and reduced the embarrassment for some subjects. However, the use of the American norms continues to produce higher T scores on some of the clinical scales. Test users need to be alerted to the elevations on these scales when interpreting the Chinese MMPI-2. Otherwise, normal Chinese subjects may be misjudged to be suffering from depressive and schizophrenic disorders. It is important to provide users of the Chinese MMPI-2 with the relevant local research literature.

An alternative approach to adjust for these cross-cultural differences is to develop local norms on the Chinese MMPI-2. By developing a normative distribution of scores based on the local population, one adopts a statistical paradigm to define psychopathology within the Chinese culture. Deviations from the population mean would be interpreted as indications of psychopathology. Interpretation strategies based on T-score elevations are borrowed from the original U.S. studies on the MMPI-2 to make clinical judgments and predictions. This approach assumes that the meaning of the T scores on the U.S. norms would be transferable to T scores of the same values on the Chinese norms, even though the raw score distributions of the two cultural groups are different. However, in the case of the Chinese norms for the original MMPI, the spread of scores on the clinical scales is reduced, resulting in lower T scores even for psychiatric patients (Cheung & Song, 1989; Cheung, Zhao, & Wu, 1992). Given that the clinical scales of the MMPI and the MMPI-2 are nearly identical, this problem is likely to remain when the Chinese MMPI-2 norms are developed. Further empirical research with Chinese clinical groups would be needed to substantiate the clinical interpretations based on the Chinese norms of the MMPI-2.

Meanwhile, the addition of the rationally derived and construct-oriented content scales to the empirically derived clinical scales in the MMPI-2 has improved the communicability and cross-cultural interpretability of the individual scales. The content scales provide additional information about the underlying psychopathological dimensions, which may be indicated by elevations on the clinical scales. They also supplement information on personality traits as well as clinical problems or activities not covered by the clinical scales (Butcher et al., 1990). For example, elevations on clinical scales 2 (D) and 8 (Sc) on the Chinese MMPI-2 may be understood in conjunction with similar elevations on content scales DEP (Depression), ANX (Anxiety), and LSE (Low Self-Esteem). Especially when used with normal subjects, the contents of these scales are more appropriate for interpretation.

A problem still remains with the cultural explanation for the elevation of scale scores for the Chinese subjects. Do the higher scores reflect more prevalent psychopathology among Chinese people or the lack of cross-cultural equivalence for some of the clinical constructs measured by the individual scales on the MMPI-2? Cheung (1985) pointed out that the higher scores obtained by Chinese subjects on some of the clinical scales of the MMPI may be explained by differences in cultural acceptance of certain behaviors or attitudes; that is, the behaviors may be considered undesirable in the American culture but desirable, and therefore not abnormal, in the Chinese culture. Thus, the higher scores obtained by normal Chinese subjects on scales 2 (D) and DEP of the MMPI-2, for example, may be a reflection of the cultural norm of modesty, imperturbability, and restraint rather than an indication of depressive features. Therefore, these items would likely be endorsed by normal subjects as well as by psychiatric patients. The lower level of elevation found on the T scores of psychiatric patients based on the Chinese norms for the Chinese MMPI support the notion that some of the items on the clinical scales do not discriminate between Chinese normal subjects and patients.

A fundamental consideration in cross-cultural assessment is whether to translate an imported instrument or to develop a new instrument indigenous to that culture. The advantage of using a translated version of the MMPI-2 is the availability of a well-established instrument with a vast amount of research data from all over the world. Despite some cultural differences, the overall cross-cultural equivalence of the MMPI-2 has been supported. Clinical applications of the MMPI-2 have confirmed its usefulness in the personality assessment of patients and prisoners. Using a comparable instrument permits cross-cultural comparisons of the personality profiles of clinical groups based on diagnostic classifications similar to those used in Western psychiatry. Using the same yardstick also facilitates communication among clinical psychologists from different parts of the world who can share their understanding of psychopathology. This practice assumes that there is basic universality in the manifestation of abnormal personality.

The assumption of cultural universality does not preclude cultural specificity in particular aspects that may not be emphasized in Western psychology. Cross-cultural differences may be observed not only in the pattern of scores on the existing personality and clinical scales, but also in terms of the domain of constructs included in clinical personality assessment. If the purpose of a personality inventory is to provide a reliable and valid assessment instrument within a particular culture rather than to investigate cultural universals, then the construction of an inventory that includes the major culture-specific personality domains in addition to the culture-comparable personality constructs may be called for. Although the MMPI was developed for use in the United States, it has since been expanded into a successful cross-cultural inventory. Working with the Chinese MMPI for the past 15 years has led us to extend our experiences to the development of an indigenous personality inventory for the Chinese people. Written originally in Chinese, the Chinese Personality Assessment Inventory (CPAI) was developed using an approach similar to that used for the MMPI-2 (Cheung, Kwok, Fan, Song, Zhang, & Zhang, 1994). The CPAI is intended to be a comprehensive indigenous personality and clinical assessment inventory parallel to the Chinese MMPI-2. In addition to clinical scales, personality scales are included to assess normal personality styles and characteristics. Studies are under way to compare patterns of results obtained on the CPAI and the Chinese MMPI-2. Until the extensive validation process of the CPAI is completed, the MMPI-2 is expected to remain the major objective personality assessment instrument used in clinical settings in Chinese societies.

References

American Psychiatric Association. (1980). *Diagnostic and statistical manual of mental disorders* (3rd ed.). Washington, DC: Author.

Boey, K. W. (1985). [The MMPI response pattern of Singapore Chinese]. *Acta Psychologica Sinica, 17*(4), 377–383.

Butcher, J. N., Graham, J. R., Williams, C. L., & Ben-Porath, Y. S. (1990). *Development and use of the MMPI-2 content scales*. Minneapolis: University of Minnesota Press.

Cheung, F. M. (1985). Cross-cultural considerations for the translation and adaptation of the Chinese MMPI in Hong Kong. In J. N. Butcher & C. D. Spielberger (Eds.), *Advances in personality assessment* (Vol. 4, pp. 131–158). Hillsdale, NJ: Erlbaum.

Cheung, F. M. (in press). *Manual of the Chinese Minnesota Multiphasic Personality Inventory (MMPI)*. Hong Kong: Chinese University Press.

Cheung, F. M., Kwok, L., Fan, R. M., Song, W. Z., Zhang, J. X., & Zhang, J. P. (1994). Development of the Chinese Personality Assessment Inventory (CPAI). Unpublished manuscript.

Cheung, F. M., & Song, W. Z. (1989). A review of the clinical applications of the Chinese MMPI. *Psychological Assessment: A Journal of Consulting and Clinical Psychology, 1,* 230–237.

Cheung, F. M., Song, W. Z., & Butcher, J. N. (1991). An infrequency scale for the Chinese MMPI. *Psychological Assessment: A Journal of Consulting and Clinical Psychology, 3,* 648–653.

Cheung, F. M., Zhao, J. C., & Wu, C. Y. (1992). Chinese MMPI profiles among neurotic patients. *Psychological Assessment: A Journal of Consulting and Clinical Psychology, 4,* 214–218.

Cheung, P. C., Conger, A. J., Hau, K. T., Lew, W. J. F., & Lau, S. (1992). Development of the Multi-Trait Personality Inventory (MTPI): Comparison among four Chinese populations. *Journal of Personality Assessment, 59,* 528–551.

Chinese Journal of Nervous and Mental Disease Editorial Committee (1986). Clinical diagnostic criteria for neurotic disorders. *Chinese Journal of Nervous and Mental Disease, 5,* 318–320.

Chinese Medical Association. (1981). The Neuropsychiatric Association diagnostic criteria on schizophrenia. *Chinese Journal of Neuropsychiatry, 14,* 96.

Dahlstrom, W. G., Welsh, G. S., & Dahlstrom, L. E. (1975). *An MMPI handbook, Volume I.* Minneapolis: University of Minnesota Press.

Dai, X. Y., Zheng, L. X., Ryan, J. J., & Paolo, A. M. (1993). [Applications of psychological testing in Chinese clinical psychology and comparisons with American data]. *Chinese Journal of Clinical Psychology, 1* (1), 47–50.

Ko, Y. H. (1978). [Clinical psychology: Psychodiagnostics (Vol. 1)]. Taipei, Taiwan: Dai Yang.

Lo, M. W. (1991). Effect of various norms on MMPI code types among Chinese subjects. Hong Kong: The Chinese University of Hong Kong, Unpublished master's thesis, Department of Psychology.

Lo, T. W. H. (1993). Discrimination between schizophrenic patients and normals using the Chinese MMPI-2 in Hong Kong. Hong Kong: The Chinese University of Hong Kong, Unpublished master's thesis, Department of Psychology.

National MMPI Coordinating Group. (1982). [The revision, employment and evaluation of the MMPI in China]. *Acta Psychologica Sinica, 17,* 346–355.

National MMPI Coordinating Group. (1989). [A user's guide for the Chinese MMPI]. Beijing: Institute of Psychology, Academia Sinica.

Song, W. Z. (1985). [Analysis of results of administration of the MMPI to normal Chinese subjects]. *Acta Psychologica Sinica, 17,* 346–355.

Song, W. Z. (1991). Use and evaluation of a modified MMPI in China. *International Journal of Mental Health, 20,* 81–93.

Song, W. Z., Cui, C. Z., Cheung, F. M., & Hong, Y.Y. (1987). [Comparison of the personality characteristics of Beijing and Hong Kong students—Content analysis on the MMPI item endorsement differences]. *Acta Psychologica Sinica, 19,* 263–269.

Tsoi, M. M., & Sundberg, N. D. (1989). Patterns of psychological test usage in Hong Kong. *Professional Psychology: Research and Practice, 20,* 248–250.

World Health Organization. (1977). Manual of the International Statistical Classification of Dieseases, Injuries, and Causes of Death. Geneva: World Health Organization.

Zhou, Y. Z., & Zhao, C. Y. (1992). [The validity of the MMPI in the clinical diagnosis of 1,422 Chinese subjects]. *Chinese Mental Health Journal, 6,* 211–213.

Zhou, Y. Z., Zhao, C. Y., & Jiang, C. Q. (1989). [Analysis of the structure validity of the Chinese version of the MMPI]. *Acta Psychologica Sinica, 21,* 266–273.

Chapter 7

Use of the MMPI-2 in Thailand

La-Or Pongpanich

The MMPI has a relatively long history of use in Thailand, having been originally translated into Thai in 1979 by Pongpanich and Butcher. The inventory was used extensively in personnel screening for military officers, medical students, and nurses, as well as for the clinical assessment of patients in several psychiatric hospitals. Given the broad success of the original MMPI in Thailand, there was a great deal of interest in adopting the revised version of the instrument into the Thai language when the MMPI-2 was published in 1989. This chapter provides a description of the procedures for adapting the MMPI-2 into Thai, describes empirical research into the application of the Thai version of the instrument with groups of normals in Thailand, and provides three illustrations of using the MMPI-2 with clinical patients in Thailand.

Developmental Procedures for the Thai Translation and Item Translation Problems Encountered

The MMPI-2 was translated into the Thai language using the same committee translation method employed in the development of the Thai version of the original MMPI. Many of the items did not require retranslation because they were not changed in the MMPI-2. Translations of new and modified items were verified by back-translation, as had been done with the original version of the MMPI. The original MMPI translation was completed while the author was studying in the United States; the MMPI-2 translation was completed in Thailand. Adaptation of the MMPI-2 into Thai was begun in the middle of 1989 and was completed at the end of that year. Eight Thai bilinguals and one American teacher worked on the translation and back-translation. James Butcher, communicating with the research team in Thailand by fax machine, checked the accuracy of the meaning of the back-translated items to ensure equivalence of the items. Problematic items were retranslated and re-back-translated until the meanings were judged to be equivalent to the English language versions. Compared with translation of the original

MMPI, we did not encounter many item translation problems in the MMPI-2 translation. The MMPI-2 was much easier to translate for a number of reasons:

1. Many items did not require retranslation.
2. We had learned from translating the original MMPI how to deal with linguistic problems in order to produce equivalent meanings involving, for example, frequency:

    > always = all the time
    > usually = almost all the time
    > often = frequently

    Other qualifying phrases required careful wording:

    > 272 "There never was a time in my life . . ."
    >   was translated "I never used to have . . ."
    > 524 "No one knows it but I have tried to . . ."
    >   was translated "In the past or the present time I have tried . . ."
    > 540 "I have gotten angry and broke furniture . . ."
    >   was translated "I used to get angry and break furniture . . ."

3. The language in the MMPI-2 is easier to understand than the language in the original MMPI because it contains fewer awkward words. No difficulties were encountered with idiomatic expressions or colloquial English.
4. No items were found to be cross-culturally irrelevant.

However, some item translation problems were encountered in the back-translation:

1. Some bilinguals in the translation process used words that generated different meanings in back-translation, for example:
    —loyal, faithful, or honest
    —little or few
    —rough or harsh
    —goal or destination
2. Some items were awkward in the English back-translation, for example:
    532 Almost all the time I feel relief after much enough crying.
    536 If I am moody I am sure that I have to have a headache.
3. Some difficulties were found with idioms or expressions, for example:
    532 "I usually feel better after a good cry."
         "good cry" was translated "cry for a long time"
    543 "Terrible thoughts about my family come to me at times."
         "come to me" was translated "come into my mind"

The items that were difficult to translate into Thai, as shown by the back-translation, were retranslated until the meanings were judged equivalent. Prob-

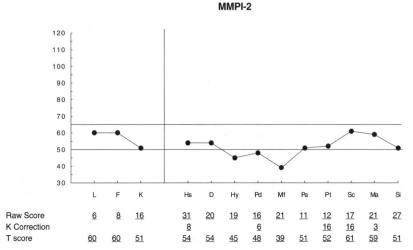

Figure 7-1. Mean MMPI-2 Standard Scale Profile of 282 Young Thai Men Applying for the Thai Army Cadet School

lematic items were discussed with James Butcher until a satisfactory translation of each one was achieved.

After the completion of the translation and adaptation process, we adapted the MMPI-2 profile, answer sheets, and scoring templates by using the scoring and administration manual for the MMPI-2 (Butcher, Dahlstrom, Graham, Tellegen, & Kaemmer, 1989) and the MMPI-2 content scale book (Butcher, Graham, Williams, & Ben-Porath, 1990). Adapting the American norms and profile sheets allowed us to begin using the MMPI-2 in Thailand and was considered to be justified because of the previous work on the original MMPI in Thailand and the similarity that Thai normals had to the U.S. norms.

Initial Research Evaluations of the MMPI-2 in Thailand

In this section we will describe a research program conducted in the Thai Army to evaluate the use of the MMPI-2 in Thailand. The program was designed to assess the suitability of candidates for various positions within the army.

Study 1

The first study to be described involved a group of 282 male applicants to the Thai Army Cadet School. All the applicants are between 16 and 20 years of age and have passed a written portion of the entrance exam that qualified them to be admitted to the Cadet School. The Thai Army Cadet School is a one-year training program that prepares the individual for entrance into the Thai Military School Program by providing academic background. The Military School Program is a

MMPI-2

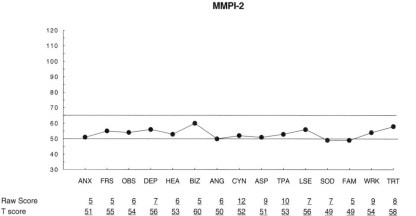

	ANX	FRS	OBS	DEP	HEA	BIZ	ANG	CYN	ASP	TPA	LSE	SOD	FAM	WRK	TRT
Raw Score	5	5	6	7	6	5	6	12	9	10	7	7	5	9	8
T score	51	55	54	56	53	60	50	52	51	53	56	49	49	54	58

Figure 7-2. Mean MMPI-2 Content Scale Profile of 282 Young Thai Men Applying for the Thai Army Cadet School

MMPI-2

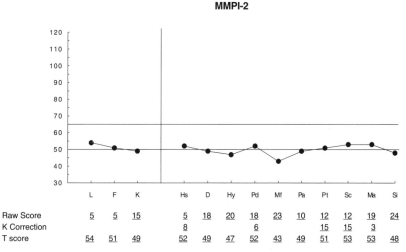

	L	F	K	Hs	D	Hy	Pd	Mf	Pa	Pt	Sc	Ma	Si
Raw Score	5	5	15	5	18	20	18	23	10	12	12	19	24
K Correction				8			6			15	15	3	
T score	54	51	49	52	49	47	52	43	49	51	53	53	48

Figure 7-3. Mean MMPI-2 Standard Profile of 1,138 Enlisted Men from the U.S. Army, Navy, Air Force, and Marine Corps

four- or five-year academic degree leading to commissioned officer status as first lieutenant or lieutenant in the Royal Thai Army. In this study, the MMPI-2 was group administered to the subjects.

The group mean MMPI-2 clinical profile of the applicants is shown in Figure 7-1, and the group mean MMPI-2 content scale profile is presented in Figure 7-2. The scores are plotted on U.S. norms. The clinical and content profiles for these Thai men are comparable to groups of normals from the United States. For example, the

MMPI-2 clinical profile shown in Figure 7-3 represents a large sample of men from the U.S. military (Butcher, Jeffrey, Cayton, Colligan, DeVore, & Minnegawa, 1990).

Study 2

The next study involved an evaluation of 66 men between the ages of 16 and 20 who have passed the written part of the entrance examination to the Thai Army Medical School. The Thai Army Medical School is a five-year academic program that leads to the commissioned rank of first lieutenant and is a medical degree granting program. The MMPI-2 was administered in small groups to individuals, most of whom were over 18 years of age. The MMPI profiles shown in Figures 7-4 and 7-5 provide the group mean profiles of the medical school entrants.

Visual inspection of these profiles reveals that the normal military personnel in the Thai Army resemble normal personnel in the U.S. military, with most of the scale scores near T = 50 and few scores exceeding the SEM. As with Study 1, the men taking the MMPI-2 in this study produced, on average, normal-range MMPI-2 clinical and content scale profiles that deviated little from the T = 50 mark that defines the mean score for the scales.

Study 3

The third study involved the evaluation of 341 career Thai Army officers who range in rank from captain to lieutenant colonel and in age from 30 to 46 years. These officers have worked in various units of the Royal Thai Army and were selected on the basis of their career achievements to study in the Army High Staff College. The MMPI-2 profiles of these officers are shown in Figures 7-6 and 7-7.

As in the previously described studies, the officers from the High Staff College produced clearly normal-range MMPI-2 scores when their scores were plotted on U.S. norms (see Figures 7-6 and 7-7). The U.S. norms appear to be an appropriate normative comparison for this study.

Clinical Applications

Following are three clinical cases that illustrate the sensitivity of the MMPI-2 to clinical symptoms and behavior in psychiatric patients in Thailand. All the patients were seen in a psychiatric treatment unit in Bangkok and were administered the Thai version of the MMPI-2. Their scores were plotted on U.S. norms.

Case 1

This is a 36-year-old married man who was employed as a practical nurse at the Veterans Administration Hospital. Before obtaining his job at the VA Hospital, he was a soldier in the Thai Army and was wounded in the arm while stationed

MMPI-2

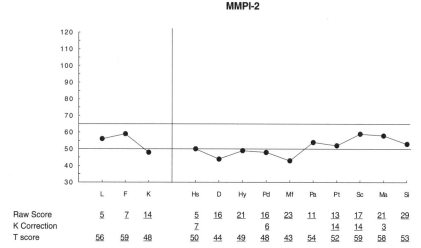

	L	F	K		Hs	D	Hy	Pd	Mf	Pa	Pt	Sc	Ma	Si
Raw Score	5	7	14		5	16	21	16	23	11	13	17	21	29
K Correction					7			6			14	14	3	
T score	56	59	48		50	44	49	48	43	54	52	59	58	53

Figure 7-4. Mean MMPI-2 Standard Profile of 66 Young Thai Men Applying for the Thai Army Medical School

MMPI-2

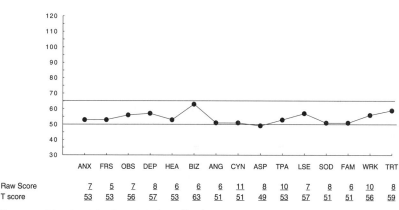

	ANX	FRS	OBS	DEP	HEA	BIZ	ANG	CYN	ASP	TPA	LSE	SOD	FAM	WRK	TRT
Raw Score	7	5	7	8	6	6	6	11	8	10	7	8	6	10	8
T score	53	53	56	57	53	63	51	51	49	53	57	51	51	56	59

Figure 7-5. Mean MMPI-2 Content Scale Profile of 66 Young Thai Men Applying for the Thai Army Medical School

in a unit along the Thai-Cambodian border. After he recovered from his wounds, he asked to be assigned to a job in the VA Hospital.

He has had a great deal of difficulty performing his job as a practical nurse and has frequently been criticized by his supervisor. He rejects authority, has objected to direction, and resents his supervisor. He has also been having considerable difficulty receiving direction from his department head and tried to change the hospital system by writing extreme letters to the newspapers to cause public pressure to force the firing of the chief of the hospital unit. He has created a nuisance with

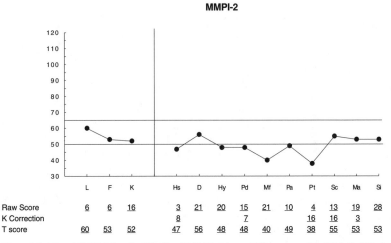

Figure 7-6. Mean MMPI-2 Standard Profile of 341 Thai Army Officers Attending High Staff College

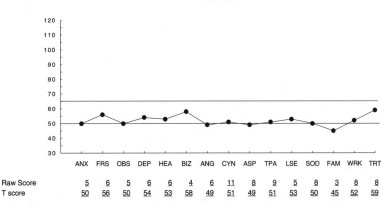

Figure 7-7. Mean MMPI-2 Content Scale Profile of 341 Thai Army Officers Attending High Staff College

his aggressive behavior and has generally been ineffective on the job. Other staff members reported that he was behaving inappropriately in the hospital. He was hyperactive, talked excessively, and said many unusual things. He tried to control and manipulate everyone around him. He became such a nuisance among his coworkers that they complained to the department head about his behavior.

His supervisor became concerned over his extreme and deviant behavior and referred him to the psychiatry department at another hospital for psychological treatment. Although he went to the hospital for the psychological evaluation, producing the MMPI-2 profiles shown in Figures 7-8 and 7-9, he refused to follow up on treatment recommendations.

MMPI-2 Interpretation

His MMPI-2 validity pattern (Figure 7-8) suggests that he has approached the test in a generally cooperative manner, producing an interpretable pattern. He seemed to understand the items and tried to present himself as having relatively few problems. However, his scores on the MMPI-2 clinical scales show a pattern that is consistent with a clinical diagnosis of paranoid schizophrenia. (See the discussion of paranoid schizophrenics in chapter 1.) He reported severe symptoms of an emotional disorder that includes thinking disturbance, possible hallucinations and delusions, and deterioration in functioning. He is likely to have great problems in interpersonal relationships. His high score on the MMPI-2 content scale BIZ supports the interpretation that he is experiencing an extreme thought disorder and bizarre thoughts. He appears to be very mistrustful and cynical about the motives of others, as shown by his high score on the CYN content scale.

The severe problems he has been experiencing on the job are reflected in his high score on the WRK scale. He tends to endorse many problems that center on work themes.

After the psychological evaluation was complete and before treatment was implemented, he left the hospital against medical advice because he believed he did not have any psychological problems, thinking that the system was all wrong. He was given a discharge diagnosis of paranoid schizophrenia.

Case 2

The 63-year-old male patient was, when tested, a politician—a representative of the Royal Thai government. He is a wealthy businessman from a province outside Bangkok and is currently married to three wives. He usually spends the first two days of the week with Wife #1, the second two days of the week with Wife #2, and the remainder of the week with his favorite, Wife #3. He came into the psychiatric outpatient unit complaining of tension, insomnia, and numerous physical complaints. Immediately preceding his visit to the clinic he believed he was having a heart attack and came to see a physician. There were no physical signs of coronary disease, and his symptoms were attributed to stress and anxiety.

Over the past few months he has been under a great deal of stress reportedly as a result of parliamentary dissensions and his quarreling wives. His three wives are having disagreement, and he feels torn between the different families. He feels that all of the spousal complaining along with the demands being placed on him by the three wives are "ruining his health." In addition to his considerable family difficulty, he is encountering stress in his government position. He has recently found himself disagreeing with the way the government is being run and has been considering returning to his hometown and resigning from his government

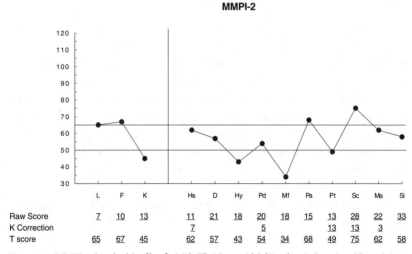

Figure 7-8. MMPI-2 Standard Profile of a Male Thai Paranoid Schizophrenic Inpatient (Case 1)

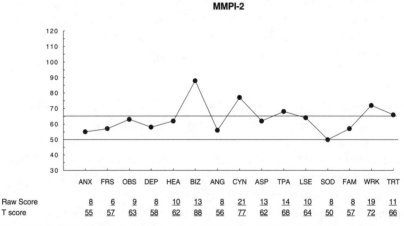

Figure 7-9. MMPI-2 Content Scale Profile of a Male Thai Paranoid Schizophrenic Inpatient (Case 1)

position. During the initial interview he appeared to be tense, worried about his physical health, and concerned that he was going to die. He was open to the recommendation that he see the psychologist because he wanted to have help in relieving his stressful situation.

MMPI-2 Interpretation

Like many medical patients in the United States who are referred by physicians, this patient produced a generally defensive profile (Figure 7-10). He appeared to

MMPI-2

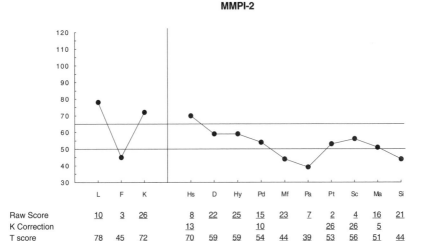

	L	F	K		Hs	D	Hy	Pd	Mf	Pa	Pt	Sc	Ma	Si
Raw Score	10	3	26		8	22	25	15	23	7	2	4	16	21
K Correction					13			10			26	26	5	
T score	78	45	72		70	59	59	54	44	39	53	56	51	44

Figure 7-10. MMPI-2 Standard Profile of a Thai Male Outpatient (Case 2)

MMPI-2

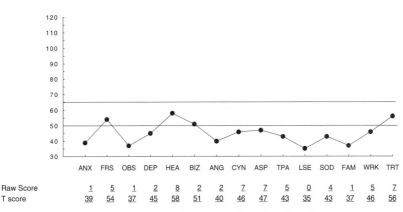

	ANX	FRS	OBS	DEP	HEA	BIZ	ANG	CYN	ASP	TPA	LSE	SOD	FAM	WRK	TRT
Raw Score	1	5	1	2	8	2	2	7	7	5	0	4	1	5	7
T score	39	54	37	45	58	51	40	46	47	43	35	43	37	46	56

Figure 7-11. MMPI-2 Content Scale Profile of a Thai Male Outpatient (Case 2)

present himself in a generally favorable way, suggesting some rather unrealistic self-views. He does not appear to be psychologically minded and is not insightful about psychological causes of problems.

His MMPI-2 clinical profile confirms that he is experiencing great somatic distress at this time. He does not appear to be depressed or experiencing a thought disorder. His problems appear to center around physical health concerns and tension. (See Figure 7-11 for the content scale profile.)

He was treated on the psychiatry unit with brief psychotherapy to reduce the amount of stress in his life. He also received antianxiety medication for his tension and insomnia. He was able, over four treatment sessions, to obtain insight into the extensive environmental circumstances that were impinging upon him. He worked with the psychologist to learn more effective ways of dealing with the pressures in his family. He resigned from the parliamentary post to be able to spend more time on his personal affairs. His discharge diagnosis was anxiety disorder with somatic symptoms.

Case 3

The patient, a 20-year-old single male, is currently a second-year student at the Royal Thai Army Military School. This young man has had quite a bit of difficulty adjusting to the rigorous routine of the military school and on several occasions has been referred to the psychiatry unit at the Army Hospital for adjustment problems. In the current hospital admission to the psychiatry unit he was reported to be experiencing extreme anxiety and uncontrollable outbursts of rage. He showed features of paranoid ideation, that is, he was very suspicious and mistrustful of people around him. The staff at the military school reported that this young man had had considerable difficulty following rules and getting along with his classmates. He also had had great difficulty accepting direction from his superiors. He was hospitalized on the psychiatry unit for the third time in two years. He remained in the hospital for three weeks during which time he received a variety of psychological and rehabilitative treatments. During his stay he was seen in individual psychotherapy and group psychotherapy. He cooperated with the psychological treatment, although on a number of occasions he lost control over his emotions and expressed extreme anger toward the staff.

MMPI-2 Interpretation

His MMPI-2 validity scale pattern (Figure 7-12) indicated that he was open and cooperative with the evaluation. His clinical and content scale profiles are likely to be good indications of his current personality functioning.

His MMPI-2 clinical scale pattern (1-7/7-1) suggests that he is presently experiencing an intense anxiety disorder with somatic concerns. He appears to be a generally maladjusted person who tends to develop physical problems under stress. He shows some tendency toward unproductive rumination and mistrust and suspicion about the motives of others.

His MMPI-2 content scale scores (Figure 7-13) suggest that he is depressed at this time and is having problems adjusting to his work environment. He appears to be an overly sensitive individual who has low frustration tolerance. He appears to have problems controlling his anger.

The treatment goals in his case were to provide emotional support and encouragement and to teach him more emotional control. The goals included allowing

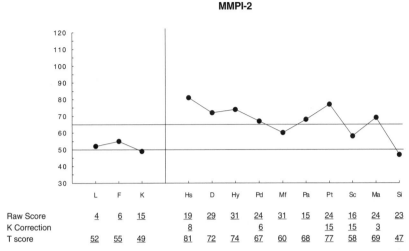

Figure 7-12. MMPI-2 Standard Profile of a Thai Male Inpatient (Case 3)

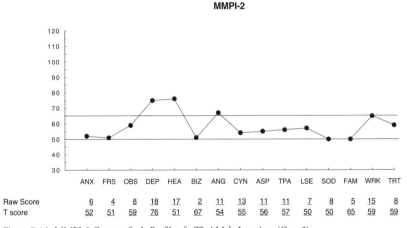

Figure 7-13. MMPI-2 Content Scale Profile of a Thai Male Inpatient (Case 3)

him to return to the military school program, which he desired to complete. Upon his discharge from the psychiatry unit, he returned to the military school and was able to adjust well to the program for a period of time. However, within a month he was having more difficulties and was referred back to the psychiatry unit for additional psychotherapy. On this occasion he was not admitted to the unit but was seen on an outpatient basis to help get him through the difficult time he was experiencing. At the last follow-up, he was continuing his school program and was making a satisfactory adjustment. His discharge diagnosis was adjustment disorder.

Practical Issues in Using the MMPI-2 in Thailand

When we began to administer the Thai MMPI-2 to psychiatric patients and normal groups, both Army personnel and civilians in and outside the Army hospital, we found no problems or resistance. Because of the extensive history of using the original MMPI in screening officer candidates, it was a natural transition to use the MMPI-2 in military personnel selection. Assessment projects have included such groups as medical students, nursing students, nursing aides, hospital employees, and new staff members at the Army hospital, and referrals of officers who have problems in their assignments. In addition, the Army officers in Army High Staff College and candidates to the Army pre-cadet school have also been screened with the MMPI-2. It is notable that most test takers find it easier to take the MMPI-2 than the original MMPI since the improved item wording eliminates some of the reading problems encountered in the original. I have been very encouraged by the usefulness of the MMPI-2 in clinical and screening programs in Thailand.

Future Goals

Many psychologists and psychiatrists in several agencies in Thailand have expressed an interest in using the MMPI-2 in their clinical work and are anxious to receive training in its use. Our future plans include developing an MMPI-2 interpretation course to teach practitioners interpretation strategies.

There are still many things to do before the MMPI-2 is completely adapted for application in Thailand. We have plans to collect a large normative sample to allow us to standardize the Thai MMPI-2 with country-specific norms. We also hope to more broadly study the translation by comparing known Thai groups with other national groups and by comparing the factor structure of the Thai version of the test with normals from other countries. Finally, we plan to develop a study to compare item endorsement percentages in normal samples of Thais with other national groups.

References

Butcher, J. N., Dahlstrom, W. G., Graham, J. R., Tellegen, A., & Kaemmer, B. (1989). *Minnesota Multiphasic Personality Inventory-2 (MMPI-2): Manual for administration and scoring.* Minneapolis: University of Minnesota Press.
Butcher, J. N., Graham, J. R., Williams, C. L., & Ben-Porath, Y. S. (1990). *Development and use of the MMPI-2 content scales.* Minneapolis: University of Minnesota Press.
Butcher, J. N., Jeffrey, T., Cayton, T. G., Colligan, S., DeVore, J., & Minnegawa, R. (1990). A study of active duty military personnel with the MMPI-2. *Military Psychology, 2,* 47–61.
Pongpanich, L. O., & Butcher, J. N. (1979). Adaptation of the MMPI in Thailand. Unpublished text.

Chapter 8

Vietnamese Translation and Adaptation of the MMPI-2

Bao-Chi Nguyen Tran

One recent movement in cross-cultural psychology involves the adaptation of American (English) psychological tests for use in other cultures. According to Brislin (1980), adapting a psychological instrument can be disadvantageous because there is the risk of missing aspects of a phenomenon that may be important or interesting in the target culture. Alternatively, advocates see many reasons for adapting a test from one culture to another (Butcher & Pancheri, 1976). A developed test has a preestablished empirical foundation. A great deal of research on the MMPI has been done and the existing data can be used for comparisons. Furthermore, developing a test from scratch can be costly in countries where psychology is still a growing field and financial resources are limited. Moreover, in deciding whether to adapt a test instrument, one needs to address issues of cross-cultural test generalization and validity (Butcher & Garcia, 1978). That is, can an instrument developed in one culture be applicable to individuals in another culture?

There have been numerous demands for translation of the MMPI-2 into various languages around the world. An important example of the need to develop a foreign language version of the MMPI-2 can be found in the United States. The influx of refugees from Southeast Asia has resulted in a subpopulation that is both at risk for developing mental health problems and also difficult to assess because of the lack of appropriate Vietnamese language assessment techniques. A large number of Southeast Asian (SEA) refugees and immigrants have resettled in the United States since the end of the Vietnam War. Between 1975 and 1985, there were 670,000 SEA refugees in the United States (Strand & Jones, 1985), with most Vietnamese resettling in California, Texas, and Minnesota. In Minnesota, more than one quarter of the 25,500 SEA refugees are Vietnamese (*Know Your Neighbors . . . the Vietnamese,* 1981). This project to develop a Vietnamese translation of the MMPI-2 was designed to develop a practical means of providing a psychological assessment instrument that could be used to assess refugees seeking mental health services.

Translation

Ervin and Osgood (1954) stress the importance of using true bilinguals for test translation. They believe bicultural experience enhances true bilinguality, so the bilingual must have lived in the culture of the target language for at least one year. The Vietnamese translation of the MMPI-2 followed the committee approach (Brislin, 1970). Two bilingual individuals who are fluent in both languages and have lived in each culture for at least eight years independently translated each item into Vietnamese.

Coincidentally, all the bilingual translators happened to speak the Northern dialect. Although the written language is the same across Vietnamese dialects, there are differences in spoken accents. Also, some words are not commonly shared among the dialects. As a result, the translators were meticulously careful to select words and phrases understood by Vietnamese of all dialects. In order to achieve an equivalent translation, the translated version was kept very close to the original version. According to Triandis, Malpass, and Davidson (1973), a perfect linguistic version does not ensure equivalence because of different word frequencies in languages. In this case, a literal translation of an item was performed whenever possible without jeopardizing its psychological meaning. In cases where a literal translation was not possible, the item was translated with as similar linguistic structure and meaning as possible. The linguistic structures of many items were modified to increase readability and understandability in Vietnamese.

Linguistic and cultural differences made some items difficult to translate. In cases where a literal translation of a verb in the past tense would change the meaning of the item, the verb was translated in the present tense. Idioms are particularly difficult to translate into Vietnamese, often resulting in a longer sentence. In cases where simple negatives translate into double negatives, creating awkwardness and obscurity, items were translated in the affirmative. In some situations, a parallel word simply does not exist in the target culture. For example, there is no Vietnamese translation for "football" because the sport is unknown in Vietnam. Fortunately, Vietnamese-Americans in the United States have developed a word for football that is phonetically adapted from the English word. Consequently, the English word football was phonetically adapted into Vietnamese as "phút bôn" (pronounced *fute-bone*).

After the MMPI-2 was independently translated into the target language by the two bilinguals, the two translators worked together to resolve any discrepancies and to establish one translated version. This translated version was then back-translated into the original language by a third bilingual. The original English version and the back-translated English version were compared for possible discrepancies. Discrepancies are bound to happen whenever a back-translation is done (Sechrest, Fay, & Zaidi, 1972), and judgment has to be exercised whether the problem is with the translation or the back-translation. After a few items were retranslated and checked for accuracy, a final form of the Vietnamese version was obtained.

After the completion of the translated version, it was necessary to test the accuracy of the translation and the validity of the translated test. A bilingual study was conducted to determine whether the Vietnamese version produced the same results as the English version for individuals who can take the MMPI-2 in both languages.

Bilingual Study

Upon completion of the translation, a reliability study of the translated version was conducted to assess the comparability of the Vietnamese form of the MMPI-2 to the English form. A test-retest study was done using 32 bilingual (11 males, 21 females) college students or recent graduates of the University of Minnesota. The mean age of the sample was 22.03 with a range of 18 to 31. The mean time of stay in the United States was 11.29 years with a range from 3 to 17 years. Because the bilinguals were young and have lived in the United States for relatively long periods of time, it was believed their fluency in English is generally better than their fluency in Vietnamese. In order to prevent subjects from guessing on the Vietnamese version by having already completed the English version, all 32 subjects were administered the Vietnamese version first. Both versions were completed within an average of 5 days with a range of 2 to 8 days.

An item analysis was performed between the Vietnamese and English responses. On average, 81.5% of the responses were endorsed in the same direction in both languages, with 50% to 99% of the responses consistent for both versions. This indicates that the item endorsement stability was high between the two versions and compares with the percentage of identical responses in English-English test-retest studies (Butcher & Pancheri, 1976). Correlation coefficients of the clinical and content scale scores were calculated for the two versions. The correlation coefficients of the Vietnamese-English scale scores are given in Table 8-1. Correlation coefficients are comparable to test-retest correlation coefficients of English-English scale scores (Table 8-1). For the validity and clinical scales, the correlations of the Vietnamese-English scores for the total sample were generally high (ranging from .51 to .87), with the exception of Hy (correlation of .35). The clinical scale with the highest correlation for the total sample was Mf. For the content scales, the correlations of the Vietnamese-English scores were slightly higher (ranging from .58 to .92). Content scales DEP and HEA had the highest and lowest correlation, respectively. When separated by gender, Vietnamese males' corre-

178   Bao-Chi Nguyen Tran

Table 8-1. Comparison of Test-Retest Correlations between Vietnamese-English Bilinguals and English-English Subjects

| Scale | Vietnamese-English | | | English-English | |
	Male N = 11	Female N = 21	Total N = 32	Male N = 82	Female N = 111
L	.72	.45	.51	.77	.81
F	.85	.85	.84	.78	.69
K	.34	.80	.63	.84	.81
Hs	.50	.69	.65	.85	.85
D	.24	.85	.62	.75	.77
Hy	.09	.53	.35	.72	.76
Pd	.80	.86	.81	.81	.79
Mf	.76	.72	.87	.82	.73
Pa	.91	.79	.85	.67	.58
Pt	.79	.88	.84	.89	.88
Sc	.94	.81	.86	.87	.80
Ma	.64	.81	.76	.83	.68
Si	.65	.84	.71	.92	.91
ANX	.90	.90	.90	.91	.87
FRS	.87	.88	.88	.84	.87
OBS	.92	.89	.89	.83	.85
DEP	.97	.90	.92	.87	.88
HEA	.36	.63	.58	.82	.85
BIZ	.91	.87	.89	.78	.81
ANG	.62	.71	.66	.85	.82
CYN	.33	.92	.75	.80	.89
ASP	.66	.89	.82	.81	.87
TPA	.53	.80	.75	.82	.79
LSE	.87	.86	.86	.84	.86
SOD	.79	.83	.79	.91	.90
FAM	.46	.87	.82	.84	.83
WRK	.87	.91	.90	.90	.91
TRT	.96	.78	.84	.79	.88

Note: Source of columns 4 and 5: Butcher, Dahlstrom, Graham, Tellegen, & Kaemmer (1989).

Table 8-2. Means and Standard Deviations of Scale Raw Scores of the Bilingual Sample (N = 32)

Scale	Vietnamese		English	
	Mean	SD	Mean	SD
L	3.75	2.14	3.91	2.51
F	9.44	4.93	8.81	6.02
K	12.47	4.71	12.16	4.44
Hs	8.59	5.42	7.03	4.77
D	21.59	4.78	20.84	5.11
Hy	22.03	5.32	19.38	5.26
Pd	18.28	5.12	18.63	5.87
Mf	29.41	5.47	28.31	6.02
Pa	13.22	4.10	12.66	4.16
Pt	20.22	8.11	18.91	8.96
Sc	23.69	10.49	21.25	11.22
Ma	20.84	5.43	19.72	6.26
Si	31.81	7.54	30.66	7.62
ANX	8.75	4.29	9.69	4.70
FRS	7.81	4.35	6.88	4.65
OBS	7.47	4.03	7.88	4.04
DEP	10.16	5.65	9.22	5.89
HEA	8.88	4.44	7.13	4.43
BIZ	6.72	4.27	6.59	4.76
ANG	8.09	3.42	7.97	3.00
CYN	13.03	5.36	13.66	5.61
ASP	9.97	4.28	10.75	4.24
TPA	11.66	3.50	11.31	3.19
LSE	8.19	4.00	7.59	4.46
SOD	8.91	3.80	8.34	4.33
FAM	8.38	3.77	8.00	4.41
WRK	12.03	5.46	12.19	6.25
TRT	11.09	3.62	9.59	4.63

Note: Source of columns 3 and 4: Butcher et al. (1989).

MMPI-2

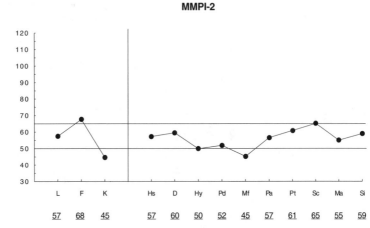

| T score | 57 | 68 | 45 | 57 | 60 | 50 | 52 | 45 | 57 | 61 | 65 | 55 | 59 |

Figure 8-1. Mean Basic Profile of Vietnamese Men (N = 94) Plotted on U.S. Norms

lations generally had a wider range of .09 (Hy) to .94 (Sc) for the clinical scales and .33 (CYN) to .96 (TRT) for the content scales. Females generally had a narrower range. For the clinical scales, correlations had a range of .45 (L) to .88 (Pt). The content scales showed a range of .63 (HEA) to .92 (CYN). Overall, the correlations between the two MMPI scores for the bilinguals in this study were comparable to other bilingual studies (Butcher & Gur, 1974).

The mean raw scores for the scales of both versions given in Table 8-2 and the mean profile configurations of validity, clinical, and content scales for the total sample given in Figures 8-1 and 8-2 show that the mean scale scores and profile configurations of the Vietnamese and English versions are comparable. Thus, the correlations between the Vietnamese and English versions are generally high, indicating that the Vietnamese translation of the MMPI-2 is a reliable alternate form.

Comparability Study

Subjects

The data for the comparability study were collected in St. Paul and Minneapolis, Minnesota. Subjects were selected based on age and Vietnamese reading level. Subjects were selected if they were between the ages of 18 and 65 and if their Vietnamese reading level was equivalent to the sixth grade level. This grade criterion is based on the fact that many older Vietnamese did not go beyond grade school, which consisted of kindergarten to fifth grade. It is assumed that anyone who has gone to high school (sixth to twelfth grade) and has completed at least the sixth grade has an adequate reading level to complete the Vietnamese MMPI-2. The questionnaires were administered in the subjects' homes. The college students

MMPI-2

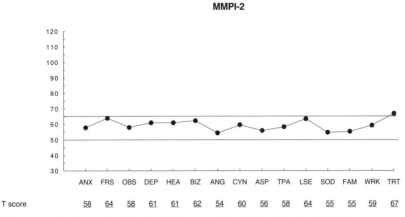

Figure 8-2. Mean Content Scale Profile of Vietnamese Men (N = 94) Plotted on U.S. Norms

who participated in the bilingual study completed the questionnaires at the University of Minnesota. Bilingual subjects taking both Vietnamese and English versions were paid $15. Subjects who completed only the Vietnamese version were paid $10. The total sample consisted of 215 subjects. The exclusion criteria included three indicators: total number of items left blank (CNS), F (raw score), and F_B (raw score). Any case where CNS > 30 or F > 25 or F_B > 25 was considered invalid and was not included in the final sample. The final sample used in the comparability study consisted of 193 subjects (94 males and 99 females).

Instructions

In order to obtain full cooperation from subjects taking the MMPI-2, considerable time was dedicated to establishing rapport with each subject by discussing issues of confidentiality, the purpose of the study, and any future benefits the study may bring to the Vietnamese community. Although the instructions are printed on the front page of the test booklets, extra time was spent explaining the instructions to subjects who were not familiar with the true-false test format. Many subjects, particularly those who were not familiar with this test format, took a long time to complete the MMPI-2 (4-5 hours). In such cases where the test administration passed 3 hours and fatigue was considered a possible factor, the test administration was continued on the next day. Although it was assumed that subjects were free of psychiatric illness, it cannot be assumed that, as a group, they were completely free of symptoms. Many subjects were recent arrivals from Vietnam, separated from their families and adjusting to a different culture. For refugees, the forced flight to a new land is traumatic in itself, not to mention the various dangers encountered by escapees, many of whom were "boat people."

Table 8-3. Age Distribution of the Vietnamese Sample

Age	Male N	%	Female N	%	Total N	%
18-20	16	17.0	24	24.2	40	20.7
21-25	18	19.2	25	25.3	43	22.3
26-30	20	21.2	11	11.1	31	16.1
31-35	6	6.4	7	7.1	13	6.7
36-40	9	9.6	8	8.1	17	8.8
41-45	6	6.4	7	7.1	13	6.7
46-50	5	5.3	11	11.1	16	8.3
51-55	5	5.3	3	3.0	8	4.2
56-60	3	3.2	3	3.0	6	3.1
61-65	6	6.4	0	0.0	6	3.1
TOTAL	94	100.0	99	100.0	193	100.0

Table 8-4. Age Statistics of the Vietnamese Sample

Statistics	Male	Female	Total
Median	28.00	26.00	28.00
Mean	33.26	30.73	31.96
SD	13.48	11.84	12.70
SEM	1.39	1.19	0.91
Minimum	18	18	18
Maximum	65	60	65
N	94	99	193

Demographic Characteristics

The demographic characteristics of the Vietnamese sample are given in Tables 8-3 to 8-8. The age distribution of subjects is given in Table 8-3 and the age statistics are shown in Table 8-4. The levels of education obtained in Vietnam and the United States are shown in Tables 8-5 and 8-6, respectively. There appears to be a higher number of people attending college in the United States than in Vietnam. This could be a result of including the bilingual college sample in the total sample. Occupation in Vietnam is given in Table 8-7 and occupation in the United States is given in Table 8-8. Occupations in Vietnam included accountants, teachers, merchants, business owners, technicians, engineers, military officers, mechanics, and students. Occupations in the United States were largely in the skilled and un-skilled categories, with more than 50% of the sample currently unemployed. This

Table 8-5. Distribution of the Vietnamese Sample by Education in Vietnam

Education	Male N	Male %	Female N	Female %	Total N	Total %
Elementary	16	17.0	16	16.2	32	16.6
High School	34	36.2	45	45.4	79	40.9
High School Grad	21	22.3	22	22.2	43	22.3
College	14	14.9	8	8.1	22	11.4
College Grad	6	6.4	0	0.0	6	3.1
Grad+	3	3.2	8	8.1	11	5.7
TOTAL	94	100	99	100	193	100

Table 8-6. Distribution of the Vietnamese Sample by Education in the United States

Education	Male N	Male %	Female N	Female %	Total N	Total %
None	29	30.9	42	42.4	71	36.8
High School	20	21.2	19	19.2	39	20.2
High School Grad	6	6.4	6	6.1	12	6.2
College	29	30.9	24	24.2	53	27.5
College Grad	6	6.3	6	6.1	12	6.2
Grad+	4	4.3	2	2.0	6	3.1
TOTAL	94	100	99	100	193	100

disproportionate level of unemployment in the sample is explained by the large number of people who were newcomers to the United States. More than 50% of the sample have been in the country for two years or less (Table 8-9). Newcomers generally needed the money offered and had time to fill out questionnaires, whereas Vietnamese who have lived here longer usually were working and did not have time to participate. Of the total sample, 54% reported that their jobs were below their ability or training. Many newcomers were undergoing ESL training or vocational or technical training or both. For this Vietnamese sample, the average man or woman was 33 years old, unemployed, attending college or vocational or technical training, and has lived in the United States for two years.

Analysis of MMPI-2 Scale Scores

Several analyses provide a comparison of Vietnamese normals with the MMPI-2 normative sample. First, the mean scores for the Vietnamese sample are plotted

184 Bao-Chi Nguyen Tran

Table 8-7. Distribution of the Vietnamese Sample by Occupation in Vietnam

Occupation	Male N	Male %	Female N	Female %	Total N	Total %
Student	28	29.7	38	38.4	66	34.3
Unskilled	25	26.6	24	24.2	49	25.4
Skilled	12	12.8	11	11.1	23	11.9
Professional	6	6.4	6	6.1	12	6.2
Military Officer	8	8.5	0	0.0	8	4.1
Unemployed	15	16.0	20	20.2	35	18.1
TOTAL	94	100	99	100	193	100

Table 8-8. Distribution of the Vietnamese Sample by Occupation in the United States

Occupation	Male N	Male %	Female N	Female %	Total N	Total %
Student	0	0.0	0	0.0	0	0.0
Unskilled	18	19.1	12	12.1	30	15.5
Skilled	16	17.0	13	13.1	29	15.0
Professional	6	6.4	7	7.1	13	6.7
Unemployed	6	57.5	67	67.7	121	62.8
TOTAL	94	100	99	100	193	100

Table 8-9. Distribution of the Vietnamese Sample by Year Arrived in the United States

Occupation	Male N	Male %	Female N	Female %	Total N	Total %
1968-1979	15	18.1	15	15.2	30	15.5
1980-1989	33	33.0	28	28.3	61	34.2
1990-1992	46	48.9	56	56.5	102	50.3
TOTAL	94	100	99	100	193	100

against U.S. norms to illustrate the relative scale elevations. Next, a factor analysis of Vietnamese MMPI-2 clinical and validity scale scores is presented. Finally, the Vietnamese subjects are grouped according to their length of time in the United States and analyzed to determine if profile elevation is related to recency of immigration.

Comparison of Profiles. The mean profile of the Vietnamese sample is plotted against the American norms (Butcher, Dahlstrom, Graham, Tellegen, & Kaemmer,

1989). The validity, clinical, and content scale profiles for males are shown in Figures 8-1 and 8-2, and for females in Figures 8-3 and 8-4. The mean T scores and standard deviations for males and females are given in Tables 8-10 and 8-11, respectively. In general, the Vietnamese profiles for males and females are within normal range, suggesting that Vietnamese normal subjects are not extremely different from the U.S. normal sample. Many of the mean scores fall close to the mean and within the standard error of measurement of the U.S. scales. The validity scales indicate that the Vietnamese were sincere and not defensive in their responses, and that they were not hesitant to endorse any distress or perceived shortcomings. Scales L and K are quite low, suggesting a cooperative test-taking attitude and careful responses to the item content. Scale 8 (Sc) and the F scale are slightly higher than the American norms. Many Southeast Asians, the Vietnamese included, consider showing self-confidence and self-praise boastful and undesirable. They tend to take pride in being humble and readily acknowledge their disadvantages rather than their fortunes. This slight elevation on scales F and Sc may be reflecting a cultural difference, since these two scales are often related to self-effectiveness and assertiveness. Of the content scales, the TRT (Negative Treatment Indicators) scale was slightly elevated, suggesting some lack of openness to mental health treatment, relative to Americans. The Vietnamese tend to have negative attitudes toward mental health treatment and generally feel uncomfortable discussing their problems with others. Thus, the average Vietnamese male or female can be characterized as expressing some problems on the MMPI-2, tending to minimize positive qualities, and generally adopting traditional gender roles. The average Vietnamese generally has negative attitudes toward mental health problems and services and is not likely to seek psychiatric treatment.

Item Difference Analysis. An item endorsement analysis shows that there are differences in endorsement between the Vietnamese and American samples. A high percentage of the items left blank by the Vietnamese are related to sex behaviors and attitudes. This is probably a cultural difference since sex is a forbidden topic of discussion in Vietnamese culture. Many unmarried Vietnamese females, perhaps also males, would be reluctant to endorse such items because premarital sex is unacceptable in the culture. Further analysis of item endorsement frequencies are shown in Appendix D. The items are listed by level of endorsement difference between the Vietnamese sample and the U.S. sample for males and females. For males, the mean level of endorsement difference is 16.65%. The items with the highest level of endorsement difference (67%) are items 399 and 558. For females, the mean level of endorsement difference is 16.32%. Item 399 had the highest level of endorsement difference (69%). In other words, this Vietnamese sample

186   Bao-Chi Nguyen Tran

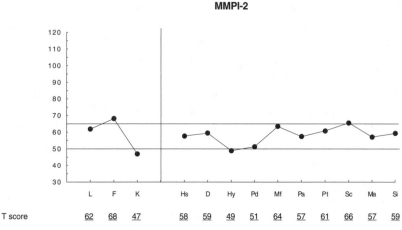

Figure 8-3. Mean Basic Profile of Vietnamese Women (N = 99) Plotted on U.S. Norms

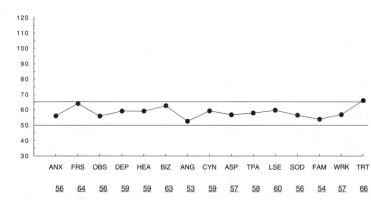

Figure 8-4. Mean Content Scale Profile of Vietnamese Women (N = 99) Plotted on U.S. Norms

differed most from the U.S. sample on items 399 and 558. Further analysis of the item endorsement differences shows that many items on which the Vietnamese responded differently from the Americans were items on the TRT scale. The item response differences shown in the extreme item analysis suggest cultural differences rather than translation problems.

Factor Analysis. An analysis of the factor structure of the Vietnamese MMPI-2 was conducted; the factor loadings for each scale are shown in Tables 8-12 and 8-13. The results of the factor analysis suggested that a four-factor solution best accounted for the variance. For the male sample, factor 1 was the general distress factor, factor 2 was the over-control factor, factor 3 was the social introversion

Table 8-10. Mean T Scores (K-Corrected) and Standard Deviations for Vietnamese Males (N = 94)

Scale	Mean T Score	SD
L	57.39	13.17
F	67.69	16.88
K	44.73	10.82
Hs	57.33	11.88
D	59.48	10.81
Hy	49.90	11.54
Pd	51.86	9.71
Mf	45.26	7.11
Pa	56.63	16.43
Pt	60.86	11.18
Sc	65.18	14.51
Ma	55.02	12.42
Si	59.01	9.50
ANX	57.81	10.94
FRS	63.99	14.89
OBS	58.01	13.43
DEP	60.90	11.13
HEA	60.93	12.01
BIZ	62.27	13.61
ANG	54.25	12.52
CYN	59.57	11.79
ASP	55.83	11.70
TPA	58.30	12.55
LSE	63.51	12.64
SOD	54.70	10.23
FAM	55.26	11.00
WRK	59.26	12.73
TRT	66.86	12.45

Note: Hs, Pd, Pt, Sc, and Ma are K-corrected T scores.

Table 8-11. Mean T Scores (K-Corrected) and Standard Deviations
for Vietnamese Females (N = 99)

Scale	Mean T Score	SD
L	61.77	14.97
F	68.11	15.48
K	46.90	11.98
Hs	57.69	13.44
D	59.41	11.59
Hy	49.03	12.65
Pd	51.25	8.63
Mf	63.49	10.36
Pa	57.36	13.28
Pt	60.82	10.16
Sc	65.58	11.23
Ma	57.20	10.85
Si	59.27	8.90
ANX	56.04	10.52
FRS	64.12	13.55
OBS	55.77	11.72
DEP	59.22	10.96
HEA	59.10	10.97
BIZ	62.63	11.62
ANG	52.61	11.76
CYN	59.29	10.47
ASP	56.81	10.57
TPA	57.94	12.80
LSE	59.71	11.04
SOD	56.37	10.41
FAM	53.88	11.63
WRK	56.85	11.48
TRT	65.95	10.10

Note: Hs, Pd, Pt, Sc, and Ma are K-corrected T scores.

Table 8-12. Factor Loadings of the MMPI-2 Basic Scales for Vietnamese Male Normals

Scale	Factors			
	I	II	III	IV
L	−.80	.11	.08	.07
F	.66	.28	.41	.14
K	−.85	.20	−.34	−.05
Hs	.42	.66	.35	.16
D	−.03	.53	.72	.09
Hy	−.18	.92	−.01	.08
Pd	.58	.50	.24	.14
Mf	−.03	.14	.12	.95
Pa	.41	.52	.17	.45
Pt	.76	.20	.53	.15
Sc	.80	.27	.43	.18
Ma	.86	.13	−.14	−.04
Si	.18	−.00	.92	.11

Table 8-13. Factor Loadings of the MMPI-2 Basic Scales for Vietnamese Female Normals

Scale	Factors			
	I	II	III	IV
L	−.17	.82	.01	.00
F	.62	−.19	.45	−.18
K	−.27	.85	−.33	−.01
Hs	.47	.15	.76	.03
D	.21	.18	.85	.16
Hy	.41	.71	.35	.20
Pd	.80	−.07	.18	.02
Mf	.05	.05	.09	.98
Pa	.72	−.13	.15	.16
Pt	.47	−.59	.58	.02
Sc	.62	−.50	.54	−.06
Ma	.60	−.62	−.09	−.02
Si	.01	−.27	.87	.03

factor, and factor 4 was the masculine/feminine factor. Similar factor structures were found for the female sample. Interpretation of these factor components suggests that the factor structures of the Vietnamese sample are similar to the factor structures of the American normative sample (Butcher et al., 1989).

Comparison of Samples According to Residency in the United States. One interesting question to consider is whether psychological distress, as measured by the MMPI-2, diminishes according to or is associated with the time of stay in the United States. Logically, it can be predicted that the longer an individual has been in the United States, the more time he or she has had to adjust, therefore the less symptom presentation could be found in his or her MMPI profile. A within sample comparison separates the total sample by the time of arrival in the country. Table 8-9 shows the three different groups of migrants: (1) those arriving during the 1970s, (2) those arriving during the 1980s, and (3) those arriving during the 1990s. Analysis of variance shows that there are significant differences between the 1970 group and the 1990 group for many scales (Table 8-14). The newcomers tended to report more distress and problems. There are fewer differences between the 1970 and 1980 groups and the 1980 and 1990 groups.

The fact that more recent immigrants show more extreme MMPI-2 scale elevation is an important finding. It suggests that more recent migrants show more symptoms of psychological stress than migrants who came to the United States several years earlier. This finding is consistent with the results of Azan (1988/1989), who found that recent Cuban immigrants had more MMPI-measured symptoms than those who migrated earlier. This finding suggests that the length of time in the United States should be considered in evaluating Vietnamese refugees with the MMPI-2.

Can U.S. Norms Be Used to Assess Vietnamese Individuals?

As we have seen, the U.S norms on many scales may provide a useful means of comparing Vietnamese individuals living in the United States. The results of the factor analysis, though limited somewhat by the relatively small sample, provide support for the idea that the MMPI-2 measures personality characteristics in Vietnamese subjects in a manner similar to the way it assesses people in the United States. However, several scales—namely F, Sc, and TRT—probably differ substantially as a result of cultural differences.

Summary

In recent years, cross-cultural psychology has seen an increase in the number of tests adapted to other cultures. The MMPI-2 has been translated into many dif-

Table 8-14. Scale Comparison of Three Refugee/Immigrant Groups (N = 193)

Scale	Significant Differences
L	
F	(1970, 1990)
K	(1970, 1990)
Hs	
D	(1970, 1990)
Hy	(1970, 1990)
Pd	
Mf	
Pa	
Pt	(1970, 1990)
Sc	(1970, 1980) (1970, 1990)
Ma	
Si	(1970, 1990)
ANX	(1970, 1990)
FRS	(1970, 1990) (1980, 1990)
OBS	(1970, 1990)
DEP	(1970, 1990)
HEA	
BIZ	(1970, 1990)
ANG	
CYN	(1970, 1990)
ASP	
TPA	
LSE	(1970, 1980) (1970, 1990)
SOD	(1970, 1990)
FAM	
WRK	(1970, 1990)
TRT	(1970, 1990)

ferent languages around the world. There has been a demand to translate the MMPI-2 into several SEA languages due to the large number of SEA refugees and immigrants resettling in the United States after the Vietnam War. Consequently, a Vietnamese version of the MMPI-2 was developed.

The translation followed the committee approach using three bilinguals. Two of the bilinguals independently translated the English version into Vietnamese. The translated version was back-translated into English by a third bilingual. The original English and the back-translated English versions were compared to assure item equivalence, and nonequivalent item wordings were discussed and resolved. Problematic items were retranslated, and a final Vietnamese version was completed only after all items were satisfactorily back-translated.

A test-retest bilingual study was conducted using college students and college graduates from the University of Minnesota. A sample of 32 bilinguals, 11 males and 21 females, took both the English and Vietnamese versions. The results of the bilingual study indicate that the Vietnamese version is a reliable alternate form of the English version. Item endorsement stability was high. Intercorrelations between the two versions for the clinical and content scales were high. In addition, the profile configurations for both versions were found to be comparable.

A comparability study for the Vietnamese MMPI-2 was conducted in St. Paul and Minneapolis, Minnesota. The total sample consisted of 193 subjects (94 males and 99 females). The mean profile of the sample was plotted against American norms. The Vietnamese profile is within normal limits and the validity scales indicated that subjects were sincere and not defensive in their responses. Scales F and Sc are slightly higher, which may be influenced by cultural factors such as the desire to appear humble and modest. The F scale may be elevated as a result of a relatively high level of stress in the Vietnamese group. New refugees or immigrants had more extreme MMPI-2 scale elevations than those who came earlier, suggesting that recency of immigration is an important factor in assessing refugees. Item endorsement analysis shows that a high number of items left blank by the Vietnamese subjects were related to sex behaviors and attitudes, which are also influenced by culture. The items that differed most on endorsement frequencies were those related to attitudes pertaining to mental health treatment. Factor analysis of the Vietnamese scores resulted in four factors, which were comparable to those of the American normative sample. In summary, the average Vietnamese male or female appears similar to the average American male or female with the exception of cultural factors such as modesty and attitudes on sex and mental health treatment.

Due to time restrictions and the limited availability of potential subjects in the Vietnamese community in Minnesota, the sample size is relatively small. It would have been desirable to have a larger sample size in the normative sample to assure test equivalence. However, preliminary results suggest that the Vietnamese MMPI-2 could be a potentially valuable instrument with Vietnamese clients since it operates psychometrically like the English language version of the MMPI-2.

References

Azan, A. A. (1989). The MMPI version Hispana: Standardization and cross-cultural personality study with a population of Cuban refugees (Doctoral dissertation, University of Minnesota, 1988). *Dissertation Abstracts International, 50,* 2144B.

Brislin, R. W. (1970). Back-translation for cross-cultural research. *Journal of Cross-Cultural Psychology, 1*(3), 198–216.

Brislin, R. W. (1980). The wording and translation of research instruments. In W. J. Lonner & J. W. Berry (Eds.), *Field methods in cross-cultural research* (pp. 137–164). Beverly Hills: Sage Publications.

Butcher, J. N., Dahlstrom, W. G., Graham, J. R., Tellegen, A., & Kaemmer, B. (1989). *Minnesota Multiphasic Personality Inventory-2 (MMPI-2): Manual for administration and scoring.* Minneapolis: University of Minnesota Press.

Butcher, J. N., & Garcia, R. E. (1978). Cross-national application of psychological tests. *Personnel and Guidance Journal, 56,* 472–475.

Butcher, J. N., & Gur, R. (1974). A Hebrew translation of the MMPI: An assessment of translation adequacy and preliminary validation. *Journal of Cross-Cultural Psychology, 5,* 220–228.

Butcher, J. N., & Pancheri, P. (1976). *Handbook of cross-national MMPI research.* Minneapolis: University of Minnesota Press.

Ervin, S. M., & Osgood, C. E. (1954). Second language learning and bilingualism. *Journal of Abnormal and Social Psychology, 59,* 139–146.

Know your neighbors . . . the Vietnamese. (1981, December). (Available from Southeast Asian Ministry, 105 W. University Avenue, St. Paul, MN 55103.)

Sechrest, L., Fay, T. L., & Zaidi, S. M. (1972). Problems of translation in cross-cultural research. *Journal of Cross-Cultural Psychology, 3*(1), 41–56.

Strand, P. J., & Jones, W., Jr. (1985). *Indochinese refugees in America: Problems of adaption and resettlement.* Durham, NC: Duke University Press.

Triandis, H. C., Malpass, R. S., & Davidson, A. R. (1973). Psychology and culture. *Annual Review of Psychology, 24,* 355–378.

Chapter 9

Development of a Hmong
Translation of the MMPI-2

*Amos S. Deinard, James N. Butcher, Umeng D. Thao,
Song Houa Moua Vang, and Kaying Hang*

Since 1975, Minnesota has experienced a large influx of Southeast Asian refugees. Over these years 70,000 individuals (Hmong, Lao, Cambodian, and Vietnamese) have moved into the state. Principal sites of residence are Minneapolis and St. Paul (Deinard & Dunnigan, 1987). Of the four groups, the Hmong have had the greatest difficulty adjusting to the relocation and assimilating into the culture of their host country. Depression and post-traumatic stress symptoms have been exacerbated by the problems they have experienced as a result of the cultural differences between their traditional values and Western expectations (Westermeyer, 1985).

Shortly after the relocation began, the Community-University Health Care Center/Variety Club Children's Clinic hired bilingual Southeast Asian staff for its mental health program to provide much-needed mental health care to these newcomers. In the early 1980s, Hennepin County Mental Health identified the clinic as the site where refugees were to receive their mental health services. These mental health services were provided as one of the primary health care programs of the clinic, in conjunction with medical and dental services.

Mental health providers at the clinic and in the community often have difficulty assessing the magnitude and, in many cases, the type of mental health problem affecting Hmong patients. Recognizing the value of the MMPI as a means of screening psychological adjustment problems or psychiatric disorders, clinic staff repeatedly stated how advantageous it would be if they had access to a Hmong translation of the instrument. They acknowledged that a Hmong MMPI might not be as definitive a resource as is the English version when used with American or other bilingual groups because many Hmong patients are not literate or hold belief systems that make using Western diagnostic schema or assessment techniques difficult. Nonetheless, the consensus was that it would be valuable to have

194

a standardized Hmong version of the MMPI-2 to provide objective information about Hmong patients' symptoms rather than having no effective means of appraising patients who cannot speak English.

Research funds were obtained from the University of Minnesota Press to develop a Hmong version of the MMPI-2. This was to be accomplished by translating the English version, back-translating the translated items to evaluate the accuracy of item wordings, refining the translation, and finally conducting a bilingual test-retest of the MMPI-2 to examine the operation of the scales in the translated form.

Test Translation Procedures

Experience of the Translators

In translating the MMPI-2 it was important to use translators who have a high degree of familiarity with both English and Hmong. The translators on the MMPI-2 translation team had considerable experience with both languages. They had lived for more than five years in each country and had attended school in both. All three translators were completing their education in the United States. One was a pre-med undergraduate student, one was a graduate student applying for (and later accepted in) medical school, and one was an advanced high school student who is fluent in both languages. Umeng (David) Thao, the translation team leader (a graduate of Brown University who entered medical school in 1994), had considerable experience with both languages and had worked at the clinic as a translator for several years. He is fluent in both Hmong and English and was recruited for this project because of his expertise in both languages.

Step One

In arriving at the working Hmong translation, it was desirable to employ two translators who independently translated the MMPI-2 items and instructions from the English into Hmong. Care was taken to ensure that linguistic equivalence was maintained as closely as possible.

Step Two

Once two initial translators had translated the MMPI-2 items, they discussed their specific item translations. When disagreement occurred, the translators discussed the possible meanings to arrive at a "best" translation. Most of the English items were easily translatable into Hmong. However, some of the items sounded awkward when translated. Fortunately, only a few of the English items had to be slightly modified to make sense in Hmong.

Some items, such as the following, were relatively easy to render into Hmong:

2. I have a good appetite.
25. I would like to be a singer.
128. I like to cook.
146. I cry easily.
201. I very much like hunting.

Other items were somewhat awkward but translatable without much modification:

11. There seems to be a lump in my throat much of the time.
13. People should try to understand their dreams and be guided by or take warning from them.
46. I prefer to pass by school friends, or people I know but have not seen for a long time, unless they speak to me first.
76. It takes a lot of argument to convince most people of the truth.
87. I have met problems so full of possibilities that I have been unable to make up my mind about them.
114. Sometimes I am so strongly attracted by the personal articles of others, such as shoes, gloves, etc., that I want to handle or steal them, though I have no use for them.
158. It makes me uncomfortable to put on a stunt at a party even when others are doing the same sort of things.
193. In walking I am very careful to step over sidewalk cracks.
199. I like science.
211. I have been inspired to a program of life based on duty which I have since carefully followed.
313. I have a habit of counting things that are not important such as bulbs on electric signs, and so forth.
436. When a man is with a woman he is usually thinking about things related to sex.
523. At movies, restaurants, or sporting events, I hate to have to stand in line.

Some items required modification in content to make sense in Hmong:

24. Evil spirits possess me at times.
72. My soul sometimes leaves my body.
198. I often hear voices without knowing where they come from.
255. I do not often notice my ears ringing or buzzing.
427. I have never seen a vision.
490. Ghosts or spirits can influence people for good or bad.

Step Three: Back-Translation

After an agreed-upon translation was obtained, an independent bilingual translator (experienced in both languages) back-translated the items from Hmong into English. This was accomplished by having the bilingual work from the translated version and translate the items back into English.

Step Four: Comparison of the English and Back-Translated Versions

When the back-translation was completed, the back-translated version was compared with the English language version to determine if the item meanings had been maintained in the translation. (Experience with back-translation of the MMPI-2 suggests that about 10% to 15% of the items fail to maintain their meanings in back-translation).

Examples of items that failed to maintain their meanings in the translation and required further translation effort were:

27. No matter how long it takes, I will be mean to someone who has been mean to me.
40. Many times when my head hurts, every part of my body hurts too.
89. I am my biggest problem.

The full team then met on several occasions to discuss the items that appeared to lose meaning in the back-translation. The questionable items were retranslated and again back-translated until the meanings were considered equivalent by the full team of translators.

Step Five: Review by University of Minnesota Press Translation Consultants

It is the policy of the University of Minnesota Press, before licensing a translated version of the MMPI-2, to obtain an external review of the translation by a linguist. The Hmong translation was reviewed and items that were thought to be questionable were discussed by the translation team. The translation was then revised according to recommendations made, incorporating suggestions that would improve the wording of the translation.

Study of Translation Equivalence

After the translation, back-translation, and linguistic evaluation phases had been completed, a study to evaluate the meaning of the test items for individuals from the Hmong culture was conducted. This study involved administering the inventory to a number of bilingual individuals to determine whether the translated MMPI-2 items operated in a psychometric manner similar to that of the English language version.

Procedures for Bilingual Testing

Thirty-five volunteers who are fluent in both Hmong and English were recruited for the study and tested according to the following procedures.

First, individuals who speak and read both English and Hmong were identified from community groups. Some of the subjects were or had been undergraduate students at the University of Minnesota and all were considered fluent in both languages. Their experience with both languages was further evaluated by examining their responses to the Language Experience Questionnaire, a biographical experience form developed to survey the range of experience the potential subjects had in the English and Hmong languages. All subjects were administered both language versions in supervised testing sessions at the clinic, in dormitories, at the individuals' workplaces, or in their homes. Volunteers were paid to participate in the study.

Second, when it was determined that a volunteer had sufficient language skill in both Hmong and English, he or she was asked to complete the Human Subjects Volunteer Form required by the University of Minnesota.

Third, the volunteers were provided the following instructions:

> We are conducting a study of the Hmong version of the Minnesota Multiphasic Personality Inventory-2 (MMPI-2), a test that has been extensively used in many other countries. The questionnaire is mostly used in mental health settings to help understand people who are seeking mental health services. We think the questionnaire will be helpful in understanding Hmong clients as well. In our evaluation of the effectiveness of the MMPI-2 with Hmong people, we need to know if the items work the same way in both Hmong and in English. We are therefore asking you to complete the MMPI-2 in both languages in two separate sessions one week apart. Do you have any questions?

Fourth, The MMPI-2 was administered in one language in the initial session. Half the subjects were administered the MMPI-2 in Hmong first; the other half English first. A record was kept of which test was administered first to ensure that both forms of the test were eventually administered. Notations on the answer sheet were made to indicate which subjects were administered English or Hmong.

The subjects were then provided the following instructions:

> Today, I am asking you to complete the MMPI-2 in (English or Hmong). Next week when you return you will be asked to complete the questionnaire in (Hmong or English). When you answer the questions to the MMPI-2 please follow the instructions provided on the booklet.

Follow-up Testing Session

Individuals were retested approximately seven days after the first administration session. They were given the other form of the questionnaire they had been ad-

Table 9-1. MMPI-2 F Scale and VRIN Scale Scores for the Five Volunteers Excluded from the Study

Subject #	LTF		LTVRIN	
	Hmong	English	Hmong	English
9	96	96	54	90
11	113	58	66	86
18	61	101	69	61
27	99	116	54	86
31	89	107	76	54

ministered earlier. As with the first test administration, the answer sheet was marked to keep track of which language was used for the retest. The subjects were provided the appropriate language MMPI-2 instructions and told the following:

Last week you were administered the MMPI-2 in _____. Is this correct?
Today, I will be asking you to complete the MMPI-2 in _____.
When you answer the questions to the MMPI-2 please follow the instructions provided on the booklet.

Results of the Bilingual Study

The F and VRIN scale scores were employed to detect problem response sets reflecting an inability to understand the items. Five subjects produced invalid protocols (F greater than or equal to 100; VRIN greater than or equal to 90) and were eliminated from the study (Table 9-1). An inspection of the scores reveals that no consistent pattern of invalidity was produced by the volunteers. That is, volunteers did not consistently have trouble with either the Hmong translation or the English-language version. Several analyses were conducted, including comparisons of group mean scale scores and Pearson Product Moment correlation analyses for the MMPI-2 scales. Finally, an item response comparison for the MMPI-2 items was conducted.

Group Mean Scale Score Comparisons

The group mean validity and clinical profiles of the volunteers for the English-language version and the Hmong-language version are plotted in Figure 9-1. The group mean profile comparison for the MMPI-2 content scales is shown in Figure 9-2. Inspection of the profiles indicates that the bilingual subjects in the study, whether they took the test in English or Hmong, produced essentially the same group mean scale scores. The MMPI-2 profiles are virtually overlapping in both comparisons. Any scale score differences obtained fall well within the standard error of measurement for the scales.

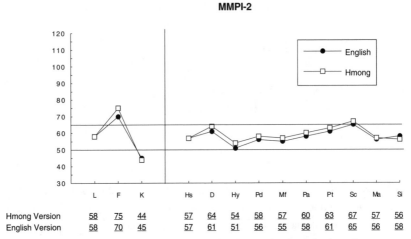

Figure 9-1. Group Mean MMPI-2 Standard Scale Profile of 30 Hmong-English Bilinguals

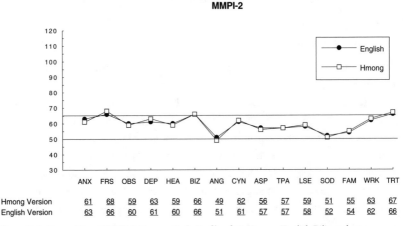

Figure 9-2. Group Mean MMPI-2 Content Scale Profile of 30 Hmong-English Bilinguals

The Pearson correlations for the Hmong condition and the English language condition are shown in Table 9-2. As expected, most of the correlations between the English and Hmong test administrations were moderate to high and serve as another indication of the equivalency between the two forms of the test.

Item Response Comparison Analysis

In addition to comparing the two test administration formats by evaluating scale score differences, we evaluated the subjects' responses to each of the MMPI-2 items in the two conditions. Item response data from the English and Hmong test

Table 9-2. Pearson Product Moment Correlations between the Hmong and English
Test-Retest Conditions

Scale	Correlations		
	Male	Female	Combined
L	0.60	0.42	0.48
F	0.53	0.51	0.47
K	0.74	0.44	0.58
F_B	0.70	0.80	0.71
Hs	0.75	0.70	0.73
D	0.78	0.83	0.80
Hy	0.64	0.60	0.60
Pd	0.50	0.30	0.40
Mf	0.54	0.49	0.64
Pa	0.75	0.59	0.66
Pt	0.63	0.59	0.61
Sc	0.66	0.60	0.62
Ma	0.59	0.12	0.38
Si	0.77	0.72	0.73
VRIN	0.24	-0.15	0.01
TRIN	0.49	0.15	0.22
ANX	0.82	0.48	0.64
FRS	0.85	0.80	0.83
OBS	0.48	0.49	0.47
DEP	0.77	0.57	0.66
HEA	0.62	0.83	0.74
BIZ	0.72	0.51	0.61
ANG	0.60	0.62	0.61
CYN	0.58	0.48	0.41
ASP	0.35	0.61	0.48
TPA	0.14	0.36	0.27
LSE	0.91	0.62	0.75
SOD	0.89	0.74	0.79
FAM	0.46	0.30	0.40
WRK	0.69	0.68	0.66
TRT	0.70	0.62	0.61

```
100.
 98. -  99.
 96. -  97.
 94. -  95.
 92. -  93.
 90. -  91.
 88. -  89.
 86. -  87.
 84. -  85.
 82. -  83.
 80. -  81.
 78. -  79.
 76. -  77.
 74. -  75.
 72. -  73.
 70. -  71.
 68. -  69.
 66. -  67.
 64. -  65.
 62. -  63.
 60. -  61.
 58. -  59.
 56. -  57.
 54. -  55.
 52. -  53.
 50. -  51.
 48. -  49.
 46. -  47.
 44. -  45.
 42. -  43.  161
 40. -  41.
 38. -  39.
 36. -  37.  120  158  261  452
 34. -  35.  31  443
 32. -  33.  168  381  438
 30. -  31.  52   71  121  151  175  277  306  318  375  397  406  458
 28. -  29.
 26. -  27.  100  142  149  239  259  298  475  517  541  566
 24. -  25.  80   89  109  113  187  273  427
 22. -  23.  63  189  202  231  315  442  481  519  523  532  551  563
 20. -  21.  3   49   55   75   78   86   87  106  116  117  129  130  171  232  286  311  325  335  341  346
            418  436  451  488  514  560
 18. -  19.
 16. -  17.  13   28   32   45   50   53   56   95  107  110  148  155  166  181  188  196  211  222  234  256
            263  267  279  284  293  309  348  353  360  364  366  368  378  388  394  407  409  411  435
            439  445  460  502  507  521  525  529  537  547  553
 14. -  15.  19   39   67   92  112  134  136  146  212  220  252  299  322  330  347  363  372  387  412  454
            510  522  540
 12. -  13.  11   26   34   70   72   90   91  104  127  154  203  207  214  233  243  287  296  300  303  305
            310  320  328  349  369  371  391  393  403  410  433  450  470  473  491  495  496  497  512
            538  543  562
 10. -  11.  5    6   15   16   17   20   24   25   30   37   40   41   48   51   60   76   88   98  124  137  144
            150  169  186  191  195  208  213  215  219  242  244  246  250  255  258  260  266  274  275
            278  281  289  292  313  314  316  327  334  337  344  351  365  370  379  384  390  395  404
            405  413  414  426  428  429  447  448  456  461  462  466  480  482  484  485  489  498  501
            504  508  509  513  524  539  544  545  554  556  558  559
  8. -   9.
  6. -   7.  1    8   12   14   21   36   42   46   57   59   61   62   65   69   74   77   82   94   97  101  103
            111  119  141  143  152  156  170  174  179  180  185  192  204  210  217  221  227  228  236
            237  251  254  268  285  291  297  301  307  308  319  321  329  331  332  338  339  345  355
            356  357  358  361  367  374  376  377  380  385  386  389  392  396  398  399  402  416  417
            420  421  425  434  437  444  469  471  474  490  494  515  528  530  531  533  534  535  549
            557  561  567
  4. -   5.  2    4   22   44   54  102  105  115  118  123  138  145  164  176  177  178  183  190  198  201
            216  230  247  248  262  283  294  333  342  354  408  422  431  441  472  477  483  506  518
            536  546  550  552
  2. -   3.  7    9   18   35   38   43   73   81   93   96  114  125  128  132  139  140  153  159  163  167
            173  182  184  199  209  225  226  229  235  240  245  249  265  269  270  271  272  280  282
            288  290  295  302  304  317  336  340  343  350  362  373  383  400  423  430  432  440  446
            449  457  459  463  464  465  468  479  486  493  500  505  511  516  520  548  564  565
  0. -   1.  10   23   27   29   33   47   58   64   66   68   79   83   84   85   99  108  122  126  131  133
            135  147  157  160  162  165  172  193  194  197  200  205  206  218  223  224  238  241  253
            57  264  276  312  323  324  326  352  359  382  401  415  419  424  453  455  467  476  478  87
            492  499  503  526  527  542  555
```

Figure 9-3. Item Response Differences (ITCOM) for Hmong-English Bilingual Subjects Taking the MMPI-2 in Both Hmong and English

administrations were used in this analysis. The item response comparison program ITCOM (see chapter 2) was employed to provide a response percentage comparison for each item in the MMPI-2. The percentage "true" for each item in English was contrasted with the percentage "true" obtained in the Hmong test administration. A response difference of 25% or more was taken as a reflection of a response difference on an item across the two test administrations (Butcher & Pancheri, 1976).

An examination of the ITCOM output summarizing the item response differences (shown in Figure 9-3) indicates that most of the item differences are within the "acceptably similar" range, that is, a response difference of less than 25% between the two groups.

The relatively few differences obtained in this comparison are probably due to the fact that some individuals shift their responses to some items over two test administrations. The most extreme item differences were further examined by the translation team to determine if item translation wording could have produced the differences. For example, the top ten differently endorsed items are listed here:

31   I find it hard to keep my mind on a task or job.
120   I frequently find it necessary to stand up for what I think is right.
158   It makes me uncomfortable to put on a stunt at a party even when others are doing the same sort of thing.
161   I frequently have to fight against showing that I am bashful.
168   I have had periods in which I carried on activities without knowing later what I had been doing.
261   I have very few fears compared to my friends.
381   I don't like hearing other people give their opinions about life.
438   I dread the thought of an earthquake.
443   I do not try to cover up my poor opinion or pity of people so that they won't know how I feel.
452   I strongly defend my own opinions as a rule.

The differences in responses were judged to result not from translation wording problems but from subjects changing their responses over the one-week testing period. Research has shown that about 13% of respondents to MMPI items in English-English test-retest studies shift their responses over a one-week period (Goldberg & Jones, 1969).

Audio Version of the Hmong MMPI-2

The primary use of the Hmong MMPI-2 at this time is for clients who presently live in the United States. Many of the individuals who experience difficulty adapting to the U.S. culture and require mental health services have neither learned English well enough to take the test nor read Hmong well enough to take a written version of the Hmong MMPI-2. Moreover, even when reading level is not a problem, as was the case in the bilingual sample, the average testing time for participants to complete the MMPI-2 in Hmong is almost twice as long as it is in

English. This problem results in part from the fact that Hmong is largely a spoken language; it has been a written language for only a few decades. Many refugees never learned to read Hmong. To provide a more useful format for administering the Hmong MMPI-2, we have developed an audiocassette version.

Future Research

In the next phase of the development of the Hmong version of the MMPI-2, two directions of study will be pursued. In the first, further evaluation of the relevance of the instrument with Hmong refugee patients will be undertaken. Symptomatic descriptions will be obtained by clinician ratings. It will then be possible to determine how the evaluations based on the MMPI-2 match the patients' behavior as described by clinicians who know them. Subjects will be administered the audio version of the MMPI-2.

In the second research strategy, we hope to accumulate a larger number of "normal" individuals to further evaluate the use of the MMPI-2 with the Hmong. Additional research and separate norms will likely be needed for a more refined clinical use of the instrument. The participants in the bilingual test-retest study were nonpatients—individuals who are "normal" in personality and well functioning. Yet their overall group mean profile on the MMPI-2 norms showed some scale elevation. These volunteers are all refugees and many are likely to be experiencing some turmoil from the refugee experience. As other MMPI-2-based research with recent refugee populations suggests (chapters 8 and 10), individuals who are recent refugees or immigrants to the United States typically report more MMPI-2-based symptoms than does the normative population. Our goal is to administer the audiocassette version of the MMPI-2 to several hundred Hmong nonpatients to provide a clearer normative picture of their response to MMPI-2 items.

Summary

Since 1975 Minnesota has experienced a large influx of Southeast Asian refugees, some 70,000 people having immigrated to the state. Many refugees have great difficulty relocating and assimilating because of the great differences between their culture and that of the host country. Many refugees experience depression and post-traumatic stress symptoms as a result of their immigration. Many also have difficulty explaining their problems to mental health practitioners because of their inability to communicate in English. For this reason, we were encouraged to develop a Hmong-language MMPI-2 to aid in obtaining objective information about patients from this group.

This translation was accomplished by rendering the English version into Hmong, back-translating the translated items to evaluate the accuracy of item wordings, and then refining the translation. Finally, a bilingual test-retest study of the MMPI-2 was conducted to examine the operation of the scales in the translated form. The translators on the MMPI-2 translation team had considerable experience with both English and Hmong. Each had lived more than five years in each country and had attended school in both. When the back-translation was completed, the back-translated version of the items was compared with the English-language version to determine if the item meanings had been maintained in the translation.

After the translation, back-translation, and linguistic evaluation phases had been completed, a study to evaluate the meanings of the test items for individuals from the Hmong culture was conducted. This study involved administering the inventory to a number of bilingual individuals to determine whether the translated MMPI-2 items operated in a manner psychometrically similar to that of the English-language version. Thirty-eight people who speak and read both English and Hmong were identified from community groups and agreed to take both versions of the MMPI-2.

The resulting MMPI-2 profiles emerging from the bilingual test-retest study are virtually overlapping. Any scale score differences obtained between the Hmong and English versions fall well within the standard error of measurement for the scales. Moreover, in a comparison of item response frequencies, we found that most of the item differences are within the "acceptably similar" range, that is, a response difference of fewer than 25% between the two groups. We concluded that the Hmong version of the MMPI-2 is linguistically equivalent to the American version.

To provide a more useful format for administering the Hmong language MMPI-2, we have developed an audiocassette version.

References

Butcher, J. N., & Pancheri, P. (1976). *Handbook of cross-national MMPI research*. Minneapolis: University of Minnesota.

Deinard, A. S., & Dunnigan, T. (1987) Hmong health care: Reflections on a six year experience. *International Migration Review*, 21, 857–865.

Goldberg, L. R., and Jones, R. R. (1969). *The reliability of reliability: The generality and correlates of intra-individual consistency in response to structured personality inventories* (Oregon Research Institute Monograph, 9, No. 2). University of Oregon, Portland.

Westermeyer, J. (1985). Mental health of Southeast Asian refugees: Observations over two decades from Laos to the United States. In T. C. Owan (Ed.), *Southeast Asian mental health: Treatment, prevention, services, training, and research* (DHHS Publication No. [ADM], pp. 65–89). Washington DC: National Institutes of Mental Health, U.S. Department of Health and Human Services.

Chapter 10

Asian American and White College Students' Performance on the MMPI-2

Stanley Sue, Keunho Keefe, Kana Enomoto,
Ramani S. Durvasula, and Ruth Chao

The United States is a multicultural society with many distinct cultural, ethnic, and racial groups (e.g., African Americans, American Indians, Asian Americans, Latinos, and European or White Americans). Great concern has been expressed over the use of assessment instruments to evaluate personality or psychopathology among culturally diverse groups for which the instruments have not been standardized or normed. Issues involving the validity of findings in general and the stimulus, conceptual, and metric equivalence of instruments are raised when the instruments have been widely used for one population but not for another (Brislin, 1993). Implicit in this concern is that populations often vary in cultural values, behaviors, expectations, and attitudes; hence, findings and conclusions drawn from one population may not be comparable with those from another population.

The Assessment of Asian Americans

Asians represent about 3% of the population of the United States and include many subgroups, such as Chinese, Japanese, Koreans, Filipinos, Vietnamese, etc. They have cultural values that differ from those of White Americans, as revealed through qualitative and quantitative research. For example, Asians in the United States are more likely than Whites to hold values and engage in behaviors that display a collectivistic and familial (rather than individualistic) orientation, respect for elders, deference to authority figures, concern over loss of face, interpersonal harmony, and achievement orientation (Bond, 1991; Sue & Sue, 1990). Considerable differences in cultural values obviously exist among different Asian American groups. For example, Japanese Americans as a group are more highly acculturated to American society than are Korean Americans. Nevertheless, Asian Americans can be distinguished from White Americans with regard to a number of cultural values and attitudes.

Given that Asian Americans exhibit cultural differences from White Americans and that psychological assessment tools have been primarily developed and used on White Americans, we have been interested in studying the performance of Asian Americans on various assessment measures, means of accurately interpreting their performances, and cultural factors that may hinder the validity of conclusions drawn from these measures. Our current research focuses on the responses of Asian Americans to the Minnesota Multiphasic Personality Inventory (MMPI).

The MMPI

The MMPI is the most widely used personality test in the United States (Graham, 1990). It has been criticized, however, because the original normative sample was unrepresentative of the general population and some of the items were outdated or inappropriate for current use. To improve the measure, the MMPI Restandardization Committee appointed by the University of Minnesota Press (Butcher, Dahlstrom, Graham, Tellegen, & Kaemmer, 1989) developed the MMPI-2. New norms for the MMPI-2 were established with a larger and more demographically representative sample. Although there was an attempt to achieve proportional representation of ethnic minority groups (see Greene, 1987; Graham, 1990), only .5% of the men and .9% of the women included in the sample of 2,600 subjects were Asian Americans (1.5% of the 1980 census were Asian-American). This small number of Asian Americans made it impossible to draw any conclusions about the group performance of Asian Americans compared with other groups.

Even on the original MMPI, little research has been devoted to Asian Americans (Greene, 1987). Some early studies using the MMPI with Asian Americans suggested that they perform differently from their White counterparts. Marsella, Sanborn, Kameoka, Shizuru, and Brennan (1975) used scale 2 of the MMPI with a normal sample of Chinese and Japanese Americans in a larger study to validate depression measures. The researchers found that the depression scale was significantly more elevated among Japanese and Chinese males than among Caucasian males. No ethnic differences were found among females. Sue and Sue (1974), testing students who used a university psychiatric clinic, found that Asian Americans had greater elevations on the MMPI than did their White counterparts. Although the MMPI profiles were similar, Asian Americans seemed to be more disturbed, having higher scale elevations. Many of the scales (L, F, 1, 2, 4, 6, 7, 8, and 0) were more elevated for Asian males than for White males, and some of the scales (L, F, 6, 7, 8, and 0) were also more elevated for Asian females than for White females. There is evidence that because of certain computational decisions in constructing the norms, the original MMPI norms were set too low, so that groups taking the original MMPI often exceeded those norms (Butcher, 1994; Pope, Butcher, & Seelen, 1993). Consistent with other research in the Sue and Sue investigation of clinic users, the Asian Americans had higher MMPI scores than did non-Asian Americans.

Looking at the critical items for somatic complaints and family problems, the researchers also found that Asian students, regardless of gender, were more likely to report somatic and family problems than were the non-Asian students. This study suggests that there may be some gender and ethnic differences in the MMPI profiles. Because of the unknown validity of the instrument with Asian Americans, Sue and Sue (1974) examined the clinical notes made by the clients' therapists. The purpose of analyzing the notes was to ascertain whether the Asian American clients who had elevated MMPI profiles were, indeed, seriously disturbed. The investigators found that therapists' descriptions of clients were related to the severity of disturbance revealed by the MMPI. They concluded that Asian Americans may fail to seek services because of the shame and stigma attached to using mental health services, because many Asian Americans may conceive of mental health and means of resolving problems in ways that militate against the use of mental health services, and because of the unresponsiveness of traditional mental health approaches to Asian cultural values (Sue & Sue, 1987). Thus, only the most severely disturbed Asians seek help, which may account for the elevated MMPI scales.

Finally, Tsushima and Onorato (1982) compared the MMPI scores of White and Japanese-American medical and neurological patients in Hawaii. The data did not reveal any significant ethnic differences in the T scores of validity or clinical scales when diagnoses were matched across ethnic groups. Significant gender effect was found across the two ethnic groups in that males scored higher than females on some of the scales (1, 2, 4, 5, 7, 8, 9) and females scored higher than males on scale 0. The results do not necessarily conflict with those of Sue and Sue (1974) because the latter study simply supported the hypothesis that among clients treated in a mental health clinic, Asian Americans are more disturbed than are Whites.

MMPI investigations with Asian populations overseas have been carried out in Hong Kong and in mainland China with the Chinese version of the MMPI. In a review of 26 studies using the Chinese-language version of the MMPI on Chinese psychiatric populations, Cheung and Song (1989) found that the translation equivalence of the Chinese MMPI had been established through numerous back-translations and modification of items. Thus, questions about the cross-cultural validity of the instrument were directed to the MMPI's conceptual and metric equivalence. The overall results of the studies demonstrated that the Chinese version adequately differentiated between Chinese psychiatric patients and normal controls. Three scales (F, 2, 8) were elevated among the normal Chinese subjects, yet Chinese psychiatric patients were elevated even higher than the baseline norm and often much higher than the American normals. The patterns of profile elevations on the Chinese MMPI for major mental disorders (e.g., schizophrenia, mania, depression, and neurotic disorders) were similar to the profile patterns of American subjects. The clinical application of the Chinese version of the MMPI seems adequate, although Cheung and Song added a cautionary note about interpreting moderate elevations on scales F, 2, and 8. With respect to metric equivalence, Cheung and Song suggested allowing for an adjustment of one additional standard deviation on scales F, 2, and 8 when predicting psychopathology among Chinese. Obviously, Chinese living in the United States may not be similar to Chinese living elsewhere. The main point is that the MMPI can be useful in clinical evaluation if factors such as cultural, metric, and linguistic differences are taken into account.

More MMPI research with Asian Americans is clearly needed. In the three studies of MMPI comparisons between Asian Americans and Whites cited earlier, the samples were limited (either college students or medical patients) and sample sizes tended to be small. Thus, generalizability of the results to the Asian American population is not known. Because all three studies were conducted on Asian-American subjects in the United States, the MMPI was administered in English in all cases and no translations were performed. However, the question of translation equivalence remains, since it is not clear whether Asian-American subjects in the studies were as proficient in English as were the non-Asian comparison subjects. There is some evidence to suggest that Asian Americans who have lived in the United States for several generations still experience some difficulty with English language mastery (Watanabe, 1973). As such, the results can only indicate possible cultural contributions to the elevation of some MMPI scales.

At least three major research efforts are needed. First, norms for Asian Americans on the MMPI-2 need to be developed. Large and representative samples, broken down by particular Asian groups, would be the most desirable. Such research is difficult, given the relatively small population of Asian Americans and the linguistic and cultural factors that may affect the validity of findings. Second, sources of bias or cultural factors that affect performance on the MMPI-2 should be identified. Third, means of controlling for bias should be devised. Dana (1993) indicates that there are four major varieties of controlling for cross-cultural bias in an instrument: (1) using "corrections" (e.g., the K scale on the MMPI was an attempt to control for defensiveness), (2) developing special norms for the different populations of interest, (3) providing adequate translations of instruments, and (4) interpreting data in a manner that takes into account the cultural background of respondents. It should be noted that the use of corrections involving the K scale has not been fruitful, especially in cross-cultural applications. Butcher and Han (1993) have developed the Superlative Self-Presentation Scale (S scale), which controls for the tendency to present oneself in a superlative manner. This scale may well have much greater validity than the K scale in cross-cultural assessment. Specific scales to detect cross-cultural differences should be developed.

The Present Study

The present study is part of a larger ongoing project investigating cultural factors associated with MMPI responses among Asian Americans. The larger project is intended to identify cultural response sets that affect MMPI performances and to construct means of correcting for these response sets. As a part of that project, the present study was designed simply to compare the responses of Asian-American and White students on the MMPI-2 and to use level of acculturation of Asian-American students as a moderator variable. If cultural factors are important in MMPI performance, we would expect within and between ethnic group differences to emerge, with less acculturated Asian Americans (LAs) and Whites showing the most discrepancy and highly acculturated Asian Americans (HAs) occupying an intermediate position on the MMPI-2 scales. In other words, if acculturation is an important variable, we would expect MMPI-2 scale scores to vary directly or indirectly with acculturation: LAs > HAs > Whites or LAs < HAs < Whites.

One hundred and thirty-three Asian-American students (62 males and 71 females) and 91 White students (37 males and 54 females) participated in the study. The students were recruited from introductory psychology classes at a large university in the Los Angeles area. Each subject received a course credit for participation in the study. The Asian-American sample consisted of 35 Chinese, 15 Filipino, 13 Japanese, 34 Korean, 23 Vietnamese, and 13 "other Asian." Asians (mean = 19.20) and Whites (mean = 20.07) differed in age, t (222) = 2.16, p < .05. The educational and occupational levels of parents were categorized and examined using chi-squares. The analysis revealed an ethnic difference in the distribution of father's education, X_2 (6) = 19.61, p < .01; the analysis for father's occupation nearly reached signficance, X_2 (8) = 14.58, p < .07. No significant ethnic differences emerged for mother's education and occupation.

A small group of students were given a questionnaire by research assistants during experimental sessions. To reduce defensiveness over completing a personality inventory, students were instructed not to write their names on the questionnaire. The questionnaire took about 90 to 100 minutes to complete.

Suinn-Lew Self-Identity Acculturation Scale

To assess the degree of acculturation, researchers administered to Asian-American students the Suinn-Lew Self-Identity Acculturation Scale (SL-ASIA). SL-ASIA consists of 21 multiple choice questions. The items deal with language use (e.g., "What language do you prefer?"), ethnic identity (e.g., "How do you identify yourself?"), ethnicity of friends and peers (e.g., "What was the ethnic origin of the friends and peers you had, as a child from 6 to 18?"), generational status, and various behaviors and attitudes (e.g., "What is your food preference at home?"). The stu-

Table 10-1. Internal Consistency Estimates for the MMPI-2 Validity
and Clinical Scales for Whites and Asians

Scale		Whites		Asians
		Group		
Lie Scale		.54		.53
F Scale		.58		.61
K Scale		.71		.72
Hypochondriasis		.44		.36
Depression		.29		.54
Hysteria		.49		.53
Psychopathic Deviate		.47		.55
Masculinity-Femininity	males	.50	males	.72
	females	.49	females	.58
Paranoia		.62		.77
Psychasthenia		.79		.83
Schizophrenia		.80		.82
Hypomania		.69		.69
Social Introversion		.63		.70

dents responded to each question on a 5-point scale ranging from 1, indicating lowest possible acculturation (or high Asian identity), to 5, indicating highest possible acculturation (or high Western identity). Students' responses were then averaged across 21 questions for a measure of acculturation. SL-ASIA was modeled after the Acculturation Rating Scale for Mexican Americans (Cuellar, Harris, & Jasso, 1980). Past research has demonstrated that the measure has acceptable reliability and validity (Atkinson & Gim, 1989; Suinn, Ahuna, & Khoo, in press; Suinn, Rickard-Figueroa, Lew, & Vigil, 1987). The coefficient alpha for the SL-ASIA in the present sample was .92, which is comparable with those derived from past studies.

Minnesota Multiphasic Personality Inventory-2

Graham (1990) and Butcher, Graham, Dahlstrom, and Bowman (1990) provided internal consistency estimates for the standard validity and clinical scales. Graham (1990) also showed that internal consistency estimates for college students were comparable to those of the MMPI-2 normative sample. In both studies, the coefficient alphas ranged from .34 to .87. In the present sample, the internal consistency estimates ranged from .29 to .80 for White students, and from .36 to .83 for Asian-American students. Table 10-1 shows coefficient alphas for the validity scales and the clinical scales for the White and Asian samples, respectively.

Past research emphasized the importance of assessing the acculturation level of ethnic minorities (Greene, 1987; Sue & Zane, 1985). Thus, the Asian-American students were divided into two acculturation-level groups based on a median split procedure. The median of the acculturation scores on the SL-ASIA for the present sample was 3.05. The results of the analyses, therefore, were based on the comparisons between the three groups: the highly acculturated Asian-American students (HAs), the less acculturated Asian-American students (LAs), and White students. To examine ethnic and gender differences on the standard validity and clinical scales of the MMPI-2, 14 analyses of variance (i.e., one for each scale, except for Masculinity-Femininity, which was analyzed for each gender) were conducted with group and gender as between-subject factors. The dependent variables in each analysis were the mean raw scores on each scale of the MMPI-2. Because our main interest was to compare the mean scores of the groups, raw scores were used as dependent variables in place of T scores (Greene, 1987; Butcher et al., 1989). If significant main or interaction effects were found on a particular scale, post hoc Scheffe tests of paired comparisons with an alpha level of .05 were conducted to reveal the specific nature of the differences.

Because ethnic differences existed on some of the demographic variables— differences that could be confounded with ethnicity—we examined whether the demographic variables were associated with each of the 14 scales. The only significant relationships were between age and the K scale and father's occupation and education and scale 4. Therefore, on the K scale and scale 4, analysis of covariance was used in which age and father's occupation and education were added as the respective covariates.

Table 10-2 shows the means and standard deviations of the MMPI-2 scales for each group. Of the 13 scales, the analyses of variance yielded eight significant group effects and five significant gender effects with only one (scale 4) showing a significant interaction effect.

Specific Group Effects

The group effects strongly and consistently supported the hypothesis that LAs and Whites would differ the most on the MMPI-2 scales. Inspection of the means in Table 10-2 shows that all cases (whether the differences were significant or not) were ordered such that LAs > HAs > Whites or LAs < HAs < Whites. Significant group effects did not emerge for scales L, K (analysis of covariance was performed, as noted earlier), 3, 5 (which was divided according to gender), and 9. Figures 10-1 and 10-2 show the mean scale scores for men and women.

On the F scale, a significant group effect was found in which $F(2, 223) = 7.06$, $p < .001$. The Scheffe comparisons revealed that LAs scored significantly higher than Whites. The group effect on scale 1, $F(2, 223) = 19.38$, $p < .001$, was one in

Table 10-2. Means and Standard Deviations for the MMPI-2 Validity and Clinical Scales for Highly Acculturated and Less Acculturated Asian-American Students and Whites

| Scale | | Group | | |
		Highly Acculturated Asians	Less Acculturated Asians	Whites
Lie Scale	M	3.03	3.40	2.93
	SD	2.20	1.98	1.94
	N	(65)	(68)	(91)
F Scale	M	7.69	9.40	5.80
	SD	6.25	6.24	4.66
	N	(65)	(68)	(91)
K Scale	M	12.75	11.93	13.76
	SD	4.48	4.95	4.65
	N	(65)	(68)	(91)
Hypochondriasis-	M	8.05	9.78	5.80
	SD	4.13	4.74	3.56
	N	(65)	(68)	(91)
Depression	M	22.25	23.62	19.35
	SD	6.62	5.72	5.14
	N	(65)	(68)	(91)
Hysteria	M	21.78	21.97	20.93
	SD	4.58	5.10	4.41
	N	(65)	(68)	(91)
Psychopathic	M	19.32	21.16	17.86
Deviate	SD	5.71	5.55	5.07
	N	(65)	(68)	(91)
Masculinity-	M	25.54 (m)	25.68 (m)	26.78 (m)
Femininity	SD	5.62	5.17	5.72
	N	(24)	(38)	(37)
	M	35.49 (f)	34.13 (f)	34.80 (f)
	SD	4.20	4.20	4.59
	N	(41)	(41)	(54)
Paranoia	M	11.71	13.41	10.65
	SD	3.84	3.82	3.33
	N	(65)	(68)	(91)
Psychasthenia	M	20.20	22.12	15.97
	SD	9.26	8.60	7.96
	N	(65)	(68)	(91)
Schizophrenia	M	20.78	24.57	16.44
	SD	10.08	11.04	9.69
	N	(65)	(68)	(91)
Hypomania	M	20.09	20.76	19.56
	SD	4.88	6.09	5.41
	N	(65)	(68)	(91)
Social	M	30.91	32.62	27.30
Introversion	SD	10.17	9.43	10.84
	N	(65)	(68)	(91)

Note: N indicates the number of sample. For the Masculinity-Femininity scale, m refers to males and f refers to females.

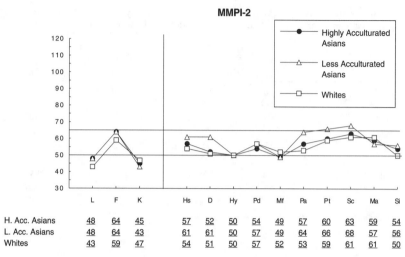

Figure 10-1. Non-K-Corrected Mean MMPI-2 Profile of College Men

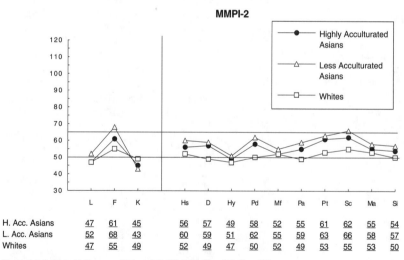

Figure 10-2. Non-K-Corrected Mean MMPI-2 Profile of College Women

which the Scheffe tests were significant for the comparisons: LAs > HAs > Whites. On scale 2, the main effect for group was significant, $F (2, 223) = 13.95$, $p < .001$. The Scheffe comparisons revealed that LAs > HAs = Whites. For scale 4, the groups differed significantly, $F (2, 206) = 4.75$, $p < .05$, such that LAs > Whites (for this scale, an analysis of covariance was performed with father's education and occupation as a covariate). A main effect was found for scale 6, $F (2, 223) = 10.26$, $p < .001$, in which LAs > HAs = Whites. Main effects of group were also found for scale 7, F (2, 223) = 10.81, p < .001, and scale 8, F (2, 223) = 11.55, p < .001. On both scales, LAs = HAs > Whites. Finally, scale 0 showed a main effect for group, F (2, 223) = 6.23, p < .01, in that LAs > Whites.

In terms of main effects for gender and specific gender differences, significant relationships were evident for the L scale [F (1, 223) = 6.79, p < .01], where F > M; F scale [F (1, 223) = 4.22, p < .05], where F > M; scale 2 [F (1, 223) = 13.07, p < .001], where F > M; scale 3 [F (1, 223) = 4, 37, p < .05], where F > M; and scale 9 [F (1, 223) = 11.46, p < .001], where M > F. On scale 4, a significant interaction effect between group and gender appeared, F (2, 223) = 4.88, p < .01.

The purpose of this study was to examine ethnic differences on the MMPI-2 and to determine if the differences are consistent with an acculturation effect. In general, the results indicated that less acculturated Asian-American students showed greater elevation on the clinical scales of the MMPI-2 profile than did highly acculturated Asian-American students or White students. In turn, highly acculturated Asian-American students had greater elevations than their White counterparts. Where significant group differences emerged on scales 1, 2, 4, 6, 7, 8, and 0, less acculturated Asian-American students and White students generally fell at the extremes, with more acculturated students in the middle. Interestingly, other recent studies suggest that refugees have higher MMPI-2 scale elavations than do members of the same ethnic group who have been in the United States longer. This was found in the case of recent Cuban refugees and Vietnamese refugees compared with Cubans and Vietnamese, respectively, who have been residing in the United States longer. These findings are somewhat consistent with those of the present study.

The results also indicate that Asian-American students had more somatic complaints, were more depressed and anxious, and feel isolated more often than Whites, regardless of their acculturation level. Moreover, as revealed by their performance on the MMPI-2, less acculturated Asian Americans had greater somatic complaints and more often perceived their environment as unsupportive than did their more acculturated counterparts.

The pattern of the MMPI-2 profiles was similar for all three groups. T scores on the validity and clinical scales were within normal range or were mildly elevated. However, the elevation was greater for the Asian Americans, especially for the less acculturated Asian Americans. Scores for females were significantly higher than those for males.

The findings may reflect a cultural response bias among Asian Americans. We predicted that if cultural factors are important in responses to the test, Asian Americans would differ from Whites, and the less acculturated Asians would show the greater difference. Results supported the prediction. Although uniform attitudes and values do not exist across diverse groups of Asian Americans, some common ways of behaving have been noted for this population. This is especially true for Asians who share Confucian values that emphasize respect for authority, close families, and formal interpersonal relationships (Dahlstrom, Lachar, & Dahlstrom, 1986). Thus, it is possible that some cultural factors may be confounded with actual psychopathology in the responses of Asian Americans to the MMPI-2. Obviously, we cannot determine the precise aspects of culture that may be important in affecting MMPI-2 responding. Furthermore, if the instrument is culturally biased, this does not mean that the MMPI-2 is not a valuable tool in cross-cultural evaluation. What it really means is that the interpretations of profiles, even similar ones, of individuals from different ethnic groups must consider how cultural factors may have influenced responses.

The findings are also consistent with Sue and Sue (1974), who found that, among users of a psychiatric clinic, Asian Americans had higher original MMPI scale elevations than did White Americans. However, the results seem to be at odds with those of Tsushima and Onorato (1982), who found that after controlling for diagnosis, Asian Americans and Whites did not differ on original MMPI scale elevations. It should be noted that the present study dealt with "normal" (i.e., nonpsychiatric) samples in contrast to Sue and Sue (1974) and Tsushima and Onorato (1982). Furthermore, the present findings suggest that ethnic differences on the MMPI are more marked among the less acculturated Asian Americans. In Tsushima and Onorato's study, their client sample was composed of Japanese Americans, who are the most acculturated among the various Asian-American groups. Under such circumstances, ethnic differences may be minimal.

The present study is limited in some ways. The sample size was small and Asian Americans represent many distinct ethnic groups. However, this study was the first to examine group differences between Asian Americans and Whites in their performance on the MMPI-2 and the relationship of acculturation and responding. Although the results are consistent with a cultural response set interpretation, we cannot rule out the possibility that they may simply reflect that Asian Americans as a minority group experience greater difficulties in their daily lives and as a result have more elevated profiles than do Whites. As a minority group, Asian Americans may experience problems such as English-language proficiency, feelings of isolation, prejudice and discrimination, culture conflicts, and so forth. It is possible that dealing with these problems takes a toll on Asian Americans' mental health despite their socioeconomic and educational resources. That is, the MMPI-2 may represent actual differences in symptoms and distress, in that less acculturated Asian Americans are under greater stress than are more acculturated Asian Americans and Whites. Nevertheless, it is precisely this inability to distinguish between a strict cultural response set interpretation and a minority group-stress interpretation that makes it imperative to conduct further studies on the validity of the MMPI-2 with Asian Americans.

We have initiated further studies to see if the cultural interpretation is valid. The larger project of which the present study is a part was initiated to identify principles that may underlie the responses of Asian Americans to self-report questionnaires such as the MMPI-2. That is, if cultural factors influence responses and if these factors can be identified, then it may be possible to control for, or take into account, cultural response sets in assessment instruments. The ultimate goal of the project is to increase the validity of measures of psychopathology that are developed in Western societies for Asian Americans. To achieve that goal, the project aims to develop scales that can systematically control for the cultural biases of Asian Americans on measures of psychopathology. It attempts to see if cultural factors can predict the responses of Asian Americans to an assessment measure. Having completed the present study, we are now examining the influence of three hypothesized cultural dimensions on responses to the MMPI-2. Shame, symptom tolerance, and cultural familiarity were identified as important cultural dimensions for Asian Americans based on the past literature (e.g., Kim, 1978; Kitano, 1976; Sue & Morishima, 1982). This second study focuses on whether ethnic differences in performance on the MMPI-2 (as found in the present study) can be explained by the cultural evaluations of the MMPI-2 items. If, for example, Asian-American respondents rate a particular item as being extremely shameful, and if few Asian Americans from the first pilot study endorsed the item, the findings may suggest that the cultural dimension of shame may be affecting responses.

In the second study, subjects are asked to rate the degree of shame, symptom tolerance, and cultural familiarity associated with each item of the MMPI-2. Because of the amount of data that needs to be collected, the study is still in progress. If the identified cultural dimensions are successful in predicting performance on the MMPI-2, we can conduct further studies to develop scales that can control for the cultural biases. For example, the S scale on the MMPI-2 can be used to understand the response set of self-presentation, and the construction of a scale for social desirability has allowed researchers to control for socially desirable responding on other assessment measures. We are hopeful that corrections for cultural response sets can be devised.

References

Atkinson, D., & Gim, R. (1989). Asian-American cultural identity and attitudes toward mental health services. *Journal of Counseling Psychology, 36,* 209–212.

Bond, M. H. (1991). *Beyond the Chinese face.* Hong Kong: Oxford University Press.

Brislin, R. W. (1993). *Understanding culture's influence on behavior.* New York: Harcourt Brace Jovanovich.

Butcher, J. N. (1994). Psychological assessment of airline pilot applicants with the MMPI-2. *Journal of Personality Assessment, 62,* 31–44.

Butcher, J. N., Dahlstrom, W. G., Graham, J. R., Tellegen, A. M., & Kaemmer, B. (1989). *MMPI-2: Manual for administration and scoring.* Minneapolis: University of Minnesota Press.

Butcher, J. N., Graham, J., Dahlstrom, W., & Bowman, E. (1990). The MMPI-2 with college students. *Journal of Personality Assessment, 54,* 1–15.

Butcher, J. N., & Han, K. (1993). *Development of an MMPI-2 scale to assess the presentation of self in a superlative manner: The S Scale.* Unpublished manuscript, University of Minnesota.

Cheung, F. M., & Song, W. (1989). A review on the clinical applications for the Chinese MMPI. *Psychological Assessment, 1,* 230–237.

Cuellar, I., Harris, L., & Jasso, R. (1980). An acculturation scale for Mexican American normal and clinical populations. *Hispanic Journal of Behavioral Science, 2,* 199–217.

Dahlstrom, W. G., Lachar, D., & Dahlstrom, L. E. (1986). *MMPI patterns of American minorities.* Minneapolis: University of Minnesota Press.

Dana, R. H. (1993, November). *Can "corrections" for culture using moderator variables contribute to cultural competence in assessment?* Paper presented at the Annual Convention of the Texas Psychological Association, Austin, TX.

Graham, J. R. (1990). *MMPI-2: Assessing personality and psychopathology.* New York: Oxford University Press.

Greene, R. I. (1987). Ethnicity and MMPI performance: A review. *Journal of Consulting and Clinical Psychology, 55,* 497–512.

Kim, B. L. C. (1978). *The Asian-Americans: Changing patterns, changing needs.* Montclair, NJ: Association of Korean Christian Scholars in North America.

Kitano, H. H. L. (1976). *Japanese-Americans: The evolution of a sub-culture.* Englewood Cliffs, NJ: Prentice-Hall.

Marsella, A. J., Sanborn, K. O., Kameoka, V., Shizuru, L., & Brennan, J. (1975). Cross-validation of depression among normal populations of Japanese, Chinese, and Caucasian ancestry. *Journal of Clinical Psychology, 31,* 281–287.

Pope, K. S., Butcher, J. N., & Seelen, J. (1993). *MMPI/MMPI-2/MMPI-A in court: Assessment, testimony, and cross-examination for expert witnesses and attorneys.* Washington, DC: American Psychological Association.

Sue, D., & Sue, S. (1987). Cultural factors in the clinical assessment of Asian Americans. *Journal of Consulting and Clinical Psychology, 55,* 479–487.

Sue, D. W., & Sue, D. (1990). *Counseling the culturally different.* New York: Wiley & Sons.

Sue, S., & Morishima, J. (1982). *The mental health of Asian Americans.* San Francisco: Jossey-Bass Publishers.

Sue, S., & Sue, D. W. (1974). MMPI comparisons between Asian-Americans and non-Asian students utilizing a student health psychiatric clinic. *Journal of Counseling Psychology, 21,* 423–427.

Sue, S., & Zane, N. W. S. (1985). Academic achievement and socioemotional adjustment among Chinese university students. *Journal of Counseling Psychology, 32,* 570–579.

Suinn, R. M., Ahuna, C., & Khoo, G. (in press). The Suinn-Lew Self-Identity Acculturation Scale: Concurrent and factorial validation. *Educational and Psychological Measurement.*

Suinn, R. M., Rickard-Figueroa, K., Lew, S., & Vigil, P. (1987). The Suinn-Lew Asian Self-Identity Acculturation Scale: An initial report. *Educational and Psychological Measurement, 47,* 401–407.

Tsushima, W. T., & Onorato, V. A. (1982). Comparison of MMPI scores of White and Japanese-American medical patients. *Journal of Consulting and Clinical Psychology, 50,* 150–151.

Watanabe, C. (1973). Self-expressions and the Asian-American experience. *Personnel and Guidance Journal, 51,* 390–396.

Part III

Spanish Adaptations for Latin America and Spain

Chapter 11

Use of the MMPI-2 in Chile:
Translation and Adaptation

Fernando J. Rissetti, Erika Himmel, and Jorge A. González-Moreno

The MMPI research program was begun in Chile in 1976 at the Catholic University of Chile as one of the components of a Students Affairs general research program. A main feature of this program was the study of the psychological characteristics of the student population. For this purpose, the feasibility of implementing an objective, group administered, computer scorable, highly reliable, and valid psychometric instrument was explored.

The study was assigned to the Student Health Department of the university, which initiated a relationship with Dr. James N. Butcher of the University of Minnesota to exchange information and obtain technical assistance. Within this context Dr. Butcher visited Chile twice, implementing a cross-cultural perspective for this research from its inception. This research program has been active for 18 years, producing a database of more than 40,000 subjects.

The research has basically consisted of the translation and adaptation of the MMPI (Rissetti, Montiel, Maltes, Hermosilla, & Fleischli, 1978; Rissetti et al., 1979a; Rissetti et al., 1979b; Rissetti et al., 1979c); and the standardization and validation of the MMPI for the university student population (Rissetti & Maltes, 1985a; Rissetti & Maltes, 1985b); and the standardization and validation of the instrument for the general adult population, including cross-cultural comparisons (Rissetti et al., 1989a; Rissetti et al., 1989b).

From the very early stages of the research program, the MMPI has been administered annually to students entering the university, providing a database for the - mental health professionals of the Student Health Department. These data have also provided a description of the epidemiological characteristics of the university student population and have made it possible to identify those at high risk for

---

To Sergio P. Olmos, M.D., our outstanding co-researcher and good friend, an exceptional person.

emotional instability who were interested in pursuing careers in which sound mental health is an important requirement (e.g., medicine, psychology, nursing, education, etc.).

As information on the psychometric characteristics of the inventory was consolidated, several prospective studies on high-risk groups among university students provided a foundation for the development of clinical support and early treatment programs for high-risk students, evidenced at the entrance MMPI screening. The MMPI has also facilitated academic decisions about students.

Studies with the Original MMPI

Translation and Adaptation of the Original MMPI

Work on the original MMPI was conducted from 1976 to 1978. An interdisciplinary committee developed the translation, producing a Spanish version by consensus. This version was back-translated by a bilingual expert, and the committee compared the Spanish version with the English original, making adjustments to the Spanish version as necessary. The final translation was revised by Dr. Butcher and Dr. Rosa Garcia, both from the University of Minnesota. The methodology employed in producing the translation was the subject of a chapter by Butcher and Clark (1979). The Spanish version of the MMPI was administered to university students, and several transcultural comparisons were made of the item endorsement frequencies of local and U.S. students (Rissetti & Maltes, 1985a).

Standardization and Validation of the MMPI

Student Populations. In 1978, a proportionally equal male-female normative sample of 3,325 students from the entire age range of the university population (16 to 25) was randomly selected. Linear T scores were computed according to the standard method recommended (Butcher & Pancheri, 1976; Rissetti & Maltes, 1985a). Subsequent administrations of the MMPI (every year since 1978) have shown the high stability of the local norms.

In 1979, factorial structure and discriminant validity in this population were investigated. For the latter, a clinical sample of 385 male and female university students under treatment at the Student Health Service was used. The factorial structure was very consistent with the factor patterns evidenced in research with other foreign populations (Rissetti & Maltes, 1985a; Rissetti & Maltes, 1985b).

The discriminant analysis revealed that the instrument diffentiated normal from abnormal subjects, confirming the transcultural stability and generalizability of the MMPI to a Chilean student population (Himmel, Maltes, & Rissetti, 1979; Rissetti & Maltes, 1985a).

Adult (Nonstudent) Populations. In 1988, the MMPI was administered to a representative sample of the Chilean population (n = 608) across several cities (Rissetti, Himmel, Maltes, González, & Olmos 1989). Sponsored by a grant from the Chilean National Council for Scientific and Technological Research (FONDECYT), the purpose of this research was to expand the use of the MMPI to the general population. Males and females were about equally represented. Item analysis was performed, reliability was estimated by Cronbach's alpha, and the factorial structure was analyzed. A discriminant analysis was performed with a clinical sample (n = 284). Linear T scores were derived for the reference population (Rissetti et al., 1989a). These studies confirmed the applicability of the inventory to the general population.

The completion of this standardization study coincided with the introduction of the MMPI-2 in the United States in 1989.

Translation and Adaptation of the MMPI-2 in Chile

The project was begun in 1991, financed by a grant from the Chilean National Council for Scientific and Technological Research (FONDECYT). The project's general objective was to translate, adapt, standardize, and validate the MMPI-2 for the Chilean population.

A literature review and experience with the development of the Chilean version of the original MMPI (TUC-l) at the Catholic University of Chile over 15 years indicated that the whole item pool of the inventory, not only the new or modified items incorporated into the MMPI-2 (Butcher, Dahlstrom, Graham, Tellegen, & Kaemmer, 1989), should be revised. Consequently, a number of modifications were made in the translation to produce a Chilean version (TUC-2) equivalent to the English original.

An item is considered to be functionally equivalent when the meaning of the response to it is the same across cultures, even when the behaviors reflected by the items are different. For instance, shaking hands in Western culture and bowing in Japan are different but functionally equivalent behaviors since they have the same meaning: a manner of greeting. Two versions of an instrument are psychometrically equivalent when they have the same psychometric properties at the item as well as scale levels. In other words, the endorsement percentages are comparable and the structures or factorial loadings are essentially the same.

Hathaway's recommendation (1970) that radical modifications not be made in the content of the inventory was followed as closely as possible in the development of the translation. This approach provides a major advantage for transcultural research in personality assessment. We made only formal and transformal modifications of the original items. The formal modifications related to making adjustments for grammatical and lexical requirements of the target language—for instance, ensuring that the stimulus (item) in Spanish is equally valid for both

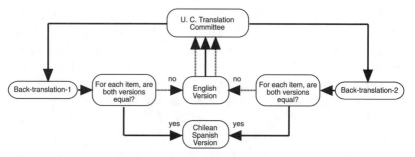

Figure 11-1. Diagram of the Translation Process for the Chilean Version of the MMPI-2

genders. Transformal modification related to making the item appropriate to the cultural context without making any radical change in the content.

On the other hand, it was important to accommodate Gough's criterion (1965) regarding maintaining the psychological rather than the literal equivalence of the original. For that reason, item translation included analysis of the scale or scales containing the item and knowledge of the diagnostic differentiation that it involves.

A multidisciplinary translation committee was formed of two psychologists, two physicians, and a master of arts in education and psychometrics. Figure 11-1 shows the procedure followed.

The process was carried out through the following stages:

1. Each member of the committee individually translated each one of the 567 items from the English original (ORI-2) into Spanish.
2. Each member's translated versions were compared by the committee, which accepted by consensus the most compatible item version according to criteria defined below.
3. This version, translated as mentioned (TUC-2), was given to two true bilingual individuals (both of them born in the United States, one a professor at a binational cultural institute in Santiago, the other a bachelor in psychology, both living in Santiago). These two individuals translated the obtained Spanish version back to English separately, producing versions BT-1 and BT-2.
4. The translation committee defined a set of rules allowing a comparison (item by item) of the BT-l and BT-2 versions with ORI-2. A summary of these rules is included in Table 11-1.

The following set of rules was formulated according to a sequential decision model.

Rule 1: When at least one of the back-translated versions was identical to ORI-2 and the other was similar, or when the back-translations were identical and

Table 11-1. Summary of Rules for Comparing Items of the English Original and Spanish Translations

Category	Classification Criteria
1	If ORI-2 = BT-1 and ORI 2 = BT-2
2	If ORI-2 = BT-1 and ORI-2 <ne> BT-2
3	If ORI-2 <ne> BT-1 and ORI-2 <ne> BT-2
4	If ORI-2 <app> BT-1 and ORI-2 = BT-2
5	If ORI-2 <app> BT-1 and ORI-2 <ne> BT-2
6	If ORI-2 <app> BT-1 and ORI-2 <app> BT-2
7	If BT-1 = BT-2 and ORI 2 <ne> (BT-1 and BT-2)
8	If BT-1 = BT-2 and ORI-2 <app> (BT-1 and BT-2)

Note: <ne> = not equal to
<app> = approximately equal to

at the same time similar to ORI-2, the TUC-2 version from which both back-translations came was accepted. In other words, when one of the situations shown by categories 1, 4, and 8 in Table 11-1 occurred, the corresponding item was unconditionally accepted.

Rule 2: When one of the back-translations was different from ORI-2, the item was examined to determine whether the discrepancy was the result of a back-translation error or an error in the TUC-2 version. Because some of the items in ORI-2 are the same as in the original version of the MMPI, it was assumed for each of those items that if its TUC-2 version was identical to its equivalent item in TUC-1, we were dealing with a back-translation error. In this case we accepted the TUC-2 version of that item. If this was not the case, it was assumed that the translation error was on TUC-2. Then the item was dealt with according to rule 3. The categories from Table 11-1 initially treated with rule 2 were 2, 3, 5, 6, and 7.

Rule 3: All items remaining after the rule 2 stages were followed were submitted to the committee for revision, to determine whether the translation error in TUC-2 was formal or related to the content of the item. In the first case, the necessary modifications were made. In the second, the item was reformulated in Spanish by consensus and again back-translated.

Throughout the translation process, committee members showed high congruence (90%) in their individual translations of the original items retained in the MMPI-2 (459 items). The convergence was slightly lower (75%) for the new items.

A large number of the back-translated items (48%) were similar to their equivalents in the American version. On the other hand, a minority (6.7%) presented significant differences in both back-translations (Table 11-2). In these cases, a hypothesis of translation or back-translation error was formulated.

Table 11-2. Summary of Rules for Comparing Back-translated Items of the English Original
and Spanish Translations

Category	Classification Criteria	n	%
1	If ORI-2 = BT-1 and ORI-2 = BT-2	53	9.3
2	If ORI-2 = BT-1 and ORI-2 <ne> BT-2	6	1.1
3	If ORI-2 <ne> BT-1 and ORI-2 <ne> BT-2	38	6.7
4	If ORI-2 <app> BT-1 and ORI-2 = BT-2	74	13.1
5	If ORI-2 <app> BT-1 and ORI-2 <ne> BT-2	63	11.1
6	If ORI-2 <app> BT-1 and ORI-2 <app> BT-2	272	48.0
7	If BT-1 = BT-2 and ORI-2 <ne> (BT-1 and BT-2)	12	2.1
8	If BT-1 = BT-2 and ORI-2 <app> (BT-1 and BT-2)	49	8.6
Total		567	100.0

Note: <ne> = not equal to
         <app> = approximately equal to

Table 11-3. Types of Decisions Made in the Translation Process

	Type of Decision			
Category	Unconditional	Modified	Second Back-Translation	Total
1	53	0	0	53
2	5	1	0	6
3	12	6	20	38
4	74	0	0	74
5	15	43	5	63
6	79	179	14	272
7	4	0	8	12
8	49	0	0	49
Total	291	229	47	567
%	51.3%	40.4%	8.3%	100%

As a result of using the aforementioned rules, it was possible to classify the items
in the following categories:

(a) unconditional acceptance
(b) acceptance with modifications
(c) acceptance after a second back-translation

The distribution of the items in each of these categories is summarized in Table
11-3. As shown, most of the items (51.3%) were accepted unconditionally as valid

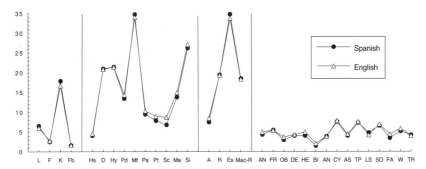

Figure 11-2. MMPI-2 Profiles of Bilingual Chilean Subjects Taking the Instrument in Spanish and English

items for the final version. Only 8.3% needed a second back-translation and 229 items (40.4%) were accepted with minor formal modifications.

Bilingual Test-Retest Study

The following hypothesis was tested: If ORI-2 and TUC-2 versions were linguistically equivalent, bilingual test-retest correlations would be of such magnitude that they would correspond primarily to measures of scale reliability. Subjects were 22 bilingual adult male and female professionals, averaging 42.1 years in age (S.D. 11.04), with relevant bicultural experience. These subjects were randomly and sequentially given the Spanish and English versions of the inventory. They then self-administered them, with over an average period of 10 days between administrations.

The profile shown in Figure 11-2 compares the mean group profiles obtained by subjects in the two test administrations. There is a virtual overlap of the two curves, particularly for the new MMPI-2 content scales.

The test-retest correlations of the scale raw scores for both administrations have a high mean correlation of about 0.80, varying between 0.96 (CYN scale) and 0.43 (Hy scale) (Table 11-4). These correlations support the scale reliability of the translation. Except for the Hy scale, these data are highly consistent with those reported in recent literature for studies of this nature (Butcher et al., 1989; Graham, 1990). These findings reveal high linguistic and psychometric equivalence of the Spanish and English versions of the MMPI-2, leading the committee to conclude that the Chilean Spanish translation was sufficiently valid and reliable to go on to the next stages of the project.

Standardization Study

Chile is a Latin American country with a population of nearly 14 million, 45% of whom live in the so-called Metropolitan Region, which comprises Santiago, the

Table 11-4. Means, Standard Deviations, and Test-Retest Correlations of the
Bilingual Spanish-English Study

Scale	Mean		Standard Deviation		
	Spanish	English	Spanish	English	Pearson
L	6.5	6.0	1.90	1.93	.573
F	2.5	2.8	2.61	2.58	.757
K	17.9	16.7	4.27	4.69	.909
F_B	1.6	1.6	2.74	1.56	.732
Hs	4.1	4.6	4.44	3.92	.880
D	21.0	20.9	6.14	4.98	.792
Hy	21.5	21.5	2.91	3.58	.428
Pd	13.5	14.4	3.88	3.91	.853
Mf	34.7	34.0	3.95	3.34	.766
Pa	9.5	10.3	2.72	2.23	.709
Pt	7.9	9.0	8.54	7.63	.945
Sc	6.8	8.7	7.78	8.01	.862
Ma	13.8	15.0	4.03	3.94	.743
Si	26.2	27.1	8.53	8.62	.954
A	7.5	8.4	8.06	8.27	.948
R	19.4	19.3	3.40	3.50	.837
Es	34.8	33.8	5.69	5.86	.895
MAC-R	18.5	18.3	3.05	2.48	.791
ANX	4.3	5.0	4.83	5.07	.900
FRS	5.5	5.4	4.60	3.69	.957
OBS	3.0	3.7	3.15	3.09	.920
DEP	4.0	4.3	4.67	3.88	.907
HEA	4.0	5.0	4.45	3.99	.885
BIZ	1.5	2.1	1.63	1.69	.728
ANG	3.9	3.9	2.82	2.45	.875
CYN	7.6	7.8	5.54	5.12	.960
ASP	4.0	4.4	3.57	3.05	.751
TPA	7.3	7.6	3.40	3.33	.734
LSE	4.8	4.2	4.91	3.83	.959
SOD	6.6	6.9	4.17	4.37	.893
FAM	3.5	4.4	3.35	3.66	.866
WRK	5.2	5.9	5.36	5.70	.944
TRT	4.2	4.1	4.09	4.08	.878

capital city, and its suburbs. The rest of the population is distributed among 12 other regions. The population is mainly white, with a low percentage of native Indians. The average schooling of the Chilean population is about seven years, and the rate of illiteracy is very low.

Normative Sample. In this study, an effort was made to gather information in the four most representative regions in the country, considering the following demographic variables: occupation, education, and ethnicity. One region is in the northern part of the country, the second is in the central part (which includes the Metropolitan Region), and the remaining two are in southern Chile. These four regions contain 80% of the total population of the country. The Metropolitan Region is urban; the remaining regions are rural and contain a representative proportion of the country's rural population.

An operational definition of normality was adopted and complemented by an empirical criterion. Normality was defined as the absence of psychopathological conditions, insofar as at the time of testing the subjects were engaged in their regular activities and were not openly manifesting maladaptive or maladjusted behavior. The empirical criterion applied excluded subjects with a raw score elevation higher than two standard deviations above the mean of the preliminary sample average (n = 3, 175) on any of the clinical scales (Dahlstrom, Welsh, & Dahlstrom, 1972). Gender composition was approximately proportional to the general population, and age ranged from 18 to 85 years. Education ranged from eight years to graduate studies.

Subjects were recruited from several institutions. People working at or related to these institutions volunteered to take the inventory and responded anonymously. A small percentage of individuals, mainly high-level executives, professionals, and older people, were contacted personally.

The subjects included undergraduate and graduate students, administrative officers, academic personnel, and elderly persons from special senior citizens programs at public and private universities; professors and students from technical postsecondary institutes; students from evening schools (mainly blue-collar workers and low-level clerical officers); members of community nonprofit organizations such as volunteers at hospitals and centers for cultural and personal development; and professionals, secretaries, and blue-collar workers from private and public enterprises.

The MMPI-2 was administered to groups ranging from 5 to 50 subjects who participated as nonpaid volunteers and answered the inventory anonymously, providing demographic information on gender, age, geographic origin, and maximum level of schooling. The test was administered by advanced psychology students trained in testing. The sessions were coordinated and supervised by an experienced psychologist.

Information was collected over 11 months from 3,175 normal subjects. The final sample was developed as follows:

1. The protocols of the 3,175 subjects were reviewed, and 224 were eliminated because of major omissions or errors in the demographic information.
2. Subjects were excluded because they did not meet the criteria of psychological normality. Nine hundred thirty-eight additional subjects whose personality characteristics met the deviant group criteria better than they did the normal group criteria, according to the psychometric model of contrasted groups on which basis the MMPI clinical scales were constructed (Wiggins, 1973; Rissetti et al., 1989a), were excluded. This decision was based on findings of the standardization study for the original MMPI on an adult Chilean population, where the discriminant analysis among the excluded group, by the same criterion, was much closer to the clinical group and significantly different from the normal subjects (Rissetti et al., 1989a). Inclusion of these statistically deviant subjects in a normative sample significantly increases the likelihood of incorporating a major bias.
3. Over-represented groups were excluded. To maintain a proportional representation of the Chilean population, in terms of demographic variables, 902 subjects from the university student population were randomly excluded.

The Chilean normative sample was composed of 1,111 subjects (522 men and 589 women). Of the males, 52.1% were under 24 years of age, 27.2% were between the ages of 25 and 34, 11.5% were between the ages of 35 and 44, and 9.2% were over the age of 45. These percentages in the female sample were 45%, 22.1%, 13.4%, and 19.6%, respectively. The mean age of males was 27.9 years (S.D. 10.8) and of females 31.9 years (S.D. 14.6). In terms of schooling, 24% of male subjects had elementary education, 44% had high school education, 9% had vocational education, and 22.6% had higher education. This distribution among the female sample was 15.5%, 37.9%, 16.5%, and 29.9%, respectively. This sample composition was considered to be approximately representative of the country's population as a whole.

Clinical sample. The MMPI was administered to 518 subjects with psychiatric pathology. This group was selected according to the same demographic parameters as was the normal sample. Their psychological abnormality was defined by the presence of some type of psychopathology at the time of taking the test, previously assessed through clinical judgment or other evaluation procedure that led to a psychiatric diagnosis and to the formulation of a treatment strategy. All subjects were undergoing some form of public or private outpatient or inpatient psychiatric or psychotherapeutic treatment at the time they took the test. Outpatient

Table 11-5. Alpha Coefficients of the Chilean Male and Female Samples on the
Validity, Clinical, and Content Scales

| | Reliability Chile | | Reliability U.S. | |
Scale	Males	Females	Males	Females
L	.63	.53	.62	.57
F	.84	.82	.64	.63
K	.75	.75	.74	.72
Hs	.81	.83	.77	.81
D	.56	.60	.59	.64
Hy	.57	.59	.58	.56
Pd	.63	.64	.60	.62
Mf	.40	.30	.58	.37
Pa	.55	.60	.34	.39
Pt	.90	.90	.85	.87
Sc	.92	.91	.85	.86
Ma	.62	.60	.58	.61
Si	.80	.81	.82	.84
ANX	.83	.83	.82	.83
FRS	.81	.81	.72	.75
OBS	.78	.77	.74	.77
DEP	.87	.87	.85	.86
HEA	.82	.83	.76	.80
BIZ	.82	.80	.73	.74
ANG	.76	.74	.76	.73
CYN	.84	.84	.86	.85
ASP	.73	.68	.78	.75
TPA	.71	.67	.72	.68
LSE	.84	.83	.79	.83
SOD	.78	.79	.80	.84
FAM	.80	.79	.78	.77
WRK	.87	.86	.82	.84
TRT	.86	.85	.78	.85
F_B	.90	.87	.72	.75
Es	.65	.70	.60	.65
A	.91	.91	.89	.90
R	.60	.54	.67	.57
O-H	.37	.19	.34	.24
MAC-R	.49	.35	.56	.45
MT	.84	.85	.84	.86

subjects were given a small allowance for transportation. Four nosological global categories were defined as being of interest in this study: Reactive or Symptomatic Neurosis; Personality Disorders or Character Disorders; Psychosis; and Other. This sample was obtained through the following steps: Fifty protocols were excluded for quality control reasons and 225 university students were eliminated to achieve a more balanced sample in keeping with the subjects' level of schooling and age. The final clinical sample consisted of 243 subjects, 109 males and 134 females. Percentages of diagnostic categories were 34.5% reactive neurosis; 36.2% personality disorders; 14.5% psychosis; and 5.8% other.

As in the U.S. restandardization study (Butcher et al., 1989), the internal consistency of scales was estimated by Cronbach's alpha coefficient, shown in Table 11-5. The coefficients for many of the scales were higher than those reported for the U.S. study (Butcher et al., 1989). They ranged from 0.30 (Mf, female sample) to 0.92 (Sc, male sample). Median coefficients were 0.80 for the Chilean male sample and 0.79 for the Chilean females, most coefficients being between 0.75 and 0.85. The new content scales have much higher consistency coefficients than the traditional clinical scales (for Chilean males, median 0.82 vs. 0.63; and Chilean females, median 0.81 vs. 0.62). The same relationship is true for the U.S. data.

Factorial and discriminant validity studies were performed. A four-factor structure was determined for the traditional clinical and validity scales, using the principal components method with Varimax rotation. Discriminant validity between the normative and clinical samples was also assessed.

One of the methods for assessing cross-cultural validity is analysis of the factor structure of the MMPI-2 across different national groups (Ben-Porath, 1990). As in the American normative sample (Butcher et al., 1989), the Chilean analysis employed a four-factor solution for the validity and clinical scales. Tables 11-6 and 11-7 show the factor loadings, explained variance, and communalities.

The first factor obtained for both male and female samples is described in the literature as General Maladjustment (Rissetti et al., 1989a; Dahlstrom, Welsh & Dahlstrom, 1975). This factor has the highest loadings on the Sc (0.93; 0.92), Pt (0.89; 0.90), F (0.78; 0.80), Hs (0.65; 0.72), and Pd (0.60; 0.67) scales. These values have the same order of magnitude as the values in the U.S. study (Butcher et al., 1989).

The second factor, also highly consistent between the samples, represents the dimension of Overcontrol, with high weights on the Hy (0.87; 0.86) and K (0.54; 0.56) scales. This is the second factor in the U.S. male sample as well, but it is the third factor in the U.S. female sample. The third factor extracted from the Chilean sample, Depression–Social Inhibition, also shows a pattern similar to other national samples, with only a slight inversion in the loadings of the most saturated

Table 11-6. Factor Analysis of the Validity and Clinical Scales for the Chilean
Male Normative Sample (N = 522)

	Factor 1		Factor 2		Factor 3		Factor 4		Communality	
Scales	U.S.	Chile	U.S.	Chile	U.S.	Chile	U.S.	Chile	U.S.	Chile
L	−.11	−.38	.48	.27	.11	.22	−.57	.17	.58	.30
F	.79	.78	.00	−.02	.11	−.04	−.01	.22	.64	.66
K	−.55	−.65	.71	.54	−.12	.05	−.05	.24	.81	.78
Hs	.70	.65	.21	.26	.34	.20	−.01	−.19	.67	.58
D	.42	.41	.30	.24	.72	.69	.08	.04	.79	.70
Hy	.16	.02	.85	.87	.07	.10	.15	−.02	.78	.77
Pd	.68	.60	.20	.32	−.10	−.28	.31	.30	.61	.64
Mf	.05	.18	.13	.47	.11	−.11	.83	−.75	.72	.82
Pa	.41	.43	.37	.50	−.01	−.17	.46	.27	.52	.53
Pt	.77	.89	−.31	−.13	.31	.05	.26	−.03	.85	.82
Sc	.87	.93	−.21	−.06	.13	−.08	.23	.05	.87	.88
Ma	.59	.48	−.19	.00	−.66	−.68	.05	−.03	.82	.70
Si	.29	.51	−.35	−.26	.79	.65	.05	.00	.83	.75

Table 11-7. Factor Analysis of the Validity and Clinical Scales for the Chilean
Female Normative Sample (N = 589)

	Factor 1		Factor 2		Factor 3		Factor 4		Communality	
Scales	U.S.	Chile	U.S.	Chile	U.S.	Chile	U.S.	Chile	U.S.	Chile
L	−.35	−.14	−.01	.29	.30	.21	−.57	.83	.54	.84
F	.67	.80	.37	−.10	.11	−.09	−.18	.08	.63	.67
K	−.48	−.64	−.63	.56	.38	−.04	−.11	−.03	.78	.72
Hs	.30	.72	.53	.28	.47	.07	−.06	.23	.66	.65
D	.08	.55	.75	.34	.46	.58	.06	−.06	.79	.75
Hy	.10	.22	−.04	.86	.91	−.04	.01	.04	.84	.79
Pd	.71	.67	.16	.32	.30	−.20	.07	−.24	.63	.64
Mf	−.17	−.04	.08	.43	.18	.22	.84	−.41	.77	.40
Pa	.44	.51	.16	.40	.37	−.25	.26	−.06	.43	.49
Pt	.58	.90	.70	−.12	.04	.06	.18	−.06	.87	.83
Sc	.77	.92	.53	−.17	.10	−.08	.04	.01	.89	.88
Ma	.83	.49	−.18	−.09	−.10	−.67	.01	.20	.73	.74
Si	.05	.51	.92	−.32	−.09	.67	.03	.02	.86	.82

Table 11-8. Factor Analysis of the Content Scales for the Chilean Male Normative Sample (N = 522)

Scales	Rotated Factor Matrix				
	Factor 1	Factor 2	Factor 3	Factor 4	Communality
ANX	0.40	0.53	0.44	0.22	0.68
FRS	0.36	0.60	0.15	0.04	0.52
OBS	0.55	0.31	0.47	0.16	0.84
DEP	0.61	0.41	0.21	0.34	0.69
HEA	0.06	0.84	0.03	0.09	0.71
BIZ	0.22	0.59	0.19	0.33	0.54
ANG	0.14	0.17	0.83	0.16	0.76
CYN	0.24	0.18	0.26	0.80	0.79
ASP	0.10	0.10	0.18	0.89	0.84
TPA	0.15	0.07	0.81	0.27	0.76
LSE	0.76	0.26	0.19	0.19	0.71
SOD	0.71	0.01	-0.02	-0.02	0.51
FAM	0.36	0.28	0.32	0.43	0.49
WRK	0.70	0.33	0.31	0.28	0.77
TRT	0.75	0.23	0.25	0.32	0.78

scales, Si (0.65; 0.67) and D (0.69; 0.58). There is high correspondence with the U.S. male sample, while it corresponds to the second factor in the female sample.

Finally, the fourth factor in the male sample corresponds to Maleness-Femaleness since it is the only scale that shows a high loading, but with the opposite sign, negative versus positive, from the U.S. sample. This change of sign is probably explained by a cultural difference. Chilean males still tend to have a more stereotyped gender identification than do U.S. males (e.g., housekeeping is considered a female activity). In the female sample, the scale with the greatest weight is L, which may be interpreted as a self-protective dimension. In the U.S. study, this factor for both samples is Maleness-Femaleness.

The present results show that, as in the previous Chilean validity study (Rissetti et al., 1989a), the factorial structure of the MMPI-2 validity and clinical scales (including Mf and Si) is highly consistent across time and culture.

The same kind of analysis was done with the new content scales. Factor loadings, communalities, and percentages of common variance are reported in Tables 11-8 and 11-9. In both samples the highest loadings for the first factor correspond to LSE (0.75; 0.79), TRT (0.75; 0.78), WRK (0.70; 0.77), SOD (0.71; 0.68),

Table 11-9. Factor Analysis of the Content Scales for the Chilean Female Normative Sample
(N = 589)

	Rotated Factor Matrix				
Scales	Factor 1	Factor 2	Factor 3	Factor 4	Communality
ANX	0.51	0.53	0.11	0.42	0.73
FRS	0.23	0.60	0.19	0.12	0.47
OBS	0.63	0.25	0.24	0.31	0.61
DEP	0.66	0.44	0.09	0.26	0.71
HEA	0.13	0.84	0.03	0.11	0.74
BIZ	0.22	0.61	0.43	0.08	0.62
ANG	0.21	0.18	0.11	0.87	0.84
CYN	0.28	0.25	0.83	0.19	0.86
ASP	0.16	0.13	0.86	0.23	0.84
TPA	0.14	0.11	0.40	0.78	0.79
LSE	0.79	0.21	0.08	0.07	0.67
SOD	0.68	0.00	0.12	-0.01	0.48
FAM	0.45	0.37	0.28	0.28	0.50
WRK	0.77	0.26	0.15	0.34	0.79
TRT	0.78	0.25	0.29	0.16	0.78

DEP (0.61; 0.66), and OBS (0.55; 0.63). This factor has been labeled Social Distress and might be associated with personality disorders, specifically in the general social and work domains. It provides complementary information to scales corresponding to the first factor on the clinical scales. The second factor also showed a high convergence in both samples. The highest loadings were found on the HEA (0.84; 0.84), FRS (0.60; 0.60), BIZ (0.59; 0.61), and ANX (0.53; 0.53) scales, which would seem to give rise to a specific factor of Neuroticism. The third factor, in the case of the male sample, could be termed Behavioral Style, with high weights on the ANG (0.83) and TPA (0.81) scales. There is a different configuration in the female sample that would point to Character Disorder, with high loadings on ASP (0.86) and CYN (0.83). The last factor in the male sample is equivalent to the third in the female and, likewise, that of the female to the third factor in the male.

In summary, the factor analysis of the content scales would seem to contribute more specific clinical and behavioral factors than does the analysis of the traditional clinical scales. The new content scales, therefore, could enrich the assessment

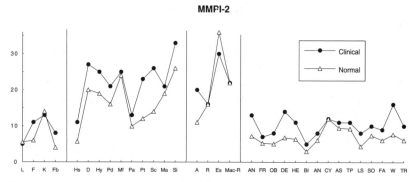

Figure 11-3. Average MMPI-2 Raw Scores for Chilean Men

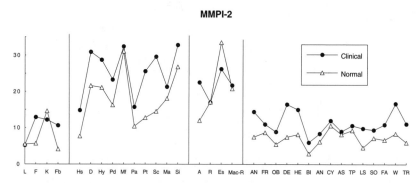

Figure 11-4. Average MMPI-2 Raw Scores for Chilean Women

potential of the new instrument. Corroboration of these findings will depend on future studies.

Discriminant validity was assessed by a multivariate statistical technique comparing the normative and clinical samples. The average profiles of raw scores for the male and female samples are shown in Figures 11-3 and 11-4, respectively. The canonical discriminant function weights and percentage of correct classification for the clinical scales are shown in Tables 11-10 to 11-12. The canonical function for males between these groups is highly significant (Wilks' Lambda = 0.6024; χ^2 = 318,85; p < 0.0001). The same conclusion holds true for females (Wilks' Lambda = 0.5202; χ^2 = 468.64; p < 0.0001).

Discriminant analysis shows that all scales present statistically significant differences between the normative and clinical samples, for both males and females. The highest canonical discriminant coefficients were found for the following scales: Pt (0.50), D (0.49), and Hy (0.41) for males; and D (0.62), Sc (0.36), and Hy (0.34) for females. When comparing these results with the former studies carried out in Chile (Rissetti et al., 1989a), a high degree of consistency becomes evident.

Table 11-10. Standardized Canonical Discriminant Function Coefficients
for the Clinical and Normal Samples on the MMPI-2 Clinical Scales

Scales	Males Function 1	Females Function 1
Hs	−0.12463	−0.22425
D	0.48753	0.62416
Hy	0.41286	0.34005
Pd	−0.01724	−0.04858
Mf	0.04103	0.03275
Pa	0.03781	0.18135
Pt	0.50062	0.13829
Sc	0.04513	0.36165
Ma	0.12119	0.08598
Si	−0.00106	−0.12781

Table 11-11. Classification Results of the Discriminant Analysis for Men

Actual Group	Number of Cases	Predicted Group Membership 1	2
Group 1	522	460	62
Normal Subjects	100%	88.1%	11.9%
Group 2	114	29	85
Abnormal Subjects	100%	25.4%	74.6%

Table 11-12. Classification Results of the Discriminant Analysis for Women

Actual Group	Number of Cases	Predicted Group Membership 1	2
Group 1	589	531	58
Normal Subjects	100%	90.2%	9.8%
Group 2	135	26	109
Abnormal Subjects	100%	19.3%	80.7%

Table 11-13. Standardized Canonical Discriminant Function Coefficients for the Clinical and Normal Samples on the MMPI-2 Content Scales

Scales	Males Func. 1	Females Func. 1
ANG	−0.02983	−0.13006
ANX	0.17497	0.31731
ASP	0.14583	0.03117
BIZ	0.02684	0.09235
CYN	−0.56810	−0.39532
DEP	0.77848	0.55043
FAM	−0.09060	0.04569
FRS	−0.15263	−0.14026
HEA	0.20035	0.24560
LSE	−0.30375	0.07145
OBS	−0.02884	−0.11040
SCP	0.07803	0.10864
TPA	0.01947	−0.11596
TRI	−0.34989	−0.21862
WRK	0.77615	0.56583

The average percentage of correct classification is 85.7% for males and 88.4% for females. For normal males the percentage of correct classification is 88.1%; for clinical males this percentage is 74.6%. Percentages for females are slightly higher: 90.2% for normal subjects and 80.7% for clinical. For both males and females there are more false negatives than false positives. These values are somewhat lower than those for the original MMPI (Rissetti et al., 1989a). It seems plausible that the pathology of the subjects in the present clinical sample was less severe.

The same analysis was performed with the MMPI-2 content scales. The results for males and females are summarized in Table 11-13. The profiles in figures 11-3 and 11-4 also show the means for both the clinical and normal samples. There are clearly significant differences between these groups for males as well as for females (males: Wilks' Lambda = 0.6053; χ^2 = 314.52; p < 0.0001; females: Wilks' Lambda = 0.5605; χ^2 = 413.60; p < 0.0001).

As noted in Table 11-13, all scales but CYN present statistically significant differences for males. For females, even CYN discriminates significantly between normal and clinical subjects. DEP and WRK outweigh all other scales. This find-

Table 11-14. Group Centroids of the Canonical Discriminant Functions
for Clinical Scale Scores of the Chilean Men

Group	Normal Subjects	Reactive Disorders	Personality Disorders	Psychosis	Others
Canonical Function 1	–0.3779	1.9082	2.1134	0.5920	1.7358
Canonical Function 2	–0.0547	–0.0846	–0.3239	2.6912	–0.2217

ing is consistent with the Social Maladjustment dimension found in the factor analysis discussed earlier. Discriminant analysis between normal and abnormal subjects seems to corroborate the proposed designation for the factor.

A discriminant analysis differentiating the four nosological groups was also performed (see Tables 11-14 to 11-17 and Figures 11-5 to 11-8). However, a note of caution is needed about this analysis because the normal groups are quite small. The standardized canonical weights for significant discriminant functions on both the clinical scales and the content scales are summarized in Tables 11-10 through 11-18. Group centroids for the clinical scales in the male sample are presented in Table 11-14 and Figure 11-5. Values for the two significant discriminant functions in the male sample were Wilks' Lambda = 0.464; χ^2 = 481.814; p < 0.0001 and Wilks' Lambda = 0.792; χ^2 = 146.516; p < 0.0001. The scales with highest weights in the first function are Pt (0.70), D (0.47), and Hy (0.48). Sc (1.36) and Pt (-0.94) outweigh all other scales in the second function.

As the figure shows, the first function maximally discriminates between normal subjects and patients with reactive as well as personality disorders, and the second function very significantly discriminates the group of psychotics. The average percentage of correct classification is 74.7%. The normal group is correctly predicted

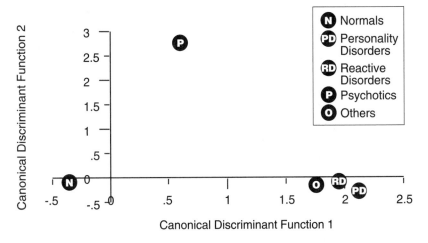

Figure 11-5. Group Centroids for Canonical Discriminant Functions for Chilean Males (Clinical Scales)

Table 11-15. Group Centroids of the Canonical Discriminant Functions
for Clinical Scale Scores of the Chilean Women

Group	Normal Subjects	Reactive Disorders	Personality Disorders	Psychosis	Others
Canonical Function 1	–0.4616	2.2420	2.1430	1.5892	1.2783
Canonical Function 2	–0.0162	–0.4542	–0.0996	1.5673	0.5905

by the MMPI-2 in 81.4% of the cases. On the other hand, the best prediction for the abnormal group corresponds to the reactive disorders.

Table 11-15 and Figure 11-6 summarize the results for females. The two significant discriminant functions (Wilks' Lambda = 0.453; χ^2 = 566.25; p < 0.0001 and Wilks' Lambda = 0.886; χ^2 = 86.26; p < 0.0001) exhibit highly significant weights for the same scales for males. The first function shows the highest coefficients for D (0.63), Hy (0.35), and Sc (0.31). The second function presents the highest weights for Sc (1.16) and Pt (-0.94). Both discriminant functions differentiate in the same direction discussed above for the male sample.

Table 11-16 and Figure 11-7 summarize group centroids of the discriminant functions for males for the content scales. Two significant discriminant functions were recognized as well (Wilks' Lambda = 0.474; χ^2 = 467.03; p < 0.0001 and Wilks' Lambda = 0.788; χ^2 = 149.25; p < 0.0001). In the first function, WRK (0.79), DEP (0.76), CYN (-0.56), TRT (-0.39), and LSE (-0.30) are the scales with the highest weights. The BIZ (0.97) scale outweighs all others in the second function. This finding is consistent with the results reported by Arbisi in his study of psychotic patients at VA hospitals (Arbisi, 1993). Likewise these results are consistent with Ben-Porath, Butcher, and Graham's findings (1991) with schizophrenics.

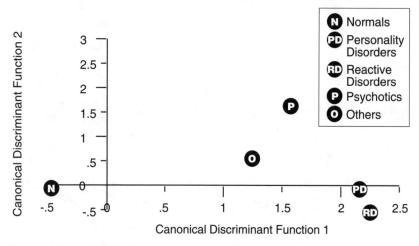

Figure 11-6. Group Centroids for Canonical Discriminant Functions for Chilean Females (Clinical Scales)

Table 11-16. Group Centroids of the Canonical Discriminant Functions
for Content Scale Scores of the Chilean Men

Group	Normal Subjects	Reactive Disorders	Personality Disorders	Psychosis	Others
Canonical Function 1	−0.3758	1.8737	1.8637	1.1771	1.6758
Canonical Function 2	−0.0269	−0.5935	−0.1265	2.6280	−0.2939

Discrimination operates in the same direction described for the clinical scales,
providing additional information for diagnostic purposes. The average percentage
of correct classification of the cases was 74.2%, and the most accurately identified
group of patients was psychotics (77.8%). The rest of the nosological groups present a fairly small percentage of correct classification, 26.1% and 45.9%.

Results for females are summarized in Table 11-17 and Figure 11-8. Two significant discriminant functions were also identified for the female samples (Wilks'
Lambda = 0.472; χ^2 = 435.47; p < 0.0001 and Wilks' Lambda = 0.849;
χ^2 = 116.84; p < 0.0001). The first function is most highly weighted on the WRK
(0.58), DEP (0.53), ANX (0.35), and CYN (-0.36) scales. In the second dimension the BIZ (0.93), ASP (0.55), ANX (-0.50), and WRK (-0.43) scales outweigh
the rest.

The average percentage of correct classification is 74.3%, and in general
these scales have a somewhat better predictive potential. Nevertheless, correct
classification for female psychotics is somewhat lower than for males. This finding must be interpreted cautiously owing to the sample structure of the clinical
groups.

Two types of norms were derived: linear T scores and uniform T scores. The

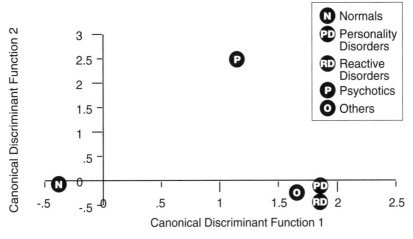

Figure 11-7. Group Centroids for Canonical Discriminant Functions for Chilean Males (Content Scales)

Table 11-17. Group Centroids of the Canonical Discriminant Functions
for Content Scale Scores of the Chilean Women

Group	Normal Subjects	Reactive Disorders	Personality Disorders	Psychosis	Others
Canonical Function 1	−0.4238	2.0846	1.8526	1.6068	1.3547
Canonical Function. 2	−0.0126	−0.3632	−0.3187	1.7947	0.7167

former are those traditionally used with the MMPI; the latter were based on a procedure for the MMPI-2 derived by Tellegen and Ben-Porath (1992) to ensure
percentile comparability of the T scores across scales.

Cross-Cultural Comparisons

Figures 11-9 and 11-10 provide mean raw score profiles of the traditional clinical
and validity scales for the Chilean male and female samples, respectively, compared
with the mean profile for the U.S. MMPI-2 normative samples. As the figures
show, the mean validity and clinical scale profiles are similar for the normative
samples of both countries. This overlapping of profiles points to a high degree of
cross-cultural convergence in MMPI-2 response patterns. An analysis of the content scales and the new validity scales also shows a very similar configuration in
the scale elevations of both samples (Figures 11-11 and 11-12). The differences
observed in some of the scales might be due to cultural differences between the
countries.

The comparison between both national samples at the item endorsement frequency level tends to corroborate the above results. In fact, only 19 extreme items

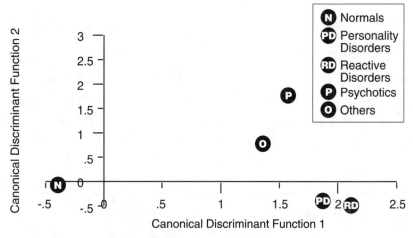

Figure 11-8. Group Centroids for Canonical Discriminant Functions for Chilean Females (Content
Scales)

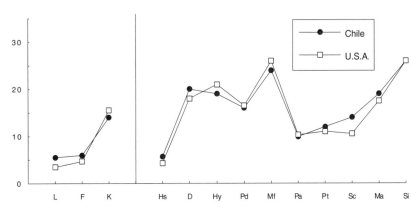

Figure 11-9. Mean MMPI-2 Clinical Profile for Chilean Normative Men (Raw Scores)

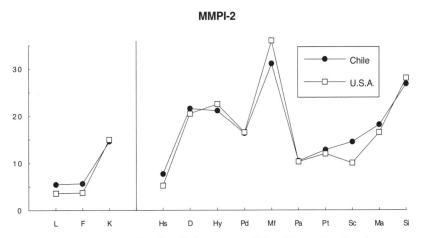

Figure 11-10. Mean MMPI-2 Clinical Profile for Normative Chilean Women (Raw Scores)

show endorsement differences greater than 30%, as can be seen in Table 11-18. These items are distributed among 15 scales, with only one or two items per scale. The low percentage of items with extreme endorsement differences provides strong support for the cross-cultural validity and equivalence of the Chilean MMPI-2 translation and the English original.

Most of these item response differences are likely due to different sociocultural behavioral patterns (e.g., voting behavior in political elections, different views about sexual freedom for women, social prestige of the military, etc.). A few differences might be attributable to the translation, without compromising the functioning of the scales involved.

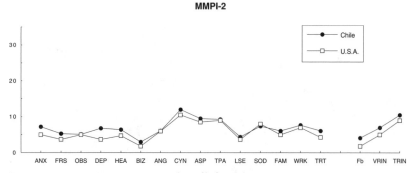

Figure 11-11. Mean MMPI-2 Content Scale Profile for Chilean Men (Raw Scores)

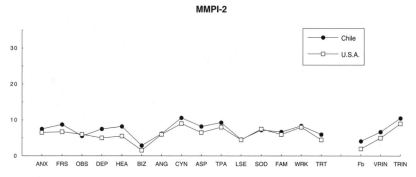

Figure 11-12. Mean MMPI-2 Content Scale Profile for Chilean Women (Raw Scores)

Case Studies

For the purpose of illustrating the cross-national validity and application of the Chilean version of the MMPI-2, we present three cases with special features.

Case 1

This case is exemplary of the international collaboration between the Chilean program and James Butcher of the University of Minnesota. This subject (female, 18 years old) participated in the experimental administration of the MMPI-2 in the Catholic University student standardization sample at the beginning of the academic year (the linear T-score profile is shown in Figures 11-13 and 11-14). The raw scores were faxed to Dr. Butcher for blind interpretation. That same day the following transcription of Dr. Butcher's report was faxed back to Chile:

> The young woman is in a great deal of distress at the moment and is presenting herself as being very seriously disturbed. This might reflect very serious psychopathology or an effort on her part to receive attention and help for immediate problems. Given that her pattern of responses is quite consistent (note the low VRIN and

Table 11-18. Comparison of "True" Item Endorsement between the Chilean Normative Sample and the U.S. Normative Sample*

Scale	L Ma	F ANX	K FRS	D WRK	Hy Es	Pa MAC-R	Pt MT	Sc
n	1 2	2 1	1 1	1 2	1 1	2 1	2 1	1
Items	232 269, 88	30, 306 415	348 447	118 525, 31	193 447	334, 286 439	331, 170 472	168

*Endorsement differences greater than 30% for both genders, alpha < 0.01.

TRIN scores suggest that she is responding in a consistent manner and not simply giving all true or false responses), it is likely that her high scores are credible and indicate severe psychopathology or extreme turmoil.

Her extreme distress centers around symptoms of depression and anxiousness. She is also reporting symptoms of a serious thinking disturbance. She is presenting very bizarre thoughts with an obsessional quality. It is likely she is experiencing symptoms of being out of control and being unable to manage her life very well at this time. She is reporting a great deal of concern over her health.

She appears to be an individual who has low self-esteem and great insecurity. She feels that she is quite incapacitated at this time and not able to manage her life very well. Her item content (critical items) should be evaluated for possible suicidal ideation.

She feels pretty hopeless about life at this time and feels that she is unworthy. It may be difficult for her to make positive changes in her life because she lacks energy and direction. However, she appears to need considerable attention and reassurance at this time because of her extreme anxiousness and low mood.

We sought an external opinion of this case because we at the university knew of the suicide of this young women through the wide media coverage given the event in Santiago. This young women had dropped out of the university a few months after entrance and committed suicide about six months later. She committed a very unusual suicide by jumping out of the seventh floor window of her family's apartment in a middle- to upper-class neighborhood, holding hands with her closest female friend.

Cases 2 and 3

These cases involve two middle-class women who are currently involved in an interdisciplinary obesity treatment program conducted by the School of Medicine of the Catholic University of Chile. Our research team was asked to provide a personality assessment as a component of the treatment strategies of the program.

The patients are a mother, 55 years of age, and her daughter, 24. Figures 11-15 and 11-16 provide the clinical and content scale profiles for the mother (case 2).

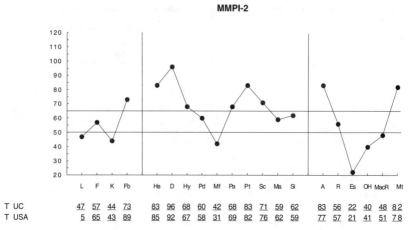

MMPI-2

	L	F	K	Fb	Hs	D	Hy	Pd	Mf	Pa	Pt	Sc	Ma	Si	A	R	Es	OH	MacR	Mt
T UC	47	57	44	73	83	96	68	60	42	68	83	71	59	62	83	56	22	40	48	82
T USA	5	65	43	89	85	92	67	58	31	69	82	76	62	59	77	57	21	41	51	78

Figure 11-13. MMPI-2 Clinical Profile of a Suicidal 18-Year-Old Chilean Woman (Case 1)

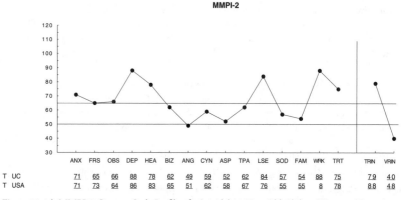

MMPI-2

	ANX	FRS	OBS	DEP	HEA	BIZ	ANG	CYN	ASP	TPA	LSE	SOD	FAM	WRK	TRT	TRIN	VRIN
T UC	71	65	66	88	78	62	49	59	52	62	84	57	54	88	75	79	40
T USA	71	73	64	86	83	65	51	62	58	67	76	55	55	8	78	88	48

Figure 11-14. MMPI-2 Content Scale Profile of a Suicidal 18-Year-Old Chilean Woman (Case 1)

This profile has extreme elevations on D (91T), Pt (79T), Es (24T), ANX (81T), LSE (69T), and WRK (79T). The analysis of the MMPI-2 critical items show suicidal risk as well (e.g., item 524). She is a housewife who suffers from morbid obesity. She has been in psychiatric treatment for several years. She lives with her husband and two children; both children are also extremely obese. She has always had a very dysfunctional relationship with her husband. The clinical history gathered by the physicians in the program shows very severe family conflict during her entire married life. The patient reported that she perceived herself as "psychologically tortured" by her mother-in-law. She reported truly traumatic experiences during her first years of marriage, due to the necessity (for economic reasons) of sharing the home with her in-laws. Clinicians describe her as a very

MMPI-2

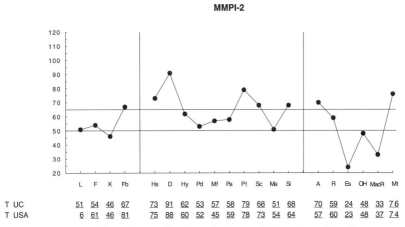

	L	F	K	Fb		Hs	D	Hy	Pd	Mf	Pa	Pt	Sc	Ma	Si		A	R	Es	OH	MacR	Mt
T UC	51	54	46	67		73	91	62	53	57	58	79	68	51	68		70	59	24	48	33	76
T USA	6	61	46	81		75	88	60	52	45	59	78	73	54	64		57	60	23	48	37	74

Figure 11-15. MMPI-2 Clinical Profile of a 55-Year-Old Obese Chilean Woman (Case 2)

MMPI-2

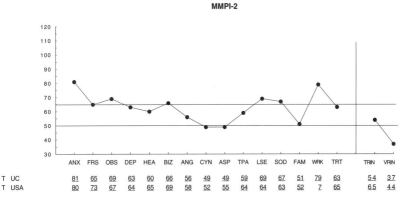

	ANX	FRS	OBS	DEP	HEA	BIZ	ANG	CYN	ASP	TPA	LSE	SOD	FAM	WRK	TRT		TRIN	VRIN
T UC	81	65	69	63	60	66	56	49	49	59	69	67	51	79	63		54	37
T USA	80	73	67	64	65	69	58	52	55	64	64	63	52	7	65		65	44

Figure 11-16. MMPI-2 Content Scale Profile of a 55-Year-Old Obese Chilean Woman (Case 2)

anxious and depressive person who increases her food intake whenever she feels unable to cope with conflicts.

The MMPI-2 profiles shown in Figures 11-17 and 11-18 provide the results for the daughter, who lives within the same family situation as her mother. She is described by clinicians as a very sweet young woman who shares the same food intake pattern as her mother. She also presents a clinical history of upper gastrointestinal bleeding and very frequent headaches. Her emotional life has been severely restricted and controlled by her father, whom she describes as "very jealous." There are extreme elevations on D (96T), Pt (83T), A (83T), Es (22T), ANX (71T), DEP (88T), LSE (84T), WRK (88T), and TRT (75T). Critical items also show a high suicidal risk (e.g., items 303 and 504).

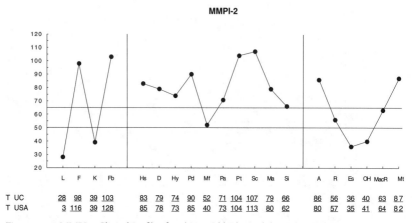

Figure 11-17. MMPI-2 Clinical Profile of a 24-Year-Old Obese Chilean Woman (Case 3)

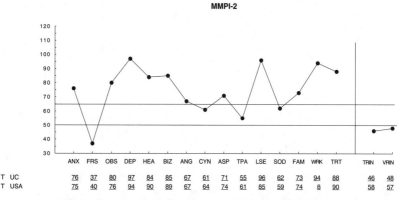

Figure 11-18. MMPI-2 Content Scale Profile of a 24-Year-Old Obese Chilean Woman (Case 3)

Current and Future Developments

At present, a longitudinal study panel on psychological maladjustment of university students is being carried out, supported by a FONDECYT grant. The aim of the study is to identify relations between the psychological status evaluated at university admission and criterion variables such as drop-out rate, psychological turmoil during the course of studies, and academic achievement. The model of adaptation being used (Vitalino, Maiuro, Russo, & Mitchell, 1989) defines psychological distress as a multivariate phenomenon comprising four critical variables: stress-provoking agents in a given situation, basic vulnerability of this personality structure (as measured by the MMPI-2), subjects' coping resources (also measured by the MMPI-2), and social support network.

A sample of 2,000 freshmen has been evaluated on two occasions during 1993 and will be followed for two more years. Another cohort of the same size, belonging to the 1994 entering class, will be included. The main hypothesis being tested is that students having high levels of distress at university admission will have at least equal levels of distress in a posterior assessment at a time of high academic pressure; a higher rate of psychological decompensation; a higher risk of low academic achievement; and higher drop-out rates than students with a lower level of initial distress. Several studies are also being done in relation to medical diagnostic and treatment programs in conjunction with the Catholic University Medical School, in areas such as obesity, epilepsy, and sleep disorders.

Conclusions

The study undertaken provides important evidence in a first approximation of the cross-cultural validity of the MMPI-2 in Chile. This statement is based on the following observations obtained from the foregoing analysis.

1. The translation resulted in a version of the MMPI-2 that is linguistically and psychometrically equivalent to the English-language version. The Chilean version has been used in a Puerto Rican study (Colon, 1993) with slight modifications—only 31 items were found to be culturally inappropriate for the local sample—and it was also used in the evaluation of the MMPI-2 in Argentina.
2. The standardization study provided significant evidence regarding the convergence of the average profiles of the Chilean and U.S. normative samples, as well as a high internal consistency of the scales, sometimes higher than those found in the original version. These data support the psychometric soundness of the Chilean version, particularly with regard to the content scales.
3. The results of the factor analysis are consistent with those reported for the U.S. sample and with the studies previously undertaken by the same team (Rissetti et al., 1989a). It should also be pointed out that the factors obtained in the analysis of the content scales contribute more specific dimensions to clinical diagnosis, and eventually could have implications for the use of the instrument in other contexts, for example, the area of organizational behavior with regard to adaptation to work and stress, and in higher education with the aim of predicting adaptation problems, or for counseling purposes.
4. The discriminant validity of the MMPI-2 in Chile (separating normals from patients) appears almost at the same level as that found in previous work done in Chile (Rissetti & Maltes, 1985; Rissetti et al., 1989a) and

also in the study by Butcher et al. (1989). Content scales contribute relevant data for discriminating between the different nosological groups, thus becoming promising scale indicators in this area. This finding is consistent with those reported in other recent studies (Ben-Porath et al., 1991).

5. The preceding conclusions reveal the likelihood of a successful transition to the Spanish version of the MMPI-2 in Chile, with the comparative advantage that the new content scales will probably broaden the use of the instrument in Chile.

References

Arbisi, P. (May, 1993). Assessing profiles of individuals with severe mental disorders. Presented at the 29th annual meeting of the MMPI-2 Workshop & Symposium, Minneapolis, MN.

Ben-Porath, Y. S. (1990). Cross-cultural assessment of personality: The case for replicatory factor analysis. In J. N. Butcher & C. D. Spielberger (Eds.), *Recent advances in personality assessment* (Vol. 8). Hillsdale, NJ: Erlbaum.

Ben-Porath, Y. S., Butcher, J. N., & Graham, J. R. (1991). Contribution of the MMPI-2 content scales to the differential diagnosis of schizophrenia and major depression. *Psychology, 3*, 634–640.

Butcher, J. N., & Clark, L. A. (1979). Recent trends in cross-cultural MMPI research and application: Chile. In J. N. Butcher (Ed.), *New developments in the use of the MMPI.* Minneapolis: University of Minnesota Press.

Butcher, J. N., Dahlstrom, W. G., Graham, J. R., Tellegen, A., & Kaemmer, B. (1989). *MMPI-2 (Minnesota Multiphasic Personality Inventory 2): Manual for administration and scoring.* Minneapolis: University of Minnesota Press.

Butcher, J. N., & Pancheri, P. (1976). *A handbook of cross-national MMPI research.* Minneapolis: University of Minnesota Press.

Colon, C. C. P. (1993). *Relationship between the MMPI-2 content scales and psychiatric symptoms with Puerto Rican college students and psychiatric patients.* Proposal for Ph.D. in psychology with specialization in clinical psychology. Centro Caribeño de Estudios Postgraduados, San Juan, Puerto Rico.

Dahlstrom, W. G., Welsh, G. S., & Dahlstrom, L. E. (1972). *An MMPI handbook: research interpretation* (Vol. I). Minneapolis: University of Minnesota Press.

Dahlstrom, W. G., Welsh, G. S., & Dahlstrom, L. E. (1975). *An MMPI handbook: research interpretation* (Vol. II). Minneapolis: University of Minnesota Press.

Gough, H. G. (1965). Cross-cultural validation of a measure of a social behavior. *Psychological Reports, 17*, 379–387.

Graham, J. R. (1990). *MMPI-2. Assessing personality and psychopathology.* New York: Oxford University Press.

Hathaway, S. R. (1970). *Research pertinent to the Spanish-American cross-validation of the MMPI.* Paper given at the 5th Annual Symposium on Recent Developments in the Use of the MMPI, Mexico City.

Himmel, E., Maltes, S. G., & Rissetti, F. J. (1979). *Validez de constructo del MMPI en la población universitaria chilena: Un enfoque transcultural.* Santiago de Chile: Pontificia Universidad Católica de Chile, Vicerrectoría Académica, Dirección de Asuntos Estudiantiles, Departamento de Salud Estudiantil, Nº9.

Rissetti, F. J., Butcher, J. N., Agostini, J., Elgueta, M., Gaete, S., Margulies, T., Morlans, I., & Ruiz, R. (1979a). *Translation and adaptation of the MMPI in Chile: Use in a university student health service*. Paper given at the 14th Annual Symposium on Recent Developments in the Use of the MMPI, St. Petersburg, FL.

Rissetti, F. J., Butcher, J. N., Agostini, J., Elgueta, M., Gaete, S., Margulies, T., Morlans, I., & Ruiz, R. (1979b). *La experiencia chilena con el MMPI*. Santiago de Chile: Pontificia Universidad Católica de Chile, Dirección de Asuntos Estudiantiles, Departamento de Salud Estudiantil. Trabajo presentado en el XVIII Congreso Interamericano de Psicologia, Lima, Perú.

Rissetti, F. J., Butcher, J. N., Agostini, J., Elgueta, M., Gaete, S., Margulies, T., Morlans, I., & Ruiz, R. (1979c). *Estudios transnacionales y transculturales con el MMPI*. Santiago de Chile: Pontificia Universidad Católica de Chile, Dirección de Asuntos Estudiantiles, Departamento de Salud Estudiantil. Trabajo presentado en el XVIII Congreso Interamericano de Psicologia, Lima, Perú.

Rissetti, F. J., Himmel, E., Maltes, S. G., González, J. A., & Olmos, S. (1989a). Estandarización del inventario Multifásico de Personalidad de Minnesota (MMPI) en población adulta Chilena. *Revista Chilena de Psicologia, 1*, 41–62.

Rissetti, F. J., Himmel, E., Maltes, S. G., González, J. A., & Olmos, S. (1989b). *Standardization of the Minnesota Multiphasic Personality Inventory (MMPI) in Chilean adult population*. Paper presented at the 24th Annual Symposium on Recent Developments in the Use of the MMPI, Honolulu, HI.

Rissetti, F. J., & Maltes, S. G. (1985a). Use of the MMPI in Chile. In J. N. Butcher & C. D. Spielberger (Eds.), *Advances in personality assessment* (Vol. 4, pp. 209–257). Hillsdale, NJ: Erlbaum.

Rissetti, F. J., & Maltes, S. C. (1985b). Validez predictiva del MMPI en la población universitaria de la P. Universidad Católica de Chile. *Cuadernos Consejo de Rectores, Universidades Chilenas, 24*, 192–203.

Rissetti, F. J., Montiel, F., Maltes, S., Hermosilla, M., & Fleischli, A. M. (1978). *Traducción al castellano del Minnesota Multiphasic Personality Inventory (MMPI)*. Santiago de Chile: Pontificia Universidad Católica de Chile, Dirección de Asuntos Estudiantiles, Servicio de Salud Estudiantil.

Tellegen, A., & Ben-Porath, Y. S. (1992). The new uniform T scores for the MMPI-2: Rationale, derivation and appraisal. *Psychological Assessment, 2*, 145–155.

Vitalino, P. P., Maiuro, R., Russo, J., & Mitchell, J. (1989). Medical student distress. A longitudinal study. *The Journal of Nervous and Mental Diseases, 2*, 70–76.

Wiggins, J. S. (1973). *Personality and prediction: principles of personality assessment*. Reading, MA: Addison-Wesley.

Chapter 12

Studies of the MMPI-2 in Argentina

Maria Martina Casullo and Lorenzo Garcia Samartino
in collaboration with Maria Elena Brenlla, Miguel A. Marquez,
and Daniel Gómez Dupertuis

The original MMPI was translated into Spanish in Argentina in 1964 by the Psychological Assessment Service of the University of Buenos Aires Vocational Guidance Department (Casullo, 1964). It was not extensively used in clinical settings but was used in personnel screening in the field of organizational psychology as well as being employed for research purposes in some national universities as a technique for clinically assessing patients from psychiatric hospitals.

With its revision and reintroduction as the MMPI-2 (Butcher, Dahlstrom, Graham, Tellegen, & Kaemmer, 1989), a new era in the history of the MMPI began internationally. We began developing the Argentine MMPI-2 in 1991 by obtaining the Spanish version developed for Chile by Risetti, Himmel, et al. (1989).

This chapter provides a general description of the adaptation procedures followed in Argentina and describes empirical research on the application of the Argentine Spanish version with general population subjects, psychiatric outpatients from J. T. Borda Neuropsychiatric Hospital (Buenos Aires), psychiatric patients being seen at a psychopathology service in a general hospital (French Hospital, Buenos Aires), psychiatric forensic research data, college students, and male applicants to an army school.

Procedures for the Development of the Argentine Version of the MMPI-2

The Argentine adaptation of the MMPI-2 was derived from the Chilean Spanish translation of the test and from a translation and back-translation developed by two bilingual psychologists working on our research team. Our work took into account both the linguistic and conceptual equivalence of the items. When these two considerations conflicted, we gave priority to conceptual equivalence.

All 567 items of the MMPI-2 were translated by the first author (MMC) and another bilingual psychologist independently. We next evaluated the accuracy and cultural sensitivity of the items and made modifications accordingly. Both translations were compared to the Chilean Spanish version; some words were changed to adapt them to "folk" or "local" verbal expressions in Argentina. The accuracy of our final adaptation was evaluated by two back-translation studies into English. The resulting translations were compared for discrepancies. Several additional steps were taken to further facilitate MMPI-2 research in Argentina.

First, a Spanish test manual (Brenlla, Diuk, & Maristany, 1992) was written to provide current information on MMPI-2 history, development, structure, and administration and scoring procedures in order to train people participating in research and university students who do not read or speak English. Second, we incorporated the MMPI-2 in the academic curriculum in a course on psychological assessment taught at the Faculty of Psychology of the University of Buenos Aires. Finally, we developed several training workshops for professional psychologists and physicians working in the psychiatric and general hospitals participating in the project, and for professionals working on the Forensic Medical Board.

Research on the MMPI-2 in Argentina

Study 1: General Population

Information was collected from an initial sample composed of 600 Argentine subjects who were friends, relatives, or neighbors of college psychology students from Belgrano and Buenos Aires, two universities in the metropolitan Buenos Aires (D.C.) area, and from the National University of La Plata, located in the capital city of Buenos Aires state. Students who had attended and passed the course on psychological assessment were invited to participate in our research group on the MMPI-2. They were in charge of inviting people to voluntarily take part in the project by answering a booklet form of the test, following the standard instructions.

Test administration was conducted individually and SES (socioeconomic status) was calculated. We began gathering data in April 1992. This report contains information collected until November 1993.

We used the following inclusion criteria:

- males and females ages 18 to 60 years
- subjects with complete elementary school education
- subjects not under psychiatric care and who had not been in treatment during the past five years
- subjects who voluntarily and anonymously wanted to participate

From a total of 600 protocols gathered in the first stage of our project, 64 were eliminated because of high raw scores (equal to or greater than two standard deviations) on scale F.

We used the following exclusion criteria:

Table 12-1. MMPI-2 Means and Standard Deviations for Argentine Women (N = 307) and Argentine Men (N = 249)

Scale	Females N = 307		Males N = 249		t*
	X	s	X	s	
Age	30.81	9.2	31.3	9.3	
L	5.12	2.3	5.7	2.4	
F	8.15	4.6	7.9	5.6	
K	14.4	3.7	14.8	4.8	
Hs	15.1	5.0	14.5	4.4	2.35
D	23.1	5.0	22.0	4.6	1.84
Hy	25.3	5.3	21.0	4.0	2.53
Pd	23.2	6.3	22.5	5.8	
Mf	31.4	4.3	27.5	5.4	3.42
Pa	10.8	3.5	10.8	4.0	
Pt	31.1	7.1	30.4	7.3	
Sc	32.7	9.3	32.8	9.8	
Ma	23.5	5.9	24.1	5.3	
Si	30.5	7.3	30.2	7.6	

* t significant 2-tail prob. ≥ 0.05 or 0.01

- subject was currently in psychiatric or psychological treatment or had been in the past five years
- item omissions of 25 or more items were verified
- the standard F scale score was 25 or higher

Applying the criteria outlined above resulted in 12% of the initial sample being eliminated.

The final Argentine sample in this first step of our project consisted of 556 subjects (249 men and 307 women), all of them living in the city of Buenos Aires and its suburban area and in La Plata city. The mean age for the male sample was 31.3 (s.d. 9.3) and for the female sample 30.8 (s.d. 9.3).

According to the calculated SES, this sample is composed of:

socioeconomic status level	%
low	10
middle	85
high	5

MMPI-2

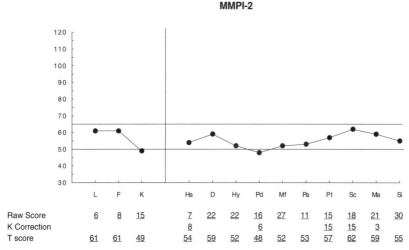

Figure 12-1. Group Mean MMPI-2 Profile of a Sample of Argentine Men from the General Population (N = 249)

MMPI-2

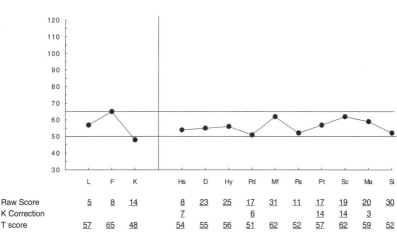

Figure 12-2. Group Mean MMPI-2 Profile of a Sample of Argentine Women from the General Population (N = 307)

All the comparisons were made on validity and clinical scales, based on K-corrected scores. All the scores are plotted on U.S. norms. Since all scoring and analyses were conducted manually, we initially completed work on the validity and clinical scales. Work on the content and supplementary scales will be reported later.

The means and standard deviations for males and females are reported in Table 12-1. We found four significant statistical differences between genders for this

Table 12-2. Comparison of Argentine Women (N = 307) with Normative Sample Women from the United States (N = 1,462)

Scale	Argentina N = 307		U.S. N = 1,462	
	X	s	X	s
L	5.1	2.3	3.5	2.0
F	8.1	4.6	3.6	2.9
K	14.4	3.7	15.0	4.5
Hs	15.1	5.0	13.6	4.0
D	23.1	5.0	20.1	4.9
Hy	25.3	5.3	22.0	4.7
Pd	23.2	6.2	22.2	4.5
Mf	31.4	4.3	35.9	4.0
Pa	10.8	3.5	10.2	2.9
Pt	31.1	7.1	27.7	5.1
Sc	32.7	9.3	26.2	5.9
Ma	23.5	5.9	19.0	4.2
Si	30.5	7.3	27.9	9.1

Table 12-3. Comparison of Argentine Men (N = 249) with Normative Sample Men from the United States (N = 1,138)

Scale	Argentina N = 249		U.S. N = 1,138	
	X	s	X	s
L	5.7	2.4	3.5	2.2
F	7.9	5.6	4.5	3.2
K	14.8	4.8	15.3	4.7
Hs	14.5	4.4	12.7	3.8
D	22.0	4.6	18.3	4.5
Hy	21.0	4.0	20.8	4.7
Pd	22.5	5.8	22.6	4.6
Mf	21.5	5.4	26.0	5.0
Pa	10.8	4.0	10.1	2.8
Pt	30.4	7.3	26.4	5.0
Sc	32.8	9.8	26.4	5.9
Ma	24.1	5.3	19.9	4.2
Si	30.2	7.6	25.8	8.5

Table 12-4. MMPI-2 Means and Standard Deviations for
Argentine College Women (N = 43) and Men (N = 51)

Scale	Men N = 51			Women N = 43	
	X	s	t*	X	s
Age	21.9	1.5		20.7	1.0
L	4.6	2.1		4.4	2.2
F	6.6	3.5		7.1	3.3
K	14.4	4.1		14.2	3.6
Hs	14.3	4.5		16.1	4.8
D	19.6	3.9	4.04	23.7	5.7
Hy	20.9	3.7	2.23	23.0	5.3
Pd	21.8	4.5		21.3	4.9
Mf	27.0	5.4	5.93	32.5	3.8
Pa	10.3	3.7		10.2	3.5
Pt	30.2	5.5		32.1	5.7
Sc	31.4	6.0		32.8	6.9
Ma	23.5	4.3		22.4	4.6
Si	27.8	6.2	2.05	30.8	8.0

* t significant 2 tail prob. ≥ 0.01 or 0.05

sample (t test), with females scoring higher on scales 1, 2, 3, and 5. In Figures 12-1
and 12-2, the means profiles are shown plotted against U.S. norms.

Data comparing normative studies of general populations in Argentina and in
the United States are reported in Tables 12-2 and 12-3. It is important to point
out that our data include only subjects living in two urban areas, Buenos Aires and
La Plata; North American data were obtained on samples from different states in
the United States.

Study 2: MMPI-2 Study of College Students

The Argentine adaptation of the MMPI-2 was administered to a group of 100
students with different majors from the National University of La Plata, who volunteered and responded anonymously. This study was coordinated by Professor
Daniel Gómez Dupertuis. Tests were individually administered. The MMPI-2
means and standard deviations by sex are reported in Table 12-4 (n = 43 women,
57 men). For this group, significant statistical differences between gender (t test)
were found for the following scales:

   3 and 5 (as for the general population sample)
   2 and 0 (women college students had higher scores than did the men)

Table 12-5. Comparison of Means and Standard Deviations for Argentine Normals (N = 553) and Argentine Psychiatric Patients (N = 156)

Scale	General Population N = 553		t*	Psychiatric Outpatients General Hospital N = 156	
	X	s		X	s
Age	31.0	9.2		34.2	16.0
L	5.4	2.3		5.4	2.5
F	8.0	4.5	5.41	13.0	4.5
K	14.6	3.6	2.98	10.9	5.4
Hs	14.9	4.5	6.84	19.8	4.9
D	22.7	4.9	8.47	28.7	5.8
Hy	23.2	5.9	6.34	27.1	5.3
Pd	22.8	5.7	6.71	27.1	5.5
Mf	-.-	-.-		-.-	-.-
Pa	10.8	3.8	6.33	14.2	3.9
Pt	30.8	7.1	8.70	37.1	6.7
Sc	32.8	9.4	7.40	40.1	8.8
Ma	23.7	5.6		22.5	7.6
Si	30.3	7.4	6.59	35.8	4.4

* t significant 2 tail prob. ≥ 0.01

Study 3: MMPI-2 Study of Psychiatric Outpatients from a General Hospital

This study was coordinated by psychiatrist Dr. Miguel Marquez, Psychopathology Service Director, French General Hospital, located in Buenos Aires city. Patients were administered the MMPI-2 (Argentine version) as part of the psychodiagnostic admissions process implemented by the Psychopathology Service (N = 156). The means and standard deviations for the MMPI-2 validity and clinical scales for the psychiatric outpatient sample and the general population sample (study 1) are shown in Table 12-5.

It is interesting to note that significant statistical differences (t test) were found between the two samples (general population and outpatients) for all scales except L, and outpatients obtained higher scores on ten scales.

The MMPI-2 data on psychiatric outpatients by gender (116 women, 40 men) are reported in Table 12-6. The different sample size reflects the usual proportion by gender of patients receiving psychiatric care in the service. Statistical differences by gender (t test) are found for scales 1 and 3, with women scoring higher (p > .05).

Table 12-6. MMPI-2 Means and Standard Deviations for Psychiatric Outpatients from
French General Hospital in Argentina

Scale	Females N = 116		t*	Males N = 40	
	X	s		X	s
Age	35.5	16.1		30.7	15.5
L	5.6	2.4		4.9	2.7
F	10.9	5.2		10.9	5.9
K	13.2	4.7		12.6	4.2
Hs	20.5	4.9	2.79	18.1	4.5
D	29.2	5.9		27.2	5.2
Hy	27.6	5.3	1.92	25.8	4.9
Pd	27.0	5.7		27.5	4.7
Mf	33.4	4.1		27.5	3.7
Pa	14.4	3.7		13.9	4.5
Pt	37.2	6.7		36.7	6.9
Sc	40.2	8.9		39.7	8.4
Ma	22.2	4.3		23.4	4.4
Si	35.9	7.7		35.5	7.4

* t significant 2-tail prob. ≥ 0.05 or 0.01

Study 4: Forensic Psychiatric Inpatients and Outpatients from a Neuropsychiatric Hospital

This study is being coordinated by psychiatrist Lorenzo Garcia Samartino, who coordinated Buenos Aires Forensic Medical Corp. (Cuerpo Médico Forense). The data collection in this inpatient psychiatric sample was carried out by psychologist V. Ferrante. All subjects are males who are in jail, with a psychiatric diagnosis that requires their referral to a special unit located in Borda General Neuropsychiatric Hospital (Buenos Aires city). The MMPI-2 was individually administered to each resident in the psychiatric unit (Figure 12-3).

The socioeconomic data indicate that 90% belong to the middle class. The means and standard deviations of the validity and clinical scales of the patients from this sample (N = 21) are shown in Table 12-7. They are compared with those of psychiatric outpatients (study 3). The forensic psychiatric patients have statistically significantly higher scores on scales L and 6 compared with the psychiatric outpatients. Figure 12-3 shows the group profile of this sample (21 male forensic psychiatric patients) plotted on U.S. norms. Table 12-8 presents data on

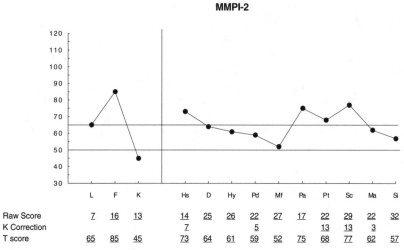

Figure 12-3. Group Mean MMPI-2 Profile of a Sample of Argentine Prison Psychiatric Patients (N = 21)

Table 12-7. MMPI-2 Means and Standard Deviations for Prison Inmates (N = 21 Men) and Psychiatric Outpatients (N = 40 Men)

Scale	Prison Inmates N = 21		t*	Psychiatric Outpatients General Hospital N = 40	
	X	s		X	s
Age	31.7	16.7		30.7	15.5
L	6.7	3.4	2.04	4.9	2.7
F	15.9	10.7		10.9	5.9
K	12.9	4.4		12.6	4.2
Hs	19.4	6.1		18.1	4.5
D	25.3	5.7		27.2	5.2
Hy	26.1	6.2		25.8	4.9
Pd	27.1	4.9		27.2	4.8
Mf	27.4	4.5		27.5	3.7
Pa	16.8	5.0	2.19	13.9	4.5
Pt	35.1	6.7		36.7	6.9
SC	42.1	10.7		39.7	8.4
Ma	25.0	5.2		23.4	4.4
Si	32.4	8.3		35.5	7.4

* t significant 2 tail prob. ≥ 0.05

Table 12-8. MMPI-2 Means and Standard Deviations for Prison Inmates (N = 21 Men) and Neuropsychiatric Hospital Outpatients (N = 41 Men)

Scale	Prison Inmates N = 21			Neuropsychiatric Hospital Outpatients N = 41	
	X	s	t*	X	s
L	6.7	3.4		6.1	2.7
F	15.8	10.7		14.6	7.8
K	12.9	4.4		11.8	4.1
Hs	19.4	6.1	1.84	17.3	5.0
D	25.3	5.7		26.2	6.9
Hy	26.1	6.2		24.2	6.6
Pd	27.1	4.9		25.5	5.2
Mf	27.4	4.5	1.93	24.9	3.0
Pa	16.8	5.0		15.5	5.0
Pt	35.1	6.7		36.3	7.7
Sc	42.1	10.7		41.4	9.8
Ma	25.0	5.2		23.4	5.0
Si	32.4	8.3		34.9	9.5

* t significant 2-tail Prob. ≥ 0.05

prison inmates (N = 21) and the men tested in the neuropsychiatric hospital outpatients group (N = 41). The study with psychiatric patients attending a neuropsychiatric hospital (Day Hospital) is being coordinated by psychologist M.E. Brenlla. The forensic psychiatric inpatients group obtains higher scores on scales 1 and 5.

We have compared data on prison inmates with those obtained from the general population sample (n = 249 men; Table 12-9). Forensic inpatients have higher scores on scales F, 1, 2, 3, 4, 6, 7, and 8.

Study 5: MMPI-2 Profiles of Young Male Applicants to an Army School

Since 1992, administration of the MMPI-2 has been an important component in the admission process to an Army school located in the suburban area of Buenos Aires city (Table 12-10). All tests were administered in group sessions. MMPI-2 K-corrected scores of the Argentine military school applicants are compared to military school applicants in the study by Pongpanich in Thailand (see chapter 7). The profiles of the Army applicants and the sample of men from the general population are compared in Figure 12-4.

Table 12-9. MMPI-2 Means and Standard Deviations for Prison Inmates (N = 21 Men) and Men in the General Population (N = 249)

	Prison Inmates N = 21			General Population N = 249	
Scale	X	s	t*	X	s
Age	31.7	16.7		31.3	9.3
L	6.7	3.4		5.7	2.4
F	15.8	10.7	3.13	7.9	5.5
K	12.9	4.4		14.8	4.8
Hs	19.4	6.1	3.43	14.5	4.4
D	25.3	5.7	2.68	22.0	4.6
Hy	26.1	6.2	3.28	21.0	4.0
Pd	27.1	4.9	2.60	22.5	5.8
Mf	27.4	4.5		27.5	5.4
Pa	16.8	5.0	3.90	10.8	4.0
Pt	35.1	6.7	2.91	30.4	7.3
Sc	42.1	10.7	3.22	32.8	9.8
Ma	25.0	5.2		24.1	5.3
Si	32.4	8.3		30.2	7.6

* t significant 2-tail prob. ≥ 0.05 or 0.01

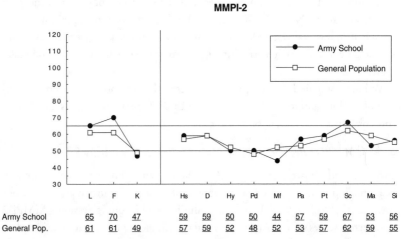

Figure 12-4. Group Mean MMPI-2 Profile of a Sample of Argentine Army Applicants Compared with a Sample of Men from the General Population

Table 12-10. MMPI-2 Means and Standard Deviations for Male Applicants to Army Schools in Argentina (N = Men) and Thailand (N = 282)

Scale	Argentina N = 689		Thailand N = 282	
	X	s	X	s
Age	17.0	1.7	15/20	n/k
L	7.1	2.7	5.8	-.-
F	10.5	6.4	7.8	-.-
K	14.2	4.4	15.8	-.-
Hs	16.4	4.8	13.9	-.-
D	21.6	3.9	19.7	-.-
Hy	20.5	5.2	19.2	-.-
Pd	23.3	4.8	22.0	-.-
Mf	22.6	3.9	20.6	-.-
Pa	11.5	4.1	10.6	-.-
Pt	30.5	5.3	27.7	-.-
Sc	35.9	8.0	32.6	-.-
Ma	22.3	4.3	23.9	-.-
Si	30.9	5.7	29.1	-.-

Summary and Discussion

This article presented several studies of the Argentine version of the MMPI-2, originally developed in Chile. Following recommendations from cross-cultural methodologists, we took into account linguistic and conceptual equivalences in modifying the translated items. Training courses on the use, administration, scoring, and interpretation of the test were organized to facilitate work with professionals on the MMPI-2 in Argentina.

The normative data on the general population included subjects from the middle socioeconomic level, all of them living in two important urban areas of the country, the cities of Buenos Aires and La Plata. Research on the validity and clinical scales has been completed. Significant differences between genders were found for scales 1, 2, 3, and 5 for the general population sample, suggesting that separate norms for men and women are needed. Women express more somatic complaints and more dissatisfaction with life situations than do men and can be seen as more demanding and self-centered. The mean Mf values suggest that Argentine women may be rejecting the traditional female role, revealing themselves as confident and assertive.

It is interesting that Argentine men and women, in comparison with U.S. normative data, obtain higher mean scores on all scales except K, 4, and 6. These differences appear to be small and most are within the standard error of measurement. There may, of course, be some culturally based personality characteristics of Buenos Aires and La Plata inhabitants, who generally are considered active, extroverted, and rebellious, with a tendency to "present an overly positive image" and to deny having psychological conflicts. The small sample size probably influenced the results.

The study conducted with college students shows differences in mean values by gender for scales 1, 2, and 5, as in the general population study. We found, for this college sample, a significant difference by gender on scale 0, but mean values are related to T scores between 50 and 65 for both sexes.

Overall, the MMPI-2 shows a clear sensitivity to psychological problems in Argentina. When mean scores from the general population sample and the psychiatric outpatient sample are compared, we see that the MMPI-2 discriminates between them on all scales except L and 9. Army school applicants show a similar profile to men from the general population sample, although they obtained higher mean scores on scales L, F, 6, 8, and 9, and lower scores on scale 5, perhaps as a result of age differences. Army applicants appear to be more conventional and moralistic, moody, dissatisfied, and action-oriented than are general population men.

We believe that the present Argentine studies of the MMPI-2 suggest a valuable role for future research and clinical personality assessment. Although the samples used in the present studies are relatively small, the MMPI-2 differentiated between normative subjects and clinical groups. Now that the MMPI-2 has been developed and the preliminary research appears promising, we consider it important to gather data on additional samples matching our population census in terms of age and socioeconomic background.

References

Brenlla, M. E., Diuk, L., & Maristany, M. (1992). *Evaluación objetiva de la personalidad.* Aportes del MMPI-2, Psicoteca Ed., Buenos Aires.

Butcher, J., Dahlstrom, W., Graham, J., Tellegen, A., & Kaemmer, B. (1989). *Minnesota Multiphasic Personality Inventory-2 (MMPI-2): Manual for administration and scoring.* Minneapolis: University of Minnesota Press.

Casullo, M. M. (1964). *Adaptación del Cuestionario MMPI, Departamento de Orientación Vocacional,* Universidad de Buenos Aires.

Risetti, F. & Himmel, E. y col. (1989). Estandarización del MMPI en población adulta chilena. *Revista Chilena de Psicología, 10,* 1, 41–61.

Shiota, N., Krauss, S., & Clark, L. (in press). Adaptation and validation of the Japanese MMPI-2.

Chapter 13

The Mexican Version of the MMPI-2 in Mexico and Nicaragua: Translation, Adaptation, and Demonstrated Equivalency

Emilia Lucio-G.M. and Isabel Reyes-Lagunes

In the late 1960s, when researchers in the United States were already calling for a revision of the original MMPI, Núñez published the MMPI in Spanish for the population of Mexico (Núñez, 1979). Concurrently with its increased popularity, professionals pointed out severe linguistic problems and cultural deficiencies with the Mexican translation that produced distortions and skewness in its interpretation (Ledwin, 1980; McCreary & Padilla, 1977; Núñez, 1987). Although specific group norms were later developed for the Mexican samples, the U.S. norms were systematically used for clinical interpretation. The studies carried out in Mexico showed that Mexicans scored significantly higher than the U.S. normative sample on scales 2 (D) and 8 (Sc) (Navarro, 1971; Núñez, 1987; Rivera & Ampudia, 1976; Rivera, 1991); Mexican female college students scored higher on the Masculinity-Femininity scale (5) (Avila, Izaguirre, & Sánchez, 1970; Casabal & Wengerman, 1974; Ampudia, Stilman, & Villanueva, 1977; Lucio & Labastida, 1993); and normal samples frequently produced psychopathological scores on clinical scales (Ampudia et al., 1977; Cárdenas, 1987; Lucio, 1976; Navarro, 1971; Núñez, 1987).

With these antecedents it was considered necessary to have a grammatically sound and culturally relevant translation of the MMPI-2 as well as Mexican norms. Since the university's goal is not only to teach but also to generate knowledge, the authors presented a research project before the Program in Support of the Postgraduate Study Divisions of the National University (UNAM), which was

We appreciate the help and interest that James Butcher has given our work with the MMPI-2 and his kindness in giving us access to American college student data and factor analysis. We recognize Luis Monzón for the development of appropriate software, Consuela Durán for her help with statistical analysis, and all graduate students who participated in the MMPI-2 research project at UNAM.

approved in 1991. It was obvious that the work had to be concentrated on the MMPI-2 and that for financial reasons we had to start with realistic goals. Consequently, based on research by Butcher and others (Butcher, Ball, & Ray, 1964; Goodstein, 1954; Butcher, Graham, Dahlstrom, & Bowman, 1990) indicating that the U.S. college sample did not differ significantly from the equivalent normative sample, it was decided to start in Mexico with UNAM students since it is the largest Mexican university situated in the largest city and comprises a heterogenous population. In addition to the college student studies, validity studies were conducted on other groups, for example, psychiatric samples in Mexico and a Spanish-speaking population in Nicaragua.

In this chapter we present the main results of the standardization and adaptation of the MMPI-2 for Mexico.

The development of the Spanish version of the MMPI-2 included the following procedures (Reyes-Lagunes, Ahumada, & Diaz Guerrero, 1967).

1. Literal Translation. A preliminary translation was developed by four bilingual psychologists and a translator. One psychologist was American, one Mexican-American, and the other three Mexican. All items were translated without referring to the Spanish translation of the original MMPI.

2. Semantic and Cultural Adaptation. This preliminary version was revised by the project researchers (a clinical psychologist and a psychologist with measurement expertise), who worked in collaboration with an expert translator, examining the semantics and syntax, as well as adapting content to culturally and clinically relevant issues.

3. External Validity. The Spanish version produced by this procedure was examined by external clinical experts on the MMPI, who worked to further develop item equivalents, obtaining an agreement of over .90 by the judges.

4. Re-Adjustment. The resulting remarks and elements of the analysis were considered by the team of researchers that developed the final Spanish version of the inventory.

5. Back-translation. The Spanish version of the MMPI-2 was translated back into English by a translator unfamiliar with the MMPI. Then the two English versions were compared, showing a high degree of agreement in item wording.

Owing to the length of the inventory and the fact that the subjects in the proposed research were to be volunteers (no funding was available to pay subjects), several different presentation forms of the inventory and designs of the answer sheets were also analyzed to facilitate responding and to obtain the cooperation of subjects to increase the reliability of the rating process.

A probabilistic representative sample was obtained through the clusters method.

Three of the schools on the main UNAM campus were selected for study: Science, Arts, and Business Administration. Students in 71 courses were tested by adjusting to their schedules and administering the test in shifts.

The original sample comprised 2,246 subjects, equivalent to 10% of the UNAM population; 254 subjects were excluded because they did not meet one or more of the inclusion factors: age (17 to 36 years old); gender stated clearly; Gough's F-K index maximum equal to or less than +9; true and false percentages no more than 80% and cannot says less than 30; TRIN (True Response Inconsistency) between 5 and 13; VRIN (Variable Response Inconsistency) maximum 13; and F scale maximum 20 and F_B scale maximum 11. The final sample was 1,920 subjects— 813 males and 1,107 females.

As a comparative group, we used the U.S. college normative sample published by Butcher, Graham, Dahlstrom, and Bowman (1990), which consisted of 515 male and 797 female students from three universities and the U.S. Naval Academy. The ages of the subjects ranged from 17 to 39 and they were obtained primarily from introductory psychology classes.

Scoring and Statistical Procedures

The answer sheets were scanned by an optical reader and scored by specially designed computer software. A subsample, 5%, was re-scored manually to test the program, obtaining 100% agreement.

A frequency analysis was performed by item and by scale; means and standard deviations by scale were obtained, and linear T scores for the Mexican sample were calculated. Then the different samples were compared through the t test. After performing these analyses, we concluded that new norms were likely to be needed for Mexico.

Results

For reasons of space we will restrict the number of results to be presented. Some of the results obtained were means and standard deviations of the basic scales of our sample, which were compared with the means and standard deviations of the college student sample obtained by Butcher et al. (1990); profiles of the sample studied; and the distribution of T scores for some of the MMPI scales.

When we compared male and female Mexican students we found significant statistical differences on all the clinical and validity scales except L and 8 (Table 13-1). The greatest differences were found on scales 2 and 5, on which females scored higher than males. On these scales the difference between means was greater than one half of the corresponding standard deviation for the scales. These results indicate that in Mexico we need separate norms for males and females. Tel-

Table 13-1. T Tests of Non-K-Corrected Raw Scores for Mexican College Student Samples
(Men, N = 813; Women, N = 1,107)

Scale	Males (N = 813)		Females (N = 1,107)			
	Mean	S.D.	Mean	S.D.	t	P
L	5.2	2.6	5.1	2.2	0.91	.001
F	5.7	3.4	4.9	3.1	5.36	.05
K	16.0	4.4	15.5	4.3	2.49	.001
Hs	6.1	3.8	7.2	4.1	−5.99	.001
D	20.1	4.7	22.4	4.9	−10.34	.001
Hy	21.1	4.9	21.9	4.9	−3.52	.001
Dp	17.4	4.3	16.5	4.2	4.59	.001
Mf	24.1	4.1	30.3	3.7	−34.65	.001
Pa	9.2	3.0	9.6	3.1	−2.83	.01
Pt	11.9	5.0	13.1	5.0	−5.20	.001
Sc	13.2	5.9	13.1	5.9	.37	
Ma	18.8	4.0	18.1	3.7	3.96	.001
Si	25.6	7.6	27.4	8.1	−4.94	.001

legen, Butcher, and Hoeglund (1993) pointed out that nongendered norms are probably not necessary in the United States.

Results also indicate that there are significant statistical differences between Mexican and American male university students on all the clinical and validity scales except scale 4 (Table 13-2). Mexican college students scored higher on scales L, F, K, 1, 2, 3, and 0. The greatest differences were found on L, 2, and 6, the differences in means being more than one half of the corresponding standard deviations obtained on these scales.

There are significant differences between the Mexican and U.S. female university students on all scales except F, 1, and 3 (Table 13-3). On scales L, K, and 2, Mexicans score higher; on scales 4 , 5, 6, 7, 8, and 9, Americans score higher. The greatest differences are on L, 2, 5, and 7, where the difference between means is greater than one-half of the standard deviation obtained for the corresponding scales. The differences between Mexican and American females are greater than those found between Mexican and American males.

Once we obtained the linear T scores for our sample, we plotted them on the American college student profiles. The comparison of the Mexican male profile with the American male profile shows a very similar pattern, except on L, 1, 2, and

Table 13-2. T Tests of Non-K-Corrected Raw Scores for Mexican College Student and American College Student Men (Mexican, N = 813; U.S., N = 515)

Scale	Mexican College Students (N = 813)		American College Students (N = 515)		t	P
	Mean	S.D.	Mean	S.D.		
L	5.2	2.6	3.3	2.2	13.76	.001
F	5.7	3.4	5.3	3.9	1.97	.05
K	16.0	4.4	14.4	4.7	6.29	.001
Hs	6.1	3.8	5.1	4.0	4.58	.001
D	20.1	4.7	17.0	4.7	11.71	.001
Hy	21.1	4.9	20.4	4.6	2.60	.01
Pd	17.4	4.3	17.8	4.8	−1.58	
Mf	24.1	4.1	25.4	5.0	−4.78	.001
Pa	9.2	3.0	10.9	3.3	−9.68	.001
Pt	11.9	5.0	14.1	7.7	−6.31	.001
Sc	13.2	5.9	15.0	9.1	−4.37	.001
Ma	18.8	4.0	20.4	4.5	−6.76	.001
Si	25.6	7.6	23.7	8.6	−4.22	.001

6, where there are differences of more than 4 T-score points (Figure 13-1). On the first three scales, Mexicans have higher scores, but on the last scale Americans score higher. The differences in scale 1 may indicate that Mexican male college students are more concerned about physical symptoms than are American male college students, and as they score higher on scale 2 (D), they might tend more to depression. The difference in scale L is not an important clinical difference but may reflect Mexican students' interest in making a good impression. Americans are apparently more distrustful, as reflected in the higher Pa score.

Comparing the Mexican female profile with the American females, we note differences of more than 4 T-score points on scales L, 2, 5, and 6 (Figure 13-2). On the first three scales, Mexicans score higher; on the last, Americans do. The greatest difference was found on scale 5, which may be influenced by cultural factors, because gender roles differ from culture to culture. The difference could also be attributed to Mexican female college students' dissatisfaction with the traditional feminine role assigned them in Mexican culture, though Mexican males accentuate their masculine role, as we see by their scores. It also may be due to the fact that Mexican women who go to the university are in some way an exception, because

Table 13-3. T Tests of Non–K-Corrected Raw Scores for Mexican College Student and American College Student Women (Mexican, N = 1,107; U.S., N = 797)

Scale	Mexican College Students (N = 1107)		American College Students (N = 797)			
	Mean	S.D.	Mean	S.D.	t	P
L	5.1	2.2	2.8	1.9	23.81	.001
F	4.9	3.1	4.9	3.6	0.00	
K	15.5	4.3	13.8	4.6	8.26	.001
Hs	7.2	4.1	6.9	4.5	1.51	
D	22.4	4.9	19.6	5.0	12.20	.001
Hy	21.9	4.9	22.2	4.8	0.44	
Pd	16.5	4.2	17.8	5.0	6.15	.001
Mf	30.3	3.7	34.9	4.2	25.28	.001
Pa	9.6	3.1	11.1	3.3	10.14	.001
Pt	13.1	5.0	16.5	7.7	11.67	.001
Sc	13.1	5.9	15.5	8.7	7.17	.001
Ma	18.1	3.7	18.8	4.5	3.72	.001
Si	27.4	8.1	26.7	8.7	1.80	

in Mexico so many women still do not pursue a university career. Elevation of scales L and 2 was found for both Mexican women and Mexican men.

It is worth noting that both profiles are within the normal range on U.S. norms; only on scale 5 do females score more than T 60, and this is not a clinical scale. These results do not confirm what was found for the original MMPI, that normal populations had elevated pathological indexes (Ampudia et al., 1977; Cárdenas, 1987; Lucio, 1976; Navarro, 1971; Núñez, 1987), but rather do confirm what was found by other authors (Avila et al., 1970; Casabal & Wengerman, 1974; Ampudia et al., 1977; Lucio & Labastida, 1992), that female college students score higher on scale 5. Our results also confirm that Mexican males and females tend to score higher on scale 2, but the difference between Mexican and U.S. college students on the MMPI-2 is not as high as the difference obtained with the original MMPI. This should be confirmed by the application of the MMPI in a representative sample of the Mexican population.

The difference between males and females in the normative U.S. population on these scales is only 4 T-score points, which is within the standard error of measurement for the scales. These results indicate that new norms should be used to

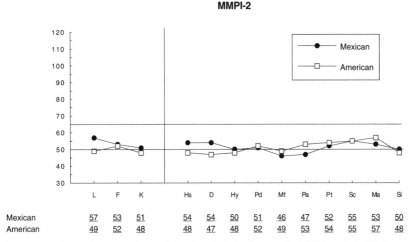

Figure 13-1. Comparison of Mexican and American Male Students on the MMPI-2 Clinical Scales

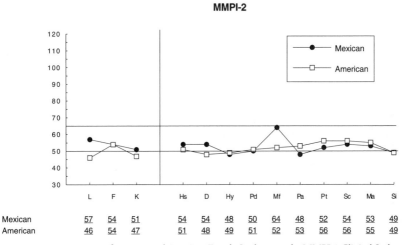

Figure 13-2. Comparison of Mexican and American Female Students on the MMPI-2 Clinical Scales

evaluate Mexican samples, but as we have not applied the test to a larger heterogeneous normative population, we can continue using American norms, because the only clinical differences are on scales 1 and 2 for males and on scale 2 for females.

Selected T-score frequency distributions from the Mexican sample were plotted against the U.S. college students' distributions and are presented in Figure 13-3. These distributions also demonstrate the similarity between the U.S. college sample and the Mexican sample.

The results also indicate that our Spanish translation is adequate for our popu-

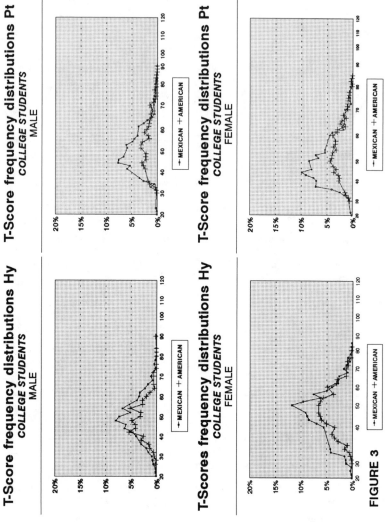

Figure 13-3. Selected Frequency Distributions of Men and Women Mexican and American College Students

lation. To confirm this, we compared our item translation with the Spanish translations for Chile and Spain and we found them quite similar, though some of the idiomatic expressions in our translation were more appropriate for our population than were those used in either of the other versions. Finally, looking at the item endorsement of the subjects, we rephrased only 12 items and slightly improved the structure of another 30.

These results show that the inventory revision and the translation and adaptation accomplished by this version are more suitable for the Mexican population than was the Núñez version of the original MMPI.

Validation Studies

To corroborate the equivalence of our version of the MMPI-2, we conducted several additional analyses: a factor analysis of the standard scales of the inventory; a comparison of students with a clinical sample; and the administration of our version to another Spanish-speaking population, Nicaraguan college students.

Factor Analysis

Several authors have discussed the role of factor analysis in personality research in general and in cross-cultural personality studies in particular. Brislin, Lonner, and Thorndike (1973) recommended the application of factor analysis in cross-cultural studies. Busse and Royce (1975) pointed out that cross-cultural communalities versus differences may be detected by factor analysis. Butcher and Bemis (1984) suggest that factor validity can guarantee that the items and scales of a measurement instrument that is adapted to a new culture generally maintain the same psychological meaning. Butcher and Garcia (1978) emphasize that factor equivalence must be demonstrated. Ben-Porath (1990) considers factor analysis to be the method of choice for assessing the invariance of measures across cultures. Previous analysis with the MMPI (Dahlstrom, Welsh, & Dahlstrom, 1975) has established two major factors when clinical scales are included—psychotic mentation and overcontrol (neurotic preoccupations)—as well as two smaller factors—gender role identification and personality disorder. Butcher and Pancheri (1976) compared the factor structure of the MMPI in Israel, Pakistan, Mexico, Costa Rica, Italy, Switzerland, and Japan. The four factors mentioned by Dahlstrom et al. (1975) were extracted in these international samples. Only Italian males did not fit the four-factor solution. In general, the factor structure of the MMPI standard scales has been shown to be relatively stable across cultures.

In this study we factor analyzed the data of our sample by gender and compared it with the data obtained by Butcher for U.S. college students (Butcher, 1992). Table 13-4 contains eigenvalues, percentages of the variance explained by each of three factors, and factor loadings of scales for men. These factors explain 63.5% of variance.

Table 13-4. Factor Analysis of the MMPI-2 Basic Scales for Male Mexican College Students

Scale	Factor			
	I	II	III	COMU.
F	.48			.59
Hypochondriasis	.67			.62
Depression	.55		.68	.78
Hysteria	.69	.55		.75
Psychopathic Deviate	.71			.52
Masculinity-Femininity	.44			.20
Paranoia	.66			.45
Psychasthenia	.76			.68
Schizophrenia	.81			.77
L		.70		.50
K		.86		.77
Social Introversion		−.48		.83
Hypomania			−.75	.74
Eigenvalues	4.14	2.47	1.63	
% of variance for	31.9	51.0	63.5	

Factor 1 is composed of scales F, 1, 2, 3, 4, 5, 6, 7, and 8, which is equivalent to the psychotic mentation factor. As can be seen, in addition to expected scales for this factor, we also find scales 2, 3, 7, and 5. The presence of scales 2, 3, and 7 in this factor may indicate cultural differences in severe psychological disturbances. The presence of scale 5 requires a more detailed analysis to understand its meaning. Scale 9, which appears in U.S. college students, does not appear in Mexican college students.

For Factor 2 the scales were L, K, and 0. This factor is similar to the overcontrol factor found by Butcher in U.S. college students. But scales 2 and 3 do not appear here because they are associated with the first factor in our sample. Scale 9 loads negatively for this factor. These results indicate that introversion and isolation might be associated with neurotic traits in Mexican males. This factor is different in Mexican and U.S. college students, because factor 2 of the Mexican sample is rather similar to factor 3 in the U.S. sample.

For Factor 3, scale 9 presents negatively with scale 2, shared with Factor 1 positively, which validates these scales. This factor has been identified by Dahlstrom, Welsh, & Dahlstrom (1975) and Butcher (1990) as personality disorders. The fact

Table 13-5. Factor Analysis of the MMPI-2 Basic Scales for Female Mexican College Students

Scale	Factor				
	I	II	III	IV	COMU.
F	.45	.68			.67
Hypochondriasis	.76				.67
Depression	.58		.64		.79
Hysteria	.76				.72
Psychopathic Deviate	.71				.54
Paranoia*	.53			.50	.58
Psychasthenia	.75				.71
Schizophrenia	.79				.75
L		−.67			.45
K		−.81			.73
Social Introversion		.44	77		.82
Hypomania			−.77		.75
Masculinity-Femininity				.93	.89
Eigenvalues	4.27	2.2	1.56	1.03	
% of variance	32.8	50.3	62.3	70.3	

that we found depression in this factor in our sample suggests that we need to perform further item analysis to establish clearer discrimination parameters. Factor 4, gender role identification, reported for other samples does not appear in Mexican male college students. Scale 5 appears in the Mexican sample on Factor 1. Our results are similar to those obtained by Butcher and Pancheri (1976) in Italian males, perhaps because Italian and Mexican cultural roots are similar.

Table 13-5 presents eigenvalues, variance percentages for each of the factors, and factorial loadings of scales for Mexican college women. These factors explain 70.3% of the variance.

Factor 1, psychotic mentation, is composed of scales F, 1, 2, 3, 4, 6, 7, and 8. This factor differs from factor 1 for Mexican male college students because it does not include scale 5, which points to gender differences in our culture. This factor is very similar to what Butcher found in U.S. college students, but in Mexican female students it also includes scales F and 7. These last two scales indicate anxiety, obsessive insecurity, and internal discomfort, traits with which psychotic mentation in Mexican women might be associated.

Factor 2, overcontrol (neurotic preoccupations), includes scales F, L, K, and 0, which are shared with factor 1. This is also a very similar factor to factor 2 in men, although scale 3 is substituted in Mexican women with scale F. This factor is also similar to that obtained by Butcher in U.S. college students, but scale L is included in Mexican women, whereas scale 7 is included in U.S. students. The fact that scale L is included in this factor in Mexican women probably means that neurotic preoccupations are associated in this group with their compulsion for making a good impression on others.

Factor 3, personality disorder, is composed of scale 9, which loads negatively, and scales 0 and 2, which are shared with Factor 1. Social introversion again shows a cultural gender pattern. This factor is very similar in Mexican and U.S. women, but 9 loads negatively in Mexican women and positively in U.S. women, which might indicate that in Mexican women the personality disorders are associated with apathy, while in U.S. women they are associated with hyperactivity and difficulty in accepting social norms.

Factor 4, gender role identification, is composed of scales 5 and 6, this last scale shared with factor 1. Because this factor is not present in Mexican males, we need to study further the item content of scale 5. Although this factor is similar for U.S. female college students, it seems to be a factor of major weight in the Mexican sample.

With respect to factor analyses of the MMPI-2, the factorial structure of our Mexican sample is similar, though not identical, to the factorial structure of the U.S. college student sample. These results support the utilization of the inventory to assess personality and also point to the fact that the adaptation and normalization of the MMPI-2 in our country resulted in a genuinely equivalent form. Subsequent studies must show if the gender differences found in this group are related to cultural factors.

Clinical Sample

One of the traditional ways of validating an instrument is to determine if it discriminates between normal and abnormal populations. We wanted to know if the Spanish version of the MMPI-2 would show such discrimination. Although the MMPI is used frequently in Mexican psychiatric hospitals, we found only one study with this kind of patient. González (1979) found significant differences between schizophrenics, depressive neurotics, and normals. Cabiya and Vélez (1989) in Puerto Rico found good discrimination between normal and psychiatric populations with the MMPI Spanish version. In other countries, authors have found elevations in the psychotic tetrad: 6, 7, 8, 9 (Pancheri, 1982; Freedman, Kaplan, & Sadock, 1982; Arbisi, 1993).

The clinical sample to which we administered the inventory consisted of 217 patients who were diagnosed as having psychotic disturbances or personality disorders, according to DSM-III-R criteria. They were inpatients at Fray Bernardino Alvarez Hospital, and San Fernando Psychiatric Hospital, Social Protection Asylum No. 4 for psychiatric patients, and the Medical-Psychiatric Unit of the South Prison, all located in Mexico City. The sample was nonprobabilistic by quota, with a deliberate effort to obtain a representative sample by including typical areas or groups of the population. A total of 17 patients were excluded from the sample for not meeting one or more of the following inclusion variables: being a resident at the date of administration of the inventory; having a psychiatric and psychological assessment performed by members of the respective institution; being controlled at the time of administration of the inventory, without delirium, confusion, depression, or agitation; not more than 15 cannot say responses; TRIN (True Inconsistency Response) between 5 and 13; and VRIN (Variable Response Inconsistency) up to 14. The final clinical sample consisted of 200 subjects. The F scale was not used as an exclusion criterion, because as Arbisi (1993) pointed out, inpatients usually score higher than 100 on F, and only in very few cases lower than 65.

Results (Palacios & Lucio, 1993) indicate significant statistical differences (p = 001) between psychiatric patients and Mexican male students on all scales except 3 and 5. The largest differences were found on scales F (t = 26.54), 8 (t = 23.15), 6 (t = 18.42), and 7 (t = 16.35). On all these scales psychiatric patients scored higher than college students.

With respect to women, we found significant statistical differences (p = 0.01) between psychiatric patients and college students on all scales except L, 3, and 5. The greatest differences were found, as in males, on scales F (t = 31.04), 8 (t = 26.57), 6 (t = 20.46), and 7 (t = 17.55).

If we compare the profile of the male psychiatric patients (Figure 13-4) with the profile for male college students, the pattern is different and elevated on the scales we would expect. The highest scale is F with a T score of 91 in psychiatric patients. With respect to clinical scales, the highest scale is 8, with a noticeable pathological score (78); scale 6 also has a score in the pathological range (69), as does scale 7. Elevation of scales 8, 6, and 7 were expected for this sample if the inventory actually discriminated. The elevation on 8 is extremely high, although the majority of patients were medicated at the time of the administration of the test. Although scale 9 is elevated beyond the normal range in the psychiatric sample, the elevation is not extreme. This fact may be due to a medication effect.

If we look at the profiles of the women (Figure 13-5), the highest scale is F, with a T score of 91. Scale 8 is the highest score of the clinical scales, with a pathological score (78). Scales 6 and 9 are also at a pathological level. Scale 7 is also elevated, but not as high as the Mf scale, whose elevation is T-66; it does not differ significantly from the students' score. The profile of female psychiatric patients is more pathological than the profile of male psychiatric patients. The elevation of

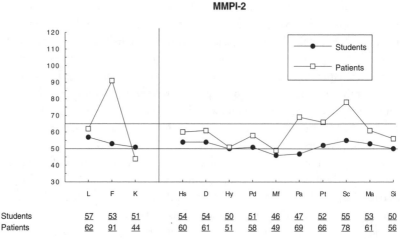

Figure 13-4. Comparison of Mexican Students with Mexican Male Psychiatric Patients on the MMPI-2 Clinical Scales

scale 9 in this group may be related to the fact, commonly observed by psychiatrists and psychologists in the hospitals, that there may be differential effects of medication for men and women.

These results show that the inventory clearly differentiates between normal and abnormal populations in Mexico, and the differences are in the expected direction. The psychotic tetrad (6, 7, 8, 9) is where we find the more outstanding differences between patients and students, as was expected and pointed out by Pancheri (1982), Freedman et al. (1982), and Arbisi (1993). Elevation on scale 8 shows severe thought disturbances, and elevation on scale 6 shows noticeable paranoid ideation of psychosis. Elevation on scale 9 indicates manic behavior, hyperactivity, euphoria, or aggressive actions. Elevation on scale 7 indicates anxiety and stress in psychotic patients. Elevation on scale F shows broad psychopathological disturbances.

In other psychiatric samples (Arbisi, 1993), a significant correlation between scale F and scales 6 and 8 has been found, so we calculated these correlations. With respect to men, we obtained a correlation of 0.78 between F and 6 and a correlation of 0.88 between F and 8. In women, the correlation between F and 6 was 0.70 and between F and 8 was 0.88. All these correlations are highly significant and corroborate severe psychopathological indexes in our sample (Palacios, 1993).

Nicaraguan College Students: Validation Study Performed by Lorena Taboada in Collaboration with UNAM

Another step we followed to validate our translation was to apply our version of the MMPI-2 to Nicaraguan college students. Nicaragua is also a Spanish-speaking

MMPI-2

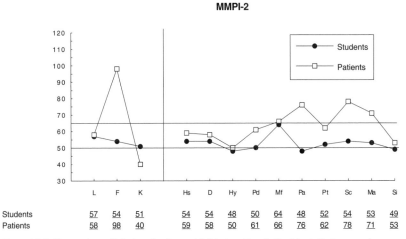

	L	F	K		Hs	D	Hy	Pd	Mf	Pa	Pt	Sc	Ma	Si
Students	<u>57</u>	<u>54</u>	<u>51</u>		<u>54</u>	<u>54</u>	<u>48</u>	<u>50</u>	<u>64</u>	<u>48</u>	<u>52</u>	<u>54</u>	<u>53</u>	<u>49</u>
Patients	<u>58</u>	<u>98</u>	<u>40</u>		<u>59</u>	<u>58</u>	<u>50</u>	<u>61</u>	<u>66</u>	<u>76</u>	<u>62</u>	<u>78</u>	<u>71</u>	<u>53</u>

Figure 13-5. Comparison of Mexican Students with Mexican Female Psychiatric Patients on the MMPI-2 Clinical Scales

country, but the culture is somewhat different from that of Mexico. In addition, there has been a severe political climate in Nicaragua due to the civil war in which they have suffered for years (Taboada, 1994).

A probabilistic representative sample from the four largest universities in Nicaragua was obtained using the cluster sampling method. The original sample included 1,085 subjects. A total of 159 subjects was discarded because they did not meet the inclusion criteria. The final sample was 926 subjects, 380 males and 546 females (see Figures 13-6 and 13-7).

The profile of the Nicaraguan male college students showed a very similar pattern to the Mexican male college students' profile, although the T scores of the Nicaraguans tended to be somewhat higher than those of the Mexicans. The profile of the Nicaraguan students tended toward normality. Differences of more than 4 T-score points were found on scales F, K, 1, 6, 7, 8, and 9. On all the scales except K, Nicaraguans scored higher, with the greatest differences on scales F and 8. The only clinical scale above statistical normality was 8.

The profile of Nicaraguan female college students also showed higher scores than those of the Mexican female college students, with the pattern very similar to that of the Mexican female students' profile. Nicaraguan female students also tended toward normality. Differences of more than 4 T-score points were found on scales F, K, 1, 6, 7, 8, and 9. The largest differences were found on scales F and 8. Scale 8 was the only clinical scale above statistical normality.

These results indicate that Nicaraguan students, both males and females, describe themselves as having more psychological symptoms, which they are ready

MMPI-2

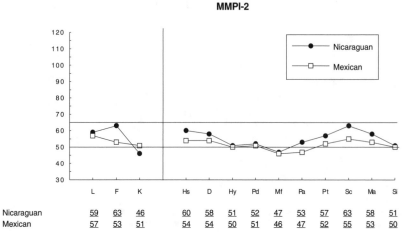

	L	F	K		Hs	D	Hy	Pd	Mf	Pa	Pt	Sc	Ma	Si
Nicaraguan	59	63	46		60	58	51	52	47	53	57	63	58	51
Mexican	57	53	51		54	54	50	51	46	47	52	55	53	50

Figure 13-6. Comparison of Mexican and Nicaraguan Male Students on the MMPI-2 Clinical Scales

to speak about, than do Mexican students. This is more accentuated in women. Butcher (1992) has pointed out that elevation on F can be related to cultural factors, because what is infrequent in one culture is not necessarily infrequent in another. Elevation of scale 1 could indicate somatic symptoms related to the climate of tension that the country was experiencing when the inventory was applied. Other chapters in this book have noted increased MMPI-2 scale elevations with stress (see chapters 8 and 10).Elevation on scale 6 indicates that Nicaraguans are more distrustful than Mexicans. The relatively high scores on scale 7 could also be related to tension and anxiety. Scores on scale 8 (Sc) indicate that they are not conventional in outlook. There is a great dispersion in the scores on scale 8 for men and women, which suggests it is necessary to analyze the scale more closely. Elevation on scale 9 indicates that Nicaraguans are more active than Mexicans, but perhaps that could be related to the fact that they need a lot of energy to adapt themselves to the climate of economic and political instability.

The results obtained with this sample suggest that the Mexican Spanish version of the MMPI-2 may be used with Nicaraguan college student groups. The differences observed could be due to cultural factors, or they may reflect real personality differences. It might be necessary for Nicaraguans to establish their own norms.

In conclusion, it is necessary to emphasize that the Spanish version of the MMPI-2 for Mexico seems to be much more adequate than the original MMPI for assessing the Mexican population. This could be both because the revised version (MMPI-2) was used and because of the more rigorous methodology followed in translating and validating the instrument.

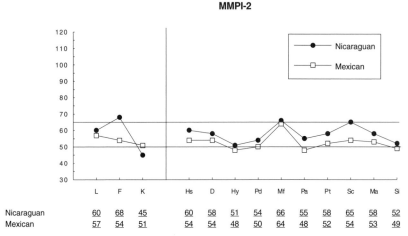

Figure 13-7. Comparison of Mexican and Nicaraguan Female Students on the MMPI-2 Clinical Scales

Although it is necessary to have norms for the Mexican population, the norms cannot be established until a normative sample of the general population is obtained. Until then, U.S. norms can be used in Mexico, because scale score differences are minimal. Scores on some scales in the Mexican population—5 and 2—seem to differ somewhat from those of Americans. The first scale is also different in the Nicaraguan students. Scale 8 is very elevated in Nicaraguan students, and this scale dispersion is rather wide in both Mexican and Nicaraguan students. Further studies must be performed with these scales.

Summary

In this chapter we presented the main results of the translation and adaptation of the MMPI-2 for Mexico. The inventory was translated following a rigorous methodology. The results obtained from 1,920 subjects (813 males and 1,107 females) indicate that the version is adequate for Mexican college students and probably for all of the Mexican population. Means, standard deviations, and T scores were calculated for the sample. We also presented a factor analysis of the basic scales of the MMPI-2. We compared our data with that obtained by Butcher et al. (1990) in U.S. college students.

The results indicate that the Mexican version is adequate not only for the Mexican population but perhaps for other Spanish-speaking countries (e.g., Nicaragua). To decide whether to use our norms or those obtained in the United States, we have to examine further the performance of the instrument in a larger normative sample of the general population in Mexico.

References

Ampudia, A., Stilman, M., & Villanueva, E. (1977). *Tendencia a la somatización en estudiantes de matemáticas (estudio comparativo entre estudiantes de matemáticas y medicina utilizando la prueba del MMPI)* [Somatization tendency in mathematics students: Comparative study between mathematics and medicine students using MMPI]. Unpublished licenciatura thesis, National University of Mexico, México City.

Arbisi, P. (1993). *Assessing MMPI-2 profiles of psychiatric inpatients.* Paper presented at the 28th annual symposium on recent developments in the use of the MMPI (MMPI-2 and MMPI-A), St. Petersburg Beach, FL.

Avila, M. Y., Izaguirre, H. C., & Sánchez, Q. C. (1970). *Normas de calificación del MMPI en adolescentes en la E.N.E.P. de la U.N.A.M.* [MMPI rating norms for adolescents in E.N.E.P. at UNAM]. Unpublished licenciatura thesis, National University of Mexico, México City.

Ben-Porath, Y. S. (1990). Cross-cultural assessment of personality: The case for replicatory factor analysis. In J. N. Butcher & C. D. Spielberger (Eds.), *Recent advances in personality assessment* (Vol. 8). Hillsdale, NJ: Erlbaum.

Brislin, R. W., Lonner, W. J., & Thorndike, R. M. (1973). *Cross-cultural research methods.* New York: Wiley.

Busse, A. R., & Royse, J. R. (1975). Detecting cross-cultural commonalities and differences: Intergroups factor analysis. *Psychological Bulletin, 82,* 128–136.

Butcher, J. N. (1992). *Factorial analysis for basic scales of MMPI-2 with college students.* Unpublished manuscript.

Butcher, J. N., Ball, B., & Ray, E. (1964). Effects socio-economic level of MMPI difference in Negro-White college students. *Journal of Counseling Psychology, 11,* 83–87.

Butcher, J. N., & Bemis, K. M. (1984). Abnormal behavior in cultural context. In H. E. Adams & P. Sutker (Eds.), Comprehensive *handbook of psychopathology.* New York: Plenum.

Butcher, J. N. & Garcia, R. E. (1978). Cross-national application of psychological tests. *Personnel and Guidance, 56,* 472–475.

Butcher, J. N., Graham, J. R., Dahlstrom, W. G., & Bowman, E. (1990). The MMPI-2 with college students. *Journal of Personality Assessment, 54* (1–2), 1–15.

Butcher, J. N., & Pancheri, P. (1976). *Handbook of cross-national MMPI research.* Minneapolis: University of Minnesota Press.

Cabiya, J., & Velez, R. (1989). Discriminative capacity of the Minnesota Multiphasic Personality Inventory with three samples of Puerto Rican population. *Avances em psicologia Clinica Latinoamericana, 7,* 105–115.

Cárdenas, Y. (1987). *Estudio de correlación entre la escala adicional del MMPI AC (Logro Académico) y promedio en una muestra representativa de adolescentes* [Correlational study between MMPI Ac (Academic achievement) additional scale and scholar grades on a representative adolescents sample]. Unpublished licenciatura thesis, National University of Mexico, México City.

Casabal, C., & Wengerman, A. (1974). *Estudio de las características de personalidad utilizando el MMPI en una muestra representativa de la generación 1973 de la Facultad de Psicología.* [Study of personality characteristics with the MMPI on a representative sample of 1973 promotion at Psychology School]. Unpublished licenciatura thesis, National University of Mexico, México City.

Dahlstrom, W. G., Welsh, G. S., & Dahlstrom, L. E. (1975), *An MMPI handbook: Research and applications* (Vol. 2). Minneapolis: University of Minnesota Press.

Freedman, A. M., Kaplan, H. I., & Sadock, B. J. (1982). *Comprehensive textbook of psychiatry.* 3rd ed. Baltimore: Williams & Wilkins.

González, L. D. (1979). *Estudio de correlación de las respuestas del Inventario Multifásico de la Personalidad de Minnesota (MMPI) de las escalas L, F, K, D y Si de normales, neuróticos depresivos y esquizofrénicos en población Mexicana.*[Correlation study of the Multiphasic Minnesota Personality

Inventory (MMPI) of L, F, K, D and Is scales in a Mexican sample of normals, depressed, neurotics and schizophrenics.] Unpublished licenciatura thesis, National University of Mexico, México City.

Goodstein, L. D. (1954). Regional differences in MMPI responses among male college students. *Journal of Consulting Psychology, 18,* 437–441.

Ledwin, A. (1980). *A comparative of the MMPI:* Spanish and culturally linguistic revision. Unpublished doctoral dissertation, United International University, San Diego.

Lucio, E. (1976). Presencia de algunas características hipocondriacas en estudiantes de medicina [Presence of hypochondriac characteristics in medical students]. *Revista de Psiquiatria,* 6 (3), 44–49.

Lucio, E., & Labastida, M. (1993). Características de personalidad que influyen en la deserción de la Carrera de Médico Cirujano de la U.N.A.M. [Personality traits associated with dropout rates of medical students]. *Revista Mexicana de Psicología, 10* (1), 44–49.

McCreary, C., & Padilla, E. (1977). MMPI differences among black, Mexican-American and white male offenders. In R. Núñez (Ed.,) *Pruebas psicométricas de la personalidad.* México City: Trillas.

Navarro, R. (1971). El MMPI (Español) aplicado a jóvenes mexicanos: Influencias de sexo, edad y nivel de inteligencia [The MMPI (Spanish) applied to Mexican youngsters: Sex, age and intelligence influence]. *Revista Latinoamericana de Psicología,* 5 (3–4), 127–137.

Núñez, R. (1979). *Aplicación del MMPI a la Psicopatología* [MMPI application to psychopathology]. México City: Manual Moderno.

Núñez, R. (1987). *Pruebas psicométricas de la personalidad.* [Personality psychometric tests]. México City: Trillas.

Palacios, H. (1993). *Análisis de la capacidad discriminativa del MMPI-2: Comparación de perfiles de pacientes psiquiátricos y estudiantes universitarios* [MMPI-2 discrimination: Profiles comparison between psychiatric patients and college students].Unpublished masters thesis, National University of Mexico, México City.

Palacios, H., & Lucio, E. (1993). *Resultados preliminares de las escalas de validez del MMPI-2 en pacientes psiquiátricos.* [Preliminary results of MMPI-2 validity scales in psychiatric patients]. Presented at the III Institutional Clinical Psychology Journeys, Fray Bernardino Alvarez Hospital, México City.

Pancheri, S. (1982). *Manual de Psiquiatría Clínica* [Clinical psychiatry manual]. México City: Trillas.

Reyes-Lagunes, I., Ahumada, R., & Diaz Guerrero, R. (1967). *Consideraciones acerca de la estandarización de pruebas en Lationamérica. Aportaciones de la psicología a la investigación transcultural* [Considerations about test standardization in Latin America: Contributions from psychology to cross-cultural research]. México City: Trillas.

Rivera, O. (1991). *Interpretación del MMPI en psicología clínica, laboral y educativa* [MMPI interpretation in clinical, industrial and educational psychology]. México City: Manual Moderno.

Rivera, O., & Ampudia, I. (1976). El MMPI en la detección precoz delas alteraciones mentales en poblaciones unioversitarias [The MMPI in the precocious detection of mental disorders in college populations]. *Revista de Psiquiatria,* 6 (2), mayo-agosto.

Taboada, A. L. (1994). *Normalización del MMPI-2 en población universitaria de Nicaragua* [MMPI-2 normalization for Nicaraguan college students]. Unpublished masters thesis, National University of Mexico, México City.

Tellegen, A., Butcher, J. N., & Hoeglund, T. (1993). *Unisex norms for the MMPI-2 and MMPI-A: Are they needed? Would they work?* Paper presented at the 28th annual symposium on recent developments in the use of the MMPI (MMPI-2 and MMPI-A), St. Petersburg Beach, FL.

Chapter 14

Use of the MMPI and the MMPI-2 in Puerto Rico

José J. Cabiya

Research with the MMPI has been slow to develop in Puerto Rico, although the instrument has been widely used clinically since the 1950s in different settings, including personnel selection, private clinical practice, forensic evaluations, child custody evaluations, and psychiatric hospitals. Not until the 1980s were the first experimental studies with the MMPI conducted on the island. As part of her master's thesis, Rodríguez (1980) administered the Spanish version of the MMPI developed by Núñez (1979) to a representative sample of 200 college students. The mean age of the sample was 21.4, with 127 females and 73 males. Her results indicated that when the original norms were applied, the students obtained T scores above 80 on all the clinical scales, with the main elevations on the Pd (100), Es (100), Pa (95), and Ma (88) scales. These extreme elevations probably resulted from poorly translated items. However, the mean T score on the F scale was 88, suggesting possible lack of cooperation with the test instructions on the part of the students.

Prewitt, Nogueras, and Draguns (1985) obtained different results with adolescents ranging from 15 to 18 years old. They administered their translation of the MMPI to 515 high school students. The number of females tested was 321 and the number of males 194. As can be seen in Figure 14-1, only the Sc scale had a T score above 70, the other main elevations being on scales 4 and 9. Although these mean T scores were much lower than Rodríguez's, they are similar to her results in that they show the same set of main elevations on the clinical scales, with the exception of the Pa scale.

Cabiya and Vélez (1989) studied how well the MMPI (Nuñez version) differentiated a normal sample consisting of 30 college students with a mean age of 22 from outpatient samples of equal sizes. We found that the clinical profile of the students was significantly lower than the profile of the outpatient sample on all clinical scales. Only the Sc scale differentiated students from the inpatients, since it was significantly higher for the latter. This was probably due to the fact that the

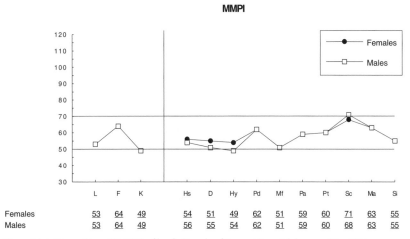

Figure 14-1. Group Mean MMPI Profile of a Sample of Puerto Rican Adolescents (N = 515)
(Prewitt, Nogueras, & Draguns, 1985)

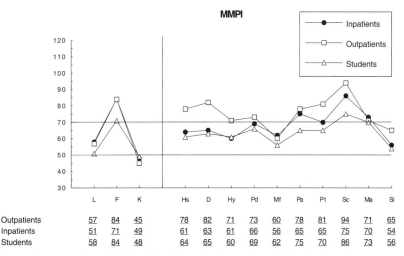

Figure 14-2. Group Mean MMPI Profile of a Sample of Puerto Rican College Students, Inpatients,
and Outpatients (Cabiya & Vélez, 1989)

inpatients had been medicated, perhaps lowering their MMPI T scores on most
scales. However, we found that the T scores of the students on the Pd, Pa, and Ma
scales were around 15 points above the expected level of 50. Moreover, the Sc scale
mean T score was above 70, as can be seen in Figure 14-2. The overall high elevation probably results from the fact that the Núñez translation had a number of
poorly translated items, resulting in different response patterns.

In conclusion, we can see that with the original MMPI, students in Puerto Rico scored significantly higher on the Sc scale, as shown in the Cabiya and Vélez (1989) and the Prewitt, Nogueras, and Draguns (1985) studies, while other scales, although elevated, were not above 70. These studies differed from Rodríguez's study in that the mean T scores on scale F for their samples were significantly lower than Rodríguez's results, which could explain her highly elevated profiles.

The overall higher scale evaluation found with Puerto Rican students is similar to evaluations found on mainland U.S. students and reflects, in part, problems with the original MMPI norms. Pope, Butcher, and Seelen (1993) pointed out that since Hathaway and McKinley (1940), in developing MMPI norms, allowed high numbers of "cannot says," the original norms were "set" too low, in contrast to requiring people to answer all or most of the items.

Research with the MMPI-2

The first study conducted in Puerto Rico with the MMPI-2 was included as part of the dissertation requirements of Cecilia Colón (1993) under my direction. Dr. James Butcher was also part of her dissertation committee. Colón (1993) used a revised version of a translation of the MMPI-2 developed in Chile. The Chilean Spanish version was evaluated by 15 licensed psychologists, and 30 items were re-translated from the original English version to Spanish by a licensed translator and then back-translated into English. This translation was then administered to 63 adult psychiatric inpatients, and 62 adult college students with a mean age of 30 years. The results indicated that the MMPI-2 clinical and content scales differentiated the two groups very well. The college students' mean T scores on the clinical scales fell between 50 and 55, except for the Mf and Ma scales, which were 59.40 and 57.39 respectively. Given the small size of the sample, the fact that these last two scales fell between 55 and 60 might not be significant. The inpatients had elevations above a mean T score of 65 on the Pa (71.43), Pt (63.56), Sc (77.56), and Ma (66.70) scales, which is consistent with their diagnosed mental disorders. All of the students' mean T scores on the content scales also fell between 50 and 55, except for the DEP scale (57.29). On the other hand, the inpatients obtained elevations on the FRS (68.89), BIZ (73.24), and TRT (67.10) scales, again consistent with their psychopathology.

In Colón's study, the mean code-type of the psychiatric sample was 6-8, which is consistent with the principal diagnoses of this sample, namely, paranoid and undifferentiated schizophrenia. Also, the only scales that correlated significantly with the symptom ratings of trained judges using the Brief Psychiatric Scale developed by Overall and Gorham (1962) were the Pa, Sc, and SOD scales. Thus, the symptom ratings suggest a clinical picture of paranoid and psychotic thought processes in an individual who exhibits discomfort in social situations.

The main reason for using the Chilean translation was that the University of Minnesota's Hispanic version was not yet published when this study was conducted. Once the Hispanic version was published, I, along with my staff, reviewed the two translations and concluded that the Hispanic version was a better translation than the Chilean for the following reasons:

1. We found that 22 items, namely, 29, 70, 84, 105, 112, 114, 127, 160, 203, 214, 235, 260, 264, 273, 275, 335, 351, 412, 431, 427, 471, and 476 seemed not to be equivalent in content in the Chilean translation.

2. We also found that 328 items had a similar meaning while 209 were almost identical. However, in our opinion, those with similar meaning were better translated by Garcia-Peltoniemi and Azán Chaviano (1993), their translation being more precise and closer to the original English. But we found that there were eight items in Garcia and Azán's Hispanic version that use idiomatic expressions not typically used by Puerto Ricans, including names of children's games. We translated those eight items from the original English into Spanish in a manner that a panel of three judges considered appropriate for use in Puerto Rico:

1. Item 99   jurada = ha dado conmigo
2. Item 101   cintillo = banda
3. Item 117   expectorado = tosido
4. Item 215   hoscas = lastimosas
5. Item 286   fuero interno = dentro de sí
6. Item 342   autobuses = guagua
7. Item 384   las casitas = mamás y papás
8. Item 426   rayuela = peregrina
                saltar la cuerda = brincar cuica

We then administered the Hispanic version with this list of items adapted to Puerto Rico to a sample of 361 first-year college students from the state university colleges of engineering and science. The students had a mean age of 18 years. The test was administered in large groups of up to 180 students. Since it was administered to large groups in a rather impersonal manner, it was expected that a number of students would not be cooperative and would answer in an invalid manner. Thus, all cases in which the F or F_B scores were higher than 80 were not included in the final analysis. The basic mean scale scores for the remaining 125 female and 158 male students are presented in Figure 14-3. The only clinical scale that was significantly higher than a full standard deviation was the Mf scale for female students (perhaps consistent with being a student in an engineering school). Also for females, the Sc and Ma scales show elevations half a standard deviation above the

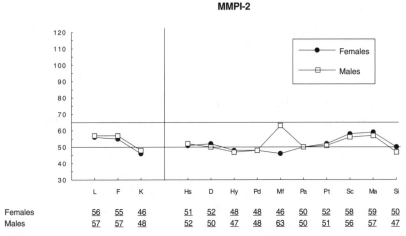

MMPI-2

	L	F	K	Hs	D	Hy	Pd	Mf	Pa	Pt	Sc	Ma	Si
Females	56	55	46	51	52	48	48	46	50	52	58	59	50
Males	57	57	48	52	50	47	48	63	50	51	56	57	47

Figure 14-3. Group Mean MMPI-2 Standard Profile of a Group of 343 College Students from State Universities in Puerto Rico

mean. The Sc and Ma scales were also found by Butcher, Graham, Dahlstrom, and Bowman (1990) to be half a standard deviation higher in female college students in the continental United States, while the Mf scale was not found to be as high as it was for the Puerto Rican females. Finally, as Butcher et al. (1990) found with male college students, our male students scored almost a full standard deviation above a T score of 50 on the Sc and Ma scales.

The content scale profiles for the remaining 251 (117 females and 134 males) cases, after dropping those with F_B scores above 80, are presented in Figure 14-4. Students scored higher than 50 on these scales, but none reached an elevation above a standard deviation from the mean except for males, whose mean T scores on BIZ hovered between 50 and 55. It should be noted that these students were in their first year and were making an adjustment to the college setting, which might cause them to be more anxious and fearful.

The frequency distribution analysis summarized in Table 14-1 demonstrates that the students obtained mean T scores on the clinical scales that fell close to the 92nd percentile, as did the normative sample of the MMPI-2 (Tellegen & Ben-Porath, 1992), with the exception of the Mf, Sc, and Ma scales. A T score of 70 on scales Mf and Sc served as a better demarcation point above the 90th percentile, while a T score of 75 was needed for the Ma scale to reach the 92nd percentile.

We conclude that research in Puerto Rico has demonstrated that the MMPI-2 is working very much as it does in the continental United States. There appears to be no need to develop new norms for Puerto Rico at the present time, although further research with a larger and more representative sample is needed to confirm this.

Of the eight items adapted to Puerto Rico, the only item that was confusing to

MMPI-2

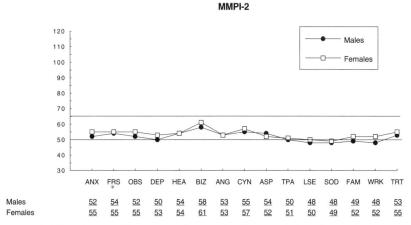

	ANX	FRS	OBS	DEP	HEA	BIZ	ANG	CYN	ASP	TPA	LSE	SOD	FAM	WRK	TRT
Males	52	54	52	50	54	58	53	55	54	50	48	48	49	48	53
Females	55	55	55	53	54	61	53	57	52	51	50	49	52	52	55

Figure 14-4. Group Mean MMPI-2 Content Scale Profile of a Group of 343 College Students from State Universities in Puerto Rico

a significant number of students was item 99. Therefore, we suggest using the Colón translation of this item, which worked well in her study. Moreover, in the comparison of item response differences between Puerto Rican and mainland U.S. college students, these eight items, except for item 284, showed a percentage difference below 25%. Overall, there were relatively few item response differences between Puerto Rican and U.S. mainland college students, as can be seen in Appendix C. In fact, only 45 items (8%) for males and 55 (10%) items for females had a percentage difference above 25%.

In conclusion, it would be more parsimonious for us in Puerto Rico to use the same Spanish version of the MMPI-2 as is used on the U.S. mainland, possibly with a specific glossary of terms explaining the slight Spanish language differences. This would be preferable to having different translations altogether and would allow for better generalizability across different investigations. Furthermore, in a future revision, Garcia and Azán might consider adding these words and phrases to their translation.

Clinical Interpretation of the MMPI-2

Two clinical cases, presented with MMPI-2 Minnesota Report interpretations, illustrate the clinical use of the MMPI-2 in Puerto Rico.

Case 1

The patient is a rather heavily built 38-year-old woman of light brown complexion. Although she dresses appropriately for her sessions, she tends to wear excessive jewelry. She was reared in San Juan by her two natural parents. She has one sister

Table 14-1. Selected Percentiles for Students on the Clinical Scales

Scale	T Score	Percentiles
Hs	65	90.8
D	65	95.8
Hy	65	94.7
Pd	65	96.8
Mf	70	93.3
Pa	65	91.5
Pt	65	91.2
Sc	70	90.1
Ma	75	92.9
Si	65	96.1

that she reported "always was the favorite of my parents and got everything she asked for." She indicated that she had always wanted to be a television reporter and to write a book. She completed a bachelor's degree in humanities and a master's degree in Spanish literature. She met her current husband in college while completing her bachelor's degree. They dated regularly for 14 years until he moved in with her six years ago. They married last year. She stated that she had waited that long to get married because, although he "was a good man with a good job," she did not want to feel "trapped" in a marital relationship. Moreover, she professed to having very high moral values and assured the therapist "that they slept in different beds" prior to their marriage.

Her sister meanwhile had married and had three daughters, but, according to the patient, "her husband got her involved with drugs, mainly cocaine." What began as casual use ended in their dealing large quantities of drugs. They eventually moved to New York City after the client tried to press charges against them for child neglect because of the way she saw the children being reared. She reported that she was so mad at her brother-in-law for getting her sister into drugs and for the harm he was inflicting upon her nieces that she "felt like killing him" many times. Six years ago they were finally arrested in New York and sentenced to long prison terms. The patient was awarded custody of the three daughters after a long and tedious legal process in which the girls were placed in different foster homes.

The patient denied any alcohol or drug abuse and has never been in therapy. She admitted that she is very compulsive about cleanliness and order at home. She reported that she needs to feel in control of those around her and gets extremely angry when she cannot "impose my will on others, especially my daughters [her

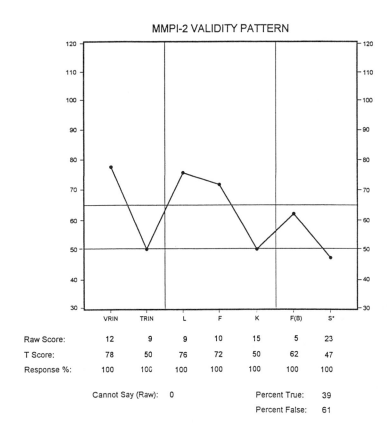

MMPI-2 VALIDITY PATTERN

	VRIN	TRIN	L	F	K	F(B)	S*
Raw Score:	12	9	9	10	15	5	23
T Score:	78	50	76	72	50	62	47
Response %:	100	100	100	100	100	100	100

Cannot Say (Raw):   0   Percent True: 39
                                Percent False: 61

*Experimental

Figure 14-5. Minnesota Report™ MMPI-2 Validity Scale Profile of a 38-Year-Old Puerto Rican Woman Being Evaluated in the Context of Psychotherapy. *Source:* The Minnesota Report™: Adult Clinical System. Copyright © 1989 by the Regents of the University of Minnesota. All rights reserved.

nieces]." In a recent incident, she became extremely upset and angry when she found a male friend of one of her daughters inside the house after she had told her that no boys could enter the house when she was out. She became so enraged that her neighbor came over to see what was happening when she heard the screams. Her oldest stepdaughter is 17 and became pregnant when she was 14. At that time

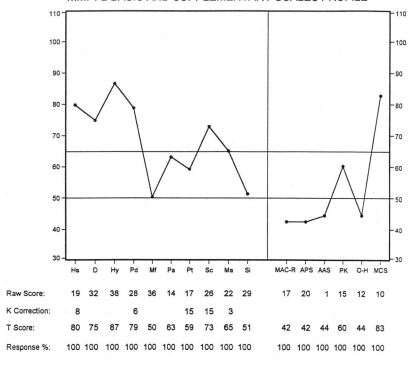

Figure 14-6. Minnesota Report™ MMPI-2 Standard Scale Profile of a 38-Year-Old Puerto Rican Woman Being Evaluated in the Context of Psychotherapy. *Source:* The Minnesota Report™: Adult Clinical System. Copyright © 1989 by the Regents of the University of Minnesota. All rights reserved.

the client told her that she would have to move in with her boyfriend as soon as the baby was born. This stepdaughter is now having severe marital problems, but the client will not take her back because she had already warned her of the consequences of getting pregnant. The client does appreciate that her oldest stepdaughter has been able to continue studying and has maintained an "A" average. She feels very frustrated at her second stepdaughter's lack of interest in school, and they have argued several times about this.

She reported that she has "never been able to get on pursuing an opportunity to

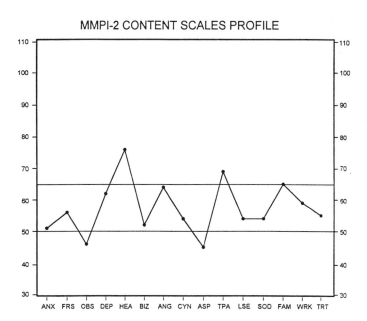

Figure 14-7. Minnesota Report™ MMPI-2 Content Scale Profile of a 38-Year-Old Puerto Rican Woman Being Evaluated in the Context of Psychotherapy. *Source:* The Minnesota Report™: Adult Clinical System. Copyright © 1989 by the Regents of the University of Minnesota. All rights reserved.

work as a reporter and to write a book" because she needs to constantly care for her stepdaughters, especially the youngest one, who is partially deaf. She spends several hours every day helping her with her homework. However, she loses her patience often and hits her with her hands when the girl does not remember something "that I taught her before and I expected her to know." The youngest daughter did tell her school social worker that her mother hits her. The social worker told the client that if the hitting continues she will report her to Social Services. The client pleaded with her not to call and told her that she will seek therapy to stop hitting her stepdaughters and to understand herself better. She entered therapy at this point.

PROFILE VALIDITY

The client has responded to the MMPI-2 items by claiming to be unrealistically virtuous. This test-taking attitude weakens the validity of the test and shows an unwillingness or inability on the part of the client to disclose personal information. Despite this extreme defensiveness, she has responded to items reflecting some unusual symptoms or beliefs. Many reasons may be found for this pattern of uncooperativeness: conscious distortion to present herself in a favorable light, lack of psychological sophistication, or rigid neurotic adjustment.

SYMPTOMATIC PATTERNS

Scales Hs, D, Hy, and Pd were used as the prototype to develop this report. Individuals with this MMPI-2 clinical profile tend to exhibit a pattern of chronic psychological maladjustment and frequently have histories of acting-out behavior, including outbursts of anger. This client seems to have a great many vague physical complaints, especially symptoms of tension, insomnia, and stomach distress. In addition, she probably has a history of medical problems, environmental stress such as job or financial troubles, and substance-use or -abuse difficulties.

Apparently emotionally immature, she is dependent and demanding and tends to become irritable when her demands are frustrated. She may appear suspicious and hostile toward professional staff.

In addition, the following description is suggested by the content of the client's item responses. She views her physical health as failing and reports numerous somatic concerns. She feels that life is no longer worthwhile and that she is losing control of her thought processes.

PROFILE FREQUENCY

It is usually valuable in MMPI-2 clinical profile interpretation to consider the relative frequency of a given profile pattern in various settings. The client's MMPI-2 high-point clinical scale score (Hy) is found in 10.5% of the MMPI-2 normative sample of women. However, only 3.7% of the sample have Hy as the peak score at or above a T score of 65, and only 2.1% have well-defined Hy spikes. Her elevated MMPI-2 profile configuration (1-3/3-1) is rare in samples of normals, occurring in less than 2.7% of the MMPI-2 normative sample of women.

The relative frequency of this profile in various outpatient settings is informative. In the NCS female outpatient sample, this MMPI-2 high-point clinical scale score (Hy) is the second most frequent peak, occurring in 17.2% of the women. Moreover, 13.3% of the outpatient women have the Hy scale spike at or above a T score of 65, and 7.5% have well-defined Hy peaks. Her elevated MMPI-2 profile configuration (1-3/3-1) is found in 8.9% of the women in the NCS outpatient sample.

Figure 14-8. Minnesota Report™ Narrative for a 38-Year-Old Puerto Rican Woman Being Evaluated in the Context of Psychotherapy. *Source:* The Minnesota Report™: Adult Clinical System. Copyright © 1989 by the Regents of the University of Minnesota. All rights reserved.

She was first seen individually in cognitive behavioral treatment directed at developing better skills in anger control, but little progress was achieved in therapy initially. The MMPI-2 was then administered to assess possible explanations for her poor progress in therapy and because she insisted that she wanted to know why she could not control her anger.

The client's approach to the MMPI-2 was to present herself in a favorable light,

PROFILE STABILITY

The relative elevation of her clinical scale scores suggests that her profile is not as well defined as many other profiles. That is, her highest scale or scales are very close to her next scale score elevations. There could be some shifting of the most prominent scale elevations in the profile code if she is retested at a later date. The difference between the profile type used to develop the present report and the next highest scale in the profile code was 2 points. So, for example, if the client is tested at a later date, her profile might involve more behavioral elements related to elevations on Sc. If so, then on retesting, emotional alienation, unusual thinking, bizarre perceptions of others, and a stronger tendency to engage in extreme fantasy might become more prominent.

INTERPERSONAL RELATIONS

She appears to be rather dependent, demanding, and manipulative in interpersonal relationships, and she may act aggressively if frustrated. She may have a tendency to be verbally abusive toward her husband when she feels frustrated.

Her very high score on the Marital Distress Scale suggests that her marital situation is quite problematic at this time. She has reported a number of problems with her marriage that are possibly important to understanding her current psychological symptoms.

The content of this client's MMPI-2 responses suggests the following additional information concerning her interpersonal relations. She feels like leaving home to escape a quarrelsome, critical situation and to be free of family domination.

DIAGNOSTIC CONSIDERATIONS

Individuals with this profile often have a long-standing Personality Disorder, with substance use or abuse as a prominent feature of their clinical pattern. They may also show elements of an Anxiety or Depressive Disorder.

TREATMENT CONSIDERATIONS

The client's long-term personality problems will probably influence treatment efforts. Antagonistic behavior may be expected in the early stages of treatment. Psychotherapy with such clients may be a long and difficult process because they tend to resist psychological interpretations and view their problems as physical. Because these individuals typically have difficulties controlling anger, they usually experience relationship problems that need to be dealt with in therapy. They also tend to blame others for their problems and see no need for personal change. Major, long-term personality changes are not likely to occur. Treatment that is focused on symptom relief without confronting major personality problems may

Figure 14-8. (continued)

but in an unsophisticated manner, while admitting to several problems. This is consistent with her behavior during therapy, since she tends to spend considerable time justifying her actions and trying to impress the therapist favorably. As therapy proceeded she became more open and admitted her low frustration tolerance, how insecure she was, and even her dissatisfaction with her husband's "passive personality." She even admitted that she "did not love him," but was quick have some success. Family evaluation and/or treatment may need to focus upon her potential to act out aggressively against other family members.

Her item content suggests some family conflicts that are causing her considerable concern at this time. She feels unhappy about her life and resents having an unpleasant home life. Psychological intervention could profitably focus, in part, on clarifying her feelings about her family.

NOTE: This MMPI-2 interpretation can serve as a useful source of hypotheses about clients. This report is based on objectively derived scale indices and scale interpretations that have been developed in diverse groups of patients. The personality descriptions, inferences, and recommendations contained herein need to be verified by other sources of clinical information because individual clients may not fully match the prototype. The information in this report should most appropriately be used by a trained, qualified test interpreter. The information contained in this report should be considered confidential.

Figure 14-8. (continued)

to point out how good he was to her and conceded that his passivity has served as a counterpart to her aggressiveness and high level of activity.

As the Minnesota Report narrative shows, the patient presents many vague physical symptoms as well as a history of acting-out behavior, including outbursts of anger, as confirmed by her own acknowledgment during therapy. She appears emotionally immature and dependent since she keeps giving excuses for not pursuing her interest in working as a reporter and writing a book. She admits that she is very demanding of all members of her family and becomes irritable very easily when any members fail to meet her expectations. Also, she admits that her problems are getting too difficult for her to handle, and that several times after a "fight" with her husband she has walked out of the house very upset without telling anyone where she was going.

She appeared very suspicious of the therapist at the beginning of therapy and mainly came because she was told that she needed to be in therapy. She does not appear to be particularly depressed and is not afraid of losing her thought processes, as suggested by the Minnesota Report. On the other hand, the report's analysis of her interpersonal relations appears to be accurate, since she is very manipulative toward others, especially toward her husband. She appears to depend a great deal on him, while at the same time she constantly demands that he be cleaner and that he keep things the way she has arranged them. As predicted by the report, she becomes easily aggressive toward him and even verbally abusive when he does not comply with her demands. The report is also extremely accurate in predicting that she will tend to leave home to escape what she calls "fights" and family domination, which was one of the main fears that led her to wait several years before marrying him.

In terms of diagnostic and treatment considerations, a personality disorder, probably a histrionic personality, needs to be ruled out. Also, her anxiety and depressed mood over her marital problems are apparent. Moreover, as predicted by the Minnesota Report, she resisted psychological interpretations and showed an antagonistic attitude on several occasions, demanding that the therapist give her quick solutions to her problems and never seeming satisfied with the psychological explanations of her problems. She also consistently blamed her stepdaughters and husband for her difficulties.

As the report suggested, progress in therapy was possible only when the focus shifted from family therapy to symptom relief, without confronting major psychological problems. It was considered important to focus on her angry outbursts at family members; doing so appeared to help her gain some insight into her personal dynamics and to control her anger. Eventually she developed strategies such as walking out of the house to cool off but telling them where she was going. Finally, the report's suggestion that therapy should also focus on clarifying her feelings toward her family did help, because eventually she concluded that even when her stepdaughters did not behave as she expected them to, she realized they had positive qualities and how much they meant to her. She also appears to value and accept her husband more for what he is and now feels more comfortable being with him.

Case 2

This 38-year-old white male of average height and weight was referred by his staff psychologist at the state psychiatric hospital. The referral was made to make a differential diagnosis, since he was presenting both psychotic and depressive symptoms. The patient was raised in San Juan with three brothers and one sister by his natural parents. He married at age 18 when he was in his first year of college. He and his wife had four children together and maintained a difficult marriage until they divorced six years later. He managed to complete a bachelor's degree in business administration and started working as an accountant for the government. When he was 30 years old he started law school. He completed the degree in 1989 but failed his licensing examination once. He held several administrative positions in the government, obtaining a good job rating until 1989 when he was fired because of problems with his immediate supervisor. He also has had a drinking problem since adolescence and admits that he has used marijuana and LSD in the past.

He was first seen by a private psychiatrist when he was 17 years old, following the use of LSD. He also visited a psychiatrist during his divorce, when he was 24 years old. His first psychiatric hospitalization was in 1989 when he was fired from his job and his girlfriend left him. His father had also died recently. At that time, he was studying for his bar examination. He was admitted to the hospital

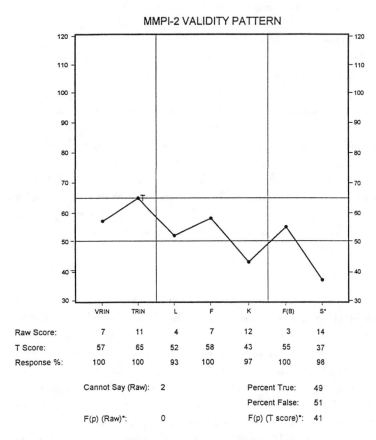

MMPI-2 VALIDITY PATTERN

	VRIN	TRIN	L	F	K	F(B)	S*
Raw Score:	7	11	4	7	12	3	14
T Score:	57	65	52	58	43	55	37
Response %:	100	100	93	100	97	100	98

Cannot Say (Raw):   2   Percent True: 49

Percent False: 51

F(p) (Raw)*:   0   F(p) (T score)*:   41

*Experimental

Figure 14-9. Minnesota Report™ MMPI-2 Validity Scale Profile of a 38-Year-Old Puerto Rican Male Inpatient. *Source:* The Minnesota Report™: Adult Clinical System. Copyright © 1989 by the Regents of the University of Minnesota. All rights reserved.

with suicidal ideation, very anxious, and complaining that other people could read his mind. He was fearful that other patients would hurt him and even "kill" him. He remained hospitalized for six weeks and then returned to his apartment under the supervision of his older brother. He got another job with the government but with much less responsibility and lower pay. He was again

MMPI-2 BASIC AND SUPPLEMENTARY SCALES PROFILE

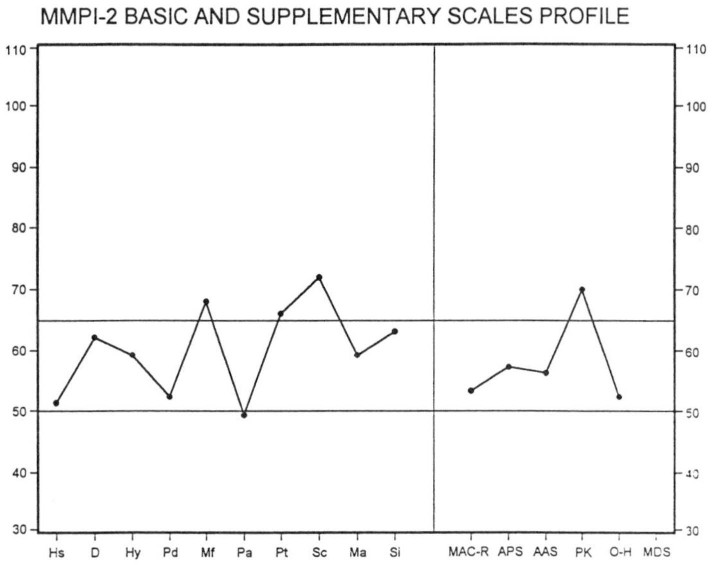

	Hs	D	Hy	Pd	Mf	Pa	Pt	Sc	Ma	Si	MAC-R	APS	AAS	PK	O-H	MDS
Raw Score:	7	24	25	19	35	10	22	27	22	37	23	26	4	20	13	*
K Correction:	6		5				12	12	2							
T Score:	51	62	59	52	68	49	66	72	59	63	53	57	56	70	52	*
Response %:	100	96	98	100	98	100	100	100	100	100	100	95	100	100	100	*

Welsh Code (new):   8'57+02-39 41/6: FL/K: Goldberg Index: 48
Welsh Code (old):   58"72'9304-61/ F-L/K?:   Henrichs Rule: Indeterminate
Profile Elevation: 58.80

*MDS scores are reported only for clients who indicate that they are married or separated.

Figure 14-10. Minnesota Report™ MMPI-2 Standard Scale Profile of a 38-Year-Old Puerto Rican Male Inpatient. *Source:* The Minnesota Report™: Adult Clinical System. Copyright © 1989 by the Regents of the University of Minnesota. All rights reserved.

hospitalized in December 1992 after slashing his right wrist with a razor blade and complaining that his fellow workers were conspiring against him. This was his second suicidal attempt prior to his most recent hospitalization. He also reported that he was worried he would lose his mind, and he appeared to be very fearful of others.

He was evaluated after four months of hospitalization, during which he continued to be very depressed over not being able to keep a job, pass the bar examination, and see his children on a regular basis. He began psychotherapy in January

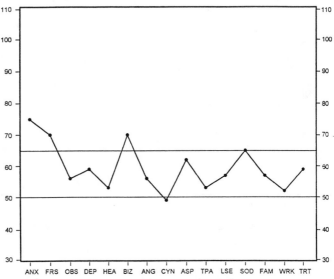

MMPI-2 CONTENT SCALES PROFILE

	ANX	FRS	OBS	DEP	HEA	BIZ	ANG	CYN	ASP	TPA	LSE	SOD	FAM	WRK	TRT
Raw Score:	16	10	7	9	6	8	8	10	13	10	7	15	8	8	8
T Score:	75	70	56	59	53	70	56	49	62	53	57	65	57	52	59
Response %:	100	100	100	100	100	100	100	96	100	100	100	100	100	100	100

Figure 14-11. Minnesota Report™ MMPI-2 Content Scale Profile of a 38-Year-Old Puerto Rican Male Inpatient. *Source:* The Minnesota Report™: Adult Clinical System. Copyright © 1989 by the Regents of the University of Minnesota. All rights reserved.

1993 but made little progress at first. The therapy was focused on helping him gain confidence in his ability to control his thoughts and "to not lose his mind." Although he did not develop good insight into his personal dynamics, he responded to symptom relief therapy directed at helping him realize that what appear to him to be hallucinations are his own thoughts and to accept that his "feelings of unreality" are something he will need to learn to live with. He remained in the hospital because he lost his apartment due to nonpayment of rent and he has no job. His relatives will not accept him at this time.

The MMPI-2 was administered when he was more stable and had responded to the supportive therapy mentioned above (see Figures 14-9, 14-10, 14-11, and

PROFILE VALIDITY

This is a valid MMPI-2 clinical profile. The client was quite cooperative with the evaluation and appears to be willing to disclose personal information. There may be some tendency on the part of the client to be overly frank and to exaggerate his symptoms in an effort to obtain help.

SYMPTOMATIC PATTERNS

The clinical scale prototype used to develop this report incorporates correlates of Pt and Sc. Because these scales are not well defined in the clinical profile (the highest scales are relatively close in elevation), interpretation of the clinical profile should not ignore the adjacent scales in the profile code. The client's profile suggests that he feels somewhat fearful and tense. He may also tend to be overideational, often feeling guilty, insecure, and inadequate to deal with life. He may have periods of intense anxiety and disorganization.

In addition, the following description is suggested by the content of the client's item responses. He has endorsed a number of unusual, bizarre ideas that suggest some difficulties with his thinking. The client's response content suggests that he feels intensely fearful about a large number of objects and activities. This hypersensitivity and fearfulness appear to be generalized at this point and may be debilitating to him in social and work situations. His high endorsement of general anxiety content is likely to be important to understanding his clinical picture.

PROFILE FREQUENCY

Profile interpretation can be greatly facilitated by examining the relative frequency of clinical scale patterns in various settings. The client's high-point clinical scale score (Sc) is the least frequent MMPI-2 peak score in the MMPI-2 normative sample of men, occurring in only 4.7% of the cases. Only 2.6% of the sample have Sc as the peak score at or above a T score of 65, and less than 1% have well-defined Sc spikes. This elevated MMPI-2 profile configuration (7-8/8-7) is rare in samples of normals, occurring in 1.5% of the MMPI-2 normative sample of men.

This profile is relatively frequent in various inpatient settings. In the Graham and Butcher (1988) sample of psychiatric inpatients, the Sc high-point score occurs in 13.8% of the males, with 13.2% scoring at or above a T score of 65 (3.8% are well defined in that high range). In the NCS inpatient sample, 9.1% of the males have this high-point clinical scale score (Sc). Moreover, 8.5% of the males in the inpatient sample have the Sc scale spike at or over a T score of 65, and 4.4% produce well-defined Sc spike scores in that range. The male inpatients in a Veterans Administration sample (Arbisi & Ben-Porath, 1993) produce this high-point peak score with 10.5% frequency. In addition, 8.9% are elevated at or above a T score of 65, and 4.9% are well-defined profiles.

Figure 14-12. Minnesota Report™ Narrative for a 38-Year-Old Puerto Rican Male Inpatient. *Source:* The Minnesota Report™: Adult Clinical System. Copyright © 1989 by the Regents of the University of Minnesota. All rights reserved.

14-12). He appeared cooperative and willing to disclose information though, as noted in the narrative report, with a tendency to exaggerate his problems in an apparent effort to ensure that he continue to receive help. The symptomatic patterns described in the report appear to fit fully with his clinical symptoms. He still appears to be hypersensitive, fearful, and generally anxious to the point that his social and work readjustment capacity has been significantly reduced. The de-

This elevated MMPI-2 profile configuration (7-8/8-7) is found in 8.2% of the males in the Graham and Butcher (1988) sample (the most frequent two-point code at or above a T score of 65), in 4.8% of the males in the NCS inpatient sample, and in 3.6% of the men in a Veterans Administration inpatient sample (Arbisi & Ben-Porath, 1993).

PROFILE STABILITY

The relative scale elevation of his highest clinical scale scores suggests some lack of clarity in profile definition. Although his most elevated clinical scales are likely to be present in his profile pattern if he is retested at a later date, there could be some shifting of the most prominent scale elevations in the profile code. The difference between the profile type used to develop the present report and the next highest scale in the profile code was 4 points. So, for example, if the client is tested at a later date, his profile might involve more behavioral elements related to elevations on D. If so, then on retesting, pronounced complaints of depressed mood and low morale might become more prominent.

INTERPERSONAL RELATIONS

He appears to be somewhat passive-dependent in relationships, and he tends to be a follower in social activities. Feelings of insecurity and fear of rejection cause him considerable anxiety at times. He has had great difficulty with relationships in the past. His personality problems may have been central in his divorce.

He is somewhat shy, with some social concerns and inhibitions. He is a bit hypersensitive about what others think of him and is occasionally concerned about his relationships with others. He appears to be somewhat inhibited in personal relationships and social situations, and he may have some difficulty expressing his feelings toward others.

DIAGNOSTIC CONSIDERATIONS

He has reported a number of psychological concerns, anxiety, and unusual thoughts that should be taken into consideration in any diagnostic formulation. His unusual thinking and bizarre ideas need to be taken into consideration in any diagnostic formulation.

TREATMENT CONSIDERATIONS

Individuals with this profile often exhibit anxiety and tension that require symptom relief. Although they may seek psychological treatment for their fears and concerns, they tend to intellectualize and ruminate a great deal and may have difficulty focusing on specific problems. Their poor social skills may become the focus of treatment.

Figure 14-12 (continued)

scription of his interpersonal relations is also extremely accurate, since he appears passive, dependent, shy, inhibited, and has difficulty expressing feelings. As suggested by the Minnesota Report, anxiety (which is probably related to his insecurity) and lack of self-confidence, together with his unusual thoughts, were considered in his diagnosis of borderline personality. His repeated suicide attempts, his pattern of intense interpersonal relationships alternating between overidealization and devaluation, and his pattern of impulsive behavior (including a buy-

He has expressed a number of specific fears with which he is concerned at this time. Behavioral therapy to alleviate these fears might be considered.

NOTE: This MMPI-2 interpretation can serve as a useful source of hypotheses about clients. This report is based on objectively derived scale indices and scale interpretations that have been developed in diverse groups of patients. The personality descriptions, inferences, and recommendations contained herein need to be verified by other sources of clinical information because individual clients may not fully match the prototype. The information in this report should most appropriately be used by a trained, qualified test interpreter. The information contained in this report should be considered confidential.

Figure 14-12 (continued)

ing spree during which he spent more than $24,000 in less than four months) confirm this diagnosis.

The treatment considerations presented in the narrative of the Minnesota Report (Figure 14-12) also appear to be valid. Once therapy was focused on symptom relief, he made good progress. He was eventually placed in a foster home where steps are being taken toward finding him new independent housing and a job. The MMPI-2 was useful in highlighting the principal areas of difficulty that were at the root of the multiple symptoms he was presenting. That is, the instrument demonstrated that his fears and poor control of his thinking processes were central to his difficulties; the apparent depression and suicide attempts appeared to be secondary to these factors. Thus, when we tried in therapy to help him develop insight into the possible dynamics of his apparent depression, no progress was made. As discussed above, progress was made only when we focused on his fears and thought processes.

References

Butcher, J. N., Graham, J. R., Dahlstrom, W. G., & Bowman, E . (1990). The MMPI-2 with college students. *Journal of Personality Assessment, 54*, 1–15.

Cabiya, J. J., & Vélez, R. (1989). Capacidad discriminativa del Inventario Multifasico de la Personalidad (MMPI) con tres muestras de poblacion puertorriquena [Discriminative ability of the MMPI with three Puerto Rican samples]. *Avances en Psicologia Clinica Latinoamericana, 7*, 105–115.

Colón, C. C. (1993). *Relationship between the MMPI-2 content scales and psychiatric symptoms with Puerto Rican college students and psychiatric patients.* Unpublished doctoral dissertation, Caribbean Center for Advanced Studies, San Juan.

García-Peltoniemi, R. E., & Azán Chaviano, A. (1993). *MMPI-2: Inventario Multifasico de la Personalidad-2-Minnesota.* Minneapolis, MN: University of Minnesota Press.

Hathaway, S. R., & McKinley, J. C. (1940). A multiphasic personality schedule (Minnesota): I. Construction of the schedule. *Journal of Psychology, 10*, 249–254.

Núñez, R. (1979). Applicacion del Inventario Multifasico de la Personalidad (MMPI) a la psico-pathology. [Application of the Minnesota Multiphasic Personality Inventory (MMPI) for psychopathology]. Mexico: El Manual Moderno.

Overall, J. E., & Gorham, D. R. (1962). The Brief Psychiatric Rating Scale. *Psychological Reports, 10,* 799–812.

Pope, K. S., Butcher, J. N., & Seelen, J. (1993). *The MMPI/MMPI-2/MMPI-A in court: A practical guide for expert witnesses and attorneys.* Washington, DC: American Psychological Association.

Prewitt, J. O., Nogueras, J. A., & Draguns, J. (1985). MMPI (Spanish translation) in Puerto Rican adolescents: Preliminary data on reliability and validity. *Hispanic Journal of Behavioral Sciences, 2,* 179–190.

Rodríguez, L. (1980). *La normalizacion del MMPI con una Muestra de Estudiantes Universitarios* [Normalization of the MMPI with a college sample]. Unpublished doctoral dissertation, Universidad de Puerto Rico en Rio Piedras.

Tellegen, A., & Ben-Porath, Y. S. (1992). The new uniform T-scores for the MMPI-2: Rationale, derivation, and appraisal. *Psychological Assessment, 4,* 145–155.

Chapter 15

The Castilian Version of the MMPI-2 in Spain: Development, Adaptation, and Psychometric Properties

Alejandro Avila-Espada and Fernando Jiménez-Gómez

This chapter is devoted to offering a description of the studies begun in Spain in 1992, whose main objective is preparing Castilian versions of the MMPI-2 and the MMPI-A and at the same time carrying out the psychometric and clinical studies necessary for laying the foundations for these versions. With this purpose in mind, a research team made up of professors and investigators from 11 Spanish universities, and coordinated by A. Avila-Espada, was formed at the University of Salamanca. Investigation by this team has been under way since 1992 in accordance with a plan to complete this project in 1995.

The MMPI in Spain: Problems and Weaknesses of the First Castilian Version

The original MMPI has not managed to achieve the prestige in Spain that it has in North America. It was first published in 1975 (and republished in 1986), and attitudes toward it have fluctuated between controversy and disinterest. Two reasons for the scant interest are the deficiencies in the first Castilian version, which will be commented upon below, and the idiosyncratic peculiarities of the Spanish public, who are not inclined to accept questionnaires as a way of giving information about themselves, especially when the questionnaires are extensive. The greatest use of the MMPI has been in personnel selection and academic counseling, though there does exist a generation of clinicians in Spain who have praised the instrument highly and have systematically included it among their assessment tools. These biases, which have hindered the instrument's development, are reflected in the normative samples used to establish the T-score tables for the MMPI.

The Castilian translation of the original MMPI contained a considerable number of items whose meaning was ambiguous, strange, or culturally or socially outdated and that also involved unacceptable biases of an ideological nature. Moreover, some of the items raised legal problems, because they possibly violate the Constitution of 1978, which protects the freedom of the individual with regard to his or her social, political, and religious ideas and guarantees both nondiscrimination on the basis of gender, race, religion, or ideology and the individual's right to privacy. As had happened in other countries, the results of psychological evaluations using the MMPI on candidates for the Barcelona Local Police Force were eventually annulled by judicial decision based on the premise that the formulation of certain items represented an assault on the individual's constitutional rights.

Another controversy existed regarding the differences between the official T-score tables authorized by the University of Minnesota for the use of the MMPI with the Spanish population and those scores known as the 1979 Norms, which were prepared by N. Seisdedos and based on a variety of Spanish samples theoretically more appropriate than those used in the first study. The University of Minnesota Spanish normative samples lacked stratification by age and geographical area and were made up largely of teenagers, university students, and subjects doing military service. In other words, they were incidental nonsystematic samples, taken chiefly at career guidance or personnel selection examinations. The norms published by Seisdedos (1979), which in the eyes of clinicians provided a more appropiate standard for the Spanish population, were never authorized by the University of Minnesota. Thus they were not included in the Spanish manual of the test but were published in a separate monograph (Seisdedos & Roig, 1986).

There is nothing especially new about the elements of dissatisfaction in Spain that made it desirable to have the original MMPI revised. They are (a) correcting formal defects and legally unacceptable content; (b) updating the instrument, including new items and new scales of interest in view of current clinical and psychopathological criteria; (c) if the test cannot be shortened, making sure it offers valuable compensations by means of more and better specific scales (18 scales were used in Spain with the original MMPI—validity, basic, and five supplementary. The number has increased threefold with the MMPI-2); and (d) taking even greater pains with controls for validity and reliablity.

All of these arguments pointed to an interest in perfecting a new version of the MMPI for Spain at a time when, after many delays, computers were finally becoming a common work tool, one that could make the most of instruments such as the MMPI that are very complex to score and interpret without computer facilities.

The Process of Translating the MMPI-2 into Castilian

The evidence described here favoring modification of the Spanish version of the MMPI is largely in agreement with the general arguments favoring revision of the original MMPI. When our research team came into contact with investigators who were working on the international versions of the MMPI-2, studies were already under way or about to be begun in at least five Spanish-speaking countries: Mexico, Chile, the United States, Puerto Rico, and Argentina. In view of this situation, one might ask: Is a new Castilian version of the MMPI really necessary? There are two replies to this question: (1) A wide range of diversity exists in the Spanish language depending on the geographical areas in which it is spoken. Bear in mind the many sociocultural communities in North America, Central America, and South America where Spanish is spoken, and their, at times, enormous sociological and linguistic distance from the so-called mother country, Spain. (2) The "distance" referred to not only affects idiomatic expressions but also demands that the consistency of psychometric norms be checked for each of the basic, content, and supplementary scales in the different geographic communities and cultures. To add even more complexity to this question, it is worth mentioning that Spain is a plural state, with economic, cultural, and linguistic diversity, which leads us to consider the fact that if the MMPI-2 eventually has a great impact among Spanish clinicians, ultimately it will be necessary to develop new versions in the other languages of the Spanish state: Catalan, Galician, Basque, and perhaps even others.

In preparing the Castilian version we have followed the guidelines for translation developed by the University of Minnesota Press. We first directly translated from English into Spanish all the items of the MMPI-2 by comparing the Castilian versions prepared by six professional psychologists (three of whom are bilingual) who were all experienced in translating scientific texts from English into Spanish. These psychologists were instructed to take equal care to maintain the original sense of the item and to make the sentences understandable for subjects from middle and low cultural levels and from different geographical locations in Spain. The problems posed by double negatives and adverbs relating to the frequency of events (frequently; usually; a few; every few days or oftener) were given special attention.

Numerous discussions on these rough versions led us to reword sentences that did not have a degree of agreement among at least four of the six translators. Once a consensus of four was reached, five psychology professors from psychological evaluation areas worked to achieve a final consensus based on the six rough drafts. This was referred to as the first Castilian version. Next, the four versions that were available to us in Spanish (Castilian, Chilean, Argentinian, Mexican) were exam-

Table 15-1. Changes Expected in the Castilian Experimental MMPI-2 Version

Where it reads	It should read
207. Me gustaría pertenecer a varios clubs o asociaciones.	207. Me gustaría pertenecer a varios *clubes* o asociaciones.
237. No me molesta tener mejor apariencia física.	237. No me molesta *no* tener mejor apariencia física.
561. Normalmente me encuentro son suficiente energía para realizar mi trabajo.	561. Normalmente me encuentro *con* suficiente energía para realizar mi trabajo.

ined jointly, and interversion discrepancies were detected and examined both for meaning and form. Discrepancies that did not result from merely cultural differences (see the following section) were corrected.

The next phase consisted of a control in which the resulting "corrected" Castilian version was submitted for examination by ten judges (professional psychologists familiar with the original MMPI). The full version was then administered to two groups of postgraduate clinical psychology students and to various subsamples of the general population, all for the purpose of appraising whether there were satisfactory indicators for three particular areas: vocabulary and reading comprehension level; detecting mistakes and confounding terms; and equivalent meaning with the MMPI original. The results of this phase allowed us to refine the first version further, revising approximately 25% of the items and constructing the second Castilian version, which was then back-translated into English and released as the experimental version, which has been and is still being used in the psychometric studies described in this chapter.

Despite the extreme care taken in the revision and in the wording of the items, after publishing the experimental version we detected printing errors in several items. These errors will be corrected in the next printing of the questionnaire (see Table 15-1).

The inverted meaning of item 237 is being taken into account in the electronic correction so that the reply to the item will not be distorted. Inevitable mistakes notwithstanding, we have managed to achieve a satisfactory basis for further refining a third Castilian version, which may become the definitive version to be used in the Spanish edition of the questionnaire.

Convergence and Differences between the New Castilian Version of the MMPI-2 and Other Versions in the Spanish Language

The most relevant and important changes in the new Castilian version with respect to previous Spanish versions have to do with the numerous modifications made in idiomatic expressions. The alterations were made to achieve an easier understanding of the items while at the same time respecting the psychological significance and overall meaning of the items. These changes affect a total of 154 items (27.16%) of the original MMPI. If we take into account the considerable number of items eliminated in the MMPI-2, as well as the new items, we find that up to 65% of the total number of items in the Castilian version of the MMPI-2 are either new or revised. The Castilian version of the original MMPI did, in fact, have many items that were inappropriately phrased, culturally biased, incomprehensible, or so ambiguous as to make responses decidedly difficult to interpret. The criteria followed in the U.S. revision of the MMPI-2 coincide with the Castilian version's deficiencies. The problematic points (bias for reasons of gender, religious beliefs, social attitudes, or purely cultural elements) have once again been taken into account in collating the four Spanish versions that have been contrasted in the hope that by doing so the phenomenon will not be repeated in the translation of the MMPI-2.

The original MMPI has already been the object of a number of Spanish translations (Butcher & Pancheri, 1976). We may note those of Costa Rica, Cuba, the Philippines, Mexico (Universidad Autónoma), Puerto Rico, and the two versions made in Spain—the version officially recognized by the University of Minnesota (TEA Ediciones) and the Spanish Army version (Central General Army Staff; Alegre Alonso et al.), the latter serving as the basis for the new scales found in the monograph prepared by Seisdedos and Roig (1986). Some time after the Butcher and Pancheri publication, a new version was prepared in Argentina (Montoya, 1977; Barbenza, Montoya, & Borel 1978), also carried out on university students.

In the preparatory phases of the Castilian translation of the MMPI-2, as we noted before, we have considered only the adaptations in Spanish that were available to us, which were those from the University of Buenos Aires (Argentina), the Pontifical University of Chile, and the Autonomous University of Mexico. On collating the three versions, we found the following: (a) great similarity in the translations and suitable adaptation of almost all items; (b) the Argentinian adaptation is the most similar to and coincident with the Castilian adaptation, although some of the greatest differences in items are found in the Argentinian adaptation; and (c) the Argentinian and Mexican adaptations did not follow the criterion of unifying the expressions of items that are phrased differently in terms of gender (male/female), a criterion that has been followed for the Castilian (not for all items) and the Chilean adaptations. The Mexican adapatation was subsequently so modified.

The most relevant discrepancies are: the lack of unanimity in the phrasing of item 443 and discrepancies in the Argentinian phrasing of items 306, 369, and

394. The remaining discrepancies in phrasing (see Appendix B) are not sufficiently relevant.

Item 443

Castilian Version:

443. *No trato de disimular la pobre opinión o lástima que me merece una persona hasta tal punto que ésta desconozca mi modo de sentir.*

Argentinian Version:

443. *No trato de disimular mi pobre opinión o lástima sobre algunas personas.*

Chilean Version:

443. *No trato de disimular mi mala opinión o lástima acerca de la gente, de manera que no se den cuenta de lo que realmente siento.*

Mexican Version:

443. *No trato de encubrir la mala opinión o lástima que me inspira una persona a fin de que ésta no sepa lo que siento.*

The phrasing of this item presents various problems. The negative wording requires complicated syntax, which makes the item difficult to understand. The Argentinian version has tried to solve the problem by simplifying the syntax, but an important part of the original meaning is lost in the process. We think the meaning of the English text is better preserved in the Castilian phrasing and thus have chosen to retain it.

Item 306

Castilian Version:

306. *Nadie se preocupa mucho por lo que le suceda a otro.*

Argentinian Version:

306. *Nadie parece comprenderme.*

Chilean Version:

306. *A nadie le importa mucho lo que a uno le pase.*

Mexican Version:

306. *A nadie le importa mucho lo que le suceda a uno.*

The Castilian version differs from the Chilean and Mexican versions in that it does not personalize in "oneself" the idea of people's lack of concern for others, thus expressing a general phenomenon. The Argentinian version continues to use the traditional wording of the first version.

Item 369

Castilian Version:

369. *Me inclino a dejar de hacer algo que deseo cuando los demás piensan que no vale la pena realizarlo.*

Argentinian Version:

369. *Me considero* capaz *de lograr lo que me propongo cuando otros creen que no vale la pena.*

Chilean Version:

369. *Soy capaz de renunciar a algo que quiero hacer, cuando los demás piensan que no vale la pena.*

Mexican Version:

369. *Tiendo a dejar de hacer algo que quiero si otros creen que no vale la pena.*

The Castilian version is more emphatic in stressing the idea of discontinuing "doing something" when it is not considered worthwhile by others, differing from the Chilean and Mexican versions in the use of colloquial idioms. We believe there is a meaning error in the Argentinian version in the use of the positive statement and in reference to capability and achievement.

Item 394

Castilian Version:

394. *Frecuentemente en mis proyectos he encontrado tantas dificultades, que he tenido que abandonarlos.*

Argentinian Version:

394. *Algunas veces me ha parecido que las dificultades se acumulaban de tal modo que no podía superarlas.*

Chilean Version:

394. *Mis planes frecuentemente han parecido estar llenos de dificultades que he tenido que renunciar a ellos.*

Mexican Version:

394. *Con frecuencia me ha parecido encontrar tantos obstáculos en mis planes que he tenido que abandonarlos.*

The Castilian, Chilean, and Mexican versions stress the idea of "quitting" in the face of difficulties, an aspect that is emphasized less in the Argentinian version. In this item, and in the previous items, we have chosen to maintain the Castilian version, at least in the empirical phase of the validation study.

Although empirical studies have begun with the Castilian version of the MMPI-2, we continue to revise the items. These adjustments do not affect the meaning of the items, but they clarify and shorten the phrasing, making the items easier to understand.

Validation

Our project of adapting the Castilian version of the MMPI-2 has included obtaining two broad samples, one of a normal population and the other of a clinical sample. The normal sample (approximately 2,000 subjects) is being constituted

Table 15-2. Spanish Normative Sample by Geographic Areas, Gender, and Age

Geographic Area	Aged 15-29	Aged 30-44	Aged 45-64	Total Males	Aged 15-29	Aged 30-44	Aged 45-64	Total Females	Total Subjects
Andalucia	71	46	53	170	68	46	58	172	342
Aragón	11	9	11	31	10	8	12	30	61
Asturias	10	8	11	29	10	8	11	29	58
Baleares	6	5	6	17	6	5	6	17	35
Canarias	16	11	10	37	16	11	11	37	75
Cantabria	5	4	4	13	5	4	5	13	27
Castilla-La M.	17	11	15	43	16	10	19	45	87
Castilla-León	27	18	24	68	24	17	28	68	136
Cataluña	56	47	52	155	54	47	55	156	310
C. Valenciana	36	27	31	94	32	28	36	99	193
Extremadura	11	7	9	28	10	7	10	27	55
Galicia	25	22	25	71	24	21	43	88	160
Madrid	46	37	38	121	46	40	42	128	249
Murcia	10	7	8	25	10	7	9	25	50
Navarra	5	4	4	14	5	4	4	13	27
País Vasco	21	17	19	58	21	17	20	58	116

from a number of samples from diverse collectives, subject to rigorous stratification criteria that, combined, reproduce the characteristics of the normal Spanish population according to 1989 census indicators, classified by gender in three age ranges: 19 to 29 years; 30 to 44 years; and 45 to 65 years. It is not possible in Spain to obtain a direct random sample; however, we have made every effort to ensure that the samples chosen are sufficiently representative. Subjects must meet the respective sample quotas (sex and age) from all the geographical areas of Spain (Table 15-2). Psychology students are excluded from the sample because bias might be introduced owing to their prior knowledge of the test and the "bad habits" they may have acquired from answering previous psychological questionnaires. In this way the sample contains subjects who, in their sociodemographic characteristics, match those of a hypothetical stratified random sample of the normal Spanish population. Each of the researchers responsible for a geographic area has formed a team of examiners, appropriately trained in the administration of the test, and has supervised the inclusion of subjects in the sample.

Similar criteria of sociodemographic representativeness were used to obtain the

Table 15-3. Reduced Normative Sample

Age	Males				Females				M&F
	19-29	30-44	45-64	19-64	19-29	30-44	45-64	19-64	19-64
Obtained	77	56	60	193	84	82	67	233	426
Remain	296	224	259	779	276	198	302	776	1555

clinical sample (not reviewed in this chapter; the final number will be 1,000 subjects) from mental health centers, outpatient clinics, and private practices in the different geographical areas of Spain. The test protocols are obtained by clinicians experienced in the administration of the test, who also fill out forms providing clinical data for each subject.

At the time this chapter was prepared, and with the intention of presenting a preview of the main psychometric indicators of the equivalence of the Castilian and U.S. versions, we took a subsample of the medical records obtained from June to October 1993, which represent approximately 25% of the total sample of the general population (normal). The composition of the subsample is described in Table 15-3 and includes subjects from the main geographical areas. It is made up of 426 normal subjects (193 males and 233 females), whose answers to the MMPI-2 have been used to carry out the initial exploratory psychometric analyses described in the following section.

Structural Characteristics of the Castilian Version with the Normal Population

Our first concern was to establish whether the Castilian version of the MMPI-2 was equivalent to the English original. Means and standard deviations for males and females in the Spanish sample were obtained for the MMPI-2 scales (Table 15-4). For most scales the average scores are higher in the Spanish sample than in the U.S. normative sample; however, the variability indicators are very similar. When they are compared by gender, both the U.S. and the Castilian descriptive statistics show the same patterns for most scales, thus enabling us to assume a satisfactory level of equivalence. Tables 15-5 and 15-6 include the most common statistical indicators (means, standard deviations, standard error of measurement, variance, coefficient of variance, minimum and maximum values, kurtosis, and skewness). Only scales F (and F_B), VRIN, Mf, BIZ, and GF show bias on kurtosis, to which Pa and R must be added in the case of male subjects. As for skewness, bias appears in practically the same scales, a result that is congruent with results from the U.S. studies. The significance of the differences in mean scores for males and females has also been estimated. Gender differences are seen particularly in the supplementary and content scales (D, PT, FRS, OBS, DEP, LSE, SOD, FAM, WRK, TRT, A, Es, MAC-R, O-H, Re, Mt, GM,

Table 15-4. Comparison of MMPI-2 Scores for Spanish and U.S. Samples

| | Castilian Sample | | | | U.S. Sample | | | |
| | Male | | Female | | Male | | Female | |
Scale	Mean	SD	Mean	SD	Mean	SD	Mean	SD
Validity Scales								
L	4.959	2.338	4.76	2.26	3.53	2.28	3.56	2.08
F	8.119	5.717	7.219	4.571	4.53	3.24	3.66	2.91
K	13.927	4.284	13.412	4.05	15.30	4.76	15.03	4.58
F_B	3.772	4.18	4.18	3.744	1.86	2.44	1.94	2.58
VRIN	7.772	3.302	8.077	3.015	5.07	2.62	5.04	2.51
TRIN	9.87	1.815	9.815	1.811	8.95	1.41	9.00	1.32
Basic Scales								
1-Hs (s/k)	7.663	5.289	8.704	4.732	4.92	3.87	5.93	4.51
2-D	21.974	5.39	23.867	4.772	18.32	4.59	20.14	4.97
3-Hy	21.637	5.034	22.21	4.768	20.87	4.73	22.08	4.72
4-Pd (s/k)	17.301	5.007	17.343	4.746	16.57	4.60	16.21	4.65
5 Mf	24.793	4.695	31.047	4.257	26.01	5.08	5.94	4.08
6-Pa	10.337	3.805	10.927	3.52	10.10	2.87	10.23	2.97
7-Pt (s/k)	14.751	8.167	16.854	8.041	11.24	6.61	12.69	7.19
8-Sc ((s/k)	16.301	9.762	16.828	9.015	11.20	7.12	11.24	7.57
9-Ma (s/k)	16.756	4.356	16.571	4.968	16.88	4.51	16.07	4.50
0-Si	28.404	9.441	28.966	8.138	25.86	8.57	27.98	9.18
Content Scales								
ANX	8.14	4.607	9.21	4.639	5.53	4.17	6.53	4.51
FRS	5.959	4.064	9.691	4.331	3.80	2.96	6.59	3.60
OBS	5.943	3.586	6.815	3.039	4.93	3.06	5.50	3.32
DEP	8.041	4.775	9.506	4.598	4.79	4.62	5.86	5.02
HEA	8.02	5.254	8.936	5.096	5.29	3.91	6.16	4.47
BIZ	3.446	3.142	3.506	3.078	2.30	2.50	2.21	2.49
ANG	6.943	3.417	7.236	3.639	5.63	3.31	5.68	3.08
CYN	11.684	4.681	11.391	4.796	9.50	5.35	8.73	5.16
ASP	10.15	4.122	9.395	3.661	7.91	4.19	6.17	3.70
TPA	9.793	3.456	9.674	3.356	8.08	3.68	7.41	3.34

continued on next page

Table 15-4 (continued)

LSE	6.881	3.79	8.258	4.021	4.25	3.69	5.16	4.24
SOD	8.124	5.068	7.172	4.15	7.65	4.77	7.53	4.80
FAM	6.166	3.867	6.888	3.813	5.32	3.52	6.14	3.77
WRK	9.622	5.965	11.185	5.317	7.30	4.98	8.51	5.45
TRT	7.824	4.824	9.043	4.501	4.70	3.71	5.02	3.98
Supplementary Scales								
A	13.845	8.211	15.95	7.761	10.02	7.10	11.64	7.90
R	17.725	4.512	17.644	4.137	15.18	4.53	16.34	3.81
Es	34.124	5.9	31.601	5.45	37.34	4.46	34.37	4.90
MAC-R	22.192	4.263	20.837	3.903	21.72	4.32	19.78	3.65
O-H	13.057	2.666	13.983	2.729	12.51	2.94	13.53	2.74
Do	15.399	3.021	15.124	3.068	16.62	2.95	16.27	2.89
Re	19.321	4.288	20.15	3.733	20.09	3.89	21.02	3.36
Mt	15.725	7.018	13.545	6.532	11.30	6.44	12.31	6.99
GM	33.684	6.222	26.498	5.995	37.87	4.87	28.83	6.51
GF	25.855	4.557	33.618	4.428	27.93	4.72	37.68	3.88
PK	11.611	7.712	11.974	6.959	8.01	5.99	8.52	6.56
PS	16.057	10.224	17.315	9.43	10.49	7.98	11.82	8.96

and GF, all with p < .01); similar tendencies are observed in Hs, ANX, and ASP (p < .05).

We have estimated to what degree age introduces significant differences in some of the MMPI-2 scales and these differences are shown in Tables 15-7 and 15-8. The men's scores for the L, TRIN, Hs, D, Pt, Si, ANX, FRS, OBS, DEP, HEA, ANG, CYN, TPA, SOD, WRK, TRT, A, MT, and PS scales increase with age; on the other hand, scores for K, Es, Do, and GM scales decrease with age. The influence of age on women's scores is slightly less, affecting only the L, TRIN, Hs, Si, FRS, HEA, CYN, TRT, and GF scales, which increase with age, and the Pd and Es scales, which decrease with age.

Likewise, we have estimated the item endorsements for both genders, which are in Appendix D. For Spanish females, 159 items are answered true by less than 25% of the subjects, whereas 92 items are answered true by more than 75%. In a similar pattern, 164 items are answered true by less than 25% of the Spanish males and 85 items are answered true by more than 75%. Items distinguishing the two national samples were examined by comparing individual item endorsement fre-

Table 15-5. Statistical Analysis of the Female Normative Sample (N = 233)

Scale	Mean	SD	Std. Error	Var.	Coef. Var.	Min.	Max.	Kurtosis	Skewn.	p*
Validity Scales										
L	4.76	2.26	.148	5.106	47.474	0	11	−.525	.237	.3739
F	7.219	4.571	.299	20.896	63.323	0	34	7.1	1.947	.0716
K	13.412	4.05	.265	16.398	30.193	4	24	−.542	.139	.2034
F_B	4.18	3.744	.245	14.019	89.569	0	20	2.25	1.407	.2926
VRIN	8.077	3.015	.198	9.089	37.324	1	20	1.375	.782	.3198
TRIN	9.815	4.811	.119	3.28	18.453	5	16	.325	.328	.7575
Basic Scales										
1-Hs	8.704	4.732	.31	22.39	54.365	0	26	.668	.886	.0328
2-D	23.867	4.772	.313	22.771	19.994	13	38	.236	.607	.0001
3-Hy	22.21	4.768	.312	22.736	21.468	11	38	−.01	.311	.2293
4-Pd	17.343	4.746	.311	22.528	27.367	7	34	.5	.654	.928
5-Mf(f)	31.047	4.257	.279	18.123	13.712	11	41	1.805	−.703	
6-Pa	10.927	3.52	.231	12.387	32.209	3	24	.701	.609	.0975
7-Pt	16.854	8.041	.527	64.66	47.712	40		−.331	.46	.0079
8-Sc	16.828	9.015	.591	81.272	53.571	2	48	.658	.893	.5627
9-Ma	16.571	4.968	.325	24.686	29.983	5	37	.601	.414	.6851
0-Si	28.966	8.138	.533	66.232	28.096	7	55	.186	.295	.5101
Content Scales										
ANX	9.21	4.639	.304	21.52	50.367	0	21	−.746	.248	.0178
FRS	9.691	4.331	.284	18.758	44.691	0	20	−.562	.18	.0001
OBS	6.815	3.039	.199	9.237	44.594	0	15	−.423	.157	.0068
DEP	9.506	4.598	.301	21.139	48.364	1	25	−.043	.496	.0014
HEA	8.936	5.096	.334	25.966	57.026	0	26	.599	.976	.1455
BIZ	3.506	3.078	.202	9.475	87.786	0	16	1.55	1.232	.8407
ANG	7.236	3.369	.221	11.354	46.565	0	15	−.791	.15	.3751
CYN	11.391	4.796	.314	22.998	42.101	1	22	−.655	−.067	.5255
ASP	9.395	3.661	.24	13.404	38.969	1	20	−.558	.017	.0459
TPA	9.674	3.356	.22	11.264	34.693	2	19	−.387	.246	.7196
LSE	8.258	4.021	.263	16.166	48.692	0	20	−.314	.428	.0003

continued on next page

Table 15-5 (continued)

SOD	7.172	4.15	.272	17.22	57.863	0	21	.267	.713	.0335
FAM	6.888	3.813	.25	14.539	55.354	0	21	.568	.73	.0537
WRK	11.185	5.317	.348	28.272	47.541	27	.114	.971	.0045	
TRT	9.043	4.501	.295	20.257	49.771	1	21	−.517	.345	.0073
Supplementary Scales										
A	15.97	7.61	.499	57.917	47.654	1	36	−.566	.34	.0059
R	17.664	4.137	.271	17.118	23.458	36	.934	.36	.8459	
Es	31.601	5.45	.357	29.706	17.247	14	45	−.049	−.385	.0001
MAC–R	20.837	3.903	.256	15.232	18.731	32	.13	.21	.0007	
O-H	13.983	2.729	.179	7.448	19.517	7	24	.5	.534	.0005
Do	15.124	3.068	.201	9.411	20.283	6	23	−.1	−.223	.3551
Re	20.15	3.733	.245	13.939	18.528	6	27	.231	−.518	.0335
Mt	17.545	6.532	.428	2.671	37.232	4	37	−.51	.213	.0059
GM	26.498	5.995	.393	35.941	22.625	6	42	−.073	−.079	.0001
GF	33.618	4.428	.29	19.608	13.172	8	41	4.522	−1.352	.0001
Pk	11.974	6.959	.456	48.43	58.118	1	38	.36	.804	.6103
PS	17.315	9.43	.619	88.927	54.463	2	46	−.145	.629	.1891

* Analysis of variance (F-test): male vs. female.

quencies across both samples. Items with endorsement percentage differences greater than 50% were identified. Only five items show differences in this range: items 48 and 94 for females and items 118, 215, and 447 for both males and females. With only these few differences, item endorsement patterns between U.S. and Spanish samples are fairly similar. The correlations of endorsement percentages are .850 for females and .871 for males, further confirming the equivalence between the English-language MMPI-2 and the Castilian version. The item endorsement patterns within genders for the Spanish samples (.911 correlation) are practically identical with the U.S. sample (.926 correlation). Appendix D reveals some cultural differences between items in the Spanish and U.S. samples, defined as those that differ by 25% or greater. With these criteria, 37 items were added to the five previously cited.

We conclude this discussion of the estimated equivalence of the Castilian version and the original English-language MMPI-2 with a correlational exploratory analysis designed to estimate the inter-scale relationships separately for each gender. The matrix of product-moment correlations of the non-K-corrected raw scores for

Table 15-6. Statistical Analysis of the Male Normative Sample (N = 193)

Scale	Mean	SD	Std. Error	Var.	Coef. Var.	Min.	Max.	Kur- tosis	Skewn.	p*
Validity Scales										
L	4.959	2.338	.168	5.467	47.154	0	11	−.469	.312	.3739
F	8.119	5.717	.412	32.689	70.419	1	32	3.872	1.753	.0716
K	13.927	4.284	.308	18.349	30.756	5	25	−.411	.104	.2034
F_B	3.772	4.249	.306	18.052	112.639	0	22	5.902	2.292	.2926
VRIN	7.772	3.302	.238	10.906	42.491	1	22	1.315	.818	.3198
TRIN	9.87	1.851	.133	3.426	18.752	4	15	.284	.057	.7575
Basic Scales										
1-Hs	7.663	5.289	.381	27.975	69.019	0	25	.388	.909	.0328
2-D	21.974	5.39	.388	29.057	24.531	9	35	−.576	.167	.0001
3-Hy	21.637	5.034	.362	25.337	23.263	11	37	−.257	.273	.2293
4-Pd	17.301	5.007	.36	25.065	28.939	7	32	.183	.543	.928
5-Mf	24.793	4.695	3.338	22.04	18.936	4	38	1.445	−0.61	
6-Pa	10.337	3.805	.274	14.475	36.806	4	28	2.307	1.059	.0975
7-Pt	14.751	8.167	.588	66.698	55.364	2	36	−.292	.648	.0079
8-Sc	16.301	9.762	.703	95.295	59.887	0	45	.066	.874	.5627
9-Ma	16.756	4.356	.314	18.977	25.997	5	29	−.242	.164	.6851
0-Si	28.404	9.441	.68	89.127	33.237	2	50	−.672	.121	.5101
Content Scales										
ANX	8.14	4.607	.332	21.225	56.599	0	21	−.47	.437	.0178
FRS	5.959	4.064	.293	16.519	68.211	0	18	−.139	.711	.0001
OBS	5.943	3.586	.258	12.856	60.332	0	16	−.416	.543	.0068
DEP	8.041	4.775	.344	22.8	59.379	0	26	.214	.702	.0014
HEA	8.202	5.254	.378	27.6	64.051	0	27	.987	1.113	.1455
BIZ	3.446	3.142	.226	9.873	91.194	0	15	2.259	1.495	.8407
ANG	6.943	3.417	.246	11.679	49.222	1	15	−.675	.227	.3751
CYN	11.684	4.681	.337	21.915	40.067	0	22	−.322	−.152	.5255
ASP	10.15	4.122	.297	16.993	40.612	0	20	−.207	−.07	.0459
TPA	9.793	3.456	.249	11.946	35.295	1	19	−.294	.087	.7196
LSE	6.881	3.79	.273	14.366	55.084	1	18	−.05	.666	.0003

continued on next page

Table 15-6 (continued)

SOD	8.124	5.068	.365	25.682	62.378	0	22	−.502	.566	.0335
FAM	6.166	3.867	.278	14.952	62.712	0	19	.036	.674	.0537
WRK	9.622	5.965	.429	35.58	61.994	0	27	−.103	.737	.0045
TRT	7.824	4.824	.347	23.271	61.658	0	22	−.124	.664	.0073
Supplementary Scales										
A	13.845	8.211	.591	67.413	59.305	1	34	−.562	.503	.0059
R	17.725	4.512	.325	20.356	25.454	7	41	2.745	.777	.8459
Es	34.124	5.9	.425	34.807	17.289	17	47	.01	−.643	.0001
MAC-R	22.192	4.263	.307	18.177	19.212	11	31	−.379	−.076	.0007
O-H	13.057	2.666	.192	7.106	20.416	6	20	−.34	.119	.0005
Do	15.399	3.021	.217	9.126	19.618	6	25	.467	−.262	.3551
Re	19.321	4.288	.309	18.386	22.193	5	28	−.341	−.352	.0335
Mt	15.725	7.018	.505	49.252	44.628	3	42	.377	.718	.0059
GM	33.684	6.222	.448	38.717	18.473	15	44	.223	−.688	.0001
GF	25.855	4.557	.328	20.771	17.627	0	41	4.658	−.766	.0001
Pk	11.611	7.712	.555	59.468	66.414	0	37	.132	.809	.6103
PS	16.057	10.224	.738	104.536	63.674	0	47	−.092	.761	.1891

* Analysis of variance (F-test): male vs. female.

the three validity and ten clinical scales shows that the Hs scale has significant correlations ($p < .001$) with almost all the scales except Mf, correlations that are significantly higher for the males than for the females ($p < .05$). A similar phenomenon of generalized intercorrelation is observed between scales D and Pd and the remaining scales (except Ma, with which, as is to be expected, D has negative correlations). In the same way, Sc and Pt correlate significantly with each other, whereas Mf (in the subsample of women) does not appear to be correlated with other scales. This high inter-scale correlation has been repeatedly demonstrated in previous studies with the MMPI and is one of the construct validity questions that needs to be reconsidered. For this reason, we have gone on to consider the grouping of the scales by factors, and to estimate the consistency of the solutions obtained with respect to those established in previous studies.

The factor analytic structure of the Castilian version of the MMPI-2 has been explored by means of a Principal Components Analysis (comparing Varimax and Oblimin rotation solutions, which are essentially coincident) starting from the intercorrelation matrices. In a first exploratory analysis we excluded validity scales L,

320 Alejandro Avila-Espada and Fernando Jiménez-Gómez

Table 15-7. Mean Differences of the Female Sample by Age Group

	Mean			p (F-test)*		
	Age Group			Age Groups		
Scale	19-29 (N = 84)	30-44 (N = 82)	45-64 (N = 67)	19-29/ 30-44	19-29/ 45-64	30-44/ 45-94
Validity Scales						
L	3.869	4.878	5.731	.01	.01	.05
F	7.429	6.866	7.388	–	–	–
K	14.036	13.183	12.91	–	–	–
F_B	3.964	3.707	5.03	–	–	.05
VRIN	7.655	8.183	8.478	–	–	–
TRIN	9.452	9.659	10.463	–	.01	.01
Basic Scales						
Hs	7.595	9.134	9.567	.05	.05	–
D	23.321	23.78	24.657	–	–	–
Hy	22.214	21.976	22.493	–	–	–
Pd	18.44	17.207	16.134	–	.01	–
Mf	30.988	31.634	30.403	–	–	–
Pa	11.31	11.122	10.209	–	–	–
Pt	16.857	16.805	16.91	–	–	–
Sc	17.286	16.22	17.00	–	–	–
Ma	17.06	16.549	15.985	–	–	–
Si	26.571	30.073	30.612	.01	.01	–
Content Scales						
ANX	8.881	9.61	9.134	–	–	–
FRS	8.929	9.427	10.97	–	.01	.05
OBS	6.845	6.451	7.224	–	–	–
DEP	9.512	9.537	9.463	–	–	–
HEA	7.667	9.5	9.836	.054	.01	–
BIZ	3.369	3.317	3.91	–	–	–
ANG	7.333	7.659	6.597	–	–	–
CYN	10.179	11.439	12.851	–	.01	–
ASC	9.143	8.939	10.269	–	–	.05

continued on next page

Table 15-7 (continued)

TPA	9.345	9.841	9.881	–	–	–
LS	8.476	7.585	8.806	–	–	–
SOD	5.988	7.768	7.925	.01	.01	–
FAM	7.06	6.878	6.687	–	–	–
WRK	11.548	10.878	11.104	–	–	–
TRT	8.226	8.793	10.773	–	.01	.05
Supplementary Scales						
A	15.881	16.171	15.836	–	–	–
R	17.262	17.695	18.06	–	–	–
Es	33.167	30.988	30.388	.01	.01	–
MaC-R	20.75	21.28	20.403	–	–	–
O-H	13.905	13.634	14.507	–	–	–
Do	15.345	15.171	14.791	–	–	–
Re	19.667	20.72	20.06	–	–	–
Mt	17.56	17.695	17.343	–	–	–
GM	27.298	26.28	25.761	–	–	–
GF	32.738	34.061	34.179	–	.05	–
Pk	12.00	12.427	11.388	–	–	–
Ps	17.289	17.561	17.045	–	–	–

*Only p < .05 and/or .01 differences.

F, and K to determine separately the clinical groupings that covaried, postulating a second order consistency. This first analysis revealed a very similar factorial structure in both the male and female groups (Table 15-9): four factors obtaining eigenvalues greater than one, which were generically labeled Psychotic (scales 4, 6, 8, and 9), representing about half the variance; three other factors, each between 10% and 15.5%, labeled Inhibited, a mixture of social introversion and depression, together with neurotic disorders; Somatoform, chiefly determined by scales 1 and 3; and, finally, the Masculinity-Femininity scale, which is independent from the rest. This structure converges with previous factor analytic studies and is congruent at the theoretical level with the repeatedly described psychotic triad and the breaking up of the neurotic triad into its two clinically significant components. We must not forget that in dealing with factorial structures detected in the scores of normal subjects, it is more likely that this will reproduce latent tendencies or indicators of "absence" of pathology than supraordered clinical syndromes.

Table 15-8. Mean Differences of the Male Sample by Age Group

Scale	Mean			p (F-test)*		
	Age Group			Age Groups		
	19-29 (N = 77)	30-44 (N = 56)	45-64 (N = 60)	19-29/ 30-44	19-29/ 45-64	30-44/ 45-94
Validity Scales						
L	4.584	4.732	5.65	–	.01	.05
F	8.169	7.125	8.983	–	–	–
K	15.065	13.75	12.633	–	.01	–
F_B	3.377	3.375	4.65	–	–	–
VRIN	7.597	7.679	8.083	–	–	–
TRIN	9.519	9.643	10.533	–	.01	.01
Basic Scales						
Hs	5.792	6.839	10.833	–	.01	.01
D	19.766	21.893	24.883	–	.01	.01
Hy	21.208	21.446	22.367	–	–	–
Pd	17.571	16.804	17.417	–	–	–
Mf	25.208	25.589	23.517	–	.05	.05
Pa	10.325	10.071	10.6	–	–	–
Pt	13.338	14.232	17.05	–	.01	–
Sc	15.571	14.982	18.467	–	–	–
Ma	17.506	15.768	16.717	.05	–	–
Si	25.312	28.571	32.217	.05	.01	.05
Content Scales						
ANX	6.818	8.232	9.75	–	.01	–
FRS	4.987	5.982	7.183	–	.01	–
OBS	5.299	5.929	6.783	–	.05	–
DEP	6.857	7.589	9.983	–	.01	.01
HEA	6.234	7.607	11.283	–	.01	.01
BIZ	3.468	2.786	4.033	–	–	.05
ANG	6.117	7.018	7.933	–	.01	–
CYN	10.792	10.804	13.65	–	.01	.01
ASC	10.273	9.607	10.5	–	–	–

continued on next page

Table 15-8 (continued)

TPA	8.61	9.929	11.183	.05	.01	.05
LS	5.74	7.143	8.1	.05	.01	–
SOD	7.182	7.982	9.467	–	.01	–
FAM	5.883	6.304	6.4	–	–	–
WRK	8.143	9.804	11.35	–	.01	–
TRT	6.117	7.786	10.05	.05	.01	.01
Supplementary Scales						
A	11.818	14.00	16.3	–	.01	–
R	17.26	17.696	18.35	–	–	–
Es	35.87	34.536	31.5	–	.01	.01
MaC-R	22.494	21.482	22.467	–	–	–
O-H	13.104	13.446	12.633	–	–	–
Do	15.909	15.714	14.45	–	.01	.05
Re	18.909	19.982	19.233	–	–	–
Mt	14.247	15.679	17.667	–	.01	–
GM	35.13	33.089	32.383	–	.05	–
GF	25.078	26.732	26.033	.05	–	–
Pk	10.662	10.607	13.767	–	.05	.05
Ps	14.132	15.304	19.2	–	.01	.05

*Only $p < .05$ and/or .01 differences.

Table 15-9. Summary of the Principal Components Analysis of the Spanish General Population

	Males	Females
Factor I – Psychotic (46.1 & 39% Variance prop.)	MA, SC, PD, (PA)*	SC, PT, PD, MA, PA
Factor II – Inhibited (15.5% & 15.8%)	SI, D, PT, HS	SI, (D), (PT), (-MA)
Factor III – Somatoform (12.8% & 12.5%)	HY, PA, (HS)	HY, D, HS
Factor IV – Gender (8.4% & 10.5%)	MF	MF

* When a scale has high factor loadings in more than one factor, the factor whose loading is lower appears in parentheses.

Table 15-10. Factor Loadings (Varimax Rotations) for 193 Normal Spanish Male Adults

Scale	Factor				
	I	II	III	IV	h²
L	−.058	**.567***	−.308	−.256	.486
F	.317	.012	**.783**	−.067	.71
K	**−.566**	.546	−.387	.084	.776
Hs	**.607**	.300	.499	.027	.708
D	**.811**	.380	.155	.158	.851
Hy	.082	**.794**	.283	.288	.800
Pd	.248	.033	**.681**	.286	.607
Mf	.073	.072	.120	**.927**	.884
Pa	.171	.404	**.615**	.261	.639
Pt	**.708**	−.186	.550	.232	.891
Sc	.526	−.067	**.780**	.157	.914
Ma	−.185	−.160	**.837**	.048	.762
Si	**.895**	−.179	−.032	−.006	.834
% Var. (cumm.)	32.1	17.7	37.3	12.9	

*Highest factor loadings are in bold type.

We later replicated the main components of the analyses described in the MMPI-2 administration manual, which included scales L, F, and K. The results are shown in Tables 15-10 and 15-11. Once again the structure coincides with that of the U.S. normal population, in which the four-factor solution, dominates the three- or five-factor solution, and the traditional differences between the factor analytic structure of the male and female samples recur. Thus, in males, scales 1, 2, 7, and 0 appear together in just one factor of "neurotic disorder," whereas in the female sample this structure splits into two factors, 2 and 0 on one hand and 1 and 7 on the other, marking the boundary between behaviors and experiences of inhibition and somatic preoccupation and neurotic indisposition in general. This delimitation might be enhanced by the usually greater rates of depressive disorders in women than in men in the general population.

At present, our psychometric studies of the Spanish normative sample continue, as do the validation studies with the clinical sample. As has been pointed out, early results offer support for the transcultural consistency of the MMPI-2, and in particular for the equivalence of the Castilian and U.S. versions, both studied with general populations of normal subjects.

Table 15-11. Factor Loadings (Varimax Rotations) for 233 Normal Spanish Female Adults

Scale	I	II	III	IV	V	h²
			Factor			
L	−.253	**.596***	.115	−.350	−.264	.625
F	**.700**	.007	−.005	−.250	.424	.732
K	−.212	.233	−.172	−.062	**−.833**	.826
Hs	.083	.593	−.001	−.067	**.701**	.854
D	.280	**.578**	.490	.139	.211	.717
Hy	.247	**.857**	−.127	.146	−.047	.835
Pd	**.851**	.084	−.037	.155	.124	.771
Mf	.019	.034	.088	**.929**	.006	.873
Pa	**.771**	.147	.030	.056	.124	.635
Pt	.538	.065	.182	.140	**.712**	.853
Sc	**.674**	−.011	−4.37E–5	−.044	.669	.904
Ma	.364	.004	**−.669**	−.072	.468	.805
Si	.106	−.019	**.840**	.031	.366	.852
% Var. (cumm.)	28.7	18.1	14.5	11.2	27.4	

*Highest factor loadings are in bold type.

References

Barbenza, C. M., Montoya, O. A., & Borel, M. T. (1978). "La tétrada psicótica del MMPI en un grupo de estudiantes universitarios. [The psychotic tetrad of the MMPI in a group of college students]. *Revista de Psicología General y Aplicada*, 150, 79–88.
Butcher, J. N., & Pancheri, P. (1976). *A handbook of cross-national MMPI research*, Minneapolis: University of Minnesota Press.
Montoya, O. A., & cols. (1977). La triada neurótica del MMPI en un grupo de estudiantes universitarios [The neurotic triad of the MMPI with a group of college students]. *Revista de Psicología General y Aplicada*, 149, 1077–1083.
Seisdedos, N., & Roig Fusté, J.M. (1986). *MMPI. Suplemento técnico e interpretación clínica*. [Technical supplement and clinical interpretation]. Madrid: TEA Ediciones.

Part IV

Adaptations in Europe

Chapter 16

The Flemish/Dutch Version of the MMPI-2: Development and Adaptation of the Inventory for Belgium and the Netherlands

Hedwig Sloore, Jan Derksen, Hubert de Mey, Greet Hellenbosch

The Flemish/Dutch version of the MMPI-2 was published at the end of 1993 (Pen Tests Publisher, 1993). It was the result of two years of fruitful cooperation between researcher-clinicians from two universities in two countries, speaking— at least for "foreigners"—the same language. In spite of this common language, we call it the Flemish/Dutch version. We will not discuss here whether it should be called the Flemish/Dutch version or the Dutch/Flemish version. To do so we would have to reconstruct perhaps five or even six centuries of the history of Europe or at least of both countries, which might dredge up old controversies and lead to new historical conflict. Let us instead say that basically our two languages are the same, but that over the years the use of that language in the two countries gave rise to some slight differences. The idea of a common version for The Netherlands and Belgium originated during a discussion in St. Petersburg, Florida, between James Butcher, Beverly Kaemmer, and the first author at an annual MMPI-workshop/symposium. The first contacts between Belgium and The Netherlands regarding this project were initiated in Kyoto during the International Conference of Applied Psychology.

Use of the MMPI in Belgium and The Netherlands

Before going into more detail about the translation and adaptation of the MMPI-2, we will briefly discuss the history of the use of the MMPI in both countries. Especially in Belgium, there has been a strong tradition of using and conducting research on the original MMPI. The first Flemish version was published in 1963 by Nuttin and Beuten. Although Nuttin claims to have remained as close as possible to the English original, in our view he did not follow the rules for translation that are generally accepted. He was strongly influenced by ideology and changed several items that related to sexual, religious, or gender-oriented preferences. Six items were never scored. For example, "I believe in a life hereafter" and "Children should be taught all the main facts of sex" remained in the questionnaire but were not scored. He developed several forms, among which were a card-form (A) and a shorter form (C, 432 items), which were the most popular in The Netherlands and in Belgium.

One of the major problems with the translation was the normative sample. It was not at all representative of the Dutch/Flemish population. Most of the subjects were younger than 30 years old and the female group was composed solely of students.

In 1970, Raymond Fowler visited the Free University of Brussels and proposed to J. P. De Waele a collaborative project involving the Roche computer-based system for the MMPI. However, De Waele, in collaboration with D. De Schampheleire and G. Van de Mosselaer, decided to develop a Flemish and a French translation, norms, and a computer system for scoring and interpretation called the BAMMPI (De Waele, De Schampheleire, & Van de Mosselaer, 1973; see Butcher & Pancheri, 1976). The test items were printed on IBM punch cards and sorted by the patients into three piles: agree, disagree, and cannot say. A very extensive scoring system and a detailed interpretation were offered. The system was used mainly in state prisons in Belgium. Some of the drawbacks were that the items were not translated in a careful way and that over time a number of minor changes were introduced. Here too, there was a problem with the norm group. It was composed of 315 normals and was a nonrepresentative sample; the majority of the subjects were students.

In the early '80s, the system was modernized by Sloore and Cluydts: The translation was redeveloped by remaining closer to the original English, the system was adapted for optical reading of the answer sheets and for use on PCs, the Nuttin norms were used, and the automated scoring and interpretation were totally reconsidered. In the past 10 years, considerable research has been conducted on the MMPI, some of the more important topics being pedophilia and incest (Sloore & Cluydts, 1985), nuclear power plant engineers (Sloore & Horrix, 1987), sleep disturbances (Cluydts, Deroeck, & Sloore, 1985), critical items (Sloore & Rouckhout, 1989), and the Morey personality-disorder scales (Sloore, 1988; Sloore & Rouckhout, 1992).

The situation in The Netherlands was different. Research, specifically reliability and validity studies, was lacking, and as a consequence the test was never completely accepted by the scientific community. However, clinical practice was totally different. Clinical psychologists in hospitals and other mental health institutions developed a comprehensive clinical expertise with the test. They were inspired both by American research and by their own clinical experience. However, insufficient validation prevented the widespread use of the MMPI.

The Flemish-Dutch Initiative

In 1991 the Flemish-Dutch MMPI-2 project was initiated. From the beginning we were committed to developing a careful stepwise translation in accordance with internationally accepted rules for translation (see chapter 2) and the rules published by the Cotan (the Commission for Test Affairs of the Dutch Institute of Psychology).

The committee approach to translation was used. Two teams of bilingual translators were formed: The Dutch team was composed of two psychologists who independently translated all the MMPI-2 items. They reached consensus through discussion. In Belgium we proceeded slightly differently. The new MMPI-2 items were first translated independently by one language specialist (Dutch-English) at the university level and by three clinical psychologists, one female, and two males. The old items that did not change were translated again by two psychologists. It took dozens of hours of discussion for the committee to try to reach a consensus.

The general principles observed were

• Remain as close as possible to the original English formulation.
• If two or more formulations are possible, choose the simplest.
• Ensure clarity of phrasing.
• Make items very readable.

At this stage of the translation process we had a Dutch version and a Flemish one, which had to be integrated. This was the moment of confrontation of the two "different" cultures. If we took into account the number of mutual jokes told on the two countries, we could expect some differences! The two Dutch psychologists and two of the Flemish psychologists formed a new committee to discuss the final formulation of all the items. All four can be considered true bilinguals; they are all familiar with psychological terminology as well as with everyday language; they all have experience with the MMPI (between three years and more than 20 years of clinical experience); and two of them had substantial bicultural experience owing to repeated stays in the United States.

The mutual jokes relate especially to differences in eating habits and the way we spend (or do not spend) money. However, when the subject was MMPI items, the cultural differences seemed rather minimal. For a very limited number of terms the use in the two countries was very different, and so we decided to include alternatives in brackets. A few examples by way of illustration: The equivalent term for "walk" in Flemish is *gaan,* while in The Netherlands it is *lopen;* to the Flemish people *lopen* means "run." "Cry" is translated in Flemish as *wenen,* and in Dutch as *huilen,* which in Belgium means "howl."

An important aspect of this last step of the translation process was that we often had very thorough discussions about the "real" or more "profound" meaning of some of the original items. If an MMPI item refers to the 'family', should we consider the nuclear family (in Dutch called *gezin*) or the family in a broader sense? If item 259 states "I am sure I am being talked about," should we interpret this in a positive or negative way? What does item 112, "I like dramatics," really mean? Should it be understood as liking plays with a dramatic story or liking to be on stage? For all the items about which we had some question concerning the exact meaning, we sent a fax with the different possible interpretations to James Butcher for consultation to determine which one to choose.

In the next step, the items were presented to potential respondents as a kind of pretest field study. The purpose was not to obtain responses but to discuss the readability of the items and to detect eventual problems in comprehending them. This step resulted in only minor adaptations, which were first discussed by the group of four.

The back-translation was done by an American psychologist who has been living and working for the past 10 years in The Netherlands. Starting from the Flemish-Dutch version, he translated all the items back into English and compared his translation with the original items. Only 12 of the 567 items had to be reconsidered.

Bilingual Test-Retest Study

In The Netherlands, research was conducted to detect any differences in the response patterns of bilinguals. Thirty-one students of English, all in their final stage of studies, volunteered to take the English and the Dutch versions. Half the subjects took the Dutch version first and the English second, and the second half the reverse. The subjects were mostly (80%) young people, between 20 and 25 years of age; 74% were female. For the 567 items, the mean stability percentage was 87%, with a range of 39% to 100%. Only eight items fell below 60%. The same items appeared to have rather low stability in the U.S. test-retest research as well.

Gathering the Norms by Telepanel

After the joint Flemish-Dutch version was completed, the normative data collection began. In Belgium this work is still in process owing to the fact that we are proceeding in a rather traditional way. A representative sample of 600 normals will be collected by gender, age, educational level, marital status, etc. Normals fitting these criteria will be asked to volunteer to take both the MMPI-2 and the Symptom Checklist-90.

The Dutch norms were gathered in a much more original way: with the help of the Telepanel of the University of Amsterdam. The Telepanel is a computer-guided data gathering system in which participating households in Holland have the loan of a computer and a modem. Interviews from the central Telepanel computer are sent to the households weekly. Members of the households can answer the questionnaires at any time convenient to them during the weekend. When they have completed the questionnaire, their answers are sent back automatically to the central Telepanel computer. The households used for the Telepanel were carefully selected to produce as closely as possible a representative sample of the whole Dutch population. The variables on which the panel was compared to the population were age, gender, province, urbanization, social relations, and professional information.

The telepanel is made up of about 1,630 households with a total of 4,300 persons. The background characteristics of these households closely correspond to the background characteristics of Dutch households generally. At the request of the second and third author, a sample was selected from these households. Age varied between 18 and 89 years, with a majority falling in the 30- 49-year-old age group (Table 16-1). Educational level varied from primary school (5%) to a scientific education (8%); 62% of the men worked in paid employment while only 29% of the women did. The majority of the women were housewives (48%). Of the selected households, 67% had a net income that varied between 1,701 and 4,200 Dutch florins per month (1 FL = U.S. $.50).

The representative sample was composed of 1,522 subjects. All subjects received a message on their PC asking whether they would be willing to answer a personality questionnaire in the last week of October 1992. More than 96% responded positively. As an incentive, a video camera was raffled off among the participants. In addition, they were told they would receive information about their scores. A total of 1,244 questionnaires filled in via the computer could be processed. This group was found to be representative of the total Telepanel population.

It is important to keep in mind that the norms were gathered using computerized test administration. Research on the differences between computer administration and "paper and pencil" administration has pointed to very small differences between the forms of administration, and as a rule, the differences were not larger than the standard error of measurement. In a meta-analysis comparing MMPI scores from 770 booklet administrations and 762 computerized administrations, Watson, Thomas, and Anderson (1992) concluded that the differences were small. On a number of scales, scores on the computerized administration were lower than the booklet scores; on average this difference was not larger than three-quarters of a T-score point.

It goes without saying that computerized administration and transmission via modem, without supervision, would not be appropriate for a clinical situation.

Table 16-1. Age and Sex Distributions of the Normative Group

Age Category	Males			Females		
	Frequency	%	Cumulative %	Frequency	%	Cumulative %
18 - 19	14	2.1	2.1	9	1.6	1.6
20 - 29	105	15.4	17.5	100	17.8	19.4
30 - 39	184	27.0	44.5	178	31.6	51.0
40 - 49	163	23.9	68.4	122	21.7	72.6
50 - 59	92	13.5	81.9	80	14.2	86.9
60 - 69	86	12.6	94.6	52	9.2	96.1
70 - 79	33	4.8	99.4	18	3.2	99.3
80 - 89	4	.6	100.0	4	.7	100.0
Total:	681	100.0		563	100.0	

The situation was rather exceptional here in the sense that all participants were very familiar with the use of a personal computer and were trained in and experienced with the use of PCs for the administration of questionnaires. At the same time, a kind of control mechanism was built in: The total time needed to fill out the questionnaire, as well as interruptions of the task, was registered. On this basis a limited number of participants were excluded from the sample.

The Dutch Norms

The Dutch normative sample responded to MMPI-2 items in a manner similar to the U.S. normative samples (see Figures 16-1 and 16-2 for the MMPI-2 standard scale scores of Dutch men and women and Figures 16-3 and 16-4 for the content scale scores for Dutch men and women). However, on the basis of the responses of 1,244 normals, separate norms were developed for women (N = 563) and for men (N = 681). As far as the validity and clinical scales are concerned, statistically significant differences (Mann-Whitney U Test) were found for scales L and K and scales 4 (Pd) and 8 (Sc). For the content scales, statistically significant differences between the sexes were found for three scales: bizarre mentation (BIZ), social discomfort (SOD), and negative treatment indicators (TRT).

Compared to the U.S. norms, the Dutch people seem to score significantly higher on L and on the validity scales generally and on scales 1 (Hs), 2 (D), 3 (Hy), and 0 (Si) (Derksen & de Mey, 1993). Americans seem to score higher on scales 4 (Pd), 6 (Pa), 7 (Pt), 8 (Sc), and 9 (Ma). As far as the new content scales are concerned, an important but not unexpected difference was found for FAM

MMPI-2

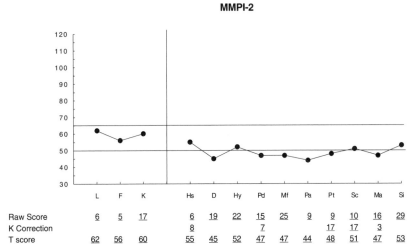

	L	F	K		Hs	D	Hy	Pd	Mf	Pa	Pt	Sc	Ma	Si
Raw Score	6	5	17		6	19	22	15	25	9	9	10	16	29
K Correction					8			7			17	17	3	
T score	62	56	60		55	45	52	47	47	44	48	51	47	53

Figure 16-1. MMPI-2 Clinical Scale Scores of Dutch Normal Men (N = 681) Compared with U.S. Normal Men (N = 1,138)

MMPI-2

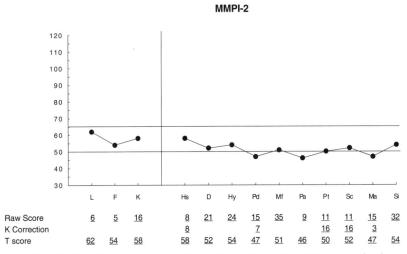

	L	F	K		Hs	D	Hy	Pd	Mf	Pa	Pt	Sc	Ma	Si
Raw Score	6	5	16		8	21	24	15	35	9	11	11	15	32
K Correction					8			7			16	16	3	
T score	62	54	58		58	52	54	47	51	46	50	52	47	54

Figure 16-2. MMPI-2 Clinical Scale Scores of Dutch Normal Women (N = 563) Compared with U.S. Normal Women (N = 1,462)

(family values), with the Dutch scores being significantly lower than the U.S. ones. In view of these results, we are convinced that it is always necessary to develop proper norms for each new translation (Figures 16-5, 16-6, 16-7, and 16-8). When the new norms are compared with the old Nuttin norms, the old norms considerably "underpathologize."

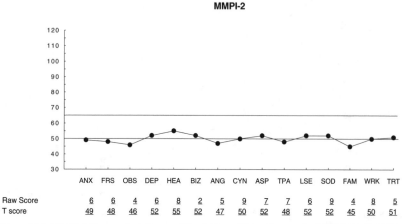

Figure 16-3. MMPI-2 Content Scale Scores of Dutch Normal Men Compared with U.S. Normal Men

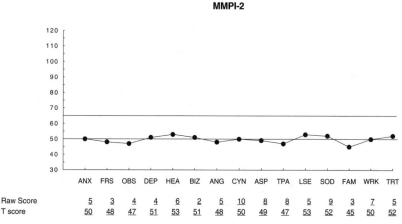

Figure 16-4. MMPI-2 Content Scale Scores of Dutch Normal Women Compared with U.S. Normal Women

As mentioned earlier, we are still constructing the normative group for Belgium. Actually, a first comparison was made on the basis of matched Flemish and Dutch samples: a small group of 105 normals was matched for gender, age, degree of education, and marital status. For both groups, statistically significant differences (Mann-Whitney U Test) were found for scales 2 (D) and 4 (Pd), non-K-corrected, the median values for scales 2 (D) and 4 (Pd) being significantly higher than the median values for the Dutch population. The total group was divided by gender, and no statistical differences were found for the male subgroup. But some differences were found for the female subgroup: For scales F, 2

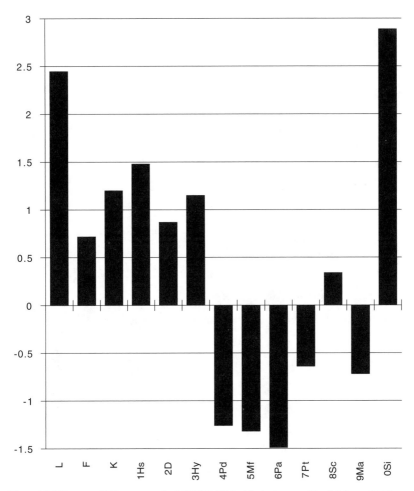

Figure 16-5. Response Differences on the MMPI-2 Clinical Scales between Dutch Men and U.S. Men

(D), 4 (Pd), 7 (Pt), 8 (Sc), and 0 (Si) the median values for the Flemish females were significantly higher. The statistically significant difference was reversed for scale K, and as a consequence, when the K-correction was applied for those scales where the correction is applicable, most of the differences disappeared. The only statistically significant differences found are for scales 2 (D) and 0 (Si). It is still too early to speculate on possible differences between Belgium and The Netherlands. The matched groups are too small, although the Dutch matching group was a representative subsample of the total norm group. As the data gathering continues, the Flemish data will be compared to the Dutch normative data to see if these tendencies hold. If these differences are confirmed, we

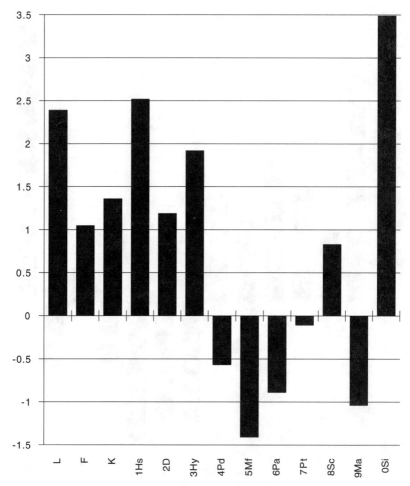

Figure 16-6. Response Differences on the MMPI-2 Clinical Scales between Dutch Women and U.S. Women

will need supplementary research to determine if they are due to cultural factors or to the questionnaire format, that is, computer administration versus paper and pencil.

Reliability Data

To estimate the internal consistency of the different scales, Cronbach's alpha coefficients were calculated for the Dutch normative sample. For the validity and clinical scales, the mean alpha for males was .6378, with a range from .4238 (Mf) to .8549 (Pt) (see Table 16-2). The mean alpha for the females was slightly lower— .6308 with a range from .3152 (Mf) to .8499 (Pt). The internal consistency esti-

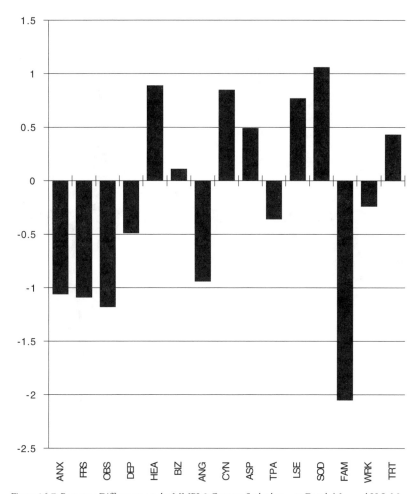

Figure 16-7. Response Differences on the MMPI-2 Content Scales between Dutch Men and U.S. Men

mates for the content scales for males vary from .6457 (FRS) to .8232 (DEP), with a mean of .7432. The mean for the females was .7447, with a range from .6419 (ASP) to .8350 (DEP). Most of these values are of the same magnitude as the U.S. values, though the Dutch values are usually somewhat smaller.

A small group of 62 females and 83 males agreed to respond to the questionnaire a second time, the interval being 18 months. The test-retest coefficients vary between .43 (Pa, males) and .88 (Sc, females) for the clinical scales, with most values superior to .70 (see Table 16-3). The test-retest coefficients for the content scales are much higher: .67 (ASP, females) up to even .91 (DEP, females). For both sets of scales the U.S. values again are slightly higher most of the time.

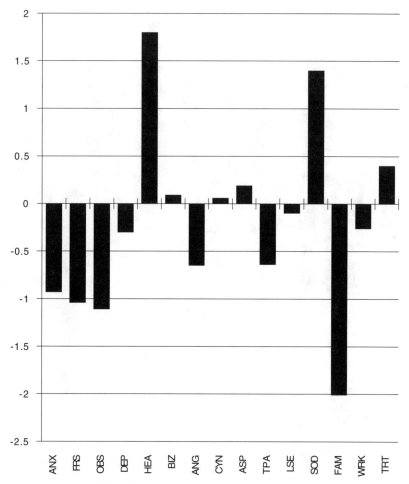

Figure 16-8. Response Differences on the MMPI-2 Content Scales between Dutch Women and U.S. Women

Other Statistical Data

The factor structure was examined separately for males and females on the basis of a principal component factor analysis (Derksen, Sloore, de Mey, & Hellenbosch, 1993). In both cases, four factors were identified explaining 72.7% and 72.8% of the variance, respectively. The results obtained are very similar to the U.S. results: a first factor that could be called general pathology, with high loadings on scale F and most of the clinical scales (1, 2, 4, 7, 8); a second factor with scales K and 3, suggesting overcontrol; factor three, a bipolar social factor (2, 9 versus 0); and factor four, scale 5 (Tables 16-4 and 16-5).

Table 16-2. Internal Consistency Estimates (Cronbach Alpha Coefficients)
for the MMPI-2 Basic and Content Scales

Scale	Items	Male		Female	
		N	Alpha	N	Alpha
L	15	679	.6054	562	.5322
F	60	672	.6171	557	.6171
K	30	672	.6806	558	.6447
Hs	32	678	.7879	561	.8049
D	57	674	.6149	561	.6491
Hy	60	672	.5763	559	.6092
Pd	50	672	.5540	561	.6304
Mf	56	667	.4238	555	.3152
Pa	40	672	.4495	559	.3924
Pt	48	674	.8539	562	.8499
Sc	78	673	.8386	558	.8353
Ma	46	672	.5013	557	.5463
Si	69	669	.7879	559	.7739
ANX	23	678	.8149	562	.8031
FRS	23	680	.6457	563	.7164
OBS	16	678	.7514	562	.7185
DEP	33	676	.8232	562	.8350
HEA	36	678	.7699	560	.7963
BIZ	23	676	.6813	561	.6797
ANG	16	679	.6761	562	.7056
CYN	23	667	.8208	557	.8278
ASP	22	674	.6624	560	.6419
TPA	19	679	.6753	561	.6430
LSE	24	675	.7477	557	.7813
SOD	24	673	.7991	560	.7688
FAM	25	670	.7367	561	.7211
WRK	33	678	.7953	561	.7841
TRT	26	678	.7486	562	.7484

Table 16-3. Test-Retest Data, Means, Standard Deviations, and Standard Error of Measurement for the MMPI-2 Basic and Content Scales on 83 Dutch Men and 62 Dutch Women

Scale	First Test		Second Test		r	Sem
	Average	Std.	Average	Std.		
Men						
L	6.06	2.46	6.13	2.74	.80	1.10
F	5.30	3.37	4.77	2.96	.71	1.81
K	16.55	4.79	16.96	4.89	.75	2.40
Hs	6.65	5.09	5.32	4.49	.81	2.24
D	19.64	5.43	19.01	4.65	.73	5.82
Hy	22.53	4.72	21.88	3.97	.52	3.28
Pd	14.89	4.02	13.99	3.87	.65	2.40
Mf	24.94	4.34	24.71	4.44	.69	2.42
Pa	8.86	2.99	8.48	2.24	.43	2.25
Pt	9.70	7.44	9.04	7.14	.86	2.78
Sc	10.40	7.39	9.06	6.18	.82	3.12
Ma	14.98	4.28	14.60	4.47	.72	2.26
Si	29.60	6.72	29.12	7.49	.79	3.08
ANX	4.61	4.11	4.05	4.18	.83	1.71
FRS	2.88	2.40	2.84	2.32	.71	1.28
OBS	3.59	3.01	3.59	3.22	.79	1.39
DEP	4.34	4.65	4.40	4.40	.80	2.08
HEA	6.75	4.68	5.99	4.22	.75	2.34
BIZ	2.65	2.75	2.18	2.11	.81	1.21
ANG	4.66	3.23	4.61	3.30	.83	1.33
CYN	9.84	5.17	9.45	5.31	.83	2.12
ASP	7.82	3.48	7.99	3.69	.81	1.52
TPA	7.54	3.83	7.66	3.79	.88	1.35
LSE	5.18	3.61	4.89	3.54	.78	1.67
SOD	9.07	3.97	8.87	4.53	.82	1.69
FAM	3.28	2.77	3.00	2.86	.70	1.51
WRK	6.94	4.88	6.29	5.02	.83	2.04
TRT	5.16	4.10	4.77	3.37	.80	1.82

continued on next page

Table 16-3 (continued)

Women

L	5.60	2.08	5.73	2.44	.67	1.20
F	4.77	3.27	4.08	2.85	.79	1.52
K	15.76	4.00	15.82	4.27	.62	2.46
Hs	7.94	5.45	7.11	5.36	.81	2.36
D	21.10	6.11	20.92	5.13	.87	2.16
Hy	23.44	6.04	23.32	5.25	.54	4.09
Pd	15.45	5.30	14.82	5.13	.84	2.09
Mf	34.44	3.78	34.47	4.06	.67	2.19
Pa	9.40	2.99	9.15	2.67	.46	2.20
Pt	11.66	6.83	10.61	6.90	.87	2.49
Sc	11.10	7.16	9.58	6.02	.88	2.44
Ma	14.26	4.19	4.23	4.10	.65	2.49
Si	32.05	6.91	31.26	7.21	.77	3.33
ANX	5.89	4.18	5.52	3.98	.88	1.47
FRS	5.52	3.55	4.97	2.87	.73	1.86
OBS	4.82	3.07	4.31	2.91	.75	1.53
DEP	6.02	5.42	5.76	5.47	.91	1.64
HEA	7.97	5.66	7.08	5.54	.75	2.85
BIZ	2.81	2.43	2.21	2.23	.79	1.10
ANG	5.35	3.18	4.66	3.03	.83	1.32
CYN	9.45	4.80	9.26	5.55	.81	2.10
ASP	6.94	3.05	6.77	3.40	.67	1.76
TPA	6.60	2.91	6.58	3.11	.75	1.46
LSE	6.58	3.89	6.15	3.45	.83	1.58
SOD	9.03	4.53	8.65	4.27	.83	1.88
FAM	4.18	3.39	3.68	3.20	.85	1.32
WRK	8.65	4.89	8.32	4.90	.84	1.95
TRT	5.94	3.56	5.87	3.84	.73	1.86

Table 16-4. Factor Loadings for the MMPI-2 Basic Scales on a Sample of 681 Dutch Men

			Factor		
Scale	I	II	III	IV	h2
L	−.28482	.43879	−.19723	.43746	.50
F	.72912	−.07853	.11387	.11307	.56
K	−.54545	.67683	−.06030	−.18479	.79
Hs	.71155	.23182	−.23972	.38300	.76
D	.67068	.31785	−.50535	.09327	.81
Hy	.36212	.81459	−.05359	.11174	.81
Pd	.64982	.27760	.37846	−.07480	.65
Mf	.43879	.20760	.02618	−.58654	.58
Pa	.49171	.34874	.34451	−.39314	.64
Pt	.89208	−.22197	−.07138	.02148	.85
Sc	.89245	−.17287	.11889	.01683	.84
Ma	.26848	−.08484	.78316	.37954	.84
Si	.50843	−.37288	−.63468	−.13960	.82
% Variance	36.7	14.9	12.8	8.3	

A week before the MMPI-2 administration, 954 panel members of the 1,244 were administered the SCL-90. The Dutch version used was developed by Arrindell and Ettema (1986) and is slightly different from the original SCL-90-R. The SCL-90 was administered to examine the correlations between it and the content scales. Some minor differences were found between men and women, and we will discuss briefly some of the correlations for the male population. All correlations are statistically significant but most are rather small. By way of example, some of the more important ones are the following: Scale ANX correlates rather highly with all the SCL-90 scales, especially with anxiety (.61), depression (.63), and the global score (.69), which is a measure of psychoneuroticism. The correlation between OBS and the SCL-90 measure of obsessive-compulsive behavior is only .49. The MMPI-2 content scale DEP correlates .66 with the SCL-90 scale of depression, and we find the same correlation (.66) with the general psychoneuroticism measure. The correlation between HEA and SOM (somatic complaints) is of the same order of magnitude (.61). ANG and HOS (hostility) seem to be measuring rather different aspects (.40). WRK correlates significantly with depression (.61), obsessive-compulsive behavior (.60), and psychoneuroticism (.67).

Table 16-5. Factor Loadings for the MMPI-2 Basic Scales on a Sample of 563 Dutch Women

	Factor				
Scale	I	II	III	IV	h2
L	-.14090	.34278	.36712	-.45407	.48
F	.72489	-.04242	-.13624	-.23887	.60
K	-.53339	.69433	.04291	.08739	.78
Hs	.72447	.22946	.27109	-.22089	.70
D	.69059	.22555	.52089	.00880	.80
Hy	.45807	.75614	.08392	-.02979	.79
Pd	.71444	.21291	-.32399	.09280	.67
Mf	.18871	.08613	.08569	.83465	.75
Pa	.52219	.41138	-.27471	.24695	.58
Pt	.88777	-.24678	.08879	.07006	.86
Sc	.89576	-.16018	-.17476	-.07675	.86
Ma	.39499	-.06971	-.73501	-.17782	.73
Si	.47497	-.44646	.64343	.09985	.85
% Variance	37.2	13.8	13.0	8.8	

Case Illustration

Gender: male
Age: 38
Occupation: unemployed former bank director
Marital status: separated

This 38-year-old man was referred to the first author for psychological evaluation by his lawyer. He was under suspicion of being the informant and organizer of the murder and robbery of a bank messenger. Belgium, being a small country where a lot of foreign currencies are exchanged, has a number of people who specialize in picking up foreign currency and exchanging it with money changers in The Netherlands to make a profit. At the time of referral he was being released from prison where he had spent one year being kept under remand. On the first consultation the MMPI was administered. Mr. X was not manifesting any signs of psychopathology, he was not in an acute state, no history of psychological or psychiatric problems was known, and he was very motivated to collaborate.

Mr. X produced a valid MMPI profile (Figures 16-9 and 16-10), responding to the items in an open and frank way, and he was willing to admit minor faults. His response pattern indicates a balance between self-disclosure and self-protection,

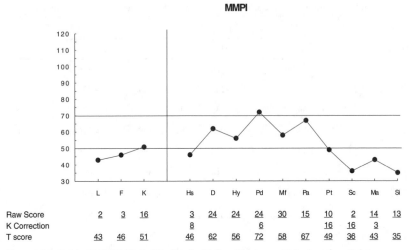

Figure 16-9. Original MMPI Clinical Profile of a 38-Year-Old Accused Murderer from Belgium

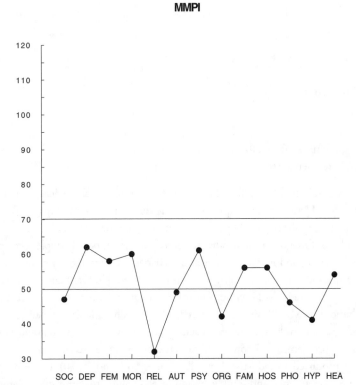

Figure 16-10. Original MMPI Wiggins Content Scale Scores of a 38-Year-Old Accused Murderer from Belgium

MMPI-2

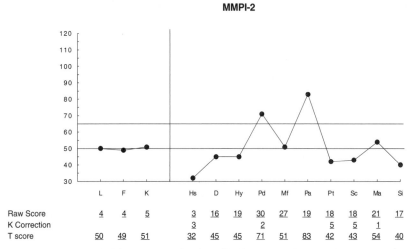

	L	F	K	Hs	D	Hy	Pd	Mf	Pa	Pt	Sc	Ma	Si
Raw Score	4	4	5	3	16	19	30	27	19	18	18	21	17
K Correction				3			2			5	5	1	
T score	50	49	51	32	45	45	71	51	83	42	43	54	40

Figure 16-11. MMPI-2 Validity and Clinical Scale Profile of a 38-Year-Old Accused Murderer from Belgium

MMPI-2

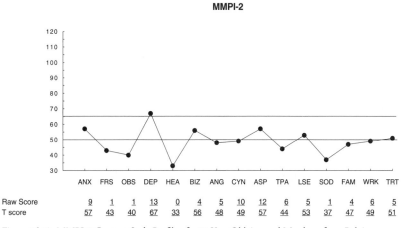

	ANX	FRS	OBS	DEP	HEA	BIZ	ANG	CYN	ASP	TPA	LSE	SOD	FAM	WRK	TRT
Raw Score	9	1	1	13	0	4	5	10	12	6	5	1	4	6	5
T score	57	43	40	67	33	56	48	49	57	44	53	37	47	49	51

Figure 16-12. MMPI-2 Content Scale Profile of a 38-Year-Old Accused Murderer from Belgium

and he seems to be well adjusted and capable of dealing with problems of every-day life. His clinical scale profile is a spike-4 (T = 72), with scale 6 (Pa) being moderately elevated (T = 67). He may show impulsive behavior, poorly controlled anger, and a low tolerance for frustration. His interpersonal relationships will likely be superficial, and he could have difficulty in intimate relationships. These aspects are confirmed by the low value on scale 0 (T = 35). The MacAndrew Alcoholism scale is elevated (raw score = 26), suggesting a substance abuse problem. The Wiggins content scales are all within normal limits, varying between T = 32 for religious fundamentalism and T=62 for depression.

Eight months later, we had occasion to administer the defendant the MMPI-2. He was still waiting for his trial, and he was kept in ignorance about the exact date of the trial. This gave him a feeling of uncertainty and a lot more tension. This legally unclear situation was also responsible for his not being able to find a job and for the fact that his girlfriend had put an end to their relationship.

Again he produced a valid profile (see Figures 16-11 and 16-12), indicating a balanced self-appraisal and effectiveness in everyday functioning. The profile configuration is of the 6-4 two-point code type. It is hard to decide to what degree the standard interpretations can be used. Compared to the first MMPI, scale 4 is of the same magnitude, but scale 6 is significantly higher. We must take into account the fact that he has been waiting for a long period for his trial and that he is denying his role in the whole affair, while others are trying to maximize his participation. This type of profile is indicative of immature, narcissistic, and self-indulgent persons who deny serious psychological problems.

Individuals with this pattern have a tendency to rationalize and transfer blame to others, while they do not accept responsibility for their own behavior. They can be somewhat unrealistic and grandiose in their self-appraisal. Most of the time, elevations on scale 4 are related to instability in personal and professional relationships. However, the case history illustrates that he was a bank director for years and that he has been married for 15 years. A closer look at the subscales reveals that scales Pd 4 (social alienation, T = 68) and Pd 5 (self-alienation, T = 68) are elevated, indicating that, owing to the circumstances, he feels lonely, unhappy, unloved, that he gets a raw deal from life, and that others do not understand him; he verbalizes regret and guilt, etc.

As far as the new content scales are concerned, nearly all scale values are within normal limits, the only exception being scale DEP (T = 67). This scale elevation probably reflects his actual state of mood, with feelings of uncertainty about the future. A reassuring fact is that scales ANG (T = 48) and ASP (T = 57) are not elevated, which is again confirmed by the case history. No loss of control under frustration or stress are known, and indeed he does not have the typical history of problematic behaviors and antisocial acts.

This particular case shows that the MMPI-2 is giving a good picture of the different aspects and problems of Mr. X. It also illustrates that the differences as far as norms are concerned between the MMPI and the MMPI-2 are relatively unimportant.

References

Arrindell, W.A., & Ettema, J.H. (1986). SCL-90: *Handleiding bij een multi-dimensionele psychopathologie-indicator*. [Manual for multidimensional psychopathology indicator]. Amsterdam: Swets & Zeitlinger.

Butcher, J. N., & Pancheri, P. (1976). *A handbook of cross-national MMPI research.* Minneapolis: University of Minnesota Press.

Cluydts, R., Deroeck, J., & Sloore, H. (1985). *Anxiety and repression in the pathogenesis of insomnia.* Paper presented at the 20th Annual Symposium on Recent Developments in the Use of the MMPI, Honolulu.

De Waele, J. P., De Schampheleire, D., Van De Mosselaer, G. (1973). *BAMMPI: The Brussels Automated MMPI.* Brussels: Free University.

Derksen, J., & de Mey, H. (1993). *U.S. and Dutch norms for the MMPI-2: A comparison.* Paper presented at the 28th Annual Symposium on Recent Developments in the Use of the MMPI/MMPI-2/MMPI-A, St. Petersburg, FL.

Derksen, J., Sloore, H., de Mey, H., & Hellenbosch, G. (1993). *MMPI-2 Handleiding bij afname, scoring en interpretatie.* [MMPI-2 handbook for administration, scoring, and interpretation]. Nijmegen: PEN Tests Publisher.

Nuttin, J., & Beuten, B. (1963). *Handleiding bij de persoonlijkheidsinventaris MMPI.* [Manual for the personality inventory MMPI]. Leuvense Universitaire Uitgaven, Leuven.

Sloore, H. (1988). MMPI and DSM-III taxonomy. Paper presented at the 23rd Annual Symposium on Recent Developments in the Use of the MMPI, St. Petersburg, FL.

Sloore, H., & Cluydts, R. (1985). *Incest and paedophilia: A comparison based on the MMPI.* Paper presented at the 9th International Conference on Personality Assessment, Honolulu.

Sloore, H., Horrix, M. (1987). *The use of the MMPI in normal groups: The case of nuclear power plant engineers.* Paper presented at the 22nd Annual Symposium on Recent Developments in the Use of the MMPI, Seattle.

Sloore, H., & Rouckhout, D. (1989). *The MMPI critical items.* Paper presented at the 24th Annual Symposium on Recent Developments in the Use of the MMPI/MMPI-2, Honolulu.

Sloore, H., & Rouckhout, D. (1992). *MMPI-2 and personality disorders.* Paper presented at the 27th Annual Symposium on Recent Developments in the Use of the MMPI, Minneapolis.

Watson, C. G., Thomas, D., & Anderson, P. E. (1992). Do computer-administered Minnesota Multiphasic Personality Inventories underestimate booklet-based scores? *Journal of Clinical Psychology,* 26, 210–214.

Chapter 17

The Norwegian MMPI-2

Bjørn Ellertsen, Odd E. Havik, and Rita R. Skavhellen

The most common purpose for translating and using instruments for personality evaluation from other countries or cultures is the desire to utilize, if possible, the empirical and interpretative body of knowledge established on the instrument in the original country. In other words, the consistency of the measures in question is implicitly assumed across the nations or cultures in question. Needless to say, this assumption may be erroneous. Basically, two possible explanations, or a combination thereof, are possible when a translated instrument yields different results in different cultures: The instruments may be different, or the cultures may be different. Slight changes in the meaning of test items, or a certain number of untranslatable terms, may mean substantial differences between the test versions, or the cultures may be different in such important aspects as attitudes, values, socioeconomic distribution, and educational systems. These problems have been thoroughly discussed in a number of publications (e.g., Berry, Poortinga, Segall & Dasen, 1992; Brislin, 1993; Butcher, 1982). Given these problems, how can we decide if instruments are reliable and valid when transferring them between cultures? There are no simple answers, but certain stringent procedures are considered important and recommended when addressing these questions. Translation and adaptation procedures have been discussed in a number of publications over the past decades (e.g., Butcher & Pancheri, 1976; Flaherty et al., 1988).

The Norwegian MMPI

The MMPI was first translated into Norwegian in 1956 by Gunvor Rand (who later became professor of education at the University of Oslo) and was used in an

We would like to express our gratitude to James N. Butcher and Beverly Kaemmer at the University of Minnesota for helpful suggestions and practical assistance throughout our work on translation and adaptation of the MMPI-2 in Norway. Both Anne Helene Skinstad and Melanie Young have contributed significantly at different stages of the project described in this chapter.

empirical study of delinquents (Rand, 1956). Anna von der Lippe, now a professor of clinical psychology at the University of Oslo, revised the translation in the 1960s. This version became the "standard" Norwegian version of the MMPI and is still in use (Lippe, 1976). The Psychology Service of the Norwegian Armed Forces became responsible for developing Norwegian MMPI norms, after having received permission to do so from the Psychological Corporation and from the Norwegian Psychological Association (Hansen, 1986). The procedures employed in translating the MMPI into Norwegian are unfortunately not available in published writing. Post hoc inspection of the item renderings does indicate, however, that the Norwegian translation is quite close to the English original in terms of the meanings of items. Thus, the majority of items that were left unchanged in the English MMPI-2 are essentially unchanged from the Norwegian MMPI to the Norwegian MMPI-2. There are, however, a few examples of substantial differences in wording and meaning between Norwegian and U.S. English MMPI items (Havik, 1993). For some items, changes seem to have been made to improve the quality of the language (items 17, 65, 177, and 220). These items, which concern relationship to parents, are worded in the past tense in the U.S. version. In the Norwegian version, they were translated to encompass both past and present tense. Interestingly, this incorrect Norwegian translation may be said to have anticipated changes made in the same items in the MMPI-2, but this does not change the fact that standard rules of translation procedure were violated. For a few other items, the meaning was changed by erroneous translation of qualifiers (e.g., item 95, "I go to church almost every week," was translated to "I go to church every week"), resulting in quite different response distributions (U.S.: True, 42%; False, 55%; Cannot Say, 0%; Norway: True, 2%; False, 98%; Cannot Say, 0%) (Hansen, 1986). Furthermore, negations were lost in three items of the Norwegian translation. Such errors underscore the need for meticulous translation, careful proofreading, and cross-cultural validation.

Several items in the Norwegian version have proved to yield differences in response distribution in spite of correct translation. One example is item 182, "I am afraid of losing my mind," which yields different response patterns in the original Minnesota sample and in Norway (True, 2%; False, 96%; Cannot Say, 2%, compared with True, 29%; False, 68%; and Cannot Say, 3%) (Hansen, 1986). Hansen (1986) further reported that a substantial, but unspecified, number of responses to items in the Norwegian normative sample showed a response distribution significantly different from the original Minnesota norms. In her pioneering study, Rand (see Lippe, 1976) found that the responses to about 20% of the items on a single scale deviated from the U.S. norms, even though the total scale scores corresponded closely to the original norms. Thus, behavioral, attitudinal, or ethical implications associated with a statement proved to be different across cultures, although the lexical meaning of the items was identical. This and other differences in the distribution of responses are not easily explained without looking more closely at cultural differences. Such considerations have been the main impetus behind decisions to develop national norms and to do cross-cultural validation studies of interpretive rules in Norway, as well as in other countries.

As part of their work on the MMPI as a selection instrument in the Norwegian Armed Forces, the Psychology Service developed Norwegian norms based on two samples. The male sample (N = 1,032) comprised military personnel (active officers, officers of the reserves, and privates), many of whom were applying for military schools and courses. According to Hansen (1986), this sample was free of behavioral problems or personality disorders, but not representative of the Norwegian male population with regard to age and education. The female sample (N = 282) was more heterogeneous, including applicants to the Peace Corps, groups paid to participate in the study, and psychology students. For both sexes, the average raw scores of the validity scales were found to be higher than in the original Minnesota normal sample. On the K scale, this difference in average scores was quite large (males, 2.75 points; females, 5.0 points), yielding higher raw scores for the K-corrected clinical scales on the Norwegian profile. However, the average raw scores of the clinical scales, for example, scales 2, 3, 6, and 0, were also higher without any K-correction. When the average raw scores from the Norwegian normal samples are plotted on the original MMPI profile sheet, the T scores for the clinical scales are 2 to 8 points above 50.

The differences between the Norwegian and the American norms may be related to several factors. It is interesting that recent American studies of normals also report higher average scores on the clinical scales compared with the original Minnesota sample (e.g., Colligan, Osborne, Swenson, & Offord, 1984). The high average K scores in the Norwegian samples may reflect younger age and higher education than that of the Minnesota sample. Furthermore, the effect of being tested in a selection setting does influence the results through the activation of defensiveness. In fact, the same phenomenon underlies the development of the new research validity scale S on the MMPI-2, which is expected to identify superlative self-descriptions (Butcher & Han, 1995). On the other hand, the differences observed in the Norwegian normative study may also reflect important cultural differences. Thus, findings showing more introversion (scale 0) and depression (scale 2) may be in accordance with Norwegian values and norms, without signifying psychopathology. Unpublished data from a study of MMPI personality disorder scales support this view (Himle & Havik, 1993). It was found that Norwegian patients (N = 428) had higher scores on the scales measuring introversion and avoidant and dependent personality traits, whereas comparable U.S. patients were characterized by more impulsivity and antisocial personality traits (Morey, Waugh, & Blashfield, 1985).

The psychodiagnostic training of Norwegian psychologists has traditionally been focused on the Rorschach. The MMPI was first introduced in the training of psychologists at the University of Oslo by Anna von der Lippe in the 1960s. However, most of the research, teaching, and postgraduate training involving the MMPI has been performed at the University of Bergen in the Department of Clinical Psychology and the Department of Clinical Neuropsychology. The clinical use of the MMPI increased markedly after 1980, when Norwegian handbooks for the interpretation of MMPI profiles became available (Havik, 1977, 1993; Lippe, 1976), and the MMPI has also gained increasing popularity as a standard procedure in connection with extensive neuropsychological evaluation.

Recently, a survey of psychological test preferences and usage among Norwegian psychologists showed that 39% of respondents were using the MMPI (Mæland, Barth, Lundal, & Sortland, 1991). The MMPI was ranked fourth among the tests in use, after the WAIS, the Rorschach, and the Bender-Gestalt. It was, however, the second most used test after the WAIS. In Norway, the MMPI has been used in the field of clinical psychology mainly for differential diagnosis and treatment planning. For a period, the Norwegian Armed Forces used it for personnel selection, but this was discarded owing to low predictive validity for this setting. The use of the MMPI in the field of forensic psychology is a controversial subject in Norway, and it is generally not recommended for use in cases of child custody evaluation.

Translation Issues

These earlier experiences with the Norwegian MMPI, as well as internationally accepted cross-cultural research procedures, were taken into account when adaptation of the MMPI-2 in Norway was being planned. It was decided to follow procedures that would ensure that the meaning of test items, and all other test material, would be as close to the original as possible. It was also decided to perform cross-cultural comparisons of item characteristics, collect data from target groups, and conduct test-retest evaluations. Such comparisons were deemed particularly important, and also particularly complicated, when approaching an instrument like the MMPI, where the clinical utility relies on empirically derived rules of interpretation of test data. The question of national norms was left open at this stage, owing to considerations discussed below.

MMPI group studies carried out in Norway have repeatedly demonstrated that the Norwegian normative data yield mean MMPI group profiles that differ from comparable studies performed in the country of origin. However, when data are analyzed using the original norms, group profiles have been shown to be strikingly similar (Bang, Skavhellen, & Ellertsen, 1993; Hjørungdal, Nielsen, & Sorteberg, 1987; Ellertsen, 1992; Ellertsen, & Kløve, 1987; Ellertsen, Værøy, Endresen, & Førre, 1991; Havik et al., 1982; Skinstad, & Mortensen, 1992). The same phenomenon has also been demonstrated for MMPI subgroups identified through cluster analyses (Løberg, 1980). The nonrepresentativeness of the Norwegian norms discussed above may at least partly account for these findings. The problem is, however, probably more basic and general, and therefore true in any country utilizing national norms. The relationships between the original norms, data from clinical samples, and the actuarial rules of interpretation are important in this connection. It seems reasonable to assume that these relationships have received unsatisfactory attention in the literature. We base this statement on experiences drawn from comparisons between the use of Norwegian norms and the use of original norms with the same subjects.

The use of a profile sheet based on more or less representative national normative data offers no guarantee that national clinical groups obtain identical profiles to those obtained in other cultures utilizing the original norms. The actuarial rules of interpretation, adhered to by most MMPI interpreters, are, however, based on research using the original Minnesota norms. It may therefore be asked what clinicians in these countries actually are doing when they produce a "national" client profile and then interpret this profile according to empirically derived rules that were developed on the basis of research performed as described. To rely on actuarial interpretation of profiles based on national norms, it would seem necessary for the instrument to have been cross-validated with regard to item analyses, normative data, and data from well-defined clinical samples, within a cross-national experimental design. The next step in this process would depend on the results obtained and would range from national adjustments of interpretive rules to discarding the national version of the MMPI or the national norms or both.

A somewhat different approach would be to cross-validate clinical group profiles, that is, compare data from national patient groups with original groups, utilizing the original norms, and recommend application of the original rules of interpretation, or modifications thereof, depending on how these comparisons came out. Actuarial interpretation according to the original rules requires that mean group profiles and scale variance are the same as, or at least convincingly similar to, that of the comparison groups. This line of reasoning has served as the basis for the first stage of the Norwegian MMPI-2 project, which was started in 1991 (Young & Ellertsen, 1991).

The restandardization of the MMPI (Butcher, Dahlstrom, Graham, Tellegen & Kaemmer, 1989), when launched, was considered long overdue by many clinicians and researchers, in spite of the fact that a number of studies had demonstrated that the psychometric properties of the original MMPI clinical scales had changed surprisingly little over 50 years. The main concern in the first publications following the release of the MMPI-2 can best be described as a fear of "throwing the baby out with the bathwater," that is, losing important parts of the scientific basis on which the original MMPI relies. (See the discussion by Dahlstrom, 1993, and the recent reply by Tellegen & Ben-Porath, 1993.) This concern was important to the Restandardization Committee, which throughout the revision made every possible effort to maintain the clinical and psychometric properties of the items contributing to the clinical scales of the MMPI (Butcher et al., 1989). It remains to be seen to what extent this goal was achieved, and these and other issues are being debated in the current literature (Graham, Timbrook, Ben-Porath, & Butcher, 1991; Helmes & Reddon, 1993; for a discussion of the bias and inaccuracy in the Helmes & Reddon critique of the MMPI and MMPI-2, see Ben-Porath, Tellegen, Graham, & Butcher, 1994). Such questions are also highly relevant to the Norwegian users of the MMPI, since the original normative data have been convincingly cross-validated and used in clinical practice and research over decades.

The Norwegian MMPI-2

The purpose of the Norwegian MMPI-2 project has been to translate and then cross-validate the inventory. Translation of the inventory was performed according to internationally accepted rules for cross-cultural translation (Butcher & Pancheri, 1976; Flaherty et al., 1988). The MMPI-2 was first translated by a group of five clinical researchers, two of whom were bilingual. Each translator presented a recommendation for the translation of each item. The group then discussed all suggestions and reached agreement. The main purpose at this stage was to make the translation as similar to the original as possible with regard to grammatical structure and the meanings of statements. The translation was then back-translated into American English by five bilinguals, one of whom was a professional translator. The group then compared each back-translation with the original MMPI-2 to identify items that were discrepant. About 10% of the Norwegian MMPI-2 items were adjusted as a consequence of this process. The resulting translation was then carefully checked by a bilingual clinician who had used the MMPI for many years. Only slight cosmetic changes were made at this stage. A review of the Norwegian MMPI-2 translation was also commissioned by the University of Minnesota Press from the University Language Center, and the translation was rated excellent, with only minor suggestions regarding 13 items (B. Kaemmer, personal communication, November 30, 1993).

The second stage of the project was to collect data from a large and heterogeneous sample of patients and from well-defined clinical groups. Clinical psychologists throughout Norway were invited to participate in the project (Young & Ellertsen, 1991). Clinicians were offered free access to the translated material and

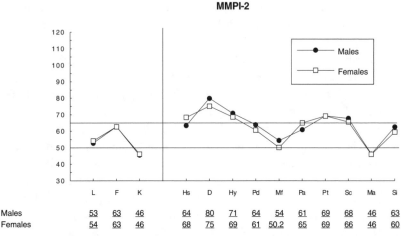

MMPI-2

	L	F	K	Hs	D	Hy	Pd	Mf	Pa	Pt	Sc	Ma	Si
Males	53	63	46	64	80	71	64	54	61	69	68	46	63
Females	54	63	46	68	75	69	61	50.2	65	69	66	46	60

Figure 17-1. MMPI-2 Clinical Profile for Groups of Depressed Men and Women Plotted on the U.S. Norms

free scoring throughout the project. In return, they participated in the accumulation of anonymous patient data for the database. In addition, selected background data were collected on all patients included in the project. These background data consisted of age, sex, problem description, and formal diagnoses (*DSM-III-R* or ICD9). No particular efforts were made to collect data from "normals" at this stage of the project.

By the end of 1993, 160 psychologists had participated in the project and about 1,400 MMPI-2 protocols had been collected. At this stage, the database started to serve as a pool of MMPI-2 data from which valid protocols on different subsamples could be extracted and analyzed. Throughout this period, valuable experience with regard to the clinical utility of the MMPI-2 was collected and reported back to the project by the participating psychologists. Such feedback has also been formalized through the participation of 10 experienced Norwegian clinicians in an evaluation project of the Minnesota Report (Butcher, 1993).

Group Studies

The Norwegian MMPI-2 project has reached a stage where the first group data analyses are being performed. As stated above, one of the purposes of the project is to compare clinical groups and individual profiles with group and case studies performed in the culture where the MMPI-2 normative data were collected. Results from the first stage of such comparisons are presented in Figure 17-1.

Patients included in Figure 17-1 were selected from the data pool on the basis of a *DSM-III-R* depression diagnosis or a detailed problem description including

MMPI-2

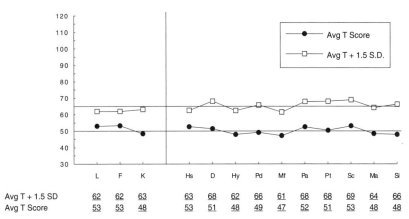

	L	F	K		Hs	D	Hy	Pd	Mf	Pa	Pt	Sc	Ma	Si
Avg T + 1.5 SD	62	62	63		63	68	62	66	61	68	68	69	64	66
Avg T Score	53	53	48		53	51	48	49	47	52	51	53	48	48

Figure 17-2. MMPI-2 Clinical Profile for a Group of Normal Norwegian Army Men Plotted on U.S. Norms

depression as the major clinical feature. As can be seen from the figure, mean profiles were strikingly similar between sexes. According to actuarial rules of interpretation, the profiles in question are likely to provide a good description of these clients' current personality functioning. Much distress, intense feelings of self-doubt, and low morale are reflected in the profiles at the time of testing. These patients typically have major problems with anxiety and depression and may also exhibit somatic problems, loss of sleep and appetite, and a slowness in personal tempo (Graham, 1990; excerpts from the Minnesota Report on this profile configuration). Thus, there was a close and clinically meaningful relationship between psychiatric diagnoses and clinical impression on one hand and actuarial interpretation of the mean MMPI-2 profiles on the other. This conclusion was further supported through feedback from the clinicians working with the patients in question.

In addition to the general data collection described above, and the informal and formal feedback from participating clinicians, several research projects have been initiated in which MMPI-2 data have been collected on carefully diagnosed and thoroughly screened patient samples. One of these studies was aimed at assessing signs of post-traumatic stress disorder in young soldiers who had experienced a traumatic hostage experience. This study included a control group that was selected on the basis of having had no somatic or psychological complaints during the past two years. The groups were matched with regard to age. Data from these young "normal" soldiers are presented in Figure 17-2.

As can be seen from the figure, both mean T scores, and the mean value +1.5 standard deviation, in the clinical MMPI-2 profile corresponded closely to T score

MMPI-2

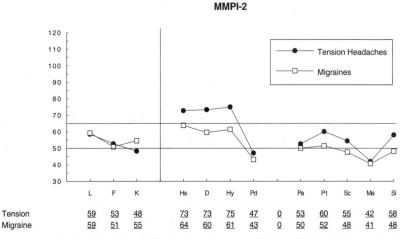

	L	F	K	Hs	D	Hy	Pd	Pa	Pt	Sc	Ma	Si
Tension	59	53	48	73	73	75	47	0	53	60	55	42	58
Migraine	59	51	55	64	60	61	43	0	50	52	48	41	48

Figure 17-3. MMPI-2 Clinical Profile for Norwegian Patients with Tension Headache Compared with Patients with Migraine Headache

50 and T score 65, respectively. Mean value of all clinical scales was actually 50.00. A preliminary conclusion is that young Norwegian males, without any signs of medical or psychological problems, obtained mean profiles close to data from the original MMPI-2 normative sample for males. Comparison of item endorsements between this normal sample and the Minnesota normative sample for males showed that a total of 25 items yielded a difference of 20% or more True responses. However, closer inspection of these items showed that most of them would be expected to be endorsed differently from a representative normative sample, owing to the fact that the life of soldiers living in a military setting is different from civilian life in a number of important ways.

In another clinical study, data were collected on patients with different headache diagnoses. Mean group profiles for tension headache (TH) and migraine (MI) are presented in Figure 17-3 and profiles for cervicogenic headache (CEH, chronic headache stemming from the neck) and cluster headache (CH) in Figure 17-4. Some important conclusions may be drawn on the basis of these four group profiles.

Patients who experience chronic headache (TH and CEH) have mean group profiles that may be described as typical "chronic pain profiles." The similarity between these profiles and MMPI-2 chronic pain profiles reported by Keller and Butcher (1991) is striking. This lends support to the conclusion that the Norwegian MMPI-2 yields group profiles in chronic pain patients that are very close to comparable MMPI-2 studies performed in the United States. It was also interesting to note that patients experiencing transient pain episodes (M and CH) showed mean group profiles well within the normal range, although scales 1 through 3

MMPI-2

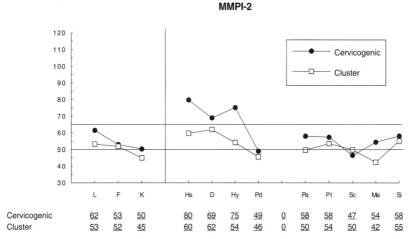

	L	F	K		Hs	D	Hy	Pd		Pa	Pt	Sc	Ma	Si
Cervicogenic	62	53	50		80	69	75	49	0	58	58	47	54	58
Cluster	53	52	45		60	62	54	46	0	50	54	50	42	55

Figure 17-4. MMPI-2 Clinical Profile for Norwegian Patients with Cervicogenic Pain versus Patients with Cluster Headache Pain

were slightly elevated. Earlier MMPI studies of migraine patients have, however, notoriously reported mean profiles suggesting pronounced psychosomatic characteristics (see Ellertsen, 1992). The results obtained using the new, as compared to the old, MMPI may be a consequence of the improved normative base of the MMPI-2. If so, we have reason to exclude migraine patients from the psychosomatic category under which they have been labeled in the literature for years, not least owing to MMPI research. It is also tempting to suggest that the MMPI-2 seems to identify fewer "false positives" than did the MMPI.

As explained above, the Norwegian MMPI-2 project also comprises a large number of clinical cases on which the Minnesota Report has been utilized and thereafter evaluated by experienced clinicians. The results from this evaluation project will be published elsewhere, but preliminary data suggest that the Minnesota Report serves as a valid tool in scoring and interpreting Norwegian MMPI-2 protocols. A case report illustrates.

Case Study

The patient was a 46-year-old female state enrolled nurse who used to work in a state prison. At the age of 42 she was violently attacked by a psychotic patient who knocked her unconscious. She reportedly has been unable to go back to work owing to severe and chronic left-sided headaches, sleep disturbances, memory problems, and reduced strength in her right arm. Repeated neurologic examinations and neuroimaging have yielded normal results. A neuropsychological examination was requested by her primary physician.

In this case, differential diagnostic considerations with regard to neurogenic

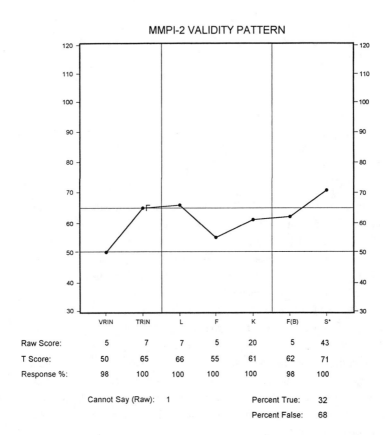

MMPI-2 VALIDITY PATTERN

	VRIN	TRIN	L	F	K	F(B)	S*
Raw Score:	5	7	7	5	20	5	43
T Score:	50	65	66	55	61	62	71
Response %:	98	100	100	100	100	98	100

Cannot Say (Raw):   1

Percent True: 32

Percent False: 68

*Experimental

Figure 17-5. Minnesota Report™ Validity Scale Profile for a 46-Year-Old Norwegian Female Patient with Chronic Headache, Sleep Disturbance, Memory Problems, and Reduced Arm Strength.
Source: The Minnesota Report™: Adult Clinical System. Copyright © 1989 by the Regents of the University of Minnesota. All rights reserved.

versus psychogenic etiology were particularly important. The patient cooperated well in the test situation, but she was slow, dysphoric, asthenic, and easily tired. She complained about headache and pain in her neck, shoulder, and right arm throughout the examination.

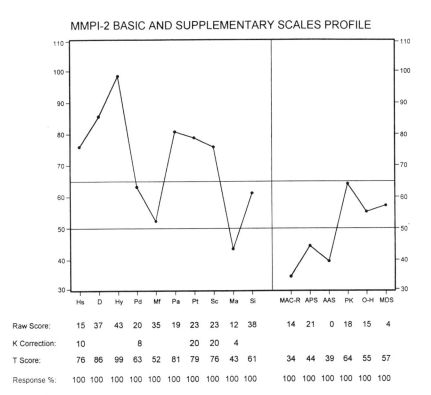

Raw Score: 15 37 43 20 35 19 23 23 12 38   14 21 0   18 15 4

K Correction: 10   8   20 20   4

T Score: 76 86 99 63 52 81 79 76 43 61   34 44 39 64 55 57

Response %:   100 100 100 100 100 100 100 100 100 100   100 100 100 100 100 100

Welsh Code (new):   3*26"7<u>18</u>'+40-5/9: L+K-F/

Welsh Code (old):   3*<u>268</u>"714'0-/<u>59</u>: KL-F/?:

Profile Elevation: 75.40

Figure 17-6. Minnesota Report™ Clinical and Supplementary Scale Profile for a 46-Year-Old Nor-
wegian Female Patient with Chronic Headache, Sleep Disturbance, Memory Problems, and Reduced
Arm Strength. *Source:* The Minnesota Report™: Adult Clinical System. Copyright © 1989 by the
Regents of the University of Minnesota. All rights reserved.

Intellectually, the patient was found to perform close to the mean level of her
age group and gender. Evaluation of memory functions showed that she had pronounced problems with sustained attention and short-term memory. Her memory
quotient was significantly lower than expected on the basis of her intellectual capacity. There were no signs of dysphasia, no apractognosia, and no other patho-
gnomonic symptoms. Evaluation with the Halstead-Reitan Battery confirmed
her attention problems and showed reduced psychomotor tempo. Otherwise, her

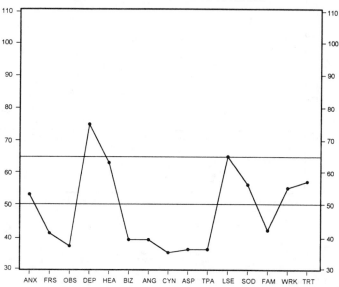

Figure 17-7. Minnesota Report™ Content Scale Profile for a 46-Year-Old Norwegian Female Patient with Chronic Headache, Sleep Disturbance, Memory Problems, and Reduced Arm Strength. *Source:* The Minnesota Report™: Adult Clinical System. Copyright © 1989 by the Regents of the University of Minnesota. All rights reserved.

test results were within normal limits. Tests of motor performance yielded results that were markedly influenced by her pain problems, and therefore problematic to evaluate, while sensory examination yielded symmetric results within the normal range. In summary, the pattern of findings from the extensive neuropsychological evaluation was more consistent with a chronic pain problem and depression than brain dysfunction.

The MMPI-2 validity scale profile for this patient is presented in Figure 17-5.

PROFILE VALIDITY

This is a marginally valid MMPI-2 clinical profile because the client may have attempted to present an unrealistically favorable picture of her personal virtue and moral values. She may feel the need to present an image of strong moral character or to deny human frailties. Her approach to the MMPI-2 items suggests a rather naive or unsophisticated self-image.

SYMPTOMATIC PATTERNS

Scales D and Hy were used as the prototype to develop this report. Physical concerns and depressed mood appear to be primary problems emerging from a somewhat mixed symptom pattern. The client feels nervous, tense, and unhappy, and she is quite worried at this time. She also appears to be quite indifferent to many of the things she once enjoyed and believes she is no longer able to function well in life. Overly sensitive to criticism, she tends to blame herself a great deal and feels that she has not been treated well. Her depressed mood is accompanied by physical complaints and extreme fatigue.

She appears to be inhibited and overcontrolled, relying on denial and repression to deal with anxiety and conflict. She may seek medical attention for her "run-down" condition, but her physical problems are likely to be related to her depressed mood.

In addition, the following description is suggested by the content of the client's item responses. She has endorsed a number of items suggesting that she is experiencing low morale and a depressed mood. She reports a preoccupation with feeling guilty and unworthy. She feels that she deserves to be punished for wrongs she has committed. She feels regretful and unhappy about life, and she seems plagued by anxiety and worry about the future. She feels hopeless at times and feels that she is a condemned person. She views her physical health as failing and reports numerous somatic concerns. She feels that life is no longer worthwhile and that she is losing control of her thought processes. She views the world as a threatening place, sees herself as having been unjustly blamed for others' problems, and feels that she is getting a raw deal out of life.

PROFILE FREQUENCY

It is usually valuable in MMPI-2 clinical profile interpretation to consider the relative frequency of a given profile pattern in various settings. The client's MMPI-2 high-point clinical scale score (Hy) is found in 10.5% of the MMPI-2 normative sample of women. However, only 3.7% of the sample have Hy as the peak score at or above a T score of 65, and only 2.1% have well-defined Hy spikes. This elevated MMPI-2 profile type (2-3/3-2) is very rare in samples of normals, occurring in less than 1% of the MMPI-2 normative sample of women.

The relative frequency of this profile in various outpatient settings is informative. In the NCS female outpatient sample, this MMPI-2 high-point clinical scale score (Hy) is the second most frequent peak,

Figure 17-8. Minnesota Report™ Narrative for a 46-Year-Old Norwegian Female Patient with Chronic Headache, Sleep Disturbance, Memory Problems, and Reduced Arm Strength. *Source:* The Minnesota Report™: Adult Clinical System. Copyright © 1989 by the Regents of the University of Minnesota. All rights reserved.

occurring in 17.2% of the women. Moreover, 13.3% of the outpatient women have the Hy scale spike at or above a T score of 65, and 7.5% have well-defined Hy peaks. This elevated MMPI-2 profile configuration (2-3/3-2) is found in 5.8% of the women in the NCS outpatient sample.

PROFILE STABILITY

The relative scale elevation of the highest scales in her clinical profile reflects high profile definition. If she is retested at a later date, the peak scores on this test are likely to retain their relative salience in her retest profile pattern. Her high-point score on Hy is likely to remain stable over time. Short-term test-retest studies have shown a correlation of 0.76 for this high-point score.

INTERPERSONAL RELATIONS

She is passive-dependent in relationships and is easily hurt by others. She is nonassertive and keeps anger bottled up, avoiding confrontation for fear of being rejected or hurt. She appears to see herself as helpless and dependent, and she relies on her husband to take care of her. Many people with this profile have marital difficulties. They typically show a diminished interest in sex and have little energy to expend on their marital relationship. Moreover, their moodiness and whining are likely to place additional strain on the marriage.

She is somewhat shy, with some social concerns and inhibitions. She is a bit hypersensitive about what others think of her and is occasionally concerned about her relationships with others. She appears to be somewhat inhibited in personal relationships and social situations, and she may have some difficulty expressing her feelings toward others.

DIAGNOSTIC CONSIDERATIONS

The most frequent diagnosis for individuals with this profile type is Dysthymic Disorder. Physically disabling conditions related to psychological stress, such as ulcers or hypertension, may be part of the clinical pattern. Her self-reported tendency toward experiencing depressed mood should be taken into consideration in any diagnostic formulation.

TREATMENT CONSIDERATIONS

She views herself as having so many problems that she is no longer able to function effectively in day-to-day situations. Her low mood and pessimistic outlook on life weigh heavily on her and seemingly keep her from acting to better her situation. Her negative self-image and sense of frustration may be very detrimental to treatment and will require attention early in therapy.

Figure 17-8 (continued)

According to the Minnesota Report, her profile was marginally valid, because she may have attempted to present an unrealistically favorable picture of her personal virtues and moral values. Further, her approach to the MMPI-2 items suggested a rather naive or unsophisticated self-image. The clinical and supplementary scales are presented in Figure 17-6 and the MMPI-2 content scale profile for the patient is presented in Figure 17-7. The full narrative of the Minnesota Report is given in Figure 17-8.

Individuals with this MMPI-2 clinical profile tend to feel quite tense and depressed and may need relief for their psychological symptoms. Perhaps the most frequent form of treatment given to individuals with this pattern is antidepressant medication. Many patients with this profile require a great deal of reassurance. They tend to lack insight into their behavior and will tolerate a great deal of tension before they will seek help. Some individuals with this profile respond to a directive, action-oriented treatment approach and possibly to assertiveness training.

NOTE: This MMPI-2 interpretation can serve as a useful source of hypotheses about clients. This report is based on objectively derived scale indices and scale interpretations that have been developed in diverse groups of patients. The personality descriptions, inferences, and recommendations contained herein need to be verified by other sources of clinical information because individual clients may not fully match the prototype. The information in this report should most appropriately be used by a trained, qualified test interpreter. The information contained in this report should be considered confidential.

Figure 17-8 (continued)

The narrative report provides information that physical concerns and depressed mood appear to be primary problems emerging from the somewhat mixed symptom pattern, and that the patient feels nervous, tense, and unhappy. She also appears to be indifferent to many of the things she once enjoyed and believes she is no longer able to function well in life. Overly sensitive to criticism, she tends to blame herself a great deal and feels that she has not been treated well. Her depressed mood is accompanied by physical complaints and extreme fatigue. She appears to be inhibited and overcontrolled, relying on denial and repression to deal with anxiety and conflict. She may seek medical attention for her "run-down" condition, but her physical problems are likely to be related to her depressed mood. The high-point two-point code of this patient (2-3/3-2) is very rare in samples of normals, occurring in less than 1% of the MMPI-2 normative sample of women.

The Minnesota Report strongly supported and confirmed the clinical impression of this patient and the conclusion from the neuropsychological evaluation. Thus, the MMPI-2 served as a valuable tool in the differential diagnostic process. It is our general experience that this is very often the case in the process of neuropsychological evaluation.

Summary

The purpose of the Norwegian MMPI-2 project has been to provide a translated version of the MMPI-2 that is as close to the original as possible in terms of grammatical structure and meaning of items. Translation and back-translation procedures adhered to yielded data indicating that this goal has been achieved to a great extent. Preliminary data from comparisons between well-defined clinical samples in the United States and Norway suggest that the original norms may be employed in Norway, possibly with minor adjustments of actuarial rules of interpretation. The question about national norms has been left open at this stage, owing to the findings reported above, but also because of logistical problems involved in employing a combination of national norms and rules of interpretation based on empirical and normative data collected in a different culture.

Further evaluation of the Norwegian MMPI-2 will comprise evaluation of a wider range of well-defined clinical samples, including control groups; item analyses comparing Norwegian samples with the original Minnesota norms; and evaluation of the Minnesota Report. It is reasonable to assume that an official Norwegian version of the MMPI-2 will be published in 1994-95.

References

Bang, U., Skavhellen, R., & Ellertsen, B. (1993, July). MacAndrew scale scores: *Relation with personality, physiologic variables and background variables in male and female substance abusers.* Paper presented at the 3rd European Congress of Psychology, Tampere, Finland.

Ben-Porath, Y. S., Tellegen, A., Graham, J. R., & Butcher, J. N. (1994). *A different perspective on developments in assessing psychopathology: A response to Helmes & Reddon.* Manuscript in preparation.

Berry, J. W., Poortinga, Y. H., Segall, M. H., & Dasen, P. R. (1992). *Cross-cultural psychology: Research and applications.* New York: Cambridge University Press.

Brislin, R. (1993). *Understanding culture's influence on behavior.* Fort Worth: Harcourt Brace & Company.

Butcher, J. N. (1982). Cross-cultural research methods in clinical psychology. In P. C. Kendall & J. N. Butcher (Eds.), *Handbook of research methods in clinical psychology* (pp. 273–308). New York: Wiley.

Butcher, J. N. (1993). *User's guide for the MMPI-2 Minnesota Report: Adult Clinical System.* Minneapolis: National Computer Systems.

Butcher, J. N., Dahlstrom, W. G., Graham, J. R., Tellegen, A., & Kaemmer, B. (1989). *Manual for administration and scoring. Minnesota Multiphasic Personality Inventory-2: MMPI-2.* Minneapolis: University of Minnesota Press.

Butcher, J. N., & Han, K. (1995). Development of an MMPI-2 scale to assess the presentation of self in a superlative manner: The S scale. In J. N. Butcher & C. D. Spielberger (1995), *Advances in Personality Assessment* (Vol. 10). Hillsdale, NJ: Erlbaum.

Butcher, J. N., & Pancheri, P. (1976). *A handbook of cross-national MMPI research.* Minneapolis: University of Minnesota Press.

Colligan, R. C., Osborne, D., Swenson, W. M., & Offord, K. P. (1984). The MMPI: Development of contemporary norms. *Journal of Clinical Psychology, 40,* 100–107.

Dahlstrom, W. G. (1992). Comparability of two-point high-point code patterns from original MMPI norms to MMPI-2 norms for the restandardization sample. *Journal of Personality Assessment, 59,* 53–164.

Ellertsen, B. (1992). Personality factors in recurring and chronic pain. *Cephalalgia, 12,* 129–132.

Ellertsen, B., & Kløve, H. (1987). MMPI patterns in chronic muscle pain, tension headache and migraine. *Cephalalgia, 7,* 65–71.

Ellertsen, B., Værøy, H., Endresen, I., & Førre, O. (1991). MMPI in fibromyalgia and local nonspecific myalgia. *New Trends in Experimental and Clinical Psychiatry, 7,* 53–62.

Flaherty, J. A., Gavira, F. M., Pathak, D., Mitchell, T., Wintrob, R., Richman, J. A., & Birz, S. (1988). Developing instruments for cross-cultural psychiatric research. *Journal of Nervous and Mental Disease, 176* (5), 257–263.

Graham, J. R. (1990). *MMPI-2. Assessing personality and psychopathology.* New York: Oxford University Press.

Graham, J. R., Timbrook, R. E., Ben-Porath, Y. S., & Butcher, J. N. (1991). Code-type congruence between MMPI and MMPI-2: Separating fact from artifact. *Journal of Personality Assessment, 57,* 205–215.

Hansen, I. (1986). A review of the Norwegian normative data on the MMPI. *Journal of the Norwegian Psychological Association, 23.* (Suppl. 1), 44–56.

Havik, O. E. (1977). *MMPI—Noen momenter for tolkning av MMPI* [MMPI—Some interpretation issues] (Report). Bergen: University of Bergen, Department of Personality Psychology.

Havik, O. E. (1993). *Klinisk bruk av MMPI/MMPI-2* [Clinical use of the MMPI/MMPI-2]. Oslo: Tano.

Havik, O. E., Barth, K., Haver, B., Mølstad, E., Nielsen, G., Rogge, H., & Skåtun, M. (1982). Psychological test findings in three categories of patients accepted for psychotherapy of short duration. *Journal of the Norwegian Psychological Association, 19,* 535–541.

Helmes, E., & Reddon, J. R. (1993). A perspective on developments in assessing psychopathology: A critical review of the MMPI and MMPI-2. *Psychological Bulletin, 113,* 453–471.

Himle, A., & Havik, O. E. (1993). [Introvert, avoidant and dependent personality traits in a Norwegian clinical sample]. Unpublished raw data.

Hjørungdal, H., Nielsen, G., & Sorteberg, V. (1987). MMPI characteristics of borderline patients. *Journal of the Norwegian Psychological Association, 24,* 372–377.

Keller, L. S., & Butcher, J. N. (1991). *Assessment of chronic pain patients with the MMPI-2.* Minneapolis: University of Minnesota Press.

Lippe, A. L. von der (1976). *Kompendium i Minnesota Multiphasic Personality Inventory* [A reader on the MMPI]. (Available from A. L. von der Lippe, Department of Psychology, University of Oslo, Norway).

Løberg, T. (1980). Comparison of Norwegian and American MMPI norms for men. *Journal of the Norwegian Psychological Association, 17,* 346–354.

Mæland, K., Barth, T., Lundal, E., & Sortland, N. (1991). Test usage among Norwegian psychologists: Results of a brief survey. *Journal of the Norwegian Psychological Association, 28,* 591–593.

Morey, L. C., Waugh, M. H., & Blashfield, R. (1985). MMPI scales for DSM-III personality disorders: Their derivation and correlates. *Journal of Personality Assessment, 49,* 245–251.

Rand, G. (1956). *MMPI som personlighetsdiagnostisk hjelpemiddel i ungdomsalderen* [MMPI as personality diagnostic method in adolescents]. Unpublished thesis, University of Oslo, Norway.

Skinstad, A. H., & Mortensen, J. K. (1992). Cross-cultural comparison of MMPI norms in alcoholics with and without a diagnosis of borderline personality disorder. *New Trends in Experimental and Clinical Psychiatry, 8,* 103–112.

Tellegen, A., & Ben-Porath, Y. S. (1993). Code type comparability of the MMPI and MMPI-2: Analysis of recent findings and criticisms. *Journal of Personality Assessment, 61,* 489–500.

Young, M., & Ellertsen, B. (1991). MMPI-2: The Norwegian version. *Journal of the Norwegian Psychological Association, 28,* 998–1002.

Chapter 18

The Icelandic Translation of the MMPI-2: Adaptation and Validation

Sölvína Konráðs

Psychology is a relatively young science in Iceland. The University of Iceland started a bachelor's degree program in psychology in 1970. Even today, there are no graduate level psychology programs available in Iceland. Before 1970, there were very few professional psychologists in the country, and those few worked in psychiatric hospitals and elementary schools. These facts explain the poverty of Icelandic psychological research, specifically field research, since such endeavors tend to be both time-consuming and costly.

Psychological instruments are not as widely used in Iceland as they are in the United States, in part because of an antimeasurement philosophy in the 1970s and '80s that had considerable influence in delaying development of psychological testing in the country. Very few psychological tests have been standardized and researched to the extent that they can be validly used, and still fewer national norms have been established.

The translation of the original MMPI into the Icelandic language was published in 1973, but other versions of that translation had been around previously. The MMPI was exclusively used in psychiatric hospitals until the early '90s when a few private clinics were established. Since then the test has gained some popularity in clinical use but less as a research instrument. The U.S. norms have been used exclusively and computer scoring systems and interpretation developed in the United States are used in the psychiatric hospitals and elsewhere. Any deviation from U.S. norms when interpreting a test has been based on clinical experience rather than empirical research.

In the past few years there has been a growing interest in psychological testing in Iceland. The population seeking psychological help is more diverse, thus their needs demand greater variety in assessment and diagnostic attention. The rationale for transferring the MMPI-2 to the Icelandic culture is primarily based on the

Table 18-1. Means, Standard Deviations, and Significance Tests for Two Groups on the Original MMPI Clinical Scales (Icelandic Translation)

Scale	Group 1 (N = 57)		Group 2 (N = 57)		F
	Mean	S.D.	Mean	S.D.	
L	5.1	2.2	5.2	2.4	.135
F	14.6	3.5	16.1	4.0	.091
K	19.4	7.3	21.7	6.9	.157
Hs	16.1	3.0	15.9	3.5	.082
D	36.1	9.3	39.9	8.0	.046
Hy	26.5	7.1	29.0	6.3	.087
Pd	28.4	5.1	29.0	5.9	.379
Mf	39.2	4.7	37.2	5.2	.081
Pa	13.3	7.0	15.1	6.9	.073
Pt	35.8	8.9	36.7	9.5	.056
Sc	37.1	5.0	40.9	5.9	.013
Ma	22.1	10.2	20.7	9.0	.097
Si	32.0	11.0	31.8	9.7	.040

growing need for an assessment and diagnostic instrument that is empirically valid. Despite the fact that the U.S.-normed MMPI has been successfully used in other cultures, elevation of scores within a normal population has been recognized for a long time. This has caused some difficulties in interpreting and evaluating clients' psychological health. Certain features of elevated scores within normal populations has been seen within the normal population in Iceland. Figure 18-1 shows the original MMPI profile of 183 men and women seeking vocational counseling in the years 1988-1993. This group was screened for psychological stability. These men and women had never been hospitalized because of psychological or mental disturbances or addiction of any kind. Figure 18-2 shows the group MMPI profile for 57 men and women seeking vocational counseling in the years 1989-1993. All the members of this group had a history of mental health problems of some kind, and 19 of them had been hospitalized more than twice. Inspection of the two MMPI mean profiles shows that they are very similar in elevation. Table 18-1 presents the means, standard deviations, and F test for significance for the group presented in Figure 18-2 and the same for a group of 57 subjects drawn randomly from the sample profiled in Figure 18-1. No

MMPI

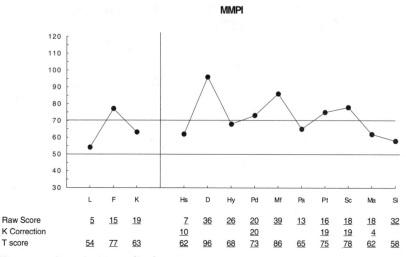

	L	F	K		Hs	D	Hy	Pd	Mf	Pa	Pt	Sc	Ma	Si
Raw Score	5	15	19		7	36	26	20	39	13	16	18	18	32
K Correction					10			20			19	19	4	
T score	54	77	63		62	96	68	73	86	65	75	78	62	58

Figure 18-1. Original MMPI Profile of 183 Men and Women Seeking Vocational Counseling in 1988-1993 in Iceland

MMPI

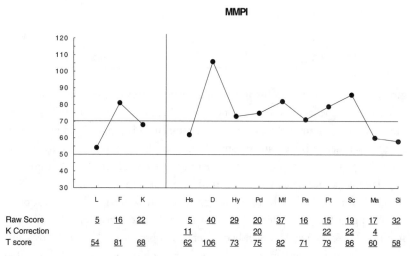

	L	F	K		Hs	D	Hy	Pd	Mf	Pa	Pt	Sc	Ma	Si
Raw Score	5	16	22		5	40	29	20	37	16	15	19	17	32
K Correction					11			20			22	22	4	
T score	54	81	68		62	106	73	75	82	71	79	86	60	58

Figure 18-2. Original MMPI Profile of 57 Men with Mental Health Problems Seeking Vocational Counseling in 1988-1993 in Iceland

MMPI-based differences were obtained. Since the original MMPI translation was never field-tested in Iceland and no research is available indicating standard measurement and standard estimate errors, it can only be concluded that the norms used for the instrument are at this time almost completely inappropriate in Iceland.

Transfer of Psychological Technology Across Cultures

The transfer of psychological technology is a delicate matter. The subject matter of psychology, human behavior, is dynamic and influenced by continuous changes in the environment and by different adaptations of individuals to their environment. The researcher has to carefully define and validate every step of the transfer procedure. The literature on cross-cultural psychology contains a large body of studies. Depression, intelligence, and need for achievement are but a few of the variables that have been studied extensively (Brislin, 1983). Cross-cultural studies have contributed to the understanding of these phenomena as well as to the transfer of technology related to these variables across cultures. The contribution is never one way. Cross-cultural research illuminates methodological issues and improves psychological theories. These theories, in turn, help scientists understand the cultural variables that affect technological transfer. Berry (1980) emphasized that the method of cross-cultural psychology involves comparing two or more naturally occurring cases that differ substantially. Thus, cross-cultural research rests on the paradox that, to compare two cultures, they must have some features in common, but to compare them to some advantage, they should differ on others. Assuming that culture is the independent variable and that there are measurable differences in psychological variables across cultures provides a sound scientific basis for transferring psychological instruments.

When researchers are validating psychological inventories across cultures, the hypothesis being tested is that there is clear similarity in the variables under study and that the inventory measures them in the same way in both cultures. The question that has to be answered through the process of test adaptation across cultures is, does the psychological instrument measure the relevant characteristics in both cultures?

Although the studies on personality measurement have a long tradition in psychology, and the literature is extensive, cross-cultural studies are relatively meager. Most of the available data on cross-cultural transfer of personality inventories suggest that at least some personality inventories developed in the United States are valid for international use. The precursor of the MMPI-2, the MMPI, has been shown to be sufficiently robust for valid international use (Butcher & Pancheri, 1976). Studies using linguistically equivalent forms of personality inventories have only recently become available. An inadequate translation of an instrument used in cross-cultural research can be a major pitfall (Brislin, Lonner, & Thorndike, 1973). Without evidence that the translation of the instrument and the instructions are adequate, translation inequivalence is always a plausible rival hypothesis that can be used to explain the results.

Equivalence is an important concept in cross-cultural research. It applies to a number of aspects and methodological procedures. Berry (1980) makes a distinction between universal characteristics and equivalent characteristics, the latter requiring an empirical demonstration. Equivalence has been defined as functional, conceptual, metric, and scalar. Demonstrating equivalences is a way of eliminating rival hypotheses and thus diminishing the likelihood of misleading interpretation of data.

The Translation Procedure

Brislin, Lonner, and Thorndike (1973) argue that the most difficult task in cross-cultural research is that of translating psychological tests and related instruments. There is a consensus in the literature that the translation procedure should involve at least three steps: (a) translation from the source language into the target language, (b) back-translation of the test into the source language, and (c) validation of the translated version. The use of metaphors, colloquial expressions, passive hypotheticals or subjective phrases, and double negatives to explain the original text or to make it more meaningful should be avoided (Butcher, 1982).

The 1973 Icelandic translation of the MMPI (Asmundsson, 1973) was not used in the development of the Icelandic translation of the MMPI-2 because it has never been field-tested. Furthermore, users of that original version have indicated that too many subjects had difficulty understanding many of the items. It was considered more desirable to translate every item of the MMPI-2 independently of the MMPI translation.

Work on the Icelandic translation of the MMPI-2 followed the guidelines outlined by Butcher (1982, pp. 34-37) as closely as possible. The initial translation was conducted in cooperation with several psychologists and teachers in the Icelandic and English languages. Two back-translations were conducted to identify discrepancies. The translation was tested for reading difficulty level and reading comprehension level to determine whether the population was able to read and interpret the meaning of the test items. The items have to be equally meaningful to all subjects regardless of their educational level.

The translation project proceeded as follows: The 567 items were divided according to transparency and straightforwardness into four categories. The most straightforward and least ambiguous items were translated first, for example, item 2, "I have a good appetite," and item 22, "No one seems to understand me." Items that are less transparent and yield some ambiguity but do not contain cultural-specific content make up the second category. The translation of the first category of items was used as a guideline when translating these items. The third category consisted of items that were very ambiguous or might be somewhat culture-specific, for example, item 193, "In walking I am very careful to step over sidewalk cracks." The items making up the fourth category were those involving difficulties in grammatical equivalence between the two languages. The translation of items in the two latter categories often yielded two or three versions that were later tested for reading difficulty and comprehension level, as well as judged by the committee for appropriateness.

The Icelandic language is Germanic in origin and is actually the Old Norse language. Owing to the isolation of the country, the language has not changed drastically since Old Norse was spoken in the Nordic countries. Because of that, the translation of modern English into modern Icelandic is cumbersome at times, particularly from a grammatical perspective.

Two back-translations were done by two independent translators. The first back-translation and the English MMPI-2 were compared for discrepancies. As a result of that comparison, 29 items were revised. The revisions consisted mainly of correcting adverbs referring to frequency of activities.

The next step involved having a committee of psychologists judge the items for appropriateness. Some grammatical revision was necessary. The second back-translation was done after the items had been tested for difficulty of reading level and reading comprehension. A comparison of the second back-translation with the English version of the MMPI-2 did not indicate any discrepancies between the two.

On the basis of the comparison between the second back-translation and the English MMPI-2, it was concluded that the Icelandic translation was ready for empirical evaluation of its validity. The field-testing was the final step in assessing the linguistic equivalence of the English version and the Icelandic version. Both versions were administered to a selected sample. The guidelines outlined by Butcher (1982) recommend using bilingual subjects in field-testing. This was not possible in Iceland. The closest group to a bilingual group would be Icelanders who have studied in the United States or have lived there for an extended number of years and still have close contact with their native culture. The bilingual sample employed was similar to the group used to validate the translation of the Strong Interest Inventory (Konráòs, 1989). The results were satisfactory. Furthermore, inasmuch as Icelanders in general are very unfamiliar with psychological testing, we thought that by testing people who were living or had lived in the United States we would eliminate to some extent the factor of unfamiliarity with psychological instruments.

Testing the Reading Difficulty and Reading Comprehension of the Icelandic Translation of the MMPI-2

As a means of testing the reading difficulty level and content comprehension of the items in the inventory, the Icelandic translation of the MMPI-2 was administered as a reading project to a group of 13- to 15-year-old students (N = 31). The last official reading exam in the Icelandic schools is given to 12-year-old students. Reading comprehension of each item was rated from zero to 10, with 10 indicating perfect comprehension. The exam had a multiple-choice format.

The items were administered according to the four categories described earlier. The first and most straightforward category, comprising 172 items, and the second group, comprising 37 items, were tested together. All but one of the students obtained a score of 10 on these items. Categories 3 and 4 were tested separately some weeks later. The results from testing category 3, comprising 209 items, were quite different. Only five students were able to answer all questions correctly; the mean score for the remaining 26 students was 6.5, with a standard deviation of 2. The testing of the fourth category, containing 149 items, showed that none of the students could answer all the items correctly. The mean score for this category was 4.6, with a standard deviation of 2.9. The results indicated that the 358 items in categories 3 and 4 had to be revised to make them more understandable. The revision mainly involved substituting more common words for less common words, replacing rare nouns with a sentence using a common verb, and rewriting items that had difficult idioms. Thus, even though the translated items transferred well through the first back-translation, revision was still necessary on the basis of the reading test results.

The revised 358 items were tested on a second group of 13- to 15-year-old students (N = 34), and the results showed 29 of them answering more than 83% of the items correctly. When one compares the results to the reading difficulty levels acceptable for different grades in the Icelandic elementary schools, the reading difficulty of the MMPI-2 Icelandic translation corresponds to a fifth-grade level. These results emphasize the importance of an objective investigation of reading difficulty level when transferring psychological instruments across cultures in order to enhance the acceptability of the test by making item content meaningful to subjects regardless of educational level.

Bilingual Study Method

Subjects and Data Collection

The subjects were men (N = 67) and women (N = 79) who had had educational or vocational experience in Iceland and the United States. Twenty-three percent of the group were Icelanders living in the U.S.; 17% of the group were U.S. individuals who have been living in Iceland for some years. The rest of the sample were Icelanders who had been working or studying in the United States for more than two years. Mean age for the sample was 31.9 years, with a standard deviation of 7.1. The individuals were contacted through various organizations and associations they belonged to, and asked to volunteer for the project.

The group was administered both the English version and the Icelandic translation of the MMPI-2 within three weeks. Six administration sessions were conducted. Half the group participating in each session was given the English version first and the Icelandic version three weeks later, and the other half got the Icelandic version first and the English version three weeks later. The mean testing time for all sessions was 96 minutes for the Icelandic version and 101 minutes for the English version.

There is always a danger, when transferring psychological instruments between cultures, that a translated item could reflect aspects of the source culture that might not be present in the target culture. This might result in the subjects' not being able to answer the item. To check whether any of the translated items were off culture, the subjects were asked to write down on a separate form the items that in their opinion did not reflect any aspect of the Icelandic culture. Only three subjects out of 148 indicated that one item, item 193, might not reflect Icelandic culture. "Walking over sidewalk cracks" seems not to be a very common superstition in Iceland.

Data Analysis

The data from the bilingual study were analyzed by inspecting means and standard deviations for the basic and content scales. Test-retest coefficients and standard errors of measurement were computed across data from both the Icelandic and the English versions for the basic and content scales. Internal consistency estimates (Cronbach Coefficient Alpha) were also computed for these scales for data from both versions. The reason for using these analyses is to determine the profile similarity between the Icelandic and the English forms of the MMPI-2, and thus demonstrate the linguistic equivalence of the two forms. Inspection of mean score differences, estimation of similarities of profiles, and computation of coefficients between parallel forms were done. Hansen (1987) also advises looking at estimates of the convergent validity of the two forms using confirmatory factor analysis to demonstrate the linguistic equivalence of two forms of psychological instruments. In this present study such analysis would not have been any more informative than the ones used. The methods used are based on generalizability theory (Cronbach, Gleser, Nanda, & Rajaratman, 1972) and are suggested to be sufficiently powerful to detect linguistic equivalence of forms of psychological instruments.

Results

To determine the linguistic equivalence of the two forms on the item level, correlation coefficients were computed for all 567 items across the 148 subjects. The coefficients ranged from .67 to 1.0. Only 20 items yielded a correlation of 1.0, the mean correlation on the item level being .84 and the median .82.

Sölvína Konráòs

Table 18-2. Means and Standard Deviations for the Basic Scales of 67 Icelandic Bilingual Men, Using Both Icelandic and English Forms of the MMPI-2

Scale	Icelandic Version		English Version	
	Mean	S.D.	Mean	S.D.
L	3.8	1.7	3.7	1.9
F	4.6	2.9	4.6	2.8
K	14.0	5.2	13.9	4.9
Hs	5.1	4.0	5.1	3.9
D	18.5	5.3	18.4	5.0
Hy	22.3	4.5	22.0	4.7
Pd	16.8	5.1	16.4	5.3
Mf	30.1	6.2	30.0	6.2
Pa	11.1	3.1	11.2	3.2
Pt	12.0	5.9	12.4	6.0
Sc	11.2	6.2	11.3	6.2
Ma	17.1	4.5	16.8	4.4
Si	26.1	9.0	25.9	9.3

Table 18-3. Means and Standard Deviations for the Basic Scales of 79 Icelandic Bilingual Women, Using Both Icelandic and English Forms of the MMPI-2

Scale	Icelandic Version		English Version	
	Mean	S.D.	Mean	S.D.
L	4.1	2.4	4.1	2.3
F	4.5	3.1	4.7	3.0
K	13.5	4.9	13.7	4.6
Hs	6.8	4.7	6.9	4.6
D	19.9	5.6	20.0	5.5
Hy	21.9	4.4	22.0	4.4
Pd	15.7	5.9	15.8	5.8
Mf	37.4	3.9	37.5	3.9
Pa	10.9	2.5	10.7	2.6
Pt	13.2	7.3	13.3	7.3
Sc	12.5	7.5	12.4	7.5
Ma	16.9	3.9	16.7	3.8
Si	27.6	9.5	27.5	9.5

MMPI-2

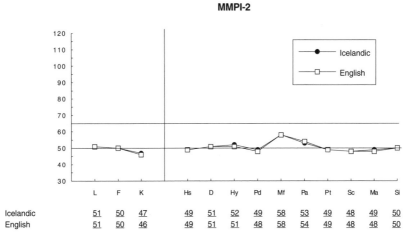

	L	F	K		Hs	D	Hy	Pd	Mf	Pa	Pt	Sc	Ma	Si
Icelandic	51	50	47		49	51	52	49	58	53	49	48	49	50
English	51	50	46		49	51	51	48	58	54	49	48	48	50

Figure 18-3. Bilingual Test-Retest Study of Icelandic Men (N = 67)

MMPI-2

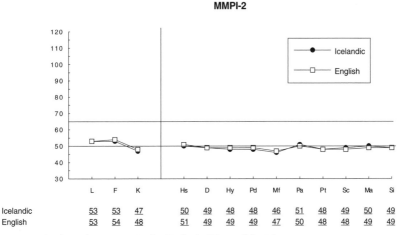

	L	F	K		Hs	D	Hy	Pd	Mf	Pa	Pt	Sc	Ma	Si
Icelandic	53	53	47		50	49	48	48	46	51	48	49	50	49
English	53	54	48		51	49	49	49	47	50	48	48	49	49

Figure 18-4. Bilingual Test-Retest Study of Icelandic Women (N = 79)

Tables 18-2 and 18-3 present the means and standard deviations for both Ice-landic males and females on the MMPI-2 basic scales for the two forms of the in-ventory. The extreme elevations of the F, D, and Sc scales that can be seen in the original Icelandic MMPI data presented in Table 18-1 are not characteristic of the MMPI-2 data. Inspection of the means and standard deviations indicate close similarity to U.S. MMPI-2 data for men and women (Butcher, Dahlstrom, Gra-ham, Tellegen, & Kaemmer, 1989) (see Figures 18-3 and 18-4). The differences between the sizes of means and standard deviations for each scale for the Icelandic

Table 18-4. Retest Correlations and Standard Errors of Measurement for the
Validity and Clinical Scales for 148 Bilingual Icelandic Adults, Using Icelandic
and English Forms of the MMPI-2

Scales	r	SEmeas
L	.79	1.23
F	.8	1.41
K	.82	1.94
Hs	.82	1.60
D	.74	2.57
Hy	.70	2.46
Pd	.77	2.39
Mf	.69	2.13
Pa	.8	2.53
Sc	.82	2.18
Ma	.85	1.92
Si	.89	2.67

Table 18-5. Internal Consistency Estimates (Cronbach Coefficient Alpha)
for the Validity and Clinical Scales for 148 Bilingual Icelandic Adults, Using
Icelandic and English Forms of the MMPI-2

Scales	Icelandic Version Alpha	English Version Alpha
L	.79	1.23
L	.7443	.7392
F	.6964	.7004
K	.7649	.7690
Hs	.7045	.6947
D	.6489	.6635
H	.6393	.6490
Pd	.7436	.7054
Mf	.5902	.5972
Pa	.5289	.5389
Pt	.8963	.9083
Sc	.9032	.9174
Ma	.6271	.5973
Si	.8706	.8701

Table 18-6. Means and Standard Deviations for the Content Scales for 67 Icelandic Bilingual Men, Using Both Icelandic and English Forms of the MMPI-2

Scale	Icelandic Version		English Version	
	Mean	S.D.	Mean	S.D.
ANX	6.1	3.9	5.8	3.7
FRS	2.8	2.5	3.0	2.8
OBS	5.3	3.1	5.3	3.4
DEP	4.9	4.2	5.1	4.0
HEA	5.7	4.9	5.5	5.0
BIZ	2.0	2.2	1.9	2.2
ANG	5.5	4.0	5.7	4.1
CYN	10.4	6.3	10.2	6.1
ASP	9.7	4.5	10.0	4.6
TPA	8.0	4.3	8.2	4.5
LSE	3.7	3.0	3.6	3.0
SOD	8.0	5.1	8.1	5.0
FAM	5.9	3.7	5.8	3.7
WRK	7.6	4.9	7.6	4.3
TRT	4.1	3.2	4.0	3.2

MMPI-2 data and the U.S. MMPI-2 data are of no interpretive significance. The two forms are considered to be linguistically equivalent.

To determine the profile similarity of the two forms for each subject, test-retest coefficients, as well as the standard error of measurement, were computed on gender-combined data for the basic scales as measured by the Icelandic and the English versions (Table 18-4). The results indicate very strong similarity between the two versions. The coefficients range from .66 for the Pa scale to .89 for the Si scale. The standard errors of measurement range from 1.23 for the L scale to 2.67 for the Si scale. In comparison, Butcher et al. (1989) report retest measures for reliability on U.S. data for males of .72 for the Hy scale to .92 for the Si scale and for females, .58 for the Pa scale to .91 for the Si scale. Standard errors of measurement for males were 1.00 for the L scale to 2.42 for the Si scale and for females 1.01 for the L scale to 2.86 for the Si scale.

The Cronbach Alpha for internal consistency estimates presented in Table 18-5, computed for both the Icelandic and the English versions, indicates satisfactory levels of internal consistency. The differences in magnitude between the coefficients for the basic scales for the Icelandic and English versions are negligible.

Table 18-7. Means and Standard Deviations for the Content Scales of 79 Icelandic Bilingual Women, Using Both Icelandic and English Forms of the MMPI-2

Scale	Icelandic Version		English Version	
	Mean	S.D.	Mean	S.D.
ANX	7.3	4.8	7.0	4.0
FRS	7.5	4.0	7.4	4.0
OBS	4.9	3.0	4.9	3.0
DEP	6.5	4.8	6.0	4.4
HEA	7.4	5.1	7.0	5.5
BIZ	2.8	3.0	3.1	2.9
ANG	6.7	3.4	6.3	3.0
CYN	12.5	6.9	11.9	7.2
ASP	9.9	3.5	10.0	3.6
TPA	8.7	3.9	9.0	4.0
LSE	4.5	4.0	4.1	3.8
SOD	10.1	5.6	9.2	5.5
FAM	7.8	4.5	8.0	4.3
WRK	9.0	6.2	9.4	6.7
TRT	5.1	4.0	5.8	4.2

Tables 18-6 and 18-7 present the means and standard deviations for the MMPI-2 content scales for males and females, respectively. No interpretable differences appear when compared to means and standard deviations computed on U.S. data (Butcher et al., 1989).

The test-retest coefficients, standard errors of measurement, and internal consistency estimates for the content scales for the Icelandic data compared with the U.S. data further support the equivalence of the MMPI-2 Icelandic translation and the inventory in the source language (Tables 18-8 and 18-9). Analyses of the data on the MMPI-2 content scales further indicate the linguistic equivalence of the two forms.

Discussion

Cross-cultural studies on psychological measures may in general be divided into two main categories: (a) studies that investigate the appropriateness of transferring psychological instruments, and (b) studies that investigate the structure of psychological variables across cultures. The procedure for developing cross-cultural

Table 18-8. Retest Correlations and Standard Errors of Measurement for the
Content Scales for 148 Bilingual Icelandic Adults, Using Icelandic and English
Form of the MMPI-2

Scales	r	SEmeas
ANX	.83	1.45
FRS	.85	1.57
OBS	.87	1.13
DEP	.84	1.67
HEA	.89	1.39
BIZ	.81	1.78
ANG	.87	1.59
CYN	.88	1.93
ASP	.86	1.66
TPA	.81	1.84
LSE	.81	1.49
SOD	.88	1.75
FAM	.84	1.51
WRK	.89	1.60
TRT	.85	1.32

studies should have at least four objectives: (a) to translate inventories into other languages and establish equivalences, (b) to provide validity data on cross-cultural usefulness, (c) to provide data to determine the universality of the original norms, and (d) to investigate how valid the inventory is with a multiethnic population in the country of origin.

Considerable effort has been made to construct culture-free tests that would eliminate cultural parameters that might influence scores on psychological measures. However, these tests have not eliminated the inventories that claim to capture cultural differences of some kind, either as known variance or as error variance. There is a certain danger involved in assuming cultural fairness, since all measures in psychology are relative across time and culture, and so are norms and inventories. Thus a test might be culture-free only for a particular population for certain periods of time and therefore become misleading or obsolete, since the error due to cultural differences is unknown.

The results of this study indicate that both the MMPI-2 basic scales and content scales for Icelandic subjects have close approximation to the psychometric properties of the U.S. samples. However, the purpose of this study was not to in-

Table 18-9. Internal Consistency Estimates (Cronbach Coefficient Alpha) for the Content Scales for 148 Bilingual Icelandic Adults, Using Icelandic and English Form of the MMPI-2

Scale	Icelandic Version Alpha	English Version Alpha
ANX	.7995	.7896
FRS	.6899	.7143
OBS	.7359	.7400
DE	.8154	.8127
HEA	.8047	.7054
BIZ	.7199	.7096
ANG	.7533	.7691
CYN	.8281	.8302
ASP	.8109	.8120
TPA	.6988	.7003
LSE	.8174	.8203
SOD	.7265	.7277
FAM	.7496	.7462
WRK	.8317	.8341
TRT	.8112	.7168

vestigate the feasibility of using the U.S. norms in Iceland, even though the Icelandic versions of the scales operate in an almost identical manner. An empirical study specifically designed to investigate cross-national comparability needs to be undertaken. The results of studying the linguistic equivalence are not to be confused with an empirical validation study.

It should be emphasized that the 148 subjects in this study are not a representative sample of the Icelandic population. It might be concluded that the similarity of the Icelandic data to the U.S. data results from the use of a highly selected sample. Using the linguistically equivalent Icelandic translation of the MMPI-2 to collect data from a representative sample should answer whether the U.S. norms can be validly used or if collection of Icelandic norms is necessary.

Future Research

We plan to obtain data from college students (N = 700) to evaluate the effectiveness of the Icelandic version of the MMPI-2 in describing college populations. Item analysis is planned to investigate the psychometric properties of the scales with Icelandic normals compared with similar groups in other countries. We also are developing a strategy to evaluate the MMPI-2 scales with clinical populations, for example, with those (1) who currently have been diagnosed as having mental disorders and have been through therapy either as inpatients or outpatients, (2) who are currently in chemical dependency treatment; (3) who three years ago were in chemical dependency treatment and today are sober, and (4) who have recently come into therapy. This evaluation phase of the project will be an important step in adapting the MMPI-2 in Iceland.

Summary

The original MMPI was translated into Icelandic in 1973 (Asmundsson, 1973). Since then the instrument has been applied extensively in clinical settings in Iceland using the norms developed in the United States. Research on the original Icelandic version of the MMPI is meager; the translation was never field-tested. Inspection of profiles reveals that the basic MMPI scales do not differentiate well between clinical and normal samples because the original norms show considerable psychopathology. Extreme elevations of scales F, 2, and 8 seem to be the rule regardless of sample characteristics.

The MMPI-2 was translated from English into Icelandic without reference to the Icelandic MMPI translation. Back-translation and investigation of reading difficulty and comprehension indicated that 294 items out of the 567 MMPI-2 items had to be revised. The revised items were again back-translated and the reading level tested. To test the linguistic equivalence of the original MMPI-2 and the Icelandic translation, both the Icelandic version and the U.S. version were administered to a "semibilingual" group (N = 148) and analyzed for profile similarity.

The results indicated that the two versions were linguistically equivalent. Inspection of the MMPI-2 T scores for the basic scales and content scales showed the Icelandic data yielding a close approximation to the U.S. norms. The extreme elevations on scales F, 2, and 8 found in the Icelandic MMPI data did not appear in the Icelandic MMPI-2 data. Further research evaluating the Icelandic version of the MMPI-2 is planned now that an equivalent form of the instrument is available in Iceland.

References

Asmundsson, G. (1973). *MMPI: Icelandic translation.* Reykjavík: University Hospitals.

Berry, J. W. (1980). Introduction to methodology. In H. C. Triandis & J. W. Berry (Eds.), *Handbook of cross-cultural psychology:* Vol 2. Methodology (pp. 1–28). Boston: Allyn and Bacon.

Brislin, R. W. (1983). Cross-cultural research in psychology. *Annual Review of Psychology, 34,* 363–400.

Brislin, R. W., Lonner, W. J., & Thorndike, R. M. (1973). *Cross-cultural research methods.* New York: Wiley Interscience.

Butcher, J. N. (1982). Cross-cultural research methods in clinical psychology. In P. C. Kendall & J. N. Butcher (Eds.), *Handbook of research methods in clinical psychology* (pp. 273–308). New York: Wiley Interscience.

Butcher, J. N., Dahlstrom, G., Graham, J. R., Tellegen, A., & Kaemmer, B. (1989). *Manual for administration and scoring: MMPI-2.* Minneapolis: University of Minnesota Press.

Butcher, J. N., & Pancheri, P. (1976). *A handbook of cross-national MMPI research.* Minneapolis: University of Minnesota Press.

Cronbach, L. J., Gleser, G. C., Nanda, H., & Rajaratnam, N. (1972). *The dependability of behavioral measurements: Theory of generalizability for scores and profiles.* New York: Wiley.

Hansen, J. C. (1987). Cross-cultural research on interests. *Measurement and Evaluation in Counseling and Development, 19,* 163–176.

Konráòs, S. (1989). *Cross-cultural validation of the lawyer and engineer scales for linguistically equivalent forms of the SCII.* Unpublished doctoral thesis, University of Minnesota, Minneapolis.

Chapter 19

The Russian Translation and Preliminary Adaptation of the MMPI-2

Victor S. Koscheyev and Gloria R. Leon

The MMPI has been used in the former Soviet Union (FSU) since the 1960s, and indeed, as in other countries, is the most widely used measure of personality. Perhaps an indication of its popularity and utility is the fact that four different versions of the MMPI exist in the FSU and are used to varying degrees. Felix Berezin, a psychiatrist, was the first in the FSU to begin work with the MMPI. A 377-item Russian language adaptation by Berezin and colleagues (Berezin, Miroshnikov, & Rozhanets; 1976) termed the MMIL (Multilateral Personality Inventory) is the most often used version. It includes all of the items used in scoring the validity and clinical scales on the original MMPI. Some items are reworded to reflect cultural differences. While there are no published studies comparing scale scores on the different Russian versions of the MMPI, the experience of Russian investigators is that there is not a great deal of concordance between the various versions.

The MMPI has been used extensively in the FSU in psychiatric evaluation, personnel selection in different industries, and monitoring the psychological health status of individuals in various high-risk jobs. It is part of the data gathered in the selection and evaluation of cosmonauts, workers in nuclear and nonnuclear power plant facilities, miners, and persons in military and other strategic positions, among others. It has also been used to monitor the functioning of persons on various expedition teams.

With regard to the space program, the Russians have been much more concerned about psychological factors in the selection and maintenance of their crews than have the Americans. In the tradition of Pavlov, psychological and physiological factors are considered to be one functional unit. Therefore, in addition to information obtained on the MMPI, other evaluations considered psychological in nature assess heart rate, blood pressure, and electrodermal activity under stressors such as simulated emergencies of the type one could experience in the particular work for which the person is being evaluated. These data are interpreted within the context of the MMPI findings. It is very rare to find scientists and clinicians conducting psychological assessments that do not include a physiological component.

Investigations Using the MMPI Conducted by the Specialized Center for Disaster Medicine Protection

Chernobyl Power Plant Operators

The Chernobyl nuclear power plant explosion is a disaster unparalleled in the history of civilian use of nuclear energy (Bunyard, 1988) with regard to its magnitude, scope, and continuing effects. The total dose of internal and external radiation was approximately 65,000 times greater than the radiation release in 1979 during the Three Mile Island accident in Pennsylvania (Matukovsky, 1990). It took nine days to contain the damaged reactor and stop the flow of radioactivity spewing from the reactor fire. More than 100,000 people were evacuated within several days after the accident, and in many areas this evacuation is permanent. The damaged fourth block of the power station in which the explosion occurred, now covered by a concrete sarcophagus, is a constant reminder to all of the terrible catastrophe that happened there and of the potential for another accident. A major personnel concern at Chernobyl, especially since the time of the disaster, is the psychological and physical health of the power plant operators, particularly those in managerial positions. This issue is particularly salient because a combination of errors by power plant personnel resulted in the 1986 explosion (Medvedev, 1990). Radiation levels in the area of the power plant for the first few years after the explosion were high, necessitating the use of protective clothing and constant monitoring of the cumulative radiation levels sustained by persons working in or near the complex. These protective procedures are still in effect.

The first author had a unique experience at Chernobyl, serving as the first medical officer following this disaster. His job was to establish sanitation and other hygienic measures for the area and to monitor the health status of the power plant and other workers sent in to contain the nuclear fire and clean up the radioactive debris. He also monitored and took measures to protect the health of the local population. As a result of this experience, he established the Specialized Center for Disaster Medicine Protection in Moscow, which is the primary center for sending response teams across Russia and the FSU in cases of technological and natural disasters. The Center has closely monitored the Chernobyl power plant operators since the time of this disaster and continues to do so. A primary evaluation tool is the MMPI.

Within the first three months after the disaster, approximately one half of the chief operators were transferred to other facilities either by personal request because of extreme stress or because significant psychological dysfunction was noted through observation and psychological testing. The MMPI protocols of the transferred workers confirmed the significant distress they were experiencing, with abnormal range scores on many of the clinical scales (Koscheyev, Lartzev, Martens, & Pukhovsky, 1987). A recent publication in which both authors collaborated presents an evaluation of the psychological status of the chief operators at the Chernobyl power plant, using the Berezin version of the MMPI (Koscheyev, Martens, Kosenkov, Lartzev, & Leon, 1993). Workers were assessed at four points: the first three months after the accident, and then at three other intervals, the last of which was 20 months postaccident. Because of the emergency situation and confusion still existing three months after the disaster, data were collected at the Time 1 period only on the chief operators who remained at Chernobyl from the time of the explosion. A control group of chief operators at the Ignalina nuclear power station in another part of the FSU (near St. Petersburg) was evaluated four months after the Time 4 Chernobyl evaluation.

This investigation was not prospective in design. The aim was to assess the status of the personnel working at the plant at these particular periods after the disaster, to evaluate their overall stress levels, and to identify and transfer individuals exhibiting significant psychological dysfunction and thus at high risk for causing accidents. Some of the workers in the different time period samples left Chernobyl after the accident, worked at other power stations for varying periods, and then returned to Chernobyl. Others remained at Chernobyl during the entire 20 months after the accident, and thus were in the groups assessed at each point.

All the chief operators in the sample had completed university level educations. The average age was 33.5 years (range, 24 to 53). Similar sociodemographic characteristics were evident in the control group. The psychological evaluation demonstrated a statistically significant increase over time in the percentage of Chernobyl workers with one or more abnormal range clinical scale scores on the MMPI (from 18.4% at Time 1 to 33% at Time 4; scale 5 was not included in this analysis). In contrast, only 10% of the control group chief operators exhibited one or more clinical scale elevations. Examination of scale score differences in the Chernobyl groups over periods 1 through 4 indicated significant changes in mean scores on six of the clinical scales. Significant increases occurred over time on scales 1, 2, 3, 4, and 8, with a significant decrease on scale 6. The significant increase in mean scores from Time 2 to Time 4 on scales 1 and 2 was particularly noteworthy. Therefore, while the mean scores on each of the clinical scales for the groups at each time period were within normal limits, there were increases in health concerns and somatic complaints, dysphoric mood or depression, somatization, conflict with others, and social alienation. There was also a relative decrease in the groups over time in vigilance or concerns about the actions of others, or how others might be evaluating them. We interpreted these findings as reflecting operators' growing fears of another accident at Chernobyl and their concerns about the impact on their health of continuing radiation exposure. However, one cannot rule out the possibility that operators who volunteered to work at Chernobyl at later time periods had relatively greater psychological dysfunction before coming to this power station. In addition, it is important in evaluating these data to bear in mind that mean scores for the group at each time interval were clearly within normal limits. Therefore, our findings reflect problems and concerns that are at subclinical levels, though nonetheless important. Our data are consistent with the demonstration of chronic subclinical dysfunction reported in studies of Three Mile Island populations (Davidson & Baum, 1986).

The extensive psychological monitoring of the Chernobyl power plant workers led to controlled research at other power stations with the same aim of monitoring the current health status of the operators. These efforts by the Center group resulted in the development of a standardized set of government requirements for psychological evaluation of personnel selected for and working in hazardous conditions such as nuclear power stations. The MMPI is a key instrument in this required evaluation battery.

Soviet-American Bering Bridge Expedition

The Specialized Center for Disaster Medicine Protection has been involved in the study of numerous expedition teams, including mountaineering and Arctic groups. One of the interests of the scientists at the Center is examining individual differences in physical and psychological capacities in highly stressful situations. In addition to the implications for personnel selection, studying these groups can provide significant information about survival in extreme conditions that could be applied to aiding and protecting persons stranded in cold environments awaiting rescue.

In 1989, researchers from three Russian and two American scientific institutes, including the Center in Moscow and the University of Minnesota, studied a subpolar expedition team. This unique expedition consisted of 12 persons, six Soviet and six U.S. members, who traveled by dogsled and cross-country skis from Siberia, across the Bering Straits, to Nome, Alaska. The Soviet and U.S. groups were each composed of three Caucasian and three indigenous members (Inuit or Chuckchi); nine members of the total group were male and three were female. An important purpose of this 61-day expedition was to increase world awareness of the plight of the indigenous peoples of this region, who live on opposite sides of an international border between the United States and the FSU. This border, which runs through the middle of the Bering Straits, was closed at the start of the Cold War, thus separating friends and family from one another and making it no longer possible to engage in commerce across the border. Therefore, in addition to the considerable physical demands of traversing an extremely cold and arduous environment on skis, the group was expected to interact with the local population along the way in the numerous villages in which they stopped. This was often fatiguing, though the interactions were an important component of the expedition.

The MMPI was one of the assessment measures used by Center scientists to evaluate the team members (Koscheyev, Roschina, & Makhov, 1994). Before the start of the trek, the Soviet participants completed the Berezin version of the MMPI and the Americans completed the U.S. version. Mean scores were evaluated, comparing male Soviet and American groups. Because there were only three females on the team, their scores were not compared according to national group. Data for two of the male Soviet members (one Caucasian and one indigenous) were not included in the group comparisons because of invalid profiles due to high scores on scale F. For both male national groups, scores on all scales were within the normal range, except for one U.S. male subject who scored in the abnormal range on scale 4. For both the Soviet and U.S. males, the relatively highest mean score was on scale 9, and the relatively lowest on scale 2. The scale scores for all of the female team members were within the normal range and consistent with the males in demonstrating high scores on scale 9 and low scores on scale 2. These data are consistent with the Multidimensional Personality Questionnaire (MPQ) findings on this group by University of Minnesota researchers (Leon, Kanfer, Hoffman, & Dupre, 1991); the highest mean scale score for the entire group was on the Achievement scale, and the lowest mean score was on the Stress Reaction scale. Inspection of individual MMPI scale scores did not indicate any differences between the Caucasian and indigenous groups.

The demonstration of personality characteristics of high energy level and low dysphoric mood are clearly adaptive for the rigors of an expedition and are consistent with those from a previous North Pole expedition (Leon, McNally, & Ben-Porath, 1989). The Bering Bridge MMPI findings are of interest in terms of their implications not only for enhancing the prediction of successful performance on expedition teams but also for selecting persons to work in other types of extreme climatic conditions. The Russian male whose MMPI profile was invalid refused to cooperate in completing daily mood measures. However, of the entire team, he scored highest on other tests administered on the trek that measured personal and situational anxiety. Therefore, even in nonclinical groups, invalid profiles can reflect psychological dysfunction. The invalid profile of the indigenous team member was not consistent with other psychometric and behavioral data that demonstrated generally good performance. It is possible that reading comprehension difficulties contributed to the invalidating F score.

Development of the MMPI-2 in Russia

As a result of the contacts made between Center and University of Minnesota investigators who worked together on the Bering Bridge study, initial discussions and more specific planning began in 1991 for collaboration on a Russian language translation of the MMPI and the collection of normative data. It was clear that the Specialized Center for Disaster Medicine Protection had extensive experience using the MMPI and a strong interest in extending this use to the MMPI-2. There also was the obvious recognition of the advantages of trying to develop a uniform MMPI measure that investigators all over the FSU could use, thus ensuring comparability of findings. The possibility of establishing direct collaboration between members of the Center and members of the University of Minnesota on this project was also of interest. As a result of trips back and forth by both authors between Moscow and Minneapolis to work out logistical details for this project, a contract was signed in December 1991 between the university and the Center for the latter to carry out the Russian language translation and standardization studies on the MMPI-2.

The research plan is as follows: After the successful completion of the MMPI-2 translation, an initial standardization sample of 300 males and 300 females will be tested. The group will include university students and persons in various work settings, ranging in age from 17 to 50. Because of the great ethnic diversity in the FSU, this investigation will focus on subjects from the relatively more homogeneous Moscow and St. Petersburg areas. Study II will consist of MMPI-2 administration to groups of female and male inpatient psychiatric patients, 100 with diagnoses of schizophrenia and 100 classified with some type of major mood disorder. Subjects will be carefully screened to rule out a history of organic brain disorder. Data from the psychiatric group will be compared to a randomly selected subset of normals obtained from the original standardization sample. Study III will be an evaluation of the factor structure of the Russian language MMPI-2, using data obtained from the psychiatric and normal groups. Comparisons will be made with the factor structure of the English language MMPI-2, separately evaluating the psychiatric and normal groups.

The translation efforts began in Moscow in 1992. A group of 15 bilingual Russians connected with the Center and from other institutes each independently translated the items into Russian. These initial efforts provided data that were sometimes difficult to synthesize in group meetings, because of the many variations in the exact wording of the items from translator to translator. Subsequently, Dr. Nicolai Pukhovsky from the Center chose a version of each item, taking into account the various translations. He then consulted with a smaller group from the Center to obtain agreement on the items. The next step involved a group of five persons who back-translated all of the items and then worked together to revise them as necessary. Following this procedure, the translation and back-translation were sent to Minnesota, where a bilingual Russian postdoctoral fellow at the University of Minnesota (Dr. Inna Koscheyev) checked through all of the items, comparing the English and Russian versions, and made minor modifications to some of the items. The changed Russian items were then sent to Dr. Alexander Prokhorov, a Russian colleague now at the University of Rhode Island, who back-translated these particular items. Final adjustments were then made in consultation with Dr. I. Koscheyev. The Russian MMPI-2 was then evaluated by the University Language Center, which evaluates all translations published by the University of Minnesota Press. The evaluation was that the Russian translation of the MMPI-2 was of very good quality, with suggestions for minor changes in a number of items.

One of the items the Moscow group had difficulty translating was item 1, "I like mechanics magazines." There are no nontechnical magazines like this published in the FSU. The meaning of a first translation was "I like popular science journals about technical subjects." When it was clear that this meaning was not precisely correct, the item was adjusted to "I like popular science journals." However, this meaning is also not precisely correct. The next version was "I like journals about automobiles." However, after further discussion we concluded that the closest equivalent, given the types of magazines available in Russia, is "I like popular science journals."

At present, initial standardization data have been collected on a group of 60 medical students, 32 males and 28 females, in their third to fourth years in the program. The age range for both the male and female groups is 19 to 24 years. Mean scores on the standard MMPI-2 validity and clinical scales are remarkably similar to those found in the U.S. standardization samples. The mean profiles for the males and females are presented in Figures 19-1 and 19-2.

The biggest problem encountered thus far in the MMPI-2 research is the fact that a country literally disappeared during the period when the research was initiated. The demise of the Soviet Union, the declaration of the independence of each of the Soviet republics, and the recent political instability in Russia have made it difficult to progress as rapidly as we would like on the data collection. However, the Center group has now reinitiated the standardization research, and it likely will not take long to collect the remaining data for the standardization sample. The Russians have typically collected data on various projects by going into an entire factory or school and testing all persons in that facility. Thus, a large number of subjects can be evaluated in a relatively short time. When the data collection on the MMPI-2 is completed, the Center group and the University of Minnesota researchers will discuss the possibility of the Center translating remaining items for

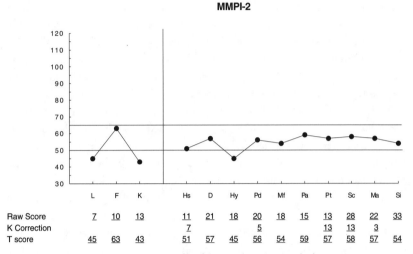

Figure 19-1. Standard Clinical MMPI-2 Profile of the Initial Russian Standardization Data on Women (N = 28)

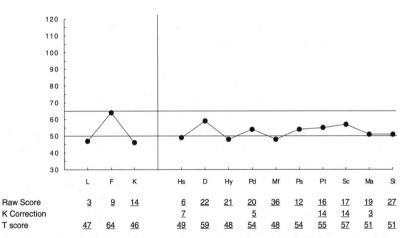

Figure 19-2. Standard Clinical MMPI-2 Profile of the Initial Russian Standardization Data on Men (N = 32)

the MMPI-A and conducting standardization studies and subsequent statistical analyses on information collected on adolescent groups. The Center group has also carried out a Russian language translation of the MPQ (Multidimensional Personality Questionnaire) and potentially can serve as the Russian center for the development and dissemination of high-quality Russian language versions of various psychological tests.

Other Projects Under Way

At the present time, we are planning to use both the MMPI-2 and the MMPI-A in projects we have submitted for funding evaluating the psychological and health status of the Chernobyl population. This research will be a collaborative project between the University of Minnesota, the Belarus Institute of Physiology, and the Center in Moscow. A comprehensive assessment of groups exposed to different amounts of radiation after this disaster is extremely important, both to carefully examine the extent of current dysfunction in groups of different ages and to assess the relationship between psychological dysfunction and physical complaints that are often associated with stress. In the aftermath of Chernobyl, the experience of various physical symptoms may be responded to with anxiety because of fears that these symptoms may be the beginning of a carcinogenic process due to radiation effects.

The Russian MMPI-2 was used to assess two cosmonauts who were part of the crew of a joint Russian-U.S. space shuttle mission to the Russian space station Mir, scheduled to take place in March 1995. Following meetings at the NASA Johnston Space Center in Houston in November 1993, the test advisory committee was enthusiastic about the existence of the Center's Russian version of the MMPI-2 and will recommend to Russian psychologists that it be used for selecting and evaluating crews for this mission. The English language version will be used by the U.S. space group.

Conclusions

There is considerable interest in the FSU in a well-translated and standardized version of the MMPI-2. The research and clinical advantages are clear. There is also a great deal of interest in using this measure in the United States and Israel. Large numbers of immigrants have arrived from the FSU in both countries, and comprehensive psychological evaluation is of extreme importance for those exhibiting psychological distress.

References

Berezin, F. B., Miroshnikov, M.P., & Rozhanets, R. V. (1976). *A method of multi-lateral personality investigation* [Russian]. Moscow: Medicine.

Bunyard, P. (1988). *Health guide for the nuclear age*. London: Macmillan.

Davidson, L. M., & Baum, A. (1986). Chronic stress and post-traumatic stress disorders. *Journal of Consulting and Clinical Psychology, 54,* 303–308.

Koscheyev, V. S., Lartzev, M. A., Martens, V. K., & Pukhovsky, N. N. (1987). Peculiarities of the psychic adaptation of the operative personnel of the Chernobyl nuclear power plant during the period of elimination of the disaster consequences [Russian]. Paper presented at the Symposium on Immediate and Remote Consequences of the Radiation Disaster in the Chernobyl Nuclear Power Plant. (pp. 866–891). Institute of Biophysics of the USSR Ministry of Public Health, Moscow.

Koscheyev, V. S., Martens, V. K., Kosenkov, A. A., Lartzev, M. A., & Leon, G. R. (1993). Psychological status of Chernobyl nuclear power plant operators after the nuclear disaster. *Journal of Traumatic Stress, 6,* 561–568.

Koscheyev, V. S., Roschina, N. A., & Makhov, V. V. (1994). Psychophysiological characteristics related to the functional state of the members of the Soviet-American Arctic "Bering Bridge" expedition. *Environment and Behavior, 26,* 166–178.

Leon, G. R., Kanfer, R., Hoffman, R. G., & Dupre, L. (1991). Interrelationships of personality and coping in a challenging extreme situation. *Journal of Research in Personality, 25,* 357–371.

Leon, G. R., McNally, C., & Ben-Porath, Y. (1989). Personality characteristics, mood, and coping patterns in a successful North Pole expedition team. *Journal of Research in Personality, 23,* 162–179.

Matukovsky, N. (1990, March 26). Catastrophe. What we learned from the Chernobyl lessons [Russian]. *Izvestia,* March 26, 1990.

Medvedev, G. (1990). *The truth about Chernobyl.* New York: Basic Books.

Chapter 20

The MMPI-2 in France

Part I by Isabelle Gillet, Mireille Simon, and Julien D. Guelfi

Part II by Julien D. Guelfi, Annick Brun-Eberentz, Claudine Monier,
Françoise Seunevel, and Liliane Svarna

The first French version of the MMPI was published in 1959. Validation studies
were carried out on the French adaptation of the test over a 35-year period, under
the direction of P. Pichot and J. Perse. Norms were developed on a representative
sample of 321 French subjects (146 men, 175 women) and were found comparable to the U.S. norms. Cultural differences were evident on certain scales (the
French usually obtaining higher scores than Americans), notably on scales L, F, D,
Sc, and Si for both men and women; Mf for men; and Hy for women. Some
significant differences appeared between men and women on the same scales in
both the French and American samples. Separate norms for men and women were
developed in France, with the exception of the Sc scale, for which common norms
were developed. Widespread use of the MMPI throughout France has confirmed
the quality of the French version. Given the overall congruence of the French and
American versions of the MMPI, the earlier French work served as a basis for the
adaptation and development of the MMPI-2.

I. Development of the French Version of the MMPI-2

Translation

The committee given the responsibility for developing the French version of the
MMPI-2 consisted of P. Pichot, J. Perse, and two ECPA (Editions du Centre de
Psychologie Appliquée) research psychologists.

The following psychiatrists at the University Paris V René Descartes, Clinique des Mal-
adies Mentales et de L'Encéphale evaluated narrative MMPI-2 reports: Mmes et Mrs les
Docteurs Aubin, Boyer, Corcos, Dardennes, Dhote, Doublet, Duneton, Foulon, Guelfi,
Guillibert, Hakim-Kreis, Hassan, Heim, Kalck, Leonard, Levy-Garboua, Matheron,
Olivier-Martin, Seror, Thibault, Vautherin, and Waintraub.

Table 20-1. Differences in Item Endorsement Frequencies between the French and U.S. Samples

Frequencies differences	Numbers of Items			
	Males		Females	
	N	%	N	%
26 and more	45	7.9	48	8.5
22-25	21	3.7	37	6.5
16-21	72	12.7	64	11.3
10-15	130	22.9	105	18.5
0-9	299	52.7	313	55.2

The 107 new and 67 modified inventory items were translated by two bilingual psychologist-translators, one an American who has lived in France for 10 years and the other a French translator who specializes in clinical psychology. Direct translations were compared and discussed until a consensus was reached on each item. Two other psychologist-translators then back-translated this first version and compared their back-translations with the American version. As a result of these comparisons, 17 items were modified. Items unchanged from the French MMPI were also reviewed with the aim of improving and simplifying them wherever possible. Thus, 180 items were reworded to make them read better in French.

Data Collection

The first experimental version of the MMPI-2 was administered to a sample population of 259 subjects (167 women and 92 men), ranging in age from 16 to 71 years (mean, 34 years; S.D., 16 years). The marital status of the sample was single, 27%; married or divorced, 30%; other or not indicated, 43%. The occupational status of the sample group was categorized as middle management, 22%; executives, 21%; college students, 30%; other or not indicated, 27%. Except for students, most of the subjects filled out the MMPI-2 during career-counseling sessions; participation in the experiment was entirely voluntary and anonymous.

Item Endorsement Frequencies. Item endorsement frequencies (IEF) from the French and U.S. normative samples (N = 2,600: 1,462 women and 1,138 men) were compared. Table 20-1 shows the item endorsement frequency differences in absolute values between French and U.S. subjects. (See also the U.S.-French item endorsement comparison in Appendix D.)

Only 45 items (7.9%) for the men and 48 items (8.5%) for the women showed differences of more than 25%, a figure considered significantly different from the results of research on the MMPI (Butcher & Pancheri, 1976). This is about the number of item differences expected by chance. These items were reviewed for item equiv-

Table 20-2. Items with Endorsement Frequency Differences of 25% or More between the French and U.S. Samples

Scale	No. of Items	French				Common (French)	
		Males		Females		Males and Females	
		N	%	N	%	N	%
L	15	3	20	5	33	3	20
F	60	2	3	2	3	1	1.5
K	30	2	7	2	7	1	3.5
Hs	32	–	–	–	–	–	–
D	57	5	9	5	9	4	7
Hy	60	6	10	5	8	4	7
Pd	50	4	8	3	6	2	4
Mf	56	4	7	3	5	3	5
Pa	40	–	–	–	–	–	–
Pr	48	2	4	2	4	2	4
Sc	78	–	–	–	–	–	–
Ma	46	1	2	2	4	1	2
Si	69	4	6	7	10	3	4

alence and clinical pertinence for the French population. During the modification phase, particular attention was paid to the two essential goals of intercultural equivalence and cognizance of cultural and linguistic differences. Sometimes it was necessary to depart from the phrasing of the English-language original to convey the underlying meaning in French. Overall, the items translated from English to French indicated a high level of item equivalence, since no notable differences were recorded in responses to 75% of the items (for women and men alike). Table 20-2 shows frequencies per scale of items with greater than 25% differences in IEF.

Excluding scale L, which contains a limited number of items, the scales that have the greatest number of items for which responses differ between the two populations are K, D, Hy, Pd, Mf, and Si for men; K, D, Hy, Pd, Mf, and Si for women; and D, Hy, Mf, Pd, Pt, and Si based on average rank scores for both men and women.

The discrepancy rate is less than 10% on all scales, in itself a highly satisfying result. However, this is but one step in the process of evaluating the content validity of the scales.

Mean Profiles of the Validity and Clinical Scales. The French raw scores on the validity and clinical scales were converted to T scores using American norms. We used a mean score difference of one standard variation (S.D. = 10) as the threshold

MMPI-2

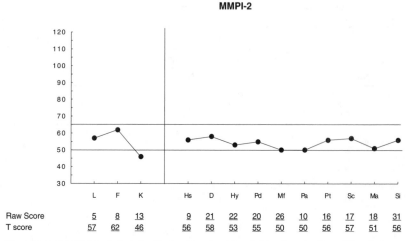

	L	F	K		Hs	D	Hy	Pd	Mf	Pa	Pt	Sc	Ma	Si
Raw Score	5	8	13		9	21	22	20	26	10	16	17	18	31
T score	57	62	46		56	58	53	55	50	50	56	57	51	56

Figure 20-1. MMPI-2 Basic Scale Profile for a Sample of French Men from the General Population (N = 92)

MMPI-2

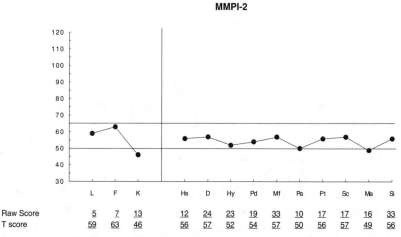

	L	F	K		Hs	D	Hy	Pd	Mf	Pa	Pt	Sc	Ma	Si
Raw Score	5	7	13		12	24	23	19	33	10	17	17	16	33
T score	59	63	46		56	57	52	54	57	50	56	57	49	56

Figure 20-2. MMPI-2 Basic Scale Profile for a Sample of French Women from the General Population (N = 167)

figure and found that scores on the F scale are significantly higher for both men and women in the French sample. Other scales indicating differences of between one half and one standard deviation from the mean score are L, Hs, D, Pt, Sc, and Si for men and L, Hs, D, Mf, Pt, Sc, and Si for women.

The French obtained consistently higher mean scores on these scales than did subjects in the United States (Figures 20-1 and 20-2). A similar tendency has been noted on MMPI-2 adaptations in several other countries.

MMPI-2

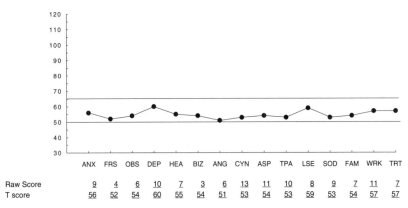

	ANX	FRS	OBS	DEP	HEA	BIZ	ANG	CYN	ASP	TPA	LSE	SOD	FAM	WRK	TRT
Raw Score	9	4	6	10	7	3	6	13	11	10	8	9	7	11	7
T score	56	52	54	60	55	54	51	53	54	53	59	53	54	57	57

Figure 20-3. MMPI-2 Content Scale Profile for a Sample of French Men from the General Population (N = 92)

MMPI-2

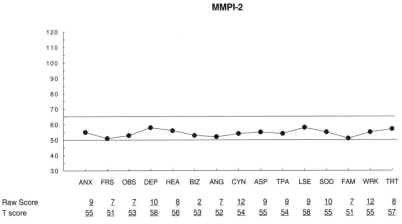

	ANX	FRS	OBS	DEP	HEA	BIZ	ANG	CYN	ASP	TPA	LSE	SOD	FAM	WRK	TRT
Raw Score	9	7	7	10	8	2	7	12	9	9	10	7	12	8
T score	55	51	53	58	56	53	52	54	55	54	58	55	51	55	57

Figure 20-4. MMPI-2 Content Scale Profile for a Sample of French Women from the General Population (N = 167)

Mean Profiles of the Content Scales. We used a mean score difference of one standard deviation (S.D. = 10) as the threshold figure and found that scores on the DEP scale are significantly higher for the male population in France (Table 20-3). Scales indicating differences of between one half and one standard deviation in the mean score are ANX, HEA, LSE, WRK, and TRT for men and DEP, HEA, ASP, LSE, WRK, and TRT for women (Figures 20-3 and 20-4).

Internal Structure of the Validity and Clinical Scales. A principal component analysis with varimax rotation was performed on the MMPI-2 scales to compare the

Table 20-3. Means and Standard Deviations of the MMPI-2 Content Scales for French Samples

	Males		Females	
Scale	Mean	S.D.	Mean	S.D.
ANX	55.7	10.9	54.8	12.1
FRS	51.7	9.7	51.4	11.8
OBS	53.5	10.5	52.9	10.7
DEP	60.4	9.5	58.3	11.9
HEA	55.1	11.5	55.6	11.8
BIZ	53.8	10.4	53.0	10.5
ANG	50.7	9.3	52.3	10.4
CYN	53.4	9.8	54.0	10.0
ASP	54.2	8.2	55.3	9.3
TPA	53.1	11.1	54.2	11.2
LSE	58.7	10.0	57.5	11.0
SOD	52.7	8.9	54.8	10.7
FAM	53.6	12.0	51.0	11.2
WRK	56.9	9.5	55.3	12.2
TRT	57.0	10.7	56.7	12.5

structure of French and American samples. Four factors were extracted following the recommendations of previous researchers (Butcher & Pancheri, 1976). Table 20-4 shows the factor loadings extracted for the French female sample.

The factor structure for women is most informative, as it appears to be almost identical to factor structures of MMPI-2 clinical scales from studies carried out in other countries, including the United States. These factors can be described as follows:

1. *Psychopathology or general maladjustment.* In France, as in the United States, this factor essentially comprises scales F, Hs, D, Hy, and Pa. Scales Sc and Pd have very high loadings on this factor (and nonnegligible loadings on other factors). The congruence coefficient is .86.

2. *Overcontrol.* As in the United States, this factor is mainly constituted by the scales F, Pd, Pt, Sc, and Ma (positive loadings), and L and K (negative loadings). The congruence coefficient is .89.

3. *Social introversion-extraversion.* As in the United States, this factor essentially concerns scales F, Pt, Sc, and Si (positive loadings) and K (negative loading). The congruence coefficient is .98.

Table 20-4. Factor Loadings on the Four Factors Extracted from the French Female Sample for the Validity and Clinical Scales

Scale	Factor 1	Factor 2	Factor 3	Factor 4
L	.14	−.62	−.20	−.24
F	.60	.42	.43	−.22
K	.06	−.52	−.75	.12
Hs	.69	.11	.46	−.09
D	.69	−.14	.56	.12
Hy	.90	−.12	−.08	.07
Pd	.63	.52	.11	.32
Mf	.13	.00	−.03	.90
Pa	.71	.18	.23	.14
Pt	.49	.32	.74	−.03
Sc	.62	.49	.53	−.08
Ma	.27	.78	−.08	−.23
Si	.21	−.09	.92	.08
Explained Variance	29.3	16.5	23.5	8.8
Global Variance	78.1			

4. *Masculinity-femininity.* This factor is mainly explained by the Mf scale. The congruence coefficient is .84.

Preliminary results were obtained on a somewhat small but sufficient female sample (N = 167). Because the results correspond closely to the U.S. results obtained on a sample of 1,462 subjects, the factorial structure of the MMPI-2 can be considered reasonably stable as well as equivalent. Results obtained from the male sample are not provided here because of the limited size of the available sample (N = 92) at the time this chapter was written.

Five scales appeared to load on a single factor: Hy and Pa (F1), Ma (F2), Si (F3), and Mf (F4). Three scales belonged to two factors: Hs and D (F1 and F3) and K (F2 and F3). For three scales less specific to a particular dimension, loadings on three distinctive factors are sufficient: Pt and Sc for factors 1, 2 and 3; Pd for factors 1, 2, and 4.

Factor Analysis of the Content Scales. A principal component factorial analysis with varimax rotation was performed on the MMPI-2 content scales. Two factors were extracted. Table 20-5 shows factor loadings extracted from the French female sample.

The first factor was made up of the scales WRK, LSE, DEP, TRT, ANX, SOD,

Table 20-5. Factor Loadings on the MMPI-2 Content Scales for the French Female Sample

Scale	Factor 1	Factor 2
ANX	.79	.39
FRS	.63	.36
OBS	.73	.43
DEP	.85	.31
HEA	.58	.35
BIZ	.34	.57
ANG	.27	.71
CYN	.37	.75
ASP	.15	.74
TPA	.11	.82
LSE	.85	.25
SOD	.79	.00
FAM	.37	.61
WRK	.86	.33
TRT	.83	.35

OBS, FRS, and HEA and can be interpreted as a factor of emotional and social maladjustment of rather neurotic symptomatology.

The second factor was composed of scales TPA, CYN, ASP, ANG, FAM, and BIZ and could be interpreted as behavioral-type disorders, with conflictual interpersonal relationships. It is interesting to note that the WRK content scale appears in the first factor and therefore seems to reflect anxious and emotive troubles manifested in difficult professional relationships, whereas the FAM content scale appears in the second factor, thus indicating troubles of an aggressive nature.

Bilingual Comparison

A test-retest reliability study was carried out using bilingual subjects. A preliminary sample of 12 persons alternatively completed the English-language and French versions at an interval of several days. Half of the sample began with the original, the other half with the French version. The limited size of the sample (8 males, 4 females) did not allow for the data to be processed separately, hence the results for the male and female samples are given together. The corrected mean profile of raw scores and standard deviations is presented in Table 20-6. No significant differences were found. However, because of the limited size of the sample, this comparative

Table 20-6. Means and Standard Deviations for the Validity and Clinical Scale Scores of 12 French Bilingual Subjects Taking the MMPI-2 in English and French

| | French | | U.S. | | |
	Mean	S.D.	Mean	S.D.	t
L	4.83	3.21	4.50	3.15	1.77
F	4.50	2.02	4.17	1.53	.63
K	17.75	4.49	18.33	4.14	.74
Hs	13.83	3.61	13.75	2.73	.20
D	19.00	4.73	20.08	4.66	1.26
Hy	23.75	3.39	22.92	2.50	1.45
Pd	25.83	2.55	24.92	2.43	1.37
Mf	32.17	6.78	30.83	6.26	1.38
Pa	8.92	1.51	9.08	1.98	.43
Pt	28.00	5.06	28.83	5.32	.89
Sc	28.42	3.34	28.08	3.45	.41
Ma	20.00	4.63	19.00	5.20	1.76
Si	21.75	5.90	23.08	6.24	1.02

study can be no more than qualitative. The Rho concordance coefficients (Spearman) are given in Table 20-7. Except for scales Sc (.43) and F (.49), the coefficients on all scales range from .53 (for Pd) to .97 (for L). Ten coefficients are equal to or greater than .60, an acceptable level of agreement between the two forms.

Discussion

The results of this preliminary study enabled us to go back over the items to evaluate discrepancies observed between the French and U.S. samples.

The committee reviewed each of the items showing differences greater than 25% between the two samples. There appeared to be two major reasons for the discrepancies: (1) The translation lacked precision and did not sufficiently define the underlying variables. In such cases, the item was revised. (2) The translation was correct from a linguistic and contextual point of view, but it appeared that a cultural difference existed. In other words, either it seemed possible to depart from the original item content to draw the items toward the scale by calling on the clinical and cultural competence of the experts to reformulate the item, or item content could not be modified and the items had to remain identical, since the results were acceptable and the creation of new "typically" French items did not appear

Table 20-7. Test-Retest Correlations (Spearman) for the
Validity and Clinical Scales of 12 French Bilingual Subjects

Scale	Rho
L	.97
F	.49
K	.71
Hs	.94
D	.60
Hy	.86
Pd	.53
Mf	.81
Pa	.62
Pt	.83
Sc	.43
Ma	.94
Si	.67

justified. Moreover, it appeared important to conserve common international item content in the MMPI-2.

Obviously, it remains to be seen whether the fluctuations observed were not simply due to sampling effects (given the limited number of subjects in each group in the French experiments). In chapter 2 of this volume, James Butcher quoted Mirza's suggestion that the task of cultural translation can be defined on three levels:

- Formal modifications: "For the most part, they are usually confined to the lexical and grammatical requirements of the new language."
- Transformal modifications: "They reshape the content to suit the new conditions without radically changing the subject matter."
- Radical modifications: "A new item is required to replace the original one when cultural differences make it impossible to retain the original form and content."

1) *Formal modifications:* In this category, the passage from American English to French necessitates changes in sentence construction, for example, the sentence is inversed or the verb form is changed from the active to the passive. Take, for example, item 91: "I have little or no trouble with my muscles twitching or jumping." Instead of becoming "Mes muscles sautent ou tressaillent jamais ou rarement," as it normally would be in French (translated

in English "My muscles twitch and jump never or rarely"), it becomes "Je ne suis que rarement ou jamais gêné par des tressaillements ou des soubressauts de mes muscles" (in English "I am only rarely or never bothered by the twitches or jumps of my muscles"). An IEF comparison shows that this formal modification in no way affects the result: American males, 89%, versus French males, 77%; American females, 89%, versus French females, 79%.

Similarly, item 255, "I do not often notice my ears ringing or buzzing," becomes "I rarely feel ringing or buzzing (noises) in my ear." The IEF on this item are American males, 78%, versus French males, 78%; American females, 84%, versus French females, 83%.

Slight formal modifications usually have little effect on the underlying meaning of the item, but they are necessary for readability and acceptability in the target language.

2) *Transformal modifications:* In this category, if the underlying meaning of the original item is to be respected, a cultural equivalent must be found as a suitable substitute. For example, item 384, "I liked playing 'house' when I was a child," should have been translated by the expression commonly used in children's games in France, "jouer au papa et à la maman," which means "playing father and mother." However, the French expression "playing father and mother" has a strong sexual connotation that could easily go beyond a simple identification with the father-mother role (scale GF). It was considered preferable to transform the item and formulate it as "playing at having a tea party" ("jouer à la dinette") to avoid any possible cultural bias. Results show that this adaptation is pertinent: U.S. males, 43%, versus French males, 34%; U.S. females, 87%, versus French females, 87%.

Similarly, item 207 on the Si scale, "I would like to belong to several clubs," could not be translated literally. The French term corresponding to the word "club" (*club*) has a strong cultural bias. It refers to the elitist practice of belonging to closed groups that are reserved for only a "lucky few" in France. It was therefore deemed necessary to conserve the social introversion value of this item by choosing a broader term that corresponds more closely to national social behavior (i.e., "association"). Results confirmed this decision: U.S. males, 32%, versus French males, 35%; U.S. females, 35%, versus French females, 34%.

Generally speaking, terms such as "parties" and "social gatherings" are difficult to translate into French because of a lack of psychological equivalence. Transformal modification always involves a risk owing to the lack of strictly equivalent words in the target language. Indeed, certain expressions, when translated in a satisfactory manner, may cover different fields semantically, leading one to wonder whether all conceptual objects have an equivalent in the other language. The translators' own intercultural knowledge must be called upon to analyze this type of modification. The homogeneity of item content can be validated only if experimental data on the subject are available in the target language.

3) *Radical modifications:* No radical transformations were necessary because U.S. and French cultures have the same general values and beliefs and produce similar behavior.

4) *Other modifications:* Relatively systematic translation difficulties from the English to the French did exist, however. Certain original items used the conditional form, but the same mood translated into French produced awkward results with extremely high IEF differences. When item 48, "Most anytime I would rather sit and daydream than do anything else," was translated using the conditional form in French, endorsement frequencies were U.S. males, 12%, versus French males, 39%; U.S. females, 12%, versus French females, 34%.

The conditional mood used in items 81 (IEF differences > 25%) and 118 (IEF differences > 20%) produced the same inflationary tendency in the French sample. In view of these results, much thought was given to the differences in psychological meaning when the conditional mood was used in the two languages. Indeed, the behavior described in these items cannot account for major differences in responses. It was therefore suggested that use of the conditional elicited a different response attitude in French subjects. In French, the conditional mood seems to lead to a more irrational, unreal projection, therefore resulting in greater endorsement, while in American English the conditional form is perceived as a probable occurrence. These observations led to a change in mode; the items were reformulated using the indicative form (the mode of likelihood in French) to elicit a more conjectural response attitude.

Items containing adverbs of frequency or intensity (qualifiers) in the original MMPI-2 systematically caused another problem. The exact linguistic translation of these adverbs (almost, at times, several times, etc.) evoke a significantly different response in French subjects than in American subjects. For example, when item 73, "I am certainly lacking in self-confidence," is literally translated, the results are U.S. males, 17%, versus French males, 64%; U.S. females, 28%, versus French females, 73%. Similarly, items 411 (IEF differences > 20%), 326 (IEF differences > 25%), 301 (IEF differences > 30%), and several others are more frequently endorsed by the French. Although there is definitely a question of cultural difference for some of these items (the French are more self-critical, and manifest a less positive attitude and less self-satisfaction), the meaning of these qualifiers is appreciably different in the two languages. Indeed, the French endorse these items even if the behavior described is not constant. The quantifying scaling aspect of the adverb bears different importance in the two cultures. The meaning of these items has thus been reinforced by offering adverbs that are less hypothetical and more categorical and absolute in the French language.

In general, the use of terms such as "to feel" and "excitement" make it difficult to adapt personality inventories to the French language. These commonly used words have widely diverse connotations in American English, yet no real equivalent in French. They must be handled with care. Very often, the meaning of such words can only be rendered into French by using a paraphrase. When a text is thus translated from American English to French there is a 20% increase in volume.

In conclusion, two more items illustrate the alchemy of the translation process and, more important, the attainable limits to which the quest for perfection may be pushed. Endorsement frequencies for item 49, "I am a very sociable person," were U.S. males, 67%, versus French males, 67%; U.S. females, 75%, versus French females, 72%. Endorsement frequencies for item 61, "I am an important person," were U.S. males, 77%, versus French males, 17%; U.S. females, 70%, versus French females, 11%.

From a linguistic point of view, these sentences are simple. The meaning lies in the two adjectives; there is no ambiguity in the syntax. Yet the results show marked differences in the responses given by the two groups. In the first case, "sociable" (for which direct translation and back-translation show complete equivalence) elicits the same percentage of endorsement. In the second, the word "important" (which has the same linguistic equivalence in both languages) is perceived very differently by the two cultures. This empirical observation serves as a reminder that, regardless of the level of perfection reached in translation, because items are samples of language they may have varying mental, social, and cultural representations.

Scale Analysis. A number of items were reworked after analysis of the experimental results to reduce some of the differences between U.S. and French scale scores. A comparison of the mean profile of the two samples appears to suggest minimal differences between French and American responding, but there were some real cultural differences nonetheless. Tendencies observed in the chapter introduction, in reference to the MMPI, still exist in the MMPI-2, to a lesser or greater degree.

The only really significant difference (a standard deviation or more) is on the F scale. Given the meaning of the F scale, this could be interpreted as a cultural difference. Because French subjects are seemingly more reluctant than their American counterparts to respond to this type of question, they are probably less conscientious and coherent in their responses. American subjects are often asked to fill out questionnaires and are therefore more cooperative and open. This hypothesis will have to be evaluated once certain items have been reworded. This same difficulty existed in the first version of the MMPI.

It should also be noted that French subjects recorded higher average mean scores on scales Hs, D, Sc, and Si. Once again, this could be the result of cultural differences; however, hypotheses about cultural differences are possible. Differences on the D scale could be due to the fact that the French admit to more suffering from mild depressive disorders than do Americans. The cultural context in France is oriented more toward pessimism (often reflected in the romantic aspects of French literature) and self-punishment (a critical attitude is often socially valued in France). Good health is not considered an integral part of the social ideal in France, as it is in the United States. The high scores recorded on scales DEP and LSE corroborate this tendency to more easily express negative mood and affect and doubts about one's own worth.

Extraversion, on scale Si, is culturally and socially acceptable in the United States, but the French do not tend to show the same expansiveness. Results of other personality tests assessing sociability and extraversion always reveal this tendency. Group activities are not held in particularly high esteem in France; individual activities play an important role in a French child's upbringing. But, as the low figure on SOD indicates, this does not cause any maladjustment, nor is it an expression of shyness.

Differences on the Sc scale are certainly due to the heterogeneity of scale content, which includes, among other things, the notion of "civility" or courtesy (inbred and more strongly developed in the American social code than in the French). The French tend to express themselves socially and emotionally in a much more impulsive and spontaneous manner, since this is considered acceptable behavior in their society. Furthermore, the results obtained on the BIZ content scale reassuringly confirm that the French generally suffer from no more hallucinations and other thought disorder problems than do Americans.

Hs scale differences could be interpreted as the French tendency to complain about being tired or being afraid of becoming ill more often than do Americans. Perhaps they more easily accept not always being in "top form," as shown on scale D. In everyday interpersonal exchanges (at cafés, department stores, the market), health is an ever present and often central topic of conversation. The importance they give to expressing fears concerning minor ills is shown on the HEA content scale.

Differences in the social behavior of the French are highlighted on the scales relevant to WRK and ASP (higher for the French female population). The higher scores on the WRK content scale are probably related as much to a lower level of self-confidence as to the slightly difficult relationships experienced with work colleagues.

These hypotheses have been postulated on the basis of the experimental results.

Of course, they can only be verified when results from the new version of the MMPI-2 have been studied on much larger samples of the population.

Structure Analysis. The factor structure analysis of French data highlights several details that are perhaps a reflection of cultural effects. The General Maladjustment factor constituted by the same scales for the French and American samples is also partly explained by loadings on the Pd and Sc scales for the French population. These undoubtedly reflect a highly cultural component in that French subjects systematically refuse to adhere to accepted social order (often evident in a highly critical attitude toward political powers and state authority). Similarly, the loading on the F scale could be interpreted as an expression of nonacceptance of "the rules of the game," even though instructions were given to reply honestly to the inventory. Overcontrol, Social Introversion, and Gender Role factors are highly comparable across cultures. These interpretations remain to be evaluated further in later studies.

Results from the preliminary study show a satisfying level of item equivalence between the two versions and suggest that the French translation can be considered a reliable version of the original. However, on completion of this study, several items were modified for purposes of standardization.

Overall, the experimental results on the French adaptation of the MMPI-2 are highly encouraging, and we anticipate similar results from the cultural and cross-cultural validation of the definitive and stable form of the 567 items.

The next step is to establish norms on a representative sample of the French general population (a need that was emphasized in the comparison of mean profiles). A test-retest reliability study will be undertaken on clinical groups to confirm not only conformity with the English-language original but also the empirical and prognostic value of the MMPI-2.

II. Preliminary French Study Comparing Data from the MMPI-2 (Computerized Report) with Clinical Opinions of Psychiatrists

General Protocol

This preliminary clinical study consisted of analyzing the opinions of psychiatrists regarding the accuracy and relevance of computerized reports obtained from 100 MMPI-2 protocols completed by psychiatric patients between January and June 1993. The study took place in two specialized psychiatric departments in Paris: the Clinique des Maladies Mentales et de l'Encéphale (CMME; Prof. Samuel Lajeunesse), which is part of the Hôpital Sainte Anne, and the Hôpital International de l'Université de Paris (Prof. Jeammet). Each psychiatrist was asked to read the computerized Minnesota Report provided by James Butcher and give an opinion of the quality of five separate sections in the report. They were asked to determine whether the information was (A) insufficient, (B) limited to "some informa-tion," (C) adequate, (D) more than adequate, or (E) extensive. The sections of the Minnesota Report evaluated were: Profile Validity, Symptomatic Patterns, Inter-personal Relations, Diagnostic Considerations, and Treatment Considerations. Following this, they were asked what percentage of the statements included in the report seemed pertinent to the patient being examined: (A) less than 20%, (B) 20 to 39%, (C) 40 to 59%, (D) 60 to 79%, and (E) 80 to 100%.

The clinicians were asked for the principal psychological symptoms of the patient and the information they considered useful and likely, which would render the report more pertinent. Finally, they were asked to give the most likely clinical diagnosis, based on the *DSM-III* or the ICD-9 (or 10).

The study was carried out on 100 patients being treated in one of the two above-mentioned facilities, either as inpatients (N = 54) or as outpatients (N = 46). A total of 22 mental health specialists, all of them psychiatrists, evaluated the 100 computerized reports. Their clinical experience varied as follows: 33 reports were analyzed by five practitioners with 4 to 6 years experience in psychiatry; 33 reports were analyzed by seven practitioners with 6 to 10 years experience, and 33 reports were analyzed by 10 practitioners with more than 10 years experience. Time spent with each patient varied from 2 to 6 hours (or more).

Following are demographics for the population studied:

Gender: 26 males and 74 females
Age: 4 patients between the age of 18 and 19 years
       71 patients between the age of 20 and 40 years
       22 patients between the age of 41 and 60 years
       3 patients older than 60 years
Sociocultural level (number of years of schooling)
       less than 10 years   N = 21
       10 to 12 years   N = 26
       13 to 14 years   N = 23
       15 years or more   N = 30

Clinical Diagnosis of Patients

The clinicians used the *DSM-III-R* or the ICD (9 or 10) to make their diagnoses, details of which are shown below. Disorders are classified by nature (Axis I or Axis II of the *DSM-III-R*) and type, that is, isolated, mixed, or complex.

Isolated disorder on Axis I, psychosis   N = 30
Isolated disorder on Axis I, depression or anxiety   N = 19
Isolated disorder on Axis I, eating disorder   N = 01

Other disorders on Axis I, somatoform or obsessional	N = 02
Isolated disorder on Axis II, personality disorder	N = 25
Mixed disorders: personality disorder + 1 disorder on Axis I	N = 22
Mixed disorders: somatoform + eating disorder	N = 01

A total of 47 patients of the 100 were considered to be suffering from a personality disorder. This appeared as an isolated disorder in 25 patients; 22 patients were suffering from an Axis I-type disorder associated with a personality disorder, either affective disorder (N = 11) or eating disorder (N = 11).

The response attitudes of the 100 patients toward the test were as follows:

Cooperative (valid profiles)	N = 20
Virtuous (inventory being completed in a systematic and excessively "favorable" way)	N = 25
Exaggeration-dramatization	N = 37
Response inconsistency (resulting for the most part in an invalid profile in regard to TRIN, VRIN, or F_B)	N = 18

Results

Of the 100 MMPI-2s completed, only 17 profiles were considered invalid and were not followed up because of an invalid note based on one of the validity scales. Of these 17 invalid MMPI-2 inventories, 11 of the patients had been diagnosed as psychotic, three had personality disorders, one was suffering from an eating disorder, another from an affective disorder, and the last from a mixed disorder (Axis I and Axis II on the *DSM-III-R*).

Thus only 83 profiles could be interpreted. We considered four reports as valid; each of them, however, included a reminder that care should be taken in interpreting the profiles obtained. The following results concern the 83 profiles on the MMPI-2 (25 males and 58 females).

The distribution of clinical diagnosis (ICD or *DSM-III-R*) on these patients is as follows:

Personality disorders	22
Mixed disorder (Axis I + Axis II)	21
Psychotic disorder	19
Affective disorder	18
Other disorder (somatoform, obsessional)	2
Eating disorder	1

The computerized reports covered the five specific sections mentioned earlier.

Clinicians' Opinions on the Profile Validity Section

On the 83 valid results, this part of the report was considered to provide:

		N	%
A	insufficient information	11	13.3
B	some information	21	25.3
C	adequate information	30	36.1
D	more than adequate information	15	18.0
E	extensive information	6	7.2

In sum, the clinicians' opinions of the validity of the 83 reports they received were favorable in 61% of the cases when in-depth, sufficient, and more than sufficient were pooled.

Clinicians' Opinions on the Symptomatic Patterns Section

		N	%
A	insufficient information	11	13.3
B	some information	23	27.7
C	adequate information	22	26.5
D	more than adequate information	22	26.5
E	extensive information	5	6.0

In sum, the clinicians' opinions of the quality of descriptions in the Symptomatic Pattern section were favorable in 59% of the cases if the categories in-depth, sufficient, and more than sufficient information were pooled.

Clinicians' Opinions on the Interpersonal Relations Section

		N	%
A	insufficient information	10	12.0
B	some information	15	18.0
C	adequate information	26	31.3
D	more than adequate information	22	26.5
E	extensive information	10	12.0

In sum, the clinicians' opinions of the Interpersonal Relations section of the 83 reports were favorable in 70% of the cases when the categories in-depth, sufficient, and more than sufficient information were pooled.

Clinicians' Opinions on the Diagnostic Considerations Section

		N	%
A	insufficient information	38	45.8
B	some information	14	16.9

		N	%
C	adequate information	17	20.5
D	more than adequate information	10	12.0
E	extensive information	4	4.8

In sum, the clinicians' opinions of the Diagnostic Considerations section of the 83 reports were favorable in 38% of the cases when the categories in-depth, sufficient, and more than sufficient information were pooled. This finding probably reflects different diagnostic practices in France and the United States.

Clinicians' Opinions of the Treatment Considerations Section

		N	%
A	insufficient information	14	16.9
B	some information	21	25.7
C	adequate information	27	32.5
D	more than adequate information	16	19.3
E	extensive information	5	6.0

In sum, the clinicians' opinions of the Treatment Considerations section of the 83 reports were favorable in 58% of the cases when the categories in-depth, sufficient, and more than sufficient information were pooled. The lower agreement between the clinicians and the computer-based reports probably resulted from different treatment orientations.

Global Evaluation of the Report. When asked to reply to the question "Globally speaking, what percentage of the affirmations contained in the report seemed to you pertinent in describing the patient?", the clinicians replied in the following manner:

		N	%
A	less than 20%	10	12.0
B	20 to 39%	17	20.5
C	40 to 59%	18	21.7
D	60 to 79%	18	21.7
E	80 to 100%	20	24.1

The overall relevance of the report to French clinicians was considered high, if categories D and E were met, and 67.5% if we consider categories C, D, and E.

Discussion

The results of the rating study seemed to show an overall congruence of the Minnesota Report in France. About one of four reports was considered perfectly satisfying. Inversely, only 32.5% of the reports were estimated at less than 40% pertinent. It should be added that several sections of the computerized reports were consid-

Table 20-8. Clinical Diagnoses of the Patients Studied in the MMPI-2 Clinical Assessment Project

Clinicians' Diagnosis	N patients	% of 83	N reports insufficient	% of 83
Depression or anxiety	18	21.7	9	23.7
Psychosis	19	22.9	10	26.3
Isolated Axis II disorder (Personality)	22	26.5	5	13.2
Isolated behavioral disorders	1	1.2	2	5.3
Mixed disorders (Axis I and II or two disorders on Axis I)	21	25.3	12	31.6
Other disorders	2	2.4	-	-
Total	83	100	38	100

ered by the clinicians to be variable in terms of appropriateness. Clinicians were less satisfied (category A) with the Diagnostic Considerations section and the Treatment Considerations section (16.9%), probably because of different diagnostic and treatment systems in France.

The sections for which most of the reports were considered valuable and providing in-depth information (category E) were the Interpersonal Relations section and, to a lesser degree, the Profile Validity, Symptomatic Patterns, and Treatment Considerations sections. The comparison between the number of reports considered highly insufficient (category A) in terms of the major diagnostic classes shows that no special diagnosis is particularly overrepresented (see Table 20-8).

Although the overall acceptability of the Minnesota Report in France was good, the ratings provided by French mental health professionals on the utility of the reports were somewhat lower than those obtained by mental health professionals in Australia (Berah et al., 1993) and in Norway (Ellertsen & Butcher, 1994) in comparable studies. These findings might reflect differences in clinical practice in different countries, different attitudes toward computers in different countries, or genuine personality differences between the French and patients from other countries. Further research will be needed to clarify this finding.

Comparison of the MMPI and the MMPI-2

A comparison between the MMPI and the MMPI-2 was carried out on 39 patients. In 17 cases, the retest took place less than three months after the first test. In 21 of the 39 cases, the MMPI-2 profile was found to be similar to that obtained on the MMPI. In 18 cases, the profile obtained was very different. It is nevertheless impossible to indicate the similarity of symptoms at the time of the two ratings, owing to the absence of a symptomatic scale on general psychopathology at testing.

The test-retest comparison at less than a three-month interval was performed only on 13 of the 17 patients (in four cases, the MMPI profile was not valid). However, the profiles obtained for these 13 cases are similar for 10 patients and different for three. This type of assessment—associated with a comprehensive psychiatric rating scale—should allow for the permanent characteristics of the subject to be distinguished from those that vary according to their state of mental health.

Conclusion

This first application of the MMPI-2 with French patients has shown that the French version of the inventory does not raise any particular problems of comprehension for patients. The percentage of computer-based reports that could not be interpreted because the subjects' attitude invalidated results on the clinical scales (17%) corresponds to the rate usually observed in documentation on this type of questionnaire in other countries. Clinicians evaluating the overall acceptability of the Minnesota Report for describing patients found pertinent information presented in the reports (68.5%). The clinicians consider the quality of the computerized reports to be better for the Interpersonal Relations, Symptomatic Pattern, and Profile Validity sections than for the Treatment Considerations and, more especially, the Diagnostic Considerations sections, perhaps because of differences in clinical practice in the two countries. This result is hardly surprising, since the answers to questions are the only elements taken into account in the reports, whereas the diagnostic study in psychopathology depends also on the history of the disorder and other important variables. This was, by the way, clearly pointed out in 1986 by J. Perse in the original French manual on the MMPI: "The MMPI profile should not be considered as being essentially oriented toward a psychiatric diagnostic. The MMPI is undoubtedly less a personality diagnostic test in the strict sense than an inventory focusing on symptoms and pathological characteristics; it is certain that these latter factors have a more universal generalization than do behaviors that depend more closely on a social context."

References

Berah, E., Miach, P., Butcher, J. N., Bolza, J., Colman, S., & McAsey, P. (1993, October). *Computer-based interpretation of the MMPI-2. An Australian evaluation of the Minnesota Report.* Paper presented at the Australian Psychological Association meetings, Melbourne, Australia.
Butcher, J. N., & Pancheri, P. (1976). *Handbook of cross-national MMPI research.* Minneapolis: University of Minnesota Press.
Ellertsen, B., & Butcher, J. N. (1994). *Adaptation of computer-based MMPI-2 reports in Norway.* Manuscript in preparation.
Perse, J. (1986). *Manuel de l'Inventaire Multiphasique de personnalité du Minnesota MMPI.* [Manual for Minnesota Multiphasic Personality Inventory]. Paris: Editions de Centre du Psychologie Appliquée.

Chapter 21

Adaptation of the MMPI-2 in Italy

Paolo Pancheri, Saulo Sirigatti, and Massimo Biondi

As Butcher and Pancheri (1976) reported, the first Italian translation of the MMPI was completed in 1948 by G. C. Reda. This version was primarily used as an experimental assessment project with a group of psychiatric patients. The original published U.S. norms were used because no Italian standardization data were available. Some years later, Nencini and Banissoni (1957) completed the official translation and adaptation of the MMPI. This version is still in use nationwide. At present, the Nencini/Banissoni translation is the only one available, and it is officially sanctioned by the American publisher and copyright holder. Since the MMPI's introduction in Italy, the official publisher has been the Organizzazioni Speciali in Florence. Three formats are presently available in Italy: standard card form, standard booklet form, and short booklet form.

Some normative data on the Italian MMPI became available in 1955, but the first national standardization for males, based on 1,564 subjects (ages ranging from 18 to 52 years), was collected by Nencini in 1958. New norms for females (638 subjects whose ages ranged from 18 to 44 years) were collected by Nencini in 1965. The samples used for the male standardization were drawn from a population of military conscripts and those for the female standardization from personnel departments of government agencies and a group of student nurses. At present, the MMPI is used for screening and personnel selection on a routine basis by several national agencies such as the Italian Army, the Italian Navy, and the Central School of State Police. Many applications could also be mentioned in the fields of clinical psychology and psychiatry; some of them will be illustrated in the next section of this chapter.

In the almost 40 years since the MMPI was introduced in Italy, it has become one of the most widely used psychodiagnostic tools. Now the time for the translation of the MMPI-2 has come because of the interest expressed by Italian psychologists and psychiatrists (Sirigatti, 1990, 1991, 1993).

Clinical Practice: From MMPI to MMPI-2

Since 1950 a number of prominent changes have occurred in clinical psychology and psychiatry in Italy. The introduction of standardized diagnostic criteria for behavioral and psychiatric disorders is one of the more important innovations. Historical terms, such as *neurosis, psychasthenia,* and *psychopathy,* which dominated the first half of the century, disappeared from the official standard nomenclature of the *DSM-III-R* and *DSM-IV.* Several terms were replaced or relocated under other categories, while new clinical entities, like somatoform disorder, were introduced. More strict criteria were introduced, in an attempt to define psychotic disorders and schizophrenia, as well as the boundaries between them. The *DSM-III* distinction between Axis I psychopathological syndromes and Axis II personality disorders, and the concept of "comorbidity" between Axis I and Axis II disorders, led to a more accurate classification of cases. The effort to develop a more precise nosology has its costs, however, in terms of greater complexity and, to some extent, in the risk of rigid, artifactual boundaries between categories, despite the evidence of psychopathological continuity in neighboring disorders.

These developments in psychiatry have a consistent impact on the clinician and on the role of the MMPI in assessing psychopathology and personality disturbances and supporting the diagnostic procedure. An interesting challenge for the MMPI-2 is evaluating basic and content scales against the latest standardized psychiatric diagnostic criteria, that is, the *DSM-IV* and the *ICD-10*. This section of the chapter will present a synthesis of the findings from our research group, which has extensively investigated the classification of MMPI profiles and clinical diagnoses since 1970.

The Problem of Psychiatric Standardized Diagnoses in the Clinical Setting

One important problem in clinical psychology and psychiatry is the use of unequivocal diagnostic criteria, both in clinical and research settings. The lack of standard criteria and the variability of diagnostic procedures and frames of reference (behavioral, psychodynamic, relational, etc.) have represented a major source of confusion and reduced reliability between clinicians, and have often led to controversial or disappointing research findings from different countries. Until a few years ago, it had been a common clinical experience that a clinical case with a well-defined MMPI profile could be differently diagnosed, even by clinicians adhering to a common general psychodynamic orientation. Another well-known example among psychiatrists is the different rates of diagnosis of schizophrenia and manic-depressive psychosis in the United States and Great Britain. In the 1960s, when common standardized criteria were not available, the same clinical cases were more easily diagnosed as manic-depressive by British psychiatrists and as schizophrenic by American psychiatrists (Cooper et al., 1972). Subsequently, the consensus on *DSM-III,* with the more restrictive Schneiderian criteria for schizophrenia, led to a reduction of the diagnosis of schizophrenia in the United States, and to the disappearance of confusing diagnoses like pseudoneurotic schizophrenia or latent or borderline schizophrenia.

Another interesting example of the consequences of standardized criteria has been the elimination of the endogenous-reactive distinction in depressive disorders. Further, in the presence of high scores on the Depression scale of the MMPI, the diagnosis of endogenous or reactive-neurotic depression was mainly, if not exclusively, based on the valuable but idiosyncratic judgment of the individual clinician. The diagnostic category of "endoreactive depression" reflected the uncertainty of doubtful clinical cases.

The Development of Standardized Diagnostic Criteria: The DSM *and the* ICD

The need to develop a common descriptive language and a consensus on a set of diagnostic criteria probably has several roots in clinical psychology and psychiatry. In the 1970s, the development of standardized criteria, such as the Feighner criteria (Feighner, Robins, Guze, Woddruff, & Winokur, 1972) and the Research Diagnostic criteria (Spitzer, Endicott, & Robins, 1978), represented a significant advancement in biological psychiatry, especially in the area of depressive and psychotic disorders. The most diffuse diagnostic criteria, however, were provided in the *Diagnostic and Statistical Manual of Mental Disorders* (the *DSM-III* in 1980, the *DSM III-R* in 1987, and the *DSM-IV* in 1994) (American Psychiatric Association, 1980, 1978, 1994) by various task forces of the American Psychiatric Association (APA), and the *International Classification of Diseases, Section of Mental and Behavioral Disorders* of the World Health Organization (WHO), especially in its latest version, the *ICD-10* (World Health Organization, 1992). Both the *DSM-IV* task force and the research group of the *ICD-10* made an effort to minimize nosologic differences in the two classifications so that data and information exchange could be increased and the risks of controversy in future epidemiological and clinical studies based on the two different systems could be reduced.

Both the *DSM-IV* and the *ICD-10* adopt explicit criteria of syndromic classification and descriptive psychopathology, minimizing theoretical assumptions for establishing diagnoses. They are different from other classification systems in medicine in not being based on supposed etiology or pathogenesis of mental and behavioral disorders. With some exceptions, such as the adjustment disorders or post-traumatic stress disorder, these mechanisms are either unknown or, at best, inadequately known.

The *ICD* of the World Health Organization deals with classification of all human diseases. For many years, its role in a series of epidemiological and transcultural studies has been pivotal. A specific *ICD* section is dedicated to behavioral and mental disorders. Of the 10 editions of the *ICD,* those that received widest acceptance were the last three. The amount of space dedicated to diagnostic criteria for mental and behavioral disorders increased with each edition. The *ICD* has been translated into almost every language. Whereas the past editions presented only a list of diseases and few concise comments, the 10th edition provides detailed guidelines and criteria for the diagnosis of various conditions.

The DSM of the American Psychiatric Association has a long history. The first edition appeared after the Second World War, but it was not well accepted. Much the same happened with the DSM-II. The 3rd edition (*DSM-III*) (American Psychiatric Association, 1980), released with a vigorous campaign in the United States, has been translated in many countries, including Italy, and has subsequently been revised (*DSM-III*-R) (American Psychiatric Association, 1987). In 1994, the 4th edition (*DSM-IV*) (American Psychiatric Association, 1994) was released. It maintains the same general frame of the *DSM-III* but with some important small innovations, mostly in the criteria for some specific groups of disorders that reflect the changes resulting from research in the past few years and from field trials of APA task forces. Many efforts were made to reduce, as much as possible, the differences between the *ICD-10* and the *DSM-IV.* It is important to note that most clinical and experimental studies currently published in specialized psychological and psychiatric journals recruit samples according to the *DSM* criteria.

MMPI and Standardized Clinical Diagnoses

When the MMPI was originally developed and validated, there were no standardized nosologic systems. Patient groups to whom the inventory was administered received diagnoses formulated by experts that reflected the clinical orientation at that time. Clinical variability was probably greater owing to the lack of standardized diagnostic criteria. It would be interesting to know what changes might have occurred in the MMPI had the original diagnostic groups been reclassified according to the present *DSM* or *ICD* nosologic criteria. However, such reclassification is not feasible. On the other hand, a comparison between a (discriminant) analysis of clinical diagnoses and MMPI profiles carried out some years ago and a similar analysis of patients with similar diagnoses carried out today but responding to *DSM-III-R* criteria is feasible, though somewhat difficult. A similar comparative study has recently been conducted at the Psychiatric Clinic of the University of Rome, during the revision of the automated interpretive-narrative MMPI system published by Pancheri et al. in 1970 at the University of Rome (Pancheri, Girardi, Bernabei, & Morgana, 1974; Pancheri & Biondi, 1989).

MMPI Profiles and Clinical Diagnoses: The First Discriminant Study (1970)

The first study carried out by our research group in 1970 assessed MMPI profiles in a sample of normal subjects and clinical diagnoses and MMPI profiles of 835 psychiatric patients referred at the Institute of Psychiatry of the University of Rome (Pancheri, Girardi, Bernabei, & Morgana, 1974). The clinical records of patients admitted for treatment to the wards of the Institute of Psychiatry between 1969 and 1971 were examined. Cases were selected for which there was an MMPI profile completed in the first four days of hospitalization before starting any treatment and before a clearly defined discharge diagnosis was made. Patients with organic brain disease or infrequent or rare diagnoses were excluded. Diagnoses were formulated by two senior staff psychiatrists according to the *ICD-8* criteria. The cases were divided into 11 diagnostic groups, plus the normal control group (Table 21-1). The final psychopathological sample was representative of the psychiatric population admitted to the Institute of Psychiatry. The relative percentage for each diagnostic group reflected the rate of pathology in the general population.

The discriminant-function program, developed by Barker (1974) at the University of Alabama, was applied to the 12 groups and included the 13 MMPI clinical and validity scales. Scores on the 11 orthogonal discriminant functions derived from the 12 original variables were used to reclassify every case in the sample. Each profile can thus be described in the discriminant space by a point whose coordinates are the values scored by the profile for each discriminant variable. Further, each group can be described by a multivariate normal distribution characterized by that point and by the variance-covariance matrix. The discriminant model was characterized by

1. Number of diagnostic groups.
2. Dimensions of the discriminant space.
3. Matrix of the centroids representing the mean profile of any group in the discriminant space.
4. Matrix of the weights allowing to pass from one point of the space of the variables to the discriminant space (see Pancheri et al., 1978, for a detailed description). When using the 13 MMPI variables, the model obtained a correct classification of 55.33% of total cases, ranging from a minimum of 29.16% (anxiety neurosis) to a maximum of 92.85% (manic excitement) (Figure 21-1).

Summarizing our findings, we can stress that this first study showed considerable correspondence between MMPI profiles and some clinical diagnoses. The correspondence was strong enough to allow the clinician to develop a program that automatically provides a descriptive sequence of most probable clinical diagnoses in the

Table 21-1. Subject Groups for the Diagnostic Model and Discriminant-Function Analyses: The 1970 Study

Diagnosis	Sample Size
Hysterical neurosis	66
Anxiety neurosis	48
Depressive neurosis	69
Obsessive-compulsive neurosis	22
Acute schizophrenia	154
Chronic schizophrenia	92
Depressive psychosis	58
Manic psychosis	14
Psychopathy (sociopathic personality)	100
Epilepsy (behavioral disorders in epileptics)	23
Chronic alcoholism	62
Normalcy	127

form of narrative output, corresponding to the examined profile, starting from the MMPI profile of a new patient. In many cases, this could represent a useful confirmation of a clinician's decision. Although the precision of the classification of the program varies according to whether symptoms and clinical picture are typical, and although it responds better to some diagnoses (those with less natural variability of symptoms) than others, it is both data-driven and empirically based. The discriminant classification system was introduced by Pancheri and colleagues in the clinical routine of the Psychiatric Clinic of the University of Rome in the late 1970s.

Based on the results of a recent second study in which we used a standardized diagnostic system, the relationship between MMPI profiles and psychiatric diagnoses appears to have changed slightly after 20 years and to have become more complex.

MMPI Profiles and Clinical DSM-III-R Diagnoses: The Second Discriminant Study (1990)

The second study was carried out according to a very similar experimental design. However, a larger sample (1,052 psychiatric cases) of patients who had completed the MMPI was evaluated. These cases were hospitalized on our ward (N = 66), referred to our outpatient facility (N = 873), came from our private practice (N = 52), or were participating in drug trials (N = 61) during the period 1983-1990, for a total of 706 men and 346 women, mean age 34.5 years, S.D. 12.6 years. The normal control group included 71 subjects, mean age 30.6 years, S.D. 9.8 years,

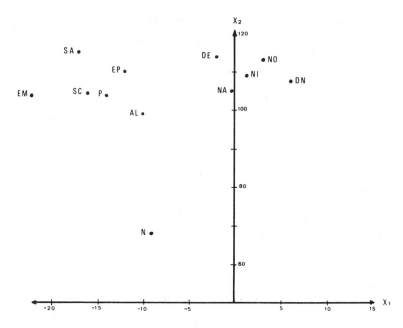

Plotting dei centroidi dei gruppi diagnostici originari nello spazio delle prime due variabili discriminanti.

EM - Eccitamento maniacale   DE - Depressione
SA - Schizofrenia acuta   N   - Normalità
SC - Schizofrenia cronica   NA - Nevrosi d'ansia
EP - Epilessia   NI - Nevrosi isterica
AL - Alcoolismo cronico   NO - Nevrosi ossessiva
P   - Personalità psicopatica   DN - Depressione nevrotica

Figure 21-1. MMPI and Clinical Diagnosis: Findings from the 1970 Discriminant Study (see text for details). The figure shows the plotting of the centroids of the diagnostic groups in the space of the two first discriminant variables: EM, manic excitement; SA, acute schizophrenia; SC, chronic schizophrenia; EP, epilepsy-related behavioral problems; AL, chronic alcoholism; P, psychopathic personality; DE, depression; N, normality; NA, anxiety neurosis; NI, hysterical neurosis; NO, obsessive neurosis; DN, neurotic depression (Pancheri et al., 1974).

referred to our outpatient service for forensic purposes and receiving a diagnosis of "no current psychopathological disorder." Doubtful cases, subjects with a past psychopathological episode, those formerly convicted of crimes, and subjects with a history of substance abuse were excluded.

Diagnosis was established by two senior staff psychiatrists (PP and MB) together with the training psychiatrist who visited the patient after examining all available data, that is, information from a psychiatric interview of about 60 minutes, a standardized patient history record (ANAM), and a mental status record (Mental Status Examination Record). The diagnosis was established according to *DSM-III* (in the 1983-1987 period) and *DSM-III-R* (in the 1987-1990 period) criteria. Patients received any possible diagnosis on both Axis I (psychopathological disorder) and Axis II (personality disorder) (Pancheri, Portuesi, Biondi, & Marconi, 1992).

The subjects bearing an Axis I diagnosis were assigned to one of the following groups:

Schizophrenic and delusional disorders, comprising all *DSM-III* subtypes of schizophrenia (catatonic, disorganized, paranoid, undifferentiated, and residual) as well as other psychotic disorders, such as delusional disorder (various types), brief reactive psychosis, and schizophreniform disorder.

Depressive disorders. This group corresponds to the affective disorder group of the *DSM-III* and also includes bipolar disorder, depressive phase, and adjustment disorder with depressive mood.

Phobic disorders and agoraphobia. The group includes simple phobia, social phobia, agoraphobia, and panic disorder, with or without agoraphobia.

Generalized anxiety disorder. This group included generalized anxiety disorder patients, as well as patients with anxiety disorder not otherwise specified, adjustment disorder with anxious mood, and post-traumatic stress disorder.

Somatoform and dissociative disorders, represented by depersonalization disorder, body dysmorphic disorder, somatization disorder, somatoform pain disorder, and adjustment disorder with physical complaints.

Personality disorders (Axis II diagnosis) were divided following the *DSM-III-R* three-cluster division (A, B, and C). Table 21-2 shows diagnostic groups, corresponding number of subjects, and their percentages.

Unlike the 1970 study, the 1990 study did not include the epilepsy and alcoholism groups. Moreover, the schizophrenia group was not divided into acute and chronic subgroups; all the schizophrenic subtypes were included in the schizophrenia and delusional disorders group, as it is described in the *DSM-III.* Conforming to the current *DSM-III* distinction, generalized anxiety and panic disorders were kept apart. Finally, unlike the 1970 study, the 1990 study included only a unified depressive disorder group, since the neurotic-endogenous distinction of depressive disorders is not any longer accepted by the *DSM.*

Discriminant analyses were performed between groups of patients classified according to the *DSM-III* and the *DSM-III-R* criteria (as shown above), using corrected T scores of the 13 scales of the MMPI as predictive variables. The procedure for analysis was similar to that of the 1970 study, except for a priori attribution of probability of belonging for every diagnostic group. Whereas in the 1970 study this probability was taken to be identical for all groups, in the 1990 study it was calculated on the real frequency of occurrence of the various diagnoses in the sample (see Pancheri et al., 1992, for details).

Table 21-2. Sample of the 1990 Discriminant Analysis Study

DSM-III Diagnostic Groups	N	Percent
Obsessive-compulsive disorder	18	1.7
Schizophrenic and delusional disorders	35	12.8
Depressive disorders	224	21.3
Phobic and agoraphobic disorders	71	6.7
Generalized anxiety disorder	86	8.2
Somatoform and dissociative disorders	58	5.5
Personality disorders, cluster A	56	5.3
Personality disorders, cluster B	104	9.9
Personality disorders, cluster C	49	4.7
Normal controls	71	6.7
Other or multiple diagnoses	180	17.2
Total	1052	100.0

Findings of the 1990 Study

Findings showed a satisfactory discrimination of the diagnostic groups. Figure 21-2 compares the percentages of correct classifications from both the 1970 and 1990 studies. With respect to the 1990 study, normalcy, depressive disorders, and schizophrenia attained the highest values. The phobic/agoraphobic group is the least defined, having a partial overlap with the generalized anxiety group and, to a lesser extent, with somatoform and depressive disorders. A certain degree of overlap is also present between the three personality disorders clusters, especially between clusters A and C, the least defined. Figures 21-3 and 21-4 show the projections of the centroids of diagnostic groups in the space of the variables expressed by the first two discriminant functions identified by discriminant analysis. As it may be observed, the generalized anxiety, phobic/agoraphobic, and somatoform disorder groups can barely be discriminated. The numbers represent the centroids of 10 MMPI clusters.

The MMPI characterization of DSM-III personality disorders is of interest: The overlap between clusters A and C and the low values of cluster B suggest a remarkable heterogeneity of the MMPI profiles of personality disorders within the clusters. A first explanation could be an overall nonspecificity of the elevation of scores on many MMPI scales within the mean profiles of the three clusters of personality disorders. A second, perhaps more likely, explanation could be that the

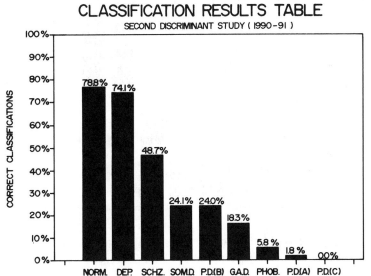

Figure 21-2. Comparison of the Percentage of Correct Classification of the Different Diagnostic Groups according to the MMPI-APAP Automated Interpretative System. First discriminant study, with patients diagnosed according to clinical diagnoses (1970); second discriminant study, with patients diagnosed according to clinical diagnoses (1970); and second discriminant study, with patients diagnosed according to DSM-III and DSM-III-R (1990) (Pancheri et al., 1992).

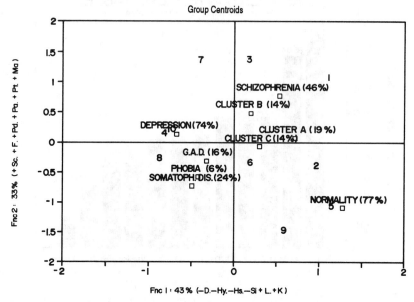

Figure 21-3. Second Discriminant Study (1990). Plotting of the centroids of the original diagnostic groups and of the MMPI clusters in the space of the two discriminant variables (Pancheri et al., 1992).

three personality disorder clusters are not clearly distinguishable through MMPI scores because they partially overlap from a psychopathological point of view. That is, the diagnostic pictures between the personality disorder diagnoses contain considerable overlap.

The relative affinity of MMPI profiles of phobic/agoraphobic and generalized anxiety disorders and their scarce discriminability on discriminant analysis could suggest that the separation-anxiety (panic disorder) and generalized-anxiety (GAD) dimensions are not clearly distinguishable through MMPI profiles, at least through the symptomatological assessment of MMPI scales. However, these findings support the common framing of separation-anxiety (panic disorder) and generalized anxiety (GAD) in the chapter on anxiety disorders in the *DSM-III*-R.

Unlike the 1970 study, findings from this study did not permit the development of a program for an automated probabilistic clinical diagnosis derived from MMPI scores.

In summary, findings of the 1990 study seem to suggest that MMPI profiles can predict *DSM-III* diagnosis in a limited number of cases: normalcy, depressive disorders, and schizophrenia. Somatoform, dissociative, phobic/agoraphobic, and generalized anxiety disorders show a remarkable heterogeneity of MMPI profiles.

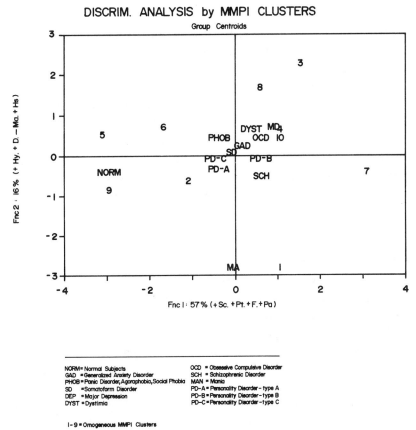

Figure 21-4. Second Discriminant Study (1990). Plotting of the centroids of the MMPI clusters and of the originary diagnostic groups in the space of the first two discriminant variables.

It is interesting that MMPI correlates of *DSM-III* personality disorders show considerable overlap among the three clusters, with the partial exception of cluster B. It could be of interest to discuss the reasons why nonstandardized, clinical diagnoses of the 1970s correlate more precisely with the MMPI than do the standardized *DSM-III* diagnoses. Are some subgroups (such as somatoform disorder and, more interestingly, the three personality disorders cluster) the result of a correct but essentially too theoretical and too speculative division and grouping? Are they more "artificial" than other more "classical" psychopathology diagnoses, such as depression or the different subtypes of schizophrenia? And finally, to what extent does the strong empirically derived structure of psychopathology inherent in the MMPI match subclassifications of cells of strictly descriptive psychopathology? These are interesting questions awaiting answer.

The Development of the Italian MMPI-2

The first problem that should be dealt with in adapting a test to a culture different from its origin concerns the linguistic aspect. However, even a linguistically perfect version does not guarantee equivalence between the original and translated versions with reference to semantic, cultural, and psychological aspects. Various procedures have been proposed for obtaining valid translations and for evaluating the equivalence between versions. These include the utilization of independent groups of bilingual psychologists, back-translation, and various types of empirical testing (Ben-Porath, 1990; Brislin, 1970; Butcher & Pancheri, 1976; Comrey, 1960; Comrey & Nencini, 1961; Poortinga, 1989; Rosen & Rizzo, 1961). However, the variety of the proposed procedures indicates that no single procedure is completely satisfactory. Therefore, using multiple strategies to test the equivalence of a translation appears to be most appropriate.

Translation: The Committee Approach

The committee approach served as the primary basis for the development of the Italian adaptation of the MMPI-2. Two independent groups were formed for the translation of the questionnaire: One was led by Pancheri, whose expertise is in psychiatry, while the other group was led by Sirigatti, whose expertise lies mainly in clinical psychology. During translation, the Italian version of the MMPI (which had been well tested) was taken into account. In particular, efforts were made to maintain the exact translation of items present in both the MMPI and the MMPI-2 to avoid introducing greater differences into the two Italian versions than were present in the two American versions. This serves to maintain continuity between the MMPI and the MMPI-2. The translations proposed by the two groups were compared and discussed to reach agreement on a preliminary version.

Pretest Field Study

This preliminary version was then presented to subject groups obtained from the normal population. After filling out the questionnaire, the subjects were asked to give a critical evaluation and suggestions relating to understandability, concreteness, and acceptability of the items. On the basis of these indications, an experimental version of the MMPI-2 was printed.

Bilingual Test-Retest

The experimental version of the MMPI-2 was presented to 30 bilingual (Italian-English) subjects who completed the Italian MMPI-2 and the U.S. version according to a counterbalanced order. The results of the bilingual test-retest study (Figures 21-5 and 21-6) confirm the substantial equivalence of the two forms.

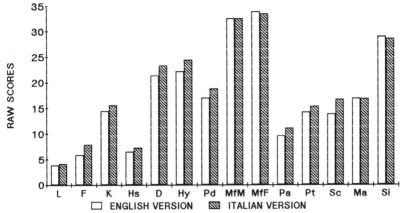

Figure 21-5. Comparison of Bilingual Test-Retest Subjects on the Basic Scales of the MMPI-2

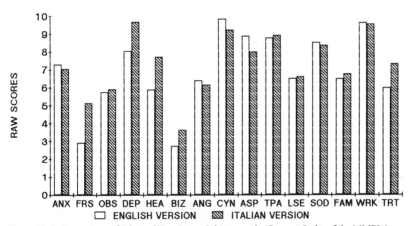

Figure 21-6. Comparison of Bilingual Test-Retest Subjects on the Content Scales of the MMPI-2

Wilks's lambda, calculated on raw scores of the control and clinical scales, was equal to .77 (chi-square = 13.07; d.f. = 14; p = .52), and the average correlation was equal to .84 ± .06. On the other hand, Wilks's lambda calculated on raw scores of the content scales was .76 (chi-square = 13.83; d.f. = 15; p = .54), and the average correlation was equal to .88 ± .04. It is interesting to note that, in some cases, the English language facility was not limited to American English but included subjects from Great Britain and New Zealand as well.

The Back-translation

The back-translation, performed by the University of Minnesota Press, supplied further useful suggestions for improving some aspects of the translation. The assessment stated, "In general, the style is good, and there are no major mistakes. However, I had the feeling that more than two people had worked on this translation. . . . I thought so because there are some inconsistencies and because as a rule the language is proper, fluent and smooth, but suddenly becomes trammelled."

Of the total MMPI-2 item pool, 62 items were judged nonequivalent in the two English versions. A new translation of these items was developed by the same back-translation procedure. Suggestions were accepted for modifications to 35 items, even though some of them replicated the translation adopted in the MMPI. For the remaining items, the modifications suggested by the back-translation were not accepted for the following reasons:

- In certain cases, the use of the double negative was suggested. This differs from the construction adopted in the MMPI and may also be difficult for psychiatric patients or subjects with a low level of education.
- At times it seemed appropriate to maintain the version utilized in the MMPI to ensure continuity between the MMPI and the MMPI-2.
- In some cases, to enable a better understanding of the item, some redundancy was preferred.
- In the case of item 477, the term "rugby" was retained instead of "soccer" because it better conveys a sport involving violent contact between players.

Reading Competence and Item Structure

Indexes of reading difficulty and comprehension were computed for each item. These indexes were based on sentence length, number of syllables, and word frequencies. For instance, the possible range of a Flesch-Vacca index starts at 0 and runs to 100. Values between 90 and 100 correspond, roughly, to a primary school level of reading difficulty; values between 0 and 30 are equivalent to college level (Vacca, 1990). The results of these analyses are reported in Table 21-3. These findings show that basic or very common words were used in the translation and that short sentences were produced. As a result, the reading skills needed to understand the Italian version of the MMPI-2 appear to be lower than the fifth-grade level.

Preliminary Data about Reliability and Scale Correlates

The experimental version of the MMPI-2 was also presented to Italian subjects from the general population (143 males and 299 females), as well as to psychiatric patients tested mainly at the Psychiatric Clinic of Rome under the direction of Pancheri (28 males and 31 females). The data were used to estimate the internal coherence of the various scales and to compare the mean basic and content scale

Table 21-3. Item Readability and Structure

Reading competency		
Flesch-Vacca Index	95	(very simple, lower than the fifth-grade)
Kincaid Index	3	(very simple)
Gunning's Fog Index	4	(reading skills needed at a fourth-grade level)
Sentences		
Number	1134	
Long ones	0	0.0%
Short ones	1022	90.1%
Words per sentence	5.9	
Syllables per sentence	11.6	
Words		
Basic	84%	
Very common	5%	
Common	2%	
Letters per word	5.9	
Syllables per word	2.0	
Mood and Tense		
Indicative present	68%	
Indicative present perfect	12%	
Indicative imperfect	6%	
Conditional present	4%	
Subjunctive present	3%	
Subjunctive imperfect	2%	

profiles with the U.S. norms. Finally, a test of the sensitivity of the MMPI-2 in identifying pathological conditions was carried out.

The Cronbach Alpha calculation (see Table 21-4) provided values for the validity, clinical, supplementary, and content scales. Internal consistency estimates observed are quite satisfactory and similar to those observed for the MMPI-2 in U.S. samples.

Mean basic and content scale profiles of the two groups (general population and psychiatric patients) are presented in Figures 21-7, 21-8, 21-9, and 21-10, plotted against U.S. norms. As far as the basic scales are concerned, the most gen-

Table 21-4. Cronbach Alphas

Scale	Males (143)	Females (299)
L	.655	.728
F	.759	.789
K	.778	.740
Hs	.746	.796
D	.558	.671
Hy	.588	.603
Pd	.602	.687
Mf	.524	.297
Pa	.484	.570
Pt	.883	.902
Sc	.880	.895
Ma	.605	.605
Si	.832	.845
A	.896	.903
R	.637	.530
ES	.684	.742
MAC-R	.446	.282
F_B	.777	.829
O-H	.418	.393
ANX	.829	.837
FRS	.782	.785
OBS	.775	.767
DEP	.848	.889
HEA	.730	.771
BIZ	.767	.769
ANG	.684	.682
CYN	.859	.847
ASP	.770	.761
TPA	.758	.696
LSE	.826	.834
SOD	.853	.851
FAM	.782	.850
WRK	.843	.858
TRT	.835	.809

MMPI-2

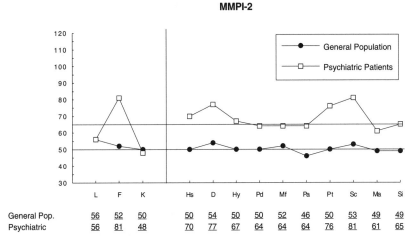

	L	F	K	Hs	D	Hy	Pd	Mf	Pa	Pt	Sc	Ma	Si
General Pop.	56	52	50	50	54	50	50	52	46	50	53	49	49
Psychiatric	56	81	48	70	77	67	64	64	64	76	81	61	65

Figure 21-7. MMPI-2 Basic Scale Profile for a Sample of Italian Men from the General Population and a Sample of Psychiatric Patients

MMPI-2

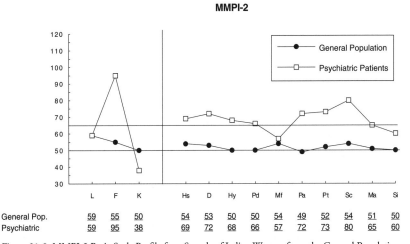

	L	F	K	Hs	D	Hy	Pd	Mf	Pa	Pt	Sc	Ma	Si
General Pop.	59	55	50	54	53	50	50	54	49	52	54	51	50
Psychiatric	59	95	38	69	72	68	66	57	72	73	80	65	60

Figure 21-8. MMPI-2 Basic Scale Profile for a Sample of Italian Women from the General Population and a Sample of Psychiatric Patients

eral observation that can be made about Italian general population profiles is that, with the exception of scale L (T score = 60 for both males and females), all mean scores fall rather close to the mean of the U.S. normative sample. In the male group, the next highest T scores are on scales F (53), D (53), and Sc (53), while the lowest one is on scale Pa (45). In the female group, the next highest T scores are on scales F (55), Mf (55), and Sc (55).

Similar observations are made when mean content scale profiles are considered.

MMPI-2

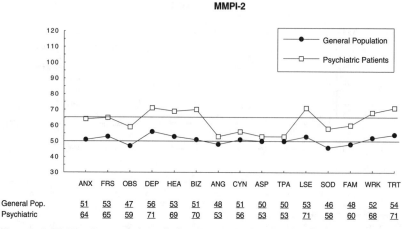

	ANX	FRS	OBS	DEP	HEA	BIZ	ANG	CYN	ASP	TPA	LSE	SOD	FAM	WRK	TRT
General Pop.	51	53	47	56	53	51	48	51	50	50	53	46	48	52	54
Psychiatric	64	65	59	71	69	70	53	56	53	53	71	58	60	68	71

Figure 21-9. MMPI-2 Content Scale Profile for a Sample of Italian Men from the General Population and a Sample of Psychiatric Patients

MMPI-2

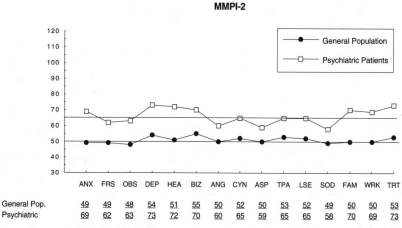

	ANX	FRS	OBS	DEP	HEA	BIZ	ANG	CYN	ASP	TPA	LSE	SOD	FAM	WRK	TRT
General Pop.	49	49	48	54	51	55	50	52	50	53	52	49	50	50	53
Psychiatric	69	62	63	73	72	70	60	65	59	65	65	58	70	69	73

Figure 21-10. MMPI-2 Content Scale Profile for a Sample of Italian Women from the General Population and a Sample of Psychiatric Patients

All mean scores fall rather close to the mean of the U.S. normative sample. The highest T scores for men are on scales DEP (56), LSE (54), and TRT (54), while the lowest is on SOD (47). In the female group, the highest T scores are on scales DEP (55), BIZ (55), TPA (53), and TRT (53).

In spite of the limited number of clinical patients in the sample and their psychopathological heterogeneity, Figures 21-7, 21-8, 21-9, and 21-10 suggest a notable difference, for both males and females, between profiles obtained from the general population and those obtained from psychiatric patients. This impression

Table 21-5. Correlations of the Basic Scales with Total Number of
Recent Life Changes (LES)

Scale	Males (52)	Females (253)
L	−.11	−.11
F	.29	.20*
K	−.38*	−.11
Hs	.51**	.21**
D	.24	.19*
Hy	.16	.19*
Pd	.18	.30**
Mf	−.01	.11
Pa	.22	.27**
Pt	.31	.22**
Sc	.41*	.29**
Ma	.28	.26**
Si	.22	.04

* p < .01
** p < .001

was corroborated by the results obtained from two discriminant analyses. For
men, Wilks's lambda, calculated on raw scores of the validity, clinical, some supplementary, and content scales, was equal to .39 (chi-square = 141.62; d.f. = 38;
p < .001). On the other hand, for women, Wilks's lambda was equal to .51 (chi-
square = 207.95; d.f. = 38; p < .001).

The Life Events Form used in the MMPI-2 restandardization and reported by
Butcher, Graham, Williams, and Ben-Porath (1990) was translated into Italian
and administered, along with the MMPI-2, to 305 subjects (52 males and 253 females). This form is a modified version of the Recent Life Events Form by Holmes
and Rahe (1967), covering significant changes in life during the six-month period
preceding subjects' completion of the MMPI-2. The data collected by this instrument were summarized by counting, for each subject, the number of significant
events reported. Pearson Product-Moment correlations were calculated between
the total number of recent life changes (LES) and the raw scores of the validity,
clinical, supplementary, and content scales. As far as Italian females are concerned
(see Tables 21-5, 21-6, and 21-7), the coefficients of correlation observed for the
various scales are similar to those reported for the U.S. sample by Butcher, Dahlstrom, Graham, Tellegen, and Kaemmer (1989), with the exception of scales
HEA, CYN, and ASP. For males, the correlations calculated for U.S. and Italian

Table 21-6. Correlations of the Supplementary Scales with Total Number
of Recent Life Changes (LES)

Scale	Males (52)	Females (253)
A	.39*	— .25**
R	−.22	−.12
ES	−.41*	−.15
MAC-R	.05	.07
F_B	.38*	.11
TRIN	.11	.05
VRIN	.20	.08
OH	−.09	−.08

* p < .01
** p < .001

groups were quite different, particularly on scales Hs, Si, FRS, HEA, and BIZ. However, one needs to take into account the small number of Italian subjects; conclusions should await data from a larger sample.

MMPI-2 Profiles and DSM-IV Clinical Diagnoses: The 1994 Ongoing Study

After the MMPI-2 became available in Italy in the spring of 1994, we began a third study in the university clinic in Rome. This study will be carried out on a large psychiatric sample including both inpatients and outpatients. The general demographic, social, and clinical characteristics of the sample will be essentially the same as in the two previous studies (except for the exclusive presence of inpatients in the 1970 study). The aims of the current study are twofold: to enhance knowledge of the MMPI-2 in an Italian psychiatric population (this is the first study in Italy with such a large sample), and to evaluate the relationship between the MMPI-2 and psychiatric diagnoses according to the new *DSM-IV* criteria. We are particularly interested in investigating the role of the new content scales for the MMPI-2. The choice of the *DSM-IV* standardized criteria, instead of the *ICD-10* criteria, derives from the tradition of our clinical unit, which adopted *DSM* criteria in 1983. Analysis of data according to *ICD-10* criteria and comparisons with other *ICD-10* studies will be possible as well, owing to the structural and formal similarity between *DSM-IV* and *ICD-10*.

The experimental design calls for a sample of 1,000 consecutive men and women inpatients and outpatients, with an age range of 18 to 70 years, suffering from psychiatric disorders as in the two previous studies. All the clinical data are collected in a standardized, computerized medical record. Information on outpatients includes history, mental status, Clinical Global Impression, self-rating

Table 21-7. Correlations of the Content Scales with Total Number of Recent Life Changes (LES)

Scale	Males (52)	Females (253)
ANX	.41*	.19*
FRS	.47**	.09
OBS	.31	.16
DEP	.34	.22**
HEA	.49**	.16
BIZ	.56**	.23**
ANG	.29	.06
CYN	.34	.03
ASP	.27	.05
TPA	.30	.07
LSE	.32	.13
SOD	.17	.02
FAM	.43*	.29**
WRK	.34	.19*
TRT	.41*	.05

* $p < .01$
** $p < .001$

scales, life stress events, and data concerning any psychopharmacological or psychotherapeutic treatment. Additional data on inpatients includes other psychometric assessments, neuropsychological assessments, routine laboratory testing, computerized axial tomography, and neuroendocrine tests.

Patients complete the MMPI-2 either before starting the psychiatric visit or within three days of hospital admission. One of four training psychiatrists, assisted by the same senior psychiatrist (MB), visits the patients. The visit lasts 45 to 90 minutes. The final diagnosis for each patient is formulated under supervision of the head of psychiatry (PP). Both Axis I and, if necessary, Axis II diagnoses, according to the *DSM-IV* criteria, are formulated. In some instances, if further medical examinations are lacking or laboratory data are needed for differential diagnosis, the final diagnosis is postponed to the next visit, after all data are available. In the case of inpatients, the procedure is similar. The MMPI-2 is completed within three days after hospital admission and before the beginning of any treatment.

Eighty cases have been collected in the first three months. We have not, as yet, performed any statistical analysis on these data. The composition of the present sample seems to have characteristics similar to those of the samples in the two pre-vious (1970 and 1990) MMPI studies. Data processing will consist of discrimi-nant analysis with MMPI-2 variables as predictive with respect to clinical *DSM*-IV diagnosis; the relationship between MMPI-2 content scales and Axis I and Axis II *DSM*-IV diagnoses, as well as MMPI-2 variables as predictive of response to drug treatment, will be of particular interest.

Conclusions

The Italian version of the MMPI-2 should be considered quite adequate from a linguistic point of view. Two independent groups worked on the translation of the questionnaire, and significant indications were collected from the pretest field study. The back-translation proved useful in improving various aspects of the Italian version. Finally, the adequacy and the accuracy of the translation was assessed by means of the bilingual test-retest technique. The bilingual study pro-vided an indication that the Italian version and the U.S. version measure the same psychological aspects. However, other studies may be needed to fully verify the equivalence of the instrument. For this reason, some adaptation studies are ongoing.

The Italian version has been administered to samples drawn from the general population and to psychiatric patients. When the scores on the various scales were evaluated against the U.S. norms, the findings showed that the majority of the mean scores fell close to the mean of the U.S. normative sample. Furthermore, profiles obtained from the general population and from psychiatric patients man-ifested clearly significant and predictable differences.

Although the Italian group produced relatively normal range profiles, when compared with the U.S. norms, it seems advisable to administer the inventory to a larger and representative sample of nonclinical subjects for the purpose of devel-oping Italian norms. The data derived from this sample will also provide useful in-formation for adaptation studies, such as checking similarity between item en-dorsement patterns or evaluating the equivalence of factor structure.

Questions concerning the external validity of the Italian version of the MMPI-2 will be examined by studying the correlates of the various scales with the Life Events Form. This goal will mainly be pursued by administering the inventory to patients with diagnosed problems in clinical settings.

From a clinical viewpoint, one of the main challenges for the MMPI-2 in the area of clinical psychology and psychiatry will be its relationship to diagnoses made according to new and increasingly used standardized diagnostic criteria, such as those of the recently issued editions of the *DSM* (*DSM-IV*) and the *ICD* (*ICD-10*). The content scales should be of prominent interest in this context. The original MMPI showed satisfactory concordance with purely clinically oriented diagnoses in psychiatric patients, while, at least in our experience, the relationship of MMPI profiles to *DSM*-III or *DSM-III*-R standardized diagnoses showed less concordance and more uncertainty. We presented findings from two discriminant analysis studies that were carried out on Italian psychiatric samples, regarding the relationships between MMPI profiles and clinical psychiatric diagnosis.

The first study was conducted in 1970 on a sample of 835 psychiatric patients. Nonstandardized psychiatric diagnoses were used. Thus, discriminant analysis used merely clinical psychiatric diagnoses, which are probably closest to the diagnoses on which the original MMPI was based. Discriminant analysis showed a fair ability to correctly classify more than half the cases, with greater precision for more typical cases (for example, manic psychosis) and with less precision for disorders with a more variably soft symptomatology, such as anxiety neurosis. However, it has been possible to construct a computer program that, on the basis of reference psychiatric diagnostic groups, classified the MMPI profile of a new case and attributed to it a given "probability to belong" to various diagnostic groups.

The second study, carried out between 1983 and 1990, adopted the standardized diagnostic criteria of *DSM-III* or *DSM-III-R* in a sample of 1,052 outpatients and inpatients and used discriminant analysis between groups of patients classified according to the *DSM* criteria, using MMPI scores as predictive variables. Results were on the whole less satisfactory than those of the 1970 study. Concordance between *DSM-III* diagnosis and MMPI profile has been detected only when considering highly typical diagnostic areas (for example, schizophrenia, depressive affective disorders, normal controls). Concordance for somatoform-dissociative disorders and for personality disorder diagnoses (Axis II) was low. The main result of this second study suggests that every *DSM-III* diagnostic group could present a sufficiently high heterogeneity of MMPI profiles, which would render difficult a precise diagnostic *DSM* classification on the basis of the scores of a single new profile. It would be interesting to discuss and clarify whether the lower productivity of MMPI profiles in orienting toward diagnosis that emerged from the 1990 study, as compared with the similar 1970 study, is to be attributed to the use of the new diagnostic categories of the *DSM-III* or to other factors.

There may be similar problems for the MMPI-2 with *DSM-IV* diagnostic subtyping. Alternatively, the interaction of the MMPI-2 with the *DSM-IV* could be more profitable than the one between the original MMPI and the *DSM-III* (and *DSM-III*-R), since the former two, as opposed to the latter, are products of the psychiatric thinking of the '90s. It would be interesting to see whether the use of the new content scales allows for better discrimination between clinical-diagnostic groups and a more precise diagnostic use of the MMPI. At present, the third study in the series is ongoing and investigates these points.

References

American Psychiatric Association. (1980). *Diagnostic and statistical manual of mental disorders* (3rd ed.) Washington, DC: Author.

American Psychiatric Association. (1987). *Diagnostic and statistical manual of mental disorders* (3rd ed. Rev.). Washington, DC: Author.

American Psychiatric Association. (1994). *Diagnostic and statistical manual of mental disorders* (4th ed.) Washington, DC: Author.

Barker, H. (1974). *Behavioral sciences statistics program library.* Minneapolis: University of Minnesota Press.

Ben-Porath, Y. S. (1990). Cross-cultural assessment of personality: The case of replicatory factor analysis. In J. N. Butcher & C. D. Spielberger (Eds.), *Recent advances in personality assessment.* (Vol. 8; pp. 27–48). Hillsdale, NJ: Erlbaum.

Brislin, R. W. (1970). Back translation for cross-cultural research. *Journal of Cross-Cultural Psychology, 1,* 185–216.

Butcher, J. N., Dahlstrom, W. G., Graham, J. R., Tellegen, A., & Kaemmer, B. (1989). *MMPI-2 Minnesota Multiphasic Personality Inventory-2. Manual for administration and scoring.* Minneapolis: University of Minnesota Press.

Butcher, J. N., Graham, J. R., Williams, C. L., & Ben-Porath, Y. S. (1990). *Development and use of the MMPI-2 content scales.* Minneapolis: University of Minnesota Press.

Butcher, J. N., & Pancheri, P. (1976). *A handbook of cross-national MMPI research.* Minneapolis: University of Minnesota Press.

Comrey, A. L. (1960). Comparison of certain personality variables in American and Italian groups. *Educational and Psychological Measurement, 20,* 541–550.

Comrey, A. L., & Nencini, R. (1961). Factors in MMPI responses of Italian students. *Educational and Psychological Measurement, 21,* 657–662.

Cooper, J. E., Kendell, R. E., Gurland, B. J., Sharp, E. L., Copeland, J. R. M., & Simon, R. (1972). *Psychiatric diagnosis in New York and London: A comparative study of mental health admissions.* New York: Oxford University Press.

Feighner, J. P., Robins, E., Guze, S. B., Woddruff, R. A., & Winokur, G. (1972). Diagnostic criteria for the use in psychiatric research. *Archives of General Psychiatry, 26,* 57–67.

Holmes, T. H., & Rahe, R. H. (1967). The social readjustment rating scale. *Journal of Psychosomatic Research,* 11, 213–218.

Nencini, R., & Banissoni, P. (1957). *MMPI forma ridotta edizione Italiana* [MMPI short form: Italian version]. Florence: Organizzazioni Speciali.

Pancheri, P., & Biondi, M. (1989). Computerized psychological assessment in Italy. In J. N. Butcher (Ed.), *Computerized psychological assessment.* New York: Basic Books.

Pancheri, P., Girardi, P., Bernabei, A., & Morgana, A. (1974). Metodo di interpretazione narrativa del MMPI. In G. B. Cassano, P. Castrogiovanni, P. Pancheri, & M. Tansella (Eds.), *Tecniche di automazione in psichiatria.* Roma: Il Pensiero Scientifico.

Pancheri, P., Portuesi, G., Biondi, M., & Marconi, P. L. (1992). Psicodiagnostica and evoluzione nosografica: La versione *DSM-III* del sistema MMPI-APAP. *Rivista di Psichiatria, 27,* 7–22.

Poortinga, Y. H. (1989). Equivalence of cross-cultural data: An overview of basic issues. *International Journal of Psychology, 24,* 737–756.

Rosen, E., & Rizzo, G. B. (1961). Preliminary standardization of the MMPI for use in Italy: A case study in intercultural differences. *Educational and Psychological Measurement, 21,* 629–636.

Sirigatti, S. (1990). *Vecchio e nuovo nel MMPI.* Convegno (La psicoterapia comportamentale e cognitiva: prospettive teoriche e sviluppi clinici), Siena.

Sirigatti, S. (1991). *Dove va l'MMPI.* XIII Congresso Nazionale della Societa Italiana di Medicina Psicosomatica, Bologna.

Sirigatti, S. (1993). *Progress Report sull'adattamento MMPI-2.* Abstracs V Congresso Nazionale di Psi-
cometria. Firenze: Organizzazioni Speciali.

Spitzer, R. L., Endicott, J., & Robins, E. (1978). Research Diagnostic criteria. *Archives of General Psychiatry, 35,* 773–780.

Vacca, R. (1990). *Comunicare come.* Milano: Garzanti.

World Health Organization. (1992). *The International Classification of Diseases, Section of Mental and
Behavioral Disorders.* Geneva: Author.

Chapter 22

The Greek MMPI-2: A Progress Note

Anna Kokkevi

The extensive international literature on the methodology of the MMPI as an objective instrument for the assessment of personality and psychopathology led to its introduction as a core element in the diagnostic procedures of patients in the Department of Psychiatry at the University of Athens. The MMPI was first translated and adapted into Greek in 1977 in the Department of Psychiatry of the Athens University Medical School. In 1978 the Greek version of the MMPI was authorized for publication by the Psychological Corporation, then publisher of the MMPI.

Since 1977, the MMPI has been administered to more than 2,000 psychiatric patients at the University of Athens. A large majority of the patients in the Department of Psychiatry are new cases and often present difficult diagnostic problems for practitioners. The MMPI is considered by the treating psychiatrists an essential aid for diagnosis and treatment decisions. Although a study on the clinical validation of the Greek MMPI is not yet completed (Adamou, Typaldov, Kokkevi, & Alevizou, 1986), the frequent referrals of patients by clinicians for psychological assessment with the MMPI are evidence of its excellent face validity. In another project, Manos (Manos & Butcher, 1982; Manos, 1985) explored the use of a second Greek version of the MMPI with psychiatric patients at the University of Thessaloniki in Thessaloniki, Greece. The MMPI was found to be a valuable clinical assessment instrument for describing psychiatric patient behavior in Greece.

The Greek version of the MMPI has also been used for more than 10 years as a screening instrument for the selection of personnel in the Greek Army. It is also used regularly as a screening instrument for the assessment of personality and likely psychopathology in obese patients attending a medical center for the treatment of eating disorders, where a multidimensional treatment program, including psychological interventions, is offered.

The MMPI is also being used extensively in research into the epidemiology of anxiety and depressive symptoms (Kokkevi, Adamou, Repapi, Typaldou, &

Stephanis, 1981; Kokkevi, 1984; Kokkevi, Typaldov, Kokossi, Katsouyianni, Adamou, 1986; Typaldou, Kokkevi, Katsouyanni, Adamou, & Kokossi, 1986), psychosomatic disorders (Zouni et al., 1979), child abuse (Tsiantis, Kokkevi, & Agathonos Marouli, 1981; Kokkevi & Agathonos, 1987), transcultural personality comparisons (Kokkevi, Typaldov, Repapi, Adamou, & Stetanis, 1981; Kokkevi, 1984), genetic studies (Alevizos, Kokkevi, Markianos, & Stafanis, 1983), drug addiction (Alevizou, et al. 1989), eating disorders (Kokkevi et al., 1989), and proneness to suicide in military draftees (Botsis, Soldatos, Kokkevi, & Lyrinzis, 1990; Botsis et al., 1991; Botsis et al., 1994).

Procedures Followed in the Translation of the Original MMPI in Greece

Two independent Greek translations were done by two translators (the present author, who has had extensive experience in the translation and adaptation of diagnostic instruments into Greek, and a psychiatrist). The official translation into the French language was also used as a guide in the translation process. The two independent translations were reviewed by a senior psychiatrist who had a long educational and professional career in both the United States and Greece. Discrepancies between the two translations were discussed and consensus was reached with the assistance of the reviewer.

Care was taken that the Greek translation be as close as possible to the original to ensure equivalence of the original and the Greek version. When the literal translation of an item posed problems of comprehension, the structure and the meaning of the sentence were retained while ensuring its natural flow in the Greek language. Synonyms and phrases with similar frequency in Greek and in English were preferred. For two items (82 and 210) in which the translation of a word or part of a phrase might not be easily understood because they were idioms, a short explanation was given in parentheses.

The Greek translation was subsequently administered in card form to 96 patients in the Department of Psychiatry. Patients were instructed to ask the psychologist administering the test any questions they had about the meaning of the items. This made it possibile to identify difficulties in comprehension of the items. Problematic items were retranslated and tested again to ensure equivalence.

The Standardization of the Original

Greek MMPI norms were developed for both adults and adolescents. The adult and adolescent data collections were not directly based on random sampling procedures, but care was taken to ensure that the samples were close to a nationally representative sample of the adult and adolescent population in Greece in terms of age distribution, gender, socioeconomic status, and geographic origin (urban, semiurban) (Kokkevi, 1984).

The standardization project started in 1979 and was completed in 1983. It took place in the frame of a large epidemiological study, conducted by the staff of Athens University, of the physical and mental health of the general population in Greece. The MMPI was administered by psychologists to small groups of adults (5-10 persons) participating in the epidemiological study. The response rate of the target population was higher than 80%. For the standardization of the MMPI with adolescents, the instrument was administered in classrooms by psychologists on the research team.

The adult normative sample was made up of two subsamples: a representative sample of 224 individuals (127 male and 97 female) from the general population, ages 18-67 years, inhabitants of a semiurban area (Salamis Island); and a sample of 317 Athenians (183 males and 134 females), ages 19-65 years, who were employees of a central bank in Athens. The sample comprised 95% of the total population of employees, irrespective of rank, at the bank.

Merging the urban and semiurban subsamples following the exclusion of participants over age 65 and invalid protocols resulted in a final normative adult sample consisting of 461 individuals. Among them, 254 were male with a mean age of 43.5 ± 8.8 years, and mean educational level of 13.4 ± 2.9 years, and 207 were females with a mean age of 36.2 ± 8.1 years and a mean educational level of 13.4 ± 2.0 years.

The adolescent normative MMPI population also consisted of two subsamples. The first was derived from the same semiurban area (Salamis Island) as the adult normative sample. The MMPI was administered in two area schools (a general orientation secondary school and a technical/vocational public school). The total school population of 309 students (155 boys and 154 girls) ages 14-19 who were present the day the test was administered participated in the study. The second subsample was derived from two secondary public schools (a general orientation secondary school and a technical/vocational one) located in an Athenean community of middle socioeconomic status. All 877 students (345 male and 532 female) ages 14-19 who were present the day the MMPI was administered participated in the study.

Merging of the urban and semiurban subpopulations following the exclusion of invalid protocols resulted in the final Greek MMPI normative adolescent sample, consisting of 1,050 (436 male and 614 female) adolescents.

The Development of the MMPI-2 in Greece

Translation into Greek

The MMPI-2 was translated into Greek in 1993 according to the following procedure:

1. The two translators of the Greek translation of the original MMPI followed the same procedures described above to translate MMPI-2 items that were changed from the original version and to translate new items. MMPI items that were identical with MMPI-2 items were retained from the original Greek translation.

2. When the initial translation was complete, the total 567 MMPI-2 items were then back-translated by an experienced bilingual professional translator.

3. Discrepancies between the English original and the back-translation were carefully considered. Items for which discrepancies resulted from an inappropriate translation into Greek were discussed with two independent bilinguals, the same senior psychiatrist who reviewed the MMPI and a psychologist who had long professional experience in both the United States and Greece.

4. After a consensus on the appropriate translation was reached, the items were back-translated by the translator who back-translated the Greek version of the original MMPI.

5. A small number of items were slightly discrepant in the back-translation because they had been more liberally translated. These items were therefore retranslated into Greek by an independent professional translator. A consensus on the most satisfactory Greek translation for these items was reached by the authors.

Overall, the MMPI-2 presented no difficulties in cross-cultural equivalence, and unchanged items remained virtually identical with the Greek version of the original MMPI.

Further Steps in the Development of the Greek MMPI-2

1. Bilingual study: A project to investigate the adequacy of the MMPI-2 translation is currently under way. Both the English orginal and the Greek version of the MMPI-2 are being administered to 30 bilinguals to test the equivalence of the two versions.

2. Greek norms: If, as expected, results from the bilingual re-test study confirm that there is equivalence of the English and Greek MMPI-2 versions, the MMPI-2 will be administered to a sample of 600 to 800 adults from the general population to obtain Greek norms. It is expected that this project will be completed by the end of 1995.

3. Validation studies: Currently, validation studies are being conducted to evaluate the utility of the MMPI-2 for assessing psychiatric patients in Greece. Patients

who have been assessed by instrumental clinical criteria typically employed in the Department of Psychiatry will be studied with the MMPI-2.

The Development of the Greek MMPI-A

The same procedures described for the translation of the MMPI-2 were followed for the translation of the MMPI-A. The MMPI-A has already been administered to a nationally representative sample of 1,400 high school students ages 13-19 years. The test was administered in classrooms under the supervision of two psychologists who are members of the research team. Normative data will soon be available for the adolescent population.

References

Adamou, N., Typaldou, M., Kokkevi, A., & Alevizou, V. (1986). *A retrospective validation study of two MMPI depressive scales in a sample of psychiatric inpatients* [Abstract F90]. Paper presented at the World Psychiatric Association Regional Symposium for Affective Disorders, Athens.

Alevizos, B., Kokkevi, A., Markianos, M., & Stefanis, C., (1983). Comparative investigation of two pairs of monozygotic twins, one with and the other without endogenous depression. In C. N. Stefanis (Ed.), *Recent advances in depression.* London: Pergamon.

Alevizou, V., Kokkevi, A., Anastasopoulou, E., Arvanitis, Y., Boukouvala, V., Ifantis, D. (1989). *Comparative personality and psychopathology assessment by the MMPI of imprisoned and treatment seeking drug abusers.* [Abstract Th.D.P.72]. Paper presented at the 8th World Congress of Psychiatry, Athens.

Botsis, A., Soldatos, C. R., Kokkevi, A., & Lyrinzis, S. (1990). Suicidal ideation in military draftees. In D. Lester (Ed.), *Suicide '90: Proceedings of the 23th Annual Meeting of the American Association of Suicidology* (pp. 294–296). Denver: American Association of Suicidology.

Botsis, A. J., Soldatos, C. R., Kokkevi, A., Lyrintzis, S., Brown, S. L., & Stefanis, C. N. (1991). Feelings of hopelessness in Greek young adults. In D. Lester (Ed.), Suicide '91: *Proceedings of the 24th Annual Meeting of the American Association of Suicidology* (pp. 203–205). Denver: American Association of Suicidology.

Botsis, A., Soldatos, C. R., Kokkevi, A., Lyrintzis, S., Liossi, A., & Stefanis, C. N. (1994). *Suicidal ideation in military personnel: Suicide and life-threatening behavior.* Manuscript submitted for publication.

Kokkevi, A., Adamou, A., Repapi, M., Typaldou, M., & Stefanis, C. (1981). Depressive symptoms in a Greek population sample: Investigation with the MMPI. In C. N. Stefanis (Ed.), *Recent advances in depression.* London: Pergamon.

Kokkevi, A., Typaldou, M., Repapi, M., Adamou, A., & Stefanis, C. (1981). The MMPI on a Greek population sample of adults and adolescents [Greek]. *Materia Medica Greca, 9,* 515–521.

Kokkevi, A. (1984). The assessment of personality characteristics of Greek adolescents with the MMPI [Greek]. Dozent thesis, University of Athens.

Kokkevi, A., Typaldou, M., Kokossi, M., Katsouyianni, K., & Adamou, M. (1986). Anxiety and depressive symptoms in a sample of adolescents [Greek]. *Encephalos, 23,* 233–241.

Kokkevi, A., & Agathonos, E. (1987). Intelligence and personality profile of battering parents in Greece: A comparative study. *Child Abuse and Neglect, 11,* 93–99.

Kokkevi, A., Maillis, A., Katsouyanni, K., Mortoglou, T., Valsamidis, S., Karamanos, B., & Toutouzas, P. (1989). *Psychological characteristics of obese patients: Assessment with the MMPI* [Abstract 680]. Paper presented at the 8th World Congress of Psychiatry, Athens.

Manos, N. (1985). Adaptation of the MMPI in Greece: Translation, standardization, and cross-cultural comparison. In J. N. Butcher & C. D. Spielberger (Eds.), *Advances in personality assessment* (Vol. 4). Hillsdale, NJ: Erlbaum.

Manos, N., & Butcher, J. N. (1982). *MMPI: A guide for use in interpretation* [Greek]. Thessaloniki: Greece University Studio Press.

Tsiantis, J., Kokkevi, A., & Agathonos Marouli, E. (1981). Parents of abused children in Greece. Psychiatric and psychological characteristics. Results of a pilot study. *Child Abuse and Neglect, 5,* 281–285.

Typaldou, M., Kokkevi, A., Katsouyanni, K., Adamou, N., & Kokossi, M. (1986). *Depressive mood and adolescent psychopathology assessed by the MMPI and teachers questionnaires in an adolescent student population.* [Abstract F]. Paper presented at the World Psychiatric Association Regional Symposium for Affective Disorders, Athens.

Zouni, M., Rabavilas, A., Kokkevi, A., Manoussos, O., Christodoulou, G., & Stefanis, C. (1979). Clinical observations, psychometric and psychophysiological findings in patients with ulcerus colitis and the syndrome of spastic bowel. *Encephalos, 16,* 5–9.

Chapter 23

Development of the MMPI-2 in Turkey

Işık Savaşır and Meral Çulha

The Turkish translation of the original MMPI has been widely used for clinical assessment in mental health settings, for personnel selection, and for research in psychopathology since its standardization in 1981. This acceptance of the MMPI encouraged us to start a project of adaptation and standardization of the MMPI-2 when the MMPI revision was complete. We think that our previous work and experience with the original MMPI will be invaluable in guiding our project. We begin this chapter with a summary of the translation, standardization, and validity studies on the Turkish translation of the original MMPI to provide background on the extensive use of the MMPI and its relevance for Turkey.

The Turkish MMPI

Translation

A version of the MMPI that was translated by Turkey's National Testing Bureau was reviewed by two bilingual Turkish psychologists (Savaşır & Turgay, 1970) and necessary changes were made. The resulting version was used with normal and psychiatric populations for about seven years. Following this experience with the instrument, all the items were again reviewed and rewritten, and a revised experimental version of the Turkish MMPI was prepared (Savaşır & Erol, 1978). During this stage, other bilingual psychologists and psychiatrists were asked to review items, especially those that were found to be very difficult to express in Turkish.

Another method used to check the translation was the bilingual retest method (Prince & Mombour, 1976). A group of 20 bilinguals were administered the Turkish translation and the English original of the test one week or 10 days apart and another group of 20 were given the Turkish version twice. Turkish-Turkish and Turkish-English correlations were examined for each validity and clinical scale. Turkish-English correlations for some of the scales compared quite favorably with test-retest correlations as well as composite English-English correlations reported in Butcher and Pancheri (1976). However, for some scales, Turkish-English correlations were considerably lower (scales F, K, 2, 6, and 8). Item endorsements of subjects who had taken the inventory in Turkish and English were compared and discrepant items were identified and modified. The modified items were checked by administering the K scale in English and in Turkish to another sample of bilinguals. The former correlation of .59 was found to be .80 in the new sample. This final form of the inventory was then printed and used in a standardization study. Items that were discrepant and difficult to translate included the following types:

1. Religious and other culturally inappropriate items.
2. Items with long and complicated sentence structure, for example, "I have at times stood in the way of people who were trying to do something, not because it amounted to much but because of the principle of the thing."
3. Items stated in the past tense, for example, "My father was a good man" (because, apparently, the equivalent tense in Turkish is less ambiguous than in English).
4. Sentences that expressed two ideas or two alternatives connected with "or," for example, "I have little or no trouble with my muscles twitching or jumping" (because Turkish use of "and" and "or" is not directly equivalent to English usage, causing particular difficulty in sentences such as this).
5. Sentences with colloquial expressions, such as "I am sure I get a raw deal from life."

Standardization

The Turkish MMPI normative sample consisted of 663 women and 1,003 men between the ages of 16 and 50. The criteria for inclusion in the study were completion of at least primary school and no history of psychiatric illness. The sample was predominantly urban, young (a majority of the sample was between the ages of 16 and 30), and more educated than the general population. Although the Turkish population as a whole was not fully represented by the sample, subsequent work done with the Turkish MMPI suggests that norms based on the sample are working well. Examination of data from studies that included normal controls of different age and socioeconomic status indicates that mean scores on MMPI scales are very similar to the normative means.

Means and standard deviations were computed separately for men and women for each validity and clinical scale. The T-score distributions were derived from the formula used in T-score generation on the original MMPI. Both K-corrected and non-K-corrected scores were computed, and profiles based on Turkish norms were developed. Finally, a comprehensive handbook for the Turkish MMPI was published (Savaşır, 1981).

A comparison of the Turkish and American norms showed that scores of Turkish subjects were generally higher than those of American subjects. Turkish males had higher scores than American males by more than one standard deviation on scales F, 5, and 8 and by up to one standard deviation on scales 2, 3, 4, 6, and 9. Turkish females had higher scores than American females on scale K and all clinical scales other than scale 0. On scales F, 6, and 8, T scores of Turkish females ranged between 60 and 70; on the other clinical scales, T scores of Turkish females ranged between 55 and 60.

Validity Studies

Comparison of Normals and Psychiatric Groups. The first study evaluated the validity of the Turkish MMPI by comparing psychiatric patients from different diagnostic groups to normals (Erol, 1982; Savaşır & Erol, 1990). One thousand psychiatric patients were first categorized into four broad diagnostic groups (neuroses, psychoses, personality disorders, and borderline) and then into specific diagnostic groups (thirteen groups, such as anxiety neurosis, depression, hysterical neurosis, etc.). The results in general were in accord with expectations. For example, male and female neurotics had the highest scores on the three neurotic scales—the neurotic triad—1, 2, and 3. The configuration of validity scales for the psychotic males and females was consistent with the common MMPI finding: low L and K scores and high F scores. Likewise, the so-called psychotic scales (4, 6, 7, and 8) were the highest for both psychotic males and females. Significant differences were also observed between specific diagnostic groups and normals despite smaller sample sizes. The highest scores for the depressives were on Depression, for hypochondriacs on Hypochondriasis, and for psychopaths on Psychopathic Deviate. An expected V configuration was obtained for conversion hysteria patients, who scored high on scales 1 and 3 and low on scale 2. Mean profiles for obsessive-compulsive neurotics showed elevations on scales 2 and 7. High psychotic scale scores (F, 6, 7, and 8) and low scores on K were observed for both male and female schizophrenics.

Factor Analytic Studies

The factor structure of the Turkish translation of the MMPI was examined to see if factor structures similar to those observed in other cultures emerged (Savaşır & Erol, 1990). The results of factor analyses for both Turkish normal males and females and Turkish psychiatric male and female patients yielded clearly interpretable factors. These factors also had common features with findings in the United States and several European countries.

The first factor for normal Turkish males and the second factor for normal Turkish females clearly resembled the psychoticism factor observed in seven national groups (Butcher & Pancheri, 1976). The factor with high loadings on the neurotic scales was obtained in normal male and female samples in Turkey. However, the second factor for the seven national groups, characterized by high loadings on scales L and K and labeled "overcontrol," was obtained only for Turkish female psychiatric patients.

When the factor structures obtained for Turkish male and female psychiatric patients were compared to the factor structures obtained for psychiatric samples in the United States, Italy, and Switzerland as reported by Butcher and Pancheri (1976), the similarities were striking. Similar factors of neuroticism, psychoticism, and overcontrol were found for Turkish female patients; the same was true for Turkish male patients except in the case of the overcontrol factor.

The clear differences found between normals and patients from different diagnostic groups, the configuration of the validity scales, and the elevations of the clinical scales in the expected directions all provide strong evidence of the cross-national validity of the Turkish MMPI. These findings are supported by the factor analytic studies, which showed similarities to factor structures obtained in different cultures.

Turkish Experience with the MMPI

Publications of norms for the Turkish MMPI and supporting evidence of validity led many researchers to use the Turkish MMPI in diverse studies. Two studies involved assessing psychometric features of the test itself. Erol (1984) compared Turkish and American response rates for each MMPI item. The objective of the study was to compare "true" and "don't know" responses to each item by a Turkish sample with those of the original American samples to establish similarities and differences. Of the 566 items, only 29% were different. These items related to health, religion, sexuality, and social attitudes. The second study involved an effort to evaluate an MMPI Short Form (168 items) in Turkey. Musabali (1990) administered the items to a sample of 320 students in Izmir. In the factor analysis of the results, five factors emerged: General Mental Health, Acting Out, Mystical Tendencies, Psychotic Disturbance, and Low Morale.

Sayilgan (1986) conducted a study at Hacettepe Hospital in Ankara to determine whether psychopathology as assessed by the validity and clinical scales of the MMPI could be faked and also whether knowledge about psychopathology and the MMPI would affect results. The MMPI was administered to a group of novice freshman psychology students and to a group of psychology graduate students knowledgeable about psychopathology and the MMPI. Both groups were directed to give responses intended to simulate psychopathology. The resulting simulated profiles were compared with MMPI profiles of female inpatients diagnosed with psychosis and thought disorder. Neither student group was successful in simulating psychopathology. The simulated MMPI profiles were easily identified using the validity scales, and no differences were found between the experienced and inexperienced student groups.

Use of the MMPI as a Research Criterion

The MMPI scales have been used as a criterion measure in the standardization of the Turkish version of several psychological instruments. Following a common practice in Western cultures, scale 2 was used to validate the Beck Depression Inventory (Hisli, 1989). The subjects were university students. The Pearson product correlation between the two scales was r = .50. In another study, with a sample of 550 students, the MMPI was used as a criterion to assess the adjustment of subjects in order to validate the Rotter Sentence Completion Test (Akkoyun, 1985). The Rotter test is a personality instrument constructed to measure the adjustment of university students. Subjects with three or more MMPI scale scores above 60 were considered "maladjusted." Students whose scale scores ranged between 40 and 60 were accepted as "adjusted." Profiles of "adjusted" and "maladjusted" male and female students were obtained. For "maladjusted" female students, the elevated scales were scales 1, 2, 3, and 7. The elevated scales for "maladjusted" male students were F, 1, 2, 3, 4, 7, 8, 9, and 0. The author pointed out that these results were similar to those obtained for normal and abnormal profiles in the MMPI validity research by Erol (1982). The distribution of Rotter scores for "adjusted" and "maladjusted" students determined by MMPI criteria determined that a Rotter score of 150 was an appropriate cut-off score to differentiate "adjusted" from "maladjusted" students. Of the female subjects identified as "adjusted" by the MMPI criteria, 74% were identified as "adjusted" using the cut-off score on the Rotter test; 68% of those identified as "maladjusted" by MMPI criteria were identified as "maladjusted" using the Rotter cut-off. For male subjects, these percentages were 67 and 83, respectively. In another study where the psychometric properties of the Turkish version of the Symptom Check List-Revised (SCL-90-R) were investigated, convergent and discriminant validities of the instrument were tested by correlations between the SCL-90-R scales and the MMPI and the Beck Depression Inventory (Dağ, 1991). The study showed significant correlations, ranging from .81 to .33, between certain SCL-90-R subscales and related MMPI scales.

Relationship of the MMPI to Diagnosis

In several studies, the relationships between diagnostic categories of the *DSM-III* or *DSM-III-R* Classification Systems and the MMPI were investigated. In one study, patients in the psychiatric department of a major Turkish hospital were diagnosed by a treatment team and assigned to five categories of the *DSM-III:* Dysthymia, Anxiety, Somatoform Disorders, Alcohol Dependency, and Schizophrenia (Sorias, 1984). Scale 8 was high for every patient group, both males and females, and scale 6 was high for all female patient groups. For Dysthymia and Anxiety patient groups, scales 2, 6, 7, and 8 were high. The only difference between the profiles of these two patient groups was that of Anxiety patients, mean scale scores being lower than for Dysthymia patients. In Somatoform Disorders, in addition to an elevated scale 8 in men and scales 6 and 8 in women, scales 2, 1, 7, 3, and 4 were elevated, as would be expected in this category of disorders. In alcohol dependency, elevation was not noticeable, including in the validity scales, with the exception of some elevated scores reflecting depressive characteristics. In Schizophrenia, for men scales 8 and 2 and for women scales 8, 6, and 7 were elevated. The author concluded that, in the Turkish culture, scale 8 of the MMPI may not be a good indicator of schizophrenic disorders as defined by the *DSM-III.* The author also concluded that elevated scores on scales 8 and 6 may be due to Turkish personality characteristics and traditional Turkish values. Of course, since this study was conducted with inpatients, scale 8 would be expected to be prominent in many patients.

In another study, the hospital files and the MMPI profiles of inpatients in the psychiatric clinic of a hospital were evaluated by three psychiatrists and diagnoses were made according to *DSM-III-R* criteria (Uluergüven, Şenol, Toplu, & Yüksel, 1988). The highest scale scores and two-point codes were obtained by patients diagnosed with major depression, paranoid schizophrenia, and bipolar disorder. The high two-point code for major depression was 1-2; for paranoid schizophrenia, the high two-point code was 6-8; and for bipolar disorder, the high codes were 6-9 and 5-9.

In a study performed on 147 inpatients diagnosed as having borderline personality disorder (BPD), histrionic personality disorder (HPD), antisocial personality disorder (APD), or narcissistic personality disorder (NPD) according to *DSM-III-R* criteria, the mean MMPI profiles of the patients were examined and comparisons made between different diagnostic categories (Dereboy, Şenol, Köse, & Yüksel, 1993). In the case of female patients, MMPI profiles showed no significant differences from diagnostic category to diagnostic category. In the case of male antisocial personality disorders patients, elevations on scales 4, 6, 8, and 9 were observed, and in male HPD patients, elevations on scales 1, 2, 7, and 0 were observed. The MMPI profiles of the male borderline patients showed similarities with the MMPI profiles of both APD and HPD patients but with significantly higher elevations. However, since the patients were also diagnosed with Axis I disorders, the results may not be clear.

MMPI Scales and Physical and Emotional Problems

Several studies have been conducted to explore the relationships between certain emotional disorders and organic illnesses and personality types as indicated by the MMPI profile. Investigations of the characteristics of the MMPI profiles of patients with affective disorders (Emil, 1990) and with schizophrenic disorders (Baycan, 1990) reveal significant findings, and the authors concluded that indeed the MMPI is as useful in assessing emotional disorders among Turkish patients as among other patient groups for which it has been validated. Kireççi (1986) compared the MMPI profiles of peptic ulcer patients and a control group. He found that female ulcer patients produced a 1-2-3-7 code type and male patients a 1-2-3 code type. In addition, the MMPI profiles of 48% of the ulcer patients showed pathology, while the profiles of only 10% of the control group showed pathological characteristics. An investigation of patients diagnosed with Behçet's disease indicated that the MMPI profiles of those patients were within the normal range (Coşkun, 1986). However, the profiles of male patients in the group showed slightly elevated scores on scale 2, and female patients showed slight elevations on scales 2 and 3.

Özmen (1991) studied the MMPI profiles of narcoleptic patients and concluded that the results supported the thesis that psychopathology observed in these individuals may be caused by the "sleepiness" that is the result of their narcolepsy.

In another study, the MMPI responses of patients with tension-type headache and with migraine headache were compared with those of a control group (Soykan, İnan, Tulunay, & Saran, 1992). The results obtained revealed that subjects in the tension-type headache group had significantly higher scores on the neurotic scales (Hypochondriasis, Depression, and Hysteria) than subjects in the control group. Migraine headache subjects had significantly higher scores on the Hysteria scale than did the control subjects.

In a study of homosexual men, the MMPI was administered to a group of young and older homosexual males and the profiles were compared to those of control groups of similarly aged heterosexual males (Çulha & Çekirge, 1989). Homosexuals showed significantly higher scores on scales F, 1, 2, 3, 4, 6, 8, 9, and 0, and the results were strikingly similar to those obtained in a study in the United States from the 1960s. The authors took particular note of the apparent similarity between social forces affecting homosexuals in the United States in the 1960s and similar forces in Turkey at the time of the study in the 1980s. The study also noted that differences between the homosexual and heterosexual groups on scales 4 and 6 were more pronounced for the younger subjects in both groups than for the older subjects in both Turkish groups investigated.

In a study of women experiencing premenstrual syndrome (PMS), the MMPI was among the instruments administered to 25 women who met the *DSM-III-R* criteria for late luteal phase dysphoric disorder, the condition often referred to as PMS (Dilbaz, 1992). The PMS group was found to convert psychological problems into somatic complaints. The MMPI results also indicated that women with PMS experienced increased physical and psychological symptomatology during the late luteal phase.

In another study, the MMPI was administered to adolescents and young adults who had attempted suicide and to a group of comparable youth (Yüksel, 1987). No significant differences were obtained between the two groups, and the investigator concluded that adolescents who do not seem to be psychiatrically disturbed may nonetheless be at risk.

Kerimoğlu (1985) obtained MMPI data from the mothers and fathers of stuttering children. Mothers of stutterers scored significantly higher on scales 8, 9, and Family than did mothers in the control group. Fathers in the control group scored significantly higher on scales L and Religion than did the fathers of stutterers.

Use of the Turkish MMPI with Alcoholics

Several MMPI studies were conducted with alcoholic patients. In one such study, inpatients in the alcoholic treatment center of the psychiatry department of a leading hospital were the sample (Uluergüven, Şeenal, & Şener, 1988). The sample was divided into four groups by age, number of years on alcohol, and starting age of alcohol consumption. ANOVA tests revealed significant relationship ($p < 0.05$) between age and scale 4, with scale 4 scores decreasing with increasing age, although the authors noted that this may also be true for the general population, as has been indicated by other research.

In a similar study, Demirbaş and Doğan (1989) obtained MMPI data from male inpatients diagnosed as alcoholic and neurotic. The MMPI results revealed elevated scales l, 2, and 3 for alcoholic patients and elevated scales 1, 2, 3, and 7 for neurotic patients. Furthermore, neurotic patients showed significantly higher scores on scales 2 and 3 (as well as 7) than did alcoholic patients. In a comparative study, Ceyhun, Palabıyıkoğlu, and Atakurt (1990) explored the effectiveness of the MAC Scale (MacAndrew Alcoholism Scale) and the ICAS (Institutionalized Chronic Alcoholic Scale). Alcoholic patients showed significantly higher scores on the MAC Scale and the ICAS than did neurotic patients ($p < 0.001$).

Use of Specific MMPI Scales

Several specific supplementary scales have been studied in Turkey. In one study, Palabıyıkoğlu, Ceyhun, Aydın, and Atakurt (1990) evaluated MMPI scales 2 and

0 and Finney's Impotence and Frigidity Scales obtained from patients diagnosed with organic and psychogenic impotency. Normal subjects and depressives with no sexual function complaints constituted two control groups. No significant differences were found between the patients diagnosed with organic impotency and those diagnosed with psychogenic impotency. In still another study, the 17-item Pn scale (Pseudoneurological scale) was administered to 75 epileptic patients to check the possibility that epileptic seizures might be psychogenic in nature in some cases (Erdinç, Dilbaz, Kutlu, Erkmen, Seber, Özdemir, & Tekin, 1990). Pn scores were compared with objective neurological data (e.g., EEG results); however, the results were inconclusive.

The MMPI was also used to measure the effectiveness of treatment modalities. Okyayuz, Berksun, and Çevik (1992) administered the MMPI to 43 patients diagnosed as psychosomatic and having neurotic disorder with somatization before and after treatment. After-treatment MMPI scores were significantly lower on scales 2, 3, 7, 8, and 0 than pretreatment scores. İnceer and Özbey (1990) obtained MMPI profiles of 10 mothers with children of below average intelligence before and after a focused, structured, and supportive group experience of 9.5 months. Scale 2 was found to be significantly lower after the experience.

Development of the MMPI-2 for Use in Turkey

The revision of the MMPI and subsequent publication of the MMPI-2 encouraged us to revise the Turkish MMPI and to develop a Turkish MMPI-2. Since considerable work was done on the translation of the original MMPI, our efforts at first were concentrated on the additional items that were included in the MMPI-2 to measure new personality dimensions or problems and the items that were rewritten (Butcher, Dahlstrom, Graham, Tellegen, & Kaemmer, 1989). In addition, we had noted that religious items posed special difficulties in the Turkish translation. Moreover, extremely rapid changes in Turkish society rendered some items obsolete, and some others were found to be intrusive and objectionable. We felt that the modification or deletion of outmoded idiomatic expressions and references to unfamiliar literary material and recreational activities was desirable and that additional items designed to provide better coverage of topics would also enrich the Turkish MMPI-2. Revisions or additions in these areas were included in our work.

The new and the revised items were translated into Turkish by the first author. Each item was then discussed by a group of three bilinguals who were familiar with both cultures, and some refinements were made. Nine items were found to be very difficult to express clearly in Turkish. Both the English and alternative Turkish translations were written and reviewed by another group of seven bilinguals. They were asked to choose the best alternative or to write their own. The initial group of three bilinguals went through the responses and decided on the final form of these items.

The revised items, printed in Turkish, were administered to 15 Turks with varying degrees of education. They were asked to read each item carefully and check whether it was easy to understand, and to write down any alternatives they had. The suggestions were carefully reviewed, and items that were checked as difficult to understand by at least three persons were rewritten.

The new MMPI-2 items were printed in Turkish and English. Twenty bilinguals were administered the Turkish and the English versions one week apart. The order of administration was varied. Sixteen items yielded low correlations (ranging between .46 and –.05). These items were rewritten on the basis of comments and suggestions provided by a group of seven bilinguals.

The resulting Turkish versions of the new MMPI-2 items were then back-translated by the second author of this chapter. The back-translated and original English items were examined by two Americans. There were some comments or questions on 18 of the items. Some questions were on the omission of "or." "Or" had been omitted from some items since it can introduce ambiguity in meaning when used in Turkish. Another comment was on the use of "I feel" instead of "I think." "I feel" is often used in Turkish instead of "I think"; thus it was decided to use "I feel" to make the items more natural. Other comments were on the use of several qualifying adjectives such as "so" versus "very" or "best" versus "much better" in accordance with common Turkish usage. Another comment pointed out the difficulty faced in translating idiomatic expressions; a particular example was "drive a hard bargain."

The new items revised in accordance with comments from the back-translation process and new versions of the revised items that previously had shown low correlations (22 items in all) were printed in Turkish and English and administered to 15 bilinguals one week apart. Examination of item correlations showed that most of these items as revised had very high or perfect correlations, except for three items, which were subsequently revised again. Following the completion of the quantitative and qualitative measures to establish equivalency summarized above, a Turkish version of the MMPI-2 is now ready to be used in a standardization project.

Standardization of the MMPI-2

The reasons for restandardization as stated by Butcher et al. (1989) are relevant for the Turkish MMPI as well. Accordingly, a restandardization project with a new sample of 1,200 subjects, 600 females and 600 males ranging from 16 to 50 years of age, is planned. An effort will be made to obtain subjects from different regions of Turkey to ensure cultural diversity. About 40 men and 40 women will be administered the inventory twice to determine test-retest reliabilities. Means and standard deviations for the new MMPI-2 scales will be computed and profiles with T-score equivalents will be developed for males and females.

Item endorsements provide clues both for cultural differences and translation discrepancies. Intercorrelations of item endorsement frequencies between the Turkish and U.S. samples will be conducted. A 20% difference in endorsement percentage will be used as the cut-off. Mean profiles for Turkish subjects will also be compared with U.S. norms.

Validity Studies

A random subset of normals from the standardization sample will be compared with groups of psychiatric patients with known diagnoses (*DSM-IV* criteria will be used), excluding patients with a history of brain disorder. Mean scale scores of the psychiatric sample will be compared to determine whether the scores differentiate between the two groups and between diagnostic subgroups. Examination of code types and the degree of similarity with U.S. codes will provide further evidence of validity.

Factor analyses will be undertaken to ascertain the factor structure of the Turkish MMPI-2 based on data obtained from the psychiatric and normal groups. Comparisons will be made with the factor structure of the American MMPI-2, evaluating psychiatric and normal groups separately.

References

Akkoyun, F. (1985). *Rotter cümle tamamlama testi—üniversite öğ rencileri formu—el kitabı* [Handbook of Rotter Sentence Completion Test for university students]. Ankara: Ankara University Press.

Baycan, N. (1990). Şizofrenik bozukluk gösteren hastaların MMPI profil özelliklerinin araştırıması [A study of characteristics of the MMPI profiles of patients with schizophrenic disorder]. Unpublished master's thesis, Uludağ University, Bursa, Turkey.

Butcher, J. N., Dahlstrom, W. G., Graham, J. R., Tellegen, A., & Kaemmer, B. (1989). *Minnesota Multiphasic Personality Inventory-2 (MMPI-2): Manual for administration and scoring.* Minneapolis: University of Minnesota Press.

Butcher, J. N., & Pancheri, P. (1976). *Handbook of cross-national MMPI research.* Minneapolis: University of Minnesota Press.

Ceyhun, B., Palabıyıkoğlu, R., & Atakurt, Y. (1990). Clinical application and predictive power of MMPI alcoholism scales in Turkish alcohol population. *Journal of Ankara Medical School, 12,* 157–163.

Coşkun, A. (1986). *Bir grup Behçet hastasının psikiyatrik yönden değerlendirilmesi* [Psychiatric evaluation of a group of patients diagnosed with Behçet's disease]. Unpublished master's thesis, Hacettepe University, Ankara, Turkey.

Çulha, M., & Çekirge, P. (1989). *A study of the MMPI profiles of male homosexuals in Turkey.* Paper presented at the 22nd MMPI Annual Conference, Honolulu, Hawaii.

Dağ, İ. (1991). Belirti tarama listesi (SCL-90-R) 'nin üniversite öğrencileri için güvenirliği [A reliability and validity study of Symptom Check List SCL-90-R for university students]. *Türk Psikiyatri Dergisi [Turkish Journal of Psychiatry], 2,* 5–12.

Demirbaş, H., & Doğan, B.Y. (1989). Alkol bağımlılarında MMPI bulguları ve bu bulguların nevroz hastalrı ile karşılaştırılması [A comparative study of MMPI profiles of alcohol abusers and neurotics]. *XXV. Ulusal Psikiyatri ve Nörolojik Bilimler Kongresi [Twenty-Fifth National Psychiatry and Neurological Sciences Congress (proceedings)]*, Mersin, Turkey, 560–564.

Dereboy, Ç., Şenol, S., Köse, S. K., & Yüksel, N. (1993). *DSM-III-R* II. Eksen Küme B kişilik bozukluğu olgularının MMPI profilleri açısından karşılaştırılması [Comparison of MMPI profiles of *DSM-III-R* Axis II Cluster B personality disorders]. *Türk Psikiyatri Dergisi [Turkish Journal of Psychiatry]*, 4, 54–59.

Dilbaz, N. (1992). Premenstrual sendromun psikiyatrik özelliklerinin MMPI ile değerlendirilmesi [Evaluation with MMPI of psychiatric characteristics of premenstrual syndrome]. *Türk Psikiyatri Dergisi [Turkish Journal of Psychiatry]*, 3, 47–55.

Emil, N. (1990). *Affektif bozukluk gösteren hastaların MMPI profil özelliklerinin araştırılması* [A study of the characteristics of MMPI profiles of patients with affective disorders]. Unpublished master's thesis, Uludağ University, Bursa, Turkey.

Erdinç, O. O., Dilbaz, N., Kutlu, C., Erkmen, H., Seber, G., Özdemir, G., & Tekin, D. (1990). Epileptik hastalarda psödonörolojik skalanın uygulanması [Assessment of the pseudoneurologic scale in patients with epilepsy]. *Anadolu Tıp Dergisi [Medical Journal of Anatolia]*, 12, 75–82.

Erol, N. (1982). *Ülkemizdeki psikiyatrik hastalarda Minnesota Çok Yönlü Kişilik Envanterinin geçerlik araştırması* [Validity study of the MMPI with Turkish psychiatric patients]. Unpublished doctoral dissertation, University of Ankara, Ankara, Turkey.

Erol, N. (1984). MMPI'ın normal Türk örneklemindeki madde analizi [Item-analysis of the MMPI normative sample]. *Psikoloji Dergisi [Journal of Psychology (Turkey)]*, 5, 24–30.

Hisli, N. (1989). Beck depresyon envanterinin üniversite öğrencileri için geçerliği, güvenirliği [Reliability and validity of Beck Depression Inventory for university students]. *Psikoloji Dergisi [Journal of Psychology (Turkey)]*, 7, 3–13.

İnceer, B., & Özbey, F. (1990). Zihinsel engelli bireylerin aileleri ile bir grup uygulaması (II) [A group experience with the families of children of below average intelligence]. *V. Ulusal Psikoloji Kongresi [Fifth National Psychology Congress (proceedings)]*, İzmir, Turkey, 159–165.

Kerimoğlu, E. (1985). Kekeme çocukların ve ailelerinin kişilik özellikleri yönünden incelenmesi [A study of the personality characteristics of stuttering children and their families]. *Psikoloji Dergisi [Journal of Psychology (Turkey)]*, 5, 15–23.

Kireçci, Y. (1986). *Peptik ülserli hastaların MMPI profil özellikleri* [MMPI profiles of peptic-ulcer patients]. Unpublished master's thesis, Uludağ University, Bursa, Turkey.

Musabali, S. (1990). MMPI-168 kısa formunun İzmir popülasyonu için maddelerinin uyarlanması çalışması [An item analysis study of the MMPI short form for the population of İzmir, Turkey]. *V. Ulusal Psikoloji Kongresi [Fifth National Psychology Congress (proceedings)]*, İzmir, Turkey, 671–677.

Okyayuz, Ü., Berksun, O. E., & Çevik, A. (1992). Psikosomatik serviste yatarak tedavi gören hastaların tedavi öncesi ve sonrası objektif ölçümler aracılığıyla değerlendirilmesi [A pre-post-treatment evaluation of psychosomatic inpatients with objective tests]. *I. Psikosomatik Sempozyumu Bilimsel Yayınları [Proceedings of the First Psychosomatic Symposium]*, Antalya, Turkey, 126–145.

Özmen, M. (1991). *Narkoleptik hastalarda MMPI profilleri* [MMPI profiles of narcoleptic patients]. Unpublished master's thesis, Istanbul University, Istanbul, Turkey.

Palabıyıkoğlu, R., Ceyhun, B., Aydın, H., & Atakurt, Y. (1990). Organik ve psikojen empotansın MMPI alt testleri ile değerlendirilmesi [Assessment of organic and psychogenic impotence using MMPI scales]. *Ankara Üniversitesi Tıp Fakültesi Mecmuası [The Journal of the Faculty of Medicine, University of Ankara]*, 43, 939–950.

Prince, R., & Mombour, W. (1976). A technique for improving linguistic equivalence in cross-cultural surveys. *International Journal of Social Psychiatry*, 13, 229–237.

Savaşır, I. (1981). *Minnesota Çok Yönlü Kişilik Envanteri—El Kitabı* [Handbook of the Turkish MMPI]. Ankara: Sevinç Matbaası.

Savaşır, I., & Erol, N. (1978). A revised translation of the Turkish MMPI. Unpublished report, University of Haceteppe, Ankara, Turkey.

Savaşır, I., & Erol, N. (1990). The Turkish MMPI: Translation, standardization and validation. In J. N. Butcher & C. D. Spielberger (Eds.), *Advances in personality assessment* (Vol. 8). Hillsdale, NJ: Erlbaum.

Savaşır, I., & Turgay, A. (1970). Translation study of MMPI on a Turkish sample. Unpublished report, University of Haceteppe, Ankara, Turkey.

Sayılgan, M.A. (1986). *Psikiyatri hastalarında olumlu temerüz amacıyla çarpıtılmış MMPI profillerinin incelenmesi* [A comparison of MMPI profiles intentionally simulated by experienced and inexperienced psychology students with MMPI profiles of a sample of psychiatric patients]. Unpublished master's thesis, Hacettepe University, Ankara, Turkey.

Sorias, S., et al. (1984). Psikiyatrik hastaların MMPI alt test özelliklerinin araştırılması [A study of MMPI scales of psychiatric patients]. *E.Ü.T.F. Dergisi [Journal of the Medical Faculty of Ege University (Turkey)], 23*, 1437–1445.

Soykan, C., İnan, L. E., Tulunay, F. C., & Saran, C. (1992). MMPI profiles of Turkish headache sufferers. In Ekbom, K., Gerber, W. D., Henry, P., Nappi, G., Pfaffenrath, V., & Teflt-Hansen, P. (Eds.), *Headache Research in Europe: Proceedings of the 1st Conference of the European Headache Federation (EHF)*, Bremen, Germany.

Uluergüven, Ç., Şenal, S., & Şener, Ş. (1988). Alkolik hastaların MMPI ölçeklerinin bazı klinik ve demografik parametrelerle ilişkisi [Relationships between MMPI profiles of alcoholic patients and certain clinical and demographic parameters]. *XXIV. Ulusal Psikiyatri ve Nörolojik Bilimler Kongresi [Twenty-Fourth National Psychiatry and Neurological Sciences Congress (Proceedings)]*, Ankara, Turkey, 650–655.

Uluergüven, Ç., Şenal, S., Toplu, A., & Yüksel, N. (1988). MMPI kod tipleri ve *DSM-III-R* tanıları [Relationship of MMPI code types and *DSM-III-R* diagnostic categories]. *XXIV. Ulusal Psikiyatri ve Nörolojik Bilimler Kongresi [Twenty-Fourth National Psychiatry and Neurological Sciences Congress (Proceedings)]*, Ankara, Turkey, 666–671.

Yüksel, N. (1987). *Adolesan intihar girişimlerinin psiko-sosyal nedenleriyle ilgili araştırma* [A study of psychosocial causes of adolescent suicide attempts]. Unpublished paper, Istanbul University.

Part V

Adaptations in the Middle East and East

Chapter 24

Development of an Arabic Translation of the MMPI-2: With Clinical Applications

Abdalla M. Soliman

In the Arab countries, psychology is associated with dealing with the mentally ill. However, a modern objective approach to understanding and ameliorating human behavior problems is often lacking. If Arab countries are to progress, they must adopt a modern, positive, and constructive approach to psychology in order to implement its goals and objectives. If this happens, there will be a need for effective psychological assessment instruments in the Arab countries.

Arab psychologists in the past have attempted to develop and adapt psychological tests. Much of the effort was spent translating foreign psychological tests. In the majority of cases, the translation process was not well defined or documented. Standardization and norming of translated instruments have rarely been adequate. The reasons for this situation are many: (1) Funds for test development are rarely available, (2) the development of a test may not be regarded as an important contribution for a psychologist to make, and (3) the public has not been aware of or accepting of the usefulness of psychological services.

The purpose of this chapter is to discuss the historical use of the original MMPI in Egypt, describe the translation of the MMPI-2 into Arabic, present a research program to evaluate the MMPI-2 assessment of Arabs, and illustrate the sensitivity of the MMPI-2 in describing clinical cases.

Several of my friends and colleagues facilitated my translation of the MMPI-2 into Arabic and the writing of this chapter. James N. Butcher encouraged me to do the translation and provided me with many resources and facilities. Without his support and advice the translation and the writing of this chapter would not have been achieved. I would like to acknowledge the assistance of Beverly Kaemmer of the University of Minnesota Press in many phases of the translation process. Louis K. Meleika provided me with copies of his publications. My friends and colleagues Shawki Galal, Roushdy Toiemah, Mahmoud Al-Naqa, and Samy Anwar made useful suggestions on the translation. Psychiatrist Talaat Matar provided the case studies and the psychiatric diagnoses for the two cases reported. My colleague Taha Amir read this chapter and made useful suggestions. Dean Sayed Kheiralla provided me with many facilities and encouragement, and I appreciate his help.

Development of the MMPI in Egypt

The Minnesota Multiphasic Personality Inventory is well known in the Arab countries. It attracted the attention of psychologists early in test development activities. The MMPI was originally translated into Arabic in the mid-1950s by three Egyptian psychologists who were graduates of major American universities: Attia M. Hana, M. Emadeddin Ismail, and Louis K. Meleika (Meleika, 1990). The test manual describing the use of the MMPI was published in 1959 as part of an edited book by Meleika, Ismail, and Hana (1959). The translators of this version of the MMPI did not describe the translation process in much detail. They used the words "adaptation" and "preparation" rather than "translation." Several questions may be raised regarding Hana, Ismail, and Meleika's version of the MMPI. For example, we do not know whether the whole test was translated by each translator independently or whether the translations were discussed by the three translators before agreement was reached on one version. Or, did the translators divide the test and each translate a third of the items? They do not report whether a back-translation was done and how this might have contributed to the final translation of the test, though it is unlikely that this developmental step was performed. Without this information, it is not possible to provide a thorough evaluation of the 1959 Arabic translation of the MMPI.

I reviewed Hana, Ismail, and Meleika's version of the MMPI (1990) and found a number of modifications or adaptations of the original English text. I will cite a few examples to demonstrate how important it is to carefully inspect a translated test before using it.

Examples of Differences between the Arabic Translation and the Original MMPI

For some items, words were added or deleted in the translation, which may have changed the meaning of the items. For other items, the meaning of the translated item was clearly different from the meaning of the original. Following are exemplary items from the original MMPI for which the Arabic translation had a different meaning. In some cases, only those parts of the translated item that diverged from the original are given.

Item No.

1   The word "reading" was added to the statement "I like reading mechanics magazines." Some people might like to look at or consult mechanics magazines, but not necessarily "read" them.

15   "things too bad" was translated "things too ugly."

22   ". . . that I cannot control" was translated "that I cannot resist."

42   "My family does not like . . ." was translated "My family is not interested."

43   "fitful" was translated "anxious."

52   "I prefer to pass by . . ." was translated "I prefer to neglect."

72   For ". . . the pit of my stomach," "the pit of" was deleted. Also, "discomfort" was translated "pains."

81   "I think I would like the kind of work a forest ranger does" was translated "I am interested in rough jobs like work in fields and forests."

108   "There seems to be a fullness in my head" was translated "I feel my head is about to explode."

110   "Someone has it in for me" was translated "Some people hide in themselves something [bad] to do for me."

225   "I gossip a little at times" was translated "I like to chat a little once in a while."

247   "I have reason for feeling jealous of one or more members of my family" was translated "I have reasons which make me oppose some members of my family."

254   "I like to be with a crowd who play jokes on one another" was translated "I like to be with a group who exchange jokes."

498   "It is always a good thing to be frank" was translated "Frankness is always appreciated."

These are only a few examples in which the MMPI Arabic translation was different from the original text. All these items could have been translated in a more readable Arabic that preserved both the meaning and style of the English original.

The Standardization of the Arabic MMPI

The original standardization group was composed of 544 male students in different colleges and universities (Meleika, Ismail, & Hana, 1959; Meleika, 1990), probably located in Cairo. According to the authors, these students were considered normal. No psychologically disturbed or clinical cases were included.

Sex Differences. Meleika (1963) also administered the MMPI to 300 female students in several colleges and universities, probably in Cairo. Means, standard deviations, and T scores were computed for each scale. The reliability was tested for each scale using Kuder-Richardson 21 and the split-half methods. For a sample of 444 male students, the Kuder-Richardson reliability coefficient ranged from .41 for the L scale to .88 for the Schizophrenia scale. The split-half reliability coefficients ranged from .52 for the Paranoia scale to .8 for the Psychasthenia scale.

The reliability coefficients using Kuder-Richardson 21 and computed for 50 female students ranged from .43 for the L scale to .88 for the Paranoia scale. Mean scale differences between the male and female samples were significant for most scales, leading Meleika to conclude that norms for males and females should be developed separately. Meleika (1960, 1966a, 1966b, 1967) conducted an empirical investigation of the validity of four clinical scales: Sc (Schizophrenia), Pd, D, and Hy (1990).

1. The Arabic version of the MMPI was administered to a clinical group characterized by the syndrome of the scale to be tested. This group was designated as the clinical group. The MMPI was also administered to a normal group that matched the clinical group with respect to age, sex, and educational and occupational status.

2. Item analysis of the responses of the two groups on the clinical scale was conducted and the items that discriminated between the two groups were included in the scale.

3. T-score tables for the new scale were developed.

4. Differences on the new scale between age, sex, and educational levels were tested.

5. The reliability of the new scale was studied.

6. Individual responses on the validity scales were studied.

7. The validity of the new scale was examined.

Reliability of the Clinical Scales

The reliability coefficients of the new clinical scales computed by Kuder-Richardson 21 formula were: for Sc (N = 51), r = .89; for Pd (N = 50), r = .49; and for D (N = 51), (r = .67). The reliability of the new clinical scales was studied using the Guttman formula, and the resulting coefficients were: for Sc, r = .88; for Hy, r = .74. The clinical groups included male and female university students. Meleika (1990) considered these reliability coefficients acceptable.

The Validity of the Original Scales

The original MMPI Pd scale is composed of 50 items. Of these, 20 items discriminated between the clinical and the normal groups at P< .05 or less, 14 items discriminated between the two groups at p < .10 and p < .20, and 16 items did not discriminate between the two groups. Meleika (1966a) included items that discriminated between the two groups at p < .05 or less and those that discriminated at p < .10 and p < .20. Thus the new Pd scale is composed of 34 of the original 50 items.

Meleika (1966b) showed that answers to Pd items that did not discriminate between the clinical and normal groups in Egyptian society can be interpreted in the context of the Arab culture. For example, item 235, "I have been quite independent and free from family rule," should be answered "True" by the Pd group; however, it was answered "False" by both normal and clinical groups. Family ties are strong in Arab societies, and one is not expected to be independent and free from family rule. Similarly, of the four items that dealt with sex behavior and attitudes, only one item discriminated between the two groups. As Meleika (1966b) proposes, it is difficult and sensitive for Arab men to talk about their feelings and attitudes toward sex and love and even more difficult for women to do so. Also, the five items concerned with self-pride and self-centeredness did not discriminate between the two groups. For item 82, "I am easily downed in an argument," 36 of the clinical group and 35 of the normal group answered "False," which expressed the two groups' tendency toward perfection. Verbal abilities are very important in Arab culture; consequently a "False" answer to this item is highly desirable.

In the case of the Hy scale, Meleika (1967) found that of the 60 items that make up this scale, only 21 items discriminated between the clinical and the normal groups at .001, .01, and .05 levels of significance. Meleika included in the new scale 2 items that discriminated at .10, 7 items at .20, and 3 items at .30 levels of significance.

In the case of the D scale, Meleika (1966a) found that of 60 items that make up this scale, 27 items discriminated between the normal and the clinical groups at .001, .01, and .05 levels of significance. Meleika included in the new scale 8 items that discriminated between the two groups at .10, and 5 items at the .20 level.

Torki (Meleika, 1990) found that of the 60 items that make up the Mf scale, only 31 discriminated between a group of 150 male students and 150 female students at Kuwait University. The difference between the means of the male and female groups was significant at the .005 level.

Meleika's research was done almost 30 years ago. Scholars living in Arab countries realize that the Arab culture of the 1990s is different from that of the 1960s in numerous ways. If such research were carried out today, results would likely be different.

Translation of the MMPI-2 into Arabic

The method adopted for translating the MMPI-2 into Arabic did not follow exactly the method proposed by Butcher (chapter 2). However, it does approximate those recommendations.

1. The translation was done by me. I am a bilingual Egyptian psychologist whose native language is Arabic. I spent slightly less than six years living in the United States as a graduate student at the University of Minnesota, and another year as a visiting scholar at the University of Georgia, along with several summers and short visits. I taught and counseled students in both Arabic and English and wrote and edited published research in both languages.

2. The translation was done in simple literary Arabic language. There is one literary Arabic language, understood, read, and spoken by all Arabic-

speaking people. It is the language of the Holy Koran. A very few words and stylistic expressions may be more popular in one Arab country than in another. The styles of Egyptian writers are popular in all Arab countries owing to the wide usage of Egyptian books, newspapers, and movies in other Arab countries.

3   After the translation was completed, it was read by a professional translator, who proposed very few changes. This translator is an Egyptian scholar, with a background in philosophy and psychology. He has 20 published books translated from English into Arabic. He lived for several years in other Arab countries. I also consulted with two professors of curriculum and methods of teaching Arabic language and a third professor of linguistics. During the process of translation, I consulted with James Butcher on several questionable item translations. The objective of this process was to ensure that the translated text is an accurate expression of the original text.

4.   The back-translation and evaluation of the Arabic translation were carried out by the University of Minnesota Press using a professional linguist. This latter process resulted in a few editorial and stylistic changes. As this chapter was being written, the Arabic translation of the MMPI-2 was approved for use by the University of Minnesota.

5.   Several dictionaries were consulted: English, English-Arabic, and dictionaries of idioms, both English and English-Arabic. When in doubt about the accuracy of a translation, I checked the meanings of words and phrases in several sources.

When reading the items in the English original, I asked myself two questions: (1) What do the authors of the text mean by this item? (2) What behavior and personality characteristic does this item measure?

Table 2-1, titled "Standardized definitions and examples for the MMPI-A," in Butcher and Williams (1992, pp. 19-20) was very helpful. I propose that this table be expanded for both the MMPI-2 and the MMPI-A. Translators of the two instruments could mark the items that did not translate directly or easily in the target language and indicate the meaning they attributed to these items and how they translated them. A cross-comparison of these items would be helpful and might clarify the meaning of some items in the original language to the benefit of the target language.

MMPI-2 Items That Were Not Easily Translated

Following are some of the items that were not easy to translate directly and needed careful study. They are referred to by their MMPI-2 item numbers, and only the part of the item that presented difficulty is given, along with the Arabic translation.

Item No.

17   "I am sure I get a raw deal from life." This is slang. It was translated "unfair treatment."

37   "At times I feel like smashing things." The word "like" here was translated "desiring" or "I feel the desire" to smash things.

55   "I sometimes keep on at a thing until others lose their patience with me" was translated "continue without stopping."

65   "Most of the time I feel blue" was translated "feel gloomy."

71   "These days I find it hard not to give up hope of amounting to something" was translated "I find it easy to give up hope of becoming successful."

74   "I do not mind being made fun of" was translated "being the object of teasing or sarcasm."

84   "I was suspended from school" was translated "dismissed from school."

93   "Sometimes when I am not feeling well" was translated "feeling that my health is not good."

99   "Someone has it in for me" was translated "Someone causes problems for me."

114   ". . . that I want to handle or steal them" was translated: "touch them by hand or."

150   "Sometimes I feel as if I must injure . . . was translated: "hurt."

155   ". . . got into trouble with the law" was translated: "committed unlawful act."

158   ". . . to put on a stunt" was translated "to do something exciting to capture attention."

161   ". . . to fight against showing that I am bashful" was translated "make an effort so that I would not look bashful."

197   "I think I would like the work of . . ." was translated "I think I could like the work of."

206   ". . . I can make up my mind . . ." was translated ". . . I can decide."

212   ". . . not because it amounted to much but because of the principle of the thing" was translated "not because this leads to big results, but because I did not like them."

221   ". . . things that are best kept to myself" was translated "things that I prefer to keep."

229   ". . . blank spells . . ." was translated "moments of unconsciousness."

244   ". . . when I am feeling low" was translated: "when I am feeling depressed."

344   ". . . for small stakes" was translated "for small benefits."

359   "I enjoy the excitement of a crowd" was translated "the excitement that I find in a crowd."

388   ". . . spells of the blues" was translated "spells of feeling gloomy."

389   ". . . to be hot headed" was translated "to have a sharp (or hot) temper."

391   ". . . to tell all about myself" was translated "to tell everything about myself."

397   "A windstorm terrifies me" was translated "makes me very afraid."

402   ". . . sleep over" was translated "postpone."

406   ". . . enjoy beating criminals . . ." was translated "enjoy defeating criminals."

416   For "I have strong political opinions," "strong" was translated literally; it means "solid opinions."

418   "It is all right . . ." was translated "It is acceptable."

419   ". . . they are catching it for something they have done" was translated "they are being punished."

421   ". . . I am not going about it in the right way" was translated "I am not dealing with it."

425   "The man who had the most to do with me . . ." was translated "The man who had the major role in my life."

428   ". . . change of heart . . ." was translated "change of interest."

440   "I usually work things out for myself . . ." was translated "deal with things by myself."

444   ". . . a high strung person" was translated "very emotional person."

469   ". . . to go to pieces" was translated "about to break down."

505   "I am so sick of . . ." was translated "I am disgusted of."

511   ". . . get high or drunk" was translated "elated or."

513   ". . . that I don't know what comes over me" was translated "what happens to me."

548   ". . . in a physical fight" was translated "a fight with hands."

In some cases, the passive voice does not read fluently in the Arabic language. Therefore, some of the MMPI-2 original items were converted into the active voice.

129   "My conduct is largely controlled by the behavior of those around me" was translated "The behavior of those around me largely controls my conduct."

138   "I believe I am being plotted against" was translated "I believe there is someone who plots against me."

144   "I believe I am being followed" was translated "I believe there is someone who follows me."

222   "Children should be taught the main facts of sex" was translated "We should teach children the main facts of sex."

The problems encountered in translating the MMPI-2 into Arabic were easily solved.

Plan for the Standardization of the MMPI-2 in the Arab Countries

The ideal plan for standardizing a psychological test in the Arab countries is to standardize the instrument in each country separately. Although in Arab countries there are similarities in beliefs, value systems, the process of socialization, and other factors that influence behavior and personality, there are cultural variations in such factors. These cultural variations are expected to be rejected in test performance. To have country and local norms for a psychological test is consistent with the recommendations of the American Educational Research Association, the American Psychological Association, and the National Council on Measurement in Education (1985) and the scientist-practitioner tradition of psychology. Moreover, conducting research with a psychological instrument in their local communities would enable practitioners to know the limits of using the instrument in diagnosing and helping clients. Such a plan is, however, ambitious. It requires financial resources and the cooperation of many researchers. This does not mean that it cannot be implemented.

James Butcher's recommendations for studies to determine the adequacy and reliability of an MMPI-2 translation into another language and the adequacy of American norms, as well as for development of norms in other countries (chapter 2), will guide my plan for the standardization of the MMPI-2 in the Arab countries. Reliability may be studied using different methods, especially the test-retest method. Both the accuracy of the translation and the reliability of the instrument may be investigated by administering the English original and the Arabic translation as alternate forms to an Arab bilingual group, randomly administering the English original to one group and the Arabic translation to another group in the first administration of the test.

Validity

The essential method for studying the validity of the MMPI-2 scales is to test the item discrimination between clinical and normal groups. For example, a group of schizophrenics with symptoms matching the Sc scale and diagnosed by an independent source (e.g., a psychiatrist, clinical psychologist, or a rating form like the Life Events Form, the Relationship Form, or the Couple's Rating Form [Butcher, Graham, Williams, & Ben-Porath, 1990]) or a combination of them may be matched with a normal group for demographic characteristics like age, years of education, marital status, geographical location, nationality, etc. The responses of the two groups to the Sc items are tested statistically to determine which items discriminated between the two groups. A decision should be made about the acceptable level of statistical significance, hence which items should be included in the new scale. Meleika (1990) found that not all the items discriminated between the clinical and the normal groups in the four MMPI scales he tested for validity. He proposed that more research might lead to reducing the number of items in the

MMPI scales, resulting in a shorter MMPI—which he seemed to prefer because he observed that test takers were usually tired and bored by the length of the MMPI. Meleika's proposal for reducing the length of the MMPI remained hypothetical; no further research was carried out to test his contention, and in 1990 he and his associates republished the translation of the MMPI they had published in 1959. Item discrimination, however, can be adopted only after careful selection of clinical and normal groups, and after several testings. Careful sampling may reduce random factors that may influence item discrimination.

A study might be conducted comparing the performance of a representative group of college students in an Arab country on the MMPI-2 clinical scales with that of American college students. If the scores of the two groups were not found to differ, this might indicate that the American norms work in that country. However, a study of the validity of each clinical scale is essential for MMPI-2 research and application.

Norms

A standardization sample from one Arab country will be selected, composed of normal males and females. The sample will be representative of age, socioeconomic and educational background, geographic location, and other strata in the country. The differences between scores for men and for women on the MMPI-2 scales will be examined, and if such differences are significant, separate norms for each gender will be developed. Item endorsement frequencies and means and standard deviations may be completed and used for the development of norms.

Illustrative Clinical Cases of the Arabic MMPI-2

In this section, two clinical cases will be examined to determine whether the Arabic translation of the MMPI-2 is sensitive in describing and diagnosing the behavior of clients seen in psychiatric clinics. The clients were seen in a psychiatric section in a hospital in one of the United Arab Emirates. Their scores were plotted on U.S. norms, and their profiles were scored and interpreted by computer using The Minnesota Report: Adult Clinical System Revised (1993).

Case 1

This is a case of a 37-year-old male patient who completed nine years of education. He is married and has five children. His nationality is United Arab Emirate. The patient came to the psychiatric outpatient clinic in one of the Emirates complaining of loss of interest in life activities and interactions, inability to enjoy life, loss of sexual desire, and feelings of being tired. He reported that he began to have these symptoms a year ago, but his condition became worse and three months ago he began to think of seeing a doctor. This happened after a fight between his son and his son's schoolmates.

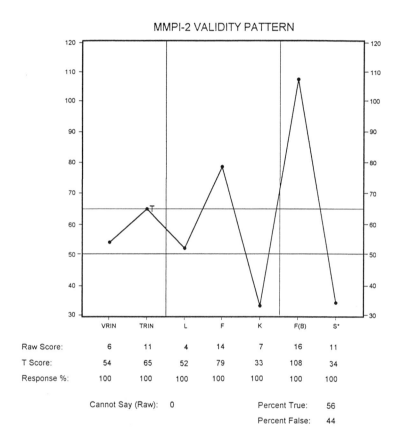

*Experimental

Figure 24-1. Minnesota Report™ MMPI-2 Validity Scale Profile of a 37-Year-Old Male Patient from the United Arab Emirates with a Diagnosed Depressive Disorder (Case 1). *Source:* The Minnesota Report™: Adult Clinical System. Copyright © 1989 by the Regents of the University of Minnesota. All rights reserved.

The patient had no previous history of psychiatric disorders, nor any relevant surgical history. No history of family psychiatric disorders was found.

The patient left school after the ninth year of his education to join the army. He worked in the army for six years, during which evaluations of his work were posi-

MMPI-2 BASIC AND SUPPLEMENTARY SCALES PROFILE

	Hs	D	Hy	Pd	Mf	Pa	Pt	Sc	Ma	Si		MAC-R	APS	AAS	PK	O-H	MDS
Raw Score:	12	37	23	29	24	18	38	40	16	54		21	24	4	33	13	10
K Correction:	4		3			7	7	1									
T Score:	59	87	54	72	46	79	89	86	43	83		48	52	56	92	52	88
Response %:	100	100	100	100	100	100	100	100	100	100		100	100	100	100	100	100

Welsh Code (new):	7<u>280</u>"64'+-13/59: F'+-L/:K#
Welsh Code (old):	2**87*<u>40</u>"6'<u>13</u>-59/ F'-L/?K:
Profile Elevation:	71.10

Figure 24-2. Minnesota Report™ MMPI-2 Standard Scale Profile of a 37-Year-Old Male Patient from the United Arab Emirates with a Diagnosed Depressive Disorder (Case 1). *Source:* The Minnesota Report™: Adult Clinical System. Copyright © 1989 by the Regents of the University of Minnesota. All rights reserved.

tive. He traveled abroad several times to enroll in training courses. Desiring to be near his family in the Emirate, he resigned his job in the army and applied for a job in the police service. In this job, he received regular promotions. His job performance was good and his relationships with his colleagues at work were excellent. He also had good family relationships. He drank alcohol for more than 10 years but was not a problem drinker. Three years ago he stopped drinking for religious reasons. He is known to be sociable, outgoing, active, and ambitious.

The following symptoms were reported during the psychiatric examination:

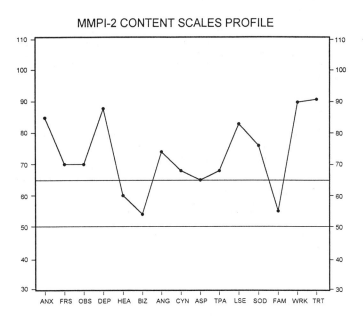

Figure 24-3. Minnesota Report™ MMPI-2 Content Scale Profile of a 37-Year-Old Male Patient from the United Arab Emirates with a Diagnosed Depressive Disorder (Case 1). *Source:* The Minnesota Report™: Adult Clinical System. Copyright © 1989 by the Regents of the University of Minnesota. All rights reserved.

insomnia, depressed mood, loss of interest, loss of sexual desire, loss of appetite, loss of weight, fatigue, helplessness, feelings of being tired, and guilt feelings.

His diagnosis was major depressive episodes.

The MMPI-2 Interpretation. The MMPI-2 was administered to the patient in January 1994. Figures 24-1, 24-2, and 24-3 contain the computerized report scores for the patient on the MMPI-2 scales; Figure 24-4 provides the computerized narrative report.

Figure 24-1 indicates that the MMPI-2 clinical scale profile is probably valid.

PROFILE VALIDITY

This client has endorsed a number of psychological problems, suggesting that he is experiencing a high degree of stress. Although the MMPI-2 clinical scale profile is probably valid, they may show some exaggeration of symptoms.

The client's item response pattern suggests that he may have answered items in the latter part of the MMPI-2 in an exaggerated manner, possibly invalidating that portion of the test. Although the standard validity and clinical scales are scored from items in the first two-thirds of the test, caution should be taken in interpreting the MMPI-2 Content Scales and supplementary scales, which include items found throughout the entire item pool.

SYMPTOMATIC PATTERNS

This report was developed using the D, Pt, and Sc scales as the prototype. A pattern of chronic psychological maladjustment characterizes individuals with this MMPI-2 clinical profile. The client is overwhelmed by anxiety, tension, and depression. He feels helpless and alone, inadequate and insecure, and he believes that life is hopeless and that nothing is working out right. He attempts to control his worries through intellectualization and unproductive self-analysis, but he has difficulty concentrating and making decisions. This is a rather chronic behavioral pattern. Individuals with this profile typically live a disorganized and pervasively unhappy existence. They may have episodes of more intense and disturbed behavior resulting from an elevated stress level.

He is functioning at a very low level of efficiency. He tends to overreact to even minor stress, and he may show rapid behavioral deterioration. He also tends to blame himself for his problems. His lifestyle is chaotic and disorganized, and he has a history of poor work and achievement. He may be preoccupied with obscure religious ideas.

PROFILE FREQUENCY

It is usually valuable in MMPI-2 clinical profile interpretation to consider the relative frequency of a given profile pattern in various settings. The client's MMPI-2 high-point clinical scale score (Pt) is found in only 4.9% of the MMPI-2 normative sample of men. Only 3.1% of the sample have Pt as the peak score at or above a T score of 65, and only 1.6% have well-defined Pt spikes. This elevated MMPI-2 profile configuration (2-7/7-2) is very rare in samples of normals, occurring in less than 1% of the MMPI-2 normative sample of men.

The relative frequency of this MMPI-2 high-point score is informative. In the NCS outpatient sample, 7.7% of the males have this MMPI-2 high-point clinical scale score (Pt). Moreover, 6.5% of the male outpatients have the Pt scale spike at or above a T score of 65, and 3.3% have well-defined Pt spike scores in that range. His elevated MMPI-2 profile configuration (2-7/7-2) is relatively common in outpatient

Figure 24-4. Minnesota Report™ Narrative for a 37-Year-Old Male Patient from the United Arab Emirates with a Diagnosed Depressive Disorder (Case 1). *Source:* The Minnesota Report™: Adult Clinical System. Copyright © 1989 by the Regents of the University of Minnesota. All rights reserved.

The F scale score (T = 79) is higher than scores on L (T = 52) and K (T = 33), indicating openness to discussing problems. Also, the client's response pattern suggests that the client may have answered items in the latter part of the MMPI-2 in an exaggerated manner, possibly invalidating that portion of the test. Caution should be taken in interpreting this part of the test.

men. It occurs in 4.8% of the men in the NCS outpatient sample. The 2-7 profile code is the second most frequent two-point code in outpatient men when both scales are at or above a T score of 65.

PROFILE STABILITY

The relative scale elevation of the highest scales in his clinical profile reflects high profile definition. If he is retested at a later date, the peak scores on this test are likely to retain their relative salience in his retest profile pattern. His high-point score on Pt is likely to show high stability over time. Short-term test-retest studies have shown a correlation of 0.89 for this high-point score. Spiro, Butcher, Levenson, Aldwin, and Bosse (1993) reported a test-retest stability index of 0.65 in a large study of normals over a five-year test-retest period.

INTERPERSONAL RELATIONS

Problematic personal relationships are also characteristic of such clients. He seems to lack basic social skills and is behaviorally withdrawn. He may relate to others ambivalently, never fully trusting or loving anyone. Many individuals with this profile never establish lasting, intimate relationships. His marital situation is likely to be unrewarding and impoverished. He seems to feel inadequate and insecure in his marriage.

He is a highly introverted and interpersonally avoidant person who feels very uneasy in close interpersonal involvements. His emotional detachment appears to be of long-standing duration. He appears to be very insecure, lacks confidence in himself in social situations, and becomes extremely anxious around other people. Individuals with this profile are typically rigid and overcontrolled, tend to worry a great deal, and may experience periods of low mood in which they withdraw almost completely from others. Personality characteristics related to social introversion tend to be stable over time. His generally reclusive behavior, introverted lifestyle, and tendency toward interpersonal avoidance may be prominent in any future test results.

His very high score on the Marital Distress Scale suggests that his marital situation is quite problematic at this time. He has reported a number of problems with his marriage that are possibly important to understanding his current psychological symptoms.

DIAGNOSTIC CONSIDERATIONS

Individuals with this profile have a severe psychological disorder and would probably be diagnosed as severely neurotic with an Anxiety Disorder or Dysthymic Disorder in a Schizoid Personality. The possibility of a more severe psychotic disorder, such as Schizophrenic Disorder, should also be considered, however.

Figure 24-4 (continued)

Figure 24-2 reports a high elevation on the D, Sc, and Si scales. Scores on the Pd and Pa scales are also elevated. The MMPI-2 profile interpretation was developed using the D, Pt, and Sc scales as the prototype. Individuals with this MMPI-2 profile are characterized by a pattern of chronic psychological maladjustment. The MMPI-2 report suggests that the client is overwhelmed by anxiety, tension, and depression; that he feels helpless and alone, inadequate and insecure; and he believes that life is hopeless and nothing is working out right.

TREATMENT CONSIDERATIONS

Individuals with this MMPI-2 clinical profile often receive psychotropic medications for their depressed mood or intense anxiety. Many individuals with this profile seek and require psychological treatment for their problems along with any medication that is given. Because many of their problems tend to be chronic, an intensive therapeutic effort might be required in order to bring about any significant change. Patients with this profile typically have many psychological and situational concerns; consequently, it is often difficult to maintain a focus in treatment.

He probably needs a great deal of emotional support at this time. His low self-esteem and feelings of inadequacy make it difficult for him to get energized toward therapeutic action. His expectation for positive change in therapy may be low. Instilling a positive, treatment-expectant attitude is important for him if treatment is to be successful.

Individuals with this profile tend to be overideational and given to unproductive rumination. They tend not to do well in unstructured, insight-oriented therapy and may actually deteriorate in functioning if they are asked to be introspective. He might respond more to supportive treatment of a directive, goal-oriented type. Individuals with this profile present a clear suicide risk; precautions should be taken.

NOTE: This MMPI-2 interpretation can serve as a useful source of hypotheses about clients. This report is based on objectively derived scale indices and scale interpretations that have been developed in diverse groups of patients. The personality descriptions, inferences, and recommendations contained herein need to be verified by other sources of clinical information because individual clients may not fully match the prototype. The information in this report should most appropriately be used by a trained, qualified test interpreter. The information contained in this report should be considered confidential.

Figure 24-4 (continued)

The general picture provided by the interpretation of the MMPI-2 clinical profile is confirmed by the case study and the psychiatric diagnosis of the client. The client's complaints of loss of interest in life, inability to enjoy life, loss of sexual desire, and feelings of being tired and hopeless are congruent with the MMPI-2 clinical profile. The psychiatric diagnosis of major depressive episodes is congruent with the elevation on the D scale.

Although it is suggested that the content scales be interpreted with caution, some of the scale elevations are congruent with the case study of the patient. Elevations on Anxiety (T = 85), Depression (T = 88), Low Self-Esteem (T = 83), Work (T = 90), and Negative Treatment Indicators (T = 51) are consistent with the client's clinical picture described in the case study.

Analysis of the MMPI-2 profile and item responses of the client are generally confirmed by the case study and the psychiatric diagnosis of the client. Therefore, this case illustrates that the MMPI-2 may be sensitive in describing behavior disorders of Arab psychiatric patients.

Case 2

This is a case of a 30-year-old male patient who was brought to the psychiatric clinic by his father three years ago for the first time. He is a Palestinian and was jobless at the time the MMPI-2 was administered. The father complained that his son had always been aggressive toward his mother. He accused her of infidelity, of having affairs with strange people. He sat alone in his room talking loudly to himself. His scholastic performance was deteriorating.

History of the Disorder

The patient's condition became apparent four years ago. At that time, his parents noticed that he isolated himself and that his behavior was inappropriate. He refused to go to school several times without any apparent reason. He expressed several health complaints and was taken several times to the clinic as a result. His behavior increasingly deteriorated, and he was brought to the psychiatric clinic.

When the patient was seen for the first time the following symptoms were reported by the psychiatrist: delusions of persecution, nonverbal auditory hallucinations, insomnia, faulty emotions with manifest incongruity of affect, and avoidance of eye contact.

Diagnosis and Treatment

The provisional diagnosis for this patient was schizophrenia. Treatment was prescribed, and the patient came to the clinic regularly. He was reported to be improving after he found a job in a drug factory. He did well for a few months, but later he stopped coming to the clinic.

One year later he was brought to the clinic by his father. The father reported that the patient left his job to resume his studies but did not go to school and began to isolate himself again. When he was seen by the psychiatrist, all the previous symptoms were present and more intense. Moreover, he reported that he was hearing voices. He was treated with phenothiazine medication. After a few days, his father returned to the clinic complaining that he was not taking his medicine.

A few months later, the patient himself came to the clinic complaining of inability to sleep and having strange ideas. Long-acting phenothiazine injections were prescribed every two weeks. The patient is currently under treatment, and his condition is fluctuating.

His parents reported that before his illness he had few friends. He was careless about how he looked and dressed. He was not willing to take much responsibility. His school achievement had been above average, but he left school in the twelfth grade after repeated failures. Failure in that grade is a stressful event for Arab

480   Abdalla M. Soliman

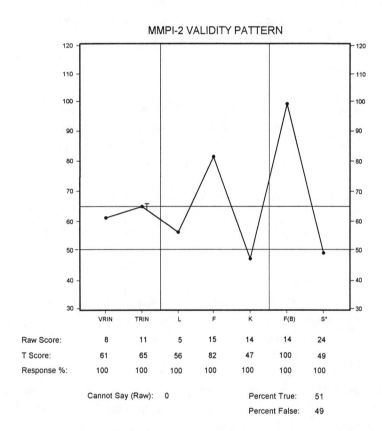

Raw Score:	8	11	5	15	14	14	24
T Score:	61	65	56	82	47	100	49
Response %:	100	100	100	100	100	100	100

Cannot Say (Raw):   0   Percent True: 51
                                 Percent False: 49

*Experimental

Figure 24-5. Minnesota Report™ MMPI-2 Validity Scale Profile of a 30-Year-Old Palestinian Man from the United Arab Emirates with a Diagnosed Schizophrenic Disorder (Case 2). *Source:* The Minnesota Report™: Adult Clinical System. Copyright © 1989 by the Regents of the University of Minnesota. All rights reserved.

students, since it determines whether students will get a grade point average that will enable them to be admitted to a university. Clinical examination revealed no physical illness. No history of mental illness or other related disorders were found in the family.

The patient's illness was diagnosed as schizophrenia.

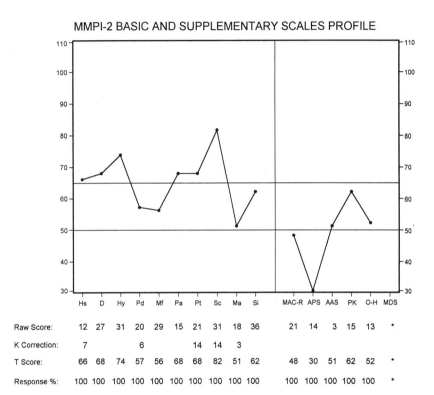

MMPI-2 BASIC AND SUPPLEMENTARY SCALES PROFILE

	Hs	D	Hy	Pd	Mf	Pa	Pt	Sc	Ma	Si		MAC-R	APS	AAS	PK	O-H	MDS
Raw Score:	12	27	31	20	29	15	21	31	18	36		21	14	3	15	13	*
K Correction:	7		6				14	14	3								
T Score:	66	68	74	57	56	68	68	82	51	62		48	30	51	62	52	*
Response %:	100	100	100	100	100	100	100	100	100	100		100	100	100	100	100	*

Welsh Code (new):   8"3'2671+0-459/ F'''+-L/K:

Welsh Code (old):   8*2"37 516'409- F'''-LK/?:

Profile Elevation: 66.80

*MDS scores are reported only for clients who indicate that they are married or separated.
Figure 24-6. Minnesota Report™ MMPI-2 Standard Scale Profile of a 30-Year-Old Palestinian Man from the United Arab Emirates with a Diagnosed Schizophrenic Disorder (Case 2). *Source:* The Minnesota Report™: Adult Clinical System. Copyright © 1989 by the Regents of the University of Minnesota. All rights reserved.

The MMPI-2 Interpretation. The MMPI-2 was administered to the patient in January 1994. Figures 24-5, 24-6, and 24-7 provide computerized report scores for the patient on the MMPI-2 scales; Figure 24-8 presents the computerized narrative report.

The validity pattern suggests that the MMPI-2 profile should be interpreted

482   Abdalla M. Soliman

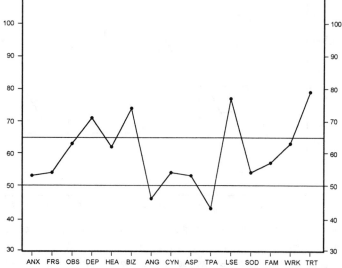

Figure 24-7. Minnesota Report™ MMPI-2 Content Scale Profile of a 30-Year-Old Palestinian Man from the United Arab Emirates with a Diagnosed Schizophrenic Disorder (Case 2). *Source:* The Minnesota Report™: Adult Clinical System. Copyright © 1989 by the Regents of the University of Minnesota. All rights reserved.

with caution. There is some possibility that scores on the clinical scales present an exaggerated picture of the client's present situation and problems. It should be noted that the F scale score (T = 82) indicates that the standard scales are probably interpretable, but that interpretation of the content scales be deferred. Nevertheless, as Butcher and Williams (1992) pointed out, high F elevations are sometimes obtained in inpatient settings and reflect extreme psychopathology. VRIN scores of less than 79 can be used to rule out the probability of inconsistent responding. For the present client, a VRIN T score of 61 suggests that his extreme F elevation

PROFILE VALIDITY

This MMPI-2 profile should be interpreted with caution. There is some possibility that the clinical report is an exaggerated picture of the client's present situation and problems. He is presenting an unusual number of psychological symptoms. This response set could result from poor reading ability, confusion, disorientation, stress, or a need to seek a great deal of attention for his problems.

His test-taking attitudes should be evaluated for the possibility that he has produced an invalid profile. He may be showing a lack of cooperation with the testing or he may be malingering by attempting to present a false claim of mental illness. Determining the sources of his confusion, whether conscious distortion or personality deterioration, is important because immediate attention may be required. Clinical patients with this validity profile are often confused and distractible and have memory problems. Evidence of delusions and thought disorder may be present. He may be exhibiting a high degree of distress and personality deterioration.

The client's responses to items in the latter portion of the MMPI-2 were somewhat exaggerated in comparison to his responses to earlier items. There is some possibility that he became more careless in responding to these later items, thereby raising questions about that portion of the test. Although the standard validity and clinical scales are scored from items in the first two-thirds of the test, caution should be taken in interpreting the MMPI-2 Content Scales and supplementary scales, which include items found throughout the entire item pool.

SYMPTOMATIC PATTERNS

This report was developed using the Hy and Sc scales as the prototype. A pattern of chronic psychological maladjustment characterizes individuals with this MMPI-2 clinical profile. The client is presenting with a somewhat mixed pattern of complaints. His symptomatic pattern may be unusual, and he may seem quite eccentric. He may cling strongly to delusional or other transcendental beliefs. Apparently rather tense and nervous, the client may have some unusual somatic complaints that he rigidly maintains even when they are challenged. He may also complain of confusion and poor memory. His adjustment is apathetic, immature, and marginal. He is likely to be experiencing delusions, hallucinations, or other symptoms of a thought disorder.

PROFILE FREQUENCY

Profile interpretation can be greatly facilitated by examining the relative frequency of clinical scale patterns in various settings. The client's high-point clinical scale score (Sc) is the least frequent MMPI-2 peak score in the MMPI-2 normative sample of men, occurring in only 4.7% of the cases. Only 2.6% of the sample have Sc as the peak score at or above a T score of 65, and less than 1% have well-defined Sc spikes. This elevated MMPI-2 profile configuration (3-8/8-3) is very rare in samples of normals, occurring in less than 1% of the MMPI-2 normative sample of men.

Figure 24-8. Minnesota Report™ Narrative for a 30-Year-Old Palestinian Man from the United Arab Emirates with a Diagnosed Schizophrenic Disorder (Case 2). *Source:* The Minnesota Report™: Adult Clinical System. Copyright © 1989 by the Regents of the University of Minnesota. All rights reserved.

is probably related to psychopathology rather than to inconsistent responding and that the clinical scales may be interpreted with some degree of confidence.

Figure 24-6 reports the client's profile for the clinical and supplementary scales, with elevations on Hy (T = 74) and Sc (T = 82). Individuals with this MMPI-2 clinical profile are characterized by a pattern of chronic psychological maladjustment.

In the NCS outpatient sample, 5.6% of the males have this high-point clinical scale score (Sc). Moreover, 4.8% of the male outpatients have the Sc scale spike at or above a T score of 65, and 2.4% have well-defined Sc scores in that range. This elevated MMPI-2 profile configuration (3-8/8-3) occurs in 0.6% of the men in the NCS outpatient sample.

PROFILE STABILITY

The relative scale elevation of the highest scales in his clinical profile reflects high profile definition. If he is retested at a later date, the peak scores on this test are likely to retain their relative salience in his retest profile pattern. His high-point score on Sc is likely to show considerable stability over time. Short-term test-retest studies have shown a correlation of 0.87 for this high-point score. Spiro, Butcher, Levenson, Aldwin, and Bosse (1993) reported a test-retest stability index of 0.61 in a large study of normals over a five-year test-retest period.

INTERPERSONAL RELATIONS

His peculiar structure of beliefs is likely to interfere with his social relationships because he tends to withdraw from people and feels distant and alienated from them. He appears to be rigid in interpersonal relationships and may be functioning at a reduced level of social effectiveness. Behavioral deterioration and lowered efficiency seem to characterize his present functioning.

He is somewhat shy, with some social concerns and inhibitions. He is a bit hypersensitive about what others think of him and is occasionally concerned about his relationships with others. He appears to be somewhat inhibited in personal relationships and social situations, and he may have some difficulty expressing his feelings toward others.

DIAGNOSTIC CONSIDERATIONS

The behaviors reflected in this profile may present some diagnostic problems. The client exhibits features of both a severe neurotic disorder (such as a Somatoform Disorder) and a psychotic process (such as Schizophrenia). Information from sources other than the MMPI-2 should be taken into account. He is likely to have a schizoid adjustment and will probably be diagnosed as having an Axis II Personality Disorder of a Schizoid or Schizotypal form.

TREATMENT CONSIDERATIONS

Individuals with this MMPI-2 clinical profile may be experiencing much tension and behavioral deterioration. Their symptomatic behavior, because it has an odd quality, might prove difficult for a therapist to understand clearly. Patients with this pattern often receive psychotropic medication for

Figure 24-8 (continued)

Analysis of the client's profile suggests some behavior characteristics that are confirmed by the case study and the psychiatric diagnosis. The Minnesota Report (see Figure 24-8) proposes that the client "may cling strongly to delusional or other transcendental beliefs." This is supported by the client's accusation of his mother having affairs with strange people, and by his talking to himself loudly when alone. The report also states that the client may have some unusual somatic com-

symptom relief. They tend not to respond well to insight-oriented psychotherapy because they resist psychological interpretation and rigidly adhere to unusual thoughts or bizarre beliefs about their health.

Individuals with this profile also find it difficult to relate to others, further reducing the effectiveness of relationship-oriented psychotherapy. Some patients with this profile respond to a directive, supportive therapeutic approach.

NOTE: This MMPI-2 interpretation can serve as a useful source of hypotheses about clients. This report is based on objectively derived scale indices and scale interpretations that have been developed in diverse groups of patients. The personality descriptions, inferences, and recommendations contained herein need to be verified by other sources of clinical information because individual clients may not fully match the prototype. The information in this report should most appropriately be used by a trained, qualified test interpreter. The information contained in this report should be considered confidential.

Figure 24-8 (continued)

plaints that he rigidly maintains even when they are challenged. This is confirmed by the case study reporting that the client expressed several health complaints.

Figure 24-7 reports the MMPI-2 content scales profile. The scale elevations are DEP (T = 71), indicating the endorsement of many mood problems; BIZ (T = 74), indicating the endorsement of many unusual thinking problems; LSE (T = 77), indicating endorsement of low self-esteem problems; and TRT (T = 79), indicating extensive endorsement of negative attitudes toward mental health treatment.

We conclude that the MMPI-2 interpretation for this client is congruent with the information provided by the psychiatric diagnosis and the case study.

The two cases suggest that the present MMPI-2 Arabic translation may have validity in assessing the psychological problems of Arabs. Further testing of this hypothesis will require a research program using representative samples from different Arab countries and careful methodology.

References

American Educational Research Association, American Psychological Association, and National Council on Measurement in Education. (1985). *Standards for educational and psychological testing.* Washington, DC: American Psychological Association.
Butcher, J. N. (1993). *User's guide for the MMPI-2 Minnesota Report: Adult Clinical System.* Minneapolis: National Computer Systems.
Butcher, J. N., Graham, J. R., Williams, C. L., & Ben-Porath, Y. S. (1990). *Development and use of the MMPI-2 content scales.* Minneapolis: University of Minnesota Press.
Butcher, J. N., & Williams, C. L. (1992). *Essentials of MMPI-2 and MMPI-A interpretation.* Minneapolis: University of Minnesota Press.

Hana, A. M., Ismail, M. F., & Meleika, L. K. (1990). *The Multiphasic Personality Inventory (Adapted from the Minnesota Multiphasic Personality Inventory by S. R. Hathaway and J. C. McKinley)*. [Arabic]. Cairo: Author.

Meleika, L. K. (1960). *The Schizophrenia scale of the Multiphasic Personality Inventory.* [Arabic]. Cairo: Al-Nahda Al-Misriah.

Meleika, L. K. (1963). Sex differences in personality traits [Arabic]. *Annals of the Faculty of Arts, Ain Shams University, 8,* 255–286.

Meleika, L. K. (1966a). The Depression scale of the Multiphasic Personality Inventory [Arabic]. Cairo: Al-Nahda Al-Misriah.

Meleika, L. K. (1966b). The Psychopathic Deviate scale of the Multiphasic Personality Inventory [Arabic]. Cairo: Al-Nahda Al-Misriah.

Meleika, L. K. (1967). The Hysteria scale of the Multiphasic Personality Inventory [Arabic]. Cairo: Al-Nahda Al-Misriah.

Meleika, L. K. (1990). *The Multiphasic Personality Inventory: Test Manual* [Arabic]. Cairo: Author.

Meleika, L. K., Ismail, M. E., &, Hana, A. M. (1959). *The personality and its measurement* [Arabic]. Cairo: Al-Nahda Al-Misriah.

Chapter 25

The MMPI-2: Translation and First Steps in Its Adaptation into Hebrew

Moshe Almagor and Baruch Nevo

Psychopathology and its assessment have been of great interest to researchers over the past century. One of the major questions has been whether psychopathology is universal or needs a unique classification and specific definition for each country or culture (Kramer, 1961; Zubin, 1969). Cultures are different in terms of language, norms, social structures and roles, and belief systems, all of which are likely to influence the understanding, clinical picture, and probably the diagnosis and prevalence of various disorders. Phillips and Draguns (1971) concluded that diagnostic criteria tend to be universal in nature. Kaplan and Sadock (1991) reviewed cross-cultural studies and reached the conclusion that certain symptoms such as anxiety, mania, depression, somatization, paranoia, and thought disturbance are universal. However, Butcher and Pancheri (1976) pointed out that diagnostic criteria are not applied and standardized in each country or even within the same country in the same way, possibly contributing to differences in prevalence of different pathologies.

The MMPI is the most widely used clinical assessment instrument in the United States and has been translated into more than 115 languages, making it the most used questionnaire in the world (Keller, Butcher, & Slutske, 1990). The MMPI was translated into Hebrew 20 years ago by Butcher and Gur (1974) and came to be widely used for clinical assessment in Israel. The Hebrew version of the MMPI is a 399-item questionnaire containing only the items that are included in the basic clinical scales.

The development and restandardization project of the MMPI-2 (Butcher, Dahlstrom, Graham, Tellegen, & Kaemmer, 1989) stimulated and encouraged

---

The authors wish to thank Professor Yossef S. Ben-Porath for his help in coordinating this project and in reviewing the manuscript.

the re-examination of the adequacy of the existing Hebrew MMPI. The publication of the MMPI-2 and increasing dissatisfaction with the Hebrew translation of some of the original MMPI items led to a decision that a new translation, as well as a new standardization project to determine the norms for the Israeli population, was needed.

To carry out these tasks, four psychologists were appointed to form a committee charged with the responsibility of supervising the translation and the standardization projects. The committee consisted of two clinical psychologists and two psychometricians, all with previous experience in translation and validation of psychological tests and measures.

Translation of the MMPI-2

Since there was a translation of the MMPI (Butcher & Gur, 1974), the committee had to decide whether to translate all the MMPI-2 items or to translate only the new and revised items. Because the Hebrew translation of the MMPI contained only 399 items, and given the concerns about the translation, the committee decided to translate the entire MMPI-2. The translation process consisted of the following steps:

Step 1. Two bilingual psychologists were given the English version and were asked to translate the items into Hebrew independently. Once this step was completed, another pair of bilingual psychologists was asked to back-translate the items into English. The original and the English back-translated item sets were then compared. Sixty-four items of the 567 were discrepant and required retranslation. These items appear in Table 25-1.

Step 2. The 64 discrepant items were subjected to the same procedure exercised in step 1, employing different psychologists. Only three discrepant items remained following this step (52, "I have not lived the right kind of life"; 62, "I have often wished I were a girl (or if you are a girl) I have never been sorry that I am a girl"; and 149, "The top of my head sometimes feels tender"). These items were translated not literally but according to their meaning in Hebrew, since there is no linguistic equivalent in Hebrew for "top of my head," and the Hebrew language differentiates between males and females so that a literal translation of item 62 would not have retained its original meaning.

Step 3. The accuracy of the translation does not guarantee that the translated items will be adequate both stylistically or grammatically. To ensure stylistic and grammatical acceptability, the items were given to a professional Hebrew-English editor for review. The editor made only slight editorial changes in item phrasing that did not require retranslation.

Step 4. Following this editing procedure, the items were again compared with the Hebrew translation and the original English to determine whether the editing

Table 25-1. Discrepant Items Found in Step 1

Item	No.	No.	No.
10	149	305	423
16	158	317	438
22	178	322	439
28	188	328	444
31	190	334	448
39	206	341	458
40	208	344	461
50	215	356	470
51	229	357	471
52	254	371	476
91	263	372	484
93	273	388	501
97	274	389	517
114	280	393	525
116	286	396	536
121	303	416	537

had changed the meaning. Two bilingual psychologists participated in this step, working independently. No items needed to be retranslated.

Step 5. The translated items were administered to a group of 30 subjects, 20 of whom were undergraduate students in psychology and 10 of whom were nonstudents. The subjects were asked to indicate whether the items were clear and easily understood. A stringent criterion was applied requiring that the item be reevaluated if it received a difficult item rating by one subject. No items were checked by the subjects as inappropriate.

Additional Translation Check: Bilingual Subjects

A further examination of the adequacy of the translation involved a study of bilingual subjects. It was assumed that the existence of between-administration differences for the Hebrew version and English original might cast doubt on the applicability of the MMPI-2 in a cross-cultural setting. A group of 52 students at the University of Haifa, consisting of 25 bilingual subjects with a mean age of 22.08 and a standard deviation of 1.41, and 27 native Israeli subjects whose mean age is 24.3 with a standard deviation of 5.41, took part in this study for a fee. All

Table 25-2. Means, Standard Deviations, and Correlations between the Two Administrations

	Bilingual					Control				
	First		Second			First		Second		
Scale	Mean	SD	Mean	SD	r	Mean	SD	Mean	SD	r
?	2.6	4.9	2.0	3.6		1.8	3.6	2.6	5.2	
L	4.1	2.3	4.1	2.3	.72	3.9	2.2	4.0	2.2	.72
F	5.9	4.2	5.4	4.4	.80	5.3	3.0	5.1	3.0	.64
K	16.1	4.5	16.5	4.8	.86	15.6	4.3	16.3	4.7	.86
F_B	2.2	3.1	2.4	3.8	.77	1.9	2.6	1.3	2.2	.81
VRIN	5.7	3.0	5.0	2.4	.42	5.6	2.4	4.4	3.0	.49
TRIN	8.2	1.2	8.5	1.4	.31	8.3	1.4	8.3	1.0	.31
Hs	9.2	3.4	7.8	3.4	.81	6.7	3.7	6.0	3.6	.65
D	23.0	5.1	22.0	6.4	.80	20.4	5.3	20.6	6.0	.91
Hy	22.3	4.0	22.2	3.9	.67	21.9	5.3	21.7	4.6	.61
Pd	17.8	5.6	22.2	3.9	.89	16.9	4.2	16.4	4.7	.60
Mf	35.0	4.3	35.0	4.7	.77	32.3	4.5	32.1	5.1	.80
Pa	11.6	3.5	10.9	2.5	.74	11.4	3.8	10.2	3.8	.87
Pt	15.7	8.2	14.6	7.8	.90	13.5	7.3	13.3	8.8	.91
Sc	15.4	9.3	14.8	9.4	.92	14.0	8.5	12.3	7.6	.79
Ma	18.0	3.7	18.4	4.7	.88	18.3	4.1	18.4	4.4	.63
Si	30.7	8.8	30.0	8.4	.90	29.1	8.2	27.6	9.7	.91
ANX	7.9	4.8	8.0	5.2	.89	6.3	4.7	6.1	5.4	.88
FRS	5.3	3.4	4.8	3.2	.73	4.2	3.4	4.0	3.4	.88
OBS	5.2	3.0	5.5	3.0	.73	4.9	3.2	5.4	3.6	.75
DEP	7.4	5.3	7.2	5.3	.92	6.9	5.8	6.1	6.1	.91
HEA	8.4	3.7	6.2	3.7	.75	5.6	3.6	4.5	3.4	.69
BIZ	4.6	3.3	3.2	3.1	.82	3.1	2.8	2.6	2.7	.68
ANG	5.9	3.6	6.1	3.7	.88	6.7	3.4	6.1	3.7	.76
CYN	10.8	5.1	10.1	5.7	.89	9.4	4.4	9.4	5.1	.71
ASP	8.9	3.9	8.4	4.7	.85	7.7	3.2	8.3	4.1	.78
TPA	9.0	3.2	9.4	3.1	.74	9.1	3.2	8.0	3.8	.69
LSE	5.7	3.3	5.8	3.4	.83	6.0	4.1	5.6	4.6	.86
SOD	7.9	5.4	7.8	5.4	.89	7.4	4.7	6.7	5.2	.92
FAM	6.5	4.5	6.3	4.9	.89	5.6	4.0	5.4	4.0	.82
WRK	10.0	4.5	10.3	5.2	.84	9.1	7.0	9.3	6.3	.88
TRT	6.4	4.3	5.2	5.2	.93	5.6	3.5	5.6	3.6	.81

the bilingual subjects spent at least five years in the United States as children and are self-reportedly fluent in both English and Hebrew. The Hebrew-Hebrew subjects were administered the Hebrew MMPI-2 twice with a two-week interval between administrations. The bilingual group was administered the Hebrew and the English MMPI-2 in a balanced order so that half of the subjects received the Hebrew version first while the other half received the English version first. The order was reversed for the second administration, two weeks later. A within-subject design was employed in analyzing the differences between the means of the basic

MMPI-2

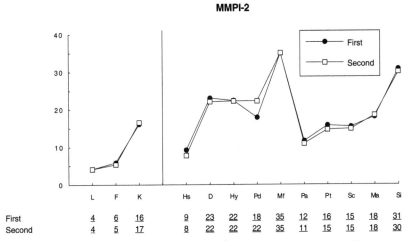

	L	F	K		Hs	D	Hy	Pd	Mf	Pa	Pt	Sc	Ma	Si
First	4	6	16		9	23	22	18	35	12	16	15	18	31
Second	4	5	17		8	22	22	22	35	11	15	15	18	30

Figure 25-1. MMPI-2 Basic Scale Scores of Two Administrations to Native and Bilingual Male Subjects (N = 26)

MMPI-2

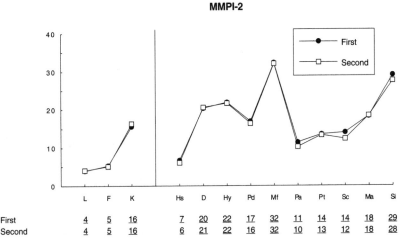

	L	F	K		Hs	D	Hy	Pd	Mf	Pa	Pt	Sc	Ma	Si
First	4	5	16		7	20	22	17	32	11	14	14	18	29
Second	4	5	16		6	21	22	16	32	10	13	12	18	28

Figure 25-2. MMPI-2 Basic Scale Scores of Two Administrations to Native and Bilingual Female Subjects (N = 27)

clinical scales and those of the content scales. Since we were interested in detecting any differences, we did not correct the alpha value for multiple comparisons. The results of the within-subject t-test analyses indicated that, for the clinical scale and content scale raw scores, there were no significant differences between the two administrations of the two groups. The means and standard deviations are presented in Table 25-2, while the graphic display of these values is presented in Figures 25-1 and 25-2. The data in Figures 25-3 and 25-4 clearly indicate the congruence be-

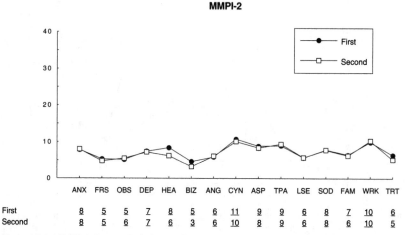

First   8   5   5   7   8   5   6   11   9   9   6   8   7   10   6
Second   8   5   6   7   6   3   6   10   8   9   6   8   6   10   5

Figure 25-3. MMPI-2 Content Scale Scores of Two Administrations to Native and Bilingual Male Subjects (N = 26)

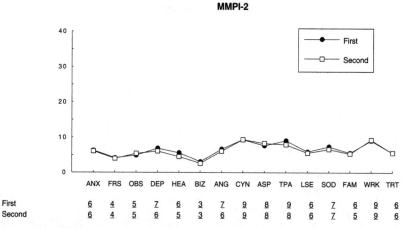

First   6   4   5   7   6   3   7   9   8   9   6   7   6   9   6
Second   6   4   5   6   5   3   6   9   8   8   6   7   5   9   6

Figure 25-4. MMPI-2 Content Scale Scores of Two Administrations to Native and Bilingual Female Subjects (N = 27)

tween the administrations. Thus, one may conclude that the Hebrew and English versions are alike.

To sum up to this point, we may conclude that the Hebrew translation of the MMPI-2 appears adequate and comparable to the English version.

Initial Psychometric Data

The next stage in the development of the Hebrew translation of the MMPI-2 was to ascertain the psychometric adequacy of the questionnaire. We included initial

Table 25-3. One-Week Test-Retest Correlations for 94 Subjects

	Administration				
	First		Second		
Scales	Mean	SD	Mean	SD	r
L	4.4	2.1	4.2	1.9	.66
F	5.9	3.9	4.7	3.5	.69
K	16.5	4.0	17.2	4.3	.76
Hs	9.0	4.5	7.4	4.5	.85
D	23.0	4.3	20.7	4.6	.65
Hy	24.5	5.1	22.4	5.0	.73
Pd	18.7	4.6	17.2	4.2	.77
Mf	34.7	3.7	33.7	4.0	.78
Pa	12.2	3.2	11.3	4.2	.50
Pt	15.1	7.2	12.7	7.8	.87
Sc	15.0	8.8	12.9	8.6	.86
Ma	18.8	3.8	18.7	4.7	.74
Si	29.0	9.0	28.3	8.2	.85
ANX	7.5	4.5	5.9	4.5	.85
FRS	4.9	3.1	4.2	3.2	.69
OBS	5.6	3.3	5.1	3.7	.84
DEP	7.6	5.2	6.4	5.2	.85
HEA	7.9	4.9	6.6	4.8	.84
BIZ	3.9	3.1	2.8	2.8	.75
ANG	6.2	3.0	5.8	3.2	.83
CYN	8.8	4.0	8.9	4.7	.79
ASP	7.9	3.4	8.1	3.8	.75
TPA	8.1	3.1	7.6	3.2	.70
LSE	6.6	3.8	5.6	3.9	.83
SOD	6.9	4.3	6.7	4.1	.89
FAM	6.0	3.8	5.3	3.6	.79
WRK	10.0	5.4	8.7	5.0	.85
TRT	6.0	4.1	5.5	3.9	.76
F_B	1.9	2.5	1.7	2.6	.55
VRIN	6.3	2.6	5.5	2.8	.43
TRIN	7.8	1.4	8.1	1.4	.32

data regarding test-retest correlations for a one-week period for Israeli college students and compared them to similar data obtained for American college students (Butcher, Graham, Dahlstrom, & Bowman, 1990). The Hebrew MMPI-2 (HMMPI-2) was administered to a group of 98 undergraduate students. Exclusion criteria based on validity scale scores (F > 100, F_B > 100, TRIN > 100, and VRIN > 80) were used to remove extremely invalid profiles. Four subjects were thus eliminated. The sample consisted of 74 women and 20 men whose mean ages were 21.75 (SD = 2.64) and 23.89 (SD = 1.91), respectively. The MMPI-2 scale scores for the 94 subjects are presented in Table 25-3.

Table 25-4. Means, Standard Deviations, and Test-Retest Correlations of the Basic Scales for American College Men and Women and Israeli College Women

	U S [a]						Israel [b]		
	Men			Women			Women		
Scale	Mean	SD	r	Mean	SD	r	Mean	SD	r
L	3.3	2.2	.77	2.8	1.9	.73	4.5	1.6	.60
F	5.3	3.9	.67	4.9	3.6	.79	5.2	3.4	.64
K	14.4	4.7	.62	13.8	4.6	.75	16.7	3.9	.76
Hs	5.1	4.0	.80	6.9	4.5	.88	8.4	4.4	.84
D	17.0	4.7	.85	19.6	5.0	.84	21.9	3.8	.61
Hy	20.4	4.6	.68	22.2	4.8	.80	23.6	4.8	.75
Pd	17.8	4.8	.82	17.8	5.0	.84	17.7	4.0	.72
Mf	25.4	5.0	.79	34.9	4.2	.84	34.9	3.3	.71
Pa	10.9	3.3	.76	11.1	3.3	.81	11.4	3.3	.67
Pt	14.1	7.7	.78	16.5	7.7	.85	13.8	7.1	.87
Sc	15.0	9.1	.79	15.5	8.7	.88	13.2	8.0	.84
Ma	20.4	4.5	.78	18.8	4.5	.79	18.6	3.4	.76
Si	23.7	8.6	.87	26.7	8.7	.91	28.7	8.0	.86

[a] Data adapted from Butcher et al. (1990).
[b] Data for Israeli subjects are the mean scores obtained in the two administrations over a one-week period.

Table 25-3 reflects an appropriate level of test-retest correlations, except for Pa, which demonstrated a relatively lower test-retest correlation. The reason for this lower correlation may be that the variance of the within-subject differences between administrations was very low. A t-test analysis for paired comparisons indicated that this hypothesis was indeed correct. The grand mean of the absolute within-subject differences between administrations was 2.3. It should be noted that a low test-retest correlation for Pa was also found in the U.S. normative data (Butcher et al., 1990).

The findings presented in Table 25-3 were compared with the data provided by Butcher et al. (1990) with respect to college students (Tables 25-4). This comparison indicates that the mean scale scores of the American and Israeli groups are very similar to each other for the respective scales. However, the means for the American college students tend to be somewhat lower than those reported for the Israeli students. Since our sample consisted mainly of women (74 of the 94 subjects were women), we decided to illustrate the differences between the

MMPI-2

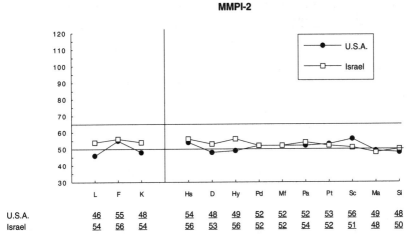

	L	F	K		Hs	D	Hy	Pd	Mf	Pa	Pt	Sc	Ma	Si
U.S.A.	46	55	48		54	48	49	52	52	52	53	56	49	48
Israel	54	56	54		56	53	56	52	52	54	52	51	48	50

Figure 25-5. Comparison of U.S. and Israeli Women on the MMPI-2 Basic Scales Based on U.S. Norms

American and Israeli women in Figure 25-3. Table 25-3 indicates that women's basic scale means follow the same pattern as indicated above. It appears that Israeli college women's test-retest correlations are generally similar to their American counterparts except for scales L, D, and Pa, which are lower than the correlations for American college women. Figure 25-3 shows that the main discrepancy between the Israeli and U.S. women is found with respect to the validity scales. Both L and K are higher in the Israeli sample. Scale Hs is also higher for Israeli women than for their U.S. counterparts.

These initial findings concerning the adequacy of the translation and the preliminary psychometric data are encouraging when the appropriateness of the English original and the Hebrew MMPI-2 version are considered. Item-content compatibility is important for both research and clinical purposes. However, clinical use of the questionnaire requires an examination of the adequacy of its norms (Butcher & Pancheri, 1976).

Standardization Project

A representative randomized sample of 500 subjects was to be drawn from the general Hebrew-speaking population of Israel. The sampling procedure was designed to match the Israeli census with respect to age, sex, education, and socioeconomic status. The latter is based on place of residence, which in Israel is highly related to socioeconomic status. The data presented here are based on a partial sample of valid profiles of 118 men and 156 women. Profiles were eliminated on the basis of the following criteria: 20 or more unanswered items; F raw score of 20 or greater; or an F_B raw score of 20 or more. These criteria are similar to those used

Table 25-5. Means of Raw and T Scores, and Standard Deviations for 118 Men and 156 Women of the Standardization Sample

Scale	Men			Women		
	Raw Scores	SD	T Scores	Raw Scores	SD	T Scores
?	3.2	4.4		3.4	4.8	
L	5.9	2.5	60	5.2	2.2	58
F	7.5	4.5	59	7.4	4.4	62
K	16.4	4.5	52	15.1	3.9	50
Hs	8.2	4.2	60	10.1	4.4	60
D	21.0	4.7	56	23.3	5.0	56
Hy	21.8	4.6	52	23.3	4.6	52
Pd	17.3	4.3	52	18.8	5.2	56
Mf	24.9	4.1	48	33.5	4.5	56
Pa	10.7	3.3	53	12.0	3.6	56
Pt	11.3	6.8	53	14.9	7.2	54
Sc	13.9	8.2	57	16.3	8.5	58
Ma	18.2	4.4	54	18.4	4.4	56
Si	28.5	7.0	53	30.6	7.6	53
ANX	5.6	3.5	50	7.6	4.3	52
FRS	4.0	3.1	51	7.3	3.8	52
OBS	4.7	3.1	49	5.8	3.2	50
DEP	6.8	5.2	55	9.0	5.9	56
HEA	7.5	4.2	56	9.0	4.5	56
BIZ	4.0	3.3	57	4.7	3.2	59
ANG	5.2	2.9	49	6.5	2.8	52
CYN	11.8	4.9	54	11.6	4.5	55
ASP	9.7	3.5	54	9.0	3.5	57
TPA	8.4	3.5	50	9.2	3.4	55
LSE	6.2	3.9	55	7.3	4.2	55
SOD	7.9	3.5	50	7.9	3.8	51
FAM	5.9	4.1	52	7.4	3.8	53
WRK	8.2	4.4	52	10.3	4.9	53
TRT	7.0	4.4	56	8.3	4.4	58
F_B	3.1	4.1	55	3.5	3.9	54
VRIN	7.3	3.6	57	7.2	2.8	58
TRIN	8.8	1.9	50	8.6	1.8	50

in the American standardization study (Butcher et al., 1989). For the purpose of illustration we converted the raw scores into T scores based on the American norms (Butcher et al., 1989), and these are presented, respectively, in Figures 25-4a, 25-4b, 25-5a, and 25-5b for the basic clinical and content scales.

An examination of Figures 25-6 and 25-7 reveals that, in general, there is good agreement between the Israeli scores and the American norms. A good agreement

MMPI-2

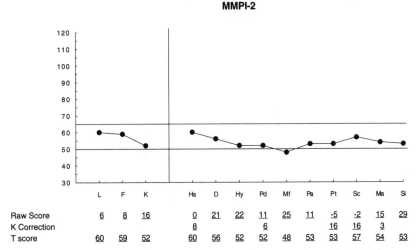

	L	F	K	Hs	D	Hy	Pd	Mf	Pa	Pt	Sc	Ma	Si
Raw Score	6	8	16	0	21	22	11	25	11	-5	-2	15	29
K Correction				8			6			16	16	3	
T score	60	59	52	60	56	52	52	48	53	53	57	54	53

Figure 25-6. MMPI-2 Basic Scale Scores of the Male Standardization Sample Based on U.S. Norms

MMPI-2

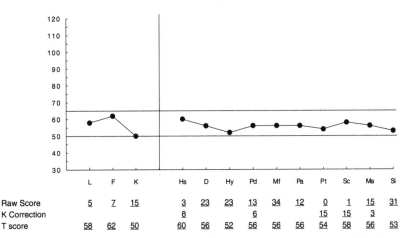

	L	F	K	Hs	D	Hy	Pd	Mf	Pa	Pt	Sc	Ma	Si
Raw Score	5	7	15	3	23	23	13	34	12	0	1	15	31
K Correction				8			6			15	15	3	
T score	58	62	50	60	56	52	56	56	56	54	58	56	53

Figure 25-7. MMPI-2 Basic Scale Scores of the Female Standardization Sample Based on U.S. Norms

is defined as a difference of five T scores or less. However, scales L, F, and Hs for both men and women deviate from this criterion. It should be noted that the findings concerning the comparison between Israeli and U.S. women college students indicates a similar pattern. These differences suggest the need for further examination of the adequacy of using the American norms with the Israeli population. At this point in the project, it seems imprudent to draw any conclusions based on this partial sample. We shall await completion of data collection.

MMPI-2

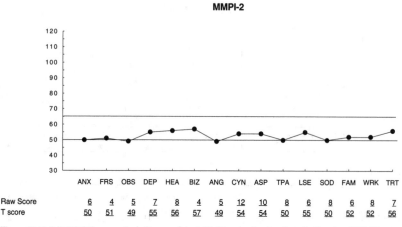

		ANX	FRS	OBS	DEP	HEA	BIZ	ANG	CYN	ASP	TPA	LSE	SOD	FAM	WRK	TRT
Raw Score		6	4	5	7	8	4	5	12	10	8	6	8	6	8	7
T score		50	51	49	55	56	57	49	54	54	50	55	50	52	52	56

Figure 25-8. MMPI-2 Content Scale Scores of the Male Standardization Sample Based on U.S. Norms

MMPI-2

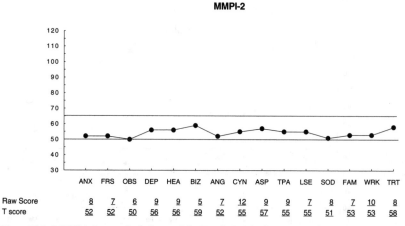

		ANX	FRS	OBS	DEP	HEA	BIZ	ANG	CYN	ASP	TPA	LSE	SOD	FAM	WRK	TRT
Raw Score		8	7	6	9	9	5	7	12	9	9	7	8	7	10	8
T score		52	52	50	56	56	59	52	55	57	55	55	51	53	53	58

Figure 25-9. MMPI-2 Content Scale Scores of the Female Standardization Sample Based on U.S. Norms

Special Populations

Results from various research projects provide the opportunity to evaluate profiles of selected groups. The first group consists of self-referred applicants to counseling services of the Technion-Institute of Technology. Data of 117 male students with a mean age of 25 and a standard deviation of 3.5 and 56 women students with a mean age of 24 and a standard deviation of 3.1 were collected. Figures 25-6 and 25-7 present the T scores (based on American norms) for the basic clinical and content scales, respectively. Table 25-6 shows the mean raw and T scores for the various scales.

Figures 25-10, 25-11, 25-12, and 25-13 have a similar code-type, 2-7-8, while

MMPI-2

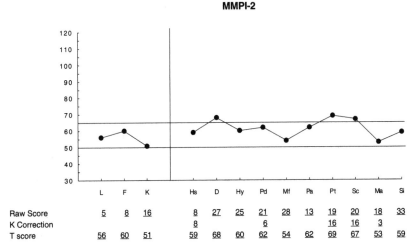

Figure 25-10. MMPI-2 Basic Scale T Scores for Male Technion Students Based on U.S. Norms

MMPI-2

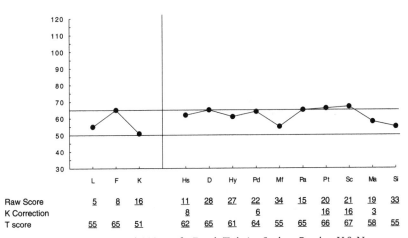

Figure 25-11. MMPI-2 Basic Scale T Scores for Female Technion Students Based on U.S. Norms

for the women there is an additional elevation on 6. These scale configurations suggest that those who turn to counseling services tend to be generally distressed, depressed, anxious, and nervous, with a self-reported lack of self-esteem. Similar code-types were found for chronic psychiatric patients (Lachar, 1974), persons suffering from post-traumatic stress disorder (e.g., Berk et al., 1989; Hyer, Woods, Bruno, & Boudewyns, 1989; Penk et al., 1989), and college students applying to counseling services (e.g., Elliott, Anderson, & Adams, 1987). The relative elevation of MDS (Hjemboe, Butcher, & Almagor, 1992) suggests the possibility of

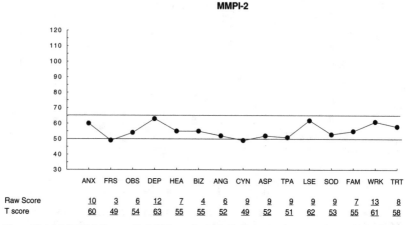

Figure 25-12. MMPI-2 Content Scale T Scores for Male Technion Students Based on U.S. Norms

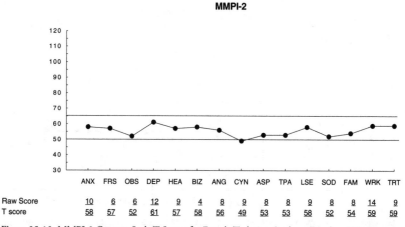

Figure 25-13. MMPI-2 Content Scale T Scores for Female Technion Students Based on U.S. Norms

marital distress or distressful dyadic relationships. It may be assumed that academic studies represent a highly stressful situation for the students that may affect their academic achievement and interpersonal relationships. This suggestion is now being extensively studied by Almagor and Friedman (1994). Our experience in using some of the supplementary scales of the HMMPI-2 indicates that some scales may need cross-validation for the Israeli population. At the beginning of the project we interpreted high MAC-R scores (raw scores > 28) as indicating possible substance abuse. The feedback coming from the therapists consistently suggested that there is no evidence of such abuse for these patients. Consequently, we deleted the scale from the standard interpretation.

Table 25-6. Means of Raw and T Scores, and Standard Deviations for 117 Men and 56 Women Applying to Counseling Services.

Scale	Men			Women		
	Raw Scores	SD	T Scores	Raw Scores	SD	T Scores
?	3.4	5.0		3.0	3.2	
L	5.0	2.2	56	4.6	2.0	55
F	7.9	4.5	60	8.2	4.0	65
K	16.0	4.8	51	15.6	3.9	51
Hs	16.4	3.8	59	18.8	4.1	62
D	26.9	6.4	68	27.6	5.8	65
Hy	25.3	4.7	60	27.1	4.6	61
Pd	27.7	4.9	62	28.1	5.0	64
Mf	28.2	4.5	54	33.9	4.6	55
Pa	13.2	4.0	62	14.6	4.0	65
Pt	35.2	3.6	69	35.8	5.8	66
Sc	35.9	7.0	67	36.9	7.9	67
Ma	21.4	7.7	53	22.2	4.3	58
Si	33.3	3.9	59	32.5	8.1	55
ANX	9.8	5.2	60	10.1	4.7	58
FRS	3.4	2.9	49	5.5	3.8	47
OBS	6.2	4.0	54	6.4	3.5	52
DEP	11.6	7.5	63	11.8	5.6	61
HEA	7.2	4.3	55	9.3	5.1	57
BIZ	3.5	2.8	55	4.2	3.2	58
ANG	6.1	3.6	52	7.6	3.4	56
CYN	9.2	4.2	49	8.5	4.0	49
ASP	8.8	3.4	52	7.5	3.3	53
TPA	8.5	3.9	51	8.3	3.7	53
LSE	8.8	5.4	62	8.8	4.5	58
SOD	9.0	4.8	53	8.3	4.3	52
FAM	7.0	4.4	55	7.6	4.2	54
WRK	13.1	7.4	61	13.7	6.2	59
TRT	8.0	5.4	58	8.8	4.7	59
MDS	4.9	2.7	63	4.9	2.5	61
F_B	3.3	3.4	56	2.9	2.9	54
VRIN	6.4	2.6	55	7.1	2.5	58
TRIN	8.2	1.4	59	8.2	1.2	59

Another special population that is of interest is applicants to clinics specializing in treating anxiety. Twenty-one men (mean age 43.6, SD = 13.2) and 25 women (mean age 40.6, SD = 10.8) applied to the anxiety clinic and filled out the MMPI-2 as part of the admission process. These patients are usually referred by psychiatrists or family physicians. Figures 25-14, 25-15, 25-16, and 25-17 depict the mean profiles for these men and women. Table 25-7 presents the mean scores and standard deviations for the various scales. Figures 25-16 and 25-17 suggest that the code-type for this group is 7-3-2-1. This code indicates the presence of both anxiety and depressive symptoms along with somatic complaints. The content scale profiles indicate

MMPI-2

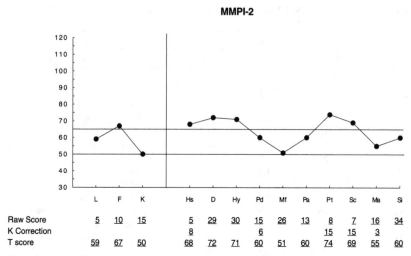

	L	F	K		Hs	D	Hy	Pd	Mf	Pa	Pt	Sc	Ma	Si
Raw Score	5	10	15		5	29	30	15	26	13	8	7	16	34
K Correction					8			6			15	15	3	
T score	59	67	50		68	72	71	60	51	60	74	69	55	60

Figure 25-14. MMPI-2 Basic Scale T Scores for Male Anxiety-Clinic Patients Based on U.S. Norms

MMPI-2

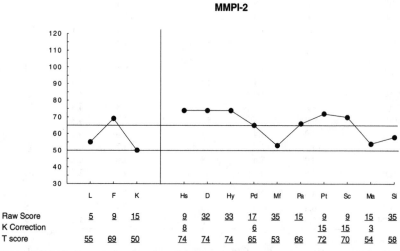

	L	F	K		Hs	D	Hy	Pd	Mf	Pa	Pt	Sc	Ma	Si
Raw Score	5	9	15		9	32	33	17	35	15	9	9	15	35
K Correction					8			6			15	15	3	
T score	55	69	50		74	74	74	65	53	66	72	70	54	58

Figure 25-15. MMPI-2 Basic Scale T Scores for Female Anxiety-Clinic Patients Based on U.S. Norms

elevation of Anxiety and Depression for both men and women and an elevation of Health Complaints for women. The simultaneous presence of these symptoms is another indication (Clark & Watson, 1991; Montgomery, 1990) of the difficulties in differentiating the two disorders. Persons complaining about feeling depressed also tend to report feeling anxious. This is borne out not only from the MMPI-2 profiles but also from the experience of the clinician heading the anxiety clinics in two major hospitals in Israel.

MMPI-2

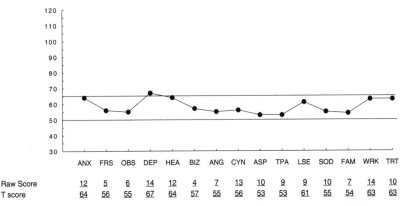

	ANX	FRS	OBS	DEP	HEA	BIZ	ANG	CYN	ASP	TPA	LSE	SOD	FAM	WRK	TRT
Raw Score	12	5	6	14	12	4	7	13	10	9	9	10	7	14	10
T score	64	56	55	67	64	57	55	56	53	53	61	55	54	63	63

Figure 25-16. MMPI-2 Content Scale T Scores for Male Anxiety-Clinic Patients Based on U.S. Norms

MMPI-2

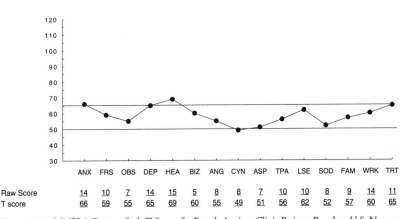

	ANX	FRS	OBS	DEP	HEA	BIZ	ANG	CYN	ASP	TPA	LSE	SOD	FAM	WRK	TRT
Raw Score	14	10	7	14	15	5	8	8	7	10	10	8	9	14	11
T score	66	59	55	65	69	60	55	49	51	56	62	52	57	60	65

Figure 25-17. MMPI-2 Content Scale T Scores for Female Anxiety-Clinic Patients Based on U.S. Norms

The study of the HMMPI-2 with special populations contributes to clinical validity of the instrument and to its usefulness in assessing and evaluating patients in different clinical settings.

Summary and Future Directions

The translation and adaptation of the HMMPI-2 proved to be quite successful. The translation process yielded an instrument that is highly comparable with the English original. Initial psychometric data indicate that the HMMPI-2 is a reliable instrument both in terms of test-retest reliability and linguistic comparability. However, data provided by the partial standardization project may indicate

Table 25-7. Means of Raw and T Scores, and Standard Deviations for 21 Men and 25 Women
Applying to an Anxiety Clinic

	Men			Women		
Scale	Raw Scores	SD	T Scores	Raw Scores	SD	T Scores
?	5.1	5.8		3.7	3.7	
L	5.7	2.1	59	4.5	2.1	55
F	10.0	6.0	67	9.2	4.6	69
K	15.3	5.1	50	15.0	4.6	50
Hs	12.4	5.2	68	16.3	5.2	74
D	29.2	6.0	72	31.9	5.4	74
Hy	29.9	4.4	71	32.5	6.2	74
Pd	21.2	4.4	60	22.6	4.9	65
Mf	26.4	4.4	51	34.6	3.5	53
Pa	12.7	3.8	60	14.8	3.7	66
Pt	22.5	11.5	74	24.2	7.0	72
Sc	22.0	12.7	69	23.5	9.4	70
Ma	19.1	3.7	55	18.1	3.5	54
Si	34.4	9.6	60	34.8	8.6	58
ANX	11.6	5.0	64	13.9	4.5	66
FRS	5.4	4.8	56	9.9	3.2	59
OBS	6.4	4.3	55	7.3	2.8	55
DEP	13.6	7.4	67	14.3	6.0	65
HEA	11.6	6.6	64	15.3	5.7	69
BIZ	4.2	4.1	57	4.7	3.7	60
ANG	7.2	3.5	55	7.5	2.6	55
CYN	12.8	5.0	56	8.4	4.3	49
ASP	9.7	3.0	53	6.5	2.2	51
TPA	9.4	3.1	53	9.5	3.4	56
LSE	8.6	4.9	61	10.1	4.5	62
SOD	9.9	5.0	55	8.4	4.0	52
FAM	6.9	3.5	54	9.0	4.2	57
WRK	14.3	8.1	63	14.3	6.5	60
TRT	9.6	4.9	63	11.1	5.6	65
F_B	5.5	5.1	65	5.3	2.9	63
VRIN	7.1	4.0	64	7.5	3.4	62
TRIN	8.2	1.5	59	9.3	1.7	60

Note: n of men = 21, n of women = 25.

the need to develop special norms for the Israeli population. A final decision will
be made when the data collection is complete.

Encouraging findings emerge from the study of special populations. Students applying for psychological counseling have an MMPI pattern similar to that obtained
with similar populations in the United States. Also, data for anxiety-clinic patients
correspond to both the clinical experience of therapists and to findings reported
elsewhere demonstrating the coexistence of anxiety and depressive symptoms.

We are conducting and planning projects that will eventually allow us to use
computerized interpretation of the MMPI-2 in Hebrew to study the validity of

various MMPI-2 supplementary scales (e.g., MAC-R). Other projects involve the study of the factorial structure of the basic clinical scales and their relations to major personality dimensions. In addition, we plan to create a national database that will promote future research on the HMMPI-2.

References

Almagor, M., & Friedman, R. (1994). *Characteristics of applicants to student counseling services in Israel.* Unpublished manuscript, University of Haifa, Haifa, Israel.

Berk, E., Black, J., Locastro, J., Wickis, J., Simpson, T., Keane, T. M., & Penk, W. (1989). Traumato-genecity: Effects of self-reported noncombat trauma on MMPIs of male Vietnam combat and noncombat veterans treated for substance abuse. *Journal of Clinical Psychology, 45*, 704–708.

Butcher, J. N., Dahlstrom, W. G., Graham, J. R., Tellegen, A., & Kaemmer, B. (1989). *MMPI-2: Manual for administration and scoring.* Minneapolis: University of Minnesota Press.

Butcher, J. N., Graham, J. R., Dahlstrom, G. W., & Bowman, E. (1990). The MMPI-2 with college students. *Journal of Personality Assessment, 54*, 1–15.

Butcher, J. N., & Gur, R. (1974). A Hebrew translation of the MMPI: An assessment of translation adequacy and preliminary validation. *Journal of Cross-Cultural Psychology, 5*, 220–227.

Butcher, J. N., & Pancheri, P. (1976). *A handbook of cross-national MMPI research.* Minneapolis: University of Minnesota Press.

Clark, L. A., & Watson, D. (1991). Tripartite model of anxiety and depression: Psychometric evidence and taxonomic implications. *Journal of Abnormal Psychology, 100*, 316–336.

Elliott, T. R., Anderson, W. P., & Adams, N. A. (1987). MMPI indicators of long-term therapy in a college counseling center. *Psychological Reports, 60*, 79–84.

Hjemboe, S., Butcher, J. N., & Almagor, M. (1992). Empirical assessment of marital distress: The Marital Distress scale for the MMPI-2. In C. D. Spielberger & J. N. Butcher (Eds.), *Advances in Personality Assessment* (Vol. 9; pp. 141–152). Hillsdale, NJ: Erlbaum.

Hyer, L., Woods, M. G., Bruno, R., & Boudewyns, P. (1989). Treatment of Vietnam veterans with PTSD and their consistency of the MCMI. *Journal of Clinical Psychology, 45*, 547–552.

Kaplan, H. I., & Sadock, B. J. (1991). *Synopsis of psychiatry* (6th ed.). Baltimore, MD: Williams and Witkins.

Keller, L. S., Butcher, J. N., & Slutske, W. S. (1990). Objective personality assessment. In G. Goldstein and M. Jersen (Eds.), *Handbook of personality assessment* (2nd ed.; pp. 345–386). Elmsford, NY: Pergamon Press.

Kramer, M. (1961). Some problems for international research suggested by observations on differences in first admission rates to the mental hospital of England and Wales and of the United States. *Proceedings of the Third World Congress of Psychiatry, 3*, 153–160.

Lachar, D. (1974). *The MMPI: Clinical assessment and automated interpretation.* Los Angeles: Western Psychological Services.

Montgomery, S. A. (1990). *Anxiety and depression.* Petersfield, England: Wrightson Biomedical Publishing.

Penk, W. E., Robonowitz, R., Black, J., Dolan, M., Bell, W., Dorsett, D., Ames, M., & Noriega, L. (1989). Ethnicity: Post-traumatic stress disorder (PTSD) differences among black, white, and hispanic veterans who differ in degrees of exposure to combat in Vietnam. *Journal of Clinical Psychology, 45*, 729–735.

Phillips, L., & Draguns, J. (1971). Classification of the behavior disorders. *Annual Review of Psychology, 22*, 447–482.

Zubin, J. (1969). Cross-national study of diagnoses of the mental disorders: Methodology and planning. *American Journal of Psychiatry, 125*, 12–30.

Chapter 26

The Persian MMPI-2

Elahe Nezami and Reza Zamani

The MMPI is the most popular clinical personality assessment procedure, with a myriad of applications throughout the world. Because of its length, several short forms were published. Early efforts to explore the effectiveness of the original MMPI in Persia used a shortened version of the instrument, the Mini Mult, consisting of 71 items. Okhovat, Barahani, Shamlou, Noeparast, and Noushirvani translated this short version into Persian in 1973 (Okhovat, 1974). The Persian MMPI has eight clinical scales; it excludes Mf and Si. Okhovat (1974) justified the exclusion of Mf based on differences between special characteristics of Iranian men and women compared to the West. The logic for excluding Si was the belief, incorrect as it turns out, that it was less reliable than other scales on the original MMPI. The number of questions in the Persian MMPI for the remaining scales are as follows: L: 5; F: 15; K: 16; Hs: 14; D: 20; Hy: 25; Pd: 19; Pa: 14; Pt: 16; Sc: 20; and Ma: 11. Eleven special keys are used for scoring the Persian MMPI. Fractions of K are added to Hs, Pd, Pt, Sc, and Ma as in the American version. Since the most widely used form of the MMPI translated and adapted into Persian is the Mini Mult, wherever we refer to the Persian MMPI, unless otherwise specified, we are referring to the Mini Mult.

Okhovat conducted the first experimental studies with the Persian MMPI that provided the basis for its further use in Iran. In a series of studies, Okhovat (1976, 1977) investigated the validity of the Persian MMPI in different clinical settings. In one of his first studies, he administered the Persian MMPI to 30 addicted inpatients between the ages of 19 and 45. Seventeen of these patients were addicted to heroin, while the rest suffered from opiate, hashish, or alcohol addiction. Similar to studies in the United States, the results of the MMPI indicated that the test successfully differentiated addicted from normal individuals. F, Pd, Pa, and Sc best distinguished the two groups. As expected, in this study L and K were higher among controls. The fact that the addicted individuals were in treatment may account for this finding. The patients were not denying their problems, while the normal individuals were more resistant and denied their shortcomings.

Okhovat (1974) found significant statistical differences between the MMPI responses of schizophrenic male inpatients and the responses of a matched normal group. The aforementioned studies are indicative of the value of the Persian translation of the MMPI in differentiating normal individuals from two clinical populations. On the basis of these two studies, the Persian MMPI became a popular diagnostic tool throughout Iran.

Since 1974 the MMPI has been used as a diagnostic tool in major psychiatric hospitals and clinics. It was used in Navy personnel selection and has also been the subject of many thesis projects. In this chapter, we present a review of the available research on the Persian MMPI.

Normative Research Studies

Okhovat (1974) did the first series of studies to obtain normative data for groups of male and female students. His normative data were based on Iranian high school (N = 637 females and 690 males) and college students (N = 321 females and 375 males). Means and standard deviations for these four groups are available. However, details about subject selection were not provided. In another study, Tavakoli Moghadam (1980) studied 500 male and 500 female high school students between the ages of 16 and 20 in an attempt to obtain normative data for this age group. The students were selected as a representative random sample of Tehran's student population. When the data were compared with Okhovat's normative data (high school students), the following results were generated. For male high school students, F and Pa were significantly different in the two studies. For females, Hs and Pd were significantly different. In the next series of calculations these data were compared with Okhovat's normative data from college students. A greater number of scales proved to be significantly different for both males and females. These differences are probably the result of sampling procedures.

Dezhkam (1993) conducted another study to obtain normative data on the general public. He collected the MMPIs of 607 men and 653 women. His subjects' ages ranged from 15 to older than 50 with education higher than that of the general public (89.5% had high school or more education). The data from this study were compared with Okhovat's normative data reported for college students. Significance tests were calculated for men and women. Scales L, F, Hs, D, Hy, Pd, Pa, and Sc were significantly different for both men and women. In addition, among men, Pt scores were also significantly different from scores reported by Okhovat (1974). These results probably reflect age and demographic differences.

Poor Hedayati (1979) studied 500 randomly selected college students between the ages of 18 and 35 (250 males and 250 females). All the subjects completed the

Persian MMPI. The normative data from this study showed significant differences between the present results and the previous normative data obtained by Okhovat. For men, scales Hy, D, Hs, F, and K were significantly different. For women, scales Hy, Hs, Ma, L, and Sc were significantly different. Ghorbani (1986) in a smaller scale study examined the MMPI responses of 50 male and 50 female high school students. The normative data from this study were compared with the normative data presented by Okhovat (1974). For male high school students, there were significant differences noted in the following scales: F, Hs, Pd, Pa, Sc, and L. For female high school students, Pd and F were significantly different from the normative data previously reported by Okhovat. When the present data were compared with Okhovat's normative data from a college population, a greater number of scales were significantly different between the two groups.

In summary, it can be concluded that several studies focused on obtaining normative data but failed to indicate an acceptable degree of concurrence. The data obtained from these studies show that, as of yet, there is not an acceptable set of normative data for the Persian MMPI to serve as norms for the instrument.

Reliability

Ghazanfari (1978) studied a group of 100 male college students between the ages of 18 and 25. The subjects were randomly selected from a total of 150 male college students enrolled in one of the departments of Tehran University. The subjects completed the MMPI in a group setting on two different occasions, one week apart. Simple correlations between the results of the MMPI on the two different occasions were significant for Ma, Sc, Pt, D, Hs, and K. However, when the common variance was taken into account, all but Pt lost their significance. The author concluded that only Pt showed significant test-retest reliability. In summary, the only available study looking at the test-retest reliability of the Persian MMPI showed questionable reliability. However, since this study used shortened versions of the MMPI scales, the resulting reliabilities are to be expected. Future research on scales should incorporate all the items on the MMPI scales if the reliability coefficients are expected to approach those obtained in other countries.

Validity Research

The complete original MMPI was translated from French to Persian and was used for Navy personnel selection between 1986 and 1989. The project focused on detecting schizophrenic patterns as well as depression. A total of 1,500 male recruits between the ages of 18 and 22 completed the MMPI. The investigators concluded that the MMPI was reliable in detecting depression among the recruits, documented by interviews and records from the student counseling center. However, the Sc scale was not found to be sensitive in detecting schizophrenic patterns in this population. The negative findings could have resulted from the fact that the Persian language MMPI was translated from the French version, which was known to have some problematic item wordings. It is important to note that in this study the French normative data were used for comparisons.

The validity of the Persian MMPI has also been the subject of several validity investigations. A series of studies examined the concurrent validity of the Persian MMPI. Nazeman (1978) evaluated the concurrent validity of the L scale of the Persian MMPI. She studied 500 college students who completed the MMPI as well as the Persian translation of the Eysenck Personality Inventory in one sitting. The EPI was used in this study since the validity of this test for Iranians was already established. She reported a significant correlation (r = 0.53) between the Lie scales of the two questionnaires. Therefore, support was provided for the concurrent validity of the L scale of the MMPI. In another study, Chegini (1981) studied the concurrent validity of the Depression scale of the Persian MMPI. Sixty-four depressed patients (32 males, 32 females) from two major psychiatric hospitals completed the MMPI as well as the Beck Depression Inventory. The author reported a significant correlation (r = .54) between the responses of the patients to the two tests, documenting the concurrent validity of the Depression scale of the MMPI.

Another series of studies looked at the validity of the MMPI as a diagnostic tool for a variety of psychiatric problems. Some of these studies point to the value of the Persian MMPI, while other studies fail to document the validity of this shortened version of the test in differential diagnoses.

Even though the MMPI scales used in the following studies were shortened, the scale scores worked well in differentiating patients from nonpatients. Khachooni (1978) studied 30 schizophrenic inpatients between the ages of 20 and 40. The subjects' education ranged from seventh grade to college level. Comparison of their responses to the MMPI with a random sample of 30 men matched for age and education showed significant differences between responses to the Sc scale. Rahimian (1978) studied a group of 100 delinquent boys between the ages of 14 and 18 and compared their responses to a random sample of high school students matched by age and education. The delinquent boys were institutionalized for a variety of crimes such as theft, drug dealing, assault, murder, etc. All the subjects completed the MMPI in groups of three to four. Significant differences between the two groups were noted for Pd. Thus, it was concluded that Pd can reliably differentiate between groups of delinquent and normal boys. Delinquent boys had significantly higher scores on F, Hy, Pa, and Sc. Dezhkam and his colleagues (Dezhkam, Bakhshee-Poor, & Roodsari, 1994) studied florid psychotics from four inpatient psychiatric wards (N = 100) between the ages of 18 and 50 with a mean age of 29. The control group consisted of 100 subjects with no history of psychiatric problems. Patients were interviewed to make sure that they met the *DSM-III-R* diagnostic criteria for schizophrenia. All the subjects completed 78 items translated from the Sc scale of the original MMPI. Item analysis indicated that 65 items differentiated the control group and the schizophrenic patients. Most of the 13 questions that did not have differential value were scored if the subject did not respond in the affirmative. The author believes that subjects might have had difficulty understanding such items. As a result they were not useful in differentiating the two groups. Four of these 13 items that were not valuable in distinguishing the patient group from the control group were related to the patient's attitude toward his family, in particular his mother. The lack of sensitivity of such items in differential diagnosis might be related to the existing differences in cultural attitudes toward family members among Iranians and individuals from other nations. It is important to note that this study used all of the 78 Sc items from the original MMPI and was able to show that, when all of the Sc items were included, the scale had acceptable diagnostic value.

There is not unanimous agreement on the validity of the Persian MMPI in the differential diagnosis of psychopathology. Even though this test differentiates normals from patient groups, it was not successful in documenting *specific* patterns that are useful in differential diagnosis. Mirzamani (1991) administered the MMPI to four groups. The first group consisted of 32 veteran patients with a PTSD diagnosis (age range 19-43) who sought psychiatric help from a veteran's clinic or hospital. The second group consisted of 32 age-matched veterans who were referred to the same center but did not have any history of psychiatric problems. The third group was composed of 32 neurotic patients who did not have a PTSD diagnosis. The last group was from a random sample of government hospital patients. Thus, the high validity scores of the first group are representative of symptom exaggeration, which might be expected from veterans with a PTSD diagnosis. In regard to the clinical scales, the first group, PTSD veterans, scored significantly higher than the other three groups on the following scales: Hs, Pd, Pa, Pt, Sc, Ma, and D. Even though such a profile differentiated the PTSD group from the other groups, it was not particularly sensitive in the differential diagnosis of PTSD.

Other studies also failed to document the MMPI's validity in differential diagnosis within patient groups. For example, Farochrooz (1974) compared three groups: 27 psychiatric patients, 27 patients with physical ailments, and 27 healthy individuals. The author reported that the MMPI was not able to distinguish between the three groups. It was concluded that the Persian MMPI in its available form did not have any diagnostic value for psychopathology in general. The shortened scales used in these studies may have limited power in differential diagnosis.

To validate the usefulness of the MMPI as a diagnostic tool for assessment of depression, Dezhkam studied a group of 30 depressed patients (based on *DSM-III-R* criteria). The patients were randomly selected from three psychiatric hospitals. The MMPI results of these patients were compared with the responses of 30 age-matched control subjects. Using a simple t-test, there were significant differences noted for the following scales: F, Hs, D, Hy, Pd, Pa, Pt, and Sc. Even though the test differentiated the two groups, it was not able to produce profiles that were mostly representative of major depression. The author concluded that this version of the MMPI was not valuable in the differential diagnosis of depression, since most of the scales were elevated.

To further evaluate the validity of the MMPI as a diagnostic tool in the assessment of psychopathology, Dezhkam administered the MMPI to a group of 40 schizophrenic patients. The results of their MMPIs were compared with responses from a group of 40 normal controls. The results indicated that several MMPI scales showed significant differences between the patient group and the controls: F, D, Pd, Pa, Pt, Sc, and Ma. The patient group scored consistently higher on all scales. However, no pattern specific to schizophrenia was detected. The author concluded that the Persian MMPI was not sensitive enough in the diagnosis of schizophrenia. He also stated that most of the items preserved in the Persian MMPI are symptomatic in nature, which might contribute to further polarization of patients from control groups without enough specificity for making a finite diagnosis. Dezhkam concluded that the low number of items in each scale might be responsible for the lack of diagnostic value of the MMPI.

In sum, the available Persian MMPI (71 items) has many shortcomings and does not seem to be a useful diagnostic tool. We do not have a reliable set of normative data. There is a scarcity of research investigating its reliability and validity. Its diagnostic value is also questionable as documented by previous research. Unfortunately, the original MMPI translators chose to translate only a portion of the item pool. It is not known whether the full version would have provided a clearer diagnostic picture. However, research on MMPI short forms in other countries (Butcher & Hostetler, 1990) suggests that short forms of the instrument do *not* produce the same clinical patterns as the full form of the MMPI. Moreover, the adequacy of early Persian MMPI translations was not demonstrated. It could well be that items on the Persian MMPI do not assess the same content as do the original MMPI items.

Development of the MMPI-2

Given the early interest in MMPI assessment methodology in Iran, we considered it important to pursue further the development of the diagnostic questionnaire in Iran. There are also a large number of Iranian immigrants to the United States and other countries who have considerable difficulty completing test questionnaires in foreign languages. Even for Iranians who are able to complete the test in English or other languages, there are no normative data or literature available to assist us in the interpretation of their profiles. Therefore, in 1993 the first author undertook the task of translating and adapting the MMPI-2.

Initially, the MMPI-2 was literally translated with the intention of producing the closest item translation. This decision was considered to be the first-line strategy, even though it was believed that the grammar and syntax of English do not have equivalents in the Persian language. First, a team of translators was recruited. Members of the translation team were chosen to meet the following criteria as suggested by Butcher (chapter 2).

1. Born and raised in Iran.
2. High school graduation and at least some college education in Iran. (An exception is noted. One of the translators had a few years of high school education in the United States.)
3. Formal education in the United States.
4. At least five years of residency in the United States.
5. Familiarity with both languages and cultures.

In the initial phase, each member of the team of translators independently translated the items into Persian. The present author compared the items from each translation and identified items with discrepancies. Discrepant items were then discussed among the translators. If there was unanimous agreement on the best translation and discrepant items, such items were then discussed by two independent translators until agreement was reached. The team discussed the appropriateness of several items for the Persian version of the MMPI-2. For example, items related to alcohol use required special attention since drinking is illegal in Iran. It was decided to keep all such items rather than substituting for them to keep the forms of the test equivalent and to preserve the meaning of the original. As a solution to deal with possibly objectionable items, the subjects were permitted not to respond to them if they chose. To further establish equivalency, the items were then translated back to English by an independent translator. The back-translated version was compared with the English version. Items that did not produce an exact match were translated again to obtain item equivalency.

In an effort to examine the exact length of time required to take the MMPI-2 in Persian, two subjects, an Iranian medical student and a homemaker, took the test. They were instructed to ask for clarification if they believed that some of the items were expressed in an awkward style. The difficulty Iranians had in understanding the Persian MMPI (71 items) was previously documented (e.g., Ghorbani, 1986). In discussions with several colleagues there was a unanimous concern about the fluency of the exact translation of some of the MMPI-2 items into Persian. Therefore, items with problematic fluency were reexamined. These items were translated again by the author and an independent translator. To get the most fluent forms of the items possible in Persian, it was decided to seek the cooperation of a faculty member of Tehran University who met all the previously set criteria for translators, except that he had been residing in Iran for the past 18 years (second author). His latest residency in Iran helped him select the most fluent items. This time the intention was to create the most fluent items while the equivalency of meaning remained intact. We translated the items that were not considered to be smoothly worded in Persian and discussed all the items to ensure accuracy in meaning as well as fluency. It is important to note that none of the original items went through any substantial alteration. An example of an adopted change is that, instead of "It is safer to trust nobody," we wrote "It is safer not to trust anybody," which sounds more fluent in Persian. The item "I seldom or never have dizzy spells" was written "I seldom have dizziness or I never have dizziness." In the item "The only interesting part of the newspaper is the comic strips" we substituted "magazines" for "newspaper," since it is not customary to have comic strips in Iranian newspapers. In another case, instead of "I am never happier than when I am alone" we wrote "I am happier when I am alone." Several other general changes were made. The first alteration is in the use of the pronoun "I" at the beginning of many of the MMPI-2 items. In Persian it is not necessary to use the pronoun at the beginning of many sentences since it is indicated by the verb form. In such sentences addition of the pronoun at the beginning of the sentence is redundant.

Research Directions for the Persian MMPI-2

A study is under way to establish the translation equivalency by administering both the English and Persian versions to 50 male and 50 female bilinguals in California. Subjects being identified are native Iranians who have been residing in the United States for at least five years and have gained adequate familiarity with both languages and cultures. Their MMPI-2 results will be compared for item equivalency to document accuracy in translation and preservation of item meaning.

Following the completion of the equivalency study, the Persian translation of the MMPI-2 will be administered to a representative sample of college students in Iran for comparison with the American college data. In this regard, the ministry of higher education in Iran has been contacted. All the major universities in Tehran, as well as universities in other major cities such as Shiraz and Tabriz, were contacted through the ministry of higher education. At this time, the authors have secured cooperation for the study at the university level. Major psychiatric hospitals' cooperation has also been enlisted for administration of the MMPI-2 to a random sample of psychiatric patients as the next stage in the validation of the instrument.

Clinical Study of the MMPI-2

Before presenting the case studies, a possible source of concern should be discussed. One of the significant factors in producing accurate results using questionnaire data such as the MMPI is the individual's level of cooperation and honesty in responding. Thus, before the new translation of the MMPI-2 can be adopted for the Iranian population, the validity of this test in this culture should be established.

Judging from previous casual observations reported in some of the aforementioned articles and the general belief among Iranian psychologists and psychiatrists, it is likely that Iranian test takers, including the student population, will be somewhat more guarded than corresponding populations in other cultures. They may mistrust the motivation behind the test or be resentful toward the testing process, which can breed further guardedness. Some of the possible reasons for the Iranians' tendency to be guarded are related to their historical, cultural, and economical background.

If the aforementioned hypothesis is true and Iranians are more guarded, then subjects might be presenting idealized characteristics in themselves while denying their shortcomings. In other words, they may show a particular pattern of responding to present a favorable personality. Therefore, it is possible that the configuration of the validity and the clinical scales will reflect this characteristic. Future research will be helpful in confirming or refuting this hypothesis.

We end this chapter with a case study and the computerized scoring and interpretive report for an inpatient at a major psychiatric hospital.

Case Study

Sex: Female
Education: High school graduate and one semester of nursing
Setting: Inpatient Mental Health Center (Roozbeh Hospital)
Date: December 1993

The patient was tested on the 30th day of her hospitalization (see Figures 26-1 through 26-4).

S.A. is a 37-year-old divorced female. The MMPI-2 was completed on her fourth hospitalization. Her first hospitalization was at age 23. Her initial symp-

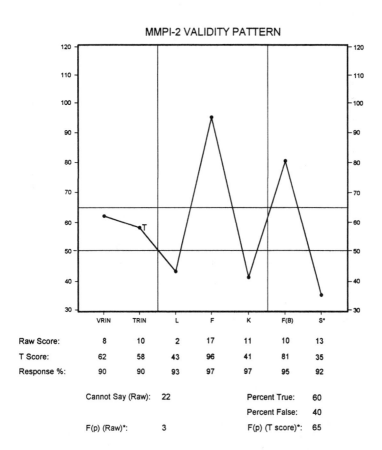

Raw Score: VRIN 8   TRIN 10   L 2   F 17   K 11   F(B) 10   S* 13

T Score: VRIN 62 TRIN 58   L 43 F 96   K 41   F(B) 81   S* 35

Response %:   VRIN 90 TRIN 90   L 93 F 97   K 97   F(B) 95   S* 92

Cannot Say (Raw):   22   Percent True: 60

                                Percent False: 40

F(p) (Raw)*:   3   F(p) (T score)*: 65

*Experimental

Figure 26-1. Minnesota Report™ MMPI-2 Validity Scale Profile of a 37-Year-Old Iranian Female Inpatient. *Source:* The Minnesota Report™: Adult Clinical System. Copyright © 1989 by the Regents of the University of Minnesota. All rights reserved.

toms included anxiety, agitation, and auditory hallucinations. Her second hospitalization was at age 25 after she gave birth to her first baby. The last two hospitalizations were at age 32 and 37. The patient reported impatience, agitation, nervousness, restlessness, and nightmares. Other symptoms included fatigue, loss of functioning, and periods of auditory hallucination. She also reported some

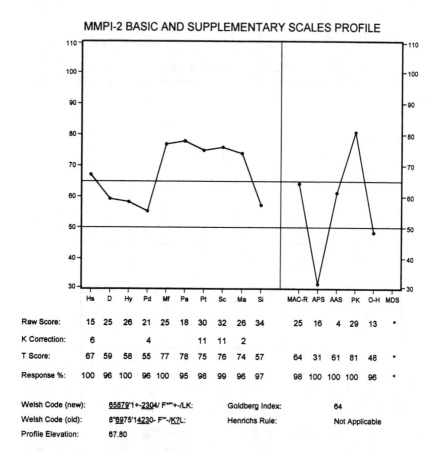

MMPI-2 BASIC AND SUPPLEMENTARY SCALES PROFILE

	Hs	D	Hy	Pd	Mf	Pa	Pt	Sc	Ma	Si		MAC-R	APS	AAS	PK	O-H	MDS
Raw Score:	15	25	26	21	25	18	30	32	26	34		25	16	4	29	13	*
K Correction:	6			4			11	11	2								
T Score:	67	59	58	55	77	78	75	76	74	57		64	31	61	81	48	*
Response %:	100	96	100	96	100	95	98	99	96	97		98	100	100	100	96	*

Welsh Code (new):	65879'1+-2304/ F*"'+-/LK:
Welsh Code (old):	8"6975'14230- F"-/K?L:
Profile Elevation:	67.80

Goldberg Index:	64
Henrichs Rule:	Not Applicable

*MDS scores are reported only for clients who indicate that they are married or separated.

Figure 26-2. Minnesota Report™ MMPI-2 Standard Scale Profile of a 37-Year-Old Iranian Female Inpatient. *Source:* The Minnesota Report™: Adult Clinical System. Copyright © 1989 by the Regents of the University of Minnesota. All rights reserved.

visual hallucinations which she believed were related to her vision. There is also some evidence of persecutory delusions. For example, she believes that her mother wanted to poison her and that her sister-in-law wants to get rid of her. According to the family, she has been negligent in child care and is not capable of caring for herself, either. There is some evidence of violence in her history. On one occasion she attacked a neighbor. On another she broke the window of her brother's house and beat up his children.

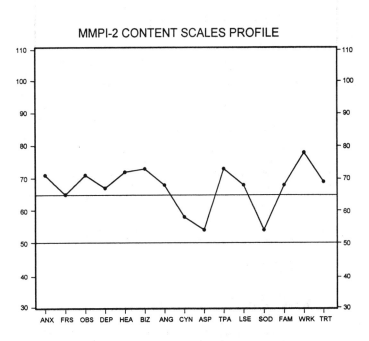

Figure 26-3. Minnesota Report™ MMPI-2 Content Scale Profile of a 37-Year-Old Iranian Female Inpatient. *Source:* The Minnesota Report™: Adult Clinical System. Copyright © 1989 by the Regents of the University of Minnesota. All rights reserved.

During the initial interview and the testing session, the patient was calm and cooperative. Her speech was normal. She was oriented to place, time, and date. Affect was mostly appropriate to the content. However, one exception was noted. The patient was smiling when she explained that her brother used to beat her up. She was not able to explain what her smile was about. She requested to take short breaks during the testing session, stating that her eyes were tired, but was able to finish the test in 2 hours and 30 minutes.

Medications at the time of testing: Eskazina, Artan, Litium, Inderal, Bipenide.

PROFILE VALIDITY

The client omitted 22 items on the MMPI-2. Although this is not enough to invalidate the resulting
MMPI-2 clinical profile, some of her scale scores may be lower than expected because of these omissions.
It may be helpful to talk with her to determine the reasons for her omissions. Many clinicians prefer to
readminister the omitted items (listed at the end of this report) to ensure the most accurate interpretation
possible.

The pattern of her item omissions should be carefully evaluated. She omitted from 10 to 15 percent of the
items on Scales TRIN, VRIN, OBS, CYN, Pa1, Ma3, and ANG1. Omitting items may result in an
underestimate of the problems measured by the affected scales. She omitted from 16 to 25 percent of the
items on Scales Ma1, CYN2, LSE2, and FAM2. Caution should be exercised in interpreting the affected
scales because scale scores are clearly attenuated by this degree of item omission. Of course, any scale
elevations above a T score of 60 should be interpreted, but it should be understood that if there are
omitted items, the score probably underestimates problems reflected by the scale.

The client has responded to the MMPI-2 items in an exaggerated manner, endorsing a wide variety of
inconsistent symptoms and attitudes. These results may stem from a number of factors that include
random responding, falsely claiming psychological problems, low reading level, a plea for help, or a
confused state. The resulting MMPI-2 clinical profile is a marginally valid indication of the individual's
personality and symptoms. The interpreter is cautioned against making clinical or administrative decisions
on the basis of this MMPI-2 protocol.

She endorsed the items at the end of the booklet in an extreme or exaggerated manner, producing a high
score on F(B). This elevated score could result from a number of conditions such as confusion,
exaggerated symptom checking, or consistently misrecording her responses on the answer sheet. The
scores on the MMPI-2 Content Scales, supplementary scales, and content component scales could be
influenced by this tendency.

SYMPTOMATIC PATTERNS

This report was developed using the Pa and Sc scales as the prototype. Her MMPI-2 clinical profile
reflects a high degree of psychological distress at this time. She appears to be tense, apathetic, and
withdrawn, and she is experiencing some personality deterioration. She seems to be quite confused and
disorganized, and she probably secretly broods about unusual beliefs and suspicions. She may have
delusions and unusual preoccupations, and she may feel that others are against her because of her beliefs.
In interviews, she is likely to be vague, circumstantial, and tangential, and she may be quite preoccupied
with abstract or bizarre ideas. This MMPI-2 clinical profile reflects a chronic pattern of maladjustment,
although she may presently be experiencing an intensification of problems. Personality decompensation,
disorganization, and thought disorder are likely to occur.

Figure 26-4. Minnesota Report™ Narrative for a 37-Year-Old Iranian Female Inpatient. *Source:* The
Minnesota Report™: Adult Clinical System. Copyright © 1989 by the Regents of the University of
Minnesota. All rights reserved.

DSM-III-R diagnoses from the hospital record:

AXIS I: Chronic Schizophrenia
    II: Schizoaffective
   III: None
    VI: Stress
     V: Decreased Functioning (no GAF was assigned to her)

Autistic behavior and inappropriate affect are characteristic features of individuals with this profile. Some evidence of an active psychotic process is apparent. She may exhibit extreme emotional behavior such as blunted or inappropriate affect or hostile, irritable outbursts. She seems to be lacking in ego defenses and may be experiencing acute anxiety. She tends to project blame for unacceptable feelings onto others. In an attempt to deal with her problems, she withdraws socially.

Her interests appear to be restricted to areas that most women do not find appealing. She actively rejects many female roles and activities, and she may be rather brusque in manner and caustic in conversation. Others may view her as aggressive, cold, and aloof. She may be rather insensitive and may seem to lack understanding of others. Interpersonally, she may be manipulative.

In addition, the following description is suggested by the content of the client's item responses. She has endorsed a number of items suggesting that she is experiencing low morale and a depressed mood. The client's recent thinking is likely to be characterized by obsessiveness and indecision. She views the world as a threatening place, sees herself as having been unjustly blamed for others' problems, and feels that she is getting a raw deal out of life.

She endorsed a number of extreme and bizarre thoughts, suggesting the presence of delusions and/or hallucinations. She apparently believes that she has special mystical powers or a special "mission" in life that others do not understand or accept. The possibility that she could act out in an aggressive manner on her delusional ideas should be further evaluated. The client attests to having more fears than most people do. She endorses statements that show some inability to control her anger. She may physically or verbally attack others when she is angry.

PROFILE FREQUENCY

Profile interpretation can be greatly facilitated by examining the relative frequency of clinical scale patterns in various settings. The client's high-point clinical scale score (Pa) occurs in 10.4% of the MMPI-2 normative sample of women. However, only 3.4% of the women have Pa as the peak score at or above a T score of 65, and only 1.9% have well-defined Pa spikes. This elevated MMPI-2 profile configuration (6-8/8-6) is very rare in samples of normals, occurring in less than 1% of the MMPI-2 normative sample of women.

The relative frequency of this MMPI-2 high-point Pa score is somewhat high in various samples of inpatient women. In the Graham and Butcher (1988) sample, Pa occurs as the high point in 21.4% of the females, the most frequent high-point score (19.1% are at or above a T score of 65, and 13.7% are well defined in that range). In the large NCS inpatient sample, this high-point clinical scale score (Pa) occurs in 10.9% of the women. Moreover, 9.9% of the females in the inpatient sample have this high-point scale spike at or over a T score of 65, and 5.4% produce well-defined Pa peak scores in that range.

Her elevated MMPI-2 profile configuration (6-8/8-6) occurs in 8.4% of the females in the Graham and Butcher (1988) sample (the most frequent elevated two-point code) and in 4% of the females in the NCS inpatient sample.

Figure 26-4 (continued)

References

Butcher, J.N., and Hostetler, K. (1990). Abbreviating MMPI item administration: What can be learned from the MMPI for the MMPI-2? *Psychological Assessment, 2*, 12–21.

Chegini, S. (1981). *An investigation on the diagnostic value of the depression scale of the Persian MMPI (Mini Mult) and the Beck Depression Inventory.* Unpublished master's thesis, Tehran Psychiatric Institute, Tehran, Iran.

PROFILE STABILITY

The relative elevation of her clinical scale scores suggests that her profile is not as well defined as many other profiles. That is, her highest scale or scales are very close to her next scale score elevations. There could be some shifting of the most prominent scale elevations in the profile code if she is retested at a later date. The difference between the profile type used to develop the present report and the next highest scale in the profile code was 1 point. So, for example, if the client is tested at a later date, her profile might involve more behavioral elements related to elevations on Pt. If so, then on retesting, intensification of anxiety, negative self-image, and unproductive rumination might become more prominent.

INTERPERSONAL RELATIONS

Disturbed relationships are characteristic of individuals with this profile type. The client feels socially inadequate and has very poor social skills. She is fearful and suspicious of other people, and she may be blatantly negative in social interactions. She tends to feel insecure in personal relationships, is hypersensitive to rejection, and may become jealous at times. She tends to need a great deal of reassurance. Individuals with this profile are quite self-absorbed and find marital relationships problematic. Marital breakup is not uncommon.

The content of this client's MMPI-2 responses suggests the following additional information concerning her interpersonal relations. She feels intensely angry, hostile, and resentful of others, and she would like to get back at them. She is competitive and uncooperative, tending to be very critical of others.

DIAGNOSTIC CONSIDERATIONS

The most likely diagnosis for individuals with this profile type is Schizophrenia, possibly Paranoid type, or a Paranoid Disorder. Her unusual thinking and bizarre ideas need to be taken into consideration in any diagnostic formulation.

TREATMENT CONSIDERATIONS

Individuals with this profile may be experiencing considerable personality deterioration, which may require hospitalization if they are considered dangerous to themselves or others. Psychotropic medication may reduce their thinking disturbance and mood disorder. Outpatient treatment may be complicated by their regressed or disorganized behavior. Day treatment programs or other such structured settings may be helpful in providing a stabilizing treatment environment. Long-term adjustment is a problem. Frequent, brief "management" therapy contacts may be helpful in structuring the client's activities. Insight-oriented or relationship therapies tend not to be helpful for individuals with these severe problems and may actually exacerbate the symptoms. She would probably have difficulty establishing a trusting working relationship with a therapist.

Figure 26-4 (continued)

Dezkam, M. (1993). *Standardization of the Persian MMPI for Iranian population.* Paper presented at the meeting of the Iranian psychologists affiliated with the ministry of health, Tehran, Iran.
Dezkam, M., Bakhshee-Poor, A., & Roodsari, A. (1994). Normalization of the Schizophrenia scale of the MMPI in an Iranian male population. *Psychological Research, 2,* 3–12.
Farochrooz, T. (1974). *Comparison of psychiatric patients, patients with physical problems, and a normal control group in Pt scale of the Persian MMPI.* Unpublished master's thesis, Rooz-beh Psychiatric Hospital, Tehran, Iran.

The item content she endorsed indicates attitudes and feelings that suggest a low capacity for change. Her potentially high resistance to change might need to be discussed with her early in treatment in order to promote a more treatment-expectant attitude.

Her item content suggests some family conflicts that are causing her considerable concern at this time. She feels unhappy about her life and resents having an unpleasant home life. Psychological intervention could profitably focus, in part, on clarifying her feelings about her family.

In any intervention or psychological evaluation program involving occupational adjustment, her negative work attitudes could become an important problem to overcome. She has a number of attitudes and feelings that could interfere with work adjustment.

Her acknowledged problems with alcohol or drug use should be addressed in therapy.

NOTE: This MMPI-2 interpretation can serve as a useful source of hypotheses about clients. This report is based on objectively derived scale indices and scale interpretations that have been developed in diverse groups of patients. The personality descriptions, inferences, and recommendations contained herein need to be verified by other sources of clinical information because individual clients may not fully match the prototype. The information in this report should most appropriately be used by a trained, qualified test interpreter. The information contained in this report should be considered confidential.

Figure 26-4 (continued)

Ghazanfari, R. (1978). *Reliability of the Persian MMPI.* Unpublished master's thesis, Tehran University, Tehran, Iran.

Ghorbani, F. (1986). *Comparison of personality in male and female high school students (15–18 years) using the Persian MMPI.* Unpublished master's thesis, Tehran University, Tehran, Iran.

Khachooni, K. (1978). *An investigation on the value of the Sc scale of the Persian MMPI (Mini Mult) for differential diagnosis.* Unpublished master's thesis, Tehran University, Tehran, Iran.

Mirzamani, M. (1991). *Patterns of responses to the F and K in the Persian MMPI among patients with PTSD.* Unpublished master's thesis, Tehran Psychiatric Institute, Tehran, Iran.

Nazeman, M. (1978). A study of the validity of the L scale on the Mini Mult. Unpublished master's thesis, University of Tehran, Tehran, Iran.

Okhovat, V. (1974). A study on the applicability of the MMPI short form in Iran. In K. Leigh and J. Noorbakshs (Eds.), *Epidemiological studies in psychiatry.* Tehran: University of Teheran.

Okhovat, V. (1978). *Personality assessment.* Tehran: Tehran University Press.

Okhovat, V. (1976). *Psychotherapy and a collection of articles.* Tehran-Iran: Payam Press.

Okhovat, V. (1976). *Special characteristics of addicted individuals.* Paper presented at the 25th meeting of the Persian Medical Association.

Poor Hedayati, A. (1979). *Obtaining normative data on the Sc scale of the Persian MMPI (Mini Mult).* Unpublished master's thesis, Tehran University, Tehran, Iran.

Rahimian, H.B. (1978). *Validity of the Persian MMPI.* Unpublished master's thesis, Alame Tabatabaye Univeristy, Tehran, Iran.

Tavakoli, Moghadam (1980). *An investigation of the diagnostic value of the Pd scale of the Persian MMPI (Mini Mult).* Unpublished master's thesis, Tehran University, Tehran, Iran.

Appendix A. Personality Characteristics
Associated with Scale Elevations

Appendix A-1. Personality Characteristics Associated with Elevations on the Validity Indicators

Validity Indicator	Characteristics
? (Cannot Say Score)	The total number of unanswered items. A defensive protocol with possible attenuation of scale scores is suggested if the raw score is more than 30.
? Percentage of True Responses	An extremely low or high true or false percentage reflects a highly distorted response pattern such as conscious manipulation or careless responding.
L (Lie) Scale	A measure of rather unsophisticated or self-consciously "virtuous" test-taking attitude. Elevated scores (above 65 T) suggest that the individual is presenting himself or herself in an overly positive light—attempting to create an unrealistically favorable view of his or her adjustment.
F (Infrequency) Scale	The items on this scale are answered in the nonkeyed direction by most people. A high score (T above 80) suggests an exaggerated pattern of symptom checking that is inconsistent with accurate self-appraisal and suggests confusion, disorganization, or actual faking of mental illness. Scores above 90 invalidate the profile.
K (Defensiveness) Scale	Measures an individual's willingness to disclose personal information and discuss his or her problems. High scores (T score above 65) reflect an uncooperative attitude and an unwillingness or reluctance to disclose personal information. Low scores (below a T score of 45) suggest openness and frankness.
F-K Dissimulation Index	This index, developed by Gough (1947), is designed to measure dissimulation—the tendency to be self-depreciative versus the tendency to enhance one's self-image. The index is the raw score of F minus the raw score of K. Scores in the plus range (over 14) suggest that the individual is making an extremely negative self-appraisal.
F_B Scale	An additional validity measure, the F_B scale, or Back Side F scale, was incorporated in the revised version of the MMPI to detect possible deviant responding to items located in the latter part of the item pool. Some subjects, tiring of taking the test, may modify their approach to the items partway through the item pool and answer in a random or unselective manner. Since the items on the F scale occur earlier in the test, the F

scale or F-K may not detect such changes in response pattern. This 40-item scale was developed in a manner analogous to the development of the original F scale, that is, by including items that had low endorsement percentages in the normal population. Within the Minnesota Report, no interpretation of the F_B Scale is provided if the T score is below T = 70 (a valid response approach) or if the profile is invalid by F scale criteria. If the F_B Scale is elevated above a T = 90 and the original F scale is valid, then interpretations of F_B are provided depending upon the level of the original F score.

Variable Response Inconsistency

The VRIN scale consists of 49 pairs of specially selected items. The members of each VRIN item pair have either similar or opposite content; each pair is scored for the occurrence of an inconsistency in responses to the two items. The scale score is the total number of item pairs answered inconsistently. High VRIN scores are a warning that the test taker may have been answering the items in the inventory in an indiscriminate manner, raising the possibility that the protocol may be invalid and essentially uninterpretable.

True Response Inconsistency

The TRIN scale is made up of 20 pairs of items that are opposite in content. If a subject responds inconsistently by answering True to both items of certain pairs, one point is added to the TRIN score; if the subject responds inconsistently by answering False to certain item pairs, one point is subtracted. A very high TRIN score indicates a tendency to give True answers to the items indiscriminately ("acquiescence"), and a very low TRIN score indicates a tendency to answer False indiscriminately (nonacquiescense). (Negative TRIN scores are avoided by adding a constant to the raw score.) Very low or very high TRIN scores are a warning that the test taker may have been answering the inventory indiscriminately, thus the profile may be invalid and uninterpretable.

The S Scale

The S scale is an empirically derived measure of a potentially invalidating response attitude—the tendency to claim extreme virtue by presenting oneself in a superlative manner. It was developed in an effort to improve our understanding of this overly positive response set. The subjects in the study were 274 male airline applicants and the MMPI-2 normative sample (N = 1,138 men and 1,462 women). A sample of 822 normal couples that had taken the MMPI-2 and had rated each other on 110 personality variables was employed to develop correlates for the scale. The S scale was initially developed by examining item response differences between airline pilot applicants, who tend to engage in superlative self-description to impress examiners, and men from the MMPI-2 restandardization normative sample. The scale was refined by using internal consistency methods to ensure high scale homogeneity. A factor analysis of the resulting 50-item scale (S) yielded five factors named Claims of "Human Goodness"; Assertion of Outstanding Adjustment; Expression of Overly Optimistic and Tension-Free Attitudes; Pleasant Collegiality; and Denial of Moral Flaws. Linear T-score conversion tables were computed for men and women separately and combined using the MMPI-2 restandardization data sets. The S scale was shown to have a number of behavioral correlates reflecting the presentation of oneself as a well-controlled, problem-free person.

Appendix A-2. Personality Characteristics Associated with Elevations on the Clinical Scales

Scale	Characteristics
1 Hs (Hypochondriasis)	High scorers* present numerous vague physical problems. The problems tend to be chronic and do not respond well to psychological treatment. High scorers are generally unhappy, self-centered, whiny, complaining, hostile, demanding, and attention-demanding.
2 D (Depression)	High scores reflect depressed mood, low self-esteem, and feelings of inadequacy. This scale is one of the most frequently elevated in clients in drug and alcohol settings. High scorers are described as moody, shy, despondent, pessimistic, distressed, high-strung, lethargic, overcontrolled, and guilt-prone. Elevations may reflect great discomfort and need for change or symptomatic relief.
3 Hy (Hysteria)	High scorers tend to rely on neurotic defenses such as denial and repression to deal with stress. They tend to be dependent, naive, outgoing, infantile, and narcissistic. Their interpersonal relations are often disrupted, and they show little insight into problems. High levels of stress are often accompanied by development of physical symptoms. (Scale 3 is the peak score among female medical patients who have no diagnosable illness.) High scorers often respond to suggestion; however, they resist insight-oriented treatment. They show little interest in psychological processes and interpret psychological problems as physical ones.
4 Pd (Psychopathic Deviate)	Among alcohol and drug abusers, this is often the highest scale in the clinical profile. Elevations measure antisocial behavior—rebelliousness; disrupted family relations; impulsiveness; school, work, or legal difficulties; alcohol or drug abuse,

etc. Personality trait disorder is likely among high scorers—
they are outgoing, sociable, and likable, but deceptive, manipulative, hedonistic, exhibitionistic, unreliable, immature,
hostile, aggressive, and show poor judgment. They often have
difficulty in marital or family relations and trouble with the
law. High scores usually reflect long-standing character problems that are highly resistant to treatment. High scorers may
enter treatment, but usually terminate quickly.

5 Mf (Masculinity-
Femininity)

High-scoring males are described as sensitive, aesthetic,
passive, or feminine. They may show conflicts over sexual
identity and low heterosexual drive. Low-scoring** males are
viewed as masculine, aggressive, crude, adventurous, reckless,
practical, and having narrow interests. Because the direction
of scoring is reversed, high-scoring females are seen as masculine, rough, aggressive, self-confident, unemotional, and insensitive. Low-scoring females are viewed as passive, yielding,
complaining, fault-finding, idealistic, and sensitive.

6 Pa (Paranoia)

Elevations on this scale are often associated with being suspicious, aloof, shrewd, guarded, worrying, and overly sensitive.
High scorers may project or externalize blame and harbor
grudges against others. High scorers are generally hostile and
argumentative, and may not benefit from treatment.

7 Pt (Psychasthenia)

High scorers are tense, anxious, ruminative, preoccupied,
obsessional, phobic, and rigid. They frequently are self-
condemning, guilt-prone, and feel inferior and inadequate.
Clients with spike 7 elevations overintellectualize, ruminate,
rationalize, and resist psychological interpretation in treatment. This scale is often elevated among individuals entering
alcohol or drug treatment and may reflect intense environmental problems and guilt over their own actions.

8 Sc (Schizophrenia)

High scorers (T = 70-80) have an unconventional, schizoid
lifestyle. They are withdrawn, shy, and moody and feel inadequate, tense, and confused. They may have unusual or strange
thoughts, poor judgment, and erratic moods. Very high scorers
(T over 80) may show poor reality contact, bizarre sensory
experiences, delusions, and hallucinations. High scorers may
have difficulty relating in therapy; they are generally unin-
formed and have poor problem-solving skills.

9 Ma (Mania)

High scorers (T = 70-75) are sociable, outgoing, impulsive,
overly energetic, and optimistic, have liberal moral views,
drink excessively, are flighty, grandiose, irritable, impatient,
unqualifiedly optimistic, and rarely "follow through." They

exaggerate their self-worth and are manipulative. Very high scorers (T over 75) may show affective disorder, bizarre behavior, erratic mood, impulsive behavior, and delusions.

0 Si (Social Introversion-Extraversion)	High scorers are introverted, shy, withdrawn, socially reserved, submissive, overcontrolled, lethargic, conventional, tense, inflexible, and guilt-prone. Low scorers are extraverted, outgoing, gregarious, expressive, aggressive, talkative, impulsive, uninhibited, spontaneous, manipulative, opportunistic, and insincere in social relations.

*Above 65 T unless otherwise noted.
**Below 40 T unless otherwise noted.

Appendix A-3. Personality Characteristics Associated with Elevations on the Supplementary Scales

Scale	Characteristics
A (Anxiety Scale) Welsh, 1956	Individuals scoring high on this scale are viewed as anxious, tense, obsessional, and generally maladjusted.
R (Repression) Welsh, 1956	Individuals scoring high on R tend to be overcontrolled. They deny problems and tend to gloss over personal frailties. They are seen as constricted and inhibited.
Es (Ego Strength Scale)	Persons who score high on the Es scale tend to have a high tolerance for stress and tend to be flexible and resilient. They tend to respond well to psychological treatment.
Do (Dominance)	High-scoring individuals tend to be viewed by others as dominant in social and interpersonal situations.
Re (Responsibility)	Individuals who score high on the Re scale tend to present themselves as socially concerned and responsible toward other people.
O-H (Over-Controlled Hostility)	People who score high on the O-H scale tend to be inhibited individuals who repress conflict or deny emotionality.
PTSD (Post-traumatic Stress Disorder)	People who score high on the PTSD scale are presenting symptoms of post-traumatic stress including hypersensitivity, anxiousness, sleeping difficulty, intrusive thoughts, and general maladjustment.
MDS (Marital Distress Scale)	Individuals scoring high on this scale are reporting relationship problems and difficulties with those intimately involved with them.

AAS (Addiction Admission Scale)	A high score indicates that the test taker is probably openly admitting to substance-abuse problems.
APS (Addiction Proneness Scale)	High scores suggest a high probability of significant problems with substance abuse.
MAC-R (MacAndrew Scale)	High scorers have been found to be prone to developing problems of addiction such as alcohol or drug abuse, pathological gambling, or other addictive problems.

Appendix A-4. Personality Characteristics Associated with Elevations on the MMPI-2 Content Scales

1. Anxiety (ANX, 23 items). High scorers on ANX report general symptoms of anxiety including tension, somatic problems (i.e., heart pounding and shortness of breath), sleep difficulties, worries, and poor concentration. They fear losing their minds, find life a strain, and have difficulties making decisions. They appear to be readily aware of these symptoms and problems and are willing to admit to them.

2. Fears (FRS, 23 items). A high score on FRS indicates an individual with many specific fears. These specific fears can include blood; high places; money; animals such as snakes, mice, or spiders; leaving home; fire; storms and natural disasters; water; the dark; being indoors; and dirt.

3. Obsessiveness (OBS, 16 items). High scorers on OBS have tremendous difficulty making decisions and are likely to ruminate about issues and problems, causing others to become impatient. Having to make changes distresses them, and they may report some compulsive behaviors like counting or saving unimportant things. They are excessive worriers who frequently become overwhelmed by their own thoughts.

4. Depression (DEP, 33 items). High scores on this scale characterize individuals with significant depressive thoughts. They report feeling blue, uncertain about their future, and uninterested in their lives. They are likely to brood, be unhappy, cry easily, and feel hopeless and empty. They may report thoughts of suicide or wishing that they were dead. They may believe that they are condemned or have committed unpardonable sins. Other people may not be viewed as a source of support.

5. Health Concerns (HEA, 36 items). Individuals with high scores on HEA report many physical symptoms across several body systems. Included are gastrointestinal symptoms (e.g., constipation, nausea and vomiting, stomach trouble), neurological problems (e.g., convulsions, dizzy and fainting spells, paralysis), sensory problems (e.g., poor hearing or eyesight), cardiovascular symptoms (e.g., heart or chest pains), skin problems, pain (e.g., headaches, neck pains), and respiratory troubles (e.g., coughs, hay fever or asthma). These individuals worry about their health and feel sicker than the average person.

6. Bizarre Mentation (BIZ, 24 items). Psychotic thought processes characterize individuals high on the BIZ scale. They may report auditory, visual, or olfactory hallucinations

and may recognize that their thoughts are strange and peculiar. Paranoid ideation (e.g., the belief that they are being plotted against or that someone is trying to poison them) may be reported as well. These individuals may feel that they have a special mission or special powers.

7. Anger (ANG, 16 items). High scores on the ANG scale suggest anger control problems. These individuals report being irritable, grouchy, impatient, hotheaded, annoyed, and stubborn. They sometimes feel like swearing or smashing things. They may lose self-control and report having been physically abusive toward people and objects.

8. Cynicism (CYN, 23 items). Misanthropic beliefs characterize high scorers on CYN. They expect hidden, negative motives behind the acts of others—for example, believing that most people are honest simply for fear of being caught. Other people are to be distrusted, for people use each other and are friendly only for selfish reasons. They likely hold negative attitudes about those close to them, including fellow workers, family, and friends.

9. Antisocial Attitudes (ASP, 22 items). In addition to holding similar misanthropic attitudes as high scorers on the CYN scale, high scorers on the ASP scale report problem behaviors during their school years and other antisocial practices like being in trouble with the law, stealing, or shoplifting. They report sometimes enjoying the antics of criminals and believe that it is all right to get around the law, as long as it is not broken.

10. Type A (TPA, 19 items). High scorers on TPA are hard-driving, fast-moving, and work-oriented individuals who frequently become impatient, irritable, and annoyed. They do not like to wait or be interrupted. There is never enough time in a day for them to complete their tasks. They are direct and may be overbearing in their relationships with others.

11. Low Self-Esteem (LSE, 24 items). High scores on LSE characterize individuals with low opinions of themselves. They do not believe that they are liked by others or that they are important. They hold many negative attitudes about themselves including beliefs that they are unattractive, awkward and clumsy, useless, and a burden to others. They certainly lack self-confidence, and find it hard to accept compliments from others. They may be overwhelmed by all the faults they see in themselves.

12. Social Discomfort (SOD, 24 items). SOD high scorers are very uneasy around others, preferring to be by themselves. When in social situations, they are likely to sit alone rather than join in the group. They see themselves as shy and dislike parties and other group events.

13. Family Problems (FAM, 25 items). Considerable family discord is reported by high scorers on FAM. Their families are described as lacking in love, quarrelsome, and unpleasant. They even may report hating members of their families. Their childhood may be portrayed as abusive, and marriages seen as unhappy and lacking in affection.

14. Work Interference (WRK, 33 items). A high score on WRK is indicative of behaviors or attitudes likely to contribute to poor work performance. Some of the problems relate to low self-confidence, concentration difficulties, obsessiveness, tension and pressure, and

decision making. Other problems suggest lack of family support for career choice, personal questioning of career choice, and negative attitudes toward coworkers.

15. Negative Treatment Indicators (TRT, 26 items). High scores on TRT characterize individuals with negative attitudes toward doctors and mental health treatment. High scorers do not believe that anyone can understand or help them. They have issues or problems that they are not comfortable discussing with anyone. They may not want to change anything in their lives, nor do they feel that change is possible. They prefer giving up rather than facing a crisis or difficulty.

Sources: Butcher, 1991; Butcher, Graham, Williams, & Ben-Porath, 1990.

Appendix B. MMPI-2/MMPI-A Translators

Arabic
Abdalla M. Soliman
United Arab Emirates University
Faculty of Humanities and Social Sciences
Department of Psychology
P.O. Box 17771, Al-AIN
United Arab Emirates

Chinese
Hong Kong
Fanny Cheung
Chinese University of Hong Kong
Department of Psychology
Shatin, N.T.
Hong Kong

People's Republic of China
Wei Zheng Song
Institute of Psychology
Chinese Academy of Sciences
P.O. Box 1603, Postcode 100012
Beijing, China

Farsi
Elahe Nezami
33981 Calle Borrego
San Juan Capistrano, CA 92675

Reza Zamani
Houshmand Tirandaz
Behrooz Bernous
Department of Psychology
University of Teheran
Teheran, Iran

Flemish/Dutch
Hedwig Sloore
Free University of Brussels
Department of Psychology
Pleinlaan 2
Brussels, Belgium 1050

Jan Derksen
PEN Tests Publisher
P.O. Box 6537
6503 GA Nijmegen
The Netherlands

French
Mireille Simon
Isabelle Gillet
Les Editions du Centre de Psychologie Appliquée
25 rue de la Plaine
75980 Paris cedex 20
France

Greek
Anna Kokkevi
University Mental Health Research Institute
Eginition Hospital
7274 Vassilissis Sophias Ave.
Athens, Greece 11528

Hebrew
Moshe Almagor
Department of Psychology
University of Haifa
Haifa, Israel 31905

Hmong
Amos Deinard
University of Minnesota
Community University Health Clinic
Box 85 Mayo
Minneapolis, MN 55455

James Butcher
University of Minnesota
75 East River Rd.
Minneapolis, MN 55455

In collaboration with
Umeng D. Thao, Song
Houa Moua Vang, and
Kaying Hang

Icelandic
Sölvína Konráðs
Hrísholti 7
210 Garðabæ
Iceland

Italian
Paolo Pancheri
5a Cattedra di Clinica Psichiatrica
30, Viale Dell 'Universita
00185 Roma
Italy

Saulo Sirigatti
Universita degli Studi di Firenze
Dipartimento di Psicologia Generale
via Nino Bixio, IA
50125 Firenze
Italy

Japanese
Noriko Shiota
Department of Psychology
Villanova University
Villanova, PA 19085

Lee Anna Clark
Department of Psychology
University of Iowa
E220 Seashore Hall
Iowa City, IA 52242

Korean
Kyunghee Han
Department of Psychology
University of Mississippi
PO Box 37
University, MS 38677

Norwegian
Bjorn Ellertsen
Melanie Young
Kari Troland
Hallgrim Kløve
Department of Clinical
  Neuropsychology
Aarstadveien 21
N-5009 Bergen
Norway

Russian
Victor S. Koscheyev
University of Minnesota
School of Public Health
Division of Environmental
  & Occupational Health
Mayo Box 807
420 Delaware St. SE
Minneapolis, MN 55455

Vladimar K. Martens
All-Russia Ctr for Disaster
  Medicine
Schukinskaya, 5
123182 Moscow
Russia

Spanish
Argentina
Dr. Maria M. Casullo
Faculty of Psychology
Tucuman 2162, 8th Floor A
Buenos Aires State
  University
1050 Buenos Aires
Argentina

Dr. Lorenzo Garcia
  Samartino
Avda Medrano 1141
1179 Buenos Aires
Argentina

Chile
Fernando J. Rissetti
MMPI-2 Research Project
Pontificia Universidad
  Católica de Chile
J.V. Lastarria 61
Santiago 1
Chile

Mexico
Dra. Emilia Lucio G.M.
Dra. Isabel Reyes-Lagunes
Facultad de Psicologia
Division Estudios de Pos-
  grado
UNAM - Mexico D.F.
Ave Nida Universidad
  #04510

Spain
Dr. Alejando Avila-Espada
Universidad de Salamanca
Department of Psychology
Avenida de la Merced
s/n 37005 Salamanca
(ESPANA)

United States
Alex Azan
Florida International Uni-
  versity
Student Counseling Center
University Park GC 211
Miami, FL 33199

Rosa Garcia-Peltoniemi
Center for the Victims of
  Torture
717 East River Rd.
Minneapolis, MN 55455

Thai
La-Or Pongpanich
Department of Psychiatry
Pramongkut Klao Hospital
Rajvidhi Rd. BKK 10400
Thailand

Turkish
Işık Savaşır
Department of Psychiatry
Faculty of Medicine
Hacettepe University
Ankara
Turkey

Meral Çulha
Koç University
Cayir Cad.
Instinye 80860
Istanbul
Turkey

Vietnamese
Bao-Chi N. Tran
1258 Capistrano Lane
Vista, CA 92083

Appendix C. Percentage
of True Responses per Item

Appendix C-1. Percentage of Women Giving a True Response to Each Item

Item	Sample 1 U.S. MMPI-2 Norm	Sample 2 United States College	Sample 3 United States Military	Sample 4 Puerto Rico College	Sample 5 Japan College	Sample 6 Korea College	Sample 7 Holland Norms
	N = 1462	N = 797	N = 186	N = 131	N = 507	N = 399	N = 563
	Butcher et al. Manual (1989)	Butcher, Graham, Dahlstrom, Bowman (1990)	Butcher et al. (1990)	Cabiya (Chap. 14)	Shiota, Krauss, & Clark (Chap. 4)	Han (Chap. 5)	Sloore, Derksen, DeMay, & Hellenbosch (Chap. 16)
1	10	4	12	12	4	11	10
2	96	93	92	89	93	78	90
3	66	46	56	69	47	40	61
4	38	13	24	21	38	28	37
5	54	42	53	42	21	44	33
6	90	94	87	93	92	86	91
7	41	45	49	33	53	55	37
8	64	58	73	60	56	51	58
9	82	81	80	80	72	29	83
10	87	94	96	67	92	84	65
11	5	3	7	9	20	28	11
12	74	73	81	63	89	17	73
13	34	33	52	47	18	33	26
14	69	71	78	75	58	68	39
15	36	41	55	23	31	34	12
16	40	56	44	33	51	62	14
17	6	7	10	3	19	11	13
18	4	4	2	4	3	21	14
19	29	48	35	52	39	68	14
20	77	79	77	63	66	70	65
21	41	59	48	31	46	82	30
22	9	17	13	15	10	35	8
23	18	43	24	44	51	68	15
24	2	4	5	5	2	14	2
25	44	47	47	38	14	33	20
26	40	43	61	44	18	41	32
27	14	20	15	24	29	30	28
28	9	18	11	18	4	26	8
29	82	91	81	67	71	54	53
30	6	12	9	52	1	9	6

Appendix C-1 (continued)

Item	Sample 1	Sample 2	Sample 3	Sample 4	Sample 5	Sample 6	Sample 7
31	13	26	7	18	18	41	15
32	18	35	38	44	26	36	12
33	64	57	63	19	65	44	52
34	81	77	85	89	91	50	80
35	37	39	28	19	32	38	22
36	6	8	9	2	7	6	6
37	38	52	39	47	45	60	27
38	28	42	18	44	43	83	34
39	14	12	15	9	12	35	21
40	7	11	6	20	17	16	9
41	56	72	52	64	86	88	37
42	3	3	3	4	7	6	4
43	77	72	84	74	63	47	88
44	13	12	8	11	7	22	21
45	87	87	89	75	93	73	77
46	23	22	13	21	25	56	17
47	84	76	88	84	83	79	58
48	12	32	18	66	32	44	10
49	75	74	81	82	77	36	81
50	47	52	70	51	36	52	14
51	96	97	98	95	97	96	80
52	12	11	20	11	14	36	12
53	25	35	31	27	13	45	20
54	5	7	10	8	8	12	5
55	37	40	29	66	28	34	26
56	34	44	35	47	28	69	21
57	68	70	81	79	76	59	53
58	56	69	75	73	81	71	42
59	11	16	10	15	4	15	10
60	3	6	4	38	0	5	1
61	77	82	88	92	33	73	33
62	74	68	69	86	80	34	80
63	32	20	48	27	24	32	28
64	73	79	75	69	59	48	54
65	9	10	11	15	17	22	7
66	2	2	2	6	2	9	2
67	72	68	78	76	54	65	51
68	14	28	23	10	37	11	5
69	39	35	41	26	17	19	37
70	32	23	10	8	34	30	35

Appendix C-1 (continued)

Item	Sample 1	Sample 2	Sample 3	Sample 4	Sample 5	Sample 6	Sample 7
71	32	40	32	7	36	47	24
72	5	4	6	15	6	14	4
73	28	35	19	18	46	66	40
74	34	29	24	13	23	35	34
75	95	94	92	93	92	82	94
76	33	36	46	54	38	52	53
77	95	96	79	79	95	94	84
78	96	95	95	89	79	79	93
79	29	27	35	45	39	33	39
80	27	28	35	24	10	21	36
81	44	60	62	69	49	74	43
82	22	30	21	24	50	58	21
83	78	66	74	64	40	36	85
84	7	8	10	6	2	2	7
85	16	32	17	20	42	54	7
86	39	74	68	82	74	48	26
87	53	64	49	47	71	90	25
88	83	90	82	71	70	62	88
89	78	72	63	63	84	98	50
90	92	95	88	95	84	76	93
91	89	88	87	79	93	59	87
92	3	5	3	11	9	6	10
93	92	94	90	78	87	89	91
94	5	10	7	8	27	57	20
95	89	87	88	85	80	34	90
96	5	12	18	5	2	9	8
97	11	10	9	18	5	13	17
98	45	64	43	65	73	74	45
99	6	5	9	11	5	10	4
100	50	34	44	53	52	49	69
101	7	8	8	24	5	20	13
102	98	99	97	97	92	83	93
103	27	22	16	15	22	44	21
104	39	42	45	40	19	25	45
105	10	12	15	11	6	5	20
106	85	78	84	82	83	31	85
107	67	64	53	60	67	63	43
108	91	95	98	98	93	85	87
109	93	90	94	97	89	59	80
110	50	61	74	63	44	87	71

Appendix C-1 (continued)

Item	Sample 1	Sample 2	Sample 3	Sample 4	Sample 5	Sample 6	Sample 7
111	9	13	9	15	13	37	7
112	68	68	58	68	71	70	20
113	70	65	70	56	52	36	51
114	1	6	3	3	3	29	1
115	64	61	72	76	46	23	74
116	36	46	33	50	38	67	36
117	86	82	90	75	93	78	88
118	64	60	58	13	74	37	56
119	79	70	70	58	46	51	97
120	73	80	81	96	90	95	92
121	77	72	79	91	93	75	91
122	82	85	82	90	83	87	77
123	30	57	33	39	56	51	17
124	25	35	34	39	24	42	21
125	88	78	83	76	88	65	90
126	98	99	97	96	96	84	95
127	58	52	28	49	73	86	64
128	76	77	69	62	76	54	66
129	26	42	30	24	66	53	37
130	38	45	30	25	58	51	25
131	43	46	45	69	27	46	46
132	78	80	81	70	65	71	54
133	4	5	53	20	3	13	3
134	8	18	15	29	15	26	13
135	30	42	27	44	55	88	16
136	36	38	32	34	48	49	32
137	58	68	65	40	77	86	23
138	2	2	3	11	5	2	2
139	87	91	87	85	96	97	71
140	73	52	66	58	66	44	61
141	91	90	96	84	90	84	74
142	94	90	95	88	83	90	91
143	56	53	48	58	54	49	65
144	1	2	4	5	3	2	1
145	11	19	18	22	10	11	12
146	46	58	33	53	47	25	48
147	15	14	5	10	8	28	8
148	48	47	56	56	78	15	41
149	12	7	9	35	4	35	23
150	5	10	7	17	6	6	1

Appendix C-1 (continued)

Item	Sample 1	Sample 2	Sample 3	Sample 4	Sample 5	Sample 6	Sample 7
151	49	45	38	77	81	94	67
152	58	57	73	61	39	30	54
153	50	67	39	44	62	63	14
154	61	47	35	44	41	77	54
155	17	20	34	23	22	9	14
156	4	8	11	5	13	56	2
157	31	31	56	38	16	20	51
158	63	60	59	48	55	46	63
159	55	65	69	74	80	77	52
160	86	85	89	88	83	73	74
161	41	38	32	47	28	66	39
162	0	1	1	2	1	1	1
163	48	52	60	53	41	18	27
164	84	77	88	82	68	17	71
165	90	93	96	86	93	74	89
166	13	28	12	55	12	35	15
167	39	38	28	29	35	52	37
168	9	19	10	13	10	55	12
169	44	75	68	53	55	91	49
170	10	12	9	34	13	41	3
171	40	36	33	8	44	26	47
172	7	16	11	16	11	10	7
173	70	55	70	56	49	12	66
174	92	82	88	85	79	70	74
175	5	10	6	15	12	25	11
176	74	69	82	66	78	44	61
177	90	89	94	83	94	51	90
178	28	34	23	43	33	47	52
179	91	91	91	80	72	81	87
180	3	5	3	11	7	34	2
181	76	73	84	63	86	89	82
182	4	6	4	5	8	32	4
183	91	92	82	73	95	96	96
184	54	25	54	42	31	5	72
185	46	49	37	53	43	66	35
186	93	92	94	81	70	67	93
187	45	38	39	31	33	59	23
188	83	93	97	89	79	46	76
189	53	77	69	61	60	18	29
190	8	14	15	45	26	45	10

Appendix C-1 (continued)

Item	Sample 1	Sample 2	Sample 3	Sample 4	Sample 5	Sample 6	Sample 7
191	38	33	35	29	38	69	18
192	97	98	97	95	97	94	95
193	9	7	9	20	17	8	14
194	44	41	54	58	31	32	64
195	10	13	10	20	14	16	6
196	61	69	45	40	62	60	54
197	17	12	23	19	20	13	6
198	2	3	8	13	3	12	1
199	63	52	63	90	40	38	40
200	42	49	52	65	36	50	55
201	3	4	22	10	11	3	1
202	19	20	23	19	12	17	18
203	91	94	84	79	91	91	76
204	90	91	95	85	89	73	86
205	66	64	52	59	22	23	43
206	75	63	75	56	77	78	72
207	35	58	51	70	70	56	30
208	72	64	70	61	81	49	67
209	38	53	42	44	39	55	15
210	98	99	95	96	93	88	85
211	26	14	44	81	23	31	36
212	24	25	20	21	28	26	24
213	42	46	37	55	53	49	48
214	63	52	59	56	50	44	35
215	17	19	10	26	16	70	44
216	2	1	1	7	2	9	11
217	53	32	28	89	38	75	96
218	24	45	35	43	43	47	47
219	58	68	69	70	34	60	59
220	11	5	15	6	11	21	29
221	27	48	41	66	41	38	34
222	89	85	81	86	88	92	90
223	82	73	87	65	63	59	82
224	81	80	88	79	89	53	63
225	28	36	41	31	32	27	26
226	40	66	61	40	34	24	50
227	42	55	65	38	30	24	31
228	2	3	3	10	6	15	6
229	5	9	8	27	27	63	4
230	73	78	80	71	42	46	57

Appendix C-1 (continued)

Item	Sample 1	Sample 2	Sample 3	Sample 4	Sample 5	Sample 6	Sample 7
231	17	28	23	56	73	72	26
232	75	56	35	15	31	46	49
233	32	43	14	25	50	73	28
234	2	3	4	8	25	3	1
235	10	7	10	5	15	13	14
236	64	52	46	37	23	41	60
237	59	46	66	68	39	41	70
238	17	21	18	27	21	20	22
239	26	23	40	76	11	19	17
240	3	5	4	15	6	2	4
241	14	22	26	42	17	19	23
242	35	58	51	27	7	25	15
243	35	31	24	29	30	54	39
244	76	82	87	64	74	94	73
245	29	28	28	26	33	46	42
246	2	4	2	10	7	4	2
247	9	5	10	8	4	8	7
248	11	14	17	26	33	5	18
249	55	56	68	47	48	25	56
250	24	22	19	17	40	54	17
251	25	53	37	48	52	29	42
252	1	2	2	2	1	4	2
253	12	14	29	29	13	37	12
254	20	28	40	44	43	45	24
255	84	80	79	79	85	48	83
256	44	50	29	24	72	85	29
257	17	37	34	30	30	20	17
258	3	4	3	9	7	11	6
259	17	27	22	43	33	23	48
260	93	95	96	83	88	84	84
261	51	40	63	57	33	42	47
262	72	63	77	70	80	54	67
263	82	80	83	91	58	63	87
264	23	35	16	13	4	4	4
265	28	32	18	31	13	54	45
266	84	82	82	90	93	95	93
267	70	82	82	69	62	87	64
268	14	33	20	68	60	62	10
269	19	37	32	85	40	59	60
270	4	4	4	11	2	3	4

Appendix C-1 (continued)

Item	Sample 1	Sample 2	Sample 3	Sample 4	Sample 5	Sample 6	Sample 7
271	46	52	46	51	52	62	26
272	11	13	23	10	4	6	25
273	18	20	11	15	16	40	12
274	28	38	31	32	58	57	40
275	59	53	41	32	31	47	68
276	96	97	98	97	96	91	94
277	19	24	24	22	27	48	14
278	84	82	85	65	79	34	76
279	48	51	35	66	39	56	14
280	81	81	87	62	89	60	69
281	4	3	4	10	5	19	7
282	6	13	5	15	9	2	5
283	40	35	61	38	63	79	44
284	50	59	58	90	44	47	69
285	49	61	44	46	43	61	30
286	27	36	46	50	49	17	46
287	14	23	17	12	5	14	5
288	14	19	11	15	14	25	7
289	46	57	35	50	42	50	38
290	54	50	33	51	28	53	33
291	4	14	10	11	13	28	2
292	35	32	26	44	19	29	31
293	25	8	19	27	16	27	31
294	5	7	4	10	1	2	11
295	83	86	83	85	89	67	83
296	13	15	16	24	14	29	11
297	62	65	65	44	36	49	37
298	12	14	18	48	5	41	10
299	15	25	12	21	21	43	21
300	11	22	10	21	6	58	4
301	20	28	12	28	27	27	5
302	39	45	35	33	39	26	21
303	3	4	5	5	7	35	2
304	54	69	61	24	36	49	39
305	36	49	46	44	33	38	50
306	9	8	9	34	18	24	22
307	11	13	17	15	4	18	12
308	13	11	7	22	23	36	6
309	31	30	30	52	54	84	21
310	11	24	15	34	19	62	6

Appendix C-1 (continued)

Item	Sample 1	Sample 2	Sample 3	Sample 4	Sample 5	Sample 6	Sample 7
311	9	16	16	26	16	41	9
312	6	13	13	15	3	5	3
313	16	22	17	25	18	52	8
314	92	88	85	73	89	89	87
315	49	46	55	37	31	50	43
316	10	28	23	34	22	31	5
317	6	6	9	18	9	22	9
318	93	91	93	90	95	76	81
319	7	13	12	25	2	8	7
320	17	27	23	27	32	47	11
321	60	49	70	56	40	45	64
322	5	8	7	12	19	42	4
323	5	7	4	10	6	24	3
324	5	12	15	20	13	20	4
325	17	29	17	22	19	33	17
326	36	38	25	32	39	50	25
327	8	18	17	29	21	43	3
328	30	40	23	44	27	62	22
329	2	4	5	15	2	4	3
330	94	96	95	88	66	49	84
331	49	49	35	54	42	57	44
332	4	6	5	9	3	6	3
333	5	10	12	9	7	3	2
334	3	5	4	6	3	6	2
335	69	57	66	27	61	70	42
336	2	2	5	7	3	6	2
337	42	27	26	24	29	52	26
338	35	42	33	41	47	85	27
339	43	60	37	43	45	66	37
340	60	77	80	79	50	42	60
341	67	69	51	45	58	93	25
342	55	41	65	54	24	21	33
343	91	91	92	89	74	72	86
344	43	39	28	34	59	15	22
345	52	65	61	86	51	78	32
346	64	44	57	67	10	22	30
347	22	31	15	16	40	64	11
348	21	37	28	50	42	71	11
349	8	6	9	19	12	23	10
350	52	57	65	82	38	63	32

Appendix C-1 (continued)

Item	Sample 1	Sample 2	Sample 3	Sample 4	Sample 5	Sample 6	Sample 7
351	42	30	25	48	44	38	29
352	71	74	80	82	57	92	75
353	83	89	88	56	79	50	22
354	82	84	81	75	81	74	69
355	1	1	3	9	1	4	3
356	33	36	55	63	31	32	39
357	46	37	47	44	52	45	8
358	17	27	28	58	12	25	21
359	59	82	78	57	12	53	27
360	82	80	87	88	65	49	81
361	2	4	8	13	6	16	10
362	59	73	49	51	71	69	37
363	76	80	80	80	80	69	62
364	26	29	13	31	37	63	24
365	74	78	84	85	83	91	67
366	11	21	23	40	8	14	19
367	28	16	20	31	8	40	48
368	25	28	16	25	46	59	17
369	45	42	23	24	37	27	39
370	78	89	89	84	80	55	76
371	10	16	12	14	58	40	8
372	67	59	72	46	47	57	68
373	39	50	39	47	26	41	12
374	38	53	66	55	45	83	51
375	31	33	25	43	40	34	21
376	13	11	11	18	28	18	48
377	30	34	18	21	74	76	18
378	39	36	30	37	18	15	45
379	14	8	11	23	34	16	8
380	16	17	16	12	56	17	10
381	9	8	11	11	24	15	7
382	24	31	24	41	31	31	16
383	91	90	92	82	71	76	95
384	87	89	80	79	79	83	71
385	40	52	62	33	70	43	60
386	47	52	51	55	34	66	50
387	3	7	4	11	4	7	2
388	64	53	69	45	69	14	66
389	15	24	23	37	20	42	10
390	48	58	51	60	65	58	31

Appendix C-1 (continued)

Item	Sample 1	Sample 2	Sample 3	Sample 4	Sample 5	Sample 6	Sample 7
391	34	35	32	48	60	49	63
392	34	21	25	26	26	33	38
393	24	41	45	52	34	46	24
394	23	28	23	24	35	35	14
395	17	25	12	39	64	63	21
396	45	59	55	74	28	44	21
397	24	17	12	38	29	16	21
398	50	64	57	46	52	49	31
399	13	25	25	31	41	29	18
400	17	35	19	24	36	44	9
401	51	73	72	74	72	58	79
402	51	39	32	31	34	70	44
403	38	48	54	57	27	27	27
404	94	95	96	85	93	95	91
405	77	73	83	68	76	54	77
406	29	42	35	51	53	63	40
407	7	9	7	26	28	9	4
408	32	38	28	40	52	40	30
409	54	69	56	44	43	77	58
410	38	34	43	40	38	34	65
411	25	37	19	26	35	38	17
412	10	16	9	16	7	3	6
413	35	28	17	46	31	50	32
414	40	42	58	76	46	85	34
415	29	38	24	63	25	46	35
416	45	26	33	51	10	15	25
417	11	23	27	17	32	11	6
418	41	57	48	56	38	59	69
419	45	62	47	42	39	78	32
420	41	42	32	47	57	74	22
421	27	32	27	24	47	29	32
422	78	90	89	76	48	75	55
423	37	46	41	20	38	61	68
424	14	28	15	34	9	12	21
425	35	30	34	22	22	27	21
426	95	93	89	81	41	54	93
427	82	81	79	63	81	52	77
428	58	68	53	47	71	65	38
429	75	64	82	82	91	60	81
430	48	57	40	50	60	95	39

Appendix C-1 (continued)

Item	Sample 1	Sample 2	Sample 3	Sample 4	Sample 5	Sample 6	Sample 7
431	3	4	4	10	4	2	8
432	14	22	19	17	12	20	12
433	51	61	47	57	64	81	55
434	29	38	47	31	32	63	52
435	17	24	10	41	43	55	18
436	29	32	38	33	50	27	27
437	62	57	70	74	43	53	49
438	55	50	52	54	58	73	35
439	39	41	38	67	72	79	70
440	65	69	71	67	50	60	72
441	21	19	19	41	35	54	25
442	68	73	59	76	72	79	73
443	27	35	42	41	28	20	21
444	28	32	31	31	61	54	25
445	35	34	52	45	8	4	26
446	38	38	18	45	24	53	44
447	14	10	11	78	70	57	13
448	18	29	20	34	53	76	11
449	73	72	67	53	62	72	34
450	3	4	2	9	11	19	3
451	15	27	12	27	26	43	8
452	65	59	67	82	57	59	69
453	41	29	39	47	42	55	55
454	4	5	5	15	6	8	4
455	83	80	83	78	76	63	83
456	79	86	79	55	82	81	47
457	22	27	10	20	52	39	26
458	59	58	48	66	29	47	33
459	80	72	80	59	81	90	72
460	55	58	76	77	56	62	44
461	57	67	53	75	53	83	75
462	51	55	62	36	40	25	63
463	6	8	7	24	5	9	4
464	34	43	28	30	33	75	27
465	25	22	26	22	33	8	22
466	34	48	37	32	55	24	18
467	56	43	52	71	32	30	45
468	8	12	7	31	29	18	8
469	31	38	20	52	6	52	26
470	36	42	48	72	60	37	43

Appendix C-1 (continued)

Item	Sample 1	Sample 2	Sample 3	Sample 4	Sample 5	Sample 6	Sample 7
471	18	28	17	50	22	12	18
472	34	37	28	79	38	42	26
473	72	71	72	66	62	63	65
474	40	30	43	44	37	35	43
474	19	33	22	41	39	64	17
476	7	12	7	8	36	30	5
477	10	33	37	15	36	12	4
478	1	2	2	8	2	3	1
479	38	43	41	49	37	69	36
480	31	26	26	34	36	40	25
481	47	51	67	67	22	26	68
482	21	33	17	34	23	66	25
483	10	16	10	24	28	45	11
484	2	9	6	20	7	19	2
485	23	32	18	38	17	70	24
486	49	56	56	56	48	56	40
487	24	30	9	9	2	0	4
488	13	24	32	44	36	56	6
489	4	3	3	5	1	1	2
490	10	8	15	27	52	64	16
491	20	25	12	23	38	39	19
492	78	78	82	79	58	62	65
493	91	88	89	82	81	85	91
494	82	79	80	79	28	87	83
495	21	11	12	31	28	84	11
496	44	22	28	47	39	40	71
497	27	19	12	29	41	17	28
498	24	21	14	21	23	31	22
499	33	37	46	35	21	48	36
500	12	9	11	18	49	23	9
501	96	92	94	85	83	91	95
502	21	18	14	14	21	46	25
503	17	21	15	19	14	25	9
504	38	30	24	58	50	60	56
505	15	28	19	30	60	31	11
506	4	10	5	11	20	15	3
507	26	38	38	44	62	81	20
508	23	26	22	27	22	47	19
509	43	49	32	50	61	82	31
510	21	24	21	26	16	25	17

Appendix C-1 (continued)

Item	Sample 1	Sample 2	Sample 3	Sample 4	Sample 5	Sample 6	Sample 7
511	9	23	6	6	2	2	2
512	24	23	29	16	13	11	19
513	23	32	25	30	14	29	10
514	74	72	64	68	82	84	78
515	11	8	10	16	11	21	11
516	3	5	4	10	8	16	2
517	2	4	3	11	29	23	4
518	21	24	28	14	30	25	20
519	36	43	35	54	27	44	36
520	2	5	4	10	6	13	2
521	62	61	68	69	40	48	41
522	49	61	61	73	39	42	56
523	47	51	49	44	52	53	60
524	5	6	2	14	5	9	4
525	13	19	11	50	38	65	30
526	4	10	5	15	41	15	4
527	8	6	10	9	2	2	6
528	6	10	9	17	13	9	12
529	25	41	33	49	23	26	29
530	1	4	3	12	16	11	1
531	14	15	27	24	13	27	7
532	68	76	68	71	57	71	53
533	40	41	27	55	38	55	28
534	62	60	69	67	46	30	66
535	61	68	76	69	62	72	66
536	25	29	31	45	7	26	28
537	24	33	46	27	25	31	12
538	40	34	58	61	71	70	28
539	7	12	8	11	15	34	3
540	4	6	5	8	3	2	4
541	78	82	72	60	69	78	43
542	56	62	52	63	28	80	41
543	21	24	17	22	19	27	15
544	2	5	5	9	24	26	10
545	44	47	28	20	60	17	26
546	14	10	7	8	16	19	19
547	69	75	66	68	63	60	62
548	7	16	13	13	5	4	4
549	11	19	51	34	7	22	7
550	16	27	22	19	26	45	3

Appendix C-1 (continued)

Item	Sample 1	Sample 2	Sample 3	Sample 4	Sample 5	Sample 6	Sample 7
551	17	23	27	43	11	27	9
552	72	70	78	81	62	58	79
553	15	20	19	38	24	71	12
554	14	22	9	31	30	40	6
555	4	8	6	19	11	14	3
556	37	39	19	43	33	50	25
557	37	31	39	29	49	34	16
558	15	12	15	50	37	57	30
559	11	13	11	21	17	44	13
560	38	30	44	54	37	34	70
561	86	80	92	86	67	73	81
562	37	37	32	27	56	17	37
563	19	13	23	24	13	15	15
564	72	71	80	67	52	56	70
565	11	11	9	24	15	20	14
566	28	47	24	21	43	82	46
567	31	17	20	34	14	43	20

Appendix C-1. Percentage of Women Giving a True Response to Each Item

Item	Sample 8 Spain	Sample 9 France	Sample 10 Chile	Sample 11 Mexico College	Sample 12 China	Sample 13 Nicaragua
	N = 233	N = 167	N = 859	N = 1107	N = 1108	N = 587
	Avila-Espada, Jimenez-Gomez (Chap. 15)	Gillet (Chap. 20)	Risetti, Himmel, Gonzalez, Olmos (Chap. 11)	Lucia & Reyes-Lagunes (Chap. 13)	Cheung, Song, & Zhang (Chap. 6)	Lucia & Reyes-Lagunes (Chap. 13)
1	6	25	14	13	5	15
2	88	83	82	91	79	84
3	54	46	57	61	75	51
4	49	34	37	18	57	28
5	50	54	60	32	58	57
6	94	82	83	91	95	81
7	45	33	60	23	67	72
8	38	27	46	42	57	53
9	80	83	80	89	61	80
10	61	66	81	57	69	56
11	13	17	20	3	12	20
12	72	73	56	59	65	43
13	33	58	46	22	50	48
14	70	52	58	74	67	73
15	22	32	39	23	27	31
16	25	32	29	18	33	36
17	27	22	14	5	36	25
18	7	9	8	3	16	17
19	14	28	34	50	64	51
20	56	62	51	74	65	63
21	29	55	39	30	35	43
22	17	13	23	7	35	33
23	30	43	32	23	21	49
24	3	1	8	1	5	6
25	28	23	44	37	19	39
26	45	62	46	21	50	40
27	46	34	40	50	27	51
28	26	16	35	17	13	41
29	56	60	67	41	46	55
30	22	12	49	6	18	23

Appendix C-1 (continued)

Item	Sample 8	Sample 9	Sample 10	Sample 11	Sample 12	Sample 13
31	27	22	45	33	31	51
32	17	21	26	26	19	46
33	40	56	55	42	61	66
34	66	80	59	75	69	58
35	35	46	35	31	14	32
36	15	15	18	5	15	17
37	24	42	47	21	31	44
38	45	62	48	38	43	51
39	26	23	25	10	29	36
40	17	13	28	20	22	58
41	63	66	49	56	65	60
42	10	13	12	4	20	28
43	67	37	76	63	44	80
44	13	16	23	8	9	50
45	81	81	66	80	83	53
46	44	24	42	35	31	47
47	70	78	64	80	52	62
48	62	34	37	23	42	44
49	77	72	67	61	28	70
50	38	34	41	29	52	43
51	83	93	79	92	82	80
52	15	66	32	7	4	29
53	37	37	35	23	12	55
54	14	9	17	6	16	24
55	53	40	50	46	19	61
56	50	49	50	39	85	71
57	76	72	64	79	53	63
58	58	55	74	66	65	72
59	11	10	42	12	14	28
60	48	20	32	15	23	34
61	14	17	64	76	11	57
62	66	83	74	78	68	67
63	27	30	27	43	46	39
64	58	51	74	65	76	75
65	15	32	32	14	26	43
66	15	6	15	8	5	13
67	61	76	71	73	49	71
68	19	37	15	7	22	22
69	17	30	30	30	18	24
70	25	31	30	21	35	28

Appendix C-1 (continued)

Item	Sample 8	Sample 9	Sample 10	Sample 11	Sample 12	Sample 13
71	48	43	63	56	37	71
72	14	11	24	8	13	34
73	26	73	27	10	44	25
74	35	28	24	21	26	27
75	98	89	89	94	84	90
76	72	67	58	56	73	86
77	76	90	68	86	68	78
78	89	83	84	89	66	88
79	39	29	32	28	35	31
80	44	43	37	16	26	21
81	79	75	64	52	75	75
82	43	47	42	23	45	46
83	73	73	70	77	75	71
84	37	6	16	6	1	8
85	19	16	22	9	14	27
86	85	31	64	90	64	88
87	25	38	30	25	68	48
88	93	83	58	85	65	72
89	52	59	64	45	60	52
90	98	88	86	94	93	88
91	80	79	66	87	70	63
92	16	19	23	9	22	22
93	90	89	77	78	79	70
94	64	35	17	8	14	30
95	77	53	72	81	69	56
96	7	8	19	3	11	17
97	15	8	20	10	17	23
98	69	43	63	47	33	67
99	13	11	26	13	10	49
100	61	62	49	74	68	65
101	7	19	20	7	12	29
102	98	91	95	98	76	96
103	41	27	33	17	25	27
104	48	47	47	33	34	44
105	21	15	22	8	9	13
106	84	86	75	73	63	77
107	57	33	45	38	79	55
108	88	92	93	98	89	97
109	84	87	91	94	70	78
110	77	68	67	70	63	86

Appendix C-1 (continued)

Item	Sample 8	Sample 9	Sample 10	Sample 11	Sample 12	Sample 13
111	22	20	25	14	17	27
112	48	77	40	59	41	52
113	54	35	48	54	58	63
114	5	2	5	2	2	5
115	63	65	54	72	50	61
116	45	48	46	35	49	50
117	70	66	71	90	72	73
118	12	38	37	10	51	15
119	75	77	81	64	54	77
120	97	93	92	97	89	98
121	84	86	72	86	85	82
122	86	75	87	66	46	83
123	55	43	34	50	30	40
124	25	29	43	42	16	77
125	83	78	68	79	85	63
126	85	63	82	42	96	47
127	80	72	67	51	78	68
128	66	69	64	68	57	70
129	44	51	49	30	32	45
130	43	60	29	26	50	49
131	48	34	41	50	41	50
132	74	45	77	70	21	64
133	13	11	19	4	48	5
134	39	13	25	10	16	19
135	54	54	55	48	48	68
136	34	60	49	38	73	41
137	23	40	36	26	74	28
138	8	5	9	2	14	23
139	88	75	78	81	66	81
140	64	56	58	58	69	43
141	84	80	68	83	85	66
142	87	92	71	94	72	83
143	65	43	55	46	60	42
144	3	2	9	2	2	8
145	14	16	23	8	13	29
146	70	50	68	56	56	67
147	24	16	29	23	32	28
148	41	43	51	54	38	47
149	28	19	28	12	21	44
150	18	7	18	5	15	13

Appendix C-1 (continued)

Item	Sample 8	Sample 9	Sample 10	Sample 11	Sample 12	Sample 13
151	69	63	83	78	68	88
152	59	57	60	67	39	63
153	38	15	50	43	34	53
154	54	58	60	44	65	69
155	9	8	26	6	15	12
156	6	20	14	12	14	28
157	30	35	49	54	62	54
158	66	47	58	60	81	63
159	53	47	54	75	68	67
160	73	66	80	59	83	88
161	49	59	49	37	53	51
162	1	0	5	1	1	1
163	30	39	36	34	20	23
164	74	63	68	84	54	66
165	77	69	79	83	73	72
166	54	16	53	45	18	53
167	44	51	45	35	52	41
168	16	29	36	23	33	39
169	37	55	53	69	12	67
170	33	33	43	28	24	55
171	32	44	29	30	40	14
172	13	20	21	16	12	35
173	51	53	50	42	35	35
174	77	78	84	91	72	91
175	14	28	20	11	38	31
176	76	63	65	80	61	57
177	85	86	75	93	87	82
178	33	29	42	40	33	59
179	86	90	76	91	92	81
180	9	22	16	10	8	33
181	83	80	67	88	81	71
182	12	20	11	4	31	16
183	88	62	76	68	88	68
184	45	40	49	54	66	59
185	60	58	62	59	71	69
186	84	70	74	83	73	75
187	31	22	41	40	36	31
188	81	73	76	91	77	69
189	62	53	54	59	24	48
190	26	17	29	23	31	24

Appendix C-1 (continued)

Item	Sample 8	Sample 9	Sample 10	Sample 11	Sample 12	Sample 13
191	45	37	46	39	34	33
192	99	90	95	98	98	98
193	20	24	62	16	45	41
194	58	57	60	70	46	47
195	13	11	31	21	17	34
196	55	67	61	42	64	73
197	10	5	13	7	25	25
198	6	1	11	4	8	17
199	71	78	64	70	73	83
200	55	41	48	72	31	62
201	2	2	11	5	21	12
202	21	19	41	14	11	34
203	90	65	46	80	61	65
204	91	90	82	88	89	83
205	58	50	62	55	51	76
206	72	66	73	73	79	73
207	41	34	44	64	32	70
208	69	53	57	65	68	61
209	48	25	57	61	12	76
210	97	98	95	99	85	97
211	33	34	69	71	74	77
212	24	29	32	23	74	35
213	67	49	72	64	75	75
214	39	48	56	30	59	42
215	79	29	56	53	65	74
216	8	8	15	5	3	21
217	92	73	78	68	39	57
218	40	32	40	28	51	45
219	46	73	74	64	23	66
220	14	8	15	4	75	22
221	20	46	52	19	19	49
222	90	76	86	98	45	95
223	67	74	68	74	85	72
224	75	66	61	82	60	58
225	21	28	34	28	40	52
226	25	38	32	56	25	51
227	34	28	49	62	46	63
228	5	7	11	8	10	34
229	17	21	31	28	20	53
230	63	40	49	56	80	65

Appendix C-1 (continued)

Item	Sample 8	Sample 9	Sample 10	Sample 11	Sample 12	Sample 13
231	66	73	64	60	81	62
232	44	46	34	61	49	21
233	45	39	41	31	44	44
234	3	8	11	0	5	9
235	25	36	31	8	13	13
236	54	41	54	38	60	48
237	77	29	68	77	75	67
238	30	20	21	14	15	29
239	38	20	72	78	60	74
240	19	20	11	11	6	24
241	25	22	45	27	35	54
242	23	24	39	10	38	49
243	30	36	38	24	61	33
244	51	71	59	72	42	74
245	24	49	21	20	37	11
246	3	5	13	2	3	9
247	20	19	9	11	8	32
248	31	13	35	52	21	52
249	48	48	44	52	55	48
250	65	23	28	25	26	19
251	36	28	37	26	25	54
252	2	2	5	4	6	17
253	22	12	31	26	26	48
254	33	32	41	42	61	68
255	78	83	61	73	58	68
256	32	34	29	23	63	28
257	24	14	27	29	50	26
258	5	5	8	4	13	17
259	45	22	32	25	22	57
260	67	91	81	93	58	92
261	47	29	61	55	62	61
262	71	71	70	83	49	74
263	90	74	82	91	56	93
264	25	25	8	9	8	13
265	38	60	44	34	34	52
266	93	95	84	96	86	89
267	86	77	70	73	37	77
268	41	40	44	37	56	58
269	65	54	78	92	31	94
270	10	5	15	4	22	12

Appendix C-1 (continued)

Item	Sample 8	Sample 9	Sample 10	Sample 11	Sample 12	Sample 13
271	48	42	49	36	44	48
272	14	8	20	10	30	21
273	47	38	37	31	45	68
274	38	41	30	22	46	47
275	47	60	55	53	43	60
276	99	92	93	98	96	99
277	17	34	42	20	34	39
278	64	54	54	71	37	45
279	64	39	61	41	59	66
280	79	57	61	66	64	58
281	12	17	13	8	66	13
282	8	8	7	6	3	6
283	35	47	68	54	47	65
284	69	77	66	60	82	82
285	48	45	57	37	41	50
286	47	64	59	39	58	65
287	17	10	13	8	6	19
288	19	11	20	12	10	28
289	30	52	32	39	55	61
290	66	54	56	54	46	63
291	8	4	18	13	19	16
292	34	30	41	23	22	55
293	25	14	25	21	10	27
294	10	8	9	2	3	4
295	73	65	68	91	58	76
296	21	30	24	9	24	22
297	62	44	67	43	33	65
298	25	24	39	21	26	49
299	31	18	36	25	35	43
300	14	11	25	17	21	37
301	53	50	46	31	28	66
302	27	29	42	25	44	38
303	9	11	15	4	12	17
304	59	68	49	42	55	66
305	55	38	58	41	48	65
306	44	33	44	20	35	47
307	24	11	27	2	24	13
308	27	12	22	22	19	31
309	42	25	54	56	33	75
310	24	23	26	15	36	32

Appendix C-1 (continued)

Item	Sample 8	Sample 9	Sample 10	Sample 11	Sample 12	Sample 13
311	15	16	28	17	29	42
312	16	10	8	3	31	12
313	29	12	27	27	19	20
314	80	85	71	93	74	76
315	36	44	37	45	28	63
316	14	17	21	10	28	31
317	32	25	32	11	36	31
318	93	71	91	98	95	96
319	6	5	17	6	9	21
320	27	28	28	12	18	35
321	72	53	65	70	75	56
322	27	6	29	10	29	36
323	9	10	17	13	19	22
324	8	10	16	8	9	19
325	34	20	34	32	27	46
326	60	63	39	34	33	51
327	12	6	19	11	18	40
328	44	42	34	16	31	45
329	8	5	14	2	5	11
330	90	91	90	90	86	94
331	75	29	81	71	50	85
332	5	8	13	2	10	5
333	5	8	11	3	10	14
334	30	6	54	30	11	63
335	56	47	56	24	60	35
336	2	1	7	1	6	8
337	26	55	32	23	41	30
338	43	44	45	27	34	49
339	38	51	44	33	48	62
340	65	65	68	70	41	72
341	48	51	59	39	64	73
342	59	14	59	22	17	48
343	93	95	88	87	78	91
344	38	23	62	40	27	36
345	67	39	74	84	57	95
346	65	54	63	57	24	64
347	19	27	22	12	35	26
348	43	23	48	26	56	45
349	5	12	22	10	26	24
350	36	14	55	56	30	69

Appendix C-1 (continued)

Item	Sample 8	Sample 9	Sample 10	Sample 11	Sample 12	Sample 13
351	43	15	48	16	84	27
352	89	83	86	84	71	92
353	58	48	51	58	52	53
354	71	63	68	77	82	74
355	5	2	10	1	14	6
356	42	48	61	33	51	52
357	40	51	64	58	42	61
358	30	25	45	26	29	48
359	71	14	80	36	60	55
360	79	60	64	87	65	81
361	7	12	12	5	14	26
362	46	39	49	41	39	60
363	78	82	81	82	89	86
364	29	34	33	13	47	34
365	86	66	78	85	75	86
366	36	19	32	16	25	31
367	31	52	51	31	27	47
368	34	26	39	26	26	52
369	34	29	38	18	52	27
370	79	83	71	87	52	84
371	15	11	15	6	17	15
372	59	50	50	45	58	45
373	54	22	46	18	28	36
374	74	62	64	68	67	87
375	48	43	41	28	31	43
376	36	17	32	13	52	28
377	36	37	31	20	30	29
378	52	49	51	31	20	50
379	9	19	22	10	18	20
380	57	47	19	34	24	54
381	24	11	27	11	19	18
382	49	16	43	26	27	53
383	92	87	84	93	70	87
384	88	87	80	86	66	75
385	45	47	41	58	41	35
386	54	45	49	38	35	56
387	3	4	18	3	6	12
388	54	48	57	63	46	53
389	44	31	38	43	56	42
390	73	51	60	68	63	81

Appendix C-1 (continued)

Item	Sample 8	Sample 9	Sample 10	Sample 11	Sample 12	Sample 13
391	49	57	52	31	86	53
392	29	28	31	29	50	64
393	35	44	39	36	22	48
394	21	35	31	11	30	29
395	38	31	39	28	61	56
396	69	37	62	60	78	86
397	52	23	42	42	59	78
398	52	46	34	40	77	48
399	60	40	38	32	82	55
400	15	25	21	14	50	20
401	55	71	53	83	55	60
402	59	17	47	43	24	57
403	39	26	47	34	42	61
404	91	95	79	91	84	82
405	60	40	56	67	58	67
406	68	26	58	50	62	63
407	6	4	21	4	24	21
408	54	55	47	35	53	54
409	69	63	59	47	64	63
410	67	65	53	42	70	53
411	34	45	28	15	43	36
412	21	13	20	2	6	10
413	69	62	65	52	13	69
414	67	66	78	74	84	83
415	64	38	57	49	52	82
416	37	21	50	30	49	48
417	13	13	21	24	13	26
418	31	35	64	70	51	67
419	57	51	49	48	70	49
420	82	76	70	56	41	76
421	42	35	29	23	55	38
422	67	33	66	76	23	83
423	54	35	27	72	44	66
424	46	25	29	21	52	25
425	27	37	37	20	36	27
426	91	90	87	92	79	64
427	85	83	70	79	62	66
428	52	48	43	39	38	49
429	90	73	73	91	58	75
430	43	53	46	32	60	43

Appendix C-1 (continued)

Item	Sample 8	Sample 9	Sample 10	Sample 11	Sample 12	Sample 13
431	11	10	12	3	8	6
432	21	27	17	8	10	14
433	68	61	49	55	43	58
434	41	35	37	33	55	41
435	33	23	37	23	49	53
436	27	36	26	4	16	21
437	89	57	78	89	88	90
438	69	35	66	60	70	87
439	80	77	75	86	79	84
440	76	42	65	71	60	67
441	40	30	55	38	66	75
442	88	84	72	81	58	82
443	31	28	46	44	49	45
444	37	38	44	32	13	44
445	36	31	36	29	55	40
446	43	51	45	35	43	52
447	82	64	79	78	76	84
448	16	32	38	23	32	40
449	70	60	80	66	65	81
450	3	8	10	2	8	10
451	27	14	29	21	28	36
452	83	77	79	82	77	79
453	40	49	39	53	65	47
454	12	17	18	4	30	20
455	86	80	72	69	86	73
456	61	40	56	61	47	68
457	21	32	27	18	45	23
458	82	34	62	58	69	76
459	79	77	58	56	85	48
460	66	43	64	69	39	67
461	81	55	80	88	43	93
462	39	63	39	48	45	50
463	8	9	25	5	11	32
464	34	34	34	18	29	41
465	12	8	29	16	8	29
466	31	29	37	27	35	39
467	45	51	60	56	54	76
468	16	10	32	15	48	38
469	33	25	43	16	29	47
470	51	26	53	41	47	72

Appendix C-1 (continued)

Item	Sample 8	Sample 9	Sample 10	Sample 11	Sample 12	Sample 13
471	30	28	32	14	11	51
472	84	29	70	77	46	89
473	67	55	67	71	59	84
474	36	47	35	56	42	36
474	31	36	35	24	53	39
476	14	15	14	4	16	10
477	14	6	18	13	17	8
478	2	2	8	0	5	3
479	40	53	45	45	37	56
480	19	23	36	26	32	41
481	58	71	73	65	56	66
482	37	33	41	24	32	45
483	25	16	22	20	45	32
484	9	5	18	6	17	20
485	34	34	37	26	41	40
486	66	59	52	48	43	50
487	8	7	12	1	1	4
488	24	22	33	26	59	55
489	1	1	8	1	3	5
490	23	22	29	11	25	33
491	27	44	38	14	42	34
492	79	68	80	85	51	81
493	88	84	83	92	89	89
494	66	65	65	84	80	67
495	24	21	27	13	70	28
496	67	58	58	62	71	56
497	45	36	33	12	40	34
498	39	38	40	16	29	41
499	62	41	53	29	46	43
500	17	17	25	8	51	27
501	97	95	85	97	88	93
502	33	28	22	8	31	21
503	18	16	18	8	30	16
504	89	62	55	47	61	58
505	23	21	27	8	30	24
506	3	10	14	4	6	11
507	28	34	40	38	65	56
508	15	24	28	7	31	26
509	58	55	53	43	47	60
510	49	38	44	30	25	29

Appendix C-1 (continued)

Item	Sample 8	Sample 9	Sample 10	Sample 11	Sample 12	Sample 13
511	3	2	7	1	2	4
512	16	22	29	13	24	29
513	41	31	41	35	42	57
514	85	77	71	68	78	78
515	7	16	21	7	21	21
516	4	11	12	4	23	17
517	8	12	10	2	28	11
518	19	10	23	9	5	20
519	53	35	51	59	49	64
520	1	7	10	2	5	8
521	47	40	60	73	39	63
522	59	55	68	74	47	70
523	60	56	65	52	64	68
524	3	6	16	4	8	9
525	34	23	52	23	44	53
526	3	7	13	4	12	32
527	3	5	8	1	3	8
528	20	13	22	5	33	32
529	41	31	35	17	21	31
530	10	1	19	8	21	15
531	31	13	42	41	47	55
532	53	49	66	77	60	85
533	53	29	50	42	49	55
534	71	47	70	77	40	70
535	72	51	68	58	75	57
536	33	29	32	12	41	35
537	40	49	44	54	48	50
538	52	62	75	64	41	91
539	7	15	17	7	23	19
540	2	1	7	2	1	5
541	65	63	75	54	89	60
542	61	40	59	41	39	63
543	23	21	29	9	34	27
544	4	4	9	2	31	8
545	49	50	44	29	33	43
546	15	7	22	6	7	13
547	72	61	59	45	27	48
548	30	8	15	6	5	12
549	25	31	21	12	9	38
550	23	22	39	31	39	50

Appendix C-1 (continued)

Item	Sample 8	Sample 9	Sample 10	Sample 11	Sample 12	Sample 13
551	29	10	34	17	15	32
552	83	78	70	81	80	76
553	21	20	32	26	28	39
554	45	34	37	13	26	34
555	12	8	21	8	19	27
556	62	41	46	39	23	55
557	15	26	40	13	51	20
558	42	32	54	25	66	48
559	23	22	23	9	28	34
560	42	37	39	33	40	30
561	87	88	81	84	86	78
562	46	40	45	28	67	40
563	35	26	50	26	38	68
564	67	57	68	84	67	73
565	24	17	21	16	22	31
566	51	44	36	61	59	77
567	43	37	53	30	46	58

Appendix C-2. Percentage of Men Giving a True Response to Each Item

Item	Sample 1 U.S. MMPI-2 Norm	Sample 2 United States College	Sample 3 United States Military	Sample 4 Puerto Rico College	Sample 5 Japan College	Sample 6 Korea College	Sample 7 Holland Norms
	N = 1138	N = 515	N = 1156	N = 184	N = 563	N = 283	N = 681
	Butcher et al. Manual	Butcher et al.	Butcher, Jeffrey, Cayton, Colligan, DeVore, & Minegawa	Cabiya	Shiota, Krauss, & Clark	Han	Sloore, Derksen, DeMay, & Hellenbosch
	(1989)	(1990)	(1990)	(Chap. 14)	(Chap. 4)	(Chap. 5)	(Chap. 16)
1	57	42	58	76	32	57	58
2	96	95	94	97	89	72	95
3	69	45	59	72	37	40	69
4	20	11	11	13	29	21	20
5	41	35	52	29	25	35	23
6	93	93	90	92	88	92	91
7	49	55	54	40	53	68	43
8	87	84	80	84	67	63	85
9	86	82	80	86	60	40	84
10	85	93	95	61	89	90	68
11	4	5	7	5	15	26	11
12	73	67	82	71	83	29	70
13	27	32	37	52	18	34	23
14	64	79	69	80	51	65	48
15	37	40	42	15	34	32	26
16	45	56	41	43	60	72	24
17	5	8	10	5	26	15	10
18	1	1	2	3	6	17	8
19	38	47	39	63	34	67	22
20	88	88	85	84	88	88	78
21	32	53	43	29	35	80	22
22	9	14	12	10	13	16	5
23	6	22	12	17	26	50	3
24	4	7	6	7	3	8	1
25	42	48	39	42	19	36	24
26	47	47	57	33	24	35	35
27	27	31	32	28	42	45	41
28	8	7	7	9	4	18	8
29	84	89	80	72	75	64	57
30	6	7	7	37	2	5	3

Appendix C-2 (continued)

Item	Sample 1	Sample 2	Sample 3	Sample 4	Sample 5	Sample 6	Sample 7
31	13	24	14	26	21	55	15
32	24	45	37	64	29	35	17
33	63	52	58	22	53	41	57
34	81	77	82	78	86	59	82
35	58	56	56	45	55	57	40
36	8	6	9	2	10	6	6
37	39	64	48	49	52	68	19
38	25	35	22	47	35	71	25
39	11	11	14	22	16	29	13
40	3	4	6	5	10	5	3
41	63	66	53	69	84	84	43
42	4	4	6	8	8	5	5
43	79	82	82	74	65	61	86
44	2	8	7	15	9	21	6
45	87	88	89	79	93	75	75
46	19	19	14	27	22	49	15
47	82	77	79	82	76	79	56
48	12	26	17	58	29	39	12
49	67	72	73	71	78	40	76
50	56	72	74	64	45	60	32
51	94	97	95	88	95	91	77
52	17	13	24	14	23	43	14
53	19	26	28	27	14	33	16
54	7	6	9	7	9	13	4
55	44	48	35	56	25	45	20
56	32	32	31	43	35	65	19
57	73	76	75	72	77	69	71
58	61	73	73	84	79	65	57
59	7	8	9	8	2	6	9
60	3	8	8	40	1	4	2
61	70	83	82	91	40	79	23
62	5	7	4	9	18	19	4
63	54	45	63	55	34	53	47
64	22	18	18	12	34	31	12
65	6	10	11	12	18	15	7
66	5	3	6	9	6	12	2
67	51	46	46	56	41	58	32
68	28	48	35	20	42	26	9
69	62	59	66	39	31	28	66
70	19	12	11	10	27	29	22

Appendix C-2 (continued)

Item	Sample 1	Sample 2	Sample 3	Sample 4	Sample 5	Sample 6	Sample 7
71	31	37	41	11	32	39	20
72	4	3	5	19	4	12	4
73	17	18	16	17	33	56	23
74	12	5	9	5	12	15	13
75	95	94	93	93	90	96	93
76	41	44	44	66	47	80	67
77	93	93	81	78	91	92	79
78	95	95	93	91	71	84	92
79	42	37	44	53	38	43	54
80	7	5	6	10	3	5	15
81	52	64	65	76	52	74	55
82	19	28	28	34	58	61	14
83	79	71	76	61	50	46	85
84	17	18	31	9	4	7	15
85	19	35	23	34	38	59	8
86	45	80	63	79	70	49	29
87	50	53	41	49	65	88	27
88	90	85	83	65	72	43	94
89	69	62	57	60	85	98	43
90	92	93	90	93	83	88	91
91	89	84	85	71	87	68	84
92	6	7	9	14	12	12	13
93	87	81	79	66	80	86	76
94	5	8	9	9	27	50	13
95	89	88	88	85	75	39	91
96	9	16	16	12	2	6	11
97	11	13	14	19	10	11	12
98	37	50	40	59	71	72	37
99	5	5	7	14	6	2	4
100	28	17	26	34	37	40	59
101	3	5	7	14	2	9	3
102	96	96	94	95	83	81	88
103	33	33	31	23	41	68	21
104	41	42	47	45	23	27	46
105	31	38	41	28	17	18	26
106	82	69	72	72	75	40	83
107	67	72	60	61	63	55	49
108	91	95	96	97	90	88	85
109	94	94	94	92	91	69	80
110	58	68	65	70	48	90	80

Appendix C-2 (continued)

Item	Sample 1	Sample 2	Sample 3	Sample 4	Sample 5	Sample 6	Sample 7
111	6	3	5	9	16	30	8
112	58	59	49	41	51	56	18
113	62	55	67	54	36	23	39
114	3	5	4	7	6	40	1
115	73	78	84	80	50	35	82
116	30	32	27	52	29	66	27
117	83	83	78	75	88	78	85
118	63	58	54	14	63	36	57
119	43	27	30	31	23	41	88
120	72	81	80	96	94	96	91
121	63	62	67	84	87	69	88
122	81	85	76	90	84	86	74
123	41	57	38	57	66	65	26
124	29	36	38	55	31	44	21
125	89	80	84	72	86	71	88
126	97	97	96	93	93	90	96
127	36	25	18	34	53	80	48
128	66	69	71	55	53	49	51
129	30	38	34	27	56	43	34
130	34	38	29	23	46	34	12
131	47	50	51	76	34	61	54
132	70	77	74	71	59	60	47
133	17	38	78	38	3	20	16
134	16	34	29	46	25	56	16
135	32	33	33	62	53	85	20
136	39	35	34	46	48	40	38
137	21	19	12	9	47	67	7
138	2	2	3	10	6	0	1
139	93	97	92	87	96	97	84
140	77	59	64	54	58	39	72
141	94	94	95	81	88	88	81
142	93	89	91	82	75	87	91
143	73	68	60	60	61	67	74
144	1	2	3	8	2	2	1
145	9	18	21	24	12	6	6
146	13	12	11	22	15	3	18
147	15	9	11	15	9	26	10
148	45	54	58	59	74	20	40
149	8	5	8	21	4	32	11
150	6	12	9	20	9	18	1

Appendix C-2 (continued)

Item	Sample 1	Sample 2	Sample 3	Sample 4	Sample 5	Sample 6	Sample 7
151	46	43	38	74	72	88	57
152	71	77	77	61	48	56	67
153	50	57	42	51	61	62	17
154	42	29	29	37	41	67	37
155	30	26	34	28	29	8	28
156	7	11	16	10	17	66	3
157	41	44	57	46	27	30	60
158	52	44	46	59	48	37	57
159	73	82	81	79	79	88	71
160	79	80	74	80	78	73	64
161	32	33	30	48	34	74	29
162	1	2	2	3	1	1	0
163	71	77	69	67	56	45	54
164	91	89	88	86	76	49	86
165	90	91	92	87	93	74	92
166	15	22	12	67	19	42	14
167	39	40	35	45	48	62	33
168	9	21	17	28	16	50	12
169	43	77	65	62	50	93	47
170	7	10	12	40	9	37	4
171	42	44	47	18	46	39	48
172	9	15	13	27	13	13	8
173	63	56	59	42	47	15	57
174	90	84	85	85	87	76	81
175	4	5	7	10	16	15	7
176	85	83	86	83	80	68	77
177	91	90	90	80	92	62	91
178	24	31	22	45	38	46	41
179	93	95	90	83	79	89	92
180	5	7	7	22	8	28	2
181	77	77	80	69	83	89	83
182	3	5	7	11	11	26	4
183	88	90	84	68	94	89	96
184	50	33	57	48	35	6	76
185	43	46	40	65	54	69	32
186	94	94	93	85	71	70	94
187	26	18	18	20	20	44	16
188	85	95	90	90	83	70	78
189	60	73	66	47	71	18	43
190	4	9	10	44	17	33	6

Appendix C-2 (continued)

Item	Sample 1	Sample 2	Sample 3	Sample 4	Sample 5	Sample 6	Sample 7
191	35	31	26	24	41	48	22
192	98	98	96	95	95	99	93
193	7	7	10	28	16	14	9
194	50	38	52	49	44	45	67
195	9	13	12	20	14	12	7
196	48	57	42	48	54	57	41
197	51	41	54	44	24	22	24
198	2	3	6	17	4	14	1
199	87	76	78	84	66	71	62
200	45	57	52	66	42	67	65
201	24	35	54	20	29	35	10
202	19	16	29	25	10	19	14
203	80	78	70	73	83	79	55
204	81	91	89	87	90	79	79
205	49	51	47	64	18	11	29
206	78	77	82	62	75	84	84
207	32	61	43	60	65	56	36
208	70	72	71	65	79	57	72
209	57	70	62	71	67	73	41
210	97	96	94	96	91	90	86
211	28	37	49	77	36	30	44
212	31	41	36	29	48	40	35
213	41	40	40	59	47	44	41
214	73	65	73	60	58	52	43
215	15	16	13	30	20	65	30
216	3	2	3	10	4	6	15
217	56	38	32	93	35	75	96
218	30	42	37	52	44	58	44
219	51	61	49	68	33	70	56
220	25	11	22	7	23	46	53
221	28	48	39	77	44	40	35
222	89	82	74	89	89	93	89
223	84	78	84	73	49	67	89
224	82	86	86	79	85	64	75
225	34	43	41	43	35	27	22
226	37	58	54	50	32	24	50
227	40	61	66	44	27	32	33
228	4	3	6	19	9	7	10
229	8	10	12	30	24	50	3
230	74	73	68	71	47	39	66

Appendix C-2 (continued)

Item	Sample 1	Sample 2	Sample 3	Sample 4	Sample 5	Sample 6	Sample 7
231	31	44	37	56	75	76	38
232	70	45	34	18	28	49	37
233	35	35	22	36	49	73	30
234	3	3	6	11	24	4	1
235	18	9	20	7	19	19	26
236	31	15	19	22	15	30	30
237	78	62	73	64	53	66	82
238	26	28	24	42	22	27	40
239	42	48	61	74	26	41	38
240	7	6	5	18	10	10	4
241	20	20	27	42	15	15	26
242	35	60	44	55	13	23	22
243	32	28	28	36	36	53	36
244	67	78	80	72	63	88	63
245	32	32	29	22	34	52	45
246	3	4	6	11	9	8	4
247	10	9	12	9	4	8	9
248	14	17	19	32	33	11	20
249	59	67	70	57	39	32	67
250	42	55	41	33	52	63	35
251	24	43	35	43	38	30	34
252	1	1	4	11	2	9	2
253	13	21	22	48	21	61	7
254	24	32	42	65	48	41	31
255	78	80	73	64	83	65	85
256	32	35	27	31	59	62	15
257	52	65	61	54	51	54	42
258	2	4	7	11	9	10	4
259	18	28	24	48	37	18	48
260	96	96	93	90	93	90	92
261	56	54	60	57	29	29	49
262	78	72	77	71	81	59	82
263	73	76	78	78	57	69	81
264	45	44	33	35	21	28	10
265	34	32	31	38	20	58	43
266	59	60	50	82	76	88	84
267	64	70	69	60	49	80	60
268	21	30	20	51	46	70	14
269	28	43	35	78	38	74	69
270	6	7	11	13	5	5	12

Appendix C-2 (continued)

Item	Sample 1	Sample 2	Sample 3	Sample 4	Sample 5	Sample 6	Sample 7
271	39	56	44	49	54	69	28
272	63	56	66	77	26	36	88
273	16	20	17	16	20	32	10
274	21	27	30	33	56	44	31
275	53	42	43	35	31	60	61
276	96	98	96	93	94	99	93
277	18	24	24	23	24	30	13
278	87	80	81	65	70	44	77
279	48	36	36	53	40	42	16
280	80	82	82	59	87	62	68
281	5	4	8	16	7	15	13
282	5	11	8	17	6	2	4
283	38	42	58	41	51	78	48
284	54	48	52	83	45	58	74
285	41	51	39	30	53	58	26
286	33	39	46	54	49	17	57
287	34	42	32	37	14	39	15
288	11	18	14	20	12	20	8
289	29	35	29	38	38	37	28
290	55	45	46	60	33	56	30
291	4	12	8	15	8	21	4
292	26	26	24	46	18	19	22
293	26	15	27	27	19	23	43
294	2	5	5	12	1	6	3
295	86	87	84	74	87	70	88
296	11	17	20	29	11	30	7
297	57	65	68	51	44	40	33
298	13	19	19	51	7	35	11
299	15	25	21	23	17	46	21
300	7	11	11	20	4	39	4
301	15	23	19	30	26	17	4
302	40	37	36	38	36	22	24
303	2	3	6	14	5	24	2
304	48	60	50	42	39	46	36
305	29	46	50	40	38	32	44
306	13	13	14	35	18	15	28
307	9	16	17	18	8	13	8
308	17	16	15	31	21	32	11
309	29	25	29	51	52	79	23
310	9	20	18	37	13	48	4

Appendix C-2 (continued)

Item	Sample 1	Sample 2	Sample 3	Sample 4	Sample 5	Sample 6	Sample 7
311	8	11	16	37	18	37	9
312	4	8	11	15	2	7	4
313	20	27	22	33	23	51	9
314	88	86	81	70	83	86	87
315	48	38	49	41	34	34	46
316	15	31	23	51	23	38	6
317	6	5	11	19	7	12	3
318	95	95	94	86	95	84	88
319	4	7	10	18	3	5	1
320	14	18	18	35	25	29	5
321	72	65	73	60	49	57	79
322	3	5	7	17	16	39	4
323	5	7	8	15	6	20	5
324	8	22	19	31	12	24	8
325	19	31	21	24	25	37	18
326	26	27	23	40	42	37	18
327	10	20	19	45	22	43	3
328	23	28	24	43	24	38	14
329	2	3	7	17	4	4	2
330	91	95	91	82	68	71	79
331	31	31	27	54	29	50	32
332	5	5	8	17	3	6	4
333	6	13	13	22	13	8	3
334	3	4	10	14	6	5	2
335	70	57	60	31	63	76	28
336	2	3	5	11	3	2	3
337	42	30	33	29	31	44	24
338	34	39	33	43	43	68	26
339	37	45	34	51	41	67	24
340	38	61	59	67	33	36	33
341	65	59	51	52	50	86	24
342	52	40	55	53	29	24	32
343	90	89	89	80	80	80	85
344	57	62	52	46	66	49	32
345	62	75	70	83	69	89	43
346	69	58	65	73	20	31	53
347	21	21	17	20	36	43	6
348	23	43	33	53	37	76	11
349	8	8	12	18	11	20	12
350	69	80	84	70	55	75	53

Appendix C-2 (continued)

Item	Sample 1	Sample 2	Sample 3	Sample 4	Sample 5	Sample 6	Sample 7
351	15	5	10	25	20	18	10
352	73	78	76	86	57	83	79
353	73	85	72	55	75	58	22
354	82	82	79	79	78	76	70
355	1	1	5	16	4	4	2
356	37	43	53	58	36	37	40
357	49	44	50	42	56	54	8
358	20	27	28	52	17	33	28
359	60	82	67	67	17	44	30
360	86	87	84	82	58	54	89
361	4	8	10	21	5	7	12
362	59	67	56	51	62	61	28
363	72	80	73	70	78	83	58
364	14	17	13	34	30	55	14
365	76	78	81	84	76	89	76
366	15	20	28	51	14	31	28
367	30	19	30	39	12	39	43
368	19	13	16	32	35	40	14
369	34	38	30	29	28	29	31
370	71	86	78	73	72	56	73
371	4	7	5	14	39	22	2
372	69	66	68	51	57	68	73
373	52	59	50	65	28	42	20
374	43	56	57	62	53	82	56
375	31	25	29	41	37	44	16
376	9	7	12	20	20	15	40
377	25	22	20	23	71	68	13
378	33	36	34	46	18	17	34
379	14	12	19	25	45	24	8
380	16	11	13	22	54	23	7
381	9	14	14	24	29	15	12
382	23	31	27	40	34	32	15
383	90	90	89	80	61	71	92
384	43	39	36	43	19	47	5
385	69	81	73	58	73	72	87
386	39	42	46	59	32	56	38
387	5	10	11	18	10	15	4
388	75	64	73	62	72	29	78
389	17	22	25	38	18	50	12
390	36	51	44	67	63	59	20

Appendix C-2 (continued)

Item	Sample 1	Sample 2	Sample 3	Sample 4	Sample 5	Sample 6	Sample 7
391	35	40	35	48	55	45	57
392	17	7	15	24	19	18	18
393	29	49	43	58	32	54	32
394	19	26	22	24	42	25	12
395	6	7	9	24	34	36	5
396	40	50	49	66	33	52	18
397	10	3	7	27	16	9	8
398	50	53	54	46	39	46	35
399	12	24	25	44	33	29	20
400	16	33	23	26	27	48	12
401	67	83	76	77	76	66	85
402	40	23	23	17	25	62	38
403	40	47	49	62	30	39	27
404	95	91	90	79	87	89	92
405	87	82	80	69	79	59	89
406	46	62	58	50	59	65	55
407	11	10	15	24	25	13	7
408	27	30	31	37	44	31	21
409	39	53	46	49	44	64	48
410	40	47	53	40	46	39	68
411	20	24	19	28	28	29	8
412	16	18	29	22	10	7	9
413	30	24	25	46	31	33	26
414	51	63	70	75	52	80	48
415	27	36	30	62	26	40	30
416	60	47	46	62	26	25	42
417	33	46	51	50	58	31	26
418	45	57	50	55	43	65	73
419	53	67	55	48	44	67	47
420	46	28	30	52	52	66	17
421	20	22	23	27	30	27	23
422	84	91	87	77	54	86	65
423	46	59	47	30	44	65	80
424	10	19	16	30	10	12	12
425	36	31	43	34	33	44	21
426	44	36	38	53	36	46	26
427	83	75	76	51	74	51	74
428	57	58	52	47	60	65	47
429	70	65	75	76	87	59	85
430	38	39	36	48	44	85	25

Appendix C-2 (continued)

Item	Sample 1	Sample 2	Sample 3	Sample 4	Sample 5	Sample 6	Sample 7
431	9	10	16	27	10	4	13
432	21	33	22	32	15	25	21
433	55	54	42	55	56	74	59
434	37	55	51	45	37	72	62
435	7	8	10	22	21	33	4
436	37	43	48	45	65	47	28
437	63	70	76	67	50	65	66
438	31	27	40	44	29	54	18
439	43	41	43	64	74	75	72
440	74	75	69	67	50	71	71
441	11	10	13	38	21	43	9
442	61	62	51	64	62	73	58
443	32	44	49	47	27	29	26
444	22	28	31	27	59	45	16
445	39	39	49	51	12	7	39
446	34	26	22	43	32	48	38
447	11	7	12	58	60	30	11
448	18	23	21	40	42	67	9
449	62	64	62	52	50	46	27
450	2	4	7	14	8	15	2
451	12	22	19	30	26	47	8
452	69	66	68	81	68	65	80
453	65	65	69	66	58	75	81
454	5	5	8	18	6	8	3
455	83	82	80	74	74	69	85
456	58	65	60	60	59	64	33
457	15	15	17	26	39	32	16
458	45	43	42	59	25	35	15
459	83	88	85	66	76	92	78
460	64	71	70	76	66	66	55
461	58	60	54	73	55	74	60
462	87	88	87	67	63	57	89
463	4	8	12	29	6	7	1
464	25	28	22	31	28	49	15
465	58	47	53	40	48	29	52
466	32	38	35	43	49	21	27
467	81	68	71	71	54	67	72
468	3	5	6	22	17	8	3
469	15	21	18	36	9	37	14
470	32	39	43	62	55	38	41

Appendix C-2 (continued)

Item	Sample 1	Sample 2	Sample 3	Sample 4	Sample 5	Sample 6	Sample 7
471	7	11	13	32	15	10	5
472	32	41	37	77	37	40	27
473	51	46	49	46	45	61	58
474	90	87	84	76	54	67	81
474	15	23	22	43	30	60	12
476	4	7	8	21	38	24	4
477	43	70	68	54	58	54	25
478	1	3	5	14	6	5	1
479	43	34	36	54	36	53	42
480	28	27	26	34	48	35	23
481	53	59	66	60	24	39	75
482	15	19	17	33	23	56	21
483	11	14	16	35	30	52	15
484	4	8	11	27	12	18	3
485	17	22	18	42	19	64	16
486	46	51	47	43	44	52	40
487	34	31	19	20	5	2	8
488	16	31	36	42	35	72	10
489	7	6	8	16	5	10	2
490	12	7	15	22	47	52	20
491	11	12	12	21	34	31	9
492	79	77	77	71	55	68	69
493	85	81	81	76	77	89	85
494	82	83	81	74	31	90	80
495	23	14	18	32	26	80	18
496	49	28	38	54	37	56	70
497	21	15	19	36	37	20	20
498	13	15	16	28	14	21	14
499	33	26	38	36	25	46	29
500	8	8	13	17	44	20	11
501	92	93	88	79	75	90	91
502	28	21	25	24	17	51	28
503	13	14	12	29	12	25	10
504	38	24	24	49	46	54	58
505	11	22	19	29	49	32	7
506	4	8	7	20	17	11	2
507	31	37	35	48	57	74	22
508	21	30	24	39	24	42	15
509	25	24	21	41	46	70	18
510	34	34	34	43	26	42	25

Appendix C-2 (continued)

Item	Sample 1	Sample 2	Sample 3	Sample 4	Sample 5	Sample 6	Sample 7
511	20	30	19	19	18	24	4
512	15	18	21	19	16	13	12
513	17	22	23	34	16	32	5
514	69	64	55	55	77	89	73
515	11	9	14	21	13	21	12
516	3	5	8	17	10	10	2
517	4	6	8	18	26	23	6
518	27	25	35	32	40	23	25
519	26	28	27	49	28	51	23
520	2	5	5	13	6	7	1
521	73	75	81	70	43	67	65
522	50	58	56	66	35	37	59
523	64	58	55	44	57	52	64
524	2	4	7	21	6	6	2
525	7	16	14	41	41	64	20
526	5	8	9	20	36	11	2
527	14	6	14	17	11	22	12
528	7	13	14	31	17	13	15
529	19	27	26	36	23	30	21
530	1	5	7	17	14	14	1
531	17	19	29	35	19	33	11
532	29	37	27	38	30	43	17
533	37	40	32	54	37	46	29
534	64	70	63	61	40	34	69
535	55	65	62	63	56	64	64
536	9	12	14	31	7	13	10
537	39	49	55	34	33	39	32
538	39	33	49	53	72	61	30
539	6	9	10	21	13	18	3
540	8	10	12	15	10	7	5
541	72	77	66	53	62	80	54
542	43	51	45	51	30	60	27
543	17	19	20	29	20	17	9
544	5	7	9	21	30	57	14
545	37	35	28	22	49	17	24
546	13	13	13	18	15	18	15
547	70	67	61	61	65	50	64
548	18	31	32	30	15	9	12
549	13	34	45	34	11	17	9
550	27	39	35	26	29	39	6

Appendix C-2 (continued)

Item	Sample 1	Sample 2	Sample 3	Sample 4	Sample 5	Sample 6	Sample 7
551	13	23	24	46	13	23	7
552	57	63	68	76	52	75	67
553	18	28	25	46	31	61	16
554	9	14	12	27	23	26	3
555	2	4	8	17	9	6	1
556	32	33	32	49	37	56	20
557	54	62	69	57	54	80	25
558	14	10	20	45	30	66	29
559	15	15	21	32	18	28	17
560	41	371	41	47	27	39	70
561	92	87	89	82	64	87	90
562	28	23	23	27	54	23	30
563	19	14	19	38	16	9	14
564	81	76	76	70	55	60	77
565	11	10	12	30	20	25	14
566	31	38	31	26	45	80	38
567	28	18	20	37	13	32	16

Appendix C-2. Percentage of Men Giving a True Response to Each Item

Item	Sample 8 Spain	Sample 9 France	Sample 10 Chile	Sample 11 Mexico College	Sample 12 China	Sample 13 Nicaragua	Sample 14 U.S. Pilots
	N = 193	N = 92	N = 758	N = 814	N = 1106	N = 372	N = 274
	Avila-Espada, Jimenez-Gomez	Gillet	Risetti, Himmel, Gonzalez, & Olmos	Lucia & Reyes-Lagunes	Cheung, Song, & Zhang	Lucia & Reyes-Lagunes	Butcher
	(Chap. 15)	(Chap. 20)	(Chap. 11)	(Chap. 13)	(Chap. 6)	(Chap. 13)	(1994)
1	41	59	63	44	20	47	74
2	91	85	91	95	81	90	100
3	51	37	52	66	72	47	100
4	32	29	17	13	32	15	3
5	37	42	52	31	51	58	19
6	93	83	86	89	95	77	100
7	48	36	64	30	74	70	30
8	72	59	68	66	74	59	99
9	80	84	78	91	64	85	99
10	63	54	86	59	66	61	100
11	5	11	16	5	13	13	0
12	72	63	78	70	65	68	99
13	28	47	41	20	42	36	3
14	73	49	58	63	72	58	74
15	24	40	38	23	27	31	3
16	29	42	40	31	36	38	16
17	39	11	12	5	38	21	0
18	6	7	5	2	15	5	0
19	12	34	30	46	70	51	22
20	73	87	67	86	72	74	99
21	26	55	37	27	35	41	4
22	14	11	17	7	31	19	0
23	12	29	16	12	9	16	1
24	4	7	8	1	4	6	0
25	35	34	41	36	16	41	19
26	40	62	42	20	55	39	30
27	47	47	45	53	26	50	3
28	25	16	26	14	13	27	0
29	56	72	64	40	45	52	68
30	16	8	47	4	11	20	1

Appendix C-2 (continued)

Item	Sample 8	Sample 9	Sample 10	Sample 11	Sample 12	Sample 13	Sample 14
31	31	28	46	30	32	42	0
32	22	22	31	37	22	55	3
33	39	57	58	40	62	60	86
34	70	79	63	81	72	64	97
35	54	70	49	50	23	45	26
36	15	11	16	5	21	17	0
37	28	43	42	27	26	39	7
38	38	61	38	33	35	37	0
39	23	35	24	10	27	32	1
40	7	10	17	12	12	36	0
41	60	82	58	61	68	65	35
42	12	9	15	5	29	31	0
43	69	32	75	65	50	76	96
44	6	13	18	12	5	39	0
45	74	82	76	83	83	64	99
46	40	32	40	31	24	41	1
47	74	74	69	77	56	64	99
48	57	39	33	19	34	38	0
49	68	67	70	64	37	72	93
50	54	46	54	38	61	55	18
51	83	84	80	88	77	81	100
52	18	71	41	18	7	37	0
53	31	26	33	19	12	42	1
54	12	8	20	5	18	17	0
55	51	46	47	45	24	54	15
56	41	47	48	34	84	65	5
57	81	74	74	79	57	66	98
58	50	64	79	71	69	77	12
59	14	13	31	8	13	20	0
60	39	17	30	14	24	28	1
61	19	11	65	68	14	46	89
62	8	12	3	2	8	2	0
63	44	38	37	64	56	61	86
64	14	22	33	23	43	31	11
65	15	27	23	10	23	26	0
66	15	11	17	10	7	16	0
67	48	57	54	60	49	67	32
68	38	50	31	21	30	28	13
69	36	60	49	34	26	32	66
70	15	25	22	12	28	17	3

Appendix C-2 (continued)

Item	Sample 8	Sample 9	Sample 10	Sample 11	Sample 12	Sample 13	Sample 14
71	40	45	65	56	33	68	12
72	15	12	21	7	10	18	0
73	15	64	20	7	34	14	0
74	13	15	8	4	22	5	3
75	93	86	89	95	86	94	99
76	77	72	69	56	77	84	7
77	79	84	70	84	66	78	80
78	90	84	82	87	63	89	100
79	41	41	46	43	48	46	44
80	28	25	21	7	6	10	1
81	77	79	75	60	78	74	10
82	33	49	46	24	31	43	1
83	75	73	75	77	75	74	97
84	42	11	38	28	3	22	3
85	20	22	23	19	20	27	2
86	74	34	61	84	59	88	61
87	24	37	35	24	58	44	8
88	93	85	54	85	69	63	91
89	50	58	64	42	59	48	29
90	95	89	89	91	91	87	100
91	76	77	70	86	75	69	99
92	20	24	27	12	32	19	0
93	76	80	70	66	64	65	75
94	54	26	16	12	13	28	0
95	71	41	75	81	69	65	100
96	7	14	17	4	12	13	3
97	14	8	20	14	14	22	0
98	62	46	52	33	30	48	10
99	16	16	30	14	10	41	0
100	50	52	42	57	66	62	48
101	6	11	13	5	9	18	0
102	97	77	91	96	75	97	89
103	44	46	35	22	33	28	13
104	51	60	42	36	31	45	8
105	24	33	45	33	29	30	14
106	84	80	75	69	62	72	97
107	56	39	53	45	75	56	56
108	90	91	93	97	89	96	100
109	90	91	90	95	76	87	99
110	81	66	74	72	64	84	9

Appendix C-2 (continued)

Item	Sample 8	Sample 9	Sample 10	Sample 11	Sample 12	Sample 13	Sample 14
111	19	18	16	9	17	14	0
112	28	65	30	43	35	46	32
113	44	33	42	51	52	54	39
114	7	4	6	3	3	8	0
115	64	71	73	80	65	78	85
116	35	39	47	28	34	40	3
117	64	67	73	83	71	73	99
118	14	43	25	12	55	15	83
119	40	47	44	31	44	55	26
120	93	93	91	97	89	98	39
121	80	77	73	87	84	75	98
122	90	76	82	64	44	76	50
123	59	53	44	63	31	53	4
124	26	33	50	46	12	70	5
125	84	72	70	80	83	64	100
126	83	60	80	44	96	60	100
127	63	50	43	29	58	39	4
128	56	61	65	60	52	67	67
129	31	49	49	27	27	40	11
130	28	57	24	22	45	39	4
131	54	49	52	55	51	52	54
132	59	47	74	55	13	60	82
133	14	11	31	15	51	18	28
134	36	10	37	29	29	29	3
135	49	59	58	52	50	72	4
136	38	59	46	38	69	42	14
137	10	11	8	8	72	13	9
138	7	11	11	3	13	15	0
139	90	80	78	83	61	83	100
140	67	65	57	59	68	44	94
141	81	87	77	90	87	77	100
142	82	90	75	95	76	85	99
143	72	54	67	62	64	42	95
144	4	7	10	1	2	6	0
145	13	12	25	8	12	24	0
146	30	24	35	18	16	24	2
147	18	13	27	17	30	20	0
148	39	42	49	58	39	54	89
149	18	14	22	8	17	29	1
150	16	11	16	8	11	11	0

Appendix C-2 (continued)

Item	Sample 8	Sample 9	Sample 10	Sample 11	Sample 12	Sample 13	Sample 14
151	59	60	70	65	66	75	18
152	61	57	69	78	46	71	99
153	34	28	45	35	39	43	26
154	37	46	43	42	44	50	9
155	13	18	36	9	30	12	35
156	10	26	19	16	15	35	0
157	39	47	62	67	70	60	38
158	57	26	46	50	74	56	39
159	66	70	71	83	76	77	97
160	61	65	73	52	78	82	95
161	50	63	43	38	50	50	7
162	1	2	6	1	1	2	0
163	48	47	60	55	49	48	89
164	82	80	75	89	64	78	100
165	78	78	84	89	76	81	100
166	60	27	61	56	14	65	0
167	52	48	53	37	42	43	8
168	22	26	41	20	32	42	1
169	42	64	56	65	12	63	43
170	32	28	42	29	21	52	0
171	40	46	27	30	39	18	32
172	9	18	23	16	11	33	1
173	52	45	49	43	40	42	89
174	77	77	83	93	80	94	100
175	12	22	16	7	30	19	1
176	81	75	76	86	74	70	99
177	88	80	75	93	89	87	99
178	30	33	44	36	36	50	3
179	88	87	82	91	94	83	100
180	9	25	17	11	10	22	0
181	76	80	76	87	82	77	98
182	6	14	13	4	38	8	0
183	86	70	70	66	90	63	83
184	54	39	52	59	66	57	90
185	59	55	60	54	70	70	11
186	83	84	81	88	77	82	98
187	21	11	27	25	28	28	7
188	87	80	80	93	77	83	99
189	47	71	61	58	39	42	43
190	20	28	31	19	24	17	0

Appendix C-2 (continued)

Item	Sample 8	Sample 9	Sample 10	Sample 11	Sample 12	Sample 13	Sample 14
191	40	43	38	30	37	33	15
192	97	85	94	99	97	97	100
193	24	21	56	14	40	39	1
194	60	55	64	70	53	46	83
195	14	15	27	18	17	27	0
196	51	54	59	38	58	66	4
197	29	28	34	15	40	31	68
198	5	3	13	3	9	12	0
199	74	77	70	81	84	92	99
200	57	49	56	75	37	69	70
201	19	11	34	17	45	40	26
202	21	21	44	18	14	37	0
203	75	54	46	65	56	50	68
204	86	87	81	88	89	84	98
205	48	47	51	48	44	65	7
206	73	66	69	78	82	77	82
207	44	35	43	64	37	68	34
208	69	70	64	69	76	62	96
209	60	54	71	71	23	87	31
210	93	91	93	98	89	99	99
211	28	32	68	70	80	74	20
212	29	46	42	29	76	34	19
213	62	49	68	57	66	62	4
214	63	54	68	49	60	64	76
215	72	22	51	38	66	67	0
216	7	7	20	6	2	18	0
217	91	74	78	65	46	67	48
218	31	28	49	26	47	45	4
219	46	74	66	69	31	72	27
220	22	13	27	11	79	26	29
221	30	46	55	22	24	51	1
222	89	80	88	98	52	94	85
223	69	70	73	74	85	80	98
224	79	72	69	86	69	68	100
225	17	34	38	29	36	59	1
226	28	46	32	57	27	55	19
227	34	42	57	62	43	57	41
228	10	7	15	6	9	25	0
229	14	17	27	23	16	42	0
230	61	46	46	61	85	61	77

Appendix C-2 (continued)

Item	Sample 8	Sample 9	Sample 10	Sample 11	Sample 12	Sample 13	Sample 14
231	76	66	64	64	84	70	32
232	34	40	33	50	46	17	51
233	40	50	46	31	44	44	3
234	6	10	14	1	5	11	0
235	22	32	33	10	15	15	0
236	32	23	24	14	48	21	11
237	80	47	73	82	70	73	95
238	26	30	29	20	26	45	3
239	51	25	81	85	68	82	64
240	30	21	18	14	9	25	0
241	27	29	49	25	32	46	3
242	32	29	42	14	40	45	14
243	29	38	40	25	49	29	5
244	47	60	49	65	42	71	75
245	26	46	22	24	39	19	44
246	6	8	16	4	4	15	0
247	16	17	12	9	9	24	0
248	28	23	36	55	24	52	3
249	48	54	62	61	58	60	98
250	76	40	44	50	31	32	23
251	28	29	37	20	22	46	2
252	5	1	7	5	6	17	0
253	16	9	39	35	36	69	1
254	31	33	49	50	65	67	4
255	76	78	64	74	64	66	96
256	19	22	27	15	61	22	5
257	63	49	57	51	63	54	73
258	4	5	15	7	19	11	0
259	52	33	42	25	19	53	3
260	85	89	85	93	74	91	98
261	53	26	62	58	69	72	57
262	77	91	78	86	64	85	92
263	82	59	80	81	52	88	59
264	48	58	26	36	32	49	9
265	36	57	51	32	31	42	8
266	87	84	78	86	76	82	88
267	79	72	72	65	31	74	42
268	40	42	55	37	59	63	3
269	61	49	72	91	34	91	6
270	11	7	16	9	35	13	1

Appendix C-2 (continued)

Item	Sample 8	Sample 9	Sample 10	Sample 11	Sample 12	Sample 13	Sample 14
271	40	34	49	32	45	49	16
272	76	62	76	77	63	84	74
273	51	27	35	28	47	67	1
274	27	39	32	17	45	40	1
275	45	52	50	43	40	49	24
276	97	95	91	99	96	98	100
277	18	25	37	17	25	30	1
278	62	61	60	74	37	52	97
279	52	29	52	33	54	52	15
280	72	75	65	69	68	63	99
281	20	14	17	13	64	15	0
282	4	7	12	6	3	6	0
283	40	53	66	52	48	61	16
284	72	79	68	65	79	77	8
285	41	36	42	25	36	42	15
286	44	48	66	44	57	59	5
287	28	23	27	21	13	35	8
288	15	13	20	11	10	27	0
289	24	39	32	28	48	50	8
290	64	66	65	55	53	66	18
291	7	3	19	10	15	12	0
292	27	29	35	22	21	51	4
293	29	18	28	24	15	29	22
294	7	9	10	1	4	3	0
295	72	71	67	88	61	76	97
296	17	26	23	14	20	24	0
297	57	45	62	43	34	63	55
298	16	21	39	20	26	40	2
299	21	15	38	22	36	34	0
300	11	11	21	8	16	25	1
301	42	42	42	27	25	61	0
302	30	26	39	22	36	31	3
303	4	7	16	3	8	8	0
304	51	60	42	41	62	63	28
305	41	33	53	33	44	59	2
306	43	30	47	21	33	49	0
307	12	14	24	3	18	8	0
308	30	10	25	18	14	25	0
309	42	29	54	55	35	71	11
310	22	16	26	14	29	24	1

Appendix C-2 (continued)

Item	Sample 8	Sample 9	Sample 10	Sample 11	Sample 12	Sample 13	Sample 14
311	13	11	30	14	27	34	0
312	10	7	15	6	29	9	0
313	23	13	27	23	21	27	3
314	85	84	71	88	70	77	99
315	37	41	39	42	25	56	20
316	21	20	25	21	32	36	0
317	12	12	22	9	26	20	0
318	93	85	91	97	94	96	100
319	5	2	17	4	7	13	0
320	14	20	24	9	13	22	5
321	70	68	67	76	81	68	88
322	17	2	26	9	15	24	1
323	14	12	15	12	9	22	0
324	12	14	25	16	8	22	0
325	26	20	35	27	25	43	1
326	43	52	31	27	31	39	1
327	20	11	23	17	14	38	1
328	31	35	32	12	26	35	2
329	7	2	15	3	4	9	0
330	84	84	84	87	85	91	92
331	62	22	72	65	45	83	6
332	7	7	22	4	12	4	0
333	8	8	16	5	11	16	0
334	27	2	45	23	13	51	0
335	56	46	62	29	60	44	93
336	3	4	12	1	5	4	0
337	35	46	34	25	36	34	9
338	37	33	40	21	33	40	3
339	36	48	39	21	45	55	7
340	38	38	59	57	25	69	50
341	47	49	49	32	59	64	23
342	49	11	53	22	26	46	59
343	86	95	87	84	82	94	97
344	51	42	57	46	40	47	39
345	65	32	79	86	67	95	51
346	67	57	70	62	34	68	19
347	13	18	22	11	32	21	3
348	38	34	56	24	43	38	2
349	11	12	22	12	23	23	0
350	42	24	61	71	38	76	94

Appendix C-2 (continued)

Item	Sample 8	Sample 9	Sample 10	Sample 11	Sample 12	Sample 13	Sample 14
351	26	4	33	4	63	12	7
352	88	85	82	79	65	89	34
353	47	46	44	53	58	46	92
354	75	65	73	75	77	83	82
355	5	0	12	2	13	3	0
356	43	46	62	31	50	47	26
357	45	53	63	59	39	65	32
358	33	26	46	27	31	47	1
359	71	25	75	37	59	61	72
360	83	80	66	91	77	87	99
361	9	18	12	4	13	19	0
362	38	38	46	41	38	54	27
363	69	67	68	77	85	84	74
364	23	23	27	8	37	24	0
365	87	70	77	86	78	91	72
366	29	29	39	21	37	32	3
367	37	45	48	40	21	47	7
368	21	21	36	15	19	39	0
369	25	36	35	13	36	19	11
370	70	78	70	81	57	83	95
371	6	8	9	2	7	3	0
372	56	64	59	55	67	60	98
373	44	38	53	37	38	53	13
374	77	58	68	71	67	82	5
375	45	33	36	22	23	37	9
376	31	12	35	12	44	23	1
377	28	41	31	17	30	26	2
378	46	49	46	27	19	39	4
379	11	17	25	14	26	27	1
380	54	38	23	36	29	50	3
381	25	11	32	15	18	21	3
382	55	29	44	29	28	45	2
383	93	75	81	94	63	85	99
384	26	34	41	49	36	47	28
385	66	72	61	68	63	53	84
386	52	40	47	38	29	52	14
387	6	9	28	9	18	18	0
388	59	55	67	72	51	62	96
389	39	24	38	36	43	40	1
390	67	50	53	60	61	75	11

Appendix C-2 (continued)

Item	Sample 8	Sample 9	Sample 10	Sample 11	Sample 12	Sample 13	Sample 14
391	44	52	47	26	61	44	5
392	9	12	17	10	85	29	8
393	32	46	45	38	26	48	4
394	21	34	29	10	22	26	0
395	16	7	26	10	25	22	0
396	59	43	61	48	34	74	13
397	23	10	25	21	67	47	0
398	36	38	39	38	31	50	49
399	52	36	41	30	73	48	0
400	15	32	28	14	80	20	1
401	72	72	67	83	49	72	92
402	54	15	36	27	71	35	15
403	40	28	48	37	29	64	3
404	91	91	81	90	37	91	97
405	65	61	66	74	84	75	99
406	71	38	62	57	68	63	20
407	9	7	29	6	62	27	2
408	44	48	35	26	23	48	5
409	47	60	50	35	44	45	9
410	61	53	53	43	47	54	26
411	18	46	27	10	67	25	2
412	27	24	27	6	40	12	0
413	55	58	56	46	15	69	3
414	79	71	79	75	13	81	25
415	60	32	58	47	82	81	2
416	49	33	59	48	45	75	39
417	40	37	47	49	64	43	47
418	42	51	63	70	28	66	24
419	63	65	52	50	55	49	23
420	77	74	60	48	66	62	4
421	33	27	30	16	33	28	3
422	62	49	69	79	37	85	93
423	63	40	33	70	37	73	12
424	33	20	26	13	46	17	1
425	24	34	35	22	31	35	26
426	32	32	29	51	46	38	38
427	83	76	64	71	28	63	98
428	56	57	50	39	53	48	5
429	91	73	79	87	42	72	97
430	39	41	47	28	59	40	3

Appendix C-2 (continued)

Item	Sample 8	Sample 9	Sample 10	Sample 11	Sample 12	Sample 13	Sample 14
431	16	21	27	15	16	18	1
432	27	39	28	14	20	23	4
433	68	63	48	46	44	59	20
434	45	48	43	37	66	45	46
435	13	5	25	10	23	22	0
436	26	38	39	10	23	33	12
437	88	60	74	90	89	94	58
438	53	25	47	38	53	64	14
439	74	88	75	86	75	86	23
440	79	42	63	75	63	65	67
441	27	15	35	22	55	50	2
442	72	77	63	71	46	79	27
443	32	23	51	40	45	49	24
444	37	25	41	23	12	36	2
445	54	34	46	32	59	53	5
446	45	49	43	29	44	45	5
447	71	54	69	66	63	73	0
448	13	37	37	18	32	35	1
449	52	54	68	61	63	68	16
450	4	9	15	1	8	6	0
451	24	13	30	17	32	34	1
452	82	76	76	87	79	87	52
453	71	72	60	76	78	72	78
454	8	10	21	4	25	13	0
455	85	76	71	77	84	73	99
456	48	30	45	53	38	65	52
457	14	26	30	11	36	19	4
458	47	27	43	42	55	56	24
459	79	79	65	65	87	62	97
460	70	54	65	74	44	78	61
461	78	60	76	82	41	87	19
462	81	89	64	78	76	81	98
463	6	7	28	6	9	31	0
464	29	25	30	12	20	30	0
465	31	29	46	34	29	54	74
466	33	28	40	26	30	37	13
467	62	55	67	72	71	86	97
468	5	5	25	5	27	16	1
469	18	15	30	10	19	26	0
470	47	32	59	48	51	70	7

Appendix C-2 (continued)

Item	Sample 8	Sample 9	Sample 10	Sample 11	Sample 12	Sample 13	Sample 14
471	14	14	27	6	6	26	0
472	74	27	65	66	36	83	6
473	63	52	64	57	51	78	13
474	82	72	69	78	68	62	98
474	29	30	34	19	43	27	0
476	10	15	17	4	12	8	0
477	61	35	58	67	38	44	57
478	3	3	11	1	5	4	0
479	47	50	51	43	42	56	12
480	19	34	36	28	34	38	4
481	68	61	74	56	53	60	58
482	38	22	40	18	28	32	0
483	25	30	29	27	46	38	1
484	13	4	24	5	19	15	0
485	33	21	43	24	36	38	1
486	65	51	51	48	37	48	12
487	12	17	27	6	1	13	0
488	28	28	41	28	60	54	12
489	6	7	17	2	8	11	0
490	13	22	29	8	19	26	2
491	17	27	31	10	38	21	1
492	72	71	75	83	48	85	95
493	83	80	75	89	89	88	93
494	67	78	68	90	78	73	99
495	24	29	35	18	72	35	12
496	68	59	55	69	74	65	77
497	39	36	32	15	37	33	1
498	25	30	33	10	25	29	1
499	48	41	50	25	40	34	8
500	15	21	26	6	53	23	0
501	94	90	82	94	84	92	99
502	49	41	29	17	49	30	1
503	16	13	25	9	24	15	1
504	72	63	51	45	56	59	6
505	15	15	29	5	24	17	0
506	2	15	16	4	3	5	0
507	39	35	42	35	66	54	3
508	16	26	24	9	32	24	4
509	41	45	41	29	33	46	6
510	53	43	54	43	31	55	12

Appendix C-2 (continued)

Item	Sample 8	Sample 9	Sample 10	Sample 11	Sample 12	Sample 13	Sample 14
511	10	5	18	4	10	17	0
512	12	11	27	12	27	29	1
513	30	18	37	27	31	47	1
514	74	70	67	58	75	69	49
515	11	17	23	10	19	17	0
516	4	4	16	2	20	10	0
517	13	11	15	4	27	16	0
518	20	13	33	15	8	32	2
519	49	35	49	48	44	54	1
520	4	8	14	2	3	6	0
521	63	53	67	75	48	72	93
522	64	54	65	67	46	60	64
523	69	65	65	52	61	67	31
524	4	3	16	3	6	5	0
525	24	15	46	15	42	41	0
526	5	2	16	5	9	24	0
527	7	15	17	3	18	18	0
528	25	14	26	4	35	27	0
529	28	24	31	14	22	26	1
530	9	3	22	8	16	14	0
531	22	12	39	40	49	60	10
532	28	18	41	50	24	53	16
533	39	29	41	35	41	51	6
534	74	53	67	74	41	67	97
535	76	45	57	51	75	58	31
536	14	16	27	6	26	21	0
537	57	66	54	70	51	68	42
538	50	54	70	59	28	88	5
539	8	15	21	6	18	13	0
540	2	7	16	3	2	12	0
541	56	63	74	48	85	69	69
542	59	39	49	32	33	49	7
543	15	14	25	11	29	27	3
544	8	13	21	7	39	24	0
545	35	51	41	23	32	44	4
546	11	5	23	7	6	15	0
547	66	67	52	40	22	40	37
548	38	12	23	18	11	21	5
549	22	33	28	16	8	38	2
550	38	22	44	34	40	48	5

Appendix C-2 (continued)

Item	Sample 8	Sample 9	Sample 10	Sample 11	Sample 12	Sample 13	Sample 14
551	28	13	37	19	15	31	3
552	67	72	62	78	77	82	71
553	21	16	32	26	32	40	2
554	33	28	28	7	16	17	0
555	6	4	15	4	7	10	0
556	65	52	50	43	27	59	2
557	28	45	58	38	63	51	69
558	37	33	58	25	56	38	1
559	22	37	30	11	32	37	1
560	48	39	38	35	33	27	75
561	87	87	86	88	84	86	100
562	55	22	42	32	65	43	7
563	33	20	45	27	32	64	1
564	75	72	72	82	72	77	97
565	18	18	23	13	20	25	0
566	37	47	36	55	60	69	4
567	39	32	49	26	41	49	4

Appendix D. MMPI-2 Item Numbers Distributed according to the Percentage Difference for a True Response between Various MMPI-2 National Samples and the U.S. Normative Group

MMPI-2 Item Numbers Distributed according to the Percentage Difference for a True Response between Various MMPI-2 National Samples and the U.S. Normative Group

100	
98 – 99	
96 – 97	
94 – 95	
92 – 93	
90 – 91	Chilean men (N = 758) vs. U.S. normative men (N = 1,138)
88 – 89	
86 – 87	
84 – 85	
82 – 83	
80 – 81	
78 – 79	
76 – 77	
74 – 75	
72 – 73	
70 – 71	
68 – 69	
66 – 67	
64 – 65	
62 – 63	
60 – 61	
58 – 59	447
56 – 57	
54 – 55	
52 – 53	
50 – 51	
48 – 49	193
46 – 47	166
44 – 45	269 558
42 – 43	334
40 – 41	30 211 331
38 – 39	118 239 525
36 – 37	88 215 232
34 – 35	71 170 203 268 306
32 – 33	31 168 231 286 348 439 472
30 – 31	415 538
28 – 29	76 112 230 241 283 353 399 414
26 – 27	60 82 135 190 213 221 253 278 298 301 358 376 413 470 485 563
24 – 25	52 59 99 151 202 254 259 305 309 356 366 374 441 463 482 488 551
22 – 23	77 81 146 217 248 299 311 322 381 387 462 468 519 531
20 – 21	20 29 46 48 84 92 113 124 134 140 157 178 340 360 382 389 395 396 405 471 474 481 484 491 498 510 513 530 567

18 – 19   8 27 28 34 58 91 120 125 129 142 183 195 218 229 244 264 266 273 277 295 351 367 407 418 427 431 435 443 444 448 451 459 461 475 483 500 505 528 536 547 554 556

16 – 17   3 44 56 63 65 72 86 93 110 116 126 141 145 164 177 185 197 199 216 227 265 310 314 317 324 325 332 341 345 368 390 393 406 424 438 454 490 499 509 544 550

14 – 15   7 13 40 51 53 80 87 95 98 100 105 107 133 139 149 167 171 172 173 194 209 219 235 255 280 284 291 300 303 307 349 357 359 397 404 417 420 422 426 457 467 469 477 494 522 524 537 539 549 553 559 562

12 – 13   11 38 39 47 54 66 69 78 137 147 156 169 175 180 186 224 246 251 258 272 281 296 319 327 329 362 364 378 391 400 410 423 450 455 456 465 473 476 495 503 504 506 512 515 516 520 529 532 555 565

10 – 11   5 23 42 45 64 94 101 111 117 121 130 150 161 163 179 182 196 198 200 201 207 212 223 228 233 234 240 245 260 270 271 274 290 312 316 320 323 333 336 355 372 379 394 398 409 412 421 437 440 478 489 493 497 501 507 517 526 546

8 – 9   9 19 22 35 36 96 97 138 144 176 206 243 267 288 292 294 308 315 328 335 337 350 352 354 361 383 385 386 388 403 408 429 430 446 466 479 480 540 543 564

6 – 7   1 6 14 17 32 75 106 127 136 143 155 158 160 165 174 208 236 242 252 261 263 282 287 304 313 330 338 377 380 411 428 432 433 434 445 449 452 487 496 518 521 542 561

4 – 5   2 12 16 18 21 24 26 33 41 43 61 74 79 83 85 89 102 109 131 132 148 153 162 188 192 210 214 225 226 237 256 257 276 279 297 318 321 326 363 371 375 402 453 464 486 492 533 545 548 552 557 566

2 – 3   4 37 49 50 55 62 67 68 70 73 90 103 108 114 123 152 159 184 191 205 220 238 247 249 250 275 289 293 339 343 384 436 442 458 508 511 514 527 534 535 541 560

0 – 1   10 15 25 57 104 115 119 122 128 154 181 187 189 204 222 262 285 302 342 344 346 347 365 369 370 373 392 401 416 419 425 460 502 523

MMPI-2 Item Numbers Distributed according to the Percentage Difference for a True Response between Various MMPI-2 National Samples and the U.S. Normative Group (continued)

100	
98 – 99	
96 – 97	
94 – 95	
92 – 93	
90 – 91	Chilean women (N = 859) vs. U.S. normative women (N = 1,462)
88 – 89	
86 – 87	
84 – 85	
82 – 83	
80 – 81	
78 – 79	
76 – 77	
74 – 75	
72 – 73	
70 – 71	
68 – 69	
66 – 67	
64 – 65	447
62 – 63	
60 – 61	
58 – 59	269
56 – 57	
54 – 55	
52 – 53	193
50 – 51	334
48 – 49	
46 – 47	231 239
44 – 45	203
42 – 43	30 211
40 – 41	166 232
38 – 39	215 414 525 558
36 – 37	439 472
34 – 35	151 306 441 538
32 – 33	31 170 286 331 353
30 – 31	59 71 213 241 268 278 413 563
28 – 29	60 112 283 356 358 406 415 420 531
26 – 27	20 27 28 77 118 168 229 298 301 317 348 374 481
24 – 25	48 76 86 88 135 217 221 230 248 322 399 468
22 – 23	34 65 87 91 107 113 129 137 141 142 146 202 255 277 305 309 345 367 389 395 418 456 459 461 510 550 554 567
20 – 21	38 40 45 47 52 81 82 92 99 125 173 190 195 224 235 254 280 299 314 359 366 405 435 448 482 488 499 537

18 – 19   7 8 12 46 58 72 98 120 124 157 186 209 253 273 311 344 357 360 376
381 382 391 397 443 463 490 491 513 522 523 530

16 – 17   51 56 95 110 111 126 134 149 164 185 194 218 219 244 265 284 307 325
372 396 398 437 444 470 475 484 494 498 504 528 551 553 555

14 – 15   2 11 22 23 29 89 93 96 117 133 140 147 172 175 177 178 179 183 208
223 256 259 264 289 291 295 300 310 349 352 354 368 387 393 404 407
408 410 424 428 451 452 454 471 485 496 507 519

12 – 13   13 36 54 55 61 66 78 94 101 105 128 136 145 150 163 180 216 251 260
279 303 315 323 329 335 378 390 422 427 462 469 483 487 500 505 559

10 – 11   14 16 39 44 53 74 80 106 115 116 156 165 171 236 246 249 257 261 270
296 313 316 319 320 324 327 337 338 361 362 375 412 417 423 438 455
501 506 509 515 524 529 533 539 547 549 565

8 – 9   3 17 32 33 37 42 49 69 83 84 97 104 127 130 139 144 155 161 169 174
176 181 191 198 201 204 207 212 226 228 233 234 237 240 245 272 281
285 308 332 340 341 355 379 394 403 426 431 434 460 477 493 516 517
520 526 534 543 546 548 556 562 566

6 – 7   5 6 10 24 26 41 50 75 85 90 103 138 160 167 182 188 200 214 225 227
288 292 333 351 364 369 370 373 383 384 388 446 449 450 476 478 479
495 497 535 536 544

4 – 5   1 18 19 57 63 114 121 122 123 158 162 184 187 197 205 220 238 242
250 252 258 275 294 297 304 321 328 330 336 342 363 365 371 400 402
409 416 419 442 457 465 467 473 474 480 489 508 512 561 564

2 – 3   9 15 21 35 70 79 102 108 109 119 131 148 152 192 206 210 222 243 262
271 274 276 290 302 312 318 326 343 350 380 386 392 401 411 421 425
429 430 432 433 436 453 458 466 486 492 511 514 518 521 532 540 541
542 552 557

0 – 1   4 25 43 62 64 67 68 73 100 132 143 153 154 159 189 196 199 247 263
266 267 282 287 293 339 346 347 377 385 440 445 464 502 503 527 545
560

MMPI-2 Item Numbers Distributed according to the Percentage Difference for a True Response between Various MMPI-2 National Samples and the U.S. Normative Group (continued)

100	
98 – 99	
96 – 97	
94 – 95	
92 – 93	
90 – 91	319 Chinese men (N = 1,106) vs. U.S. normative men (N = 1,138)
88 – 89	
86 – 87	330
84 – 85	
82 – 83	
80 – 81	295
78 – 79	277 322
76 – 77	355
74 – 75	
72 – 73	361 454 463
70 – 71	364 521 541
68 – 69	318 468 554
66 – 67	314 404 536
64 – 65	515 547 563
62 – 63	278 281 343 366 372 383
60 – 61	450 524 561
58 – 59	282 321 336 435 438 455
56 – 57	61 132 276 335 388 393 400 407 502
54 – 55	220 331 495
52 – 53	56 211 231 371 441 475 489 497
50 – 51	137 215 296 405 412 422 431 467
48 – 49	291 559
46 – 47	273 350 362 421 557
44 – 45	212 392 448 462 471 505 508 552
42 – 43	484 520 542
40 – 41	254 304 332 341 437 492 566
38 – 39	29 100 268 285 365 406 465 474 476 479 482 501 514
36 – 37	1 69 76 122 222 297 337 375 414 427 452 478 493 503 526
34 – 35	35 133 182 209 283 303 349 370 389 408 433
32 – 33	17 19 78 139 193 267 305 363 385 447 500
30 – 31	49 136 169 306 403 449 477 555
28 – 29	43 157 256 270 300 359 428 459 507
26 – 27	25 77 81 92 164 175 185 239 271 274 280 310 317 360 391 411 424 445 456 472 551
24 – 25	7 42 47 152 203 213 232 244 253 307 329 344 354 386 387 397 419 446 498 544
22 – 23	9 22 48 60 64 93 112 127 158 163 168 173 260 287 312 315 327 345 351 356 416 444 457 460 496 534 539

20 – 21	55 88 95 102 106 121 151 189 190 201 219 263 298 311 381 384 506 530 532 546 565
18 – 19	10 31 109 135 161 272 289 358 377 399 418 481 519 523 550
16 – 17	39 51 57 65 73 120 124 142 184 186 218 236 243 258 266 395 398 409 429 464 483 516 517 529 543 556
14 – 15	2 13 18 20 84 86 91 128 147 165 170 255 262 302 309 369 373 376 396 415 443 453 473 480 488 504 535 560 564
12 – 13	4 8 36 37 82 117 134 178 214 224 230 241 261 264 294 347 401 417 426 436 461 469 470 533 537 538 558
10 – 11	5 15 38 52 54 74 89 104 111 113 123 130 138 153 176 196 197 226 248 250 257 279 292 299 316 323 325 380 413 425 439 486 511 513 528 540
8 – 9	11 12 14 16 26 34 40 58 70 75 87 94 107 115 118 140 143 149 156 174 195 200 204 210 217 229 233 275 313 328 334 348 352 402 420 423 434 458 491 499
6 – 7	53 59 72 79 98 101 110 125 141 148 188 198 208 237 245 269 284 290 320 333 340 342 353 367 390 394 442 494 509 567
4 – 5	3 28 30 41 45 46 50 83 99 116 131 150 180 181 202 205 206 207 221 228 242 252 293 339 374 379 382 410 430 432 451 490 512 527 548 562
2 – 3	6 21 23 32 44 62 63 66 67 68 71 96 97 105 108 129 145 146 154 159 167 171 172 177 183 187 191 194 199 225 227 234 235 240 251 265 286 288 338 368 378 466 485 487 522 545 549 553
0 – 1	24 27 33 80 85 90 103 114 119 126 144 155 160 162 166 179 192 216 223 238 246 247 249 259 301 308 324 326 346 357 440 510 518 525 531

MMPI-2 Item Numbers Distributed according to the Percentage Difference for a True Response between Various MMPI-2 National Samples and the U.S. Normative Group (continued)

100	
98 – 99	
96 – 97	
94 – 95	
92 – 93	
90 – 91	Chinese women (N = 1,108) vs. U.S. normative women (N = 1,462)
88 – 89	
86 – 87	
84 – 85	
82 – 83	
80 – 81	
78 – 79	
76 – 77	
74 – 75	
72 – 73	
70 – 71	
68 – 69	399
66 – 67	61
64 – 65	220 231
62 – 63	281 447
60 – 61	
58 – 59	
56 – 57	132
54 – 55	422
52 – 53	391
50 – 51	56 212 558
48 – 49	211 215 495
46 – 47	49 278 488
44 – 45	133 222 395 414 441
42 – 43	268 351 547
40 – 41	76 254 346 389 439 468
38 – 39	342 376 424 500 507
36 – 37	19 29 122 136 193
34 – 35	173 219 239 244 260 348 397 475 483
32 – 33	43 47 169 175 213 257 267 284 396 400 406 410 435 456 531
30 – 31	17 48 78 81 157 164 203 286 317 353 525 562 566
28 – 29	163 189 297 374 421 544
26 – 27	7 22 77 112 182 209 218 232 243 255 263 273 306 370 398 402 434 437 454 492 496 517 528
24 – 25	25 86 119 168 185 295 310 312 322 419 453 537
22 – 23	35 67 82 102 106 109 142 190 262 350 413 415 443 457 487 491 504 521 534 550

20 – 21	9 60 69 95 127 139 186 224 241 299 311 315 362 364 383 384 408 427 428 445 516 530
18 – 19	4 10 31 42 55 88 91 92 100 128 135 151 152 158 174 201 256 270 272 274 314 316 340 349 356 378 388 405 411 485 513 563
16 – 17	2 13 38 65 73 89 120 137 147 153 165 237 275 280 360 392 407 426 429 460 465 518 523 536 539 542 559
14 – 15	39 40 51 57 63 87 115 117 170 205 217 226 229 253 264 277 291 293 298 321 323 344 366 390 438 444 448 461 484 490 499 503 505 535 555 556 557 567
12 – 13	18 20 27 30 34 53 93 98 107 110 113 116 118 130 138 159 161 167 176 184 210 225 233 269 292 305 307 343 347 355 358 361 363 386 430 436 451 452 472 473 497 519 543 553 554
10 – 11	26 54 75 146 148 150 156 199 200 248 258 261 279 296 300 325 327 373 381 404 409 418 442 458 470 482 502 515 541 545 565
8 – 9	3 12 15 36 41 46 52 58 68 72 74 94 111 121 124 134 149 187 197 202 221 228 245 285 287 289 301 303 330 334 335 372 380 433 449 476 481 501 508 526 532 533 552
6 – 7	8 11 16 21 37 62 79 84 96 97 129 141 188 195 198 230 265 283 290 308 332 369 371 394 423 462 471 477 486 511 546
4 – 5	1 5 6 28 44 50 71 99 101 104 140 143 154 166 172 178 180 181 191 206 208 214 227 236 252 259 288 302 324 333 336 339 345 357 379 401 403 412 416 431 432 440 446 450 455 459 463 464 478 498 509 510 514 527 529 564
2 – 3	14 23 24 33 45 59 64 66 70 83 85 103 108 125 126 131 145 155 160 177 183 194 196 207 223 234 235 240 242 250 266 271 282 294 309 313 318 319 326 329 341 382 387 393 417 467 469 474 493 494 506 520 522 524 540 548 549 551 560
0 – 1	32 80 90 105 114 123 144 162 171 179 192 204 216 238 246 247 249 251 276 304 320 328 331 337 338 352 354 359 365 367 368 375 377 385 420 425 466 479 480 489 512 538 561

MMPI-2 Item Numbers Distributed according to the Percentage Difference for a True Response between Various MMPI-2 National Samples and the U.S. Normative Group (continued)

100	
98 – 99	
96 – 97	
94 – 95	
92 – 93	
90 – 91	Dutch men (N = 681) vs U.S. Normative men (N = 1,138)
88 – 89	
86 – 87	
84 – 85	
82 – 83	
80 – 81	
78 – 79	
76 – 77	
74 – 75	
72 – 73	
70 – 71	
68 – 69	
66 – 67	
64 – 65	
62 – 63	
60 – 61	
58 – 59	
56 – 57	
54 – 55	
52 – 53	
50 – 51	353
48 – 49	
46 – 47	61
44 – 45	119
42 – 43	335
40 – 41	112 217 269 341 357
38 – 39	384
36 – 37	
34 – 35	264 423 449
32 – 33	153 232 279 373
30 – 31	100 214 259 359 362 376 458
28 – 29	220 410 418 420 439 557 560
26 – 27	29 47 76 89 184 197 487
24 – 25	50 55 121 199 203 266 272 286 290 297 344 434 456
22 – 23	87 110 113 130 132 391 396 481
20 – 21	16 37 41 200 205 284 342 496 504 550
18 – 19	5 25 35 67 68 107 120 157 287 337 345 385 401 416 422 426 477 541

16 – 17   10 14 19 51 86 163 178 189 194 209 211 256 293 302 346 350 390 453
511 542

14 – 15   27 77 109 123 128 137 160 201 215 218 238 285 305 306 347 363 375
398 425 429 558

12 – 13   26 45 56 79 103 127 135 141 191 216 225 226 242 245 280 304 330 339
348 354 366 367 374 377 403 411 430 438 513 525 532 545 556 567

10 – 11   15 20 21 64 71 85 93 151 185 187 210 251 257 271 274 278 283 301 313
428 452 464 492 552

8 – 9   49 80 94 102 115 124 139 174 176 183 230 235 249 263 265 275 281 316
320 326 328 338 358 361 380 382 399 406 409 427 436 448 460 467 470
474 490 507 510 521 522 528 533 535 538 543 544

6 – 7   7 11 18 32 33 43 63 73 83 92 108 118 122 131 167 171 173 181 188 196
206 221 224 227 228 231 241 248 250 253 254 255 261 268 270 273 299
308 309 318 321 327 352 379 394 408 412 417 419 443 444 465 473 482
486 488 508 509 531 537 547 548 551 554 566

4 – 5   13 17 22 44 46 58 69 82 88 91 104 105 129 140 146 147 148 150 152 154
156 158 164 169 192 202 207 212 219 223 229 233 237 239 243 244 260
262 267 277 292 296 310 340 343 349 351 368 372 389 400 407 413 431
433 446 451 459 466 472 480 483 489 495 499 505 514 534 549 563 564

2 – 3   6 8 9 12 23 24 30 31 36 39 52 53 54 57 59 66 70 75 78 81 84 95 96 111
114 116 117 142 145 149 155 159 161 165 168 170 175 180 190 193 195
204 208 234 240 258 276 288 295 298 300 315 317 319 333 356 360 369
370 371 381 383 388 393 397 402 404 405 414 415 421 424 435 437 440
441 442 454 455 461 462 463 471 475 491 494 500 503 506 512 517 518
519 526 527 529 539 540 546 553 559 561 562 565

0 – 1   1 2 3 4 28 34 38 40 42 48 60 62 65 72 74 90 97 98 99 101 106 125 126
133 134 136 138 143 144 162 166 172 177 179 182 186 198 213 222 236
246 247 252 282 289 291 294 303 307 311 312 314 322 323 324 325 329
331 332 334 336 355 364 365 378 386 387 392 395 432 445 447 450 457
468 469 476 478 479 484 485 493 497 498 501 502 515 516 520 523 524
530 536 555

MMPI-2 Item Numbers Distributed according to the Percentage Difference for a True Response between Various MMPI-2 National Samples and the U.S. Normative Group (continued)

100	
98 – 99	
96 – 97	
94 – 95	
92 – 93	
90 – 91	Dutch women (N = 563) vs. U.S. normative women (N = 1,462)
88 – 89	
86 – 87	
84 – 85	
82 – 83	
80 – 81	
78 – 79	
76 – 77	
74 – 75	
72 – 73	
70 – 71	
68 – 69	
66 – 67	
64 – 65	
62 – 63	
60 – 61	353
58 – 59	
56 – 57	
54 – 55	
52 – 53	
50 – 51	
48 – 49	112
46 – 47	
44 – 45	61
42 – 43	217 341
40 – 41	269
38 – 39	357 449
36 – 37	153
34 – 35	137 279 346 376 541
32 – 33	50 359 456 560
30 – 31	14 259 423 439
28 – 29	29 87 89 214 391 401 418
26 – 27	16 47 215 232 335 373 410 458 496
24 – 25	15 25 107 132 178 189 297 396
22 – 23	10 187 199 205 209 218 342 362 422 434
20 – 21	5 67 76 110 157 163 191 194 242 271 290 344 345 350 367 385 416 428 438 481 487 521 557

18 – 19	41 64 100 113 119 120 151 174 184 220 224 264 284 285 286 302 398 420 461 504 545 566
16 – 17	51 139 141 230 251 265 337 384 390 466 525
14 – 15	19 27 35 57 58 94 121 135 203 256 272 301 304 305 363 425 453 532 542 558
12 – 13	20 33 56 73 86 109 123 130 140 160 164 176 200 210 245 274 280 306 318 351 354 374 377 419 437 462 492 509 513 523 533 537 538 550 556
10 – 11	18 21 37 43 45 55 77 79 105 115 128 129 149 185 197 211 226 227 237 309 326 330 347 348 375 403 406 460 467 495 567
8 – 9	13 26 44 68 71 80 85 118 143 216 231 239 241 260 266 275 278 287 289 313 328 338 361 366 368 382 394 400 411 430 445 459 472 486 503 544 551 554
6 – 7	2 8 11 17 32 38 39 46 49 62 83 92 97 101 103 104 127 147 148 154 170 171 175 181 188 196 213 221 248 250 267 273 288 293 294 299 300 308 315 320 339 356 365 369 378 379 380 402 414 415 424 429 440 443 446 448 451 464 470 473 477 480 488 490 507 511 522 528 531 543 547 552
4 – 5	3 7 53 63 88 102 108 122 124 134 136 150 152 169 173 179 183 193 195 204 207 208 228 233 235 236 238 243 254 261 262 263 268 277 283 292 310 314 316 321 327 331 343 352 358 383 389 392 395 399 409 412 417 421 427 431 433 441 442 452 457 469 482 502 505 508 510 512 514 529 534 535 539 546 549 561 563
2 – 3	23 31 40 48 60 65 69 70 78 91 96 99 111 117 125 126 131 142 146 155 156 159 161 166 167 168 190 192 201 206 225 244 247 258 276 281 291 296 298 312 317 323 333 349 355 364 370 371 381 386 388 397 404 407 408 413 426 432 436 444 463 465 474 475 476 479 489 498 499 500 517 527 536 548 553 559 564 565
0 – 1	1 4 6 9 12 22 24 28 30 34 36 42 52 54 59 66 72 74 75 81 82 84 90 93 95 98 106 114 116 133 138 144 145 158 162 165 172 177 180 182 186 198 202 212 219 222 223 229 234 240 246 249 252 253 255 257 270 282 295 303 307 311 319 322 324 325 329 332 334 336 340 360 372 387 393 405 435 447 450 454 455 468 471 478 483 484 485 491 493 494 497 501 506 515 516 518 519 520 524 526 530 540 555 562

MMPI-2 Item Numbers Distributed according to the Percentage Difference for a True Response between Various MMPI-2 National Samples and the U.S. Normative Group (continued)

100	
98 – 99	
96 – 97	
94 – 95	
92 – 93	
90 – 91	French men (N = 92) vs. U.S. normative men (N = 1,138)
88 – 89	
86 – 87	
84 – 85	
82 – 83	
80 – 81	
78 – 79	
76 – 77	
74 – 75	
72 – 73	
70 – 71	
68 – 69	
66 – 67	
64 – 65	
62 – 63	
60 – 61	
58 – 59	61
56 – 57	
54 – 55	52
52 – 53	
50 – 51	
48 – 49	95
46 – 47	43 73
44 – 45	350 439
42 – 43	447
40 – 41	342
38 – 39	
36 – 37	38 126
34 – 35	231 359 422
32 – 33	3 440
30 – 31	10 76 82 161 232 237 261 345
28 – 29	8 107 113 230 413 420 456 465
26 – 27	48 81 135 158 203 278 301 326 353 405 411 416 467 537
24 – 25	39 100 163 190 266 284 335 399 402 504
22 – 23	21 23 68 130 132 153 197 219 265 380 559
20 – 21	13 27 65 94 118 120 136 169 170 180 268 269 362 388 408 409 414 509 521 549 556

18 – 19	41 80 92 102 104 129 143 156 173 175 183 214 217 221 274 279 432 448 458 474 483 554 558
16 – 17	63 117 125 168 239 306 341 354 377 378 391 393 400 442 487 491 498 566
14 – 15	14 26 31 56 60 71 121 127 151 152 160 187 193 212 223 233 235 240 245 259 263 283 286 295 296 302 344 361 366 367 373 374 383 390 394 446 475 497 511 518 538 545 552
12 – 13	7 29 35 46 87 91 103 111 123 139 140 155 165 166 174 185 192 201 206 220 262 264 297 304 328 346 352 398 403 410 419 426 431 488 500 502
10 – 11	2 6 12 44 50 51 78 86 89 99 137 146 164 176 177 182 184 186 189 199 224 256 273 287 289 290 318 339 348 351 424 434 457 460 476 490 496 506 532 534 535
8 – 9	4 25 28 47 72 75 77 98 101 110 116 138 167 172 178 191 213 222 226 229 236 241 248 254 267 281 293 298 331 356 364 384 406 412 433 443 449 477 481 492 499 510 519 525 533 539 541 544 546 557 564
6 – 7	11 17 18 33 40 53 59 62 66 67 70 83 84 93 112 133 134 141 144 149 157 179 195 196 204 210 215 234 242 243 244 247 260 277 294 308 310 313 315 317 320 323 324 330 358 360 365 370 382 389 418 421 423 427 438 450 452 453 455 471 479 480 482 495 515 517 520 528 536 548 562 565
4 – 5	19 37 42 45 88 96 119 122 124 128 150 154 171 188 194 200 211 216 238 246 249 251 253 271 280 285 300 303 305 307 314 316 321 337 343 349 357 363 371 372 387 392 401 404 407 415 417 441 445 454 459 466 472 485 486 493 494 505 507 508 512 522 529 531 542 550 561 567
2 – 3	1 9 15 16 22 24 30 32 34 36 55 58 69 74 85 90 97 105 106 109 115 131 142 145 147 148 159 181 202 205 207 209 218 227 228 250 257 258 282 288 292 311 312 319 332 333 336 347 368 369 375 376 379 381 385 396 425 429 430 435 437 444 461 462 463 468 478 501 526 530 543 547 553 555 560
0 – 1	5 20 49 54 57 64 79 108 114 162 198 208 225 252 255 270 272 275 276 291 299 309 322 325 327 329 334 338 340 355 386 395 397 428 436 451 464 469 470 473 484 489 503 513 514 516 523 524 527 540 551 563

MMPI-2 Item Numbers Distributed according to the Percentage Difference for a True Response between Various MMPI-2 National Samples and the U.S. Normative Group (continued)

100
98 – 99
96 – 97
94 – 95
92 – 93
90 – 91   French women (N = 167) vs. U.S. normative women (N = 1,462)
88 – 89
86 – 87
84 – 85
82 – 83
80 – 81
78 – 79
76 – 77
74 – 75
72 – 73
70 – 71
68 – 69
66 – 67
64 – 65
62 – 63
60 – 61   61
58 – 59
56 – 57   231
54 – 55   52
52 – 53
50 – 51   447
48 – 49
46 – 47
44 – 45   73 359 422
42 – 43
40 – 41   43 342
38 – 39   350 439 456
36 – 37   8 95 286 405
34 – 35   38 76 107 113 126 153 269 353 402 420
32 – 33   132 230 265
30 – 31   81 94 237 278 301 380
28 – 29   183 232
26 – 27   118 203 235 268 284 326 351 399 410 413 414
24 – 25   13 23 82 129 135 136 280 306 367 374 416 458 481 491 504 537
22 – 23   26 29 48 64 65 68 130 170 175 186 187 236 261 318 335 360 391 408
           440 521 538
20 – 21   3 10 25 27 117 120 160 164 165 168 217 245 273 331 344 362 393 401
           411 438 549 554

18 – 19	89 110 137 161 180 208 221 295 297 317 354 532
16 – 17	14 17 60 80 92 140 156 158 173 182 205 229 240 296 341 369 372 373 388 389 442 465 473 475 487 494 510 542 558 566
14 – 15	1 20 21 56 87 127 151 174 184 193 199 214 219 224 227 277 304 356 395 448 479 496 498 534 541 564
12 – 13	2 11 50 53 78 100 101 116 123 139 143 167 172 185 194 197 209 215 222 254 274 281 298 310 328 337 345 352 375 394 403 432 446 449 452 454 460 462 482 490 509
10 – 11	41 42 71 91 111 125 141 169 176 188 242 247 256 266 293 302 320 346 361 378 424 428 433 444 457 470 471 485 486 492 517 518 525 533 535 557 559
8 – 9	6 7 16 31 33 35 36 39 62 69 86 104 112 121 131 155 159 163 190 206 211 218 223 241 263 279 303 338 339 358 364 365 366 382 396 400 409 415 421 441 453 476 480 488 497 499 507 513 516 523 539 547
6 – 7	28 30 40 45 47 72 74 75 102 109 122 128 133 149 192 196 213 216 233 234 239 249 267 283 289 309 311 314 316 321 363 377 385 392 418 419 431 434 435 436 469 474 483 493 502 505 506 511 522 528 529 545 546 550 551 552 563 565 567
4 – 5	4 15 18 22 37 54 57 66 67 77 83 90 99 105 124 134 145 146 148 157 171 177 181 212 228 244 259 271 276 285 287 292 312 313 315 323 324 332 340 343 347 349 357 370 376 379 383 398 426 430 437 445 450 466 467 472 477 500 515 520 536 553 555 556
2 – 3	32 44 49 51 55 63 93 96 97 98 119 138 142 150 154 166 220 226 238 246 248 251 257 258 260 264 272 282 288 294 299 305 319 325 327 329 330 333 334 348 381 386 390 406 407 412 417 423 425 429 455 459 461 463 468 484 489 512 514 526 527 540 544 561 562
0 – 1	5 9 12 19 24 34 46 58 59 70 79 84 85 88 103 106 108 114 115 144 147 152 162 178 179 189 191 195 198 200 201 202 204 207 210 225 243 250 252 253 255 262 270 275 290 291 300 307 308 322 336 355 368 371 384 387 397 404 427 443 451 464 478 495 501 503 508 519 524 530 531 543 548 560

MMPI-2 Item Numbers Distributed according to the Percentage Difference for a True Response between Various MMPI-2 National Samples and the U.S. Normative Group (continued)

100	
98 – 99	
96 – 97	
94 – 95	
92 – 93	
90 – 91	Japanese men (N = 563) vs. U.S. college men (N = 515)
88 – 89	
86 – 87	
84 – 85	
82 – 83	
80 – 81	
78 – 79	
76 – 77	
74 – 75	
72 – 73	
70 – 71	
68 – 69	
66 – 67	
64 – 65	359
62 – 63	
60 – 61	
58 – 59	
56 – 57	
54 – 55	
52 – 53	447 494
50 – 51	
48 – 49	377
46 – 47	242
44 – 45	
42 – 43	61 380
40 – 41	490
38 – 39	346 538
36 – 37	422 500
34 – 35	133 227 481
32 – 33	205 371 379 439 474 521
30 – 31	82 231 272 373 444 476 534 562
28 – 29	14 25 69 115 127 137 151 152 219 223 249 274 287 340 360 383 526
26 – 27	50 169 226 230 309 330 395 445 487 505
24 – 25	78 121 256 261 350 420 440 457 462 525
22 – 23	9 26 55 89 186 239 264 368 419 429 436 491 492 497 504 509 522 544 549 561
20 – 21	83 98 100 105 110 135 148 163 234 267 297 304 352 384 416 437 480 507 517 542 558 564

18 – 19	4 17 21 41 94 104 113 129 132 263 378 432 434 448 458 501
16 – 17	8 12 32 43 64 128 131 157 179 197 232 248 254 266 268 321 393 394 396 403 443 470 483 537 548
14 – 15	13 29 70 73 84 96 142 200 229 233 244 257 326 347 351 370 381 391 398 407 408 418 423 449 467 518 541 545
12 – 13	19 37 53 81 87 88 95 102 111 120 136 154 164 188 220 265 290 298 357 364 375 376 390 392 397 417 435 459 468 469 477 495 511 514
10 – 11	1 5 11 27 52 62 63 86 90 175 191 199 235 275 278 286 322 324 342 353 358 369 386 414 415 441 466 550 551 552 560 565
8 – 9	3 34 65 103 107 112 123 130 134 167 173 185 190 193 225 237 243 259 262 283 292 299 305 307 316 341 343 372 385 388 399 409 412 421 424 455 496 506 510 530 535 554 557
6 – 7	2 15 40 49 58 59 60 68 74 106 125 141 143 145 156 178 181 182 194 201 202 208 212 213 214 222 228 238 288 296 300 310 311 312 320 325 335 345 348 356 366 367 400 401 413 446 453 456 475 486 508 513 532 566
4 – 5	6 10 16 18 23 24 30 36 39 42 45 67 71 75 92 108 117 118 119 124 126 138 153 158 168 183 203 207 210 215 221 240 241 246 247 251 258 269 276 279 280 282 291 293 294 306 308 313 315 319 328 338 339 344 354 362 389 404 411 430 450 451 460 461 471 472 482 484 488 493 502 515 516 527 528 529 536 539 555 556 567
2 – 3	7 28 31 46 48 51 54 56 66 76 77 80 85 91 97 101 109 116 146 150 155 159 160 165 166 171 172 174 176 177 184 187 189 192 196 206 209 216 217 218 245 250 255 260 270 271 281 284 285 289 301 303 314 317 327 331 332 334 349 355 361 363 365 374 382 402 405 406 425 428 433 438 452 463 478 479 485 503 512 524 533 546 547 553 559 563
0 – 1	20 22 33 35 38 44 47 57 72 79 93 99 114 122 139 140 144 147 149 161 162 170 180 195 198 204 211 224 236 252 253 273 277 295 302 318 323 329 333 336 337 387 410 426 427 431 442 454 464 465 473 489 498 499 519 520 523 531 540 543

MMPI-2 Item Numbers Distributed according to the Percentage Difference for a True Response between Various MMPI-2 National Samples and the U.S. Normative Group (continued)

100	
98 – 99	
96 – 97	
94 – 95	
92 – 93	
90 – 91	Japanese women (N = 507) vs. U.S. normative women (N = 1,462)
88 – 89	
86 – 87	
84 – 85	
82 – 83	
80 – 81	
78 – 79	
76 – 77	
74 – 75	
72 – 73	
70 – 71	359
68 – 69	
66 – 67	
64 – 65	
62 – 63	
60 – 61	447
58 – 59	
56 – 57	
54 – 55	
52 – 53	426
50 – 51	242 494
48 – 49	61
46 – 47	
44 – 45	231 490
42 – 43	205 371 422
40 – 41	377 500
38 – 39	380 395
36 – 37	151 230 538
34 – 35	219 346 542
32 – 33	25 226 304 469 505
30 – 31	148 264 330 396 439 526
28 – 29	236 283 297 444 458 481 487
26 – 27	83 268 340 379 409 429 445
24 – 25	4 26 119 129 227 232 309 373 391 448 457 476 507 517 558
22 – 23	53 104 186 234 256 263 275 290 419 497 522 536
20 – 21	5 29 64 82 88 121 127 169 267 274 344 403 492 504 511 521
18 – 19	69 80 100 131 152 179 229 248 250 265 285 287 350 368 378 383 385 386 407 418 424 435 436 440 470 513 525 529 532 544 557 562 564

16 – 17   11 12 50 56 78 94 110 166 189 208 262 300 305 342 343 352 376 381
388 399 416 441 468 495 496 499 519

14 – 15   13 28 34 41 67 115 118 132 140 157 159 188 206 209 254 284 289 315
339 345 351 357 358 360 408 420 421 437 446 461 462 485 534

12 – 13   14 17 20 21 55 58 59 62 79 89 113 130 135 181 190 199 200 207 239 279
286 292 308 328 366 372 397 398 415 453 483 488 491 509 530 541 545
547 549 551 561

10 – 11   15 30 70 73 81 85 90 96 117 120 124 125 136 146 161 163 193 194 223
266 306 312 319 322 325 341 353 384 406 432 449 464 465 467 480 482
506 512 514 548

8 – 9   7 9 19 23 27 31 32 33 43 68 98 116 137 145 164 168 171 176 197 202
211 224 235 244 249 272 280 293 298 307 321 347 364 367 370 374 412
417 423 425 438 459 473 486 501 510 537 552 554

6 – 7   22 35 37 40 45 47 57 60 65 74 84 87 93 95 102 105 142 147 154 173 184
185 196 201 210 213 217 220 221 233 237 257 259 260 261 294 302 316
331 349 375 390 393 394 434 443 450 466 471 474 475 479 493 503 518
535 546 556 560

4 – 5   16 42 44 63 71 91 92 97 106 139 150 153 156 158 172 177 187 191 225
241 245 255 273 282 288 299 310 313 318 320 335 338 348 356 365 369
389 392 402 410 414 455 456 508 527 543 553 559 565 566

2 – 3   6 8 10 24 46 49 52 72 75 76 101 107 108 112 114 122 126 133 134 138
149 155 160 167 174 175 180 182 183 203 204 212 214 215 218 222 228
246 258 269 270 277 278 281 295 303 317 327 329 332 333 334 337 354
361 362 387 404 405 411 413 428 430 433 452 460 463 477 484 489 498
502 515 516 528 531 533 539 540 555 567

0 – 1   1 2 3 18 36 38 39 48 51 54 66 77 86 99 103 109 111 123 128 141 143 144
162 165 170 178 192 195 198 216 238 240 243 247 251 252 253 271 276
291 296 301 311 314 323 324 326 336 355 363 382 400 401 427 431 442
451 454 472 478 520 523 524 550 563

MMPI-2 Item Numbers Distributed according to the Percentage Difference for a True Response between Various MMPI-2 National Samples and the U.S. Normative Group (continued)

100	
98 – 99	
96 – 97	
94 – 95	
92 – 93	
90 – 91	Korean college men (N = 283) vs. U.S. college men (N = 515)
88 – 89	
86 – 87	
84 – 85	
82 – 83	
80 – 81	
78 – 79	
76 – 77	
74 – 75	
72 – 73	
70 – 71	
68 – 69	
66 – 67	495
64 – 65	
62 – 63	
60 – 61	
58 – 59	
56 – 57	558
54 – 55	127 156 189 309
52 – 53	135
50 – 51	544
48 – 49	95 137 215 525
46 – 47	377 430 509
44 – 45	151 448 490
42 – 43	9 88 94 115 485 566
40 – 41	161 164 173 205 229 253 268 488
38 – 39	12 73 154 233 359 364 402 420 483
36 – 37	38 76 89 217 242 278 283 475 482 507 534
34 – 35	87 103 114 116 148 220 226 230 249 322 388 439
32 – 33	49 56 82 113 163 231 348 360 441 445 553
30 – 31	31 46 52 69 86 269 370 462 502 504
28 – 29	23 106 168 177 227 266 300 310 338 389 395 487 496 538
26 – 27	21 111 149 170 184 187 256 265 311 341 346 353 368 374 438
24 – 25	29 83 85 109 186 188 190 243 261 297 313 330 340 427 435 451 514
22 – 23	2 68 98 100 110 118 134 167 185 224 286 327 339 347 405 416 446 447 519 548 556
20 – 21	8 11 19 43 105 128 140 152 166 180 182 245 272 280 299 303 367 433 464 474 481 499 522

18 – 19	34 39 41 133 155 197 275 331 335 375 378 383 449 465 479 491 545 557
16 – 17	16 18 70 91 107 132 147 165 169 191 218 225 264 274 295 298 308 342 373 401 414 434 444 457 466 469 476 477 517 527 547 549 564
14 – 15	1 14 27 102 104 119 120 157 176 178 208 236 255 302 304 305 337 345 371 386 400 417 443 461 473 531 565 567
12 – 13	7 25 26 44 45 48 50 62 64 67 145 181 204 214 251 262 271 273 296 323 344 349 351 379 380 425 455 500 508 515 552 554 559
10 – 11	4 28 32 33 74 78 81 84 96 131 175 198 200 222 223 235 244 257 259 267 281 284 290 318 320 326 328 357 365 366 392 409 412 426 442 450 453 484 503 505 513 537
8 – 9	15 58 63 66 72 123 124 125 146 174 219 221 250 252 254 282 291 293 321 343 369 376 384 385 390 403 410 413 418 432 458 480 492 493 510 521 530 539 542
6 – 7	17 51 53 54 57 79 108 121 126 141 150 158 159 160 179 193 194 206 210 211 239 248 258 260 263 277 279 285 292 301 316 317 325 354 356 358 362 397 398 423 424 428 429 431 494 498 511 523 532 533
4 – 5	3 37 60 61 65 90 92 93 101 117 129 130 136 153 171 199 207 213 216 228 232 237 240 241 246 315 333 350 352 387 391 393 399 411 415 421 422 436 437 440 459 460 489 497 512 516 546 563
2 – 3	10 13 22 30 47 55 59 71 75 97 99 112 138 142 172 202 209 270 287 288 289 306 307 319 324 355 363 372 396 404 406 407 454 468 478 501 506 518 520 524 526 529 540 541 543 555 560
0 – 1	5 6 20 24 35 36 40 42 77 80 122 139 143 144 162 183 192 195 196 201 203 212 234 238 247 276 294 312 314 329 332 334 336 361 381 382 394 408 419 452 456 463 467 470 471 472 486 528 535 536 550 551 561 562

MMPI-2 Item Numbers Distributed according to the Percentage Difference for a True Response between Various MMPI-2 National Samples and the U.S. Normative Group (continued)

100	
98 – 99	
96 – 97	
94 – 95	
92 – 93	
90 – 91	Korean women (N = 283) vs. U.S. normative women (N = 1,462)
88 – 89	
86 – 87	
84 – 85	
82 – 83	
80 – 81	
78 – 79	
76 – 77	
74 – 75	
72 – 73	495
70 – 71	
68 – 69	
66 – 67	
64 – 65	
62 – 63	
60 – 61	164
58 – 59	189
56 – 57	12 490
54 – 55	229 309
52 – 53	9 95
50 – 51	215 553
48 – 49	151 156 278
46 – 47	94 106 135 188 330 447 448 525
44 – 45	231 283 558
42 – 43	173 217 226 338 377 414 507
40 – 41	38 205
38 – 39	49 115 177 310 353 388 395 426 430 439 485
36 – 37	29 168 191 300 538
34 – 35	46 62 127 163 256 322 340 348 364 370 441 566
32 – 33	146 148 230 242 250 255 347 420 464 482 488 509
30 – 31	64 73 83 109 154 190 227 233 249 264 303 313 360 368 374 402 435 445 462 475 487 504 534 545 559
28 – 29	82 88 91 113 149 161 170 180 268 359 427 483 502
26 – 27	34 86 87 89 110 152 182 224 298 453 479 567
24 – 25	11 23 43 52 56 111 176 186 251 277 308 311 327 337 341 344 367 371 434 466 481
22 – 23	21 39 85 103 114 118 128 243 253 265 269 328 346 413 438 444 539

20 – 21   19 116 184 187 273 280 304 320 342 378 403 406 433 477 508 511 544 562

18 – 19   22 90 119 137 165 204 245 274 286 293 295 299 302 343 352 389 405 459 476 496 517 522 542 550 554

16 – 17   18 41 68 69 76 78 102 104 169 181 185 211 220 254 257 263 281 297 306 317 323 349 419 424 451 455 461 471 492

14 – 15   2 4 25 31 45 81 100 120 126 147 158 167 175 199 206 208 223 291 296 318 369 383 386 391 396 398 401 422 423 443 446 450 465 469 480 491 500 529 533 547 564

12 – 13   33 48 63 65 75 101 125 159 160 174 178 228 244 266 284 326 335 345 361 365 392 412 417 457 467 512 514 515 521 531 548 552

10 – 11   7 10 24 27 44 53 57 72 98 108 129 136 155 157 171 179 210 221 232 236 260 271 282 305 354 363 416 458 484 498 499 516 556

8 – 9   6 20 28 37 61 132 133 134 140 145 194 196 198 214 216 219 225 248 262 287 312 324 331 351 357 373 379 385 400 409 415 440 473 494 520 546 565

6 – 7   1 3 8 15 16 55 66 70 71 74 79 80 84 105 123 124 130 139 141 166 172 222 235 258 272 275 276 288 289 333 339 350 366 376 381 384 394 442 468 530 555 561

4 – 5   17 40 54 93 99 117 143 150 153 183 192 237 239 259 267 279 294 307 315 319 321 325 336 356 362 393 399 429 436 437 456 460 470 472 474 503 506 526 527 532 535 540 541 551 560

2 – 3   5 14 26 30 36 42 47 58 67 77 96 97 112 121 122 195 202 203 207 209 213 218 240 241 247 252 261 290 292 316 355 358 372 408 418 421 425 428 431 432 454 489 493 497 505 513 523 524 536 537 543 549 557 563

0 – 1   13 32 35 50 51 59 60 92 107 131 138 142 144 162 193 197 200 201 212 234 238 246 270 285 301 314 329 332 334 375 380 382 387 390 397 404 407 410 411 449 452 463 478 486 501 510 518 519 528

MMPI-2 Item Numbers Distributed according to the Percentage Difference for a True Response between Various MMPI-2 National Samples and the U.S. Normative Group (continued)

100	
98 – 99	
96 – 97	
94 – 95	
92 – 93	
90 – 91	Mexican men (N = 814) vs. U.S. normative men (N = 1,138)
88 – 89	
86 – 87	
84 – 85	
82 – 83	
80 – 81	
78 – 79	
76 – 77	
74 – 75	
72 – 73	
70 – 71	
68 – 69	
66 – 67	
64 – 65	
62 – 63	
60 – 61	
58 – 59	447
56 – 57	
54 – 55	
52 – 53	126
50 – 51	
48 – 49	29 269
46 – 47	118 242
44 – 45	359 439
42 – 43	
40 – 41	100 496
38 – 39	248
36 – 37	37 239
34 – 35	10 50 166 331
32 – 33	194 211 353 436
30 – 31	309
28 – 29	87 160 335 541
26 – 27	21 26 68 107 184 197 217 221 266 285 341 362 511 538 547
24 – 25	7 16 69 121 183 271 339 369 380 472 487 557
22 – 23	27 132 133 151 153 157 163 215 251 297 373 413 429 459 461
20 – 21	3 89 122 231 237 256 272 287 367 420 437 452 504 508 519 531 537
18 – 19	8 63 71 135 170 196 200 201 254 304 334 338 342 348 397 400 409 428 432 434 542 549

16 – 17   14 15 43 85 98 112 120 130 155 213 214 218 222 284 328 344 394 419 464 505 566

14 – 15   61 67 93 139 171 189 225 253 257 262 302 357 374 389 391 398 411 426 535 552 558

12 – 13   13 25 33 46 76 96 154 169 173 203 212 229 230 244 280 305 307 356 385 412 414 418 422 441 456 465 466 483 529 532 545 548 563

10 – 11   23 73 84 103 124 129 137 145 181 190 274 283 290 316 321 345 347 372 384 393 403 415 423 430 438 453 462 469 473 518 556

8 – 9   9 32 40 49 51 77 78 99 128 147 174 185 219 238 240 245 264 273 281 293 306 320 330 333 350 364 365 378 388 390 405 425 433 442 470 474 479 493 510 522 528 543 562 567

6 – 7   22 24 28 31 35 48 53 60 66 79 83 95 104 111 123 142 143 146 158 186 187 193 249 255 268 277 278 288 289 310 324 354 399 421 424 445 492 494 512 514 523 536 540 546 554 564

4 – 5   5 6 34 41 44 45 52 62 64 72 81 82 86 92 94 105 110 113 116 119 127 131 134 141 148 150 156 161 178 179 180 195 199 216 223 232 233 241 250 252 261 263 267 282 286 292 294 301 313 315 317 322 323 325 337 340 343 346 349 360 361 370 371 376 377 383 386 402 406 407 408 410 427 431 443 444 448 451 455 457 467 471 475 489 495 498 502 503 506 509 513 533 534 550 551 559

2 – 3   1 4 12 17 20 30 38 55 56 57 58 80 90 91 108 114 115 136 149 165 167 175 176 177 188 202 204 205 207 208 210 228 234 243 258 259 260 270 279 291 296 299 300 308 311 312 314 318 319 327 336 363 368 375 379 382 392 395 396 417 435 446 449 450 460 463 476 477 478 481 484 485 486 488 491 500 507 516 517 520 526 527 530 539 553 560 565

0 – 1   2 11 18 19 36 39 42 47 54 59 65 70 74 75 88 97 101 102 106 109 117 125 138 140 144 152 159 162 164 168 172 182 191 192 198 206 209 220 224 226 227 235 236 246 247 265 275 276 295 298 303 326 329 332 351 352 355 358 366 381 387 401 404 416 440 454 458 468 480 482 490 497 499 501 515 521 524 525 544 555 561

MMPI-2 Item Numbers Distributed according to the Percentage Difference for a True Response between Various MMPI-2 National Samples and the U.S. Normative Group (continued)

100	
98 – 99	
96 – 97	
94 – 95	
92 – 93	
90 – 91	Mexican women (N = 1,107) vs. U.S. normative women (N = 1,462)
88 – 89	
86 – 87	
84 – 85	
82 – 83	
80 – 81	
78 – 79	
76 – 77	
74 – 75	
72 – 73	
70 – 71	
68 – 69	447
66 – 67	
64 – 65	
62 – 63	
60 – 61	
58 – 59	
56 – 57	126 211
54 – 55	239 269
52 – 53	
50 – 51	29 118
48 – 49	242
46 – 47	359
44 – 45	439
42 – 43	137
40 – 41	100 472 496
38 – 39	16 87 248
36 – 37	10 217
34 – 35	215
32 – 33	151 231 335 362 373 414 437
30 – 31	27 37 237 341 353 538 547
28 – 29	21 184 194 221 428 436 487 541
26 – 27	89 107 160 196 251 256 264 304 309 339 423 429 474 531
24 – 25	73 153 183 285 328 334 369 397 398 413 430 453 456 464 529
22 – 23	7 26 50 63 85 157 200 214 230 297 331 409 411 452 469 511
20 – 21	23 68 76 262 302 321 357 400 461 466 477 505 537 542
18 – 19	15 122 130 163 189 199 213 229 283 289 316 342 345 347 389 441 508 545 557

16 – 17   8 41 71 86 93 98 120 166 170 218 271 274 364 380 394 459 504 519 534 536

14 – 15   3 12 33 64 121 155 181 203 236 254 261 266 280 287 320 338 351 367 372 374 377 386 403 412 419 420 422 432 471 481 518 543 566

12 – 13   46 49 53 80 129 173 222 233 253 293 306 346 418 467 503 521 522 558 563 564 567

10 – 11   5 13 22 25 62 77 83 113 115 116 132 139 145 152 159 165 176 185 206 226 244 263 273 278 279 307 308 312 348 352 371 388 390 401 415 425 438 455 460 491 502 512 535 548 552

8 – 9   1 9 32 35 40 43 48 57 60 74 81 96 99 104 110 112 117 128 134 147 174 186 190 193 195 205 209 225 245 257 267 292 305 310 392 406 410 421 442 443 457 475 476 482 486 499 554 562

6 – 7   30 31 45 55 61 66 78 82 95 119 123 124 135 140 141 143 148 164 169 171 178 191 202 207 227 238 240 243 247 255 282 288 296 298 318 319 323 327 330 333 340 354 360 365 385 399 405 424 433 448 449 451 462 465 485 492 497 506 509 510 526 549 551 553

4 – 5   4 20 38 44 47 51 52 56 59 65 67 69 72 88 92 103 105 106 109 114 131 142 149 150 156 168 177 180 197 216 219 228 232 241 249 268 277 281 290 294 295 300 313 314 317 324 326 332 337 343 349 366 375 378 382 387 391 393 402 404 407 416 434 445 483 493 494 498 501 514 525 527 528 530 539 540 546 550 559 561 565

2 – 3   2 6 14 17 19 24 34 36 39 58 70 84 94 108 146 154 167 182 187 188 204 212 224 234 246 250 252 259 260 265 272 286 301 322 325 329 356 363 368 370 376 379 381 383 384 395 408 427 440 446 450 463 468 478 479 484 488 489 490 495 513 517 520 524 544 560

0 – 1   11 18 28 42 54 75 79 90 91 97 101 102 111 125 127 133 136 138 144 158 161 162 172 175 179 192 198 201 208 210 220 223 235 258 270 275 276 284 291 299 303 311 315 336 344 350 355 358 361 396 417 426 431 435 444 454 458 470 473 480 500 507 515 516 523 532 533 555 556

MMPI-2 Item Numbers Distributed according to the Percentage Difference
for a True Response between Various MMPI-2 National Samples and
the U.S. Normative Group (continued)

100	
98 – 99	
96 – 97	
94 – 95	
92 – 93	
90 – 91	Military men (N = 1,156) vs. U.S. normative men (N = 1,138)
88 – 89	
86 – 87	
84 – 85	
82 – 83	
80 – 81	
78 – 79	
76 – 77	
74 – 75	
72 – 73	
70 – 71	
68 – 69	
66 – 67	
64 – 65	
62 – 63	
60 – 61	133
58 – 59	
56 – 57	
54 – 55	
52 – 53	
50 – 51	
48 – 49	
46 – 47	
44 – 45	
42 – 43	
40 – 41	
38 – 39	
36 – 37	232
34 – 35	
32 – 33	549
30 – 31	201
28 – 29	
26 – 27	227
24 – 25	217 477
22 – 23	169
20 – 21	211 283 305 340 488
18 – 19	50 86 127 239 254 414 417
16 – 17	157 226 356 402 420 443 537

14 – 15   84 222 341 350 374 393 416 434 487 504 514 548 557

12 – 13   32 58 61 77 81 89 119 134 140 143 145 148 154 233 236 244 264 279
286 366 399 406 410 412 433 437 446 481 531

10 – 11   3 5 10 13 21 26 41 71 105 106 115 202 203 207 221 249 251 275 297 324
335 348 436 442 445 467 470 496 538 551 552

8 – 9   4 12 37 53 55 63 70 82 87 93 112 118 120 124 137 151 153 156 159 168
187 191 199 204 242 253 257 266 274 290 296 307 310 311 316 327 337
345 358 389 390 396 401 403 438 444 463 505 518 521 523 545 547 550
567

6 – 7   8 9 23 49 52 68 88 96 104 107 110 152 158 184 189 190 196 200 218 225
230 231 241 259 269 277 278 298 299 312 314 319 333 334 359 361 370
384 386 387 400 405 409 424 425 426 427 431 451 460 471 474 475 479
484 512 513 522 525 528 529 530 535 541 553 555 558 559

4 – 5   7 14 15 16 17 27 29 33 44 46 48 60 64 65 67 69 85 91 94 101 108 113
117 121 122 125 128 129 130 131 132 136 147 155 160 167 170 171 172
173 174 182 183 188 198 206 209 212 224 229 237 243 248 255 256 258
261 263 267 270 271 291 300 301 302 303 317 320 322 329 331 344 346
347 349 351 355 365 369 377 379 381 382 385 398 404 407 408 413 418
428 429 440 450 453 461 465 472 476 478 483 493 495 499 500 501 507
509 516 517 524 526 533 536 539 540 544 562 564

2 – 3   2 6 11 20 22 24 25 35 38 39 40 42 43 45 47 54 57 59 74 75 76 78 79 83
90 92 97 98 99 100 102 103 116 123 142 144 146 150 161 163 164 165
166 175 178 179 180 181 185 192 193 194 195 197 205 210 215 219 220
228 234 235 238 240 245 246 247 252 260 265 272 280 281 282 284 285
287 288 292 294 295 304 308 313 323 325 326 332 336 339 342 352 354
360 362 368 373 375 376 380 388 392 394 395 397 415 419 421 422 430
435 441 448 454 455 456 457 458 459 464 466 468 469 473 480 482 490
492 497 498 502 506 508 515 520 532 542 543 554 561

0 – 1   1 18 19 28 30 31 34 36 51 56 62 66 72 73 80 95 109 111 114 126 135 138
139 141 149 162 176 177 186 208 213 214 216 223 250 262 268 273 276
289 293 306 309 315 318 321 328 330 338 343 353 357 363 364 367 371
372 378 383 391 411 423 432 439 447 449 452 462 485 486 489 491 494
503 510 511 519 527 534 546 556 560 563 565 566

MMPI-2 Item Numbers Distributed according to the Percentage Difference for a True Response between Various MMPI-2 National Samples and the U.S. Normative Group (continued)

100	
98 – 99	
96 – 97	
94 – 95	
92 – 93	
90 – 91	Military women (N = 186) vs. U.S. normative women (N = 1,462)
88 – 89	
86 – 87	
84 – 85	
82 – 83	
80 – 81	
78 – 79	
76 – 77	
74 – 75	
72 – 73	
70 – 71	
68 – 69	
66 – 67	
64 – 65	
62 – 63	
60 – 61	
58 – 59	
56 – 57	
54 – 55	
52 – 53	
50 – 51	
48 – 49	133
46 – 47	
44 – 45	
42 – 43	
40 – 41	232 549
38 – 39	
36 – 37	
34 – 35	
32 – 33	
30 – 31	127
28 – 29	86 374
26 – 27	154 477
24 – 25	110 157 169 217
22 – 23	50 70 227 356 369 385 537
20 – 21	26 32 226 254 283 290 340 393 401 446 460 481
18 – 19	13 15 58 81 201 211 233 236 275 286 359 402 413 414 434 488 538 556
16 – 17	63 77 155 189 196 207 242 253 257 337 341 351 403 417 445 496 545

14 – 15   4 89 107 152 159 188 205 221 239 256 331 344 443 487 497 504 535

12 – 13   57 76 96 146 163 225 241 249 251 261 267 269 272 279 316 350 364 366
377 397 399 416 457 470 499 507 522 531 533

10 – 11   3 38 46 61 74 103 112 147 151 153 167 194 200 218 219 243 244 265
289 305 321 324 326 342 358 362 365 370 396 422 458 462 469 498 509
514 551 567

  8 – 9   7 8 10 14 35 52 55 68 73 80 115 119 120 124 130 143 148 161 176 181
183 185 222 284 292 301 327 345 352 367 368 378 389 392 420 430 436
437 442 491 495 529 564

  6 – 7   12 19 21 23 31 43 48 49 53 67 79 100 104 108 118 128 134 137 140 145
156 165 171 187 190 197 198 203 215 224 230 231 237 248 264 268 273
280 291 293 298 304 307 308 311 312 314 315 320 328 333 339 346 347
348 361 375 384 398 405 406 411 418 426 429 435 440 449 464 472 486
502 518 521 534 536 541 546 548 550 552 560 561

  4 – 5   2 16 17 22 34 41 44 47 54 62 83 87 90 105 117 125 129 136 141 158 164
172 174 177 178 202 204 209 212 213 214 220 223 250 255 259 262 277
285 302 310 319 353 360 363 372 386 388 395 408 410 415 423 428 432
433 461 467 480 482 484 485 490 492 505 512 542 543 553 554 562 563
566

  2 – 3   1 6 9 11 18 24 25 28 30 36 45 51 64 65 69 75 84 91 93 94 97 98 99 114
116 121 123 131 132 135 144 149 150 160 191 208 210 229 234 260 266
274 276 287 288 296 297 299 303 317 322 329 335 336 338 355 371 376
379 381 390 391 400 404 409 419 427 438 441 444 447 448 451 452 453
466 474 475 479 493 494 501 503 511 513 520 523 524 525 527 528 530
544 547 555 557 565

  0 – 1   5 20 27 29 33 37 39 40 42 56 59 60 66 71 72 78 82 85 88 92 95 101 102
106 109 111 113 122 126 138 139 142 162 166 168 170 173 175 179 180
182 184 186 192 193 195 199 206 216 228 235 238 240 245 246 247 252
258 263 270 271 278 281 282 294 295 300 306 309 313 318 323 325 330
332 334 343 349 354 357 373 380 382 383 387 394 407 412 421 424 425
431 439 450 454 455 456 459 463 465 468 471 473 476 478 483 489 500
506 508 510 515 516 517 519 526 532 539 540 558 559

MMPI-2 Item Numbers Distributed according to the Percentage Difference
for a True Response between Various MMPI-2 National Samples and
the U.S. Normative Group (continued)

100	
98 – 99	
96 – 97	
94 – 95	
92 – 93	
90 – 91	Nicaraguan men (N = 372) vs. U.S. normative men (N = 1,138)
88 – 89	
86 – 87	
84 – 85	
82 – 83	
80 – 81	
78 – 79	
76 – 77	
74 – 75	
72 – 73	
70 – 71	
68 – 69	
66 – 67	
64 – 65	
62 – 63	269 447
60 – 61	
58 – 59	
56 – 57	253
54 – 55	415
52 – 53	215 232 331
50 – 51	166 273 472
48 – 49	118 334 538
46 – 47	211 301
44 – 45	170 563
42 – 43	76 86 254 268 309 439 531
40 – 41	124 135 239
38 – 39	231 248 374 390 413 441 470 488 566
36 – 37	44 71 99 126 207 306 397 399
34 – 35	100 229 259 278 380 396 525
32 – 33	29 40 56 140 168 193 345 438
30 – 31	32 69 143 203 209 305 340 414 437 513 547
28 – 29	8 31 151 156 327 461 474 519 537
26 – 27	42 48 88 110 120 178 185 241 286 298 311 335 353 358 423 463 473 483 556
24 – 25	10 60 61 82 95 125 171 172 183 200 225 292 325 403 532 549 552 558
22 – 23	3 27 45 46 53 81 93 94 163 221 251 266 283 284 382 389 451 507 553 559

20 – 21   7 39 52 65 89 91 149 169 173 197 213 219 228 272 289 316 322 368 408
418 427 459 485 487 504 509 510 528 550 567

18 – 19   28 47 155 157 161 189 195 196 202 226 238 240 274 299 300 339 393
442 452 471 526 544 551

16 – 17   5 6 17 34 58 67 141 180 201 205 227 252 261 280 288 323 352 357 366
367 385 395 406 407 420 443 448 482 496 498

14 – 15   20 30 72 77 101 145 175 176 216 218 224 247 263 304 310 317 324 348
349 361 365 369 376 410 416 435 444 445 460 490 500 512 533 560 562
565

12 – 13   19 35 38 51 59 92 112 119 121 123 134 138 164 186 190 230 245 246
255 277 296 326 328 363 370 379 381 386 387 388 392 405 468 475 479
495 497 517 530 536

10 – 11   1 22 23 54 55 66 97 98 106 107 116 117 129 132 139 146 179 198 217
236 242 250 256 267 271 281 290 295 314 333 344 356 364 417 446 455
458 469 480 484 491 522 543

8 – 9   11 13 21 26 36 64 85 111 113 137 142 148 154 165 208 214 233 234 258
265 291 302 308 315 319 320 337 372 391 421 428 431 434 440 454 494
554 555

6 – 7   2 14 15 16 57 63 74 78 87 109 153 184 262 270 297 303 313 329 338 342
350 375 378 394 409 424 426 449 453 456 462 481 492 505 515 516 529
539 542 545 561

4 – 5   4 12 18 49 79 83 84 90 96 103 104 108 114 115 122 130 131 144 147 150
158 159 167 174 177 182 194 199 222 223 237 244 260 264 275 279 312
321 343 362 383 384 400 401 402 404 411 412 419 433 436 450 457 464
465 466 467 476 489 518 520 527 540 564

2 – 3   24 33 41 43 62 70 73 80 127 136 160 187 188 191 204 210 212 235 243
257 276 293 336 351 355 429 430 432 478 486 493 502 503 508 511 523
524 534 535 541 546 548 557

0 – 1   9 25 37 50 68 75 102 105 128 133 152 162 181 192 206 220 249 282 285
287 294 307 318 330 332 341 346 347 354 359 360 371 373 377 398 422
425 477 499 501 506 514 521

MMPI-2 Item Numbers Distributed according to the Percentage Difference for a True Response between Various MMPI-2 National Samples and the U.S. Normative Group (continued)

100	
98 – 99	
96 – 97	
94 – 95	
92 – 93	
90 – 91	Nicaraguan women (N = 587) vs. U.S. normative women (N = 1,462)
88 – 89	
86 – 87	
84 – 85	
82 – 83	
80 – 81	
78 – 79	
76 – 77	
74 – 75	269
72 – 73	
70 – 71	447
68 – 69	
66 – 67	
64 – 65	
62 – 63	
60 – 61	334
58 – 59	
56 – 57	215
54 – 55	232 397 441 472
52 – 53	76 124 415
50 – 51	40 126 211 273 538
48 – 49	86 118 229 239 254 374 563 566
46 – 47	301
44 – 45	170 231 268 309 439
42 – 43	99 345 399 414 488
40 – 41	166 241 248 259 396 525 531
38 – 39	31 71 135 151 209 278 286 306 380 395
36 – 37	27 44 56 110 253 298 331 435 461 470
34 – 35	45 65 173 207 335 406 413 420 513 550
32 – 33	28 48 95 149 193 213 228 284 311 327 390 438 459 471 558
30 – 31	7 10 12 23 53 60 81 137 140 168 178 180 322 353 358 392 426 468 507
28 – 29	32 72 172 251 299 305 325 382 423 437 519 526
26 – 27	29 89 91 171 175 203 300 368 389 418 463 528 537 549 567
24 – 25	22 42 46 55 82 94 120 125 141 156 163 195 225 265 283 317 348 361 393 482 553
22 – 23	19 34 38 39 47 93 98 101 157 169 183 185 221 224 247 280 372 403 408 448 483 490 555 559

20 – 21   61 138 146 199 200 214 218 227 240 277 292 310 316 352 366 451 467 475 487 504 522 523 547 554 565

18 – 19   17 54 92 111 129 145 164 165 186 216 245 274 279 308 320 339 356 367 369 391 443 479 481 484 541 556

16 – 17   30 51 52 58 59 77 112 176 190 236 252 255 256 314 323 349 350 427 444 454 458 469 485 498 509 532 557

14 – 15   3 11 13 20 69 100 109 116 132 143 187 188 198 202 242 258 288 289 303 315 319 324 326 328 338 351 357 376 407 410 417 442 446 452 491 494 500 516 530 533 551

12 – 13   2 18 96 97 107 117 147 159 182 196 233 238 291 304 337 340 365 375 384 404 434 460 473 496 539

10 – 11   4 8 36 66 85 88 123 127 130 134 142 161 179 205 208 212 220 223 226 261 263 264 272 363 378 388 405 411 421 424 455 456 480 499 515 536

8 – 9   6 68 78 106 150 154 177 197 201 219 230 237 257 270 281 290 296 329 333 354 364 381 386 387 401 409 425 428 436 449 505 510 517 534 560 561

6 – 7   37 62 63 74 80 83 108 113 128 131 139 144 204 222 234 246 249 267 295 312 336 341 342 344 370 379 394 402 433 450 453 464 495 497 506 520 529 542 543 544

4 – 5   1 14 15 16 24 25 35 41 49 50 57 70 75 87 90 104 114 121 136 152 155 181 184 189 191 217 250 266 287 313 321 347 355 359 371 383 385 419 422 430 445 465 466 474 511 512 514 524 535 548 552

2 – 3   5 9 21 33 43 64 73 79 102 105 115 119 153 160 167 194 206 235 243 244 262 271 276 293 297 307 318 373 398 400 416 431 440 476 477 478 492 493 501 508 562

0 – 1   26 67 84 103 122 133 148 158 162 174 192 210 260 275 282 285 294 302 330 332 343 346 360 362 377 412 429 432 457 462 486 489 502 503 518 521 527 540 545 546 564

MMPI-2 Item Numbers Distributed according to the Percentage Difference for a True Response between Various MMPI-2 National Samples and the U.S. Normative Group (continued)

100	
98 – 99	
96 – 97	
94 – 95	
92 – 93	
90 – 91	Puerto Rican men (N = 184) vs. U.S. normative men (N = 1,138)
88 – 89	
86 – 87	
84 – 85	
82 – 83	
80 – 81	
78 – 79	
76 – 77	
74 – 75	
72 – 73	
70 – 71	
68 – 69	
66 – 67	
64 – 65	
62 – 63	
60 – 61	
58 – 59	
56 – 57	
54 – 55	217
52 – 53	
50 – 51	447
48 – 49	
46 – 47	
44 – 45	118 166
42 – 43	
40 – 41	211
38 – 39	
36 – 37	472
34 – 35	1 190 269 284 558
32 – 33	10 48 60 254 298
30 – 31	30 33 151 170 353 366
28 – 29	68 135 221 423 441
26 – 27	3 71 131 171 189 232 239 253 309 311 335 415 496
24 – 25	15 21 327 358 397 420 427 470 504 525 541 563
22 – 23	76 121 183 241 250 266 280 306 331 385 413 439 459 551
20 – 21	13 69 88 116 193 229 259 268 272 285 292 316 351 367 399 462 463 471 475 479 483 485 497 519 538 565
18 – 19	32 112 124 185 213 304 310 368 419 484 495 528 536 553 567

16 – 17   19 29 72 79 100 149 152 227 228 255 279 314 320 344 362 364 375 386 389 390 392 395 396 426 431 438 446 448 458 468 477 509 524 531 556 559

14 – 15   7 26 37 77 93 120 128 130 158 161 169 173 178 180 184 198 201 206 215 238 248 278 286 290 297 308 317 328 329 346 355 356 359 372 403 407 416 422 435 452 469 476 482 490 501 503 523 533 537 544

12 – 13   16 38 81 91 134 141 172 179 205 212 231 240 281 293 295 296 322 326 330 332 342 361 370 376 379 404 405 406 414 445 449 454 461 498 506 513 515 516 517 526 530 539 545 550 552 554 555 566

10 – 11   35 39 56 58 63 67 83 103 105 107 129 136 137 146 163 177 194 218 245 249 252 257 267 303 319 334 348 349 350 363 378 380 381 383 424 428 429 434 450 457 474 478 487 488 489 499 507 511 527 543 560

8 – 9   43 45 46 50 51 55 61 84 98 99 101 117 125 127 138 139 143 150 154 181 186 196 199 200 202 216 226 234 243 264 294 300 318 323 324 333 336 343 345 352 369 382 387 391 393 408 430 440 451 455 486 491 494 500 508 510 514 520 522 529 534

6 – 7   5 25 44 66 82 92 97 111 132 142 144 145 147 153 168 182 191 195 208 219 222 224 236 244 246 258 260 265 270 271 274 275 282 301 305 312 313 325 339 340 341 365 371 373 374 398 400 401 402 410 465 480 492 505 518 547 564

4 – 5   9 12 20 22 23 36 42 47 57 64 78 80 87 96 119 122 126 140 148 167 175 188 203 204 214 220 223 242 256 273 276 287 321 338 360 384 409 411 412 417 421 456 460 466 493 521 540 546 557 561 562

2 – 3   2 4 17 18 27 28 31 41 62 65 70 89 95 104 106 108 109 110 114 115 155 157 159 164 165 187 192 197 230 235 237 261 263 288 289 291 299 307 315 354 357 394 418 425 436 437 442 443 464 467 502 535

0 – 1   6 8 11 14 24 34 40 49 52 53 54 59 73 74 75 85 86 90 94 102 113 123 133 156 160 162 174 176 207 209 210 225 233 247 251 262 277 283 302 337 347 377 388 432 433 444 453 473 481 512 532 542 548 549

MMPI-2 Item Numbers Distributed according to the Percentage Difference for a True Response between Various MMPI-2 National Samples and the U.S. Normative Group (continued)

100	
98 – 99	
96 – 97	
94 – 95	
92 – 93	
90 – 91	Puerto Rican women (N = 131) vs. U.S. normative women (N = 1,462)
88 – 89	
86 – 87	
84 – 85	
82 – 83	
80 – 81	
78 – 79	
76 – 77	
74 – 75	
72 – 73	
70 – 71	
68 – 69	447
66 – 67	211
64 – 65	
62 – 63	
60 – 61	
58 – 59	
56 – 57	217
54 – 55	
52 – 53	239
50 – 51	
48 – 49	269
46 – 47	118
44 – 45	304
42 – 43	472
40 – 41	30 232
38 – 39	33 199 558
36 – 37	
34 – 35	48 268 298 414
32 – 33	60 71 151 353
30 – 31	190 242 284 335 358 456 470 525
28 – 29	21 137 149 171 196 231 467 504
26 – 27	10 55 166 226 256 306 356 423 439 538 545 566
24 – 25	29 341 350 359 409 415 416 496 560
22 – 23	3 16 131 153 169 170 237 264 309 346 362 441 452 471 541
20 – 21	35 130 241 275 297 345 397 419 428 487 488 495 551
18 – 19	15 62 68 76 79 88 100 121 123 129 183 221 229 233 244 280 293 351 366 369 385 398 413 427 429 449 453 460 462 468 477 490 553

16 – 17   20 73 74 77 87 93 101 120 184 189 194 200 227 254 259 261 278 339
407 435 437 463 466 481 511 536 567

14 – 15   13 70 115 128 133 203 236 253 279 285 286 314 347 367 379 395 396
422 469 474 533 549

12 – 13   7 34 45 85 119 158 193 207 248 260 267 292 302 317 319 342 348 349
372 377 389 391 426 459 464 522 565

10 – 11   12 61 64 72 132 134 179 181 186 198 240 263 287 308 310 311 327 329
375 382 384 393 400 404 411 445 454 484 497 518 519 552 555 562 563

8 – 9   1 4 25 31 32 40 41 47 49 53 57 67 69 81 86 89 91 97 113 138 148 159
161 167 178 209 213 223 249 266 296 315 324 330 352 354 355 360 361
383 388 402 403 406 421 425 458 461 475 480 483 500 515 521 524 529
530 531 550 554 559

6 – 7   11 36 63 78 82 92 96 99 103 109 117 139 140 141 150 157 165 168 177
180 187 195 197 201 204 206 215 216 228 230 238 246 257 262 270 274
281 289 316 321 325 326 357 365 376 399 410 417 424 430 431 434 443
446 457 478 479 485 493 501 507 512 517 523 528 534 537 547 561

4 – 5   2 14 17 19 27 37 58 65 66 80 106 107 116 122 124 136 143 146 147 152
164 175 185 188 191 205 212 214 225 234 250 251 258 273 288 299 305
322 328 331 336 344 370 380 387 392 394 405 420 432 433 438 448 450
473 476 502 514 516 520 526 532 544 556 564

2 – 3   8 22 38 39 43 51 56 83 84 94 95 102 104 108 110 111 114 125 126 127
135 142 144 145 154 155 156 160 174 176 192 208 210 218 219 235 243
245 247 272 277 282 283 291 294 307 312 313 323 332 337 340 343 364
368 371 373 374 381 386 390 408 440 442 455 489 491 499 503 505 510
513 527 540 543 546 548 557

0 – 1   5 6 9 18 23 24 26 28 42 44 46 50 52 54 59 75 90 98 105 112 162 163 172
173 182 202 220 222 224 252 255 265 271 276 290 295 300 301 303 318
320 333 334 338 363 378 401 412 418 436 444 451 465 482 486 492 494
498 506 508 509 535 539 542

MMPI-2 Item Numbers Distributed according to the Percentage Difference for a True Response between Various MMPI-2 National Samples and the U.S. Normative Group (continued)

100	
98 – 99	
96 – 97	
94 – 95	
92 – 93	
90 – 91	Spanish men (N = 193) vs. U.S. normative men (N = 1,138)
88 – 89	
86 – 87	
84 – 85	
82 – 83	
80 – 81	
78 – 79	
76 – 77	
74 – 75	
72 – 73	
70 – 71	
68 – 69	
66 – 67	
64 – 65	
62 – 63	
60 – 61	447
58 – 59	
56 – 57	215
54 – 55	
52 – 53	
50 – 51	61
48 – 49	94 118
46 – 47	
44 – 45	48 166 231
42 – 43	472
40 – 41	399
38 – 39	380
36 – 37	60 76 217 232
34 – 35	17 250 259 269 273 374 504
32 – 33	382 415 556
30 – 31	112 306 331 390 420 439
28 – 29	29 86 266 414
26 – 27	19 69 81 87 127 301 350 465 562
24 – 25	33 84 98 170 278 334 353 406 413 437 554 557
22 – 23	10 100 110 163 197 240 376 389 405 422 424 438 482 487 519 558
20 – 21	27 46 80 120 134 213 244 362 396 410 429 461 502 510 535 548
18 – 19	31 89 95 113 117 123 161 268 284 341 467 477 486 496 497 528 537

16 – 17   1 3 16 28 121 135 146 153 155 160 185 190 193 225 326 352 381 384
            388 408 423 441 445 485 509 525 541 542

14 – 15   8 20 77 82 92 223 248 267 281 309 322 335 348 366 375 398 402 444
            470 475 481 483 494 499 522 551 563

12 – 13   4 15 38 39 45 53 91 111 126 141 151 165 167 168 174 189 199 200 207
            230 256 272 295 305 308 310 358 372 378 386 397 421 425 426 433 451
            452 473 488 498 513 538 567

10 – 11   30 34 37 43 51 56 58 63 66 68 71 72 93 99 103 104 107 122 128 132 137
            140 142 149 150 173 186 194 214 249 257 260 263 286 302 315 327 351
            359 365 395 412 416 419 436 442 446 449 456 511 521 534 550 552

 8 – 9   14 42 57 65 115 131 152 164 175 226 239 275 280 290 323 328 347 364
            369 373 391 392 409 434 480 484 507 517 529 530 549

 6 – 7   9 21 23 25 26 36 47 55 59 64 105 130 148 159 178 227 228 229 241 245
            247 254 274 287 296 299 312 316 317 325 330 337 344 354 356 367 417
            431 432 435 453 460 471 474 476 491 492 500 518 527 559 560 565 566

 4 – 5   2 5 18 22 35 40 44 54 70 78 83 88 90 109 114 116 125 138 145 154 158
            176 179 180 184 187 191 195 201 203 204 206 210 216 219 233 235 251
            252 253 264 270 279 288 289 294 300 311 324 329 355 357 361 401 404
            440 448 459 462 464 479 505 508 514 523 531 536 540 547 553 555 561
            564

 2 – 3   32 41 50 62 67 73 75 96 97 101 106 119 124 133 139 144 147 156 157
            171 177 182 183 188 196 198 202 209 212 220 221 224 234 237 242 243
            246 255 258 261 265 283 291 293 298 303 304 307 313 314 318 321 332
            333 338 342 343 345 349 360 363 368 371 377 379 383 385 393 394 407
            411 418 450 454 455 458 463 468 469 478 493 501 503 506 512 520 524
            533 539 543 544

 0 – 1   6 7 11 12 13 24 49 52 74 79 85 102 108 129 136 143 162 169 172 181
            192 205 208 211 218 222 236 238 262 271 276 277 282 285 292 297 319
            320 336 339 340 346 370 387 400 403 427 428 430 443 457 466 489 490
            495 515 516 526 532 545 546

MMPI-2 Item Numbers Distributed according to the Percentage Difference for a True Response between Various MMPI-2 National Samples and the U.S. Normative Group (continued)

100	
98 – 99	
96 – 97	
94 – 95	
92 – 93	
90 – 91	Spanish women (N = 233) vs. U.S. normative women (N = 1,462)
88 – 89	
86 – 87	
84 – 85	
82 – 83	
80 – 81	
78 – 79	
76 – 77	
74 – 75	
72 – 73	
70 – 71	
68 – 69	447
66 – 67	
64 – 65	
62 – 63	61 215
60 – 61	
58 – 59	94
56 – 57	
54 – 55	
52 – 53	118
50 – 51	48 472 504
48 – 49	231
46 – 47	86 269 399
44 – 45	60
42 – 43	380
40 – 41	166 250 420 439
38 – 39	76 217 406
36 – 37	374
34 – 35	81 137 306 413 415
32 – 33	27 301 424
30 – 31	84 134 232 499 554
28 – 29	87 259 273 389 397 410 437 510
26 – 27	8 10 29 110 260 268 317 331 334 414 558
24 – 25	33 89 98 120 123 135 146 213 214 244 326 353 366 382 390 396 461 556
22 – 23	69 127 170 322 348 376 395 408 458 496 548 557 566
20 – 21	17 20 46 82 112 151 248 278 286 442 525
18 – 19	38 77 129 163 173 190 237 284 305 341 352 441 452 456 497 513

16 – 17   25 28 30 55 56 71 80 113 117 149 218 240 267 279 289 299 325 337 350
375 405 423 433 435 482 486 487 494 519 529 531 537 563

14 – 15   15 16 19 31 34 37 47 64 103 174 185 187 194 223 226 235 238 308 328
345 373 381 391 409 421 429 438 470 483 498 509 521 528 532 549

12 – 13   3 21 23 39 51 53 66 92 95 111 126 150 153 160 165 200 219 229 233 239
242 254 256 275 290 298 302 307 310 313 314 315 321 335 358 359 362
365 378 419 434 451 462 465 471 475 480 490 502 523 533 538 541 551
559 565 567

10 – 11   4 40 43 67 79 88 100 105 107 128 164 193 209 230 236 241 247 251 253
265 274 295 309 312 320 354 369 388 393 412 418 422 440 460 467 481
485 488 514 522 535 552 562

8 – 9   2 11 22 36 42 50 54 57 62 72 91 99 104 109 116 133 140 143 147 155
161 168 171 175 182 184 186 189 199 205 227 263 266 281 296 338 356
368 372 402 411 416 425 431 444 454 468 505 508 512 530 534 536 555

6 – 7   41 65 70 78 90 121 138 141 142 148 154 169 172 180 181 191 196 197
207 211 216 221 224 225 249 255 257 270 303 311 329 357 377 386 428
432 476 484 491 511 517 550 553

4 – 5   1 5 6 7 26 45 63 68 83 97 114 119 122 125 130 131 132 167 177 178 179
198 243 245 261 283 288 291 294 300 304 316 323 327 330 339 340 342
344 355 361 371 379 385 392 401 426 430 443 446 455 473 474 477 500
515 527 542 545 560 564

2 – 3   9 12 18 35 49 52 58 73 75 85 93 96 108 136 144 145 156 158 159 176
183 188 192 195 202 204 206 208 220 228 258 264 271 272 276 277 280
282 287 324 343 347 349 360 363 364 367 394 398 400 404 417 427 436
448 449 463 466 469 479 489 493 495 503 507 518 524 543 544 547

0 – 1   13 14 24 32 44 59 74 101 102 106 115 124 139 152 157 162 201 203 210
212 222 234 246 252 262 285 292 293 297 318 319 332 333 336 346 351
370 383 384 387 403 407 445 450 453 457 459 464 478 492 501 506 516
520 526 539 540 546 561

Contributors

Moshe Almagor is senior lecturer at the University of Haifa, Israel. He completed his B.A. in psychology, sociology, and anthropology in 1972 at Tel-Aviv University, his M.A. in rehabilitation psychology in 1981 at Bar-Ilan University, and his Ph.D. in clinical psychology at the University of Minnesota in 1983. Dr. Almagor is director of the clinical psychology graduate program at the University of Haifa. He is also the director of the Laboratory for Family and Behavior Therapy and Research at the University of Haifa.

Alejandro Avila-Espada is professor of personality, psychological assessment, and treatment in the Department of Psychology at the University of Salamanca. His major publications include *Picodiagnóstico Clínico* [Clinical Psychodiagnosis] (Eudema, 1986, rev. ed. 1992) and *Evaluación en Psicología Clínica. Vol. 1: Proceso, Método y estrategias psicométricas* [Clinical Psychological Assessment. Vol. 1: Process, Method and Psychometric Strategies] (Amaru, 1993).

Massimo Biondi is currently a research assistant in psychiatry at the Institute of Psychiatry and Psychosomatics at the University of Rome in Italy. Professor Biondi received his M.D. from the University of Rome and has been an active researcher in psychosomatics, psychometrics, cognitive psychotherapy, personality disorders, and psychoendocrinology. He has published 10 books and more than 100 articles in psychiatry and psychology.

Maria Elena Brenlla is a psychologist on the Faculty of Psychology of the University of Buenos Aires. She received a scholarship at the University of Buenos Aires to conduct research on the MMPI-2.

Annick Brun-Eberentz is a clinical psychologist at the CMME, Hôspital Sainte Anne, specializing in eating disorders, psychometrics, and patients and parents groups.

James N. Butcher is professor of psychology in the Department of Psychology at the University of Minnesota. He received an M.A. in experimental psychology in 1962 and a Ph.D. in clinical psychology in 1964 from the University of North Carolina at Chapel Hill. He was awarded Doctor Honoris Causa from the Free University of Brussels in 1990. He is a member of the University of Minnesota Press's MMPI Consultative Committee. Currently he is the editor of *Psychological Assessment* and serves as consulting editor for numerous other journals in psychology and psychiatry. He is a fellow of the American Psychological Association and of the Society for Personality Assessment.

José J. Cabiya was born in San Juan, Puerto Rico, in 1954. He obtained his B.A. degree from the University of Puerto Rico at Rio Piedras in 1972 and his doctoral degree in clinical psychology from the State University of New York at Albany in 1983. In 1981 he completed his clinical internship in the Framingham Youth Guidance Center in Massachusetts providing psychological services to a Hispanic community. He also worked for several years with Hispanics in Albany. He has been practicing for more than 10 years in Puerto Rico as a clinical psychologist in private practice. He has been director of the Psychology Department of the State Psychiatric Hospital in Puerto Rico and has taught in the Caribbean Center for Advanced Studies in San Juan, a professional school of psychology, since 1983. Dr. Cabiya has conducted research with the MMPI since 1985 and currently is conducting research with the MMPI-2, including studies of a Puerto Rican penal population and victims of armed assault. His future research includes the study of a representative sample of the Puerto Rican population to assess if the U.S. MMPI-2 norms are valid for Puerto Rico.

Maria Martina Casullo, a psychologist, is professor of psychology at the University of Buenos Aires and academic secretary of the Faculty of Psychology at the university. She is a member of the Argentine Council of Scientific and Technological Researchers (CONICET). She received her psychology degree from the University of Buenos Aires, and she completed the Ph.D. program in counseling psychology at Ohio State University in 1964. Currently she is a member of ICP (International Council of Psychologists), APA (American Psychological Association), and IACCP (International Association for Cross-Cultural Psychology).

Ruth Chao received her Ph.D. in education from the University of California, Los Angeles, and was a research associate at the National Research Center in Asian American Mental Health, working under the direction of Dr. Stanley Sue. She is now assistant professor at Syracuse University in the Department of Child and Family Studies. Her interests are in the role of culture in child development and in exploring alternative conceptualizations and models for describing Asian American parenting. Currently she is conducting research on European American and East Asian parenting in relation to academic achievement and study skills.

Fanny M. Cheung was born in Hong Kong. She received her B.A. in psychology at the University of California, Berkeley, in 1970 and her Ph.D. in psychology at the University of Minnesota in 1975. She is currently a reader in the Department of Psychology at the Chinese University of Hong Kong and the coordinator of its Graduate Studies in Clinical Psychology Program. She is a past president of the Hong Kong Psychological Society and was president of the Division of Clinical and Community Psychology of the International Association of Applied Psychology from 1990-94. She initiated the translation and adaptation of the Chinese MMPI in Hong Kong in the late 1970s. The Hong Kong version was used as the blueprint for the Chinese version in the People's Republic of China. Her collaborations with Professor Weizheng Song on the Chinese MMPI and MMPI-2 have been extended to the development of the Chinese Personality Assessment Inventory (CPAI). Her major research areas are personality assessment, Chinese psychopathology, and gender studies.

Lee Anna Clark received a B.A. in psycholinguistics and an M.A. in East Asian studies from Cornell University. She holds a Ph.D. in clinical psychology from the University of Minnesota. She was on the faculty at Southern Methodist University for nine years and currently is professor of psychology at the University of Iowa.

Meral Çulha was born in Ankara, Turkey. She received an M.A. in clinical psychology and, from the University of Minnesota, a Ph.D. in counseling psychology. Dr. Çulha's experience includes test development and validation for the Study of Personal Attributes, Columbia University; personnel administration at the United Nations Population Fund; teaching, research, and private practice; and organizational counseling. She authored, with D. E. Super, the original Work Salience Inventory, the Word-Processing Interest Inventory, and the Role Expectations Questionnaire. As an associate professor, she taught several graduate level courses at Bogazici University in Istanbul and acted as a supervisor and trainer in the research project on Preschool Education and Development and Mother Education. Dr. Çulha joined the staff of the Student Counseling Services of Iowa State University in 1987 as a staff psychologist and coordinator of research and program evaluation. She is currently working on the application of the Correspondence Model—a research-based theoretical model developed at the University of Minnesota by Professors Lloyd Lofquist and René Dawis—to practice in a cross-cultural context. Dr. Çulha was recently on sabbatical leave in Turkey to teach, help set up a Student Counseling Center at Bogazici University, and work with Dr. Işık Savaşır on several MMPI projects, including the standardization of the Turkish translation of the MMPI-2.

Amos S. Deinard is associate professor in the Department of Pediatrics at the University of Minnesota and director, since 1984, of the Community-University Health Care Center/Variety Club Children's Clinic, a neighborhood-based outpatient clinic of the University of Minnesota Hospital and Clinic. Dr. Deinard received an undergraduate degree in chemistry from Harvard University in 1957 and his M.D. degree from the University of Minnesota (1962). He did an internship in pediatrics at the University of Minnesota Hospital (1962-63), a residency in the Department of Pediatrics, University of Minnesota (1963-65), and a fellowship in the Department of Pediatrics, University of Minnesota (1965-69). He joined the faculty of the Department of Pediatrics at the University of Minnesota in 1969. From 1969 to 1984 he was pediatric consultant to the Bureau of Maternal and Child Health, Minneapolis Health Department.

Hubert de Mey is associate professor in the Department of Clinical Psychology and Personality at the University of Nijmegen in The Netherlands and holds a Ph.D. His interests are in behavioral theory, especially Skinner's contribution, and in personality research.

Jan Derksen is associate professor in the Department of Clinical Psychology and Personality at the University of Nijmegen in The Netherlands and holds a Ph.D. Currently, his major research interest is the assessment of personality disorders. He has a private practice as a psychoanalytic psychotherapist.

Ramani S. Durvasula is currently a doctoral student in clinical psychology at the University of California, Los Angeles. As a student working with the National Research Center on Asian American Mental Health, she has studied the severity of psychiatric disorders in Asian outpatient populations, mental-health issues of Asian Indians, and breast cancer in Asian women.

Bjørn Ellertsen is professor in the Department of Biological and Medical Psychology, Clinical Neuropsychology Section, at the University of Bergen, Norway. He holds a Ph.D., teaches clinical neuropsychology in the psychology program at the University of Bergen, and supervises clinicians and researchers in the field. His major research interests are in clinical neuropsychology, personality psychology, pain syndromes, and applied psychophysiology. He leads the Norwegian MMPI-2 project.

Kana Enomoto is a graduate student in clinical psychology at the University of California, Los Angeles. She has been a researcher at the National Research Center on Asian American Mental Health. Her research interests are Asian American personality, acculturation, and ethnic identity.

Isabelle Gillet is a clinical psychologist who, since 1989, has been in charge of research and test development for les Editions du Centre de Psychologie Appliquée in Paris. She has developed the French adaptations of several instruments, including the K-ABC, 16 PF 5, and MMPI-2. She has several publications and has developed a training program for psychologists.

Daniel Gómez Dupertuis, a psychologist, is professor of experimental psychology in the Department of Psychology at La Plata State University.

Jorge A. González-Moreno is director of student affairs at the Pontificia Universidad Católica de Chile. He is a general physician and at present is director of the Student Health Service at the University. He has extensive medical experience with college students and has participated in MMPI studies since 1988.

J. D. Guelfi is professor of psychiatry at the Université René Descartes Paris since 1984. He worked for 15 years with Professor Pierre Pichot, who introduced psychological testing in psychiatry to France. He has published, alone or in collaboration, more than 280 papers or books. His major publications are three psychiatric textbooks, a case book, a book on the methodology of clinical trials in psychiatry, and two books on standardized clinical assessment in psychiatry. Professor Guelfi was the coordinator-in-chief of the French translation of the *DSM-III* and *DSM-III-R* and coordinator of the translation of the *DSM-IV.* He is also editor-in-chief of *European Psychiatry,* the journal of the Association of European Psychiatry (Elsevier). His main interests are in psychopharmacology, the methodology of clinical research, personality disorders, and assessment.

Kyunghee Han has an M.A. in child studies from Sookmyung Women's University in Seoul, Korea, and a Ph.D. in personality psychology from the University of Minnesota. She is currently a visiting professor of psychology at the University of Mississippi where she conducts research in cross-cultural psychology and works on the standardization and validation of the Korean MMPI-2.

Kaying Hang came to the United States with her family in November 1976. Originally sponsored in Georgia, they did not remain there because there were no existing Hmong communities. They went to Providence, Rhode Island, then moved to Wisconsin, and now reside in St. Paul, Minnesota. She will be entering her fourth year at Brandeis University in Waltham, Massachusetts, majoring in sociology and minoring in legal studies. She has completed the premedical program and hopes to attend medical school in the near future.

Odd E. Havik is professor of clinical psychology in the Department of Clinical Psychology at the University of Bergen and holds a Ph.D. He teaches psychodiagnostic and psychotherapeutic procedures in the clinical psychology program at the University of Bergen. His major research interests are psychodiagnostic methods in personality assessment, short-term psychotherapy, and health psychology, the latter focusing on psychological factors in the course and outcome of myocardial infarction.

Greet Hellenbosch is research fellow in the faculty of psychology at the Free University of Brussels, Belgium. She holds an M.A. and is preparing her Ph.D. dissertation on the construction of personality disorder scales for the MMPI-2.

Erika Himmel received an M.A. in measurement and evaluation in psychology from the University of Columbia. She is professor of measurement and statistics at the Pontificia Universidad Católica de Chile. Her research is in measurement and evaluation in psychology and education, and she has published about 30 publications in the past 10 years. She has conducted large educational assessment programs for university student admission programs and with primary and secondary educational systems. She has been involved in MMPI research since 1976.

Fernando Jimenéz-Gómez is professor of psychodiagnosis in the Department of Psychology at the University of Salamanca. He holds a Ph.D., and his major publication is *Introducción al Psicodiagnóstico de Rorschach y Láminas Proyectivas* [An introduction to the Rorschach Test and Projective Cards] (Amaru, 1993).

Keunho Keefe was born in Seoul, South Korea. She received her Ph.D. in social development from Purdue University in 1989. She is currently a postdoctoral fellow with the National Research Center on Asian American Mental Health in the Department of Psychology at the University of California, Los Angeles. Her major research is the various aspects of adjustment of Asian American adolescents, including peer relationships, school adjustment, and substance abuse.

Anna Kokkevi was born in Athens, Greece. She received an academic degree from the University of Paris (Sorbonne) and received her Ph.D. from Athens University in 1967. She is currently associate professor in the University Mental Health Research Institute, Eginition Hospital, in Athens. Dr. Kokkevi is an active researcher in the area of personality assessment and is president of the European Congress of Psychology.

Sölvína Konráòs was born in Iceland in 1948 and obtained her Ph.D. in psychology from the University of Minnesota in 1987. She has been a member of the faculty in psychology at the University of Iceland since 1985. Since 1992 she has also practiced as a counseling and consulting psychologist in Iceland.

Victor S. Koscheyev was professor at the Institute of Biophysics in Moscow and founder and first director of the Specialized Center for Disaster Medicine Protection in Moscow. He received the M.D. degree from Irkutsk Medical School in Siberia and a Ph.D. in disaster medicine from the Institute of Biophysics in Moscow. His research interests involve human thermoregulation, protection of persons in extreme environments, and radioactivity effects on health, particularly after the Chernobyl disaster. He currently is a senior fellow in the Division of Environmental and Occupational Health in the School of Public Health at the University of Minnesota.

Steven S. Krauss received his B.S. in psychology from the University of Iowa and Ph.D. in clinical psychology from the University of Minnesota. He is currently assistant professor in the Department of Psychology at Villanova University.

Gloria R. Leon is professor of psychology and former director of clinical psychology at the University of Minnesota. Her research interests include the general area of stress and coping; personality stability in the face of traumatic life circumstances, including environmental disasters; and the prospective development of eating disorders.

Emilia Lucio-G. M. was born in Mexico City. She is professor of clinical psychology at the National University of Mexico (UNAM), where she has taught for more than 25 years. She completed her professional, M.A., and Ph.D. studies in psychology at UNAM. She is a specialist in personality assessment and psychotherapy. She has been working with the MMPI since 1975 and has published several articles. She is author of the book *Integración de Estudios Psicológicos* [Integrating Psychological Test Reporting] and has presented several papers at the National and International Congress. She was chair of clinical psychology in the Department of Graduate Studies at UNAM and has a clinical practice in psychotherapy and personality assessment with children, adolescents, and adults.

Miguel A. Marquez is a psychiatrist and forensic medical doctor. He graduated from the Faculty of Medicine of the University of Buenos Aires and is currently director of the Psychiatric Service of the French Hospital in Buenos Aires and forensic psychiatrist on the Federal Forensic Medical Board. He is professor of psychopathology in the Department of Psychology at the Argentine Catholic University.

Claudine Monier is a clinical psychologist at the CMME, Hôspital Sainte Anne, specializing in psychometrics.

Baruch Nevo is an associate professor at the University of Haifa. He received a Ph.D. from the Hebrew University of Jerusalem in 1972 and chairs the graduate program in occupational psychology at the University of Haifa. From 1983 to 1987, while on leave from the University of Haifa, he became one of the founders and the first director of the National Inter-University Institute for Testing and Evaluation. Professor Nevo's main areas of interest are applied psychological measurement, testing and evaluation in education, and human intelligence.

Elahe Nezami was born in 1959 in Tehran. She received her B.A. from the University of Massachusetts in 1981. She has an M.A. degree in clinical and counseling psychology from the University of Houston. Her second M.A. degree and her Ph.D. in clinical psychology, completed in 1993, are from the University of Southern California.

Paolo Pancheri is professor of psychiatry at the Institute of Psychiatry of the University of Rome. Professor Pancheri has been an active researcher and practicing psychiatrist since he obtained his M.D. and residency in psychiatry. He has published 28 books and more than 300 scientific articles, many of which are on the MMPI. His active research areas include psychopharmacology, treatment of schizophrenia and affective disorders, the use of computers in psychiatry, and the establishment of computer networks in clinical practice and research.

La-Or Pongpanich is chief of the Psychology Service in the Department of Psychiatry at the Army Pramongkut Klao Hospital and a lecturer in psychology at Army Medical College and Army Nursing College in Bangkok, Thailand. Since 1981, she has collaborated with Dr. James N. Butcher to translate and adapt first the original MMPI and then the MMPI-2 into Thai. She has also used the MMPI as the standard test for screening, clinical assessment, and research with military and civilian groups.

Isabel Reyes-Lagunes received a Ph.D. from the National University of Mexico (UNAM) in 1982, where she has been professor for more than 20 years. A specialist in social psychology, cross-cultural psychology, and measurement and evaluation, she is author of more than 30 scientific articles. Professor Reyes-Lagunes was chair of the Graduate School of Psychology at UNAM for four years and has held positions in several scientific associations, both national and international. At present she is the chief editor of the *Revista de Psicología Social y Personalidad.*

Fernando J. Rissetti is a psychologist trained at the Pontificia Universidad Católica de Chile. He has conducted the MMPI research program there since 1976 and has collaborated with Dr. James N. Butcher since that time. He has published several articles on this research in Chile. He has been a member of the Society for Personality Assessment since 1990. He has taught courses on personality assessment in three Chilean universities and was nominated in 1990 for the Distinguished Psychologist Award, given by the Chilean Psychological Association.

Lorenzo Garcia Samartino is a medical doctor and psychiatrist. He received his M.D. degree from the Faculty of Medicine of the University of Buenos Aires. Currently he is a forensic psychiatrist at Buenos Aires Federal Forensic Medical Board. He is also professor in the Department of Psychology at the Argentine Catholic University and in the Department of Legal Medicine at the Faculty of Medicine of the University of Buenos Aires.

Işık Savaşır was born and raised in Turkey. She attended Middle East Technical University in Ankara. She received a Fulbright scholarship and attended Southern Illinois University at Carbondale, receiving M.A. and Ph.D. degrees in clinical psychology. She completed a clinical internship at the University of Kansas Medical School. Currently she is professor in the Department of Psychology and the Department of Psychiatry in the Faculty of Medicine at Hacettepe University in Ankara. She serves as chair of the doctoral program in clinical psychology. Professor Savaşır has long been involved with research on the MMPI and published (with Nese Erol) a study on the clinical validity of the MMPI in Turkey. She collaborated on the Turkish translation of the MMPI-2 with Meral Çulha.

Françoise Seunevel is a clinical psychologist at the CMME, Hôspital Sainte Anne, a specialized center for children and adolescents in psychometrics and psychotherapy.

Noriko K. Shiota was born in Tokyo and grew up in Tokyo and Boston. She holds a B.A. in psychology and East Asian studies from Sophia University and a Ph.D. in clinical psychology from the University of Minnesota. She is currently a staff psychologist at Friends Hospital in Philadelphia and teaches in the Department of Psychology at Villanova University.

Mireille Simon is a psychologist at the Université René Descartes. Since 1983 she has been in charge of the Research and Test Development Department at les Editions du Centre de Psychologie Appliquée in Paris. She has collaborated for 10 years with Professor Pierre Pichot's research team in the field of applied psychiatry. Since 1978 she has served as a psychotherapeutic consultant at Mutuelle Generale de l'Education Nationale Mental Health Center. She has been a member of the scientific committee of the *European Review of Applied Psychology* since 1990.

Saulo Sirigatti is professor of psychology at the University of Florence where he directs the Section of Health Psychology. He graduated from the University of Florence and received his M.A. in psychology from Fordham University and a Ph.D. in psychology from the New School for Social Research. At the University of Sienna he taught clinical psychology and directed the Institute of General and Clinical Psychology of the School of Medicine and the Clinical Psychology Section. He has done extensive research in the fields of social and clinical psychology.

Rita R. Skavhellen is research associate in the Department of Biological and Medical Psychology, Clinical Neuropsychology Section, at the University of Bergen, Norway. She holds a Ph.D., and her research interests include personality psychology, substance and alcohol abuse, pain syndromes, and clinical psychology. She is coordinator of the Norwegian MMPI-2 project.

Hedwig Sloore is professor on the faculty of psychology at the Free University of Brussels and director of the Department of Personality and Social Psychology. He holds a Ph.D., and his interests are personality assessment and personality disorders.

Abdalla M. Soliman is professor of psychology and chair of the Department of Psychology at United Arab Emirates University. He received his Ph.D. from the University of Minnesota in 1967. He has taught at Ain Shams University, Cairo University, and Kuwait University and was a counseling psychologist and consultant to the dean of students at American University in Cairo. In 1985-86 he was visiting scholar at the Torrance Center for Creative Studies at the University of Georgia. Dr. Soliman is a member of the American Psychological Association, the American Counseling Association, and other scientific and professional organizations and has been serving as editor, consulting editor, and advisor to several journals. His publications include books, monographs, chapters, and articles on research methods, counseling, personality, and creativity.

Weizheng Song was born in Zhejiang province, China, and graduated from the Beijing Normal University in 1955. She is professor in the Institute of psychology at the Chinese Academy of Sciences. She has made major contributions in the areas of medical psychology and personality assessment, especially in the introduction, revision, and application of the MMPI in the People's Republic of China since psychology was resumed as a scientific study in the late 1970s. She established the National MMPI Coordinating Group to facilitate research and training in the use of the Chinese MMPI and MMPI-2. She is currently a member of the Standing Committee and deputy secretary-general of the Chinese Mental Health Association and chairperson of the Chinese Youth Mental Health Committee.

Stanley Sue is professor of psychology at UCLA and director of the National Research Center on Asian American Mental Health, an NIMH-funded center. He received a B.S. degree from the University of Oregon (1966) and a Ph.D. degree in psychology from UCLA (1971). Prior to his faculty appointment at UCLA, where he was also associate dean of the Graduate Division, he served for 10 years on the psychology faculty at the University of Washington and from 1980-1981 was director of clinical-community psychology training at the National Asian American Psychology Training Center in San Francisco, an APA-approved internship program. His research has been devoted to the study of psychopathology among, and delivery of mental health services to, culturally diverse groups. His work documented the difficulties that ethnic minority groups experience in receiving adequate mental health services and offered directions for providing culturally appropriate forms of treatment.

Liliane Svarna is a clinical psychologist at the CMME, Hôpital Sainte Anne, specializing in psychometrics. She teaches at the Ecole des Psychologues Praticiens, Université Catholique.

Umeng Thao was born in Vientiene, Laos, in 1971. His family came to the United States in July 1976 and resided in Providence, Rhode Island, for six years before moving to the Midwest. He graduated from Brown University in 1993 with a B.A. in human biology, specializing in health and disease. He is now attending the University of Minnesota School of Medicine. He would like to become a primary-care provider to communities such as the Hmong.

Bao-Chi Nguyen Tran was born in Saigon, Vietnam. She immigrated to the United States and settled in Minnesota in 1975. She is a graduate of the University of Minnesota with a B.A. in computer science (1988) and an M.A. in clinical psychology (1992). Her special interests are in anxiety disorders, trauma, and cross-cultural mental health. She was in clinical practice at Ramsey Clinic and the Center for Victims of Torture and is planning to return to school to pursue her interest in cross-cultural mental health.

Song Houamoua Vang was born in 1975 in Laos. From 1978 to 1988 he lived in the refugee camps of Banvinai in Thailand. His family arrived in St. Paul, Minnesota, in September 1988. He recently graduated from high school and is currently studying business at St. Thomas University.

Reza Zamani received his B.A. from the University of Tehran, and his Ph.D. from the University of Minnesota in 1974. He presently is on the faculty at the University of Tehran in Iran.

Jianxin Zhang was born in Beijing, China, and received his B.A. from the Department of Psychology at Beijing University. He received his M.Phil. from the Department of Psychology at the Chinese University of Hong Kong and is now a Ph.D. candidate there studying with Dr. Fanny Cheung. He is also an assistant professor affiliated with the research group led by Professor Weizheng Song at the Institute of Psychology at the Chinese Academy of Science. He is responsible for the translation, revision, data collection, and analysis of the Chinese MMPI-2 in the People's Republic of China.

Index

(Note: t following a page number indicates a table; f, a figure.)

item characteristic curve (ICC), 56,59
item response function (IRF), 56–57
methods of measurement, 50–59
Cui, C. E., 139
Çulha, Meral, 536, 647
on MMPI/MMPI-2 in Turkey, 448–60
Cultural (anthropological) approach to abnormal psychology, 9
Culturally appropriate norms, development of, 39–40
Culturally problematic expressions, in translation, 33
Culture
culture-bound items in MMPI-2 and MMPI-A, 33–35
research across language or cultural boundaries, 6
Cynicism (CYN; content scale), characteristics suggested by, 531

D (Scale 2; Depression), characteristics suggested by, 527
Dahlstrom, J., 211
Dahlstrom, L. E., 274
Dahlstrom, W. G., 267, 273, 274
Davenport, F., 53
Davidson, A. R., 176
de Mey, Hubert, 48, 648
on Flemish/Dutch version of MMPI-2, 329–49
De Waele, J. P., 330
Decentering test items, 27–28
Defensiveness (K) scale, characteristics suggested by, 525
Deinard, Amos S., 535, 648
on Hmong translation, 194–205
Demirbas, H., 455
DEP (Depression; content scale), characteristics suggested by, 530
Depression, cross-cultural manifestations of, 5–6
Depression (DEP; content scale), characteristics suggested by, 530
Depression (Scale 2; D), characteristics suggested by, 527
Derksen, Jan, 48, 535, 648
on Flemish/Dutch version of MMPI-2, 329–49
Dezhkam, M., 507, 509, 511
Diagnostic and Statistical Manual of Mental Disorders (DSM-III), 150, 418–19
Differential item functioning (DIF), 58–59

Difficult-to-translate idioms, 32, 99, 176
Difficult-to-translate items, 34
in Arabic, 468–70
in French, 404–7
in Hmong, 197
in Korean, 99
in Russian, 391
in Turkish, 449, 456, 457
in Vietnamese, 176
Direct translations, as first procedure, 35–37, 36t
Dispositional timidity, 19
Dissimulation (F-K) index, characteristics suggested by, 525
Do (Dominance supplementary scale), characteristics suggested by, 529
Doğan, B. Y., 455
Dominance (Do) supplementary scale, characteristics suggested by, 529
Double negatives, in translation, 35
Draguns, J. G., 7–9, 284, 286
Drasgow, F., 50
DSM-III. See Diagnostic and Statistical Manual of Mental Disorders
Durvasula, Ramani S., 648
on Asian American/white college students' performance, 206–18
Dutch version of MMPI-2. *See* Flemish/Dutch version of MMPI-2

Editions du Centre de Psychologie Appliquée (ECPA), 395
Edwards Personal Preference Schedule (EPPS), 138
Egli, E., 28
Ego Strength scale (Es) supplementary scale, characteristics suggested by, 529
Egypt, MMPI in, 464–67
clinical scale reliability, 466–67
standardization of Arabic MMPI, 464–66
translation differences from original, 64–65
validity of original scales, 466–67
Ellertsen, Bjorn, 536, 649
on Norwegian MMPI-2, 350–67
Ellis, B. B., 59
Emics. *See* Etics vs. emics
Enomoto, Kana, 206, 649
EPQ (Eysenck Personality Questionnaire), 137–38, 509
Equivalence. *See also* Cross-cultural equivalence, establishing